HEALTH CONSEQUENCES OF ACUTE AND CHRONIC MARIHUANA USE

HEALTH CONSEQUENCES OF ACUTE AND CHRONIC MARIHUANA USE

MADELAINE O. MAYKUT

Health Protection Branch, Health and Welfare Canada,
Ottawa, Ontario

PERGAMON PRESS

OXFORD · NEW YORK · TORONTO · SYDNEY · PARIS · FRANKFURT

U.K.	Pergamon Press Ltd., Headington Hill Hall, Oxford OX3 0BW, England
U.S.A.	Pergamon Press Inc., Maxwell House, Fairview Park, Elmsford, New York 10523, U.S.A.
CANADA	Pergamon Press Canada Ltd., Suite 104, 150 Consumers Road, Willowdale, Ontario M2J 1P9, Canada
AUSTRALIA	Pergamon Press (Aust.) Pty. Ltd., P.O. Box 544, Potts Point, N.S.W. 2011, Australia
FRANCE	Pergamon Press SARL, 24 rue des Ecoles, 75240 Paris, Cedex 05, France
FEDERAL REPUBLIC OF GERMANY	Pergamon Press GmbH, Hammerweg 6, D-6242 Kronberg-Taunus, Federal Republic of Germany

First Edition 1984

Library of Congress Cataloging in Publication Data

Maykut, Madelaine O.
Health consequences of acute and chronic marihuana use.
"Published as supplement no. 1 (1984) to the review journal Progress in neuro-psychopharmacology and biological psychiatry."
1. Marihuana — Physiological effect. 2. Marihuana — Toxicology. I. Title. [DNLM: 1. Cannabis — metabolism. 2. Cannabis Abuse — complications. 3. Cannabinoids — pharmacodynamics. QV 77.7 M469h]
QP801.C27M38 1984 616.86'3 84–13990

British Library Cataloguing in Publication Data

Maykut, Madelaine O.
Health consequences of acute and chronic marihuana use.
1. Cannabis 2. Cannabis—Physiological effect
I. Title
615'.7827   QP801.C27
ISBN 0-08-031984-X

Published as Supplement No 1 (1984) to the review journal *Progress in Neuro-psychopharmacology and Biological Psychiatry.*

Printed in Great Britain by A. Wheaton & Co. Ltd., Exeter

Contents

Foreword   1

General Introduction   2

I.   Short Summary of Health Aspects of Marihuana Use

   1. Introduction   3
   2. Chemistry and Metabolism   3
   3. Clinical Effects
     (i) Acute Effects   4
    (ii) Chronic Effects   4
   4. Possible Therapeutic Benefits   5

II. Discussion of Health Effects of Marihuana Use

   1. Introduction   6

   2. Chemistry and Metabolism   7
      Abstract   7
     1. Introduction   7
     2. Chemical Content of Cannabis   7
     3. Cannabinoid Analysis   8
     4. Cannabinoid Metabolism   10
     5. Summary   13
     6. Figures   14

   3. Known and Possible Clinical Effects
     Introductory Remarks   28
    A. Chromosomes, Cell Metabolism, Immunity   29
       Abstract   29
      1. Introduction   29
      2. Medical Genetics   30
        (a) General Aspects   30
        (b) Genetic Modifications   30
      3. Immune System   31
        (a) Cellular and Humoral Immunity   31
        (b) Development of Immunological Status   32
        (c) Immunodeficiency Diseases   32
        (d) Hypersensitivity Reactions   33
        (e) Immunosuppressants; stress   34
      4. Marihuana Effects   34
        (a) Genetic Effects - Chromosomal Aberrations   34
        (b) Cell Metabolism - Effects on Macromolecular (DNA, RNA, Protein) Synthesis   37
        (c) Effects on Cellular (T-cell) and Humoral (B-cell) or Antibody Mediated Immune Systems; and on Phagocytic Pulmonary Alveolar Macrophage System   39
      5. Discussion and Summary   45
      6. Figures   48

    B. Reproductive System   59
       Abstract   59
      1. Introduction   59
      2. Reproductive Physiology   60
      3. Marihuana Effects in the Male   61
        (a) Testosterone   61
        (b) Spermatogenesis   63
        (c) Gynecomastia   64
      4. Marihuana Effects in the Female   65
        (a) Hormonal and Ovulatory Effects 65
        (b) Placental Effects   66
        (c) Maternal Milk Content   66
        (d) Fetal Toxicity   67
      5. Summary   71
      6. Figures   73

C. Central Nervous System 81
   Abstract 81
   1. Introduction 82
   2. Marihuana Effects on the Brain 82
      (a) Distribution of Marihuana in the CNS 82
      (b) Gross Pathology 82
      (c) EEG (Cerebral Cortical Activity; Limbic System) Studies . 84
      (d) Effects on Nerves 87
   3. Psychopathology and Psychiatric Aspects of Cannabis Intoxication or
      Marihuana's Capacity to Impair Brain Function 87
      (a) Acute Emotional Responses to Cannabis 87
          (i) Acute Panic Anxiety Reaction 87
          (ii) Transient Mild Paranoid Feeling 88
          (iii) Toxic Delirium or Acute Brain Syndrome (Toxic Psychosis or
                Poisoning) 88
      (b) Prolonged Psychological Effects (Chronic Organic Brain Syndrome) . 88
          (i) Psychotic (Pathological Organic CNS Response) 88
          (ii) Non-Psychotic 91
               Flashbacks 91
               Amotivational Syndrome and Personality
               (Neuropsychological) Changes 92
      (c) Aggressive Behaviour 94
      (d) Classification of Psychiatric Conditions 98
          (i) Drug Dependence 99
          (ii) Non-Psychotic OBS (Organic Brain Syndrome) 99
          (iii) Psychosis or Psychotic OBS 99
          (iv) Schizophrenic-Type + (i) or (ii) or (iii) 99
   4. Psychomotor Function or Performance 99
   5. Tolerance and Dependence 102
   6. Summary 104
   7. Figures 106

D. Cardiopulmonary System 128
   Abstract 128
   1. Introduction 129
   2. Pulmonary System Disorders 130
   3. Cardiovascular System Dysfunction 131
   4. Marihuana Effects on Pulmonary System 133
      (a) Smoke Constituents 133
      (b) Acute Effects 137
      (c) Chronic Effects 138
      (d) Pulmonary Defense System Effects 141
      (e) Discussion and Summary 144
      (f) Figures D_1 147
   5. Marihuana Effects on Cardiovascular System 164
      (a) Acute and Short Term Effects 164
      (b) Possible Mechanism of Action 166
      (c) Chronic Effects 171
      (d) Cardiac Toxicity 174
      (e) Interactions 178
      (f) Discussion and Summary 182
      (g) Figures D_2 188

E. Field Studies 233
   Abstract 233
   1. Introduction 233
   2. In Jamaica 233
   3. In Greece 235
   4. In Costa Rica 236
   5. Discussion and Summary 237

III. General Summaries 240
   Abstract 240
   1. Chemistry and Metabolism 240
   2. Chromosomes, Cell Metabolism, Immunity 242
   3. Reproductive System 245
   4. Central Nervous System 246
   5. Cardiopulmonary System 249

IV. **Conclusion and Final Comments**   252
     Abstract   252
   1. Introduction   252
   2. Marihuana Hypoxic Effects   252
   3. Secondary CVS Adrenergic Reflex Response   253
   4. Metabolic and Hormonal Alterations   254
   5. Altered Blood Glucose Control   255
   6. Adrenergic Blocking Effects   259
   7. Final Statements   260
   8. Final Conclusion   261
   9. Figures   262

V.   **References**   278

VI. **Author Index**   293

VII. **Subject Index**   301

Foreword

A few attempts were made to write for the lay public which was an oversimplification so that scientists questioned statements made. A semi-lay-scientific effort was made when semantics caused some scientists to misinterpret the intended conclusions and implications. It was decided to do an original research literature search to find out why certain alleged controversies existed looking into the conditions of reported investigations such as subjects studied, materials used including potency, dose, route and/or mode of administration, frequency and duration of dose(s) used, previous drug(s) use, and state of health of subjects studied. Also clues were sought in an attempt to explain the varied body system effects of marihuana looking for a common thread (mechanism) tying all the system alterations together. It should be kept in mind that each of the sections discussed could, in themselves, result in an extensive review. In order to try to cover as much of the marihuana research area as possible within a reasonable period of time, representative papers have been reviewed depicting only part of the available massive literature. Clinical investigations were stressed and where such were lacking, basic and animal research were reported noting clinical implications (if possible) which should be watched for clinically. It is hoped that the presentation is adequately conveyed to anyone interested in the cannabis field to help them make decisions in whatever discipline the reader may be involved as well as to raise questions for future research pursuits.

The actual review begins with a short discussion on chemistry and metabolism of marihuana followed by a more detailed portion beginning with the cellular metabolic effects due to marihuana use and ending with metabolic effects in the body (in the conclusion and final comments section). Even though therapeutic aspects of marihuana use have been mentioned in the short summary preceding the review, time did not permit discussion of this area per se but mention of some therapeutic possibilities have been indicated in the different systems presented as were drug interactions. Each section in the discussion segment of the review has its own table of contents beginning with an abstract and an introduction, followed by normal physiological function of the system being considered prior to presenting marihuana effects and ending with a summary including some comments. The graphs illustrated in this review are adaptations from published reports to help visualize some cannabis effects; details being found in the respective papers. General summaries (overview) are provided at the end of the detailed review as well as final comments (including metabolic effects and hypotheses to explain varied effects) in the conclusion with a short concise final conclusion. The term THC used in this review refers to delta-9-tetrahydrocannabinol unless otherwise specified while benzpyrene alludes to benzo(a)pyrene.

General Introduction

The term marihuana is derived from the Mexican (Latin American) word maraguanquo, signifying an inebriant plant. It is the popular name for a plant, Cannabis sativa, also known as hemp, and a common name of a drug prepared by drying the leaves and flowering tops of the plant which contain chemicals known as cannabinoids. The Greek and Latin name cannabis originated from the Assyrian Kunnapu (from Assyrian words qunubu and qunabu meaning "a way to produce smoke") and hemp is from the same root. The hemp plant thrives practically in any climate and has long been cultivated in the Central United States for its fibre (rope, linen) and seed (birdseed, oil for quick-drying paint). Resin (richer in cannabinoids) exuded by the marihuana plant may be dried to produce hashish, 1 gram of which is effectively equivalent to 5-10 grams of marihuana. However, there is wide intersample potency variation of both preparations. Cannabis materials are smoked or ingested by various cultures and subcultures to induce psychotomimetic effects such as euphoria, hallucinations (may be a symptom of overdose similar to alcohol hallucinations), drowsiness and other mental changes. Usually, the plant is cut, dried, chopped and incorporated into cigarettes. The cannabinoid believed responsible for most of the characteristic psychological effects of marihuana is l-delta-9-tetrahydrocannabinol (Δ^9 THC). Cannabis was formerly used as a sedative and analgesic. Marihuana was essentially banned in 1937 with the passage of the Marihuana Tax Act in the U.S.A. which required physicians to pay a tax for a licence to prescribe marihuana. The use of cannabis was prohibited in Canada through its inclusion in the Schedule of the Opium and Narcotic Drug Act, 1923. Presently, Canada is obliged by the "Single Convention on Narcotic Drugs 1961" to limit the production, distribution, and use of certain forms of cannabis (flowering tops, resin or hashish, plant, extracts and tinctures) to medical and scientific purposes. Therapeutic use by physicians is not prohibited by Canadian federal law as long as the drug is obtained from a licensed (legal) source of supply (LeDain, 1972).

The Narcotic Control Regulations make provision for authorization to be given by the Minister to purchase, possess and administer cannabis for scientific purposes. Section 47 of the Regulations provides as follows:

(1) Where he deems it to be in the public interest and the interests of science, the Minister may authorize in writing,

    (a) any person to purchase and possess, a narcotic, and

    (b) notwithstanding section 38,

        (i) any person to administer that narcotic to an animal, and

        (ii) any practitioner of medicine to administer that narcotic to a person,

    for the purposes and subject to the conditions set out in the authorization.

(2) The Minister may, at any time, revoke the authorization referred to in subsection (1) and require any person in possession of a narcotic pursuant to that authorization to deliver the narcotic to the Minister or his agent.

The Minister also has a discretion to authorize the cultivation of marihuana for scientific purposes.

I. Short Summary of Health Aspects of Marihuana Use

I. 1. Introduction

The controversy which exists over the health hazards of cannabis use may be due to:

(1) difficulty in proving or disproving health hazards in man from animal studies which use large doses over a short period of time;

(2) use of relatively small doses of the drug intermittently by young healthy individuals thereby underestimating the potential health effects in older or high risk segments of the population;

(3) use with licit (tobacco, alcohol) and illicit drugs making it difficult to distinguish health effects due to one substance;

(4) prejudices (for or against) by the investigator (emotional issue).

Cannabis should be considered as any other active substance with desirable and undesirable health effects, weighing the benefits vs risks depending on the purpose of its final use (therapeutic vs social use). Presently it is difficult to do a cost-benefit analysis of risks as is done with therapeutic agents.

Health hazards associated with cannabis use remain to be <u>fully</u> determined. Some do exist. Continued studies are therefore necessary before the relative importance of health effects to the social user can be determined (e.g. a long time was necessary to determine the ill effects of accepted social drugs; tobacco, alcohol). <u>If</u> cannabis is to be a social drug, legal constraints are necessary against producing injury or death to others as with alcohol (driving while intoxicated).

Where the older individual uses alcohol (and does not consider it a drug), the younger person uses cannabis. The public should really be discouraged (educated) from using cannabis as well as alcohol and tobacco; at least moderation should be stressed which would minimize health hazards. The possibility of any therepeutic usefulness of cannabis (or its derivatives) should be investigated in the same way as any new therapeutic agent.

I. 2. Chemistry and Metabolism

Cannabis is not a single pure substance but contains several cannabinoids making it difficult to determine its mechanism of action (how it works). It is of variable potency. Potency depends upon the degree of refinement of the plant (stems yield products less potent than the leaves), the time or date of harvest, whether it is a drug plant producing a more potent substance than hemp used for its fibre, a good growing area, and yields. The average marihuana cigarette delivers 5-20 mg Δ^9 THC (major active ingredient) with recently reported increasing potency of 30 mg or more. Smoking a marihuana cigarette results in a 50% loss (approximately) of THC by smoke escaping into the air or exhaled from the respiratory dead space. Rapid absorption occurs with onset of effects noted in seconds/minutes with a duration of 2-3 hours (post 1 cigarette) vs oral THC with an onset of 0.5-2 hours and a longer duration of action (5-6 hours). The amount of cannabinoids absorbed by the lungs depends on how long marihuana smoke is held in the lungs. It is unknown if one type of cannabinoid is absorbed more readily or metabolized in the lung tissue. The metabolism of Δ^9 THC occurs in the liver.

Following the metabolism of marihuana, a metabolite (breakdown product) appears in the urine in the form of carboxy-THC for several days after a single dose (it also appears in the blood). The presence of this metabolite in the urine for 3-4 days is a clue to regular use of > 1 cigarette/week. This urinary metabolite (also known as THC-11-oic acid) may be found 1.5 hours after smoking a marihuana cigarette. Techniques of radioimmunoassay and thin layer chromatography are being used to detect these substances. The THC in plasma may be detected for 30-60 minutes following a marihuana cigarette, lasting for 4 hours. However, the plasma THC disappears faster than the clinical effects (impairment) disappear. It is important to find the range of plasma and urinary concentrations of THC and/or carboxy-THC consistent with <u>psychomotor impairment</u> for forensic purposes (e.g. <u>driving</u>). In the state of California in the United States of America, there is increasing evidence that drivers involved in accidents have been under the influence of alcohol and marihuana. Drugs with CNS depressant effects are additive (e.g., marihuana, alcohol, sedatives). Marihuana is retained in the body fat, but it is unknown how long it remains biologically active. Under stress, fat is broken down but it is unknown whether the drug is released. Early <u>detection</u> is important to discourage use, before marihuana becomes a custom as with alcohol and tobacco. Detection is important at the site of <u>automobile accidents</u>.

I. 3. Clinical Effects

The parameters of risk of cannabis use have not been adequately explored as with alcohol because the <u>clinical significance of some of the laboratory findings are unknown</u>. Modest research studies have been done on healthy male human volunteers and not on those with poor health, older individuals, nor female subjects, thereby leading to a biased conclusion that the drug is safe. The drug is being used by the young, adolescents, when they are developing their personality, intellectual capacity, and psychosocial skills. The effects of chronic intoxication on these parameters are unknown.

(i) Acute Effects

(a) Biphasic perceptual and <u>psychic changes</u> appear as a euphoric "high" (hilarity) followed by drowsiness. There may be altered time (slowing) sense, less discriminant hearing, sharper vision with visual distortions, depersonalization, difficulty in concentrating and thinking (impairment of learning, memory, and intellectual performance), and dreamlike states.

(b) Correlated with the appearance and duration of the psychic effects are the <u>physiological effects</u> of increased pulse rate with a slight increase in blood pressure in the supine position with blood pressure decrease upon standing followed by orthostatic hypotension with syncope in some individuals, decreased platelet aggregation, pupil constriction, conjunctival reddening, decreased intraocular pressure, decreased muscle strength, psychomotor impairment, bronchodilation (increased diameter of lung air passages), respiratory depression, dose-dependent pulmonary antibacterial defense system effect of alveolar macrophage phagocytic impairment, a trend to decreased airway clearance by cilia, and increased appetite with increased food intake (especially sweets); a carbohydrate metabolic disturbance being observed as decreased glucose tolerance (a pancreatic function test).

(c) <u>Psychopathological</u> or acute emotional responses have been observed as an

(1) acute panic anxiety reaction and transient mild paranoid feelings; and as an

(2) acute brain syndrome (toxic delirium, toxic psychosis, poisoning) with potent material(s) manifested as clouding of mental processes, disorientation, confusion, memory impairment.

(ii) Chronic Effects

These are less certain and may be considered as potentially serious to individuals and society necessitating well planned research in this area.

(a) <u>Cell metabolism</u> and <u>chromosome</u> (represents metabolism in nuclear area of cell) alterations could influence reproduction, growth, genetic transmission of abnormalities.

(b) Depression of the <u>immune</u> response could increase susceptibility to disease including infections and cancer especially in those with borderline immunological competence; hypersensitivity (allergic) reactions occurring in those with allergic diathesis.

(c) <u>Endocrine</u> (gonadotropins, sex hormones) alterations may affect fertility and reproductive outcome. Possible undesireable fetal effects (behavioural teratogen; non-specific malformations) may occur due to maternal marihuana use during pregnancy (as with alcohol and tobacco) as well as due to paternal use (sperm alteration). Decreased testosterone (male sex hormone) levels may lead to inadequate sex differentiation in the male fetus if the mother smokes marihuana or affect the sex maturation and growth of the child. Preliminary human reports revealed decreased birth weight and physical features reminiscent of the fetal alcohol syndrome in some newborn infants due to maternal marihuana use, and, pubertal arrest associated with heavy marihuana use in a male youth.

(d) Possible impairment of <u>brain function</u> similar to alcohol may only become apparent after longer use. Possible brain damage has been observed as reversible EEG (electrical activity on the surface of the brain) dose-related changes. Deep implanted electrodes have shown persistent changes, the signifance of which is unknown with respect to behavioural or functional effects.

(e) Prolonged intoxication or heavy use may lead to development of <u>psychiatric</u> conditions such as

(1) flashbacks or spontaneous recurrence(s) of feelings similar to actual drug effects, or

(2) an amotivational syndrome, or

(3) psychoses (disorder of the mind) due to frequent high drug doses; marihuana use to be avoided in controlled schizophrenics whose illness may be exacerbated.

(f) Impaired (dose-related) <u>psychomotor</u> function may affect driving ability; THC having a stronger effect on estimation of time (overestimation) and distance than alcohol.

(g) Development of <u>tolerance</u> with prolonged use occurs as does moderate <u>psychological</u> (psychic) and mild <u>physical</u> (physiological) <u>dependence</u> (withdrawal effects) which may lead to some becoming cannabinolics (similar to alcoholics), the prevalence of which is unknown. Nor are predictors known, but psychologically troubled are more at risk. Acute effects (such as increased pulse rate, altered blood pressure, bronchodilation, respiratory depression) are attenuated due to tolerance development which is not a metabolic drug tolerance but may be a functional or adaptive tolerance.

(h) Possible <u>lung damage</u> may occur due to

(1) smoke (as with tobacco) and inefficient removal of particulate matter leading to bronchitis, emphysema or lung cancer, or

(2) contamination by paraquat, a herbicide used in Mexican crop spraying to destroy plants (defoliant), with the possibility (probability?) of developing an edematous, hemorrhagic lung ending up in fibrosis which could be lethal; contamination with infectious organisms being detrimental to immuno-suppressed (increased risk of infection) cancer patients in whom pulmonary infection could be fatal.

(i) Possible deleterious effects in <u>heart disease</u> may occur in conjunction with increased carboxyhemoglobin due to smoke.

I. 4. Possible Therapeutic Benefits

Medical usefulness has been reported in:

(a) Glaucoma. The increased intraocular pressure which may lead to blindness has been decreased with a topical application of THC in an oily vehicle.

(b) Alleviation of nausea and vomiting (antiemetic) due to cancer chemotherapy but undesirable side effects such as hallucinations upon repeated use have been reported for some cannabinoid homologues (e.g. Nabilone, a homologue of cannabinol).

(c) Other potential therapeutic uses reported include: antiasthmatic (bronchodilator); tranquilizer, sedative-hypnotic, antianxiety and antidepressant; analgesic, antipyretic and antiinflamatory; antispasmodic; anticonvulsant or antiepileptic; treatment of alcoholism and narcotic detoxification; antineoplastic (antitumor) and immunosuppressant; antifertility; appetite stimulant; antihypertensive; antidiarrheal; antibacterial; antitussive; anti-peptic ulcer.

Therapeutic usefulness of a drug will depend upon whether it is better than any other existing drug and whether the desirable effects outweigh (or can be separated from) the undesirable effects (in this case, the mental effects). The disadvantages of natural cannabis include variation in potency and unreliable shelf-life. A desirable new drug with beneficial effects but less THC undesirable effects should have the following characteristics: persistent therapeutic effect for chronic conditions, non-tolerant, safe, effective, and without deleterious side effects (such as increased heart rate, undesirable psychological effects, lung irritation).

II. Discussion of Health Effects of Marihuana Use

II. 1. Introduction

To place the following discussion in perspective, some general comments on research, including definition of some terms, shall be made.

Social, as it relates to human society, refers to the interaction of an individual and a group, or the welfare of human beings as members of a society. Welfare is to "fare well" in prosperity (economic), well-being (medical), and happiness (psychologic). A social disease (or problem) is a disease whose incidence is directly related to social and economic factors e.g., tuberculosis, alcoholism (substance misuse). Disease in a social sense means dis ease that an individual experiences in society in the form of anxiety and frustrations. If the individual cannot cope with these frustrations then an undesirable behaviour (psychological) may ensue in the form of misusing drugs giving rise to dis ease of the body or impairment of performance of vital functions. Pathological drug use (pharmacological and toxicological effects) has social, psychological and physical determinants, keeping in mind that all individuals have an innate breaking point (individual variation). In short, dis ease with society (social; anxiety, frustrations) leads to dis ease of body (biomedical) and mind (psychological; behaviour). Thus many disciplines are necessary to attempt to solve any problem.

Animal studies are quite pertinent to social problems. If animals are studied more closely in their environment to observe how they handle their social (behaviour) problems we may learn something from them. In fact, animals have more common sense than some human beings for it is difficult to get an animal to drink (alcohol) itself to destruction without prior conditioning. The purpose of animal studies is primarily to:

(a)   rule out poisonous substances before new compounds are tried in man;

(b)   study useful pharmacological effects and note toxicities which should be watched for when finally used in man and may not necessarily appear in man (i.e. species specific);

(c)   conduct studies that are not ethically feasible in man, i.e., a human being is not subjected to unnecessary dangers or harm (such as purposely developing addicts) while an attempt is being made to solve a problem.

Presently a good animal model is lacking thereby making it difficult to extrapolate animal results to man.

Good controlled clinical studies require time and patience because of the difficulty encountered in obtaining an appropriate patient population for clinical investigation. Not only should effects found in animals be watched for but clinical acumen is necessary to pick up differences, i.e., effects not seen in animals or effects opposite to those found in animals. For example, headaches cannot be detected in animals. Also, an antifertility drug in animal studies proved to be a fertility drug in the human subject.

While the social ills are being corrected (which takes a long time; history is a witness to this) which hopefully may decrease the number of new disease entities in time, it is also necessary to clear up established dis ease illnesses, prevent their progression, find means to predict susceptible individuals and prevent their induction. If someone did not undertake research, we would not have our daily conveniences (electricity, telephone) nor give life to diabetic individuals (insulin). What research really means to to re search for something that is already there in nature for us to find and to use intelligently for the good of man even though some of it may become misused or abused because of so-called human nature peculiar to the human race. Thus a decision for a particular need must be based on a common sense approach to and execution of research.

Until mental frustrations of living in our society are removed, individuals will seek escape (in the form of drugs including alcohol) which does not solve an existing problem but very often leads to destruction (of self) of a functional society. The preservation of man or survival of society depends upon good brain function to make decisions and health to reproduce healthy offspring.

II. 2. Chemistry and Metabolism

Contents

	Abstract	7
1.	Introduction	7
2.	Chemical Content of Cannabis	7
3.	Cannabinoid Analysis	8
4.	Cannabinoid Metabolism	10
5.	Summary	13
6.	Figures	14

Abstract

Chemical composition of cannabis, methods of (cannabinoid) detection, and cannabinoid metabolism are discussed briefly.

Keywords: analysis, cannabinoids, chemistry, metabolism, plants.

Abbreviations: beats (bts); cannabichromeme (CBC); cannabicyclol (CBL); cannabidiol (CBD); cannabigerol (CBG); cannabigerol monomethyl ether (CBGM); cannabinol (CBN); cannabis (C); carboxy-Δ^9 tetrahydrocannabinol (C-THC); degrees north (°N); delta-8 or 9-tetrahydrocannabinol (Δ^8 or Δ^9 THC); dichloro-diphenyl-trichloro-ethane (DDT); electrocardiogram (ECG); 11-hydroxy-Δ^9 tetrahydrocannabinol (11-OH-Δ^9 THC); gas-liquid-chromatography-mass spectrometry (GLC-MS); gram (gm); heart rate (HR); homogeneous enzyme immunoassay (EMIT); hour(s) (hr); intramuscular (IM); intravenous (IV); Linnaeus (L); minute(s) (min); multiple ion detector (MID); nanogram (ng); oral (p.o.); picogram (pg); radioimmunoassay (RIA); thin layer chromatography (TLC).

1. Introduction

Cannabis is a natural plant product containing many substances in varied proportions being comparable to tobacco in this respect vs alcohol which is a single compound. The chemical properties of cannabis and its metabolism are important, serving as an aid in attempting to understand the reported varied and controversial pharmacological actions and clinical outcomes as well as helping to determine dosage schedules for therapeutic uses of cannabinoids and derivatives.

2. Chemical Content of Cannabis

The cultivation, extraction and analysis of cannabis sativa was described by Doorenbos and colleagues in 1971 (Doorenbos et al., 1971). Various marihuana seed types give rise to several variants of plants. Seeds germinate in less than a week when the soil is moist. Plants grow as rapidly as 2 feet/week resulting in 3-25 foot plants at maturity (Fig. 1). Plants mature in August, September, and October after 3 to 5 months growth. According to many botanists, all plants of the genus Cannabis belong to one species, C. sativa (commonly known as marihuana) (Small et al., 1976) even though some report that there are at least 3 species (C. sativa, C. indica, C. ruderalis). The so-called 3 species are really subspecies and varieties (Small, 1977; Small and Cronquist, 1976) as depicted in the diagram (next page) with fibre and drug (strains) plant (wild and cultivated) varieties.

Depending upon the percent concentration of Δ^9 THC (delta-9-tetrahydrocannabinol) and CBD (cannabidiol), there are at least 3 phenotypes (Small and Beckstead, 1973; Small et al., 1975); type I containing mostly THC while type III has mostly CBD with type II having a high content of both THC and CBD (slightly more) which may be a hybridization between phenotypes I and III strains. A fourth phenotype (IV) has been reported to contain trace amounts of CBGM (cannabigerol monomethyl ether). Loss of potency of marihuana occurs with conversion of Δ^9 THC to cannabinol (CBN) via air oxidation while exposure to light leads to loss of cannabinoids (Petersen, 1976; 1980). Δ^9 THC and CBD are present as acids which are products of biosynthesis. Δ^9 THC is stable in ethanol solution (5%), propylene glycol or sesame-oil diluent.

Cannabinoid content is similar in female and male (more slender) plants (Fig. 2) of phenotype I while in phenotype II and III strains, female are more potent (re THC) than male plants (Small et al.,

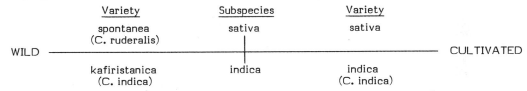

Cannabis Plants: Cannabis sativa (species)

Fibre type or strain; northern plants (north of latitude 30°N). Fibre in blast of stem or bark; oil in fruits (seeds); high CBD (non-intoxicant) content.

Drug type or strain; southern plants (south of latitude 30°N). Intoxicating resin (terpenoid chemicals called cannabinoids with high THC (psychotomimetic) content) in epidermal glands on upper surface of leaves and flowering parts.

1975); the cannabinoid content decreasing in plant parts in the following order: bracts, flowers, leaves (Fig. 3), small stems, large stems, roots and seed. A positive correlation exists between total number of epidermal capitate glands and total cannabinoids per leaf and bract, with glands in the latter containing almost all of the cannabinoids present while those on the leaf having only part of the cannabinoids detected which may be present in one other leaf tissue; the specific site for plant cannabinoid synthesis remaining unknown (Turner et al., 1981). The cannabinoid content is determined more by heredity (genetics) of the plant than climate. It is also related to type of plant, time of harvest, and plant part used. There are individual plant differences in content within a given variant. However, after several generations of growth, the cannabinoid profile tends to drift from the resin type (more THC) to the fibre type (less THC) in temperate climate and vice versa in hot climates. The number of cannabinoids and other chemical substances identified in marihuana continues to increase; the grand total of plant natural cannabinoids estimated to be at least 37 (Mechoulam et al., 1976). A more recent report (Turner et al., 1980) indicates that cannabis sativa L. contains 421 compounds with 61 known cannabinoids which belong to the terpenophenolic chemical class (widely distributed in nature). Cannabis preparations from different geographic locations may have different cannabinoid biogenesis resulting in the growing number of cannabinoids isolated. The potential effects of each substance should be considered. Several cannabinoids (THC, CBD, CBG) have been shown to inhibit incorporation of leucine and uridine into protein and nucleic acids of animal brain cortex slices, and inhibit lymphocyte transformation (CBL) (see section on chromosomes, cell metabolism, and immunity); CBN having 1/10th the psychotomimetic activity of THC while the activity for Δ^8 THC is slightly less than for Δ^9 THC. Antibacterial activity has been reported for CBD and CBG; the latter (CBG) decreasing the rate of absorption and excretion of pentobarbital. CBN possesses anticonvulsant (as does CBD), anti-inflammatory, and immunological properties as well as potentiating THC effects. Other known compounds found in cannabis include nitrogenous compounds (20); amino acids (18); proteins, glycoproteins, and enzymes (9); sugars and related compounds (34); hydrocarbons (50); simple alcohols (7), aldehydes (12), ketones (13) and acids (20); fatty acids (12); simple esters and lactones (13); steroids (11); terpenes (103); non-cannabinoid phenols (16); flavinoidglycosides (19); vitamins (1); and pigments (2). The presence of sterols and triterpenes is of concern because of the possible conversion to carcinogenic hydroperoxides and hydrocarbons. The tar content of cannabis smoke is comparable to that of tobacco smoke (about 5% on leaving a 30 mm butt). Phenols found in the mainstream of cigarette smoke come from the carbohydrate (decarboxylation) content of flue-cured tobacco leaf. This also applies to smoked marihuana. The physiological effects of phenols in tobacco smoke have revealed cocarcinogenesis and ciliostasis which should be watched for in habitual marihuana smokers. Phytosterols which are precursors of carcinogenic hydrocarbons in smoke have been found in tobacco and marihuana smoke (Adams and Jones, 1975).

3. Cannabinoid Analysis

Cannabinoid metabolism in man and animals is complex necessitating specificity in assay procedures for cannabinoids. The quantification of cannabinoids in human blood is difficult because of the small amounts present. This is due to tissue uptake and a large volume of distribution of THC and its metabolites (Lemberger, 1976; Lemberger et al., 1971). Chloroform has proven to be useful in extracting marihuana samples for analysis with methanol extracting cannabinoids from tissues completely (Doorenbos et al., 1971; Schoolar et al., 1976). The preferred method for qualitative and quantitative identification of cannabinoids is a GLC-MS combination (gas-liquid-chromatography-mass spectrometry) which monitors (sensitive detection by MS) the compounds as they leave the column (separation of compounds by GLC) (Mechoulam et al., 1976) The method is used in routine chemical structure elucidation and identification helping to determine the geographical origin of illicit marihuana samples

(Petersen, 1976; 1980). The characteristic slightly sweet odour of marihuana is due to volatile essential oils identified by GLC-MS. GLC-MS has been used for quantitative estimation of Δ^9 THC in experienced marihuana users, 11-hydroxy-Δ^9 THC, and CBN (Fig. 4). Following intravenous administration of 4-5 mg Δ^9 THC in experienced marihuana users, peak plasma levels of Δ^9 THC (50-60 ng/ml) were seen at the 10-20 minute period coinciding with maximum psychotomimetic activity. The amount of 11-OH-Δ^9 THC (metabolite) in plasma was 1/20-1/25th (2-3 ng/ml at peak level with 0.5 ng/ml after 24 hours) that of Δ^9 THC and the CBN amount was insignificant. Elimination of Δ^9 THC from the blood is biphasic; initially being rapid (15-40 minutes) followed by a slower rate up to 24 hours (Lemberger et al., 1971; Wall et al., 1976b) when 3-5 ng/ml THC was still found in plasma. Where measurements (via GLC-MS) were determined earlier following various routes of THC administration (IV, inhalation or smoking, oral) in marihuana (infrequent to frequent) users, the peak THC plasma levels occurred at 3 minutes, > 200 ng THC/ml plasma following intravenous injection (5 mg THC/2 min.) and < 100 ng/ml after smoking (1 cigarette with 19 mg THC) while oral ingestion (1 cookie with 20 mg THC) resulted in a peak (6 ng/ml) at the 1 hour period; the order of peak plasma levels obtained being IV > smoking > oral routes (Hollister et al., 1981). Plasma THC concentrations correlated with degree of subjective "high" (peak at 30 min. post IV, smoking; 2 hours post p.o.) and conjunctival hyperemia or reddening of eyes, a clinical sign of cannabinoid use (peak at 3 min post IV, smoking; 1-3 hr post p.o.; persisting with plasma THC levels > 5 ng/ml). Tachycardia (average increase ranging from 26 to 40 bts/min), another sign of use, occurred at lower plasma THC concentration (4.5 ng/ml) after oral ingestion (vs 45 and 100 ng/ml post smoking and IV respectively) indicating the possibility of active metabolite(s) contributing to pharmacological activity. THC is less bioavailable following the oral route because it reaches the liver directly being metabolized to various metabolites, while following smoking or IV routes, cannabinoids enter the blood directly (via lungs with smoking) flowing through the left side of the heart being pumped to various organs (including the brain) before entering the liver thereby resulting in quicker onset of action (correlating with plasma levels). Mass fragmentography (addition of multiple ion detector; MID) increases the sensitivity (to 0.3 ng/ml) of MS for ng or pg levels (ng or nanogram = 1 billionth gram or 1×10^{-9} gm; pg or picogram = 1 trillionth gm or 1×10^{-12} gm) (Nordqvist et al., 1976; Ohlsson et al., 1976). This would permit following the THC level for 12-24 hours after smoking (Fig. 5) correlating it with physiological and psychological effects. This method has been used in studying (cross-over design at weekly intervals) interactions of ingested (cookies) THC 20 mg with 40 mg CBD, 40 mg CBN and placebo in 12 marihuana experienced men (18-40 years of age) via plasma cannabinoid level determinations; the sensitivity for CBD and CBN being 30 pg and 0.1 ng/ml respectively (Agurell et al., 1981). Peak plasma THC level was 5 ng/ml at the 1 to 2 hour period, decreasing to 1 ng/ml at 10 hours with a similar peak level for CBD which fell off more rapidly resulting in a 0.4 ng/ml level at 10 hours without influencing the pharmacokinetics of THC. Slightly higher plasma levels occurred with THC and CBN, both peaks being similar (9 ng/ml) with 10 hour levels of 0.8 and 0.3 ng/ml respectively. Another method for quantifying plasma CBD (abundant in hashish and fibre type cannabis) is by formation of fluorinated high molecular weight compound (dipentafluorobenzyl CBD) which is then analysed by GC (gas chromatography) equipped with an electron-capture detector (Jones et al., 1981). THCBD (tetrahydro CBD) is used as an internal standard, being added prior to plasma extraction which is a necessity. The detection limit for CBD was 50 ng/ml. Another modification of chromatography, HPLC-MS (high pressure liquid chromatography-mass spectrometry), has been used to quantitatively measure Δ^9 THC in human specimens (plasma, breath, saliva, bile, brain) being accurate over a range of 1-100 ng/ml (Valentine et al., 1976). Following the smoking of one cigarette (10.8 mg THC, 2.16 mg CBN, 0.9 mg CBC, 0.63 mg CBD) by 11 moderate marihuana smokers, peak plasma levels (15.3-66.7 ng THC/ml) were noted at 15 minutes with detection of Δ^9 THC in breath and saliva during the first 60 minutes. Brain and bile levels were higher than in plasma of post-mortem samples. Radioimmunoassay (RIA) methods are used for screening purposes (qualitative) for cannabinoids as a group with a detection limit of 1 ng/ml (Marks et al., 1976; Willette, 1976); being applicable to blood, urine and saliva analyses. Evidence of prior cannabis use is indicated by urinary THC metabolites since lipophilic THC is not excreted by the kidney; the RIA technique detecting these cannabinoids in marihuana smokers for several days after exposure (Chase et al., 1976). By combining RIA (screening) with HPLC (separation), cannabinoids in blood and urine may be quantified for forensic purposes (Law 1981; Law et al., 1979). Using this method, plasma CBN elimination curve was found to be similar (biphasic) to the parent compound THC and not to the monohydroxylated metabolites, indicating that CBN is not a true metabolite but a thermal degradation product of THC arising during smoking. In the occasional marihuana smoker, 1 cigarette (containing 19.8 mg Δ^9 THC) gives rise to a peak Δ^9 THC plasma level (10-130 ng/ml) at the 15-30 minute period being undetectable at 1-2 hours; 11-nor-9-carboxy-Δ^9 THC or carboxy-Δ^9 THC (C-THC), a metabolite, peaks at 30-60 minutes persisting for several (3) hours (Gross and Soares, 1976). Following 3 cigarettes, THC (peak of 100-260 ng/ml) may be detected in plasma up to 3 hours and C-THC up to 48 hours (Fig. 6). Urinary analysis reveals absence of drug levels prior to smoking one cigarette which yields detectable amounts of C-THC (up to 60 ng/ml) up to 48 hours. Chronic marihuana smokers show detectable urinary levels of C-THC (17-123 ng/ml) prior to using 1 cigarette following which great increases occur in C-THC levels at the 2-4 hour peak period (Fig. 7). Metabolism of THC occurs more rapidly in the chronic user than in a naive individual noted by a shorter plasma half-life of THC (28 hours vs 57 hours in naive) and greater renal excretion of metabolites during first 2 days post IV THC (Fig. 8) (Lemberger et al., 1971). Biological levels may, therefore, indicate single substance use just prior to testing or multi-use several days earlier. That is, if THC is not detected in plasma, then marihuana was not smoked within the previous hour. Whereas, if only C-THC is present, then distant exposure may be suspected (Gross and Soares, 1976). A dose-response (subjective "high", HR from ECG) study (double-blind, cross-over design) in 6 experienced marihuana (6-13 years use with current 4-13 cigarettes/month) users (3 men, 3 women; 26-32 years of age; abstinence 7 days pre study) who smoked (at weekly intervals) 3 different potencies (strengths corresponding to street marihuana of 1.32, 1.97, 2.54% THC) of (slightly less than 1 gm) marihuana cigarettes (1/14-18 min) determined plasma THC and 9-carboxy metabolite levels via RIA verified by GLC-MS in 5% of blood samples (Perez-Reyes et al., 1982). The degree of responses ("high", tachycardia) and plasma cannabinoid levels varied proportionately with potencies of marihuana cigarettes smoked (especially between low and high doses); the smoking pattern not being altered by the potencies studied. THC consumed was 9.7, 12.8, and 16 mg with less cigarette consumed with increasing potency; the unsmoked cigarette portion containing the original THC concentration. Peak plasma THC concentration (100-163 ng/ml) was reached at 7-8 minutes after beginning smoking with peak plasma 9-carboxy THC (34-50 ng/ml) levels occurring at 20-28 min period. The peak pharmacological effects appeared at 20-33 min interval, peak tachycardia preceding the peak "high" by 2-3 minutes. A lack of correlation is apparent between plasma THC concentration and pharmacological effects which appear to be more closely related to plasma carboxy-THC levels which were also found in pre-study abstinent period. Carboxy-THC was shown to be deficient in pharmacological effects following IV metabolite to 3 subjects. Women tended to have higher plasma THC concentration (127%) with less physiological (90%) and psychological (77%) effects than men. Another method used in general urine (50 ul) screening for cannabinoid use is EMIT homogeneous enzyme immunoassay for THC and metabolites (detection range of 0.5-10 ug/l) revealing (Fig. 9) peak cannabinoid excretion at 2-6 hours post exposure (one marihuana cigarette; THC content?) with high level duration of up to 24 hours; frequent users having higher basal metabolite levels than peak values of infrequent users (Rubenstein, 1979). Another means of detecting and quantifying cannabinoids in urine is by utilizing a specific chemical reaction between cannabinoids and diazonium salts giving azo compounds which are chelated to a metallic salt (such as gallium) resulting in fluorescent compounds. The fluorescent intensity emitted by the chelates is then measured against a standard (Bourdon, 1976). A simple means of detecting marihuana use is by analysis of saliva or fingertip washings rather than blood. Cannabinoid detection is evident in saliva 1-2 hours after smoking a cigarette with 2.8 mg THC (Just et al., 1974; 1976), and in fingertip washings 1-3 hours using a TLC (thin layer chromatography) and MS techniques. TLC has been used to detect THC-11-oic acid (carboxy-THC) a major urinary cannabinoid metabolite (both conjugated and unconjugated), found in man 1.5 hours after smoking a marihuana cigarette (16-18 mg THC), thereby providing another screening procedure for determining marihuana use (Kanter et al., 1982a; b). Positive results have been obtained one week after admission to treatment programs; 28 days in one user (20-30 marihuana cigarettes/day/3 months). Geographical origin of cannabis products has been determined by TLC and gross physical appearance of materials (Baker et al., 1980). A simple rapid (one minute) sensitive specific field test for ($\leq$ 1 mg) marihuana (and products) uses a dry reagent microcolumn coated with Fast Blue B salt which remains stable to environmental factors such as light, air and moisture; spectrometry confirming suspected material (Lau-Cam and Piggitola, 1979). Presently it is not possible to interpret cannabinoid levels in terms of intoxication as with alcohol and other drugs (Petersen, 1976).

4.   Cannabinoid Metabolism

Smoked marihuana appears to have at least four cannabinoid constituents which are Δ^9 THC (delta-9-tetrahydrocannabinol), CBD (cannabidiol), CBN (cannabinol) and CBC (cannabichromeme). Psychotomimetic properties appear to be due to Δ^9 THC. Plasma levels of Δ^9 THC and metabolites correlate with physiological changes seen following the smoking of a cigarette with 10.8 mg Δ^9 THC, 2.16 mg CBN, 0.9 mg CBC, and 0.63 mg CBD. (Valentine et al., 1976). The major active principle of marihuana (Δ^9 or Δ^1 THC) was isolated in pure form, structure elucidated, and synthesized in 1964 (Mechoulam, 1973). The rhesus monkey has been used as a suitable model for testing (IV administration) most cannabis effects except euphoria and hallucinations. Activity variations observed in THC homologues are not due solely to lipid solubility but rather to orientation of the molecule within the receptor site area. Δ^9 THC (or Δ^1 THC) has a fairly high molecular weight of 302 and no nitrogen atom. This differs from other drugs of abuse which have nitrogen enabling formation of water-soluble salts. This problem of water solubility makes it difficult to give well defined doses in clinical trials. However, standardization of smoking methods have resulted in dose related responses.

Oral activity of THC in humans has been noted to be 2-3 mg (Edery et al., 1971). Smoking results in 50% THC being absorbed into the blood stream (50% destroyed on smoking with some cannabinoid acids surviving the smoking process) with a maximal plasma THC concentration of about 100 nanograms/ml appearing at the 5 minute interval following approximately 5 mg THC (Fig. 10). The

Structural Formula for THC

- Δ^9 or Δ^1 THC (delta-9 or delta-1 (depending upon which numbering system is used) tetrahydrocannabinol);

- Δ (delta) refers to double bond position;

- Δ^8 or Δ^6 with double bond (=) between 8-9 or 1 - 6 positions.

bioavailability following smoking THC is ten times greater than when ingested as seen by a maximal plasma concentration of around 10 nanograms/ml, usually 1-1.5 hours (may be up to 5 hours) post 20 mg THC taken orally (Agurell et al., 1979). Δ^9 THC binds readily to human plasma proteins (lipoproteins). Thus only a small amount of free Δ^9 THC is necessary for activity. In animals rapid clearance occurs from the blood to liver, fat, brain, spleen, lung, kidney, and reproductive tissues. Following chronic dosing, accumulation takes place in the fat and liver. Maximum total cannabinoid concentrations reached in various organs 2 to 4 hours after acute (1 dose) 2 uCi I.M. $^{14}C-\Delta^8$ THC (at C-11) in rodents were 70 ng/gm liver tissue, 26 ng/gm epididymal fat, 18 ng/gm lung tissue (at one hour), 7 ng/gm spleen tissue, 6 ng/gm brain tissue, 4.5 ng/gm peripheral blood, and 2 ng/gm gonadal tissue (Nahas et al., 1981). Chronic dosing (3 to 6 injections/14 days) resulted in increasing cannabinoid concentrations in liver from 28 to 40 ng/gm tissue, in fat from 40 to 90 ng/gm with blood, brain and testis levels remaining essentially constant at 6-8, 4-6, and 3-4 ng/gm tissue respectively. It was suggested that relatively low plasma cannabinoid concentrations may not correlate with tissue concentrations thereby making it difficult to correlate plasma levels with pharmacodynamic effects. High hepatic cannabinoid levels may be due to metabolites while liposolubility may lead to high fat levels with accumulation accounting for the long biological half-life of cannabinoids. Isotope studies have revealed THC in the milk of animals as well as in the urine and feces of suckling infants. Autoradiographic studies in animals revealed drug accumulation in salivary glands, adrenal gland (with hormonal producing cortical cells) and brain (especially structures involved in processing visual and acoustic information and in motor control) (Just et al., 1976). THC content of cannabis smoke may not be the sole ingredient following smoking. Pyrolysis (chemical change due to heat) of cannabis, i.e. smoke, gives rise to various new known and unknown compounds which may or may not be pharmacologically active. It has been shown that CBD is partially converted to THC and CBN (Kephalis et al., 1976; Salemink, 1976).

The metabolism of Δ^9 THC, Δ^8 THC, CBD, and CBN (in marihuana smoke) in man occurs in the liver via the major route of hydroxylation (by hepatic microsomal oxygenase or drug-metabolizing enzyme) to active 11-hydroxy metabolites (excreted in the feces via bile) followed by further oxidation to carboxylic (11-nor THC-9 carboxylic acid or carboxy THC or THC-11-oic acid) and polar (polyhydroxy) acids found mainly in plasma and urine with some in feces (Burstein and Kupfer, 1971; Wall, 1971; Wall et al., 1976a). A slower minor route may occur simultaneously involving hydroxylation at the 8α, 8β, or side chain positions (Wall and Brine, 1976). Metabolite composition varies with species (animal, human) studied and experimental conditions. Sites for transformation of THC occur in heart and lungs of animals, although the metabolism is not as extensive as in the liver (Harvey and Paton, 1976). The proportions of metabolites (major and minor) may vary indicating differences in metabolism in organs that are metabolically active. More than 50 metabolites have been found and identified (Braude, 1976). Hydroxylation of the side chain of major metabolites has shown behavioural change in animals which may suggest higher psychotomimetic activity than the parent compound (THC). However, whether these metabolites are significant in man is unknown (Agurell et al., 1976). Hydroxylation at the 11-position appears to be partly responsible for the psychological (euphoria) (Fig. 11) and pulse rate effects of cannabinoids in man (Lemberger et al., 1976), and analgesia in animals (Wilson and May, 1976). Δ^9 THC and 11-hydroxy-Δ^9 THC (metabolite) are considered to be equipotent in that equal doses of each produces similar effects in man with the 11-hydroxy metabolite disappearing from the plasma compartment at a faster rate (Fig. 12). The metabolite penetrates the brain faster (observed in animals) than the parent compound which may account for a quicker onset of action (subjective "high" feeling, increased heart rate) for the metabolite (Fig. 13; 14). However, Δ^9 THC is more potent in that a lower brain concentration is required for marihuana-like effects (Perez-Reyes et al., 1976). The intact monkey brain is capable of metabolizing Δ^9 THC to 11-hydroxy metabolite as noted by higher venous (vs arterial) radioactivity blood levels (Fig. 15) following THC (labeled) intraventricular injection indicating a slow release of drug (radioactivity) from the brain and a higher proportion of metabolite in venous blood due to metabolite formation in the brain (Ben-Zvi et al., 1976).

The pattern of THC metabolism in men and women is the same following IV (4-5 mg/20-25 min in 7 subjects), p.o. (20 mg in 6 subjects) or smoking by water pipe or reefer (10-20 mg with 40% inhaled resulting in 4-8 mg THC) routes (Wall and Perez-Reyes, 1981). Equal amounts of plasma THC and active 11-OH metabolite (6-8 ng/ml at 2-3 hours) were found after oral intake with 11-nor-THC-9 carboxylic and polar acids being the major plasma constituents (65-70 ng/ml), while after IV and smoking routes the 11-OH metabolite was a minor constituent (1/10th of THC which peaked at 60 ng/ml), the major constituents being 11-nor and polar acids (which are formed from 11-OH-THC). The plasma half-life post IV and oral THC was found to be around 30 hours. The major urinary metabolites are 11-nor-THC-9 carboxylic and polar acids; 10-15% of total dose being excreted/72 hours. The main excretion route is via feces with 11-OH-THC being the major component together with carboxylic and polar acids; 35% of total dose excreted/72 hours. It is thought that side chain hydroxylation is not a significant factor in THC metabolism. Related cannabinoids follow the THC metabolic pattern. Plasma levels and systemic availability (area under curve values) following IV deuterium labelled ($^2H_3$) THC (5 mg/2 min) were similar in heavy (at least 1 x/day use) and light (not more than once per month use) users while after smoking 10 mg THC (8.6-9.9 mg/3 min), systemic availability was greater in heavy (27%) than in light (14%) users due to more efficient smoking by heavy users who preferred higher plasma drug levels (Ohlsson et al., 1982). Plasma clearance was calculated to be 760-1190 ml/min (liver plasma flow of 800 ml/min) with elimination half-life of THC being > 20 hours (based on 72 hours determinations). It was felt that metabolic tolerance to THC was not evident as indicated by the IV data. Minimal changes noted in THC metabolism (using 2 mg radiolabelled ^{14}C-THC IV/2 min) post chronic oral THC (30 mg q4h/12 days followed by placebo/6-8 days in 6 (one with 20 mg THC dose) experienced male volunteers who had smoked 11-40 marihuana cigarettes/week/average 5-8 years) vs pre-chronic phase (placebo/9 days) could not account for reversible tolerance development (acute effects assessed via smoking 1 gm cannabis cigarettes with 2.2% THC/8-10 min pre, during and after the chronic oral phase) to cannabinoid pharmacological effects (cardiovascular tachycardia, psychological subjective "high", and hypothermic (fingertip temperature) effects) indicating a possible functional or adaptive tolerance rather than a metabolic one (Hunt and Jones, 1980). Plasma THC time course was essentially unaltered with tolerance development, which increased average metabolic clearance, apparent initial volume of distribution, and metabolic half-life resulting in slightly lower plasma THC levels; the time course for plasma metabolites being unaffected with percent of IV dose excreted in urine decreased (lipophilic cannabinoids being highly protein-bound). Lack of metabolic tolerance to marihuana had been reported in rodents (Siemens and Kalant, 1974).

As noted above, THC binds readily with plasma lipoproteins (97%). It is taken up by tissues and metabolized completely by the liver rapidly; both THC and metabolites concentrating in the lungs, liver, myocardium, adrenals, spleen, and fat. The half-life of THC (time required for half the amount of the drug to be eliminated) in tissues (post IV THC) is reported to be 7 days (due to slow release from tissues) indicating accumulation in the body; daily dosing/27 days leading to a 10-fold increase in accumulated body THC vs a single dose. By 5 days, 15-17% of the dose appears as metabolites in the urine and 40-45% is biliary excreted in the feces with a 15% entero-hepatic recirculation of biliary metabolites. The slow elimination of metabolites with a half-life of 50 hours (vs IV metabolites which are rapidly excreted) is due to the slow rate determining return of THC from deep compartments to plasma (Garrett, 1979). Clinically urinary cannabinoid excretion persisted for at least 3 weeks following supervised abstinence from chronic marihuana use (1-6 joints/day; potency?) in 7 polydrug (alcohol, amphetamines, barbiturates, cocaine, diazepam, hallucinogens, heroin, methadone, methaqualone) using psychiatric patients screened for cannabinoids using an EMIT assay (Dackis et al., 1982). CBN may be an intermediary (?) in THC metabolism. Whereas, CBD may interfere with the metabolism(inhibition) of THC and 11-hydroxy-THC accounting for the different activities of crude cannabis extracts. This has been seen in animals as decreased metabolite formation in the liver, a dose-dependent inhibition of biliary excretion of THC metabolites, and accumulation of unchanged THC in the lungs (Siemens et al., 1976). Exposure to other drugs and environmental contaminants (DDT) may alter THC metabolism (stimulate) as well as induce its own metabolism by repeated administration (animal studies).

Antibodies specific for small molecules (haptens) can be produced by immunization with conjugates consisting of a given hapten covalently linked to carrier molecules such as proteins. Active immunization with Δ^9 THC-0-hemisuccinate-porcine γ-globulin (a THC-protein conjugate i.e. cannabinoid-CONH-protein) was found to neutralize the depressant effect of Δ^9 THC on motor activity in animals (Mechoulam et al., 1976). This may prove useful in treatment of marihuana addiction or amotivational syndrome by making an individual resistant to the effects of marihuana. The principle of immunization has been used to develop immunoassay techniques (above) for determining cannabinoids in body fluids.

5. Summary

From the above one may deduce that marihuana is not a simple pure substance as alcohol. There is only one species of marihuana plant (cannabis sativa) with 2 subspecies which have wild and cultivated varieties.   Cannabinoids (61 known) in marihuana may be biologically active (such as interferring with nucleic acid and protein synthesis) with (THC) or without (CBD, CBG) psychoactivity. Cannabinoid content may be analysed by GLC-MS, mass fragmentography, electron-capture gas chromatography and HPLC-MS techniques with qualitative screening of biological fluids (for cannabinoids) being accomplished by immunoassay methods (RIA; EMIT) and TLC. Detection of plasma THC indicates recent (previous hour) marihuana use while the presence of only C-THC (carboxy-THC) suggests exposure several days earlier.   Urinary cannabinoids are evident for several days after marihuana exposure; chronic users having detectable levels prior to current exposure. THC has been detected in saliva, breath, and fingertip washings (1-3 hr) following smoking using TLC. Various routes of THC administration (IV, inhalation by smoking, oral) yield plasma levels which are related to onset, degree and duration of clinical effects ("high", pulse rate, conjunctival reddening) taking into consideration rate of absorption, distribution and metabolism of administered drug. The degree of pharmacological responses and plasma cannabinoid levels attained vary in a dose related manner depending upon the potency (% THC) of marihuana smoked; the peak pharmacological effects correlating with peak plasma carboxy-THC (inactive metabolite) levels. CBD does not influence THC pharmacokinetics while CBN (thought to be a thermal degradation product of smoking marihuana) potentiates peak plasma THC levels.

Marihuana is usually smoked as a cigarette weighing 0.5 to 1 gm with 1-2% THC (5-20 mg); increased potency of 3% or more being reported in recent years. The dried resin (exuded from marihuana plant being richer in cannabinoids) or hashish (5-10x potency of marihuana) is often mixed with tobacco and smoked. Loss of potency occurs following exposure to air, light, humidity, and high temperature. Approximately 50% THC (psychoactive component) is lost by smoking marihuana with a bioavailability of 10x oral route and psychoactivity 4x oral route. This difference in THC bioavailability may be due to orally administered THC reaching the liver directly where it is metabolized to metabolites, whereas smoking (inhalation; similar to IV effects) introduces cannabinoids into the lungs entering the bloodstream which courses through the left side of the heart reaching organs (including brain) before passing through the liver thereby resulting in quicker onset of action (correlating with plasma cannabinoid levels) with smoking vs oral ingestion. THC binds with plasma lipoproteins (97%) and is metabolized mainly in the liver being distributed to various tissues (lungs, heart, spleen, adrenals, fat, brain and gonads). A similar pattern of THC metabolism occurs in men and women; THC being hydroxylated to 11-OH-THC which is oxidized to carboxylic (11-nor-9 carboxy THC or THC-11-oic acid) and polar (polyhydroxy) acids found in plasma, urine and feces. Plasma constituents include THC, 11-OH-THC (especially after oral intake), carboxy THC and polar acids; plasma THC half-life occurring around 30 hours. The major urinary metabolites are carboxy THC and polar acids which are also found in feces (major route of excretion) where 11-OH-THC is the major component. Metabolic tolerance to THC has not been evident; reversible pharmacological tolerance development perhaps being functional or adaptive. The water insoluble THC (due to lack of nitrogen atom in molecule) accumulates in the fat depots of the body with a half-life of 7 days; the complete elimination of one dose requiring 30 days and a "steady state" (elimination = absorption) being reached after 4 weeks daily administration. Enterohepatic recirculation of metabolites encourages their retention; the 11-hydroxy metabolite having active (equipotent to THC) pharmacological properties.

Metabolites produced in the lungs differ from those produced by the liver indicating that effects of the drug may depend upon the route of administration (smoking vs oral ingestion) (Petersen, 1976; 1980). Interactions occur between marihuana constituents (cannabidiol, cannabinol) and Δ^9 THC (principle psychoactive ingredient) in animals. Thus different varieties of cannabis with different compositions as well as different effects may be only partly related to the biological THC level. Accumulation of metabolites (conjugates of palmitic and stearic acid) appear in tissues with repeated exposure to cannabinoids, the biological significance of which is unknown. At the present time it is difficult to determine which substance should be measured (by simple technique comparable to the alcohol breathalyser test because both parent compound(s) and metabolites are pharmacologically active) and correlated with a consistent response (e.g. performance impairment). This is important for forensic purposes (impaired driving). Pharmacokinetic investigations are therefore necessary for each type of marihuana preparation and each new substance discovered, correlating the various biological substance levels (plasma, urine) with their pharmacological and toxicological properties. Attempts are being made in this direction. However it may be difficult to correlate cannabinoid plasma levels with pharmacodynamic effects because such levels may not reflect tissue concentrations.

II. 2. Chemistry and Metabolism

List of Figures

Fig. 1.   Marihuana plantation   15
Fig. 2.   Cannabis plants   16
Fig. 3   Cannabis leaf   17
Fig. 4.   Plasma cannabinoid levels in marihuana users   18
Fig. 5.   THC plasma levels   19
Fig. 6.   Plasma THC and C-THC   20
Fig. 7.   Urinary C-THC   20
Fig. 8.   Renal excretion of metabolites   21
Fig. 9.   Cannabinoids in urine   21
Fig. 10.   Plasma THC levels post smoking or oral intake   22
Fig. 11.   THC and metabolite effects   23
Fig. 12.   Plasma THC or 11-OH-THC radioactivity levels   24
Fig. 13.   Psychological effects   25
Fig. 14.   Percent heart rate increase   26
Fig. 15.   THC metabolism in animal brain   27

Fig. 1.   Marihuana plantation at the Central Experimental Farm, Ottawa,
II.2   Canada in 1970. Plants exceeding 3m (10 ft) were present.

             Courtesy of Dr. E. Small, Agriculture Canada.

Fig. 2.   Plants of cannabis. The male (left) is usually more delicate and begins
II.2   to wither, like the plant shown here, after the pollen is shed.   The
             female (right) is more robust and lives until killed by frost.

Courtesy of Dr. E. Small, Agriculture Canada.

Fig. 3.
II.2

Leaf of cannabis. Marihuana leaves are "compound", composed of several leaflets, usually of an odd number (7 in this example), "palmately" arranged (radiating from a central point).

Courtesy of Dr. E. Small, Agriculture Canada.

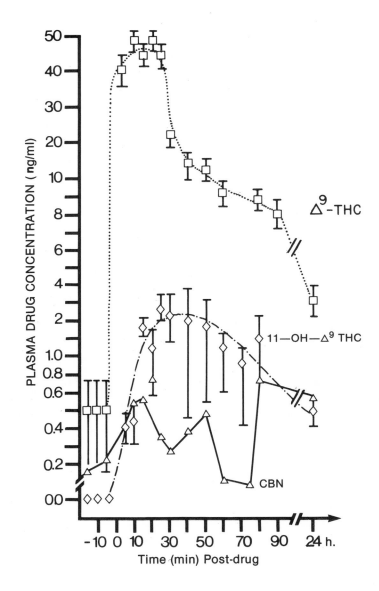

Fig. 4.   Plasma cannabinoid levels post IV THC (4-5 mg) in experienced
II.2   marihuana users.

Adapted from Wall et al., 1976b.

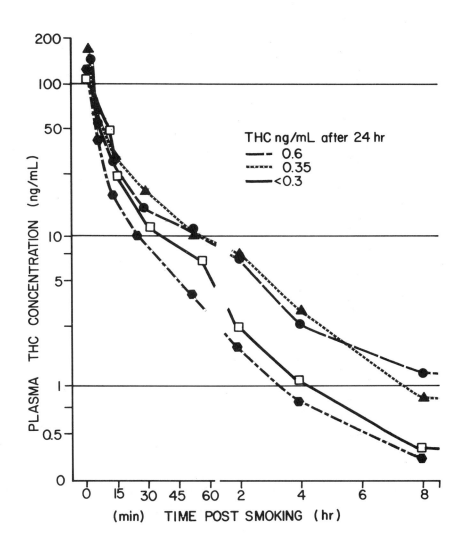

Fig. 5.   THC plasma levels after smoking THC (8.3 mg).
II.2
               Adapted from Ohlsson et al., 1976.

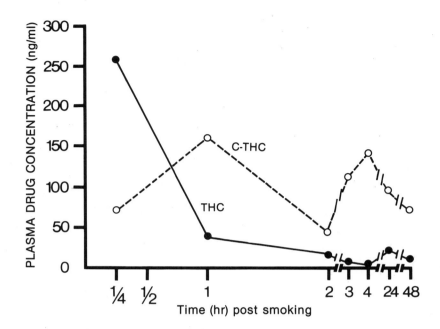

Fig. 6.   Plasma THC and C-THC (carboxy-THC; metabolite) post (smoking) 3
II.2   marihuana cigarettes (2.2% THC/cig.) in occasional marihuana users.

Adapted from Gross and Soares, 1976.

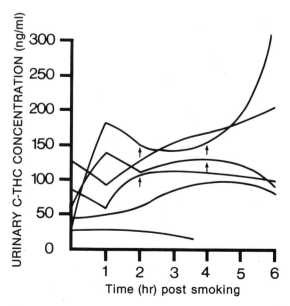

Fig. 7.   Urinary C-THC (ng/ml) in 6 chronic marihuana users post one mari-
II.2   huana cigarette with 2.2% THC (additional cigarette at arrow).

Adapted from Gross and Soares, 1976.

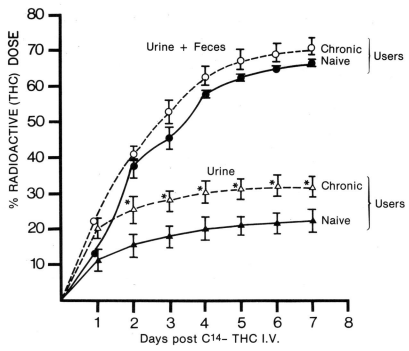

Fig. 8.   Renal excretion of metabolites post IV ^{14}C-THC in naive and chronic
II.2   marihuana users.

Adapted from Lemberger et al., 1971.

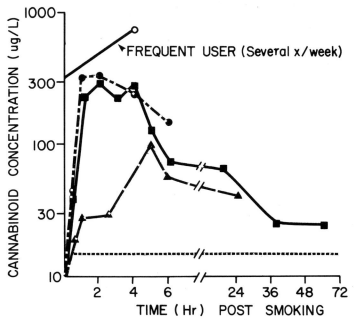

Fig. 9.   Cannabinoids in urine after smoking one marihuana cigarette in 4
II.2   marihuana users.

Adapted from Rubenstein, 1979.

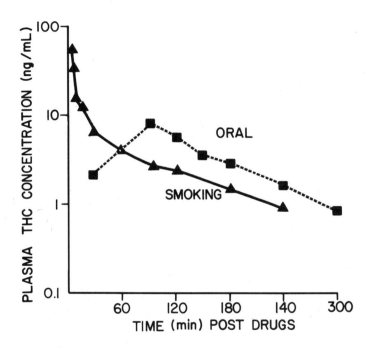

Fig. 10.   Plasma THC levels post smoking 5 mg and oral 20 mg THC.
II.2
                Adapted from Agurell et al., 1979.

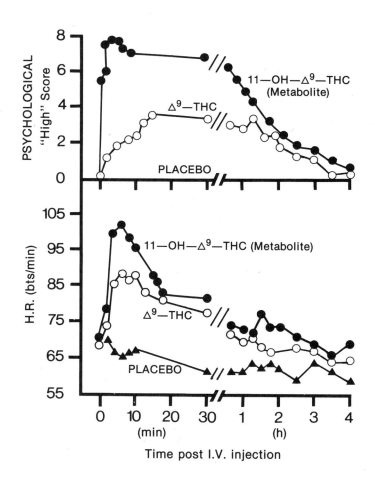

Fig. 11. THC and metabolite effects post 1 mg IV in 6 casual marihuana users.
II.2

Adapted from Lemberger et al., 1976.

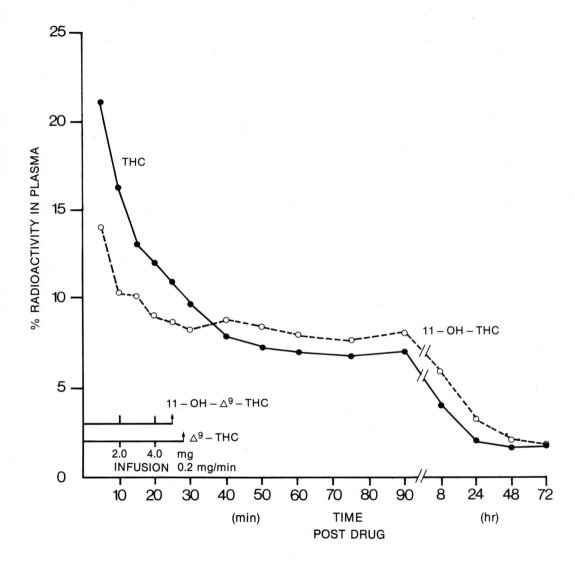

Fig. 12.
II.2   Plasma radioactivity levels post 5 mg (average) IV THC or 11-OH-THC
in 20 marihuana users.

Adapted from Perez-Reyes et al., 1976.

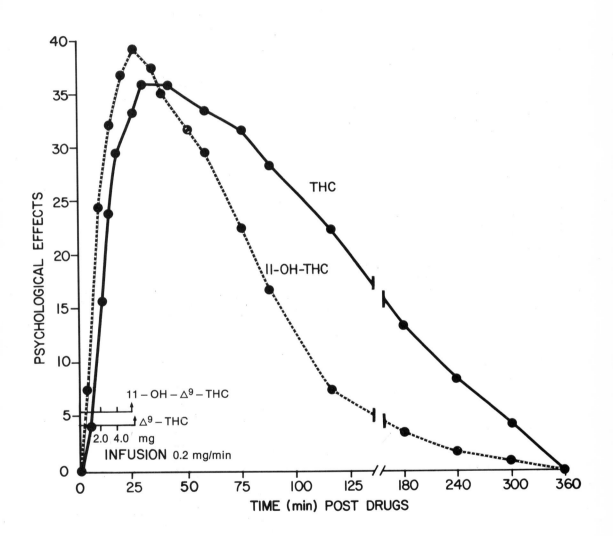

Fig. 13.   Psychological effects post IV THC or 11-OH-THC reported by mari-
II.2   huana users.

            Adapted from Perez-Reyes et al., 1976.

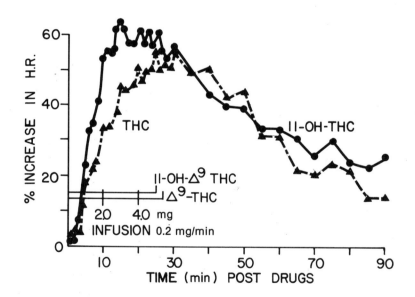

Fig. 14.   Percent heart rate increase post IV THC or 11-OH-THC in marihuana
II.2   users.

              Adapted from Perez-Reyes et al., 1976.

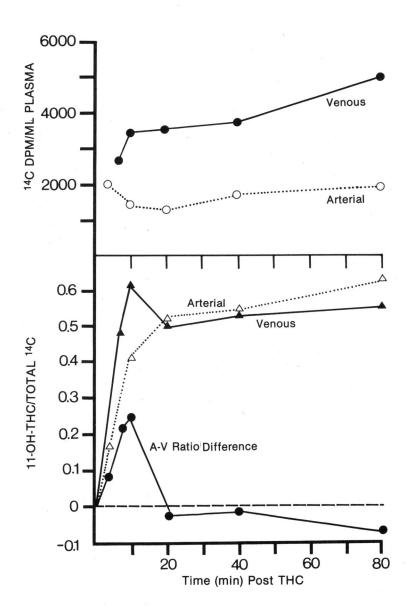

Fig. 15.   THC metabolism with formation of 11-OH-THC (metabolite) in
II.2   monkey brain post intraventricular labeled THC injection.

Adapted from Ben-Zvi et al., 1976.

II. 3. Known and Possible Clinical Effects

Introductory Remarks

As noted in the chemistry and metabolism section, marihuana is not a simple substance but a mixture of several cannabinoids, the potency of which varies with the plant source. With the synthesis of the major psychoactive component, Δ^9 THC, the results of investigations (animals and man) have been comparable with respect to marihuana-like effects. In the main, the following sections will deal with these investigations keeping in mind that knowledge (pharmacological including toxicological) is still lacking regarding other components in marihuana as well as various compounds produced by smoking. That is, interactions between the various substances have not been completely assessed.

The discussion begins and follows through with cellular effects of marihuana and possible clinical implications in the genetic system (chromosomes), immunological system (T and B cells), reproductive system (sperm cell; endocrine function), CNS (including ultrastructure alteration), followed by pulmonary and cardiovascular systems which are necessary to maintain the above systems (in a healthy newborn individual with genetic endowments including potential intelligence) and ending with some field studies looking for chronic cannabis effects in healthy individuals (whole organism). Each section discusses normal physiology as well as some relevant known pathological changes in order to place varied alterations brought about by marihuana into clinical perspective. In several controversial areas relatively detailed accounts of research are presented with respect to subjects studied, material (marihuana, hashish, THC) and dose used, schedule or regimen followed, so as to better understand the various outcomes reported, placing them into proper context with respect to each other when comparing and assessing results. Graphs illustrated in the sections are adaptations (to help visualize some marihuana effects) from published reports as noted; details to be found in the respective publications. Following the discussions, an overview of each area is presented in the form of general summaries leading into conclusion and final comments which include metabolic effects (adequate functioning of liver (metabolism; including pancreas) and kidneys (excretion of by-products of metabolism) necessary to maintain well-being of an individual) with a hypothesis to explain the multi-system cannabis effects and ending with a final provocative precise conclusion.

II. 3. A. Chromosomes, Cell Metabolism, Immunity

Contents

	Abstract	29
1.	Introduction	29
2.	Medical Genetics	
	(a) General Aspects	30
	(b) Genetic Modifications	30
3.	Immune System	
	(a) Cellular and Humoral Immunity	31
	(b) Development of Immunological Status	32
	(c) Immunodeficiency Diseases	32
	(d) Hypersensitivity Reactions	33
	(e) Immunosuppressants; stress	34
4.	Marihuana Effects	
	(a) Genetic Effects - Chromosomal Aberrations	34
	(b) Cell Metabolism - Effects on Macromolecular (DNA, RNA, Protein) Synthesis	37
	(c) Effects on Cellular (T-cell) and Humoral (B-cell) or Antibody Mediated Immune Systems; and on Phagocytic Pulmonary Alveolar Macrophage System	39
5.	Discussion and Summary	45
6.	Figures	48

Abstract

1. Medical genetics and the immune system are discussed briefly prior to presenting marihuana effects in these areas (including cellular metabolism).

2. Chromosomal aberrations observed in chronic marihuana users represent altered cellular metabolism in the nuclear area.

3. The clinical significance of the reported varied changes in immune system components is presently unknown but may be important in individuals with borderline immunological competence.

4. Allergic (hypersensitivity) reactions to marihuana may occur in those with medical histories of allergy (incidence?); an occupational immediate type allergy having been reported.

Keywords: alveolar macrophage, cell metabolism, chromosomes, genetics, immunology.

Abbreviations: antibodies (IgA, IgC, IgE IgG, IgM); bone marrow lymphocytes (B-cells); cannabidiol (CBD); cannabinol (CBN); central nervous system (CNS); chromosome arms - short (p), long (q); cubic millimetres (cu mm); delayed type hypersensitivity (DTH); deoxyribonucleic acid (DNA); dinitrochloro-benzene (DNCB); effective dose for 50% population (ED_{50}); 11-hydroxy-THC (11-OH-THC); eosinophilic chemotactic factor (ECF); fetal alcohol syndrome (FAS); focus forming virus (FFV); Friend leukemia virus (FLV); gamma (γ); grams (gm); group (GP); immunoglobulin (Ig); intraperitoneal (IP or i.p.); intratracheal (IT); intravenous (IV); kilogram (kg); lethal dose for 50% population (LD_{50}); lipopolysaccharide mitogen (LPS); lymphocytic leukemia virus (LLV); lysergic acid diethylamide (LSD); mercaptopurine (MP); micro (μ); migration inhibition factor (MIF); milligram (mg); mixed lymphocyte culture (MLC); molar, moles (M); nanogram (ng); per os or oral (p.o.); percent (%); phytohemagglutinin (PHA); radioactive elements or isotopes (^{3}H, ^{14}C); red blood cell (RBC); reticuloendothelial system (RES); ribonucleic acid (RNA); sex chromosomes - female (2X), male (XY); sheep red blood cells (SRBC); slow reactive substance of anaphylaxis (SRS-A); staphlococcus (staph); subcutaneous (SC); systemic lupus erythematosus (SLE); tetrahydrocannabinol (THC); thymus-dependent lymphocytes (T-cells); ultra violet light (UVL); white blood cell (WBC).

1.   Introduction

A great deal of concern has been expressed over possible biological implications of cannabis effects on immunity, chromosomes and cell metabolism. Chromosomal and cellular metabolic altera-tions could influence reproduction, growth, and genetic transmission of abnormalities while depression of the immune response could increase susceptibility to disease (infections, cancer) and/or prevent tissue rejection following transplant surgery. In order to understand the implications of research results in this area, medical genetics and the immune system will be discussed briefly.

2.   Medical Genetics

(a)   General Aspects

Genetic factors (or genome established at conception) interact with environment (internal and external) to shape individual development. The genome may be altered by mutation (inheritable alteration of gene) via environmental changes. Most diseases have a genetic element which varies from a slight role in bacterial diseases found in the more susceptible male (therefore not being entirely environmental), to specific genetic defects (mongolism); the varying proportions of genetic and environmental factors (between the two extremes) yielding birth defects and metabolic disorders. Hereditary transmission occurs with duplication of DNA molecules which make up the genes (basic units of heredity) and supply the genetic code (regulates cell metabolism and development by controlling RNA synthesis). Cellular (or protein) function depends upon the amino acid composition of proteins which is determined by the sequential order of components in RNA. Chromosomes (rod-shaped in cell nucleus), which bear the many genes, number 46 in each cell (23 pairs) including one pair of sex chromosomes. In each cell nucleus, the female has 2X chromosomes and the male, 1X and 1Y. The two members of a pair of sex chromosomes are not identical (heterologous); the larger X chromosome being responsible for many hereditary traits and sex determination while the Y chromosome is different structurally and in size (smaller) with genes determining only the male sex. The other 22 pairs of chromosomes (autosomes) have pairs identical in shape, size, and genetic loci (homologous). Genes, arranged in linear order along chromosomes, have their own specific loci, the number and arrangement of which on homologous chromosomes are identical and are called alleles. There are 2 alleles for each kind of gene (one on each chromosome of a pair) which, if identical, denote a homozygote; a dissimilar pair, heterozygote. A dominant gene is present on only one chromosome; a recessive gene in both members of a chromosome pair (or single X of a male or XO female). A gene located on the X-chromosome is X-linked, otherwise it is autosomal.

(b)   Genetic Modifications

Genetic alterations are classed as:

(i) "mendelian" or single gene mutations with inherited recognizable patterns

(ii) polygenic or multifactorial inheritance; interaction of genetic mutations and non-genetic (environment) factors without a predictable pattern, and

(iii) chromosomal aberrations or abnormalities; abnormal number and structural defects.

A brief discussion of examples of the 3 types of genetic changes ensues.

(i) A single gene defect is responsible for osteogenesis imperfecta (an autosomal dominant disorder) a connective tissue abnormality affecting many structures in the body. There are more than 2000 identified conditions for which mathematical predicted risks of producing affected offspring can be made.

(ii) Multifactorial inheritance is exemplified by a large number of congenital anomalies with a continuously distributed variable with a threshold separating affected from normal individuals. The affected have a predisposition (liability genes) to a condition representing the sum of genetic and environmental factors. For example, neural tube defects (myelomeningocele; spina bifida (defect in spinal column with absence of vertebral arches) with protrusion of cord and membranes) have a higher incidence in certain geographical areas, although, the environmental agent has not been identified. The human has a great capacity to vary in genotype (genetic or hereditary constitution) and phenotype (visible properties of an organism due to gene-environment interaction). Phenotypically similar conditions may be due to different mutations (heterogeneity), non-genetic factors or combination of both. Concern is growing regarding the teratogenic effects of drugs taken during pregnancy. For example, a large amount of maternal alcohol ingestion during pregnancy increases the risk of an FAS infant (fetal alcohol syndrome; severe intrauterine growth retardation and malformations). Thus, the cause of a problem and future risk is established via a thorough family history including possible environmental teratogens. Many forms of cancer are another example of multifactorial inheritance, though little is known about the genetics of most types. It is felt that most malignancies occur in genetically predisposed individuals exposed to environmental carcinogens (many unknown). In carcinoma of the breast, daughters of similarily affected women are at higher risk than the general population. Immunologic deficiency diseases (inherited a-and dys-γ-globulinemias) increase the risk of lymphoid system malignancies (lymphomas and leukemias which may have variable chromosomal anomalies). The incidence of various mutations in different populations is important since the risk of a particular disorder depends on the frequency of a particular gene in the population, differing in various racial and ethnic groups (Tay-Sachs disease is more frequent in a particular Jewish population (East European) vs non-Jews].

(iii) Precision of cytogenetic diagnosis has been increased by enabling identification of each chromosome by a banding technique (staining process). Chromosome preparations are made from cultured cells (obtained from human cells (including circulating lymphocytes) and tissues] which are stimulated to divide (by PHA; phytohemagglutinin, a bean extract) arresting the mitosis (by colchicine) during metaphase when chromosomes are best seen. The number of chromosomes may be abnormal (Down's syndrome or mongolism with an extra chromosome 21 or trisomy 21) with variants such as translocation of an additional chromosome or mosaic of 2 cell lines (normal and 47 chromosomes), the proportion of which may vary in tissues (intelligence depends on the proportion of trisomy 21 cells in the brain). A structural defect may occur in a chromosome (absence of short arms "p" of chromosome 5 in cat-cry syndrome; "q" is the long arm of a chromosome). The Barr body or sex chromatin mass in female somatic cell nuclei is the genetically inactivated second X-chromosome. X-chromosome anomalies are relatively benign vs autosomal disorders (Down's syndrome) due to the inactivation of an extra X-chromosome or absence of X-chromosome (Turner's syndrome). Most syndromes associated with chromosome anomalies occur only once in a family with optimistic prognosis for future offspring except in Down's syndrome (with or without a translocation) when maternal age is important. Chromosomal anomalies are often accompanied by infant low birth weight, congenital anomalies and failure to thrive.

3.   Immune System

(a)   Cellular and Humoral Immunity

The general biological function of the immune system includes resistance to disease (e.g. cancer), prevention of tissue transplantation from one individual to another, and capability of causing diseases by injuring normal tissue. When the immune system becomes hyperactive, hypersensitivity (allergic) disorders including autoimmune diseases may develop; an underactive system results in immunodeficiency diseases or growth of malignant cells. Immune responses occur as humoral (associated with circulating antibodies (produced by bone marrow B-cells or lymphocytes) in body fluids] and cell-mediated (delayed immunity under control of thymus-dependent lymphocytes or T-cells), both reacting with specific antigens when plasma cell and activated T-cell mediators are formed respectively. The T-cell mediated (cellular) immune system, which is dependent on the presence of the thymus at birth, is responsible for delayed skin tests, delayed hypersensitivity (injury to host tissue), graft rejection, and is an important defense against malignant cells and infections (viral, fungal, and some bacterial). T-cells make up 70% of circulating blood lymphocytes and can be detected by observing rosette formation (RBC^s around lymphocytes) when sheep RBC^s are mixed with lymphocyte preparations. Macrophages (phagocytes; engulf foreign material) are necessary for processing and presenting all antigens to T-cells. Upon first contact with antigen, some T-cells become activated T-cells being responsible for cellular immunity or host tissue injury (hypersensitivity or exaggerated response to antigen after prior exposure); others become memory cells, increasing the cell numbers to react with a specific antigen; and some become helper or suppressor cells regulating the production of antibody by B-cells. Defects in suppressor T-cells may result in autoimmune diseases (decreased suppressor activity) and immunodeficiency diseases (excessive suppressor activity). Short-lived (15 days) B-cells, which produce immunoglobulins (Ig; serum protein antibody which protects against viruses and bacterial pathogens including toxins) comprise 30% of blood lymphocytes, being morphologically similar to T-cells and detected by immunofluorescent technique using fluorescein-labelled anti-immunoglobulin. The first interaction of antigen and antibody or primary immune response, results in some B-cells becoming memory cells while others become antibody-synthesizing plasma cells (chiefly IgM). A subsequent encounter with the same antigen, or secondary (booster) immune response results in a large amount of IgG antibody (capable of crossing the placenta) being produced. Some antibody production requires the presence of T-cells. Humoral immunity may be active (antibody stimulated by antigen exposure) or passive (via serum γ-globulin (IgG) fraction, i.e. preformed antibodies from another individual). The immune system may be represented schematically as follows:

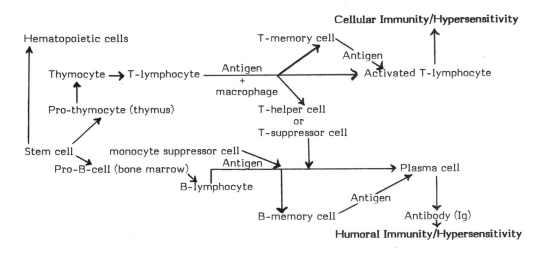

The process by which antibody production leads to immunity (or hypersensitivity) involves the combining of antibody with antigen which initiates complement activity important for host defense (or may result in normal tissue injury seen as hypersensitivity reactions).

A closely related immune function lies in the bactericidal activity of pulmonary alveolar (air cells of lungs) macrophages.

(b)   Development of Immunological Status

The delivery of a baby from its in-utero sterile environment into an antigenic world stimulates the development of specific immune mechanisms which are still relatively deficient in the young infant. The thymus gland (considered to be the mediator of tolerance to "self" antigens which develop during fetal and perinatal life) increases in size rapidy "in-utero" with a more gradual increase until puberty, involuting during adult life. The capacity of T-cells to respond to antigen stimulation occurs at the end of the first trimester of pregnancy. This parallels the sequential appearance of immunoglobulins during maturation. The neonate's immunity to various diseases depends on IgG antibodies received from the mother via placenta occurring mostly in the third trimester of pregnancy; a premature infant of less than 34 weeks gestation could have a severe IgG deficiency. Only IgG crosses the placenta. At birth, serum IgG levels begin to decrease being lowest at 3-6 months of age, a time of greatest susceptibility to serious infections (meningitis). Adult Ig levels are achieved at varying ages being 1 year for IgM and about 8 years for IgG.

(c)   Immunodeficiency Diseases

Immunodeficiency diseases may be physiological (immature perinatal system), specific (B and T-cell defects) or non-specific (complement deficiencies), and are characterized by increased susceptibility to various infections with consequent severely acute, recurrent, and chronic disease (e.g. congenital anomalies, recurrent infections, bronchitis); defects or deficiencies may be single, combined, partial or complete. They may be primary disorders, genetically determined (with or without intrauterine stress such as rubella infection) or, secondary to other diseases such as the nephrotic syndrome with renal loss of γ-globulin as well as to toxic drug reactions with pancytopenia (reduction of all blood cells) due to bone marrow and lymphoid tissue suppression. Replacement therapy (fetal thymus and bone marrow implants, γ-globulin) has been used to replace functional deficits of primary disorders. Antibiotic treatment is used once infection develops; some require continuous antibiotic and γ-globulin therapy to minimize recurrent infections. If onset of infection occurs before 6 months of age then cell-mediated defect is suspected; if after 6 months of age, a humoral defect may be responsible. The causative infectious organisms provide clues such as recurrent pneumococcal infections suggesting splenic disorders (vs ordinary childhood susceptibility to infections as otitis media, tonsillitis). The spleen aids in resistance to infection since it is the site of specific antibody production by B-cells and is part of the RES (reticuloendothelial system) clearing microorganisms from the plasma. The size of lymphoid and RES organs (lymph nodes, tonsils, adenoids, spleen, liver) are also clues as are the presence or absence of the thymus gland, and laboratory tests with respect to blood counts (lymphocyte count of > 2000/cu mm in normal cell-mediated immune system) and calcium levels (decreased in thymic hypoplasia). In delayed hypersensitivity skin tests which involve intradermal skin injection (0.1 ml) of antigen, induration and erythema occur at the test site at 24-48 hours if T-memory cells for the antigen are present; while the ability to develop cell-mediated immunity may be tested with DNCB (dinitrochlorobenzene, an antigen not previously encountered), a sensitizing dose followed by a test dose, applied to the skin resulting in a contact dermatitis indicating T-cell immunological competence. In-vitro tests for cellular immunity and presence of T-memory cells include lymphocyte transformation to lymphoblasts following antigen addition to patient's lymphocytes (for functional capacity or T-memory cells) and occurrence of rosette formation noted earlier (for presence of T-cells). Primary non-specific immunodeficiency disorders involve impairment of the phagocytic system due to decreased number of phagocytic cells or functional cell deficits due to complement (protective role against infection) deficiencies resulting in impaired chemotaxis and adherence, impaired chemotaxis due to WBC defects, and failure to kill phagocytized bacteria due to intracellular enzyme or lysosomal defects.

(d) Hypersensitivity Reactions

Hypersensitivity reactions may be considered a pathological process brought about by the specific interaction of an antigen (exogenous or endogenous) and an antibody (humoral) or sensitized lymphocytes (activated T-cells). In other words, hypersensitivity is an exaggerated response to antigen following prior exposure to antigen leading to tissue damage. Diseases which may ensue range from hay fever (exogenous antigen without systemic morbidity being limited to respiratory and ocular mucosal surfaces) to SLE (systemic lupus erythematosus; endogenous antigen in own tissue with multisystemic morbidity) as well as drug reactions. There are also antibodies to host tissues without known pathological significance but with diagnostic value, e.g., antibody to heart tissue following myocardial infarction or heart surgery. Hypersensitivity reactions resulting in immunological injury may be classified into 4 types:

    (i) Immediate type or allergic, atopic or inherited (asthma, rhinitis), anaphylactic, stinging insect, food and drug reactions due to release of pharmacologically vasoactive substances (histamine, SRS-A (slow-reactive substance of anaphylaxis) and ECF (eosinophilic chemotactic factor)) from IgE-sensitized (previously sensitized or exposed) basophils and mast cells post specific antigen contact causing vasodilation, increased capillary permeability, smooth muscle contraction, and eosinophilia. This is seen clinically as urticaria, angioedema, hypotension and spasm of bronchial, gastrointestinal, or uterine masculature. Diagnostically, a positive wheal-and-flare reaction usually occurs 15-20 minutes after a test extract of suspected material (pollen) is applied directly to scarified skin.

    (ii) Cytotoxic (cell lysis) reaction or hemolytic anemias (may be penicillin or drug induced), incompatible transfusion, SLE, and early acute graft rejection occurring when antibody (complement-fixing) reacts with antigenic components of cell or tissue. The presence of antibody (Ig) or complement on cell or tissue may be detected by direct antiglobulin and anti-non-γ-globulin tests or by fluorescent microscopy via direct immunofluorescent technique while indirect techniques are used to determine specificity of the circulating antibody. Coombs test (direct anti-globulin test) demonstrates whether RBC^s are coated with antibody (autoimmune hemolytic anemia).

    (iii) Soluble immune complex toxic reaction is due to circulating antigen-antibody deposition in vessels or tissues, or, acute inflammatory reaction brought about by complement activation by antigen-antibody complex with WBC migration and, release of lysosomal proteolytic enzymes and permeability factors in tissues. The outcome of this complex formation depends on the proportion of antibody:antigen. With relative excess of antibody, complexes precipitate near the site of antigen (in joints of rheumatoid arthritis) or become non-toxic if phagocytized by macrophages, while antigen excess, results in soluble complexes giving rise to systemic reactions or being deposited in various tissues. Clinical conditions include serum sickness due to serum, drugs, or viral heptatitis antigen (allergic reaction seen as urticaria, swelling, eruption, arthritis, fever, lymphadenopathy); SLE; rheumatoid arthritis; polyarteritis; bronchopulmonary aspergillosis (due to molds); glomerulonephritis and renal disease associated with infections. Vasculitis raises the suspicion of a Type III reaction supported by direct immunofluorescent techniques indicating the presence of antigen, Ig, and complement in the area.

(iv) Delayed (T-cell mediated not antibody in serum) or tuberculin-type reaction is brought about by sensitized or activated lymphocytes (T-cells) following antigen contact by means of a direct cytotoxic effect (or tissue damage) or via release of lymphokines from T-cells affecting the activity of macrophages, skin reactive factor and includes lymphotoxin. Perivascular lymphocytes and macrophages characterize this inflammatory reaction which may be seen clinically as contact dermatitis (including topical drug use), allograft rejection, granulomas due to intracellular organisms, thyroiditis and encephalomyelitis post rabies vaccination. Diagnositic tests include skin tests (delayed hypersensitivity for presence of T-memory cells to antigen) and patch test for allergen causing contact dermatitis and, MIF (migration inhibition factor) assay for presence of activated T-cells.

Hypersensitivity to drugs occurs following one or more exposure(s) without incident and at low doses (below therapeutic and idiosyncratic doses) with restricted clinical features of skin rashes (urticaria), serum sickness, unexpected fever, anaphylaxis, as well as eosinophilic pulmonary infiltrates. Large protein (polypeptide) drugs (e.g. glucagon m.w. 3500) can stimulate specific antibody production, with most drugs (smaller molecules) or metabolites acting as haptens which must combine firmly with a protein (serum or tissue) to form an antigenic complex prior to antibody formation. In autoimmune disorders the immune system produces autoantibodies to endogenous antigens resulting in tissue injury. Genetic factors may play a role regarding predisposition to a particular disease (SLE) which may be provoked by environmental factors (viral infection, drugs, UVL tissue injury).

(e) Immunosuppressants; Stress

Immunosuppressive agents, used to control (graft) rejection reaction (due to antigenic differences) suppress all immunological reactions as well as metabolism of rapidly dividing cells which may result in overwhelming infection leading to death in transplant recipients. Once grafts are established, small doses maintain them. Chemical and viral carcinogens may suppress immune response. Deficient cellular (T-cell defect in Hodgkin's disease) and humoral (abnormal B-cells in multiple myeloma) immunities may be associated with recurrence and dissemination of tumors. Large tumor masses may be decreased by surgery, radiotherapy or chemotherapy to allow immune mechanisms to be effective. Since many tumors release antigens into the circulation, early diagnosis may be possible via an immunological approach as well as monitoring for tumor recurrence post treatment. Surgical trauma and stress in normal patients transiently depress measureable "in-vitro" parameters of cellular immunity including "in-vivo" cutaneous delayed hypersensitivity response (Slade et al., 1974). However, the "in-vitro" tests do not completely reflect "in-vivo" capability noted by the progressive decrease in cutaneous delayed hypersensitivity (in-vivo) responses (returning to normal by 9th post-operative day with complete return of cutaneous activity by 3 weeks) even after the number of T and B-cells had been restored (within 24 hours of surgery) and lymphoblast transformation ("in-vitro" tests) was returning to normal (by the 5th-6th post-operative day).

4. Marihuana Effects

(a) Genetic Effects - Chromosomal Aberrations

Cytogenetic studies examining human chromosomes have been used to assess genetic effects via "in-vitro" and "in-vivo" culture systems (the former using lymphocyte cultures to which substances, e.g. marihuana, are added; the latter examining lymphocytes, including DNA content, from substance or marihuana users).

Structural chromosomal abnormalities were sought in cultures of leukocytes (white blood cells) from 56 psychoactive drug (27 males, 29 females) and 16 control non-drug (7 males, 9 females) users who denied recent exposure to irradiation (including X-rays) or viral infection; 12 of the controls never used drugs with 4 having used amphetamine or marihuana very lightly more than one year previously (Gilmour et al., 1971). Seven with irradiation history were studied separately to test the evaluation method. Drug users were divided into 5 groups consisting of 13 light marihuana users (1-2x/month with occasional use of librium in 2 subjects), 11 phenothiazine treated (up to 900 mg chlorpromazine daily/up to 7-12 years; some used other drugs as antiparkinsonian, mild tranquilizers) psychiatric patients (schizophrenics), and 3 groups of heavy users (of 2 or more drugs) of various combinations of marihuana, heroin and amphetamine with or without LSD, being divided into 10 mainly amphetamine users (1 had used LSD), 11 heroin addicts, and 11 subjects using various drugs (7 had used LSD), with heavily used marihuana (10x-daily/month) being common to all. In this double blind retrospective study, the heavy polydrug using and psychiatric patient groups had an increased incidence of chromosomal aberrations in a few individuals per group, each with more than 2 aberrant cells/50 cells examined, the increase being much smaller than in the irradiated group. The light marihuana users and controls had a similar low incidence of some aberrations with no more than one aberrant cell. The effect of any one drug or pattern of drug use on aberration incidence could not be established. There were actually 12 individuals with multi-aberrations which included 3 in the phenothiazine group (highest drug level and severe psychotic illness for which hospitalized/long term), 3 amphetamine group, 4 heroin addicts and 2 heavy marihuana (without LSD) users; the latter 9 using more than one drug with 7/9 being heavily drug dependent. It has been suggested that factors other than the actual drug(s) common to drug users may be responsible for chromosomal damage (e.g. viral infection including hepatitis in drug users (unreliable medical histories) or, possibility of a genetic or biochemical (endorphin) defect). To avoid problems encountered in a retrospective study, a prospective study is preferable when blood samples may be obtained prior to and at various intervals following drug use, but may be unethical with abuseable (illegal) drugs. The structural chromosomal aberrations seen in drug users have been sporadic and no clone or subpopulation of cells with the same abnormality has been observed as seen with irradiation. Thus lymphocyte precursors in drug users do not appear to be affected. The occasional aberrations noted above were in somatic cells so that inferences cannot be drawn re meiotic chromosome effects or transmission to progeny; also the presence of isolated structural rearrangements is without proven clinical significance for the host. Another double blind retrospective study (Stenchever et al., 1974) of healthy college students including 49 marihuana users (29 males, 20 females; 17-34 years of age; duration of marihuana use 6 months to 9 years with the most recent use of 30 days to 5 hours pre study) and 20 controls (12 males, 8 females; 13-52 years of age; no drug use, except occasional aspirin, nor irradiation in the previous 6 months; few used nicotine and most, caffeine) evaluated peripheral blood lymphocyte cultures with respect to chromosomal breaks and abnormal forms. Users had an average of 3.4 (0-8) cells with breaks/100 cells vs controls with 1.2 (0-5) cells with breaks (Fig. 1); with spontaneous chromosomal breakage rate of 1-2% which increased with viral infection. Differences were not evident between heavy (> 2x/week) and light (≤ 1x/week) marihuana users (3.8 vs 3.2 cells with breaks/100 cells); mixed drugs (barbituate, amphetamine, tranquilizers, mescaline, LSD, heroin) and marihuana + caffeine vs marihuana only (3.7 for mixed vs 3.1); and males vs females (3.7 vs 2.9). Abnormal chromosome configurations were noted in a greater number of user cells vs controls but the difference was not significant. Both isochromatid and chromatid breaks were observed with equal frequency indicating that both pre and post chromosome division periods (cell cycle) were affected by drug. Perhaps DNA replication is affected denoting that marihuana may be a mutagen. It appears that marihuana use (ingredient(s) or metabolite(s) responsible unknown) may cause chromosomal breaks in lymphocytes of users irrespective of frequency of use (latter differs from above report); other body cells probably affected similarly. Clinical implications of chromosome breaks may include neoplasms and teratogenesis noted with persistent chromosomal damage due to irradiation or certain disease states (Fanconi anemia, ataxia telangiectasia). The possibilities can be determined only by long term observation of a large number of marihuana users.

Some of the variables which may influence cytogenetic observations include purity of marihuana, THC content, actual dose, multi-drug use, nutritional state, and, hepatitis or other viral infections. A study (Nichols et al., 1974) was undertaken in 30 healthy male volunteers (21-35 years of age) with previous marihuana experience (duration not stated) who abstained for one week prior to the study (also excluding other drugs) when they received daily oral preparations (equivalent to 20 mg THC) of hashish (CBN, CBD, THC) or marihuana extract (THC only), or synthetic THC or placebo for a period of 5 to 12 days (short term). Post treatment chromosome damage noted in peripheral blood leukocytes did not differ appreciably from pre-treatment levels. However, such a negative result could indicate a persistent change due to the previous marihuana experience. In a group of 15 male (25-69 years of age) heavy hashish users (daily/10-30 years) vs 15 normal male controls, irregular mitoses was observed with chromosome aberrations of asymmetrical Gp A chromosomes (length change in short or long arms of chromosome, the latter due to addition or deletion of genetic material), dicentric chromosomes, breaks and numerical aberrations (hypo and hyperploidy) (Miras et al., 1978). These chromosomal alterations resemble those seen with chemicals and irradiation. It was pointed out that if such damage persists then neoplasia and teratogenesis could be more prevalent in hashish users. In a controlled study of heavy marihuana smoking, 5 male (22-32 years of age) chronic marihuana users (at least 10 cigs/week/min. 6 years, no other abuseable drugs used nor exposure to irradiation or viral infection) smoked an average of

14 marihuana cigarettes (0.9 gm cigarette with 2% THC, smoked to butt length of less than 0.2 gm)/day/28-29 days following a drug free period of 22-32 days with a post (drug free) smoking period of 18-23 days (vs 7 healthy controls without a history of marihuana use, 21-23 years of age) (Morishima et al., 1979). Blood samples were collected during all 3 time periods for metaphase and anaphase chromosome preparations. Metaphase preparations revealed an increased incidence of hypoploid cells (nuclei with less than 30 chromosomes vs normal 46 chromosomes) during heavy smoking vs controls and vs pre and post smoking periods without a significant increase in these cells in the latter 2 periods from control. However a higher incidence occurred in the post smoking period than in the pre period which may be due to the differences in the number of abstinent days (18-23 days vs 22-32 days); during the post smoking period the incidence of normal metaphases (more than 31 chromosomes) was returning to control levels. There was an absence of chromosomal breaks (with chromatid breaks in < 1% cells in both smoking and control groups) or segregational errors (smokers similar to controls) in anaphase preparations. It appears that heavy marihuana smoking can increase the incidence of hypoploid cells which return to normal baseline with abstinence (> 10 days). In an earlier study (Morishima et al., 1976), addition of 6.4×10^{-6} M THC (40-70% inhibition of ^{3}H-thymidine cell uptake) or 1.5×10^{-4}M olivetol (chemical structure similar to C-ring of cannabinoids and 10-20% inhibition of ^{3}H-thymidine incorporation) to normal lymphocyte cultures of healthy individuals resulted in induction of hypoploid nuclei which implies that a large number of cells in the DNA synthesis period have less than the euploid DNA content leading to a decreased ability of cells to incorporate ^{3}H-thymidine (i.e. protein synthesis or growth). In a later "in-vitro" study, natural cannabinoids (THC, CBD, CBN) were added to cultures containing lymphocytes from healthy adult male individuals which were then incubated for 72 hours (Henrich et al., 1980). The cells were harvested without mitotic arrest agent exposure; those in metaphase, anaphase, or telophase of nuclear division being photomicrographed for double-blind examination for normal or abnormal (segregational error) mitoses. Control-cultures revealed spontaneous segregational errors of 1.34% with an average mitotic index of 2.2%; most errors appearing as bridge formations (anaphase and telophase) or anaphase lags. THC (3.2×10^{-6} M concentration giving peak incidence) treated cultures (not with CBD nor CBN) had a higher segregational error incidence (3.54%) vs paired controls (1.11%) especially the abnormalities of anaphase lags and unequal segregations in bipolar divisions; mitotic indices being without significant difference. Such segregational error induction by THC indicates a chromosomal mutagen with abnormalities probably being due to disrupted spindle and microtubular formation. Therefore THC may be considered a mitotic poison. Another "in-vitro" study (Leuchtenberger et al., 1973 a,b) used human lung explants (normal lung tissue from surgical male patients, 45-56 years of age, who had pulmonary tumors or from a healthy young man of 25 years of age, killed in an accident) exposed to fresh marihuana (1.8 gm cigarette with 0.6% THC) smoke (4 puffs/day/4-10 days) or, whole fresh smoke or smoke from gas vapour phase of a tobacco cigarette (Kentucky standard; 2 puffs/day/4-20 days); puff vol of 25 ml at intervals of 58 secs; control cultures without exposure. Following exposure (1-45 days) chromosomal behaviour was observed during mitosis. Differences from control were noted for both marihuana and tobacco smoke exposed cultures. Mitosis and DNA synthesis were decreased with cytotoxic effects noted 1-4 days following substance exposure (tobacco > marihuana effects which may be due to differences in smoke delivery or sidestream being greater for marihuana thereby less smoke reaching the culture). Surviving cells from both exposures showed increased size of cytoplasm, nucleoli, and nuclei, with increased DNA content. Following exposure (1-45 days) mitotic abnormalities were evident from the abnormal chromosomal behaviour observed during metaphase (tripolar, large spindle) and anaphase (lagging and breakage of chromosomes); the frequency of mitotic abnormalities being 20-30% in exposed cultures vs 0-3% in controls. The early decreased DNA synthesis and mitosis were increased at later periods (7-45 days post exposure vs 1-4 days) with irregular or disorganized growth pattern. Other non-lethal alterations included decreased number of cells with euploid complement of chromosomes and DNA content (i.e. disturbance of genetic equilibrium of cell population). It appears that both marihuana and tobacco cigarette smoke produce similar abnormalies in DNA metabolism (Fig. 2), mitosis and growth in fibroblast cells of human adult lung explants as well as alterations in DNA and chromosomal complement. The unanswered question is whether the cells with abnormal DNA and chromosomal complement are responsible for subsequent atypical growth which may represent an early stage in malignant transformation. This possibility was followed-up by further experiments with lung cultures from animals (mice, hamster) and humans (fetal, adult) exposed (from short-term to 2-8 months) to puffs (8-25 ml. vol) of fresh cigarette smoke (tobacco, tobacco + 0.5 to 1 gm marihuana, or marihuana alone 1.8 gm (0.4, 0.6, 4.0% THC)) (Leuchtenberger and Leuchtenberger, 1976). Following exposure, time sequential changes were observed from 6 hours to more than 1 year later noting cytological and cytochemical (DNA) alterations. Assessment of possible malignant transformation in lung cultures were carried out by injecting cells from the cultures subcutaneously into mice and examining the developed tumors histologically for malignancy. The addition of marihuana to tobacco increased abnormalities in mouse lung epithelioid cells above that of tobacco used alone being partly due to THC seen as earlier and more marked alterations with increasing concentration of THC. Similar atypical growth was produced in human lung culture with tobacco or marihuana smoke, the latter producing more severe alteration to DNA content and number of chromosomes. DNA synthesis and mitosis were first inhibited (cytoxic effect; stage I) followed by abnormal cell morphology and mitosis

with irregular abnormal growth (stage II) leading to an increased number of dividing cells with variable number of chromosomes and DNA content (disturbance of genetic equilibrium of cell population); marihuana showing a tendency to a lower number of chromosomes and DNA content vs tobacco. Both whole smoke and gas vapor phases from marihuana or tobacco cigarettes enhanced malignant cell transformation of hamster lung cultures. The two stages noted above were followed by more irregular growth of abnormal fibroblasts with crisscross and piling up indicating malignant transformation of cells (stage III). This was confirmed when cells from these cultures, injected into mice, resulted in development of fibrosarcomas vs control cells (the latter showing similar transformation with aging; spontaneous). Thus marihuana smoke may contribute to the development of premalignant and malignant lesions in cultured lung cells suggesting a possible (human probability?) pulmonary carcinogenic role similar to that found with tobacco. Human epidemiological data is necessary before any definitive statement can be made. Some preliminary work with mice or cultured mouse testis exposed to marihuana smoke revealed a decreased number of spermatids with the normal haploid amount of DNA with some spermatids exhibiting reduced variable amounts of DNA. Marihuana smoke may thus have the capacity to alter heriditary material in germ cells (<u>mutagenic potential</u>). The marihuana components responsible for the above effects are unknown.

Chemical analysis of marihuana smoke condensate from Mexican marihuana (2.8% THC) revealed mutagenic and carcinogenic chemicals (similar to tobacco) which are products of pyrolysis of cannabinoids (Novotny et al., 1976). In an Ames test (a short term bioassay for potential mutagenic and carcinogenic effects) smoke condensates from marihuana cigarettes were estimated to be mutagenic (similar to tobacco) requiring liver enzymes for their activation (Busch et al., 1979). Mutagen intake may be estimated from tar yields of cigarettes, being 17 mg/cigarette for tobacco and 40-56 mg/cigarette for marihuana (due to absence of filters and smoking to a minimum butt length). Thus tar intake from one marihuana cigarette is approximately 1.5 high-tar or 100 low-tar tobacco cigarettes (mutagenic hazards being similar for marihuana and tobacco). Another study showed that combustion of cannabis cigarettes (327 mg cigarette with 7.89% cannabis resin, 0.36% THC, 1.14% CBD, 0.82% CBN) produced benzpyrene (1.06 ng/mg cigarette), a known carcinogenic agent in tobacco smoke, which is not present in unsmoked plant material (Repetto et al., 1979). Smoke condensate (194 mg/ml or 5.7 µg benzpyrene/ml) injected subcutaneously into newborn rats produced mesenchymal (cells give rise to connective or supporting tissue, smooth muscle, vascular endothelium, blood cells) type tumors in offspring from normal healthy female animals while offspring from chronically exposed cannabis females died early within 10 days of the injection. An "in-vitro" study (Shahar, 1975) of the THC (0.03 - 0.6 mM) effect on the kinetic morphlogy of human and bull sperm (cinematography and transmission electrom microscopy) revealed decreased sperm motility with weak beating of the tail (or none at all, depending upon THC concentration), progressive movement being almost non-existent, and swelling of the mid portion of the sperm (location of all mitochondria (principal energy source of cell)) where ultrastructural membrane changes (disintegration) occurred especially of the mitochondria with rupture of outer membranes and cristae (folded inner membrane). THC appears to have an affinity for cellular membranes due to its interaction with lipoprotein fractions. This has been borne out by observations of lymphocyte lipid changes (total lipids and phospholipids) noted 30-60 minutes following (not prior to) hashish smoking in 15 chronic heavy hashish smokers vs 15 healthy control subjects (Kalofoutis et al., 1978). Analysis of phospholipids revealed changes in phosphatidyl compounds with increased concentrations of choline and inositol components, and decreased serine and ethanolamine; the first three compounds being essential phospholipids for cell membrane function. These changes in phospholipid concentrations may be related to fluctuation in the immune ability of lymphocytes, by affecting lymphocyte membrane enzyme mechanisms.

(b) Cell Metabolism - Effects on Macromolecular (DNA, RNA, Protein) Synthesis

The smoking of a marihuana cigarette with 18.9 mg THC by chronic users has yielded a plasma concentration of 250 ng/ml (7.95×10^{-7}M). Since THC accumulates following successive doses, the effect on macromolecular synthesis was considered to be essential. In normal human dipolid fibroblasts (from fetal foreskin), human and mouse neuroblastoma cells, Δ^9 THC (10^{-5} M) inhibited (Fig. 3; 4; 5) the incorporation of radioactive (^{3}H, ^{14}C) precursors (thymidine, uridine, leucine) into DNA, RNA (40-50% inhibition of nucleic acid synthesis; minimal effect of 11-17% inhibition with 3.2×10^{-7}M THC concentration) and protein (30-40% inhibition of protein synthesis; no effect with 3.2×10^{-7} M THC) (Blevins and Regan, 1976). This inhibition was found to be due to a 50% reduction in macromolecular precursor pool size with the rate of transport of precursors into the cell and DNA repair synthesis (after UV or ionizing radiation damage to DNA) remaining essentially unaltered. The reduction in pool size could not be explained; a suggestion being made that the lipid soluble THC interacts with the cell membrane making it more permeable (leaky) thereby resulting in a smaller macromolecular precursor pool size vs untreated cells. The possibility also exists that precursors may be altered or biosynthesis prevented by THC blocking the synthesis of DNA or giving rise to abnormal DNA with permanent modification which may be compatible with cell life but transmissible to subsequent generations;

modifications resulting in mutagenesis and carcinogenesis. The possible damage to the DNA molecule followed by corrective DNA repair mechanism resembles antineoplastic alkylating agents and ionizing radiation effects.

"In-vitro" tests using mixed lymphocyte culture (MLC) or PHA (phytohemagglutinin) were performed in 51 young marihuana smokers (average age 22 years) who had used only cannabis products (average 4x/week; potency unknown) for an average of 4 years; patients with impaired T-cell immunity (60 with cancer, 20 uremia, 24 renal allograft recipients with iatrogenically induced immunosuppression following 1 to 4 year drug therapy); and 81 healthy controls (average age 44 years) (Nahas et al., 1974). Both tests are used to assess functional capacity of T-cells indicating presence of T-memory cells; the former test (MLC) using donor cells (allogenic antigens) and the latter PHA (mitogen) as stimulators of lymphocytic transformation to lymphoblasts (blastogenic response), the transformation being measured by H^3-thymidine uptake by the lymphocytes. Both test systems showed similar decreases in thymidine uptake in marihuana smokers and patients vs normal controls indicating inhibition of "in-vitro" blastogenesis which may be due to DNA synthesis impairment. Thus the decreased immune response found in marihuana smokers was found to be similar to patients with T-cell immunity impairment. Blastogenic inhibition using PHA on normal human lymphocytes, was obtained with THC begininning with 1.6 µM concentration being complete with 20 µM. Since thymidine uptake indicates protein synthesis (growth) the possibility exists that this blastogenic inhibition may be due to DNA (deoxyribonucleic acid; in cell nucleus (chromatin, chromosomes), molecular basis of heredity) synthesis impairment. Cultivated (72 hours) lymphocytes from 4 marihuana smokers revealed a decreased number of cells during DNA synthesis and an increased number of chromosomal breakages, the latter finding suggesting a possible alteration in the genetic equilibrium of T-cells. These possibilities were investigated further (Nahas et al., 1977). It was found that lymphocytic biosynthesis of DNA (as measured by thymidine incorporation) was reversibly impaired by natural cannabinoids and metabolites of THC (all of which have the C-ring of olivetol) as well as by aspirin and caffeine (both of which required higher concentrations than for cannabinoids) which may be due to cell membrane effects of THC inhibiting transport of precursors necessary for macromolecular (DNA, RNA, protein) synthesis (or perhaps making precursors unavailable for synthesis; see final comments section). This has also been suggested by a more recent report (Desoize et al., 1979) of a non-specific THC membrane effect (at concentrations equivalent to heavy chronic use) related to the drug's liposolubility vs acute psychotropic effect due to specific receptor site interaction in the CNS. That is, the greater the liposolubility, the greater the cytotoxic effect which is also observed with other fat soluble psychotropic drugs (Fig. 6; 7; 8) as anesthetics and tranquilizers (Banchereau et al., 1979). The metabolism of cultured lymphocytes was altered by THC noted as decreased glucose consumption with a corresponding decrease in lactate excretion (Fig. 9) and coincident slower growth rate or lowered protein synthesis (Fig. 10). It appears that THC decreases glucose utilization by cells as well as discouraging protein synthesis (the latter observed with other psychotropic drugs noted above (Fig. 6; 7; 8; see final comments section). It was suggested further (Nahas et al., 1974) that during the lymphocytic transformation process (blastogenic response) following mitogen (PHA) stimulation, the dividing cells may be more sensitive to THC inhibitory effects and that the THC-induced segregational errors of chromosomes may also be due to impairment of macromolecular synthesis. These ideas were tested in studies investigating the effects of cannabinoids on cell proliferation (associated with immunological response, tissue regeneration including wound healing, erythropoiesis, and gastro-intestinal epithelial lining cells replacement) and on macromolecular biosynthesis responsible for cell division which involves modification in gene expression, which in turn led to the examination of cannabinoid effects on structural and functional properties of the genome (Mon et al., 1981 a, b; Stein et al., 1979). The results revealed that both psychoactive (Δ^9-THC, Δ^8-THC, 11-OH-Δ^9-THC) and non-psychoactive (cannabinol or CBN) cannabinoids (1-40 µM) inhibit cell growth rate by 8-55% (dose-related) with a dose-dependent decreased incorporation of radioactive (^{3}H) thymidine, uridine, and leucine into macromolecules (DNA, RNA, and protein respectively) in intact cells with a comparable decrease in acid soluble intracellular precursor pools thought to be due to transport inhibition across the cell membrane. The degree of psychoactivity was not related to the cellular proliferative effect as noted by the order of decreasing potency being Δ^8-THC, 11-OH-Δ^9 THC, CBN, and Δ^9 THC with a larger amount of Δ^8 THC found in the nucleus of the cell. The growth inhibition of 30-40% was reversed 48 hours following cessation of treatment. The noted biochemical effects reflect alteration in gene expression. Thus cannabinoid effects on macromolecules which comprise the genome (chromosomes with their genes) were studied with respect to structure (composition) and function (metabolism). Chromatin (genome in cells) is a nucleoprotein complex made up of DNA, and, histone and non-histone chromosomal proteins. Histone chromosomal proteins parcel DNA into nucleosomes (seen as beads on a string under the electron microscope) and may repress genetic sequences while non-histone chromosomal proteins may be involved in genome structure and various enzyme activities as well as determining availability of genetic sequences for transcription. The four cannabinoids did not alter the relative composition (structure) of histone or non-histone chromosomal proteins but did decrease rates of synthesis and/or turnover (function); psychoactivity being unrelated to the effects. These alterations imply possible impairment of gene expression necessary for regulation of cell proliferation and for biological viability.

The post-translational (formation of protein molecule from information in messenger RNA) modification of chromosomal proteins by acetylation and phosphorylation of histones, and phosphorylation of non-histone chromosomal proteins may be partly responsible for determining the availability of genetic sequences for transcription (transfer of genetic information to messenger RNA) and is important for structural and functional properties of the genome. Cannabinoids were found to interfere (decrease) with histone acetylation and phosphorylation, and phosphorylation of total chromosomal proteins implying possible alteration in genome structure and function. It appears that the four cannabinoids (irrespective of psychoactivity) decrease the proliferative capacity of cells due to impairment of essential macromolecular biosynthesis brought about by the alteration in the modification of gene expression or in structural and functional properties of the genome. Reference (Issidorides, 1979; Stefanis and Issidorides, 1976) has been made, in the section on reproduction (spermatogenesis), to lymphocytes obtained from chronic hashish users (who did not show clinical immunological incompetence) which showed alteration in histone (chromosomal basic nuclear protein which maintains chromatin structure) ratio with reduction of arginine and an increase in lysine denoting transcriptional arrest (repression of genome expression seen as condensed chromatin) and implying a possible underresponse to antigenic stimulation reported as decreased cell-mediated immunity. Thus, with chronic marihuana use, alteration of cellular metabolism is particularly evident in the nuclear area observed as altered chromatin. However, a correlation between cellular metabolic changes and overt pathology has not been established which may be a matter of drug concentration, pattern or frequency of use (continuous, intermittent) and genetic background.

(c) Effects on Cellular (T-cell) and Humoral (B-cell) or Antibody Mediated Immune Systems; and on Phagocytic Pulmonary Alveolar Macrophage System

"In-vivo" and "in-vitro" techniques have been used to evaluate the presence and functional competence of T- and B-cells (as in evaluation of immunodeficiency disease) as well as of pulmonary alveolar macrophages (bactericidal or phagocytic activity) in marihuana smokers and in animals exposed to marihuana and/or THC (active psychoactive component in marihuana).

Active rosetting T-cells (1/3rd of T-cell population form rosettes with sheep RBCs at room temperature post short incubation) and immune rosettes of B-cells (9-15% of B-cell population, with complement receptor, with sheep RBCs in presence of complement and antibody) were studied in 23 healthy chronic marihuana smokers (use 1-7x/week/1-8 years; THC concentration unknown) and 23 normal controls (non-marihuana) in their 20s, both groups using tobacco daily and some alcohol use (Cushman et al., 1975; Gupta et al., 1974). The marihuana group (except 2) denied other illicit drug use 2 weeks prior to the study. In some chronic marihuana smokers, a depression of T-cell forming rosettes was observed. Even though the physiological significance of T-cell active rosettes is unknown, it is felt that these T-cells are active in immunological reactions thereby raising the possibility of T-cell functional disturbances in chronic marihuana users. In 5/23 marihuana users the percent of B-cell rosettes was low although the group average was similar to the control group. Delayed hypersensitivity skin tests using 4 different antigens intradermally in 16 marihuana using subjects resulted in a variable outcome; some reacted to only 1 antigen, others not reacting to any. A positive reaction indicates the presence of T-memory cells for the antigen tested. Thus some T-cells are depressed which may be due to cellular effects noted above, while other T-cells may still be immunologically competent. The question is, are the latter cells adequate to counteract infection, carry out immunological tumor surveillance and subserve graft rejection? A follow-up study with 35 marihuana (potency unknown) smoking students (average 22 years, using about 6 joints (1-16)/week during the previous 3 months; duration of marihuana use about 4 years (1-8) averaging 3x/week use) and 34 controls (average age 30 years) investigated early (active) and total (late) T-lymphocyte sheep cell rosetting "in-vitro" properties (Cushman and Khurana, 1976). Of the 35 marihuana users, 71.4% had abnormally low levels of active rosettes vs control subjects. The levels correlated with the time of last marihuana use; a longer interval being associated with normal percent of active rosettes (Fig. 11). Very little difference between the 2 groups was noted in the late rosette formations. The decrease in active rosette formation in marihuana smokers was not due to T-cell decrease in the peripheral blood, indicating a sub-population of T-cells (perhaps 10%) being affected by marihuana use. Rosette formation was not influenced by tobacco, alcohol, nor aspirin. Clinical and immunological significance of rosette tests are unknown (Hong and Horowitz, 1975), but it has been suggested that those with impaired cell-mediated immunity (cancer, acute viral not bacterial infections, uremia) are likely to have lowered active T-cell rosette formation (Wybran and Fudenberg, 1973). The number of active rosette forming cells (15% being lower limit of normal) appear to correlate with the clinical status of cancer patients. A low number in high risk families (e.g. gastrointestinal carcinoma) may indicate a predisposition to disease. Lepromatous (nodular) leprosy is an example of a disease state (Nath et al., 1974) which is accompanied by a change (decrease; correlating well with positive bacillary load) in active rosette formation (2 hour T-cell incubation) without a change in total rosettes (24 hour incubation; total T-cell population) with increased number of B-cells (especially in those with decreased total T-cells) which persists even after drug therapy.   The significance of T-cell rosette formation abnormalities in marihuana smokers is unknown since clinical evidence is lacking for T-cell deficiency disorders occurring in marihuana smokers. Another study (confirming the above) was undertaken to determine if any relation existed between time of blood sampling and alteration in T-cell "in-vitro" test responsiveness in male chronic marihuana smokers (22-26 years of age) who smoked at least once a week for at least one year (no other drugs were used) and in matched normal controls; both groups having some individuals who smoked tobacco cigarettes (Petersen et al., 1976).   "Street" marihuana used by 13 chronic marihuana smokers revealed a decreased number of T-lymphocyte forming rosettes compared with 8 matched non-marihuana using controls as well as a slight decrease in PHA stimulation response (though not statistically significant), the latter indicating a possible decrease in T and/or B memory cells.   In 3 subjects, who abstained from marihuana for 3 weeks, 24-72 hour post smoking blood sampling vs pre-smoking sampling disclosed decreased rosette formation in 2/3 individuals with decreased PHA stimulation response in 1 subject. Marihuana cigarettes (1.45% THC) with 10 mg THC smoked by 6 chronic marihuana users (following 3 week abstention) resulted in decreased T-cell rosette formation in all subjects at 2-6 hours after smoking which persisted for 24 hours in 2 individuals with an increase seen in 1 subject (Fig.   12); 2 subjects showing an increase following placebo cigarette smoking.   A decreased PHA stimulation response was observed in 2 individuals using 2 and 6 hour blood samples with one subject showing decreased activity at the 24-48 hour period; activity was normal by the 8th day following smoking.   Thus marihuana appears to affect T-cell function transiently (individual variation) with the possibility of affecting T-memory cells in some individuals.   Hospitalized chronic marihuana smokers (10 males, aged 18-30 years, smoked marihuana at least twice a week, with normal physical and laboratory tests) took part in a THC study (2-3 week abstinent) in which T and B cell rosette formations were determined prior to, during, and 2 weeks following a 4 week period of smoking daily an average of 5-12 cigarettes (20 mg THC/cigarette) vs 6 non-marihuana using, non-hospitalized healthy men (18-45 years of age) (Cushman and Khurana, 1977).   Early T-cell rosette formation was decreased in THC smokers vs controls who had no change; both groups revealed no change in WBC, percent circulating lymphocytes, B-cell rosettes (complement receptor), and late T-cell rosettes.   It appears that THC smoking individuals had a decreased capacity to form early rosettes, the immunological significance of which is unknown, although, patients with decreased cell-mediated immune function (cancer, certain infections, immunosuppressive therapy) may show decreased T-cell rosette formation.

Divergent observations have been noted by several investigators.   One group (White et al., 1975) reported that long term marihuana (potency unknown) smoking in healthy individuals did not alter mitogen-induced (PHA, pokeweed) blastogenic response of lymphocytes indicating unaltered functional status of blood (T and B) lymphocytes or unimpaired immune response capabilities.   Marihuana was used on an average of 3.4x/week/4.8 years by 12 healthy smokers, age 19-32 years, who had smoked at least once during 48 hours prior to testing; 12 matched controls had never used marihuana.   Another group (Kaklamani et al., 1978) investigating hashish smokers did not observe impairment of lymphocytic response to PHA or to rosette formation.   Twelve chronic hashish smokers (40-45 years of age) with duration of 20 year use via nargileh pipe (using up to 100 gm crude hashish/time) participated in this study with 15 healthy non-drug using controls.   The experimental hashish resin contained 1.6% THC; 20 gm was smoked via pipe over a 15 minute period, blood specimens being collected 30-60 minutes later.   A third study (Rachelefsky et al., 1976) reported that short term (64 days) chronic marihuana use in a hospital setting did not adversely affect T and B lymphocytes of young healthy adults.   Taking part in this study were 12 healthy chronic marihuana smokers aged 21-28 years (6 heavy users of 1/d/previous 6 months; 6 moderate users of 3-6x/week/6 months; also used alcohol, tobacco, other drugs 2-3x) who smoked at least one (average was 5.5) 900 mg marihuana cigarette (2.2% THC)/d/64 days following 12 days abstinence with 1 week of non-smoking at the end of the 64 day period followed by resumption for 9 days, discharge being 3 days later, and non-hospitalized normal matched controls who had not used marihuana.   Immunological tests were not influenced by the number of cigarettes smoked per day prior to or during the study.   T and B cells were initally decreased, increasing toward normal by the 63rd day. IgE levels increased in 4/8 patients tested by day 55 without apparent allergic manifestations (such as urticaria, wheezing).   The differing reported results may be due to methodological differences such as temperature (37°C vs 4°C) and time (1 hour vs 3 days) of incubation of lymphocyte cultures, type of serum (calf vs human) used in culture media; blood sampling time (minutes, several hours vs 48 hours) since last marihuana use; cell population (total vs sub or active) studied; method of smoking (cigarette vs water pipe) and depth of inhalation; quality of marihuana (potency) used as well as concomitant use of other drugs; and state of health of individual including genetic background.

A preliminary study in 17 (8 males and 9 females, 18 to 38 years of age with 5 males and 1 female hospitalized for clinical illness) marihuana smokers (frequency use of 1/month to once daily) with less than one month since last use, revealed humoral antibodies (positive indirect Coombs test) to cannabis in 15/17 smokers without a definite relation to clinical disease (Shapiro et al., 1974).   That is, cannabis is an antigen capable of eliciting a humoral immune response.   A follow-up study (Shapiro et al., 1976a) was undertaken in 34 male marihuana smokers (who used the drug > 20x, 10 subjects not having used it during the previous 6 months) without clinical disease and 34 non-marihuana using controls (all subjects 18-30 years of age) to identify the antigens in marihuana and determine if any relation exists between immunological response and production of subclinical disease (abnormal laboratory tests). The marihuana (extract from cannabis sativa leaves 50 mg) used in the tests contained 1.2% Δ^9 THC, 0.11% CBN, 0.6% CBD, and 0.04% Δ^8 THC. Positive antibody responses to marihuana occurred in all 34 marihuana using subjects but not in the control; all but 2/34 marihuana users responded to the marihuana components (0.1 µg) (two did not react to CBD, nor to CBN in 1/2; 1 control had positive response to Δ^9 THC). This indicates that marihuana and its components are antigens capable of inducing antibody production. The antigen-antibody specificity response was confirmed in 6 positive sera by absorption studies with marihuana and its components, generally removing the specific antibody or decreasing the reaction (i.e. antigen is able to absorb or remove antibody against self). Pre-absorbed sera with marihuana rendered it immunologically unreactive to marihuana and all components except CBN antigen. The class of protein coating the RBCs (using monospecific antisera) was variable with IgG,C, IgM noted in all 6 tested sera with IgA in 2/6 sera. Abnormal routine laboratory tests occurred in 22/34 marihuana smokers (65% with >1 abnormal tests including reticulocytosis in 7, decreased serum haptoglobin in 8, decreased serum Ig in 9, and abnormal liver function in 10) and in 9/34 controls (26% with one abnormal test). It was suggested that antibody production against marihuana antigens may be associated with subclinical laboratory abnormalities with uncertain relationshp as to whether it is causal or casual.

An animal study (Daul and Heath, 1975) using 3 different exposures to THC in marihuana smoke/6 months (high level with 22.4 mg THC/smoke at 3 smokes/day, 5 days/week; medium level of 1 smoke/day, 2 days/week; low level with 4.4 mg THC/smoke at 1 smoke/day, 5 days/week) in 6 rhesus monkeys (1 on high, one on medium, 3 on low dose levels with 1 control) resulted in decreased plasma IgG and M levels at high and medium doses without a change in total plasma protein levels indicating an absence of hypoproteinemia (ruling out one cause for decreased Ig) and a decreased "in-vitro" lymphocyte blastogenic response to all dose levels (returning to normal response levels, 1-2 months following cessation of smoking) vs pre-drug levels. There were differences in magnitude of lymphocyte response to various mitogens used, indicating differences in circulating subpopulation of cells which represent only part of the total immunocompetent cell pool. These changes were not evident at the 3 month period. The clinical significance of these changes with respect to immunological competence could not be assessed. The ability of Δ^8 THC and CBN (2 components in marihuana) to modify DTH (delayed-type hypersensitivity) response to SRBC (sheep red blood cells) in mice was studied (Levy and Heppner, 1978-79) using varying drug doses (Δ^8 THC 10-125 mg/kg; CBN 100 mg/kg) and regimens of single or multiple (4 days) subcutaneous doses prior to or following sensitization (immunization) to SRBC. The patterns of alteration in the development of DTH were dissimilar; Δ^8 THC produced a moderate decrease in DTH peak response (13-33% from control) with multiple dosing during the pre-sensitization period with a 24 hour delay in the response with post-immunization administration, while CBN decreased the response by 60% following multiple dosing during the post-immunization period. The degree of DTH suppression with the 2 drugs was considered to be only slight to moderate vs known immunosuppresive agents (cyclophosphamide, prednisone, azathioprine). Since different batches of marihuana vary in their component composition (which may produce different responses noted in this study as well as diverse reports in the literature), it was suggested that the effects of each component found in marihuana including their interactions on the immune system be investigated; the type of cells being affected (e.g. helper cells, a subclass of T-cells) may be different or specific for marihuana or for each component. The importance of age or maturity of an individual with respect to THC effects on the immune system was examined in animals (mice, 4 and 14 weeks of age; THC 10-40 mg/kg IP/4-8 days) (Pruess and Lefkowitz, 1978). Younger (vs older) animals responded to THC by decreased body and spleen weights with decreased number of splenic cells with higher concentration THC during the short exposure period; decreased cellular immunity (splenic lymphocytes); greater decrease in humoral response (synthesis of circulating antibody, IgG antibody production); and decreased rosette formation with both T and B-cells. It appears that age of the animal influences THC response. Suggested possible explanations for the age phenomenon re THC effects were:

(i) developing cells being affected more than mature cells;

(ii) the THC interaction with lipid phase of the cell membrane responsible for pharmacological properties (immunosuppression) may be altered with age due to membrane changes which may modify the binding capacity of the drug;

(iii) the younger system may be less able to develop a compensatory mechanism for restoring normal immune response; and

(iv) changing cell population and alteration of certain T-cells occurs in aging mice.

A possible role of age and sex hormones in immunological maturation and regulation has been suggested by an animal study of autoimmunity using a certain strain of mouse which develops a spontaneous disorder resembling human SLE (systemic lupus erythematosus) an autoimmune disease occurring predominantly in women (Melez et al., 1978-79). The results from the pre and post pubertal castration studies in both male and female animals, with and without hormone treatment, revealed that hormonal effects on the immune system was greatest in early life; the presence of testosterone (male sex hormone) discouraging the development of the autoimmune process. It may be that sex hormones are a part of an interrelated complex immune-endocrine system. Possible regulatory roles (which may be normal physiological effects) for male sex hormones (androgens; testosterone) may be to maintain suppression (suppressor T-cells) of the autoimmune process vs female sex hormones (estrogens) which may decrease suppressor effects (enhance helper cell effects). Thus if testosterone levels are altered (decreased, noted in the reproduction section), especially prior to and during adolescence, by marihuana or THC, the male individual may become more susceptible to autoimmune disease (such as SLE).

The basic pharmacological THC action on the immune system was investigated in animals using mice given THC orally (25-200 mg/kg) as a single dose or daily dosing for a period of 7-16 days (Munson et al., 1976). The functional (phagocytic) activity of RES (reticuloendothelial system; fixed macrophage system of Kupffer cells in the liver not alveolar and splenic macrophages) was slightly but erratically altered (no dose-response relationship) with suppression of T ("in-vivo" increase in skin allograft survival by 21-42% vs vehicle treated control of 16.2 days and "in-vitro" decreased blastogenic response by splenic cells) and B (decreased antibody titer by 72% vs vehicle treated control to SRBC or sheep red blood cells at the highest THC dose and blastogenic suppression of B-cells using LPS or lipopolysaccharide mitogen) lymphocytes as well as a decrease in spleen size by 30% with the highest dose and and a decreased number of splenic (up to 46% at highest dose with return to normal levels 48 hours post drug) and peripheral (33-65% below control value of 6,469/mm^3 16 hours post drug) nucleated cells; the last three parameter responses occurring only with single dose exposure. Tolerance to immunosuppression was not evident with 16 days of THC treatment. Possible mechanisms for THC immunosuppressive activity include a direct inhibition of cellular metabolism with a change in lymphocytic population (decreased number of cells) and THC release of adrenal steroids (decrease immune response). THC may represent a new class of immunosuppressive agents vs 6-MP (mercaptopurine), a potent immunosuppressant (an antimetabolite also used in WBC neoplastic diseases such as lymphocytic and granulocytic leukemias) which increased graft survival by 45% in the above study following 25 mg/kg IP/11 days. THC was also observed to suppress proliferation of neoplastic tissues in animals using various tumor systems with different growth characteristics and etiologies (Lewis lung adenocarcinoma similar to human solid tumors being very metastatic; leukemia L1210 used as screen for drugs for human leukemia; FLV or B-tropic Friend leukemia virus with at least 2 different viruses (LLV-lymphocytic leukemia virus and FFV-focus forming virus) used to screen drugs for antiviral and antitumor properties, noting spleen size, monitoring the leukemia and noting survival time of the animals) without altering normal bone marrow cells ("in-vitro" toxicity) (Harris et al., 1976). Following tumor inoculation into mice, daily oral THC (25-200 mg/kg) treatment began 24 hours later for a period of 10 days or until dealth. Δ^9 THC inhibited primary Lewis lung tumor growth by 30-75% with increased life span of 22-36% (especially at the 100 mg/kg dose) vs vehicle treated control. Δ^8 THC and CBN also inhibited growth and prolonged survival time while CBD enhanced growth without altering life span. The inhibiting property of tumor growth was significant within the first 2 weeks following inoculation, diminishing at 3 weeks, with tumor size approaching control values by the 30th day (tolerance or resistance developed with repeated medication). Cyclophosphamide, an alkylating nitrogen mustard compound, at 20 mg/kg, increased survival time by 33% with a 20% decrease in body weight. THC (50-200 mg/kg p.o.) did not increase the life span of animals with L1210 leukemia but decreased FLV induced splenomegaly by 71% with a 200 mg/kg dose (vs 90.2% with 0.25 mg/kg actinomycin D, a natural antibiotic product). In the "in-vitro" systems of isolated cells, Lewis lung cell uptake of ^{3}H-thymidine was inhibited by 2.5×10^{-6}M Δ^9 THC, Δ^8 THC, CBN but not by CBD which occurs at 2.5×10^{-4}M concentration. Only Δ^9 THC showed some selectivity in its ability to inhibit tumor cells (DNA synthesis inhibited by 55% in Lewis lung and L1210 leukemic cells) without affecting normal bone marrow cells which required a higher drug concentration. The antineoplastic activity does not appear to be related to behavioural properties since CBN was found to be effective. Immunosuppression caused by cannabinoids was also found to be unrelated to CNS activity; 1-methyl Δ^8 THC and abnormal Δ^8 THC (reversal of 2 attached groups in Δ^8 THC) with minimal CNS activity, were more potent in suppressing humoral and cell-mediated immunity than Δ^9 THC in "in-vitro" cell systems (Smith et al., 1978). Cannabinoids lack anti-inflammatory activity(?) indicating a direct action on immunocompetent cells. Cannabinoid effects on macromolecular synthesis (inhibition) with immunosuppressant and antineoplastic activity resemble chemotherapeutic agents used in neoplastic disease which are both immunosuppressants (prevent transplant rejection) and antiproliferative agents (tumor inhibiting properties with acquired resistance in some, such as alkylating agents and antimetabolites, thought to be due to increased activity of the DNA repair system), as well as having effects on the reproductive system as amenorrhea in women and spermatogenesis impairment in men (other cellular effects being cytolytic, mutagenic, carcinogenic, teratogenic as well as inhibition of protein and nucleic acid synthesis and function); the difference being that at certain concentrations of THC, normal bone marrow cells are not affected (depressed as seen with antineoplastic agents). This could lead to the development of a new class of therapeutic agents (organ transplantation, autoimmune disease, neoplasms) without CNS activity and lower toxicity. An animal (rat) study (Johnson and Wiersema, 1974) has implicated a metabolite (11-OH-THC) of THC as being responsible for inhibition of bone marrow myelopoiesis (granular leukocytes of blood developed from myelocytes or marrow cells) with accelerated lymphocyte maturation following intravenous administration of a high dose of THC (50 mg/kg). The question remains whether the suppression of proliferative neoplastic tissue is species specific and/or tumor specific in humans keeping in mind that the entire population of neoplastic cells must be eradicated for a desired cure vs antimicrobial therapy which relies on the immune mechanism playing a major role in treatment of infections. An "in-vivo" cannabinoid (Δ^9 THC, Δ^8 THC, CBD; 200 mg/kg) animal (mouse) study revealed inhibition of Lewis lung DNA synthesis 3 hours after intraperitoneal drug administration but was not apparent at 24-48 hours following oral intake (Friedman, 1977). Another "in-vivo" animal (mouse) study (Tucker and Friedman, 1977) using murine L1210 leukemia cells (from peritoneal cavity) showed that 3 hours after i.p. 200 mg/kg cannabinoids (Δ^9 THC, Δ^8 THC, CBD, abnormal CBD, CBN, 11-OH-Δ^9 THC) DNA synthesis was inhibited with the maximum or peak inhibitory effect being reached at 1.5 hours post drug injection; Δ^8 THC, 11-OH-Δ^9 THC, and CBD being the most potent inhibitors. Following a single injection of Δ^9 THC, inhibition of DNA synthesis was approaching control values at the 24 and 48 hour periods vs Δ^8 THC which retained its inhibitory effect for the same time periods. Twenty-four hours following two injections (24 hours apart), Δ^8 THC displayed inhibition vs stimulation of DNA synthesis by Δ^9 THC (tolerance or tumor resistance). Inhibition of both RNA and protein synthesis by Δ^8 and Δ^9 THCs was similar to their inhibition of DNA synthesis (without affecting O_2 consumption (respiration) in L1210 cells (Tucker and Friedman, 1979). Fewer cells were obtained from the peritoneal cavity of animals treated with Δ^8 and Δ^9 THCs at least 24 hours previously. THC (Δ^9) was found to inhibit (dose related) cell growth in mouse neuroblastoma cells with a corresponding dose-dependent decrease in macromolecular synthesis (DNA (most sensitive), RNA, protein); the site of growth interference observed as nuclear morphological changes of condensed nuclear material (electron microscopy) (Carchman et al., 1979). Rat glioma cells were found to be more refractory to growth and macromolecular synthesis inhibitory effects of THC. This may indicate that some cannabinoids may be active only against some rapidly growing tumors (by inhibiting DNA synthesis). Dividing cells in a malignancy are more susceptible to chemotherapy, attacking the cell cycle at different phases depending upon the agent used.

The possibility of increased susceptibility (including toxicity) to infections due to cannabis use was investigated in rodent (mice) studies. Animal (6 different mouse strains; male and female animals) mortality was enhanced with THC (pure, red oil or marihuana distillate) combined with bacterial endotoxin (various purified LPS or lipopolysaccharide preparations) such that, for example, a nonlethal dose (2.5 mg/kg IP) of E. coli decreased the LD50 (dose fatal to 50% test animals) of THC in mice (from 350 to 150 mg/kg IP, i.e. more toxic) (Bradley et al., 1977). However this hyperadditve lethality was not evident in animals made refractory (tolerant, resistant) to THC or LPS by prior repeated administration of these substances. This type of lethality in mice, occurs with other compounds (antineoplastic drugs, steroid hormones) which are often immunosuppressant inhibitors of protein or RNA synthesis. The possibility of enhanced toxicity in man may exist with (e.g. food borne) gram negative bacteria (serving as an LPS source) in non-tolerant marihuana users. Host resistance to gram positive bacteria (listeria monocytogenes) was decreased (dose-dependent) by immunosuppressive (of delayed-type hypersensitivity to sheep RBC; ED_{50} for all cannabinoids tested approximated 100 mg/kg SC) doses of cannabinoids (38-200 mg/kg IP THC) in mice (Fig. 13) similar to flumethazone (potent immunosuppressant steroid which decreases host resistance to infections) while resistance to herpes simplex virus type 2 (HSV-2) was lowered with THC (lying betwen flumethazone and cyclophosphamide (alkylating immunosuppressant antineoplastic agent) effects) but not with marihuana extract (20% THC) (Morahan et al., 1979). Assessment of host resistance to both pathogens (IV) (infectious in mice and men; macrophages and T-cells involved in elimination of microorganisms) was done by noting the LD_{50} changes in cannabinoid treated vs control animals. The decreased host resistance appeared to be due to immunosuppressive properties rather than CNS effects since both CBD and 1-methyl Δ^8 THC, with immunosuppressive properties without CNS activity, also decreased host resistance. Susceptibility of human marihuana users to various infectious diseases has not been established.

However, a hypersensitivity (exaggerated response to antigen following a previous exposure leading to tissue damage) reaction (anaphylactic; allergic response of immediate type) has been reported in the human (Liskow et al., 1971). A female patient with an allergic (to ragweed) history developed anaphylactoid type symptoms (nasal and pharyngeal pruritus, lacrimation, nasal congestion, dyspnea, wheezing/20-30 minutes, gradually subsiding) after smoking one marihuana cigarette; a second attempt lead to similar symptoms. Her previous exposure to marihuana smoke was at parties (not smoking herself) when no ill effects were felt (probably dose-related). Marihuana intoxication by passive inhalation (contact high) has been documented by detection of urinary cannabinoid metabolites in a naive control placebo smoker living on a hospital ward with a group of heavy marihuana smokers taking part in a study (necessitating controls being housed separately in a marihuana study) (Zeidenberg et al., 1977). Since the above female patient had an earlier exposure to marihuana smoke prior to her first attempt of smoking the plant, her allergic diathesis probably set her up for a hypersensitivity reaction to marihuana. A direct skin test (scratch test) with marihuana solutions (with 1.35% and 0.03% THC) resulted in a positive wheal and flare (erythema) reaction (vs 9/10 controls) with 1.35% THC marihuana solution, indicating the possible presence of IgE sensitized mast cells. The immunological basis for this response was confirmed by a passive transfer test in which the patient's serum was injected intradermally into a non-allergic individual to whom the antigen (marihuana and THC (1.35% with some exocyclic THC) solutions) was applied (as in the direct skin test) to the test sites 48 hours later. A positive reaction was obtained with marihuana solution (1.35% not 0.03% THC) and the purified THC solution (vs control sites) indicating a passive transfer of cutaneous sensitivity due to skin sensitizing antibodies. These tests established the diagnosis of marihuana allergy and identified the offending allergenic substances (for this individual) as marihuana (with 1.35% THC) and purified THC. It appears that allergic reactions (various degrees of mild to serious anaphylactic responses) to marihuana may occur in individuals with medical allergy histories, since one control subject (noted above), who had a history of seasonal rhinitis and mild symptoms of coryza, lacrimation, and pharyngeal pruritus when using marihuana, responded positively to the direct skin test with marihuana solution (1.35% THC). Such individuals may avoid marihuana use if the allergic reaction is unpleasant or severe enough. The incidence of marihuana allergy is unknown (nor are the responsible marihuana constituents), although a preliminary survey (at that time) of marihuana users in a psychiatry clinic revealed that 4/30 individuals had similar respiratory symptoms (to the female patient) while smoking the plant. CBD and cannabicyclol elicited a positive cutaneous response (scratch test) in the female patient. An occupational immediate type allergy to hemp (cannabis sativa) pollen and hashish in a 26 year old criminological technician appeared as conjunctivitis, rhinitis, and urticarial eruptions on lower arms and hands (Lindemayr and Jäger, 1980). An intense positive reaction (rubbing test) was elicited with pollen rich hashish.

Marihuana or THC (and metabolites) specifically may act as a hapten noted in chemistry section (Mechoulam et al., 1976) covalently linked to protein (binds readily with plasma lipoproteins (Wahlqvist et al., 1970)) forming an antigenic conjugate capable of producing antibodies (noted earlier; Shapiro et al., 1974, 1976a). Antigens may enter the body via bronchopulmonary system with its highly developed lymphatic system where local immune response(s) may occur. Chronic environmental exposure to various substances, alone or in combination (sulphur dioxide, carbon, pollution, cigarette smoking) may modify defences, eventually decreasing immune response(s) (stimulation occurs initially, i.e. a biphasic response) to inhaled antigen(s) increasing susceptibility to disease (infections, cancer) (Nulsen et al., 1974). An immunosuppressive THC effect was observed in rodents immunized with sheep red blood cells noted as decreased splenic cellularity and antibody synthesis (Lefkowitz and Chiang, 1975). IT (intratracheal) (also IV, IP) innoculation of SRBC (sheep red blood cells) has elicited antibody producing cells in the lungs, spleen, blood and mediastinal lymph nodes; the principal site of antibody production occurring in the spleen followed by lymph nodes with some in the lungs (Thomas et al., 1973). In normal non-smoking (control) animals, both IgM and IgG/IgA antibody forming cells were detected following the first and second (12 days after first) IT inoculations. With tobacco cigarette smoking (30 king size filter cigarettes/day/26 weeks with a ratio of 1/7 re smoke/air at a puff volume of 35 ml) immune response was modified in the organ systems; the degree of decreased response being related to the distance that an organ is from the primary point of antigen (smoke) entry (primary response in lungs virtually annulled with reduced and short-lived response in spleen and nodes; all secondary responses variably decreased). With cessation of cigarette (tobacco) smoking (16 weeks without exposure following 42 weeks of exposure), recovery of the humoral (antibody) immune system occurs in animals (Thomas et al., 1974). Since human epidemiological data have indicated a lowering of risk re disease development with cessation of smoking, it has been suggested that this recovery may be due in part to restoration of immune function. Perhaps a similar recovery may be anticipated in marihuana smokers provided that the point of "no return" has not been reached.

Another aspect of the immune system involves pulmonary alveolar macrophages with bacteri-cidal activity against inhaled organisms and particles. A functional study of alveolar macrophages was conducted in marihuana (4 males, 4 females, aged 20-27 years, with 2-26 marihuana cigarette years i.e. 1 marihuana cigarette/day/year or equivalent), tobacco (2 males, one female, 20-28 years of age, 0.2-0.5 pack years with one having smoked a total of 100 cigarettes) and non (2 males, 2 females, 20-28 years old) smokers (all with negative chest X-ray and normal pulmonary function) with a morphological study being carried out in marihuana and non-smoking groups (Mann et al., 1971). The material studied were cells and acellular matter removed from lungs by bronchopulmonary lavage under local anesthesia noting the volume, size and ultrastructure of macrophages, and the ability of glass adhering macrophages to phagocytize heat-killed Candida albicans (yeast-like fungal organism; patients with leukemia, organ transplants, or those receiving immunosuppressive or antibacterial therapy are prone to Candida septicemia). In the morphology study, the volumes of cellular and acellular material as well as the diameter of macrophages were similar in marihuana and non-smokers with a decreased number of macrophages and an increased number of other cells (probably replacing the decreased macrophages) in marihuana vs non-smokers. The opposite has been reported in tobacco smokers; greater volume and number of macrophages. The structure of cytoplasmic inclusions in marihuana smokers was found to be similar to that reported in tobacco smokers. Functionally, an increased number of macrophages from marihuana and tobacco smokers adhered to glass vs non-smokers (probably indicating a difference in net negative surface charge) but no difference was evident with respect to the capacity of the adherent macrophages to phagocytize C. albicans. Thus it appears that functionally the defensive capacity of alveolar macrohages was not decreased but fewer cells were recovered from marihuana smokers vs non-smoking controls. An animal study (Drath et al., 1979) investigating the functional characteristics of alveolar macrophages from animals exposed to marihuana (2.2% THC) or tobacco for 30 days revealed that both substances did not compromise alveolar macrophages with respect to their ability to ingest particulate challenge of staph. aureus. At the end of the 30 day exposure period, weight gain of animals was less with both marihuana and tobacco exposure (vs controls) which may be due partly to stress induced by the exposure regimen; the lower weight gain with tobacco may be due to nicotine appetite suppressing effect vs the potential marihuana appetite stimulating effect. Certain animal data differed from the above human data in that no difference (from controls) was observed in the number of recovered macrophages or in glass adherent properties for the two substances (may be due to species difference, period of drug exposure, drug quality, and other drug use). Other animal studies re phagocytic impairment are noted in pulmonary system section.

5. Discussion and Summary

Clinically some polydrug and marihuana (including hashish) users have shown irregular mitosis with chromosomal abnormalies (breaks, hypoploidy (nucleus with less than 30 chromosomes; normal 46), hyperploidy) in cell nuclei similar to that seen with chemicals and irradiation; abstinence (> 10 days restoring cells to normalcy. If damage persists, possible (probability?) clinical implications of chromosomal alterations include neoplasms, transmission of permanent new mutations to one half of the offspring as well as teratogenesis, being more prevalent in chronic heavy drug (including marihuana) users. THC was found to be capable of inducing hypoploidy in cell (from healthy individuals) cultures indicating a decreased ability of the cells to synthesis proteins or enzymes (growth, inborn errors of metabolism). THC induced chromosomal segregational errors in normal human cultured lymphocytes suggesting it to be a chromosomal mutagen or mitotic poison. Human and animal cells exposed to marihuana and tobacco cigarette smoke had similar outcomes. At first, DNA synthesis and mitosis were inhibited (cytotoxic effect), followed by abnormal cell morphology and mitosis with irregular abnormal growth (disturbing genetic equilibrium of cell population) proceeding to more irregular growth of abnormal cells or malignant transformation of cells (confirmed by development of malignant tumors following injection of the cells into animals). The possibility exists that cells with abnormal DNA and chromosomal complement were responsible for subsequent atypical growth which may represent an early stage in malignant transformation in humans. The products of pyrolysis of cannabinoids contain potential mutagenic and carcinogenic chemicals (tars, benzpyrene, similar to tobacco, which are capable of producing tumors in newborn animals from healthy mothers and causing death in newborns from chronically marihuana exposed mothers. Some preliminary data has indicated that marihuana smoke may alter hereditary material in animal germ cells (mutagenic potential) observed as a decreased number of spermatids with normal haploid amount of DNA with some spermatids having decreased variable amounts of DNA. Exposure of human sperm to THC resulted in decreased motility with swelling of the mid-portion of the sperm containing mitochondria (principle energy source for cell), the outer and inner membranes of which were ruptured. THC appears to have an affinity for cell membranes due to its interaction with lipoproteins, leading to changes in phospholipid (essential for cell membrane function) concentrations which may be related also to fluctuations in immune ability of lymphocytes by affecting membrane enzyme mechanisms.

The inhibitory effect of THC on macromolecular (DNA, RNA, protein) synthesis was found to be due to a reduction in the precursor pool without altering either precursor transport rate into the cell, or DNA repair synthesis. The decreased pool size may be due to THC interaction with cell membrane resulting in leakage (more permeable) or alteration of precursors with modification of DNA leading to possible mutagenesis and carcinogenesis which may be transmissible to future generations. Cannabinoids (irrespective of psychoactivity) decreased cell proliferation via impairment of macromolecular bio-synthesis altering the genome (chromosomes with their genes). Alteration in cell metabolism particularly evident as altered chromatin (condensed; transcriptional arrest) in the nuclear area has not been correlated with overt pathology (e.g. altered immunity). The possible damage to DNA followed by corrective DNA repair resembles antineoplastic alkylating agents and ionizing radiation effects.

In normal healthy patients, stress (such as surgical trauma) may transiently depress cellular immunity, the "in-vitro" tests (T and B cells, lymphoblastic transformation) underestimating the "in-vivo" capability (cutaneous delayed hypersensitivity response) which takes longer to return to the previous baseline level. Some immunological tests have shown similarities between marihuana smokers and patients with T-cell (cellular) immunity impairment. Some T-cells (sub-population) may be depressed (due to cellular effects noted above) while other T-cells may still be immunologically competent. The question is, whether the latter cells are adequate to counteract infections, carry out immunological tumor surveillance, and subserve graft rejection? The clinical status of cancer patients appears to correlate with the number of active rosette forming T-cells (15% being the lower limit of normal). A low number in high risk families (e.g. gastrointestinal carcinoma) may indicate a predisposition to disease. Marihuana appears to affect T-cell function transiently with THC affecting early (active) rosette formation. The significance of abnormal T-cell rosette formation in marihuana smokers is unknown since clinical evidence of T-cell deficiency disorders is lacking. Cannabis is an antigen capable of eliciting a humoral immune response (antibody production) which may be associated with subclinical laboratory abnormalities (significance?). Allergic reactions to marihuana may occur as a consequence of certain occupations or in those with medical histories of allergy (incidence?). Animal studies have shown that the initial antibody stimulation may be followed by depression of this immune response with chronic drug exposure increasing susceptibility to disease. Enhanced toxicity or decreased host resistance to bacterial infections occurred in non-tolerant (to marihuana) animals due to immunosuppressive property. Such susceptibility to infectious disease has not been established in non-tolerant human marihuana users. Decreased immunity (cellular and humoral) occurred with THC especially in younger (vs older) animals. The presence of testosterone in early life appears to deter the autoimmune disease process. Any alteration (decrease) of the male sex hormone by marihuana or THC (noted in reproduction section) during pre and adolescent periods may render the male individual more susceptible to autoimmune disease (e.g. SLE). Since sources of marihuana have varying compositions of various components (e.g. THC, CBN, CBD) the effects of each component (and their interactions) should be studied including effects on the various cells (e.g. subclass of T-cells; helper cells) making up the immune system. Besides immunosuppression, THC suppressed proliferation of neoplastic tissue (as did Δ^8 THC, CBN, but not CBD) to which resistance developed with repeated doses but without affecting normal bone marrow cells (at certain THC concentrations); the antineoplastic property being unrelated to behavioural property. Thus THC resembles chemotherapeutic agents used in neoplastic disease (which however depress bone marrow cells). Some cannabinoids may be active only against some rapidly growing tumors (by inhibition of DNA synthesis). It is unknown whether suppression of proliferative neoplastic tissue is species specific and/or tumor specific in humans. With respect to pulmonary alveolar macrophages (bactericidal activity), fewer cells were recovered from the lungs of marihuana smokers (vs non-smokers) with unaltered functional defensive capacity (phagocytic impairment noted in pulmonary system section).

Since both animal and some human studies have revealed a decrease in T-cells, the clinical significance of which is unknown, questions regarding possible clinical effects should nevertheless be considered. Is the decrease in T-cells a clinically significant one, or is adequate function still present in healthy individuals vs marginally immunologically affected individuals? If marihuana suppresses only cell-mediated immunity leaving the humoral immunity intact, then defense against many bacterial infections may be preserved. Does a genetic predisposition exist which may be provoked by an environmental factor (virus, drug) leading to a possible primary immunodeficiency disease, or, is the lymphopenic state due to a suppression of bone marrow and lymphoid tissue brought about by a cytotoxic drug result in a secondary immunodeficiency disease? Would hypersensitivity reactions (allergies, cytotoxic hemolytic anemias, serum sickness, autoimmune disease or autoallergy) become more prevalent? Antibodies that may be formed against marihuana may be without pathological significance and may be useful diagnostically in detecting marihuana use. (Chronic alcoholics exhibit marked increase in serum Ig levels which may be due to inhibition of T-suppressor cells which are sensitive to toxic agents or due to increased antigenic stimulation of lymphoid tissue as a result of disturbed liver function.) Is the suppression of T-cells a non-specific one seen with central nervous system depressant drugs (marihuana, alcohol)? Is a partial immunological tolerance being developed whereby a substance normally capable of inducing an immune (cellular) response, fails to do so? Since the T-cell defect was noted in street drug users vs hospital ward users, may such a defect be stress-related? The decrease in T-cells may possibly lead to an increased incidence of some (cell-mediated deficient) tumors as well as possible enhancement by blocking antibodies. Malignancy itself suppresses immune responses leading to secondary immunodeficiency states, and, deficient cellular and humoral immunities are associated with recurrent and disseminated tumors. Thus using cannabis in the treatment of nausea and vomiting of cancer chemotherapy does not seem to be logical because the drug's partial immunodepressant effect may add to the chemotherapeutic immunosuppression and to an inefficient immune system in the cancerous patient, although THC and CBN (not CBD) have shown antineoplastic properties in animals (perhaps a general decrease in growth or synthesis). It is unknown whether the constituents in marihuana responsible for the decrease in T-cells are similar or different from those responsible for beneficial effects in cancer patients. Such knowledge would lead to a desireable synthetic drug for alleviation of chemotherapitic side effects seen in cancer patients. However the partial immunosuppressive effects of marihuana may be beneficial in tissue transplantation by avoiding late cell-mediated rejection (vs early rejection by humoral antibodies). Should the humoral system (antibodies) also be suppressed (as indicated in some studies) then a possible increase in tumors may occur due to the lack of humoral antibodies as well as increased occurrence of bacterial infections but avoid early rejection of tissue transplants. Is the suppression of B-cells (Ig deficiency) a direct one or an indirect one via increased suppressor T-cell activity by virtue of decreased helper T-cell activity?

Some of the things to watch for clinically regarding possible inheritable alterations following marihuana use include:

(a) abnormal birth weight, congenital anomalies, and failure to thrive in newborns from marihuana-using mothers which may indicate possible chromosomal anomalies,

(b) increased incidence of infection during first 6 months of age pointing to a possible cell-mediated defect while after 6 months of age, a humoral defect may be suspected, and

(c) cases of leukemia may reveal chromosomal alterations and/or immunodeficiency disease(s).

Clinical features associated with immunodeficiency include:

(a) those frequently present with high degree of suspicion such as chronic infection, more than expected recurrent infection, incomplete clearing of infection and unusual infecting agents,

(b) those frequently present with a moderate degree of suspicion such as skin rash (candida, eczema), chronic diarrhea, recurrent abscesses and osteomyelitis, hepatosplenomegaly, and growth failure, and

(c) those of specific disorders such as eczema, partial albinism, telangiectasia, tetany, cartilage-hair hypoplasia, short-limbed dwarfism, thrombocytopenia, ataxia, and idiopathic endo-crinopathy.

Immunodeficiency diseases are classed as antibody (B-cell) deficiency, cellular (T-cell) deficiency, combined B and T-cell deficiency, phagocytic dysfunction and complement abnormalites. Should some marihuana users be observed to be more susceptible to infections, then possible genetic defect(s) (or predisposition) must be determined; if present, is it familial or a new mutation? A predisposed (genetically) individual and an environmental factor (marihuana) may lead to varying problems (cancer, degenerative disease, teratogenicity depending upon the genetic defect or damage (mutation) caused by an environmental agent). The immunological status and possible genetic alterations in chronic marihuana smokers remains to be established.

From the foregoing, it may be seen that many questions remain to be answered before any conclusive statement can be made with respect to marihuana effects on the immune and genetic systems and their implications. The possibility exists that the immunosuppressant and antineoplastic effects (without depressing normal bone marrow cells) of THC noted in animals may lead to the development of a new class of therapeutic agents (organ transplantation, autoimmune disease, neoplasms).

II. 3. A. Chromosomes, Cell Metabolism, Immunity

List of Figures

Fig. 1.   Chromosomal breaks   49
Fig. 2.   DNA in chromosomes   49
Fig. 3.   Total intracellular ^{3}H-thymidine uptake   52
Fig. 4.   Total intracellular ^{3}H-uridine uptake   50
Fig. 5.   Total intracellular ^{14}C-leucine uptake   51
Fig. 6.   Psychotropic drug effects on ^{3}H-thymidine uptake   53
Fig. 7.   Psychotropic drug effects on ^{3}H-thymidine uptake   54
Fig. 8.   Psychotropic drug effects on ^{3}H-thymidine uptake   53
Fig. 9.   Glucose consumption and lactate excretion   52
Fig. 10.   Cellular growth rate   55
Fig. 11.   Early active rosette formation   56
Fig. 12.   T-cell number and PHA stimulation response changes   57
Fig. 13.   Host resistance to gram positive bacteria   58

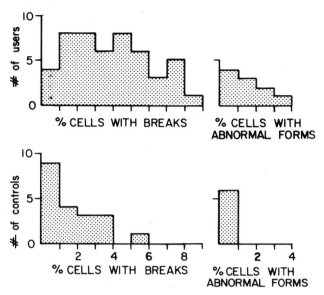

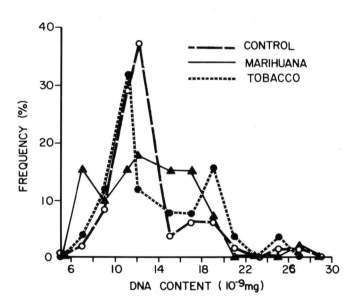

Fig. 1.
II.3.A
Chromosomal breaks and abnormal configurations in marihuana users and control subjects.

Adapted from Stenchever et al., 1974.

Fig. 2.
II.3.A
Amount of DNA in chromosomes (telophase) of fibroblastic cells from a control adult human lung transplant and from fibroblastic cells following fresh marihuana and tobacco smoke exposures.

Adapted from Leuchtenberger and Leuchtenberger, 1976.

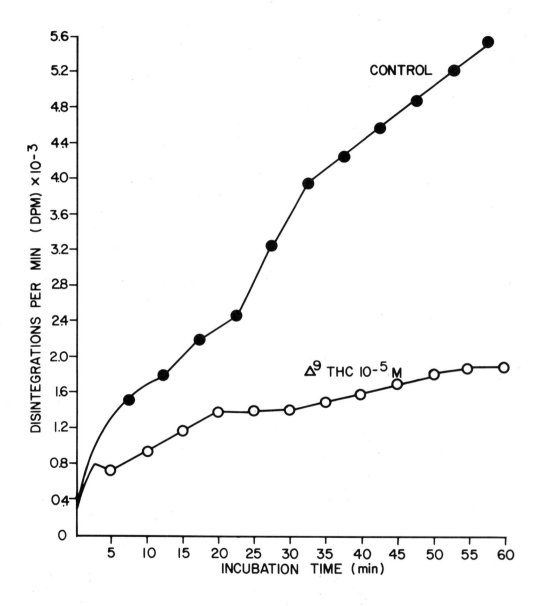

Fig. 4.   THC effect on total intracellular ^{3}H-uridine uptake (intracellular free
II.3.A ^{3}H-uridine + ^{3}H-uridine incorporated into RNA) vs incubation time in
                normal human diploid fibroblast cells.

Adapted from Blevins and Regan, 1976.

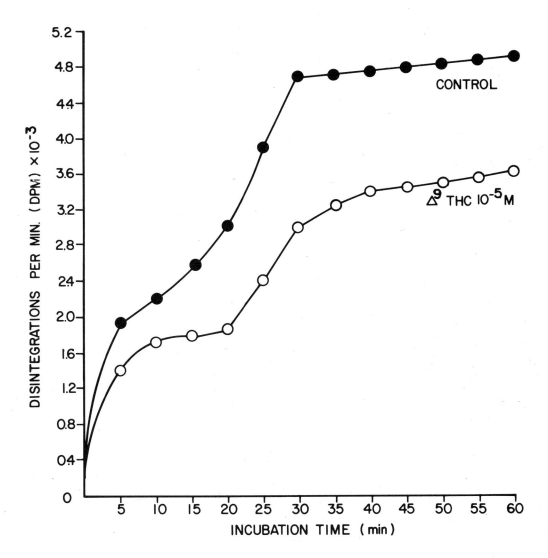

Fig. 5. THC effect on total intracellular ^{14}C-leucine uptake (intracellular
II.3.A free ^{14}C-leucine + ^{14}C-leucine incorporated into protein) vs incubation time in normal human diploid fibroblast cells.

Adapted from Blevins and Regan, 1976.

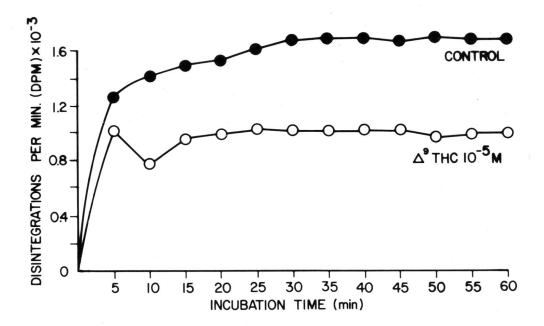

Fig. 3.   THC effect on total intracellular ^{3}H-thymidine uptake (intracellular
II.3.A   free ^{3}H-thymidine + ^{3}H-thymidine incorporated into DNA) vs incuba-
             tion time in normal human diploid fibroblast cells.

             Adapted from Blevins and Regan, 1976.

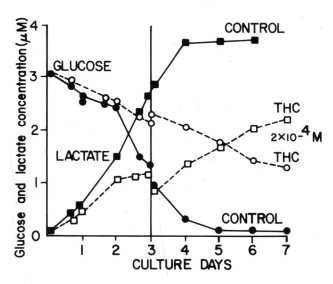

Fig. 9.   THC effect on glucose consumption and lactate excretion in lympho-
II.3.A   cyte cultures.

             Adapted from Banchereau et al., 1979.

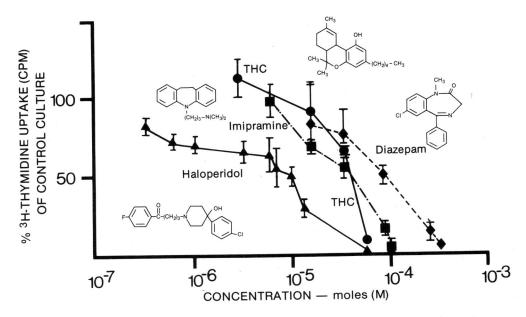

Fig. 6.   Psychotropic drug effects on ³H-thymidine uptake by cultured (3 days)
II.3.A   lymphocytes stimulated with PHA (phytohemagglutinin; lymphocyte
            transformation to lymphoblasts).

Adapted from Banchereau et al., 1979.

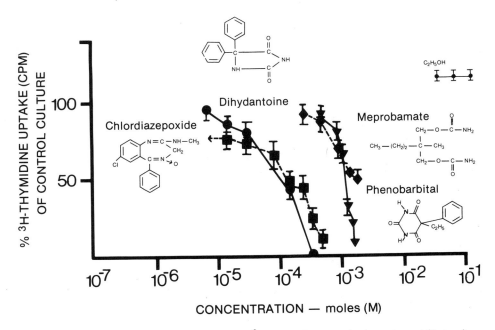

Fig. 8.   Psychotropic drug effects on ³H-thymidine uptake by cultured (3 days)
II.3.A   lymphocytes stimulated with PHA (phytohemagglutinin; lymphocyte
            transformation to lymphoblasts).

Adapted from Banchereau et al., 1979.

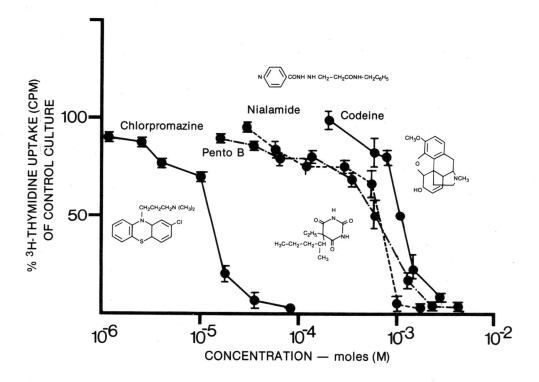

Fig. 7.   Psychotropic drug effects on ^{3}H-thymidine uptake by cultured (3 days)
II.3.A   lymphocytes stimulated with PHA (phytohemagglutinin; lymphocyte
             transformation to lymphoblasts).

             Adapted from Banchereau et al., 1979.

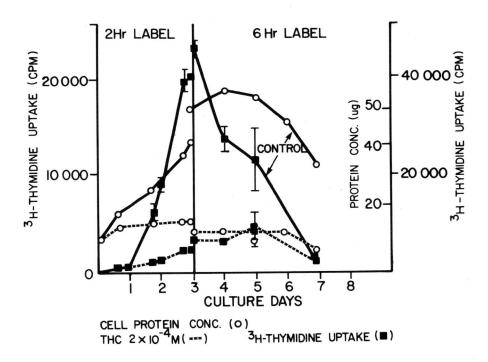

Fig. 10.   THC effect on cellular growth rate determined by ³H-thymidine
II.3.A   uptake and cellular protein concentration per culture.

Adapted from Banchereau et al., 1979.

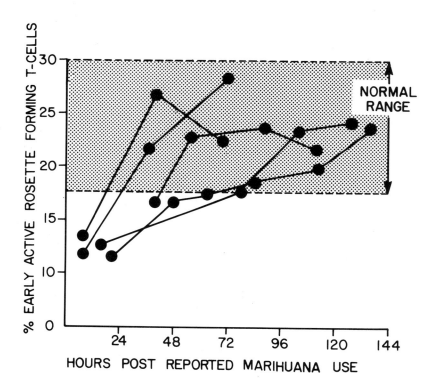

Fig. 11.
II.3.A   Active rosettes in chronic marihuana smokers post marihuana use.

                 Adapted from Cushman and Khurana, 1976.

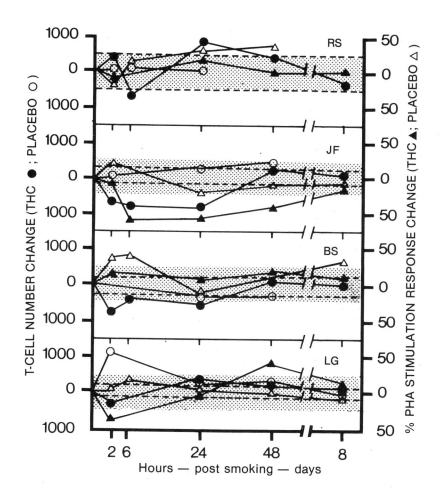

Fig. 12.
II.3.A

T-cell number and PHA stimulation response changes post marihuana
(10 mg THC) or placebo cigarette smoking (shaded area and dashed
lines indicating 2SD from mean for T-cell and PHA responses respectively).

Adapted from Petersen et al., 1976.

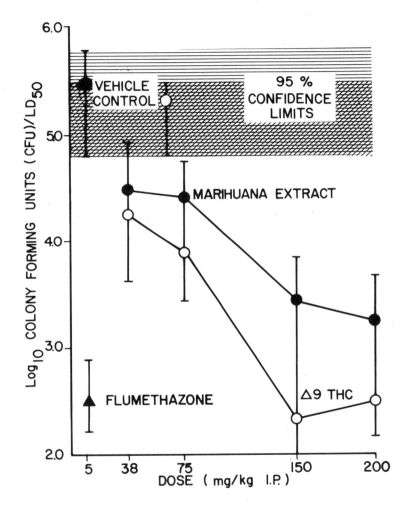

Fig. 13.   Cannabinoid (vs. flumethazone, vehicle, control) effects on host resis-
II.3.A   tance to gram positive bacteria (listeria monocytogenes).

             Adapted from Morahan et al., 1979.

II. 3. B. Reproductive System

Contents

	Abstract	59
1.	Introduction	59
2.	Reproductive Physiology	60
3.	Marihuana Effects in the Male	
	(a) Testosterone	61
	(b) Spermatogenesis	63
	(c) Gynecomastia	64
4.	Marihuana Effects in the Female	
	(a) Hormonal and Ovulatory Effects	65
	(b) Placental Effects	66
	(c) Maternal Milk Content	66
	(d) Fetal Toxicity	67
5.	Summary	71
6.	Figures	73

Abstract

1. Human reproductive physiology is discussed in order to understand endocrine alterations produced by marihuana use in males (affecting testosterone levels and spermatogenesis with possible gynecomastia development) and females (affecting ovulation, placenta, maternal milk, and the fetus).

2. Marihuana may affect reproductive function (and outcome) or fertility by inhibiting gonadotropin (LH, FSH) secretions at the hypothalamic level, altering reproductive hormonal production (testosterone, estrogen, progesterone) and maturation of reproductive cells (sperm, ovum); potential clinical implications being presented.

Keywords: marihuana reproductive system effects, prenatal maternal marihuana exposure effect, reproductive cell effects, reproductive hormonal synthesis.

Abbreviations: adenosine monophosphate (AMP); adrenocorticotrophic hormone (ACTH); cannabichromene (CBC, CBCH); cannabicyclol (CBCy); cannabidiol (CBD); cannabigerol (CBG); cannabinol (CBN); carbon monoxide (CO); carboxyhemoglobin (COHb); cardiovascular system (CVS); central nervous system (CNS); crude marihuana extract (CME); deoxyribonucleic acid (DNA); dimethylheptyl (DMH); 11-hydroxy-THC (11-OH-THC); electroencephalogram (EEG); every-hour(s) (q-h); female chromosomal complex (XX); follicle stimulating hormone (FSH); growth hormone (GH); human chorionic gonadotropin (HCG); interstitial cell stimulating hormone (ICSH); intramuscular (IM); intraperitoneal (IP); intraveneous (IV);   kilogram (kg); LH-releasing hormone or factor (LHRH or LHRF); luteinizing hormone (LH); male chromosomal complex (XY); microgram (μ g); milligram (mg); nanogram (ng); per os or oral (p.o.); pregnant mare's serum (PMS); radioimmunoassay (RIA); subcutaneous (s.c.); tetrahydrocannabinol (THC); triiodothyronine (T_3); thyroxine (T_4).

1. Introduction

Possible impairment of reproductive endocrine function raises concern with respect to fertility and reproductive capacity, fetal development, growth, and sexual differentiation and maturation. In order to understand the significance of any endocrine (hormonal) alterations that may occur following marihuana use, human reproductive physiology shall be presented briefly including regulation of synthesis and secretion of sex hormones (androgens in the male; estrogens in the female) as well as their effects, which together with gonadotropins (in the CNS; anterior pituitary hormones) are involved in spermatogenesis and oogenesis (formation and maturation of the sperm or egg)   (Murad and Gilman, 1975; Kolodny, 1975; Rose, 1975).

2.   Reproductive Physiology

The embryonic gonad (sexual gland) has the potential of developing into a testis or an ovary depending upon the chromosomal complex (XY (male) or XX (female)); both glands being responsible for hormonal and reproductive functions.   The testis, ovary, and adrenal cortex (of adrenal gland near anterior medial border of kidney) synthesize androgens (male sex hormones), the biosynthesis of which and interrelation with female sex hormones (estrogens) is exemplified in the following schematic presentation:

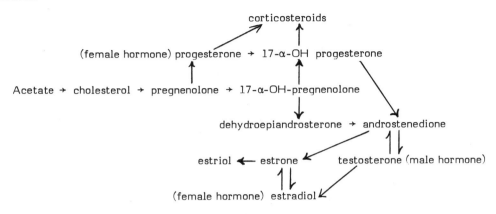

Testosterone (potent natural steroid and male hormone) is synthesized and secreted by interstitial Leydig cells while spermatogenesis (which may be impaired by drug toxicities) occurs within seminiferous tubules in the testis. Puberty begins in most males between the ages of 10 and 15 years (the initiation of which is unknown).   Regulation of testicular function is under the direct control of LH (luteinizing hormone, in males referred to as ICSH or interstitial cell stimulating hormone) and FSH (follicle stimulating hormone), both of which are increased during puberty and are anterior pituitary gonad-otropins secreted by the pituitary gland (governing endocrine glands of the body) located at the base of the brain.   LH stimulates the testis to increase the synthesis and release of testosterone; FSH participates in the growth and maturation of seminiferous tubules, and in conjunction with increased testosterone, is considered to be necessary for the induction of spermatogenesis.   Testosterone is responsible for the appearance of secondary male sexual characteristics, enlargement of sexual organs, and accelerated linear growth characteristic of normal pubertal development; in the female, androgens from the ovary (without virilizing effect) are thought to be necessary for normal growth and distribution of body hair.   A testicular-pituitary feedback mechanism exists whereby synthesis and release of hormones are modulated.   That is, a fall in serum testosterone level is followed by an increase in circulating LH which, in turn, stimulates the testis to synthesize and secrete more testosterone; a raised testosterone level decreases pituitary release of LH. FSH regulation is unknown, although the possibility of estrogen playing a role in males has been suggested. Following damage to seminiferous tubules, FSH levels are increased but not LH.   A hypothalamic or LH-releasing hormone (LHRH) stimulates the pituitary to synthesize and release LH, and, apparently is necessary for normal male gonadal function. Thus, in man, a hypothalamic-pituitary-testicular axis exists.   The testes secrete testosterone daily averaging 7 mg for a 70 kg man; females produce 0.5 mg. via conversion of precursors secreted by the ovaries and adrenal cortex. Adult male plasma testosterone levels vary greatly with a normal range of 0.3-1.4 μ g%. Most of the plasma hormone is bound to globulin (98%); the free hormone (2% with half-life of 10-20 minutes) being available to act on target tissues. Greater binding occurs in women, infants, children, and older men (6th-7th decade). Newborn boys and girls have essentially the same testosterone level (may be slightly higher in boys) which increases greatly in boys at puberty (2-3x/18 month period), gradually decreasing with age (60-90 years of age → decrease of 25-60% of 20-40 age levels). Testosterone is secreted episodically resulting in individual diurnal variation in plasma concentration (as much as 40% variation during the day) indicating that the time of blood sampling from a particular individual for testosterone determination is important.   Radioimmunoassay techniques are used to measure testosterone plasma levels. Depending on the antibody (globulin or albumin conjugate) used, cross-reactivity may occur with other androgens (especially dihydrotestosterone) thereby overestimating plasma values by 30-50%. Male sex hormones are metabolized in the liver and excreted in the urine as androsterone. Hormonal imbalance may result in abnormal conditions in both males and females (and vice versa). The adrenogenital syndrome in girls (hyperfunction of the adrenal cortex with excessive output of adrenal androgens resulting in pseudohermaphrodism and virilism) implies that excess testosterone present during fetal development may affect future behaviour; this has been demonstrated in animals (a small amount of testosterone given to a developing female fetus resulted in neonatal sterilization, failure to ovulate in adulthood, and increased male mounting behaviour). Animal research has indicated that appropriate levels of testosterone during crucial periods of brain development are necessary for normal adulthood behaviour associated with male sexual and aggressive conduct. The Klinefelter syndrome in males (due to one or more extra X chromosomes) or male hypogonadism with varying degrees of eunuchoidism, reveals lower than normal serum testosterone levels. In post-pubertal males, marked prolonged testosterone deficiency leads to decreased frequency of shaving and regression of secondary sexual characteristics. Castration in males and females leads to increased LH levels whereas exogenous testosterone decreases LH, and, periods of stress (surgical, psychological) decrease testosterone levels without significantly decreasing LH. Drugs such as phenothiazines and opiates alter (lower) LH secretion thereby decreasing testosterone plasma levels. Strenous exercise produces transient elevations of androgen levels.

Just as the testes secrete testosterone (also small amounts of estrogens) and are involved in spermatogenesis, the ovaries in the female secrete various hormones essential to reproductive tract cyclic function and take part in ova production. In the ovary, the ovarian follicle secretes estrogen (estradiol) whereas the corpus luteum (a mature ovarian follicle which has discharged its ovum) secretes progesterone and estrogen, both hormones being influenced by the pituitary gonadotropins, FSH and LH, which in turn are controlled by the hypothalamus sensitive to the feedback levels of circulating ovarian hormones. Disruption of the control mechanisms (dysfunction or disease) leading to abnormal ovarian function may be seen as disturbed menstrual pattern or sexual development, or as fertility problems. FSH brings about the rapid growth of the ovarian follicle with an oocyte (egg) while LH stimulates estrogen secretion by the follicle; this maturation beginning during the menstruation phase. The rising estrogen level leads to the preparation of the reproductive tract for receipt of spermatozoa. Both FSH and estrogen levels peak just prior to LH release (or cyclic surge) which induces ovulation (discharge of mature ovum from follicle) occurring at mid-cycle (usually the 14th day of a 28-day cycle) leading to the development of a corpus luteum which remains active for 14 days (noted as elevated basal body temperature). Progesterone is now secreted (in the presence of continued estrogen secretion) reaching a maximum at 21-22 days of the cycle when implantation of a fertilized ovum may occur in the prepared uterus (brought about by the two hormones). With a successful conception, the fertilized ovum secretes HCG (human chorionic gonadotropin) which maintains the corpus luteum until the placenta begins to secrete adequate supplies of estrogen and progesterone (large amounts found in urine during pregnancy). If conception does not occur, the corpus luteum regresses rapidly resulting in decreased levels of estrogen and progesterone, and menstruation ensues. Removal of ovaries leads to uterine atrophy and low sexual function. As noted in the above schematic diagram, estrogens are formed from androgenic precursors which are found excessively in pathological conditions of virilism and hirsutism seen in the Stein-Leventhal syndrome (or polycystic ovarian disease). Estrogens (bound to globulins in the blood) are metabolized in the liver and excreted in the urine as estriol, estrone, and estradiol (as glucuronides and sulphates), the daily excretion at mid-cycle being 25-100 µg vs 2-25 µg/day for males; near the term of pregnancy, the placenta excretes 30 mg/day (radioimmunoassay techniques being used to measure the hormone levels). Estrogens are responsible for changes in girls at puberty (beginning around 12 years of age).

A hypothalamic-pituitary-testicular/or ovarian axis has been established. FSH is essentially involved in the development of ova in the female or spermatozoa in the male, while LH is concerned with female (estrogen and progesterone) or male (testosterone) hormonal production. Both FSH and LH (in the anterior pituitary gland) are controlled by a hypothalamic releasing hormone.

3.   Marihuana Effects in the Male

(a)   Testosterone

It has been suggested that alteration in male reproductive physiology may occur following chronic intense use of marihuana due to its central action in the hypothalamus or pituitary gland (Kolodny et al., 1974). A dose related (0, 5-9, more than 10 joints/week) depression of plasma testosterone (radioimmunoassy determinations; average control 742, smokers with lower use 503, and with higher use 309 ng/100 ml) was observed in a study with 20 young (18-28 years of age) healthy males who used only (except alcohol use which was not more than 415 ml or less than 14 oz/week) marihuana (purity and potency unknown) at least 4 days/week (weekly intake of 5-18 joints) for a minimum of 6 months (6-20 months) vs a control of similar age and cigarette smoking habits but non-marihuana users. Testosterone levels were increased with cessation of drug use (by 57-141% 1 week post drug) or HCG administration during marihuana use (by 121-269% vs a normal 50% response), the latter indicating a normal Leydig-cell reserve. Even though pituitary hormones, LH and FSH, were within normal limits, FSH differences occurred between the two marihuana using groups (the lower intake group having higher

FSH levels than the higher intake group) which, together with decreased testosterone levels (which may be secondary to central depression) may account for oligospermia seen in 6/17 individuals (35%) (sperm counts of less than 30 million/ml semen with the higher using group having lower counts than the lower using group). There was a correlation between the sperm counts and plasma testosterone as well as with FSH concentration. Sexual function was normal in most subjects except for 2 individuals reporting impotence, one of whom recovered normal function 2 months following cessation of marihuana use (the other did not wish to discontinue drug use). A mild gynecomastia (enlarged breasts) noted in one subject (present in early adolescence prior to marihuana use) revealed a slight increase in plasma prolactin (an anterior pituitary hormone which stimulates lactation in mammary glands). The above study demonstrated impaired spermatogenesis and decreased plasma testosterone level. In a subsequent study by the same group (Kolodny et al., 1976), subjects (13 males, 21-27 years who took part in the above chronic study) were used as their own controls, and the purity and potency of the drug was known (natural marihuana with 2.2% THC). Individuals were hospitalized for 94 days to avoid other drug use confirmed by screening urines. Marihuana was not used one week prior to hospitalization nor during the initial eleven days in hospital. The purpose of this study was to determine the acute effects of smoking one or 3 standarized 900 mg marihuana cigarettes on plasma testosterone level over a 3 hour period. Acute effects were studied at the beginning of the smoking period and following 9 weeks of daily smoking. The normal range of testosterone levels in fasting plasma samples ranged from 380 to 980 ng/100 ml in 18-65 year old males. Confirmation of findings found in chronic users noted above were obtained. Plasma testosterone levels decreased (by 35% from 779 to 505 ng/100 ml) within 3 hours (Fig. 1) of smoking one marihuana cigarette (as well as smoking 3 cigarettes). Weekly blood samples revealed significantly lower testosterone levels after 5 weeks of daily smoking vs the initial abstinent period. Stimulation with HCG promptly increased the testosterone output indicating that the Leydig cells were not grossly impaired. Plasma LH levels were also lowered (Fig. 2) at the 3 hour interval but not FSH levels. It appears that the central effect (hypothalamus or pituitary or both) of marihuana is responsible for decreased (secretion) testosterone level while spermatogenic disruption may be a direct gonadal effect. Animal studies (Dalterio et al., 1978) support this hypothesis. That is, THC induced decrease in plasma testosterone levels is due to the inhibition of pituitary LH release and to the direct effect on testicular responsiveness (impaired) to LH stimulation. Plasma FSH levels were also lowered in animals suggesting a possible mechanism for impairment of spermatogenesis of chronic cannabinoid exposure. A direct gonadal effect has been intimated by findings of a dose-related inhibition of testosterone and protein synthesis in rodent testicular Leydig cell (in-vitro) preparations by low concentrations (0.15 - 150 µM) of various cannabinoids (Δ^9 or Δ^8 THC, 8-ß-OH-THC, 11-OH-THC, CBN, CBD and a water soluble derivative of THC or SP-111A) (Jakubovic et al., 1979). Acute and chronic THC in rodents inhibited testosterone production in testis microsomes (List et al., 1977). Inhibition of Leydig cell testosterone production by THC and CBN in the presence of LH occurred at the pre-pregnenolone step in biosynthesis via inhibition of cholesterol esterase which provides precursor cholesterol for steroidal hormone synthesis (Burstein et al., 1978a; b). The order of potency of various major natural occurring cannabinoids in decreasing testosterone production was found to be CBG > CBD > CBCy > CBN > THC > CBC (Burstein et al., 1980) indicating the importance of knowing cannabinoid content of cannabis preparations used by individuals. Acute alcohol effects (Kolodny et al., 1976) do not affect testosterone nor LH levels vs chronic effects which decrease testosterone with a high incidence of azoospermia (lack of sperm) in chronic alcoholics. Thus, marihuana and alcohol differ in their acute effects on plasma testosterone levels. Since the chemical structure of THC is similar to cholesterol, the possibility exists that it may enter the biosynthetic process of sex hormones, perhaps displacing some of the cholesterol, or, via secondary adrenergic effects affecting carbohydrate metabolism such that cholesterol becomes unavailable (noted as increased esterified cholesterol concentration in animal testes due to inhibition of cholesterol esterase which in turn may be due to decreased protein synthesis) for hormonal (inhibition of animal testosterone production) biosynthesis (see final comments section re metabolic effects), thereby decreasing hormonal production. It appears that cannabinoids may have both indirect central and direct gonadal effects. The significance of the above changes (which may be temporary or perhaps permanent with chronic use) is not clear but possible or potential implications of decreased testosterone levels include:

(a) decreased aggression,

(b) interference with sexual differentiation during the critical period of fetal development (first trimester of pregnancy),

(c) delay onset or completion of puberty including normal skeletal growth pattern, secondary sex characteristics, with potentially adverse psychosocial and sexual maturation,

(d) possibly affect spermatogenesis (partially interdependent on testosterone production) especially in those with mild oligospermia or partial suppression of FSH, leading to infertility, and

(e) those with marginal reproductive function may find difficulty in conception or some impotence.

Pubertal arrest has been associated with heavy marihuana smoking (at least 5 joints/day since 11 years of age) in a 16 year old boy (chief complaint of short stature and delayed puberty) (Copeland et al., 1980). Testicular growth appeared to be normal (serum FSH levels in prepubertal range of 1.9 m IU/ml) but serum testosterone level was low (16-32 ng/dl) thought to be due to LH (< 2.9 m IU/ml) inhibition while a bone age of 13 years was not due to growth hormone deficiency. Abstinence from marihuana for 3 months prior to follow-up at 17.5 years of age revealed a testosterone level of 394 ng/dl, an LH level of 5.7 m IU/ml, an FSH level of 2.5 m IU/ml and growth velocity of 7.8 cm/year.

(b) Spermatogenesis

In discussing human spermatogenesis, it should be noted that an average of 70 days is necessary for a single generation of cells to come to maturity. Monthly follow-up of 6 (2 spermatogenic cycles) to 9 months is therefore necessary to accurately assess drug effects (Kolodny et al., 1976). Approximately 10% of normal adult males have idiopathic oligospermia. Alteration in number of sperm (stress may decrease the count) is usually associated with diminished motility and abnormal morphology (form, shape, structure) seen with inflammation of various parts of the genital tract.

Following 4 weeks of smoking 8-20 marihuana cigarettes (2% THC) daily (preceded and followed by 4 weeks of no smoking), 16 healthy chronic marihuana users (18-29 years of age) showed abnormal (morphologically) sperm (first week post smoking), decreased motility (4th week of smoking), as well as decreased sperm concentration by 35% and total sperm count without change in semen volume during the 5th and 6th weeks (1st and 2nd weeks post smoking) of the study (Hembree et al., 1979). Sustained decreased sperm concentration occurred in 12/16 individuals with 11 subjects showing low values at the end of the study. Loss of motility response (during and post smoking) to cyclic AMP and phospho-diesterase inhibitor, theophylline, (response to assay system correlates with fertilizing capacity of sperm) indicates that sperm produced during marihuana exposure may have structural or biochemical functional defects due to Sertoli cell (cells in testicular tubules to which spermatids attached during spermiogenesis or nurse cells) dysfunction. A returning to normal conditions (more than 100×10^6 total sperm count, normal motility and morphology) was noted by the end of the study; 40 days hospitalization and cessation of smoking accomplishing normal motility. There was no sustained decrease in LH, FSH, or testosterone plasma levels, although acute intermittent suppression is possible as noted above. Beside the possible (latter) hormonal effect on spermatogenesis, a direct cannabinoid effect on the germinal epithelium of the seminiferous (carry semen) tubules in the testes may occur during spermiogenesis (morphogenesis; spermatid to spermatozoa) affecting sperm production. It is unknown whether such abnormalities would affect reproductive capacity and/or fetal development. A dose-related seminiferous tubular degenerative effect with sperm maturation interference has been seen in rodents (rats) treated with Turkish marihuana, CBD, or CBCH (cannabichromene) (Rosenkrantz and Hayden, 1979). The induction of testicular damage was associated with CBD (more potent) or CBCH (not seen with THC or placebo). Together with the observed delayed lethality (of 4 weeks), caution was advised as to the use of marihuana variants with high CBD or CBCH content. The relative toxicity of cannabinoids on sperm morphology in rodents (mice) was found to be THC > CBN > CBD (Zimmerman et al., 1979).

One explanation for altered human spermatogenesis may be the cellular cannabis effect on a particular metabolic pathway in the nuclear area involving nucleoproteins. In chromatin (gene carrier) within the nucleus of a cell, DNA (molecular basis of heredity) is specifically bound to low molecular weight proteins (5-20,000) with dibasic amino acids (especially lysine and arginine) called histones and protamines (the latter with a lower molecular weight and basicity). During spermatidic development, histones are extensively modified by enzyme mechanisms being gradually replaced by newly synthesized protamines. Protamines are found in the nuclei of normal mature spermatozoa. In 15 infertile oligospermic patients (24-38 years of age) with normal serum gonadotropins and testosterone (vs 15 controls, 23-33 years of age), protamines were not detectable, only histones, with testicular biopsy material revealing spermatidic arrest (Silvestroni et al., 1976). This suggests a maturation defect of spermatogenesis during spermatidic maturation seen as a lack of substitution of histones by protamines in the nucleus of the sperm cell thought to be responsible for the infertility in these men. Cellular effects (assessed blindly) of chronic hashish (4-5% THC) use was studied in a group of 34 apparently healthy Greek men (average of 40 years) who had used hashish for an average of 25 years duration, 2-6x/day with 3-8 Gm/day dose vs 18 matched controls (Issidorides, 1979; Stefanis and Issidorides, 1976). No other drugs were used except for tobacco and irregular social alcohol use. In most spermatic cell nuclei of users, the decrease in arginine-rich histones was counterbalanced by an increased lysine-rich fraction indicating arrest in spermatic cell maturation. Chronic cannabis use may, therefore, interfere with the sperm's final differentiation via impairment of transition of histones to protamines. A similar alteration in histone ratio was noted in peripheral blood cells (lymphocytes) with the implication of possible under-response to antigenic stimulation (i.e. inhibition of immune response). However, a compensatory mechanism may override the initial suppressed immunological response avoiding any clinical manifestations of a decreased immune response. Testosterone may be involved in the lowered arginine content. During sperm maturation, testosterone is necessary to induce changes in nuclear proteins. Since cannabis decreases testosterone, then protein synthesis may be indirectly affected (also see final comments section). This would also apply to the blood cells since sex hormones affect cell maturation in the bone marrow differentially. The observed abnormalities of sperm heads was due to altered acrosomal (cap-like structure covering 1/2 to 2/3 sperm head) morphogenesis (including absence of acrosomes). The shape of the sperm head and structure of the acrosome, which are species specific and genetically controlled, determine the sperm's capacity for fertilization and normal embryogenesis. Shaping of the head is related to properties of arginine-rich proteins (histones or protamines), synthesis of which is associated with the onset of chromation condensation. The abnormalities (spermatidic maturation arrest, altered acrosomal morphogenesis, incomplete chromation condensation in sperm heads) noted in users are probably due to the low protamine content brought about by depletion of arginine by cannabis. Preservation of an individual or species is brought about by brain mechanisms (adaptive behaviour), fertile sperm, immune reaction, and antibacterial activity, of which, two peripheral systems (sperm and blood cells) have had a common metabolic coordinating process affected. That is, a common metabolic disturbance (with respect to histones) may exist in various tissue cells of chronic users (see final comments section). The possibility exists that a similar metabolic or chemical modification may occur in the brain. Presently, it is unknown whether these findings have potential health significance for cannabis users with respect to functional abnormalities, since there appears to be a lack of a positive correlation between cellular metabolic changes and overt pathology.

(c) Gynecomastia

Gynecomastia is the enlargement of breast glandular tissue in the male (sometimes secreting milk) due to hormonal activity. This tissue reaction is a common transient occurrence in normal adolescence. Some of the varied causes of this phenomenon include testicular insufficiency and intersexual states; testicular, pituitary or adrenal feminizing tumors; liver cirrhosis (circulating estrogens not inactivated); and iatrogenic causes due to hormonal (estrogens for prostatic carcinoma) and drug administration (steroidal therapy with digitalis; amphetamines, chlorpromazine, meprobamate). Reports have appeared in the literature implying that marihuana may be another substance responsible for drug-induced gynecomastia. In 14 young male patients (mid-20 age), gynecomastia developed following heavy (not defined) marihuana use (average 5 year duration) (Harmon and Aliapoulios, 1972; 1974). Excluded were pubertal onset of gynecomastia, various associated disorders, and use of hormones or mammotrophic drugs. Abstinence from marihuana in 3 patients resulted in decreased breast tenderness and size. Post-operative pathological examination of excised excessive breast tissue (requested by 3 patients) revealed typical ductal proliferation of gynecomastia. Animal experiments were undertaken to investigate the possible marihuana-induced gynecomastia. THC (1 mg/kg S.C./13-21 days) stimulated the development of male rat breast tissue (Fig. 3) which was consistent with the above clinical findings. A possible CNS marihuana effect via pituitary prolactin (lactation inducing hormone) release or a direct mammary effect was suggested. In a U.S. army population in Germany where the incidence of cannabis use was nearly 50%, 11 patients (average age 20 years) with idiopathic (cause unknown) gynecomastia requiring mammaplasty were compared with matched controls to determine if an association exists between cannabis use and gynecomastia; none was found (Cates and Pope, 1977). Sex hormone levels were not determined nor were laboratory tests conducted for controls. Cannabis (potency unknown) use was slightly more frequent (1.6 vs 1.3x/week) and of shorter duration (25 vs 29 months) in patients vs controls within the previous 6 months. The acute intravenous effect of single doses of THC and 11-OH-THC vs placebo on serum prolactin was evaluated (double-blind, cross-over study) in 6 casual marihuana smokers (not defined) abstinent for 1-4 weeks (Lemberger et al., 1975). In 2/6 subjects, serum prolactin concentration increased (doubled) at the 2 hour period but was not evident at 4 hours (Fig. 4). It was concluded that there was a lack (?) of an acute THC effect on serum prolactin. Male animals, intraperitoneally injected with THC (40 μg, 4 and 16 mg/kg) or estradiol (female sex hormone) (40 and 400 μg/kg) showed increased serum prolactin levels with 16 mg/kg THC and 40 μg/kg estradiol (Daley et al., 1974). In a clinical study noted above (Kolodny et al., 1974), neither gynecomastia nor elevated prolactin levels could be found. However three patients (2 students, 21 and 25 years of age; one prisoner, 30 years of age) with a 2 to 5 year cannabis smoking history (occasional by the 2 students) developed gynecomastia with prolactin levels higher than age-matched controls (70.8-85.6 vs 40.6-43.8 ng/ml); various known causes for gynecomastia being ruled out (Olusi, 1980). The apparent discrepencies may be due to dose and potency of the drug used as well as to the frequency of use and the endocrinological state of the individual.

4. Marihuana Effects in the Female

(a) Hormonal and Ovulatory Effects

Studies using female animals have shown that THC alters reproductive hormones and inhibits ovulation. A recent study in female primate animals reported on THC effects on gonadotropin levels (LH and FSH), ovarian function and menstrual cycle, and target organ tissues of the female reproductive system (uterus, vagina) (Smith et al., 1979). Single intramuscular doses of THC (0.625, 1.25, 2.5 and 5 mg/kg) vs vehicle in ovariectomized animals inhibited the gonadotropins (LH and FSH) by 50-88% (Fig. 5; 6) lasting 6-24 hours (depending on THC dose) occurring at the level of the hypothalamus (since LHRF released LH and FSH from the pituitary in the presence of THC). Changes did not occur with the 0.3125 mg/kg dose. Daily THC (2.5 mg/kg) administration during the luteal phase of the menstrual cycle (second half of the cyle) in normal primates affected the subsequent cycle (Fig. 7) observed as absence of ovulation (anovulatory cycle) associated with alteration in LH and progesterone levels (subnormal). That is, the cyclic surge of LH necessary to trigger ovulation was blocked. No evidence was found for any direct estrogenic or antiestrongenic activity for THC since:

(a) THC (2.5 mg/kg/14 days) in ovariectomized animals did not cause proliferation of glandualar epithelium in the endometrium of the uterus, nor maturation of vaginal epithelium normally seen with estrogenic activity, and,

(b) THC, cannabidiol, or marihuana extract did not compete with estrogen for estrogen receptor sites in the uterus (i.e., no antiestrogenic activity).

In adult female rodents, a high acute dose of THC (50 mg/kg IP-rat) given during estrous (heat) significantly reduced both serum LH (8.7 vs 385 ng/ml for controls) and prolactin (23.1 vs 171.7 ng/ml for controls) levels (Chakravarty et al., 1975). Daily injections (IP) of cannabis extract (1 mg/day in mice; 5 mg/day in rats) for 64 days resulted in cessation of ovarian follicular cyclic activity evidenced from vaginal smears and by the absence of corpora lutea in the ovaries (i.e. no ovulation) (Dixit et al., 1975). DMH (dimethylheptyl) homologues of THC and other cannabinoids (some without psychotropic activity) showed potent inhibitory ovulation activity in pro-estrous rodents by suppressing pre-ovulatory LH surge with a possible direct ovarian effect (Cordova et al., 1980). Other CNS drugs inhibiting ovulation include barbiturates, chlorpromazine, morphine, and reserpine. Disturbances in the estrous cycle of rodents (observed via vaginal smear) by cannabis sativa resin and smoke condensate was seen as shortening of estrous and lengthening of diestrous (sexual quiescence) indicating possible diminished fertility (Lares et al., 1981). In small rodents, dose-dependent suppression of pregnancy occurred with long term (70 days) oral THC or CME (crude marihuana extract) equivalent to human moderate and heavy marihuana use; a 30 day recovery period allowing for normal pregnancies to occur in 80% of previous failures (Kostellow et al., 1980). Short term (8 days) CME treatment did not affect PMS-HCG-induced ovulation (synchronized estrous cycles by pregnant mare's serum - human chorionic gonadotropin regimen) but did delay entry into proestrous (preparatory physiological changes for estrous) with the highest dose (75 mg/kg) decreasing serum progesterone during the luteal phase and inhibiting female receptivity to males.

A preliminary human study (Marihuana and Health, U.S. report, 1980) attempted to assess chronic marihuana effects on ovulatory status or hormonal patterns. Women in their twenties took part in this study consisting of 26 chronic marihuana users (self-reported marihuana use at least 3x/week for a minimum duration of 6 months; potency of marihuana unknown) and 16 non-using controls. The users also drank alcohol more frequently than controls. Abnormal menstrual cycles were noted for a greater proportion of time in users (vs controls) in the form of anovulatory cycles (failure to ovulate) or inadequate luteal phase (shortened potential fertility period) which could contribute to female infertility. Hormonal alterations in the users were observed as slower post-ovulatory increase in progesterone with lower peak concentration, lower prolactin levels, and higher testosterone levels. These data appear to be consistent with available animal data. The decrease in luteal phase progesterone levels concurs with "in vitro" inhibition of progesterone synthesis (Burstein et al., 1979) by THC and CBN in isolated rat luteal cells; the ovary is thought to be affected directly, the site of inhibition being the release of cholesterol (precursor) from its ester storage pool. Should decreased prolactin levels occur in the post-partum (after childbirth) period, then impairment of lactation and nursing may occur. Cholesterol esterases were inhibited by THC in various rodent organs (adrenal, testis, luteinized ovary, liver) altering steroid hormone production (Burstein et al., 1978a). Since progesterone synthesized by the corpus luteum maintains pregnancy, a possible abortive effect may occur in rodents. In animals, marihuana has been shown to stimulate the pituitary-adrenal axis (Barry et al., 1970; Dewey et al., 1970) which may explain the increased testosterone levels in marihuana using women (in normal women a large fraction of testosterone production is of adrenocortical origin). Secretion of ACTH was stimulated as was diuresis. This also occurs with intoxicating doses of ethyl alcohol.

From the above, it appears that reproductive function or fertility may be affected by chronic intensive marihuana use in young men and women due to THC inhibitory action on gonadotropin (LH, FSH) secretion mediated via the hypothalamus, observed as altered (decreased) sex hormone production (testosterone, estrogen, progesterone), and decreased sex cell production or maturation (sperm, ovum), as well as adrenal (stimulatory) effects (possibly via secondary adrenergic effects noted in CVS section).

(b) Placental Effects

Viviparous animals bear living young which derive nutrition directly from the mother via the placenta which is an outgrowth of the embryo and include mammals which nourish the born young with milk secreted by the mammary gland.   The degree of placental transfer for any drug is directly proportional to the free drug concentration in the maternal plasma. During pregnancy, animal studies have demonstrated placental transfer of THC to the fetus where it is concentrated in fatty tissues including the brain. THC has also been found in the milk of nursing primate mothers which transports the drug to the feeding young. Oral THC (2 mg/kg) given to female pregnant rats throughout pregnancy (from day 3 of pregnancy) resulted in 21.4 ng THC and metabolites per gram of pup tissues (with a total amount of 553 ng/average pup at birth) indicating placental transfer (Vardaris et al., 1976). There was a transient alteration in social behaviour. Teratogenicity was not evident at this drug level but altered behavioural effects were seen as slower learning of avoidance behaviour in the offspring from the drug group at 21 days of age as well as a permanent increased competitiveness which may be part of a maturation process. In pregnant dogs (near parturition or delivery), 30 minutes (peak behavioural change) following an intravenous injection of radioactive THC (0.5 mg/kg), radioactivity distribution (µg THC + metabolites/gm tissue or ml fluid) in peripheral tissues was similar to non-pregnant dogs with radioactivity being found in chorionic fluid, amniotic fluid, and all fetal tissues (Martin et al., 1977). The concentration of radioactivity found in the placenta was 30% of the maternal plasma level, being only slightly higher than that found in most fetal tissues. The highest concentration was in the adrenal glands of mothers and fetuses, with liver being next in order for the mothers and fat for the fetuses. Even though similar concentrations occurred in the fat of both mothers and fetuses, in relation to other tissues, maternal fat had the lowest concentration and fetal fat the highest. Concentration in the fetal testes was similar to adult male dogs. Distribution was similar in maternal and fetal brain with levels being higher in the former, as expected. That is, evaluation at the 30 minute period is only one point along a pharmacokinetic time-concentration curve.   The curves (when established with more time interval studies) may prove to be similar with a shift of the fetal curve to the right with respect to time sequence of events, explaining the difference in levels of radioactivity found in the mother and fetus. A larger percent of the radioactivity in fetal brain was due to unchanged THC, being slightly higher (due to an immature liver) than in maternal brain where the predominate metabolite was 11-OH-THC (not seen in the fetal brain). A correlation was established between radioactivity concentration and phospholipid levels in the brain.   It has been suggested that accumulation and slow release of lipid soluble cannabinoids in phospholipids (in glial cells and myelin in the brain) may be responsible for prolonged duration of pharmacological and behavioural effects of THC. Another example demonstrating placental transfer was observed during simulated marihuana smoking (500 mg cigarette with 1.4% Δ^9 THC) in the maternal and fetal guinea pig (Singer et al., 1973). Changes were noted in maternal, fetal and newborn heart rates, and, in brain wave (EEG) patterns. Maternal heart rate progressively increased with onset at 2-6 minutes and a duration of 18-96 minutes. Fetal heart rate decreased lasting 8 minutes with recurrence of the bradycardia 8-40 minutes post smoking period (Fig. 8). Newborns at 9 hours of age responded by a decrease in heart rate in 3 neonates, an increase in one (largest) animal, and a recurrent bradycardia in two. During the smoking period, EEG changes were not evident in the mother whereas the fetus showed slow frequency, high voltage activity. Following the smoking session, the maternal EEG changed to low frequency, high amplitude activity for up to 24 hours while the fetus had higher frequency, lower voltage activity for 50-90 minutes duration. Exposure to smoke resulted in slow shallow respirations in the mother due to irritant nature of the smoke. Mothers and newborns were active during the control or pre-smoking period, noticeably disturbed during smoking, and sedated (relatively immobile, unreactive to stimuli) in the post-smoking period which lasted for 90-120 minutes indicating adequate lung absorption of the drug.

(c) Maternal Milk Content

Lactating primates placed on chronic oral doses of THC (2 mg/kg) at 2-5x/week schedule, when infants were 2 weeks old, received a tracer dose of ^{14}C-THC (16 µCi at 8 and 20 week periods) to follow the passage of THC in the body (Chao et al., 1976). There was no difference in the milk volume from the THC and control (no drug) mothers, nor in weight gain of their infants. Maximum excretion of total radioactivity via the milk occurred 2 hours after drug intake and declined steadily over the next 24 hours (Fig. 9). During a 24 hour observation period, 0.2% labelled THC appeared in the milk with 42% being excreted in the feces and 1% in the urine. Infants (3-6 months of age) who suckled for 6 hours following tracer THC dose, excreted 0.12% of the mother's dose in the feces and 0.01% in the urine for 18 hours post suckling. The time course of secretion of THC and metabolites into the milk of primates is similar to plasma where peak concentration occurs 2 hours post oral ingestion and 10 minutes post smoking. THC and CBN were identified in the milk agreeing with reported plasma content; some metabolites with unknown chemical structures were also noted. Human nursing mothers (2) smoking marihuana daily (by pipe 1-7 x/d; potency?) concentrated THC (8 x plasma level) in their milk (up to 340 ng/ml) which was absorbed by the baby resulting in infant fecal excretion of 347 ng THC, 67 ng 11-OH-THC and 611 ng carboxy-THC (from higher intake mother); 11-OH-THC and carboxy-THC also being found in maternal plasma and milk (Perez-Reyes and Wall, 1982).

(d) Fetal Toxicity

Morphogenesis or differentiation of cells and tissues begins in the early embryonic stage of development resulting in established form and structure of the body. The human embryonic period occurs from one week following conception to the end of the second month of pregnancy when the developing organism in the uterus becomes a fetus until birth. The neonatal period is the first 4 weeks of life, after which the neonate becomes an infant until an erect posture is assumed (12-14 months of age) and childhood begins. Exogenous substances ingested by the mother during pregnancy (prenatal period) may be embryo or fetotoxic, and/or teratogenic. A terotogen is an agent that causes abnormal development seen as developmental (congenital) malformations observed as abnormal growth and structure or serious deviation from the accepted norm. Organogenesis in humans begins about the 20th day of gestation continuing through the 3rd month. Biochemical and finer morphological differentiation occurs during the second trimester with the last three months being devoted to growth and further biochemical development. Risk of morphologic anomalies is greater during the period of greatest organ development (1st trimester especially days 20-90). Drugs as well as environmental factors (pollutants, stress, noise) could interact to increase teratogenic response without visible maternal toxicity.

Cannabis effects on endocrine glands (Rosenkrantz and Esber, 1980) studied in animals (rodents treated for 14-180 days with oral THC 2-50 mg/kg (1-10 mg/kg in pregnant and lactating animals) or marihuana smoke exposure for 14 days with 0.7-4 mg/kg THC equivalent to human inhalation of 0.1-5 mg/kg THC) measuring circulating hormones (via RIA) revealed

a)   a dose-related decrease in testosterone with 14 day treatment,

b)   decreased thyroxine (T_4) and triiodothyronine (T_3) following oral intake; inhalation altering only T_3 levels with 14 day treatment,

c)   increased LH, FSH, and estrogens at higher doses (not progesterone) with treatment during gestation (days 6-17) and lactation except for a decrease in LH with small drug doses during gestation; non pregnant animals having hormonal levels in concert with ovarian events of increased FSH with follicular growth and increased LH with corpora luteal growth, and,

d)   during the 180 day oral chronic phase, decreases in LH, FSH (in males), and GH (growth hormone) only at 90, 14, and 28 (and 180) day periods respectively; other periods usually showing increases.

Oral CBD (30-300 mg/kg/90 days with 30 days recovery) treatment in monkeys increased FSH serum level after treatment and recovery (at higher doses in the latter period) with a slight increase in LH after the recovery phase in male animals. Testosterone was decreased at the 90 day period with the highest dose while progesterone increased after treatment and recovery (the latter effect also occurring in females). An earlier report revealed increased T_4 levels with subchronic CBD treatment. It appears that cannabis impairs hormonal balance in animals, the degree and direction depending upon the cannabinoid, dose, route, duration, sex, species and physiological state; such imbalance contributing to gonadal and reproductive malfunction.

Oral THC (2.4-4.8 mg/kg equivalent to moderate-heavy marihuana use) given daily over a 5 year period to 5 female and 3 male primates did not appear to affect reproductive potential such as cyclic endocrine changes (normal plasma estrogen, progesterone and testosterone) nor conception (Sassenrath et al., 1979). It was pointed out that interindividual variability may have overshadowed any THC-related endocrine effects. However, a reproductive loss (offspring not surviving to 6 months of age) of 42% occurred vs 10% in a control drug-free group of female primates, both groups mated with undrugged males. The deficit remained the same when drugged fathers were mated with drugged and undrugged females. The drug status of the mother appears to be more of a determining outcome factor. The distribution (non-specific) of loss occurred throughout pregnancy and parturition (first trimester to early infancy) irrespective of parity (number of children previously borne) of the mother at various stages of development as "in-utero" resorption, abortion, fetal deaths; at term as still births and neonatal deaths; and as postnatal infant deaths (reminiscent of tobacco smoke effects). Higher THC doses in females resulted in greater losses earlier in pregnancy as resorption and abortion rather than later fetal, neonatal or infant deaths. During pregnancy, weight gain for drug treated females was less than the control group. Some pathological changes noted in neonatal and infant deaths included hydrocephalus, inguinal hernia, ectopic pancreas, and, umbilical and myocardial degeneration. Two infants with hydrocephalus were offspring of a THC and a control mother mated with the same drug treated male in different birth years. Placenta from drug treated females had gross morphological and vascular abnormalities being massively infarcted not seen in the control mothers. Viable progeny from THC treated parents were grossly normal with a significant decrease in birth rate of male infants who were also smaller. Subtle behavioural differences from control noted during the first year of life were hyperactivity and over-responsiveness to environmental stimuli with lack of appropriate cautiousness to a novel environment and inappropriate adaptability to a peer social environment (over-stimulation and assertiveness). Thus, the pattern of reproductive deficit due to a chronic moderately large THC dose indicates embryonic and fetal toxicity without characteristic specific consistent congenital anomalies (i.e. no reproducible pattern of congenital malformations). Survivors appeared morphologically normal with altered autonomic and behavioural responsiveness to visual, auditory, and social environmental stimuli. Chronic THC exposure of males did not result in significant reproductive loss vs exposed females. Birth weights of male infants born to THC treated females were less than those from controls, not seen in female offspring. It is known that a greater vulnerability of male conception to adverse pre-, peri- and neonatal influences occurs in primates (including man). The pathological basis for increased reproductive loss is unknown. It may be due to impairment of maternal support for the fetus noted as placental and hormonal alterations, and lack of maternal weight gain during pregnancy.

Similar findings have been reported in two rodent species (rat, mouse) receiving marihuana by inhalation (smoke) and orally (Rosenkrantz, 1979). Marihuana smoke (from marihuana cigarettes with 2.8% THC) contained 0.8, 2.6, or 3.8 mg/kg THC correlating with dose-related THC plasma levels of 73-297 ng/ml (also reported in man) and COHb levels of 21-60%; exposures (via automatic smoking machine) occurring during the critical phase of organogenesis from 6 to 15 days of gestation. Oral THC doses were 12.5, 25, and 50 mg/kg for rats and 5, 15, 50, 150, 300 and 600 mg/kg for mice, with 2 (for mice) to 5 (for rats) oral treatments around 7 to 9 days of gestation being sufficient to induce embryotoxicity (fetal absorptions) at doses equivalent to heavy chronic marihuana use in man. Behavioural changes brought about by marihuana smoke exposure were dose-related CNS-inhibitory effects (to which tolerance developed) noted as ataxia, dyspnoea, and inactivity in the first 2 hours with rapid recovery by the 3rd hour. Oral THC resulted in dose-related decrease in voluntary activity to which tolerance developed in 3-4 days; high doses (75-300 mg/kg) revealed considerable intoxication and mortality. The fetocidal effect in mice was related to vaginal bleeding due to interrupted development of fetoplacental circulation and deranged hormonal balance. Carbon monoxide may contribute to the cidal effect since it was observed that cannabinoid extracted marihuana (used as a placebo) generated about 30% more CO inducing cyanosis, tremors, convulsions and lethality. Dose-related teratogenic effects were not evident. In a pilot study in which dams received 1, 5, or 10 mg/kg THC orally throughout 21 days of gestation, the offspring showed a dose-related hypersensitivity with 25% responding with involuntary vertical (popcorn) jumping. THC given to these pups resulted in CNS inhibition.

In large and small rodents, the incidence of pregnancy was decreased; vaginal bleeding being related to a high incidence of abnormal pregnancies (Fleischman et al., 1980). A high incidence of whole litter resorptions (14-100%; leaving no trace of implantation in some animals) and fetal mortality (15-100%) occurred after 2-5 oral non-toxic THC doses in dams (12.5-50 mg/kg rat; 150-600 mg/kg mouse/gestation days 6-15); the greatest embryotoxic fetal (rat) sensitivity to THC occurring between 7 to 9 gestation days. Prenatal (gestation day 3 to parturition) oral marihuana extract (150 mg/kg/d; 30% THC, 2% CBD, 2% CBN) or alcohol (6 gm/kg/d; 30% w/v) intake resulted in decreased rodent pup birth weight persisting into the neonatal period (21 days; nursed by non-treated dams) with increased postnatal mortality noted in the marihuana group; female body weights remaining below normal at 11 weeks of age (Abel et al., 1980). Maternal weight gain during pregnancy (normal gestation length) was decreased which may be due partly to decreased food and water intake with marihuana or alcohol treatment. Rotarod (motor) performance was decreased (dose-related) in female offspring (75 days of age) from such marihuana treated dams (Abel, 1979). Cannabis resin (54.9% THC, 19% CBD, 14% CBN) in pregnant rodents (4.2 mg/kg resin I.P./d/gestation days 2-6) produced lower birth weight offspring with poorer growth rate, affecting behavioural development observed as impaired emotionality and learning capacity (Kawash et al., 1980). Hashish (3% in food; 1% THC with more than 1% of CBN and CBD) during lactation (increasing intake from 40 mg to 100 mg/kg THC/day) in small rodents resulted in decreased weight and weight gain in sucklings (4-15 days of age) suggesting malnutrition which may be due to decreased or inadequate maternal lactation and/or a direct drug (in the milk) effect on the pups; a retarded development of eye opening being observed (Frischknecht et al., 1980). In small rodents, 50 mg/kg oral CBC (without its own effect) antagonized 50 mg/kg oral THC perinatal effects of decreased postnatal viability (associated with higher incidence of cannibalism) and impaired male reproductive behaviour at maturity with decreased seminal vesicle weights, indicating the significance of knowing the cannabinoid composition of marihuana used which may help to explain the varied reported reproductive results (Hatoum et al, 1981).

Other rodent (mice) studies investigating teratological effects of THC given to pregnant animals produced "in-utero" deaths, decreased fetal weights and fetal abnormality of cleft palate (Mantilla-Plata et al., 1975). Embryocidal (decreased litter size) and fetocidal effects were related to dosage and day of administration; resorption occurring if drug (THC 50 mg/kg IP) was given (acutely or chronically) during early (day 8-10) not late (day 12-14) organogenesis. Growth retardation susceptibility occurred during gestation days 10-16 (late organogenesis). Cleft palate resulted from single doses of THC (300 mg/kg) given on gestational days 12 and 14 as well as from multi doses of 75, 80 and 100 mg/kg during days 6-15. It was pointed out that apparent discrepencies in toxicological outcome of marihuana intake is not only due to variation in potencies of plant material but also due to vehicle used and route of administration. Lower plasma and tissue THC concentrations were obtained with corn oil vehicle vs Tween and saline, and, after p.o. administrations vs i.p. or i.v. routes. Also, when embryo and fetal lethality are high, abnormal fetuses reaching term are reduced because many malformed conceptus die early and are resorbed. This was confirmed by another rodent (mice) study using single THC exposures (3-400 mg/kg via IV, SC, and oral intragastric routes on gestational days 7-11) during pregnancy (Joneja, 1976). Fetal weights were decreased with all 3 routes of administration. Malformations were not evident following IV injection, some occurred after SC injection, with definite teratogenic response post intragastric route with large doses (400 mg/kg) noted as cleft palate and skeletal developmental defects. An indirect THC effect may occur by means of interference with gastrointestinal function producing fetal skeletal deformities seen following 24 hour fasting during pregnancy. Teratogenic effects of cannabis extracts have been investigated in rabbits (vs untreated controls) using capsules of cannabis resin extract with 44 mg THC (Δ^8 and Δ^9 THC in 5:1 proportion) for p.o. administration of 1 or 2 capsules (15 or 30 mg/kg)/day/8 days (from 5th to 12th day post implantation) resulting in a total amount of 360-720 mg, the dose being equivalent to that used by habitual marihuana users (Fournier et al., 1976). Preliminary findings revealed

(a) the presence of 7-OH metabolite in the urine from treated pregnant animals indicating intestinal absorption of the drug explaining the slight drowsiness noted during the first few days of treatment;

(b) following cesarian section delivery of offspring, a decreased number of living fetuses and corpora lutea in ova; increased number of resorption nodules and macerated fetuses; congenital defects including lack of skull dome and dorsal spine (with neural tube present), eventration (protrusion of bowels from abdomen), harelip with cleft palate, and hip subluxation (partial dislocation), present in 8/133 living fetuses (5.3% vs 0.8% control) with a higher number of abnormalities occurring in the 15 than 30 mg/kg treated group; and,

(c) following normal spontaneous pup delivery, a decreased number of normal offspring especially with the 30 mg/kg group; increased neonatal and postnatal mortality; decreased pup weights at 4 days and 1 month of age vs control; and congenital malformations of spina bifida (defect in bony encasement of spinal cord) and harelip with cleft palate.

A similar rabbit study (Cozens et al., 1979) using crude marihuana extract suspended in sesame oil with 3% THC, 15% CBN, 2.5% for each of CBD, CBC, was given in 0.2 and 1.0 ml/kg/day/days 6-18 of gestation (reported to be equivalent to 3 mg THC/kg/day, 15 mg CBN/kg/day with 2.5 mg/kg/day for both CBC and CBD) with 1 ml sesame oil/kg/day used in control animals. Pregnant animals lost weight during treatment. Fetal weights were decreased, thought to be partly due to decreased ossification or immaturity of skeletal structures with more anomalies being noted in the thoracic skeleton. Fetal corneal and lenticular opacities occurred with 1 ml/kg dose. Cannabinoids (50 mg/kg THC or CBN or CBD ingested 3 x/wk/5 wks corresponding to a human oral dose of 4 mg/kg equivalent to 3 marihuana cigarettes with 1% THC/cigarette) in male adult rodents (mice) reduced fertility and increased chromosomal abnormalities which were also noted in untreated male offspring (Dalterio et al., 1982). CBD treated males impregnated less females with more prenatal and postnatal deaths occurring. THC and CBN increased fetal loss; CBN animals having lower testicular weights and plasma testosterone levels with higher plasma gonadotropins (LH and FSH; perhaps a feedback response to lowered testosterone levels). Following 5 daily cannabinoid treatments (including CME (crude marihuana extract) 25 mg/kg instead of CBD), chromosomal rearrangements in male chromosomes (ring and chain translocations) were found with increased aneuploidy (monosomy, trisomy) and polyploidy (4N) especially with THC and CME treatments. The THC group had a higher frequency of unpaired sex chromosomes in metaphase 1 stage. Single doses of THC or CBN (100 mg/kg) or CME 50 mg/kg depleted cells in metaphase 1 (CME > THC > CBN). Male offspring of THC and CBN treated males had reduced fertility or abnormal litters in the form of congenital malformations or birth defects (exencephaly, spina bifida, exteriorized intestines) as well as chromosomal rearrangements associated with small testicular size. Reproductive effects appear to be transmissible, i.e., mutational changes have occurred (note also in chromosome section). Therefore acute or chronic (non or psychoactive) cannabinoid exposure affects fertility and spermatogenesis in male rodents inducing chromosomal aberrations with genetic mutations as well as altering gonadal endocrine function (testosterone and gonadotropin hormonal levels) and testicular weight. The contribution to maternal and fetal toxicities by various components of marihuana (other than THC) has not been fully explored.

The effects of prenatal cannabis exposure on behaviour (some noted above) of the developing progeny has been studied in pregnant rats exposed to cannabis (1.1% THC) smoke from 0.6 gm plant cigarettes during gestational days 1-19 (maximum exposure to 3.3 mg THC/animal) (Fried, 1976). It was observed that these animals had a greater number of resorptions vs a control group and lower birth weight offspring who exhibited reduced EEG activity at 9 days of age and delayed physical development seen as delayed incisor eruption and eye opening. Pups (exposed prenatally to cannabis) nursed by experimental mothers were lighter and smaller even at 2 months after weaning (at 20 days of age) while those raised by control mothers eventually caught up to control pups 1 month after weaning, indicating prenatal placental transfer and nursing effects of the drug. Tolerance (to repeated IP injections of THC 4 mg/kg q 48 h beginning at 100 days of age) developed more rapidly in offspring exposed to cannabinoids during lactation vs controls and those prenatally exposed to the drug. The postnatal effect with only pre-pregnancy drug use (19 days) by female rodents was slower incisor eruption with a trend to litters containing more male than female offspring; the latter effect also observed with adult male pre-pregnancy drug treatment (Fried and Charlebois, 1979). Drug intake by female animals prior to and during gestation did not affect offspring as drug taken only during the gestational period (noted above as less active smaller pups with delayed development) indicating tolerance development in the dams leading to lesser pharmacological/toxicological effects. In mice, oral THC or CBN (50 mg/kg) during late pregnancy (day 20) and early lactation (6 days post partum) altered weight regulation and pituitary-gonadal function suppressing adult copulatory activity (androgen-dependent behaviour) in male offspring suggesting that male reproductive functional development may be affected by psychoactive and non-psychoactive constituents of marihuana (Dalterio and Bartke, 1979). Perinatal THC exposure resulted in increased weight in adult males, decreased testicular weights, increased LH plasma levels with slight decrease in testosterone levels while CBN only depressed FSH levels indicating that THC and CBN may have different effects on pituitary-gonadal function. A possible direct cannabinoid effect on the fetal testis may exist since a) THC and CBN (in-vitro) affected testicular steroidogenesis by interfering with testicular cholesterol esterase, an enzyme necessary for the production of testosterone precursors (Burstein et al., 1978a;b) and b) short term THC (in-vivo) exposure resulted in the accumulation of esterified cholesterol in the testis with concomitant decrease in peripheral testosterone levels (Dalterio et al., 1978). It has been suggested that THC and CBN exposure during sexual differentiation may have a combination of effects on the fetal testis, pituitary and hypothalamus with early exposure resulting in altered reproductive function and copulatory behaviour in male mice. That is, cannabinoid induced hormonal changes during critical perinatal sexual differentiation period may result in permanent alteration in male reproductive function and in development of CNS sexual dimorphism mediating copulatory behaviour. Maternal cannabinoid exposure (THC, CBN) in rodents may interfere with sexual differentiation in male offspring due to decreased fetal androgen production (600 control vs treated 460 pg testosterone/gm fetal tissue on gestation day 16) (Dalterio and Bartke, 1981).

In drug evaluation of reproductive toxicity, systematic tests of behaviour should be a prerequisite. Previous research in animal behavioural teratology has revealed the following working principles (Vorhees et al., 1979) indicating that marihuana may be one of the psychotropic drugs classified as behavioral teratogens:

(a) agents that are teratogens of the CNS are also behavioural teratogens even when given at doses below which major malformations are induced in any members of the litter,

(b) the pattern of behavioural effects is dependent on the stage of development at which the agent is administered,

(c) the period of fetal susceptibility to effects producing behavioural abnormalities is broader than that for producing malformations of the CNS, even though the period of maximum susceptibility is similar to that for morphological susceptibility of the CNS,

(d) agents which are teratogenic to non-CNS structures are not behavioural teratogens,

(e) genotype (species) interacts with the agent in determining the behavioural effects,

(f)   the extent of the behavioural effects is dependent on the dose of the agent,

(g)   some agents that are behavioural teratogens are apparently not structurally teratogenic, and,

(h)   some behavioural teratogens may be called "pure", in that they can produce behavioural abnormalities without accompanying alterations in growth or other physical measurements of postnatal vitality.

In humans, 2 papers have implicated LSD and marihuana as possible teratogens. One (Hecht et al., 1968) reported malformation of a child's arm as right terminal transverse acheiria (absence of hand); the stump having several vestiges (representing digits). The mother took LSD (amount unknown) prior to and during early pregnancy, stopping the drug with realization of pregnancy, but continuing to smoke cannabis prior to and during pregnancy. During the first trimester of pregnancy other drugs were used to control nausea. At the time of conception the father was using LSD and smoking cannabis. Maternal chromosome studies revealed no chromosomal breakage (not done in father who committed suicide nor in child because permission was refused). The other report (Carakushansky et al., 1969) described an infant with terminal transverse deficit or portions of fingers of the left hand (absent nails and shortened 4th and 5th fingers, i.e. missing phalangeal bones), syndactyly (webbing between 2nd, 3rd, and 4th fingers) of the right hand with shortened fingers, webbing between 2nd and 3rd toes of the right foot and talipes equinovarus of the left foot (club foot). It was believed that the mother was exposed to LSD and cannabis during pregnancy. The baby's chromosomes had no breaks. A prospective study of mothers-to-be (Fried, 1980) with marihuana use during pregnancy ranging from 1 joint/week to 50 joints/week revealed a dose-response relationship with respect to prenatal marihuana effects on the offspring. If more than 5 joints/week was used by the mother, the infants produced were irritable, tremulous, had high pitched cries with behavioural impairment to stimulus indicating an altered immature, nervous system. These effects were independent of cigarette and alcohol use, and resembled narcotic and alcohol effects. Further studies in a total updated sample of 420 pregnant women (Fried, 1982) revealed in 8 heavy marihuana smokers during pregnancy (> 5 joints/week), a shortened gestation period (< 39 weeks in 5/8 women) and decreased maternal weight gain (< 10 kg in 4/8 women). Four heavy users reported > 100 joints/week use in the year before pregnancy. Infants revealed altered visual responsiveness at 2-4 days of age with neonatal symptoms abating by 30 days of age. Developmental impairments (mental, motor, behavioural assessments) were not evident in 7 one year old infants born to women having smoked > 2 joints marihuana/week prenatally. A preliminary epidemiological study (Greenland et al., 1982) of marihuana (regular use ranging from 3.8 during the first trimester to 1.4 x/week at one week pre-delivery; potency?) effects during (course and outcome) 35 pregnancies (vs 36 matched non-user controls; some of both group (more in users) using alcohol and tobacco) revealed a shortened gestational period (Greenland, personal communication), precipitant labour (< 3 hr duration) as well as prolonged labour, and meconium staining (57% vs 25% control) by newborns with some infants requiring resuscitation. During pregnancy the marihuana group had a greater tendency toward anemia, less weight gain and intrauterine growth retardation. Meconium is a sticky greenish black material which is usually passed by the infant within 24 hours of birth containing lanugo hair, squamous epithelial cells from swallowed amniotic fluid and intestinal secretions. Meconium staining indicates passage in-utero into amniotic fluid because of perinatal asphyxia possibly due to placental insufficiency or dysfunction possibly brought about by the maternal hypotensive effect of marihuana, i.e. fetal distress. Asphyxia leads to hypoxia which may permanently damage the CNS. Asphyxiated infants are prone to hypoglycemia because of increased utilization of glycogen stores via anaerobic glycolysis. Potential harmful effects in newborn infants have been reported in women who used marihuana (potency ?) during pregnancy (vs non-users) delivering babies of lower average birth weight (possible fetal growth retardation; probability?) with physical features reminiscent of the fetal alcohol syndrome in some infants (Hingson et al., 1982). Marihuana smoking of < 3 x/week resulted in infants being lighter weight by about 3 oz. (95 gm) vs non-users (similar to > 1 pkg tobacco cigarettes/day use) while with > 3 x/week use, infants were about 5 oz (139 gm) smaller than normal (taking into account other drug use including alcohol, tobacco and caffeine). From the few human reports available, it appears that prenatal marihuana use affects progeny similarily to other psychotropic CNS depressent drugs.

5.   Summary

Gonadal and reproductive malfunction appears to be the outcome of hormonal imbalance. Reproductive function or fertility may be affected by chronic marihuana use by means of THC inhibition of gonadotropins (LH, FSH) via the hypothalamus seen as decreased sex hormone release (testosterone in the male, estrogen and progesterone in the female) the production of which may be affected directly by THC via unavailability of precursor cholesterol (see final comments section), decreased sex cell maturation (male sperm, female ova) and adrenal (stimulatory) effects. Reproductive deficit due to chronic moderately large THC dose appears as embryonic and fetal toxicity, due partially to altered placental circulation, with non-specific congenital anomalies. In male animals, acute and chronic oral cannabinoid (non and psychoactive) intake resulted in chromosomal alterations with fertility and reproductive problems in male offspring suggesting transmissible mutational changes. In humans, delayed onset of puberty and of normal skeletal growth pattern has been associated with heavy marihuana use in a male youth revealing hormonal imbalance; a 3 month abstinence from drug use resulting in normal hormonal levels and increased growth.

Animal studies (keeping in mind species differences in behaviour and physiology) indicate that the possibility exists that human female marihuana exposure to amounts commonly used may be associated with increased risk of reproductive loss, with surviving infants being at increased risk for subsequent behavioural and developmental abnormalities with possible (probability?) risk of physical abnormalities. It may be difficult to recognize fetal marihuana effects in the human population because viable offspring may not have apparent physical abnormalites nor any consistent teratological pattern in "in-utero" death, and, the variability in embryo-and fetotoxicity may terminate pregnancy early on one occasion, but proceed to full term on another occasion. A pure behavioural teratogen (without overt congenital malformations) may be difficult to uncover in the human; behavioural deficits usually being recognized only at school age at which time it may be difficult to establish a causal relationship with prenatal drug use. One must keep in mind a) the delayed clincial recognition of the "fetal alcohol syndrome" which is at one end of the spectrum of fetal alcohol effects and b) the teratogenic hazard of thalidomide (phocomelia; defective development of arms and/or legs) which had a greater effect in humans than in animals. Thus, reported teratological effects produced by marihuana, alone or in combination with other drugs, should not be ignored since dose, intake route, frequency and duration of use, period of pregnancy, species, and genetic (strain) background are important factors. If a drug is teratogenic in any animal species at a dose below maternal toxicity, then the possible hazard of teratogenicity in humans should be considered which includes not only death and morphological change but also functional and behavioural deficits. Physicians should be alert to the possibility of the emergence of a peculiar pattern of deficits. Drug plasma level determinations would make comparisons more meaningful with respect to dose-response relationship(s) since metabolic rates may vary among species as well as between individuals within a species. Drug-induced teratogenic effects are related to fetal drug concentration indicating that alterations in maternal pharmacokinetics can significantly alter the production of fetal abnormalties (Evans et al., 1975). It is possible that a continuum of prenatal toxic effects exists which may be similar to that seen with alcohol and tobacco ranging from behavioural aberrations to major malformations. Any drug which prevents the fullest expression of genetic character either anatomically or behaviourally, must be used with extreme caution in pregnant women, if at all. Pregnancy is not recognized until at least 20 days after fertilization implying that many embryos could be exposed to the risk of malformation prior to such recognition. Thus contraindication of a drug during pregnancy is not enough for prevention of fetal teratogenic effects. Preliminary human pregnancy outcome data confirms some of the animal toxicity findings such as decreased birthweight and some physical anomalies in some newborn infants.

II. 3. B. Reproductive System

List of Figures

Fig. 1.   Plasma testosterone levels   74
Fig. 2.   Plasma LH levels   74
Fig. 3.   Breast tissue stimulation   75
Fig. 4.   Serum prolactin   75
Fig. 5.   Ovariectomized LH levels   76
Fig. 6.   Ovariectomized FSH levels   77
Fig. 7.   Menstrual cycle alteration   78
Fig. 8.   Placental drug transfer   79
Fig. 9.   Maternal milk content   80

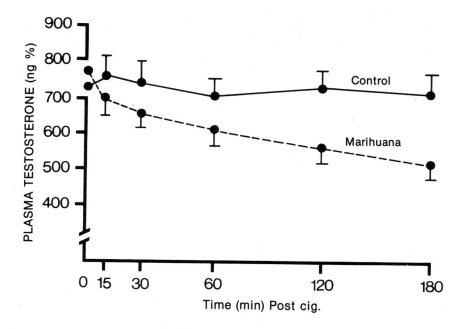

Fig. 1.   Acute effect of smoking one marihuana cigarette (2.2% THC) on
II.3.B   plasma testosterone levels over a 3 hour period in 13 regular mari-
               huana users.

               Adapted from Kolodny et al., 1976.

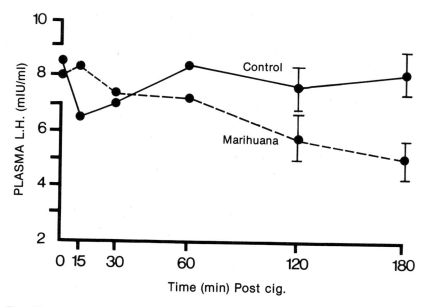

Fig. 2.   Acute effect of smoking one marihuana cigarette (2.2% THC) on
II.3.B   plasma LH levels over a 3 hour period in 13 regular marihuana users.

               Adapted from Kolodny et al., 1976.

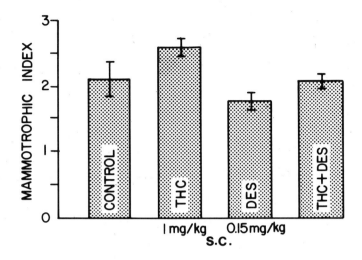

Fig. 3.   Stimulation of male animal breast tissue. DES (diethylstilbesterol)
II.3.B

Adapted from Harmon and Aliapoulios, 1974.

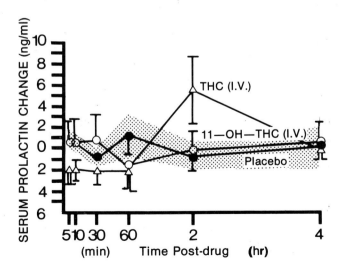

Fig. 4.   Serum prolactin change from control post THC, THC metabolite, and
II.3.B   placebo.

Adapted from Lemberger et al., 1975.

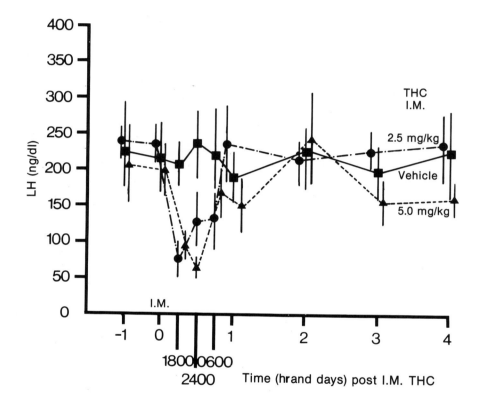

Fig. 5.   LH levels post IM THC in ovariectomized primate animals.
II.3.B
               Adapted from Smith et al., 1979.

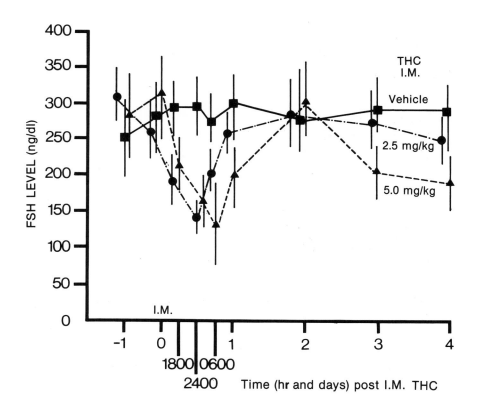

Fig. 6.   FSH levels post IM THC in ovariectomized primate animals.
II.3.B
                 Adapted from Smith et al., 1979.

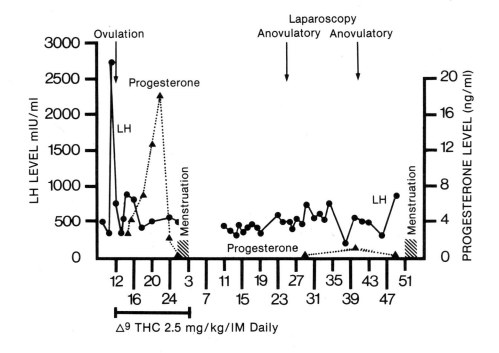

Fig. 7.   THC during luteal phase in normal female primates affecting subse-
II.3.B   quent menstrual cycle.

Adapted from Smith et al., 1979.

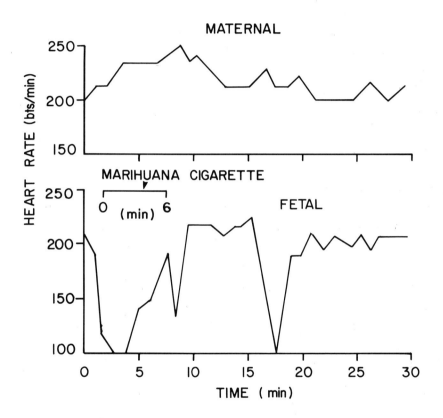

Fig. 8.   Heart rate changes post one marihuana cigarette.
II.3.B

Adapted from Singer et al., 1973.

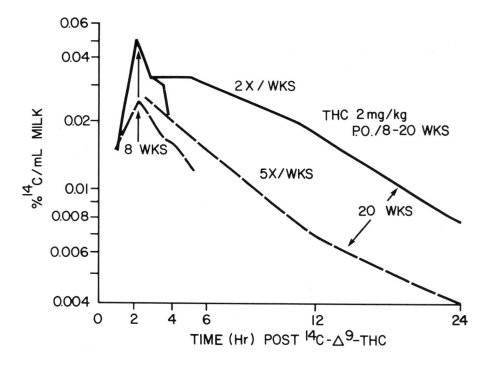

Fig. 9. ^{14}C in milk from lactating animals post chronic oral THC (2 mg/kg/8-
II.3.B   20 wks).

Adapted from Chao et al., 1976.

II. 3. C. Central Nervous System

Contents

Abstract   81
1. Introduction   82
2. Marihuana Effects on the Brain
    (a) Distribution of Marihuana in the CNS   82
    (b) Gross Pathology   82
    (c) EEG (Cerebral Cortical Activity; Limbic System) Studies   84
    (d) Effects on Nerves   87
3. Psychopathology and Psychiatric Aspects of Cannabis Intoxication or
    Marihuana's Capacity to Impair Brain Function
    (a) Acute Emotional Responses to Cannabis
              (i) Acute Panic Anxiety Reaction   87
             (ii) Transient Mild Paranoid Feeling   88
            (iii) Toxic Delirium or Acute Brain Syndrome (Toxic Psychosis
                   or Poisoning)   88
    (b) Prolonged Psychological Effects (Chronic Organic Brain Syndrome)
              (i) Psychotic (Pathological Organic CNS Response)   88
             (ii) Non-Psychotic
                   Flashbacks   91
                   Amotivational Syndrome and Personality
                   (Neuropsychological) Changes   92
    (c) Aggressive Behaviour   94
    (d) Classification of Psychiatric Conditions   98
              (i) Drug Dependence
             (ii) Non-Psychotic OBS (Organic Brain Syndrome)
            (iii) Psychosis or Psychotic OBS
             (iv) Schizophrenic-Type + (i) or (ii) or (iii)
4. Psychomotor Function or Performance   99
5. Tolerance and Dependence   102
6. Summary   104
7. Figures   106

Abstract

1. Brain function is discussed briefly.

2. Cannabinoid induced pathology (gross and microscopic) of the brain is presented including EEG alterations and psychopathology including aggressive behaviour.

3. Impairment of psychomotor performance following marihuana use may lead to accidents when operating machinery.

4. Tolerance develops to marihuana effects with reports of psychological and mild physical (physiological) dependence.

Keywords: behaviour, cannabis, central nervous system, cerebral pathology, psychomotor function, psychopathology, tolerance and dependence.

Abbreviations: alpha (α); area under the curve (AUC); blood alcohol concentration (BAC); California Psychological Inventory (CPI); cannabidiol (CBD); cannabinol (CBN); carbon monoxide (CO); cardiovascular system (CVS); central nervous system (CNS); cerebrospinal fluid (CSF); computerized transaxial tomography (CTT); cycles/second (Hz); electroencephalogram (EEG); for example (e.g.); gram (gm); growth hormone (GH); heart rate (HR); hemoglobin (Hb); Intelligence Quotient (IQ); intramuscular (IM); intravenous (IV); kilogram (kg); lysergic acid diethylamide (LSD); microgram (μg or mcg); milli (m); milligram (mg); Minnesota Multiphasic Personality Inventory (MMPI); nanogram (ng); organic brain syndrome (OBS); per os or oral (p.o.); percent (%); radioimmunossay (RIA); rapid eye movement (REM); slow wave sleep (NREM); short (or long) term store (S or (L)TS); State-Trait Anxiety Inventory (STAI); tetrahydrocannabinol (THC); that is (i.e.); twice (or three) times a day (b. (or t.) i.d.).

1.   Introduction

The brain (with 15 billion neurons or nerve cells) operates using chemical and electrical messages (Swanson, 1975-76). It is in charge of interpreting sense reports (Fig. 1) and maintains stable perception.   Upsets in the way the brain translates sense messages can fragment our perceptions. Dynamic equilibrium or "steady state" is maintained by controlling the diversity of sense reports helping to get a better picture of the world. In order to function properly the brain inhibits much of the received information, i.e., does not pay attention to messages unimportant to the task at hand even though it is aware of them. Some drugs (hallucinogens) prevent the brain from blotting out some of the information received. On the other hand, facilitation enables daily activities to be carried on, with alertness to any danger signals (e.g. mother's alertness to baby's cry in distant part of the house). Central nervous system drugs (e.g. alcohol) "dull the senses" thereby disabling the brain to facilitate important information or send messages to take action. For some chemicals, a "blood-brain barrier" exists (i.e. slows absorption) to help avoid disruption of information processes. In infants, this barrier does not develop until the second year of life, making their central nervous system more vulnerable to drug effects. Chemical states of the brain may alter electrical impulses. When neurons or brain cells fire at random, convulsions may ensue as seen in epilepsy (inherited) or with some drugs (hallucinogens, major tranquilizers). The irregular nerve firings in an epileptic do not harm the brain's reasoning capacity other than during a seizure which can be controlled. The brain is not fully understood. It is known that it has the ability to inhibit and facilitate information which may be related to chemical and electrical processes.   The transfer of external information through physiological transducers into the electrical language of the nervous system is a complex process which may be altered by the addition of exogenous chemicals.

2.   Marihuana Effects on the Brain

(a) Distribution of Marihuana in the CNS

The concentration of marihuana in the brain may be partly governed by an active transport process in the choroid plexus (Agnew et al., 1976). The choroid plexus is a network of blood vessels in the brain cavity (ventricles) which regulates intraventricular pressure by absorption and secretion of cerebrospinal fluid (CSF). Distribution of marihuana in the CNS of animals (monkeys) at various time periods following intravenous (IV) injection of different doses of radioactive THC has been studied by means of autoradiography (production of an image on photographic film by radiation from a radioactive substance injected into tissue which is in close contact with the film) (McIsaac et al., 1971). Behavioural effects were also noted. In man, maximum effects following IV administration appears within 15 minutes with a duration of action of 4-6 hours. The amount of unchanged THC found in the animal brain at the 15 minute period was 77% with a decrease to 51% at 4 hours, paralleling the decrease in behavioural effects. The dose-response (behavioural) effects in animals were similar to those observed in man. At a low dose of 2 mg/kg THC IV, the animals sat quietly, unaware of their surroundings, losing their natural aggressiveness, which corresponded to anxiolytic and euphoric action accompanied by disruption of time perception in man.   At a moderate dose of 10 mg/kg, stimulation was evident with marked motor incoordination, catatonic-like positions assumed after jumping about and perhaps hallucinations; in man, stimulation and talkativeness may lead to hallucinations depending on the dose. At a high dose of 30 mg/kg, marked sedation and pronounced motor incoordination peaked at the 1 hour interval, subsiding in 8 hours when over-reaction occurred to external stimuli; man reveals incapacitation of cognititve and motor function.   Behavioural effects may be related to drug distribution in the brain.   High concentrations of THC were found in the following areas at the 15 minute period: frontal cortex (general association area) and hippocampus (early recall memory with superimposed temporal orientation), the two areas interacting thereby associating stimuli into a temporal context which may account for distortion of time sense; amygdala which may be related to anxiolytic and euphoric effects; lateral geniculate nucleus which connects with the visual pathway may be one locus for hallucinations; and cerebellum which may be related to motor incoordination. Drug concentration decreases with time over a 24 hour period when very little radioactivity remains and behavioural effects have disappeared. From the above there appears to be a relation between distribution of THC in the brain, its rate of metabolism and behavioural effects.   Since marihuana is able to enter the brain with apparent alteration in neurological function, the duration of undesirable effects and possible permanency are of importance.

(b) Gross Pathology

Neurological effects noted above have been perceptual, cognitive, and mood changes indicating alteration in nervous system activity (Petersen, 1976). The logical starting point would be a gross examination of the brain for structural damage before proceeding to study possible subtle changes in order to explain the observed neurological manifestations of marihuana. Some studies have been carried out without fully resolving the issue of structural damage. A British study (Campbell et al., 1971) reported on cerebral ventricular size in 10 young men (18-28 years of age) who smoked marihuana (amount and potency unknown) regularly for a varied period (3-11 years) and in a control group of 13 (7 male, 6 female) of comparable age (15-25 years) because ventricular size increases with age. Subjects from both groups were being investigated for neurological symptoms or cerebral function. The control group complained of headache, loss of consciousness, or syncope and did not develop any neurological illness on follow-up. The drug group consisted of: 4 individuals complaining of headache, memory loss, or behavioural changes; 5 were under treatment for drug abuse; and the tenth was an LSD (lysergide) overdose hospital admission. They all used cannabis regularly as well as other drugs, especially LSD and amphetamine. Radiological examination of the cerebral ventricles (lateral and third) was accomplished by means of air or pneumoencephalography. This technique involves making X-ray films of the head following the injection of air or gas (oxygen) into the subarachnoid space permitting visualization of cerebral ventricles. The lateral and third ventricle measurements in the drug group were significantly different from the control group suggesting cerebral atrophy indicating irreversible brain damage. Other causes of cerebral atrophy in the young were ruled out. Such ventricular changes may be found in the 7th or 8th decade. Alcoholism may lead to cerebral atrophy. However, only one patient had used alcohol heavily. In this pilot study it was difficult to relate marihuana history to total dose or extent of cerebral atrophy thereby leading to several other studies. Two have used CTT (computerized transaxial tomography) which is an accurate non-invasive brain scanning technique for visualizing the anatomy of the brain by means of a series of narrow beamed X-ray slices which are processed via a computer enabling reconstruction of slices and brain. One such study (Co et al., 1977) utilized 12 young men ranging in age from 21-28 years with varied occupations and education who used marihuana at an average of 5-20 joints/day with occasionally 35 joints/day for a period ranging from 5-9 years of regular heavy use. The potency of marihuana used was unknown. A control group of 34 men (20-30 years of age), suspected of neurological disorders but found to be normal, were included for comparison purposes. Except for 2 individuals in the drug group, other drugs used were especially LSD, amphetamine, mescaline; others included barbiturates, peyote, psilocybin, cocaine, opiates, and glue sniffing. Even though no neurological nor intellectual impairment was evident, two subjects had a psychiatric history of treatment for depression and one had an antisocial personality history. The CTT scans read blindly by neuroradiologists, did not show evidence of cerebral atrophy. It was suggested that extensive exposure to cannabis does not necessarily result in cerebral atrophy. However, the potency of the drug may have been low (unknown). The other CTT study (Kuehnle et al., 1977) involved 19 young healthy men (21-27 years of age) who were considered to be heavy users of marihuana, all of whom had used alcohol, while some also used amphetamines (11/19), hallucinogens (10/19), barbiturates (6/19) and heroin (4/19). A control group was not included. To confirm the heavy use of marihuana, the subjects smoked 1 gm marihuana cigarettes containing approximately 20 mg THC each for a period of 21 days. The intake of THC varied from 50-150 mg/day and on occasion 400 mg/24 hour period. The usual average number of cigarettes smoked per day ranged from 2.5 to 7.5. The CTT scans of this group did not show any structural brain damage. It was suggested that this finding does not rule out the possibility of subtle impairment of brain function which could not be assessed by CTT scanning of the brain. Another non-invasive technique for examining the brain grossly is by means of echoencephalography used in a Greek study (Stefanis et al., 1976). This method makes use of reflected ultrasound in examination and measurement of internal structures (ventricles) of the skull and in diagnosis of abnormalities. A group of 47 regular cannabis users had smoked hashish for an average period of 23 years on a twice to three times daily basis with an average intake of 2-6 gm hashish/day containing 4-5% Δ^9 THC (80-300 mg THC/day). A control group consisted of 40 subjects. Both groups had 3-4 years schooling with an average age of 40 years, smoked tobacco, and used alcohol socially (not alcoholic). Eight in the cannabis group and two in control had enlarged livers which were related to the degree of alcohol use. Psychopathology (mental abnormality) was found in 18/47 (38%) cannabis group and 7/40 (17%) control. Echoencephalograms of the 3rd ventricle (width) were found to be within normal limits in both groups. However, the way in which hashish is smoked in Greece by means of a water pipe leads to active principles of cannabis (Δ^9 THC, CBD, CBN) being retained by the pipe (Savaki et al., 1976). Thus, the THC dose in the above study (Stefanis et al., 1976) may not have reached the lungs of the chronic smoker. This is likely since 24 of these chronic users took part in an experimental study, smoking cigarettes containing 3 gm marihuana with 2.6% THC, 2-4 gm Greek hashish with 4-5% THC, 100 mg pure THC in a marihuana placebo and a 3 gm marihuana placebo (all mixed with tobacco) revealing pulse rate changes with the active substances to which tolerance usually develops in chronic users. Also chronic users probably regulate their dose to obtain a self-satisfying effect that does not upset the autonomic equilibrium as noted by the fixed dose experimental situation above (changes) vs 'ad libitum' use (less change). In non-human primates (baboons), oral cannabis (2-10% with 1.38-1.5% THC) in food for several weeks to 8 months did not reveal structural brain damage (no cortical atrophy nor ventricular enlargement) nor neuropathological lesions in necropsy material examined under the light microscope (Ames et al., 1979). Cannabis in food was avoided if possible or intake decreased leading to varied weight responses (increase or decrease) depending upon initial cannabis dose and regimen used. Cannabinoids in serum varied from 10 to 510 ng/ml and in urine from 110 to 2245 ng/ml. Behaviourally, the animals became lethargic and apathetic. Varied biochemical changes suggested glucose utilization defect.

From the above 4 clinical studies dealing with gross pathology of the brain, the following points were noted.

(1) All cannabis users were polydrug users.

(2) The amount and potency of the material used chronically was not well-defined. Each batch of cannabis may be different with respect to percent and potency of active ingredients. The way in which cannabis is smoked (cigarettes, water pipe) as well as pattern of smoking may vary the concentration of active principles reaching the lungs.

(3) The state of health and neurological status of an individual was varied.

The study findings may be compared to those found with tobacco and alcohol with respect to development of certain toxic effects. That is, not everyone who smokes tobacco develops lung cancer, nor everyone who drinks alcohol develops Wernicke-Korsakoff Syndrome, or cerebral atrophy, or give birth to a baby with fetal alcohol syndrome. The possibility exists that those with marginal neurological function may perhaps be affected more readily than healthy individuals. Certain individuals may have a predisposition to, or undesirable sensitivity to regular drug use resulting in a disease diathesis. For example, chronic high doses of hydralazine (antihypertensive agent) may give rise to disseminated lupus erythematosus (inflammatory connective tissue disease) in a small percent of patients. A dose-response relationship should be established in healthy and varied ill individuals. That is, what dose, frequency, duration of use is necessary to produce deleterious effects, and, are there differences in different populations with different racial and genetic backgrounds. More importantly, blood concentration of active components and/or their metabolites would indicate that the drug(s) has entered the body and may also indicate altered metabolism (e.g. due to liver damage).

(c) EEG Studies

Brain activity or functional condition of the brain and vigilance (behaviour) may be assessed by electroencephalography (EEG), an objective neurophysiological measure. EEG records electrical currents (brain waves noting frequency and amplitude) developed in the brain by means of electrodes applied to a) the scalp, b) the surface of the brain (intracranial EEG) or c) placed within the brain (depth EEG). EEG is a summation of the electrical activity in the brain indicating cerebral activity. It is useful in localizing intracranial lesions, brain tumors, and distinguishing between diffuse and focal brain lesions in epilepsy. Normal vigilance is characterized by predominance of α-rhythm (frequency band of 8-13 Hz (cycles/second)). With decreased vigilance (sleep) wave amplitude is increased and basic rhythm slows down (decreased frequency) leading to synchronization of EEG. Whereas increased vigilance (watchfulness) is indicated by decreased amplitude and increased frequency denoting desynchronization of EEG. In organic brain disease, the most common change in EEG is slowing down of the basal rhythm. Besides classifying cerebral pathology, EEG may be used to classify cerebral effects of psychoactive drugs from characteristic EEG changes or profile.

Socially used doses of cannabis result in EEG effects of short duration. Small doses of THC show sudden EEG changes in vigilance from arousal to drowsy states. With increasing doses, psychodysleptic (induce dream-like or delusional state of mind) properties are intensified. The specific EEG profile (scalp-recorded) for the active principle (Δ^9 THC) in cannabis with acute and chronic use consists of increased α-activity, decreased β-activity, and decreased mean frequency (sychronization). These effects are dose dependent (7.5-180 mg THC) with respect to intensity and duration of action, as are the behavioural or mood (euphoria or "high") and physiological (increased heart rate) parameters. Tolerance develops to all these effects. With chronic use euphoria is followed by dysphoria. A feeling of pleasantness increases with the heart rate up to 102 beats/minute but becomes unpleasant at heart rates over 120 beats/minute. The EEG profile of cannabis is similar to that of a low dose of alcohol leading to a classification of a central euphoriant with the psychotropic group of psychodysleptics with morphine-like and hallucinogenic properties (Fink et al., 1976).

High doses of oral marihuana or THC (70-210 mg/day/2 weeks in marihuana users who had used 1-2 cigarettes/day) have produced a unique effect on EEG sleep pattern. The time spent in low voltage EEG (tonic) occurring in association with rapid eye movement (phasic) is a measure of REM (rapid eye movement) sleep. The tonic and phasic processes are not perfectly correlated and may be differentially affected by drugs. Rapid eye movement of REM sleep is decreased by THC and marihuana as is the duration of REM with some increase in slow wave sleep (NREM) (Fig. 2). Some tolerance develops to REM effects. Cessation of drug results in a "rebound" effect on REM especially on eye movement vs REM duration with a decrease in NREM. The greater decrease in eye movement vs REM duration during drug use also occurs with barbiturates and other sedative-hypnotics including benzodiazepines. This may be related to the sedative effects of the drugs. However, fast activity induced by these sedative-hypnotics during REM sleep was not seen with THC, although marihuana elicited such a response in 2/4 individuals tested. The functional and biological significance of alteration in sleep pattern due to cannabis is presently unknown. However, the behaviour observed with a high dose of THC was one of sedation and lethargy noted in performance changes on motor and cognitive tasks, symptom check lists, and ward behaviour ratings. Marked tolerance was evident following 5-6 days with 210 mg doses daily seen as improved test performance and belief that doses were lowered or placebo given. Drug withdrawal resulted in more alert but irritable behaviour. The effect of THC on human sleep pattern appears to be somewhat similar to lithium. Lithium given to patients with affective disorders (manic depressive illness) in therapeutic doses results in decreased eye movement activity and increased NREM, the latter being greater than that found with THC. Also, there is no rebound effect with lithium. It has been suggested that the efficacy of THC be tested in the treatment of bipolar (episodes of both mania and depression) depressed patients. In unipolar (recurrence of either mania or depression) patients, larger doses of THC produce dysphoria which may be used as a diagnostic test to distinguish between bipolar and unipolar depression (Feinberg et al., 1975; 1976). Sleep disturbances (difficult to fall and stay asleep) produced by abstinence following chronic marihuana use reported by users has been substantiated by other studies; such disturbances perhaps contributing to continued drug use. A primate (monkey) study using oral THC 1.2 mg/kg/60 days depressed slow wave sleep (stage 3 and 4 with excessive delta EEG activity) beginning 7 days after drug administration persisting during the 30 day recovery period; the decreased slow wave sleep being compensated by increased stage 1 drowsy sleep and awake time (Adams and Barratt, 1975). A human investigation revealed sleep disruption (increased sleep latency and wake time after sleep onset with decreased slow wave sleep compensated by increased non-REM stage 2 or light sleep) during a 12 day recovery period following cessation of oral THC 20 mg/12 days; return to baseline levels being established at the 70 day post drug period (Freemon and Al-Marashi, 1977).

In order to understand the implications of the findings obtained with depth EEG studies, a brief description of the limbic system in the (lower fifth) brain will be presented first. The brain is made up of 3 basic cerebral types (Fig. 3) differing in structure, chemistry and organization (MacLean, 1970). These are: 1) reptilian or brain stem, responsible for instinctive (survival) behaviour (and regulator of vital functions of body), 2) old mammalian (paleocortex) or limbic brain surrounding the brain stem (like a cap or limbus) having an important role in emotional behaviour and motivation (contains opiate receptors); and, 3) new mammalian (neocortex) brain (thinking cap) with the capacity for symbolic (written and spoken) language. The 3 subdivisions of the limbic cortical system or ring are linked by 3 pathways to the brain stem (Fig. 4). The lower part (hippocampus; memory formation) of the ring connected with the amygdala insures self-preservation (survival). The upper part connected to the septum is involved with pleasure and the preservation of species. These 2 pathways interconnect with the olfactory (sense) pathway. The third pathway bypasses the olfactory apparatus and involves the visual aspect of socio-sexual behaviour. It connects with the prefrontal cortex which provides insight and foresight necessary for our welfare. With limbic dysfunction as with irritative lesions (e.g. psychomotor epilepsy), abnormal discharges are accompanied by symptoms seen in endogenous and toxic psychoses. These include emotional and mood disturbances, feelings of depersonalization, distortions of perception, alteration of time sense and paranoid states. Sclerosis (hardening) of the hippocampus has often been involved in seizure discharges in limbic epilepsy with perceptual alterations and hallucinations involving any one of the sensory systems. It has been suggested that all sensory systems feed into the hippocampal formation. The hippocampus is thought to be an unstable structure with the lowest seizure threshold making it vulnerable to stressful situations which could result in paranoid states. Because of it's peculiar blood supply and location in the cranium, it is vulnerable to mechanical injury, vascular insufficiency and infection. In a recent report (Goldman et al., 1975) animals who were intravenously injected with 1 mg/kg THC showed reduced blood flow to the hippocampus as well as decreased cardiac output. This could modify the function of the hippocampus. An interesting chemical property of the hippocampal formation is that testosterone may be bound to the neuronal cells which may be the receptors for the gonadal hormone (Altman and Das, 1975; MacLean, 1970). From the above it may be seen that any damage (mechanical or chemical) to the limbic system would have far reaching effects on emotional behaviour, motivation, and even possible hormonal disturbances.

Depth EEG studies in patients with various disorders have revealed a correlation between altered emotion, as seen in marihuana users, and brain activity which is not elicited by other substances such as tobacco, amphetamine, and alcohol. An anatomic-physiologic relation has also been established to explain sensory perception which accompanies changes in emotion (Heath, 1975). Similar studies were undertaken in animals (rhesus monkeys) to permit rigid control (e.g. no polydrug use) and learn about acute and chronic effects of marihuana and THC on brain function and behaviour (Heath, 1976). Electrodes were implanted in sites associated with emotion (septal area (pleasure, psychotic behaviour), hippocampus and amygdale (rage and fear)), sensory relay nuclei, and nuclei with reservoirs for specific chemical transmitters. Doses of smoked marihuana and intravenous THC used corresponded to heavy, moderate, and light smokers (7, 1, and 1/2 joint/day respectively) for a 6 month period. Heavy and moderate smoking of active marihuana as well as THC resulted in acute behavioural changes with notable changes in brain activity which persisted (chronic) following regular use vs inactive marihuana use and light smokers. The acute behavioural effect was one of decreased awareness (drowsiness) confirmed by scalp EEG which lasted for one hour following smoking of marihuana. Depth EEG electrodes recorded consistent changes in sites associated with emotion. The THC effect was seen as slow activity and/or high amplitude spiking which was pronounced in the septal area with catatonic behaviour resembling data from severely disturbed psychotic patients. With changes recorded from the sensory relay nuclei, the animals behaved as though hallucinating. Nuclei associated with chemical transmitters were also affected. At the 3 month period of regular moderate and heavy marihuana smoking or intravenous THC, evidence of irreversible or permanent changes in brain function in areas associated with emotion was noted throughout the weekend when drug was not given. Re-introduction of the drug resulted in a different type of brain activity similar to the pattern of a drug dependent individual receiving temporary relief from deprivation by taking more drug. These changes, which were recorded by the implanted electrodes but not by scalp electrodes, persisted for 7-8 months following cannabis exposure. Two heavy smoking animals (one with an implanted electrode and the other an intact control) died of respiratory complications during the study (3 1/2 and 5 1/2 month period). Smoking at very low doses did not elicit detectable effects on brain function or behaviour, nor did smoking of inactive marihuana display EEG changes. Animals were sacrificed at 7-8 month periods following canabis exposure and tissues removed from the brain (e.g. septal area) where altered brain activity (EEG) was noted (Harper et al., 1977). Light microscopy did not reveal morphological changes. However, electron microscopy revealed ultrastructural synaptic (axodendrite) changes seen as accumulation of electron opaque material in the synaptic cleft and in the pre and post synaptic region with widening of the cleft (27% above control) and clumping of synaptic vesicles (contain chemical neurotransmitters) in the presynaptic bouton. These changes were absent in the control animals. Patients with neurological disorders show dense material within the cleft which may be a chemical or molecular change. This also occurs with thiamine and vitamin E deficiencies, and lithium toxicity. Widening of the cleft is considered to be a specific phenomenon because the widths are similar within the brain. Aggregation of synaptic vesicles have been produced by ischemia, toxins, and neuropathies. The modification of the fine structure of the synapse may be related to the mechanism of impulse transmission across the synapse explaining the EEG changes. Other ultrastructural changes noted (Myers and Heath, 1979) include low volume density of components in a cell, and various degrees of fragmentation and disorganization of rough endoplasmic reticulum which reflects the metabolic state of the cell (protein synthesis).

A follow-up controlled study in primates using marihuana (smoked; 2.45% THC) and THC (IV 0.69 mg/kg) vs controls (placebo marihuana; unexposed) giving plasma THC levels (Fig. 5) comparable to those found in human marihuana smokers, confirmed the above results (Heath et al., 1980). That is, chronic EEG changes were observed especially in the septal area, hippocampus, and amygdala with changes at the synapse (correlating with persistent EEG changes), destruction of rough endoplasmic reticulum, and development of nuclear inclusion bodies (significance? however, a larger number appeared to occur with greater cellular functional and ultrastructural alterations). The changes (absent in controls) occurred during chronic treatment (1-3 joints/day/5 days/week/6-8 months) persisting for 1-8 months post treatment indicating possible permanent brain function and structural alterations. Thus, regular moderate-heavy marihuana use appears to produce persistent changes in the limbic structures in the brain. Since the limbic cortex (including the septal area, amygdala and hippocampus) is involved with emotional states including motivation as well as psychotic symptoms (disorder of thinking, feeling and perceiving; a mental disease), then damage (mechanical or chemical) could conceivably lead to psychopathological states which have been described following marihuana use.

An attempt has been made to define specific EEG characteristics (different functional brain states) relating to cannabis induced psychopathology (visual hallucinations, body image disturbances, attention and thought disturbances, dysphoria, depersonalization, derealization, euphoria) (Fig. 6) (Koukkou and Lehmann, 1976; 1978). Oral THC (200 ug/kg) (which caused increased pulse rate) was used in 12 infrequent cannabis users (not more than 3x) who had abstained for the previous 3 months and had not used other drugs except alcohol. Scalp EEG measurements were taken prior to and following drug intake at various time intervals up to 3 hours with the subjects signalling occurrences of THC experiences. Subjective effects were noted by means of a questionnaire pre and post drug use. Pre-drug EEG which reflects individualistic psychophysiological characteristics, indicated predisposition to THC induced body image disturbances and euphoria. Post-drug EEG in periods without experiences indicated a tendency to THC induced experiences. EEG, prior to and following THC, showed higher resting alpha frequencies in those with frequent visual hallucinations and body image disturbances (Fig. 7), both of which could be clinically distinguished from the EEG (Fig. 6) indicating different electrophysiological mechanisms. During THC experiences slower alpha and more theta frequencies appeared (which may be a prerequisite for hallucinations), similar to that seen in initial drowsiness EEG and in some schizophrenics. It has been suggested that the increased tendency to hallucination under THC may be a neurotic trait (fast resting alpha frequency) with a possible(?) relation to a schizophrenic condition noted as fast beta activity during hallucinations. From the above, it appears that there are electrical brain activity characteristics which indicate a predisposition to subjective drug effects of THC; the slower theta frequencies and higher alpha frequencies in resting EEG predisposing to visual experiences (Fig. 8).

(d) Effects on Nerves

A new neurological finding has been reported (Coleman et al., 1976) in 43 young (16-34 years of age) chronic ($>$ 10 days use/month/$>$ 1 year) medium-heavy (6 joints/day) marihuana users complaining of frontal and temporal headaches suggesting an ocular etiology. Visual examination revealed an apparent permanent unilateral paralysis of the superior oblique muscle of the eye. This muscle is solely innervated by the trochlear or 4th cranial nerve. This nerve is the longest cranial nerve with the fewest number of fibres being the least myelinated of the cranial nerves. Its nucleus is on the opposite side of the brain in the gray matter of the midbrain at the level of the inferior colliculus. Distribution of marihuana in the monkey brain (McIsaac et al., 1971) has shown high concentration of THC in the gray matter of the frontal cortex and midbrain (superior and inferior colliculus). Thus, the possibility exists that marihuana may affect the trochlear nerve or its nucleus adversely.

Nerve conduction (sensory and motor) studies in the peripheral nervous system were undertaken in 12 male casual (use 12x/month/5 years) and 15 heavy (42 cigarettes/month/5 years) marihuana smokers (Di Benedetto et al., 1977). Over a 3 week experimental period, the casual users consumed an average of 54 cigarettes and the heavy users 120; each 1 gm cigarette containing 2% THC. Initial (basal) evaluation of these subjects revealed minor sensory nerve conduction abnormalities in 21 subjects mostly as decreased action potential (amplitude). These abnormalities were thought to be due to other drug use such as alcohol, hallucinogens (LSD), amphetamines, heroin, and barbiturates which are known to produce peripheral neuropathies following prolonged use. Motor nerve function was normal. Experimental marihuana use for 3 weeks resulted in 10/21 subjects continuing to have abnormal values. As a group, deterioration of the peripheral nervous system was not evident. This could be due to forced abstinence from other drugs during the experimental period as well as to good nutrition. Differences could not be detected between casual and heavy marihuana users.

3. Psychopathology and Psychiatric Aspects of Cannabis Intoxication or Marihuana's Capacity to Impair Brain Function

(a) Acute Emotional Responses to Cannabis

Psychopathology or adverse psychological reaction is the study of psychological (mental (psyche, mind) and emotional (behaviour) processes; conciousness, sensation, ideation, memory) dysfunction occurring in mental disorders or in social disorganization, i.e., causes and nature of mental disease. Hypochondriacal individuals (morbid anxiety about health and severe mental depression) are thought to be more prone to react adversely to psychoactive drugs (Petersen, 1976). It appears that the mental set (expectation) as well as individual biological drug response rather than setting (physical environment) may influence reactions (Hollister et al., 1975; Smith, 1978). There are a variety of potential acute emotional responses to cannabis.

(i) Acute Panic Anxiety Reaction

The most common adverse psychological reaction to marihuana by relatively inexperienced or naive individuals to potent material is acute panic anxiety reaction due to acute drug intoxication in which anxiety is expressed to transient drug induced distortions of reality such as feelings of impending death and/or loss of mental function. In clinical trials of oral THC for analgesic efficacy or therapeutic use in cancer patients with chronic pain, a 20 mg dose resulted in some patients becoming extremely anxious to the dysphoric effect of losing control over thought and action which persisted for 3-4 days in some. This indicates that older individuals cannot accept mental changes due to a medication (Noyes et al., 1975). When moderate users of marihuana were premedicated with intravenous THC (0.02-0.04 mg/kg doses giving a subjective "high") for oral surgery involving the surgical removal of impacted 3rd molar teeth under local anesthesia (2% lidocaine with 1:100,000 epinephrine), anxiety states were greatly increased (Fig. 9) (Gregg et al., 1976b). It appears that THC combined with mild surgical stress (Fig. 10) in healthy individuals may lead to psychophysiological complications. More intense autonomic response (decreased blood pressure with syncope) occurred with the psychic response which was preceded by tachycardia. Dysphoria predominated over euphoria with various degrees of psychotic-like paranoic thought. This may be due to distortion of pain perception without analgesic effect on pain threshold with noxious stimuli being more painful; increased autonomic and visceral arousal; absence of overt behavioural signs of distress due to depersonalization; and time disintegration resulting in fear with respect to surgical procedure. The patients did not wish to submit to future surgery with THC premedication.

(ii) Transient Mild Paranoid Feeling

Another common reaction is a transient mild paranoid feeling experienced by those who have a paranoid defense mechanism which may help prevent acute anxiety reactions (Naditch, 1974). Pre-existing psychopathology may predispose individuals to adverse psychological reactions as indicated by those who had high scores on a schizophrenia subscale of the MMPI (Minnesota Multiphasic Personality Inventory) as well as degree (rate) of drug usage independent of psychopathology. It appears that acute adverse reactions may be the result of overwhelming psychological defenses. Those high in regression (defensive ego mechanism) may use psychoactive drugs as a regressed way of handling personal problems. More disturbed people are attracted toward stronger drugs. Use of drugs for therapeutic purposes (which may be associated with underlying psychopathology leading to increased difficulty in functioning or reflect current life stress(es) with immature or inefficient coping with problems) to solve life problems and as response to peer pressure may be related to the development of acute adverse reactions, which experience in turn may produce changes in psychopathology (Naditch, 1975).

(iii) Toxic Delirium

Toxic delirium, otherwise known as marihuana acute brain syndrome, is an acute reaction of the brain to high doses and/or potency of an exogenous toxin (in this case, cannabis). Such an intoxication is characterized by clouding of mental processes with disorientation, confusion, memory impairment, emotional lability, fluctuating sensorium, loss of insight and reality, poor concentration, impaired thinking, rambling verbalization, increased suggestibility, inappropriate fearfulness and apprehension, paranoid misinterpretations, delusions, illusions, and hallucinations; with physiological dysfunction of hyperactivity, restlessness, tremors, slurred speech, difficulty swallowing, failure in rapid movement, staggering gait, and sleeplessness (Halikas, 1974). A moderately-severe marihuana toxic type psychosis was reported in two male children (3 and 11 years of age) from Nigeria (Binitie, 1975). The 3 year old had been given puffs of hemp by a soldier. The immediate effect was profuse perspiration, restlessness, sleeplessness, and overactivity. The acute effect disappeared in one day with persistence of restlessness, destructive behaviour, and sleeplessness for 4 months. Complete recovery was evident at the end of one year. The 11 year old was given hemp to smoke by an older brother. Five months prior to hospitalization, it was noted that the boy talked nonsense, was restless, danced in the streets, unable to sit still or sleep, and refused food. He had difficulty understanding, frequently repeating words 2-3x to obtain full meaning. Following treatment for 3 months, he became well. The 3 year old exhibited a behaviour disorder with an acute episode followed by a longer lasting illness; the 11 year old, an organic toxic psychosis with perseveration (repitition of words) and difficulty in comprehension. The 2 cases demonstrate reversible cerebral damage and indicate that high doses of smoked hemp may be accompanied by a toxic psychosis. In another report of cannabis poisoning in a 4 year old girl (Bro et al., 1975), dark brown residue found in the front teeth was identified as cannabis resin. Analysis of the urine yielded cannabinols (21 mmoles/l). The child had eaten some cannabis resin (1.5 gm with 150 mg THC/gm). The symptoms and signs, consisting of alternate states of stupor and excitement with inappropriate laughing and ataxia, as well as decreased temperature and respiratory rate and increased blood sugar (116 mg%), subsided in about one day. In an oral surgery group of patients, noted above (Gregg et al., 1976b), premedicated with intravenous THC, the predominant mood experienced was dysphoria with psychotic-like swings from dysphoria to euphoria, transient panic and paranoia, depersonalization, time disintegration, and perceptual illusions, all of which were intensified by the stress of surgery.

(b) Prolonged Psychological Effects or Chronic Organic Brain Syndrome

Reports have appeared indicating prolonged undesirable psychological effects including psychotic (a severe emotional illness which may lead to mental derangement with defective contact with reality) and non-psychotic (personality or neuropsychological changes, amotivational syndrome, flashbacks) reaction states.

(i) Psychotic

There is increasing clinical evidence for a specific pathological organic response in the CNS to cannabis. A group of uniform symptoms (indicating a common toxic agent) unrelated to psychological predisposition has been reported (Kolansky and Moore, 1972). That is, mental or psychic changes (cerebral functioning) will occur in those (normal, adolescent in conflict, neurotic) individuals who smoke marihuana (potency of material as well as frequency and duration of use being important factors) regularly, thought to be due to chemical (THC) damage to brain cells. Reported characteristic symptoms in 13 adults (20-41 years of age) who smoked marihuana and/or hashish regularly (from 3-10x/week to daily use for 6 months to 6 years) included apathy with sluggish mental and physical responses; loss of interest in goals and personal appearance; considerable flattening of affect which could be easily disrupted when supply of cannabis threatened, giving way to irritability or outbursts of irrational anger; reversal of sleep cycle (sleep during day and wakeful at night); and headaches. Symptoms and signs of mental confusion, slowed time sense, difficulty with recent memory, and inability of completing thoughts during a conversation resulting in confused responses, indicate organic (reversible biochemical and/or persistent structural) cerebral change.

In an American army population in West Germany, 720 hashish smokers were medically and psychiatrically assessed over a 3 year period (Tennant and Groesbeck, 1972). Casual smoking of less than 10-12 gm hashish (5-10% THC)/month in small intermittent doses resulted in minor respiratory ailments (rhinopharyngitis or "hash throat") without adverse mental effects. Personality disturbances were evident in 110 individuals using more than 50 gm hashish/month (50-600 gm/3-18 months), all of whom, known as "hashaholics" (smoking several times a day and rarely using other drugs), exhibited chronic intoxication (similar to depressant drug dependent individual) manifested as apathy (no interest in self or job performance); dullness; lethargy with mild to severe impairment of judgement, concentration, and memory; intermittent episodes of confusion and inability to calculate; and slowed speech. Violence was not apparent though social and legal difficulties were frequent. With the addition of alcohol or other psychoactive drugs to hashish use, panic reactions, toxic psychosis and schizophrenic reactions occurred. Hashish use was discontinued in 23/110 patients with 10 of these subjects continuing to show residual symptoms (similar to organic brain damage) of intermittent episodes of memory loss, inability to concentrate and calculate, and confusion. These residual symptoms were also seen in 3/9 soldiers observed prior to, during, and after hashish use of 50-250 gm/month/3-12 months. Of the remaining men who continued to smoke, 70 were given a premature discharge because they were unable to function adequately in a working capacity. Treatment of acute psychosis which had developed in 115 hashish smokers was not successful progressing to a chronic phase similar to chronic schizophrenia. Three of these patients had used only hashish at high doses for 1-10 days, exhibiting hallucinations, delusions, paranoia, withdrawal, and inappropriate affect. There was evidence of pre-existent latent schizophrenia. Thus high doses of hashish may induce chronic psychosis similar to a schizophrenic reaction in predisposed individuals. The other 112 patients had used hashish (25-200 gm/month/3-6 months) and other drugs (hallucinogens, amphetamines, alcohol). All 115 patients were returned to the U.S.A. for long term psychiatric hospital treatment. During 1967-1971, the number of schizophrenic reactions/year increased from 18 to 77. If the average marihuana cigarette weights 0.5 gm with 1% THC then to obtain the equivalent THC dose noted above, it would be necessary to smoke 500-6000 marihuana cigarettes/month.

In an American air force population stationed in Thailand where potent marihuana (THC content unknown) was available, 5 cases of prolonged psychosis asociated with marihuana use were referred for psychiatric evaluation (Kroll, 1975). Marihuana use varied from 4-5 cigarettes/day/2 months to heavy use/3 years. Individuals with depressed feelings attempted to stay "high" or "stoned". Marihuana appeared to be potentially hazardous for emotionally unstable men indicated by premorbid personalities of 4 of these patients (borderline or schizoid). The drug was hazardous for the borderline adolescents who only superficially managed to resolve conflicts surrounding dependency or sexual identity. Risk of marihuana use was greatest in prepsychotic individuals. Those diagnosed later as schizophrenic reported paranoid reactions to occasional or casual use of local potent material. It was suggested that a Thai marihuana provocative test might be developed for prepsychotic personalities. Transient psychotic episodes often went unreported because symptoms cleared rapidly and because of the punitive policy toward drug abuse by the air force.

Clinical experience gained in India with respect to various potencies of cannabis preparations and duration of use giving rise to psychotic symptoms were reported in 200 patients (190 men, 10 women, average age 31 years, 114 occasional users, 62 with a family history of alcoholism or drug abuse) from a drug addiction clinic representing 11% of the patient population admitted over a 5 year period (usually self-referred) (Chopra and Smith, 1974). The least potent preparation, marihuana, was smoked while bhang was used as a beverage. The next potent preparation, ganja was smoked in pipes as was the most potent, charas (similar to hashish). Most patients had taken a large intoxicating dose of cannabis prior to admission resulting in an "alcohol blackout" type of amnesia lasting from a few hours to several days. The most common incapacitating psychotomimetic reaction was an acute confusional state often developing into a full blown toxic psychosis. The most common symptoms were sudden onset of confusion (with delusions, visual hallucinations, and emotional lability), temporary amnesia, disorientation, depersonalization, and paranoid symptoms. Individuals (68 or 34%) without a previous history of personality or mental disorders, recovered from their acute toxic psychosis within a few hours or days. Those (132 or 66%) with a previous history of psychiatric disorders (schizoid, sociopath, unstable personality, overt psychosis) had symptoms lasting for several weeks following which the underlying psychopathology became more evident with prevalent schizophrenic and paranoid symptoms. Some relapsed into previous drug symptoms reminiscent of LSD-type "flashbacks". Physical findings included injected conjunctivae, tachycardia, moderate blood pressure increase, dry mouth, increased appetite (some with anorexia, nausea, vomiting), epigastric pain, diarrhea (or constipation), chronic cough, emphysema, and asthmatic wheezing. Some neurological findings were ataxia, pupil dilation with occasional photophobia and nystagmus. Following clinical discharge, re-use of cannabis resulted in recurrent development of acute toxic psychosis (3-year follow-up). Psychotic reactions were more frequent with more potent preparations with which duration of use was also less; naive subjects often reacting to one dose. The average daily dose at the time of psychotic reactions was 5-10 gm (THC content unknown) with average duration of drug use prior to onset of reaction being 3-40 weeks depending on the potency of the preparation used. The more stable individuals used cannabis for social purposes vs relatively unstable individuals who used the drug as an escape mechanism for emotional problems; the younger patients taking it for pleasure and intoxication while the older individuals took it for the relief of stress or as a substitute for alcohol or opium.

Another clinical report from India (Thacore and Shukla, 1976), attempted to differentiate cannabis psychosis (paranoid type in 25 men, 18-42 years of age) from paranoid schizophrenia (25 men, 16-50 years of age) on the basis of initial clinical symptoms. Heavy cannabis use (THC content unknown) for more than 5 years consisted mainly of bhang (several grams/day in 4-6 divided doses) with occasional use of charas and ganja (by 6 subjects). Those with cannabis psychosis exhibited significant behavioural differences in the form of violence and odd bizarre behaviour. Most were in a panic state (some elated and boisterous) with disorganized behaviour not seen in schizophrenia. Both groups had auditory hallucinations with visual hallucinations occurring only in cannabis psychosis. Thought disorder was prevalent in schizophrenia while those with cannabis psychosis had rapidity of thought and flight of ideas with insight into the nature of their illness (i.e. contact with reality). Short term antipsychotic treatment of cannabis psychosis with phenothiazines resulted in complete recovery, relapse occurring with return to drug use. Cannabis dose was increased gradually until eventual development of a psychotic reaction, the genesis of which is unknown. It is postulated that tolerance develops until a "saturation" point is reached when further dosage increase leads to decompensation of mental functioning resulting in a psychosis similar to a functional psychosis vs toxic psychosis indicated by the absence of confusion and memory disturbance.

Clinical and patients' subjective experience with chronic marihuana use (7 months - 5 years) in 60 (50 men, 10 women) young adults (including adolescents, 13 to 28 years of age) revealed prolonged perceptual-cognitive disturbance of varying degrees with development of a paranoid reaction (including severe delusional and hallucinatory behaviour) with potential for psychotic decompensation (Lutz, 1979). An initial group of 4 patients showed schizophreniform derangement associated with frequent marihuana use (daily/2-4 years, potency unknown) which began with gradual personality changes and paranoid development (noted by teachers and parents). Of these, 3/4 had abnormal EEG findings in the left mid-temporal area of the brain. Of the group of 60 patients, only 5 had previous psychiatric histories. In a group of non-marihuana smoking patients of 16 (paranoid thought disorder; similar age group), 14 had family histories of mental illness. This could mean that there is a causal relationship between marihuana smoking and paranoid thinking disorder. In the group of 60, subtle personality changes prior to psychiatric symptoms included loss of motivation (apathy, indifference), decreased goal-directed activity (loss desire to work), social stagnation, inability to concentrate, and academic failure (arousal of parental concern seeking consultation). Psychiatric symptoms included perceptual-cognitive disturbances (affecting time, space, self, others), mental disorganization (flight of ideas), incoherence, depersonalization, hallucinations in all perceptual areas (visual, auditory, tactile, gustatory, olfactory, somatic-kinesthetic) with paranoid (thought disorder) development (reflected in widened blood pressure amplitude seen in untreated paranoid illness). Treatment consisting of termination of drug use, small doses stelazine (1 mg b.i.d. - 2 mg t.i.d.), and supportive psychotherapy, resulted in gradual disappearance of paranoid behaviour (several months - 2 years), the length of recovery being correlated with frequency and duration of marihuana use. It was felt that those with pre-existing mild or subclinical disturbance and marginal psychological adjustment were at increased risk to develop definite neuropsychological deficits following marihuana exposure. Prolonged tissue storage (fat) may explain insidious onset of behavioural changes and prolonged perceptual and behavioural deficits following cessation of drug use, and, may be responsible for long term organic brain damage. Thought disorder may be induced by exogenous (psychotomimetic chemicals or endogenous (schizophrenia) substances, and appear to result from subcortical CNS activity malfunction leading to disruption of subcortical-cortical homeostasis.

Several (four) schizophrenic patients, who were well-controlled with antipsychotic medication, had exacerbation and deterioration of their psychotic process following the moderate use of marihuana (Treffert, 1978). Such patients should be alerted to the possible undesireable interaction between their illness and marihuana (comparable to patients taking Parnate, an MAO inhibitor for depression, being alerted to the special hazards of foods with a high tyramine content found in aged cheese and fermented food). That is, psychotic patients (irrespective of etiology) run the risk of relapse and exacerbation of a well-controlled illness by moderate amounts of marihuana. Abstinence from marihuana leads to improvement and stabilization. Marihuana use appears to be correlated with recurrence of psychotic symptoms indicating that schizophrenic patients cannot use marihuana safely. Marihuana may also pose a risk to individuals predisposed to developing psychiatric disorders. From a single occasion of marihuana smoking by individuals with mild to moderate underlying psychopathology (functioning normally without known psychiatric illness), long lasting adverse effects were observed as functioning on a lower level for several months with greater psychopathology (Gersten, 1980). Marihuana, together with environmental stress, appeared to precipitate the development of psychiatric disturbances (schizophrenic thought disorder; psychosis with severe obsession) in emotionally vulnerable (prior difficulties such as ego deficit) individuals. Depersonalization, often described during acute marihuana intoxication, has occurred months after marihuana use (ranging from an overall marihuana cigarette use of only 2 cigarettes to daily use) initiated by stressful life situations (Szymanski, 1981). It was felt that such occurrences may serve as a subconscious defense mechanism against intolerable anxiety in some (anxious) individuals (some with family histories of substance abuse suggesting genetic or family dynamics influence).

The relevant features of a cannabis psychotic effect (to be differentiated from schizophrenia) include the following (Paton et al., 1973):

(1) fragmentation of thought, distractibility, inability to select relevant material, recent memory impairment, all of which may occur with ordinary doses becoming apparent when sustained mental effort is required; this type of impairment resembles nonsequential thinking of schizophrenia, however, where the cannabis user plays games with thoughts and feelings offering some rationalization for sequence of thought, the schizophrenic does not feel the need to do this;

(2) confusion, disassociation, and depersonalization;

(3) paranoid thought ranging from a tendency to be suspicious to paranoid thinking and actions often accompanied by intense anxiety, though mood fluctuation occurs abruptly;

(4) incongruity of affect such as laughing or weeping without apparent cause;

(5) hallucinations with high doses and free visual imagery;

(6) withdrawn, preoccupation with "milieu interieur", resembling withdrawal in catatonia or treated schizophrenics with large doses of chlorpromazine or by lobotomy, i.e. a flatness of affect.

The duration of mental reaction often correlates with duration of marihuana use and recovery time. Sufficiently high doses of cannabis may produce a schizophrenic-like psychotic state in any subject, the pattern of response being related to the personality structure. Cannabis may elicit a graded and reversible form of mental state showing many features of a natural psychosis. Variation in the patterns of disturbed behaviour or overlapping symptoms in a mental disorder make it difficult to arrive at a categorized diagnosis.

(ii) Non-Psychotic

The causality of non-psychotic prolonged reactions remains unresolved because it is difficult to distinguish between antecedents and consequences of marihuana use.

Flashbacks

Flashbacks are spontaneous recurrent feelings and perceptions similar to the original drug effect which have been reported in frequent and infrequent marihuana users and are not necessarily related to LSD (acid) use (Stanton et al., 1976). The etiology of the various degrees of these experiences is unknown and treatment is apparently not necessary. It is unclear whether flashbacks are a result of high drug doses or are hallucinatory experiences of prepsychotic personalities. They may be (a) marihuana induced following a bad LSD experience thought to be a psychological reaction to stress, (b) due to a persistent biochemical effect of marihuana, or (c) due to a disorganization of sensory processes and attention systems by marihuana.

Amotivational Syndrome and Personality Changes

Excessive use of drugs for pleasure may decrease motivation (incentive, drive). Whether cannabis has any specific capacity for inhibition of motivation is still highly controversial, although any neural damage in the limbic system (noted earlier) might explain possible decrease in drive. The picture of "amotivational syndrome" reported following chronic use of high doses of marihuana is one of apathy and depression with lack of clear goals, flattening of affect, and mental confusion, thought to be an intercurrent (passing) psychiatric syndrome seen in, for example, a college population; i.e. depression concurrent with marihuana use (Halikas, 1974).

An Egyptian study was undertaken to determine the level of functioning of male chronic cannabis users compared to non-users (Souief, 1976b). Twelve objective psychological tests (with 16 test variables) were administered to a prison population of 850 regular long term cannabis users incarcerated for hashish use (15-50 years of age, average 39 years and duration of use 5-30 years) and to 839 non-users (15-50 years of age, average 33 years). The drug users usually smoked a water pipe, twice daily with 0.5-1.0 gm hashish per sitting with a THC content averaging 3% (1.9-3.6%). Those representing an urban city population numbered 460 vs 454 controls and rural areas (or prisons) 390 vs 385 controls. Both groups contained individuals who were illiterate as well as those with various levels of education. The various modalities tested were speed of psychomotor performance, distance and time estimations, immediate memory, and visuomotor coordination. Users were slower in all speed tests (performed more slowly); overestimated distance; memory span for digit backwards was significantly different from controls; and less accurate performance occurred in visuomotor coordination tests. Therefore, controls showed superior performance in speed and/or accuracy tasks. Certain combination of intake, level of literacy and residence showed a better drug effect than others. It was postulated that the lower the non-drug level of proficiency in tests of cognitive and psychomotor performance or abilities, the smaller the psychological deficit following chronic drug use. This was confirmed by test results indicating less function impairment with chronic cannabis use in illiterates, rural residence, and older subjects. That is, the lower the level of literacy, and/or nearer to ruralism, and/or older the subject, the less detectable is the psychological impairment associated with drug use. Perhaps such individuals have low levels of arousal (alertness) which may be the key or central psychological process responsible for the outcome(s). Lower scores were obtained in the younger better educated users. Those under 25 years of age had statistically different intellectual function from the over 35 year age group. Impairment of cognitive skills due to chronic use was detected mostly during adolescence when intellectual growth is still present. Intellectual abilities are known to peak in the early 20's and decline thereafter. From the above it may be seen that if users and controls were selected only from one stratum of the population (e.g. illiterates), then differences would have not been evident. This could explain some of the controversial (opposite) results seen in the literature as well as conclusions reached by some, that moderate use produces no injurious effects on the mind (Carlin and Trupin, 1977), questioning however, the possibility of differential effects of chronic use on vulnerable individuals. The latter study included 10 normal marihuana smokers (average age 24 years; average education 14 years) who had used marihuana daily for an average of 5 years, and a matched control group of non-smokers.

In order to determine long term psychological effects of cannabis, 9 psychological tests were given to 50 (mostly illiterate men) heavy cannabis users from India (half smoked charas, half drank bhang) with an average daily intake of 150 mg THC over a 4-10 year period, and to 25 matched controls; age ranged from 16-45 years (average 30) (Mendhiratta et al., 1978). The tests were performed following at least a 12 hour drug free period to avoid acute effects. Users were significantly differentiated from controls in 8/9 tests, with duration and heavy use being important factors. Cannabis users were found to react more slowly, have poorer concentration and time estimation, higher neuroticism, and greater perceptuo-motor disturbance. Charas smokers were the poorest performers with poor memory, decreased psychomotor activity, and poor size estimation.

In an academic select group of university men, personal and social implications of drug use were studied (Mellinger et al., 1976). There was a high prevalence of drug use in 1970 with more frequent marihuana use occurring among polydrug users. Marihuana use was experimental, casual, or recreational vs habitual or compulsive use. The goal was to identify characteristics or patterns of use likely to produce an amotivational syndrome. Marihuana use was not substantial over an extended period of time but continuity and multi drug use was related to frequency of marihuana use. It was found that the probability of school drop-out in drug users (in this sample of 950 freshmen) was no higher than expected, given background characteristics, value orientation, and academic motivation as freshmen except if parents were less educated and if marihuana use progressed to multidrug use when the likelihood of dropping out increased. Poor relation with family and alienation from the larger society was associated with low academic motivation, school drop-out, and drug use. Perhaps some moderate users (as alcohol users) may be less able to cope with drug use creating problems or impairing capabilities to cope realistically or constructively with life, i.e., less goal oriented and less equipped to achieve goals. It appears that drug use has an indirect effect on school drop-out via association with low academic motivation. Men using (or had used) drugs as freshmen were more likely than non-users to become permanent drop-outs.

In another college population of 1380 students in the same period (1970), the relation between use and psychosocial adaptation as well as academic performance was subjectively investigated over a 3-year period (1970-1972; data being obtained from 1133 students in 1971 and 901 in 1972) (Brill and Christie, 1974). There was no difference between users and non-users with respect to grade point average or education achievement except that users had more difficulty in deciding on career goals and dropped-out to reassess goals. A smaller percent of regular users (use more than 5x/week) sought advanced or professional degrees vs occasional (use less than twice/week) or non-users. With longer duration of marihuana use, worsening of emotional state was more likely to be reported (6% with 1 year use; 20% with more than 7 year use) which may indicate that regular use may be deleterious to mental health or that those with emotional difficulties tend to use marihuana longer. There were 12.3% users who experienced worsened academic performances and 8.6% poorer physical health leading to decreased or stopping drug use. Use decreased with increasing age. With increasing years of use, the reported beneficial effects on adaptation was decreased. It was felt that this group of students used marihuana for relaxation, getting high, and socializing similar to that which is sought with alcohol. It has been suggested that dropping out of school may be due to loss of motivation or intellectual function as noted in poor academic adjustment and reassessing of goals by regular users. With respect to intermittent to moderate marihuana use (average more than 6x/month/2-3 year period) in 40 college students (20 on drug, 20 controls used alcohol, age 18-21 years, good point average), insignificant adverse effects on intellectual function and perceptual-motore skill has been reported (Hall et al., 1975-76).

The lack of agreement with respect to marihuana effects on behaviour led to a study to determine whether several levels of motivation would differentially decrease acute marihuana effects (Pihl and Sigal, 1978). Male volunteers (112; 18 to 30 years of age) took part in this study with 14 subjects in each of 8 groups under 2 drug conditions (either marihuana or no drug) and 4 motivation conditions. Performance measurements included time perception, complex or choice reaction time, and a paired association memory task. In the drug groups, 4 marihuana cigarettes (each with 0.5 gm marihuana with 0.8% THC) were smoked by pairs of subjects (passing the cigarette between each other) over a 20 minute period resulting in consumption of 1 gm marihuana or 8 mg THC. The results revealed overestimation of time, increased reaction time and less accurate memory task in marihuana groups. The non-drug groups improved with motivation vs marihuana groups who did not. The apparent lack of response to incentives indicates a possible interaction between acute low dose marihuana effects and motivation, and, may be related to an antianxiety property of marihuana (Gale and Guenther, 1971) which is thought to be responsible for its habitual use (i.e. a reinforcing property of a more relaxed state and tolerable painful or stressful states).

This antianxiety property was confirmed by a psychoanalytic case report (Wallace, 1978) focussing on the immediate after effects of marihuana use in a 32 year old laborer who had smoked marihuana daily for about 10 years, using ocasionally 2 joints/day. The immediate after effects consisted of a "high" with intense day dreams followed by lethargy, tiredness, time dragging feeling, and work made much more difficult (even though earlier in treatment reported that work was made tolerable). The day after marihuana use, a tranquilizing effect occurred with a decrease in pleasant and unpleasant effects as well as in ambition and drive, with a let-down feeling associated with recognition that fantasies were unreal which led to an immediate impulse to repeat the "high" and to decrease motivation to tolerate delays involved in pursuing goals of reality. Discontinuance of drug resulted in increased psychic discomfort, with a peak effect at 4 days, gradually subsiding by the 9th to 10th day, during which time earlier frustrations were re-lived. The immediate "high" substituted for the pursuit of satisfaction in reality and provided a temporary escape from internal conflicts. The tranquilizing effect accounted for regular marihuana use to relieve painful boredom and reinforce defenses against anger by suppressing all affects (psychic defense); the latter in turn contributing to boredom, making it a vicious cycle. The withdrawal symptoms reaching a peak in 4 days and tapering off in a week indicates an addictive quality of marihuana. The above confirms the statement that heavy marihuana use is correlated with a loss of interest in conventional goals and development of a kind of lethargy.

The tranquilizing or lethargic effects occurring on the day following marihuana use is further exemplified in another study (Babor et al., 1976) in which moderate (smoke more than 5x/month) and heavy (daily use/1-2 years) users showed lowered activity levels one hour following intake with increased sleep time for several days after heavier consumption thought to be due to the half-life of THC. Volunteers (21-27 years of age) were observed prior to, during, and after 21 days of free access to 1 gm 2% THC marihuana cigarettes. Male marihuana users were compared with a control group of casual alcohol drinkers (less than 1 oz/day; 4-10x/month). It was estimated that the moderate marihuana smokers absorbed 15-30 mg THC/day and the heavy users, 30-60 mg/day. The investigators felt that there was only limited support for the amotivational syndrome but that repeated self-administered marihuana over a concentrated period of time may produce lethargy and decreased activity on the day following drug intake. It was suggested that this delayed reaction may be associated with the gradual elimination of active metabolites from the body.

Since marihuana effects on behaviour are considered to be inconclusive, a study was undertaken in which the following individuals took part (Salvendy and McCabe, 1975). Four groups of 10 male volunteers each (average 20 years of age, weight 73.7 kg) consisted of those who never smoked marihuana, those who did previously (2-5x/week) but stopped 11-19 months earlier, and those who smoked marihuana habitually (average 4.7x/week). The latter group smoked either placebo or marihuana, 30 minutes prior to performance tests measuring manipulative and coordination skills found in industrial and occupational skills. The marihuana contained 1.4% THC with 13 mg THC/cigarette smoked. Marihuana smokers (past and current users) had lower performance than those who had never used the drug; with smoking prior to the tasks decreasing performance further (Fig. 11). This could mean that marihuana smoking negatively affects both acquisition and initial performance of manipulative and coordination skills while those who had previously used the drug performing less efficiently than non-users. Greater coordination impairments (especially in more difficult tasks) in experienced marihuana users (21-42 years of age; 2-100 x/past year use) vs a naive (25-59 years of age; non-users) group (8 males and 8 females in each group) were observed in another (double-blind) study (Milstein et al., 1975) where perceptual-motor coordination (horizontal and vertical grooves, hand maze task, hand steadiness; significant difference), motor ability (finger and toe tapping; no difference) and visual perception (speed of stimulus recognition; no difference) were measured prior to and following marihuana (600 mg of 1.3% THC/30 min) or placebo marihuana (0.1% THC) smoking via a smoking device (34% THC retained by smokers). Subjective measures consisted of intoxication state (conjunctival redness, memory loss, ability to carry on coherent conversation, affective state changes) assessed by the observer, PAS (primary affective scale measuring anger, arousal, depression, fear, happiness) presented to each subject and individuals identifying substances received. Observable intoxicated state occurred in 11 experienced and 9 naive individuals without changes in PAS with subjects able to identify the marihuana state. It appears that acute marihuana intoxication, especially in the experienced users, impairs behaviours requiring higher order integration and processing (perceptual-motor performance effects) vs simpler behaviours requiring limited processing (motor ability and visual perception noted above) which may be minimally affected. Thus tasks requiring good coordination or cognitive processes should be avoided by intoxicated individuals. Also physical work capacity (measured by a submaximal bicycle ergometer test) was altered (decreased) by marihuana (1.4 gm with 18.2 mg THC) smoking (vs marihuana placebo and control; double-blind study) through a hand made glass pipe by 18 users (average 23.1 years of age) as were resting HR (increased) and resting systolic and diastolic blood pressures (increased) (Steadward and Singh, 1975).

An attempt was made to assess the psychological characteristics of college marihuana users especially those pertaining to the amotivational syndrome (Wagner and Romanik, 1976). Three matched groups, each with 30 college students (17 males, 13 females), were comprised of marihuana users, multi-drug users, and abstainers. Comparisons were made across 24 Hand Test scores for pathological (maladjustment, withdrawal), environmental (involvement) and aggressive (interpersonal responses directed to giving pain, hostility, or aggression) effects. Marihuana users scored higher on the exhibition variable indicating an exhibitionistic effect. Abstainers were significantly different from the drug-using groups in variables of acquisition (exert oneself to obtain goal), active (psychological investment in achievement) and environmental. This suggests that college drug users are less inclined to exert effort to accomplish environmental goals. Such subjects would be less willing to extend themselves to acquire status, knowledge and power, and less involved in constructive accomplishment. It appears that comparative lack of environmental orientation is characteristic of student drug users (polydrug or only marihuana use). Results are consistent with an amotivational hypothesis of passive inward turning attitude developed with marihuana smoking, withdrawing from challenge of life. This tendency is characterized by apathy, loss of effectiveness and a decreased capacity of willingness to accomplish future plans. However the results do not necessarily imply a cause-effect relationship because it is difficult to tell whether amotivated students are predisposed to turn to drug use or whether drugs themselves produce subsequent lack of motivation (may be both). The overt aggressiveness measurement (aggression and acting out) was not significantly different between the groups.

(c) Aggressive Behaviour

Concern has been raised with respect to marihuana use and criminality as well as the association between marihuana intoxication and hostile human behaviour. In order to understand and intelligently discuss agressiveness, which covers many behavioural patterns, a general definition is in order and may be stated as specifically oriented behaviour directed toward removing or overcoming whatever is threatening the physical and/or psychological integrity of a living organism. This includes maintenance of internal homeostases, and, species self-preservation but not different kinds of aggression

(Valzelli, 1978). Organized neural systems in the brains of animals and man subserve aggression in the presence of a particular stimulus. This aggression is stimulus bound. For example, a wild animal in its natural environment operates via predatory aggressiveness to capture its usual prey for its feeding behaviour vs a laboratory animal which has food made available. Therefore, biological aggressiveness is a behavioural means for achieving different goals. Aggressiveness may also be considered as a goal directed behaviour with deep biological roots. This natural force is released by frustration or any impulse linked to species and self-preservation. Aggressiveness thus supports and assures success of impulses or needs via a series of graduated behaviour patterns ranging from simple consolidation of supremacy to destructive outbursts. It is not a single entity and different types of aggressive responses may vary in intensity depending on various factors of genetic, endocrine, instinctive, frustrative, learning-dependent, and socio-cultural order. Different kinds of aggressive responses with different physiological bases, each defined by a stimulus situation triggering it, may be differentiated into the following:

(a) predatory (due to presence of a prey)

(b) competative or inter-male (social rank or choice of female in same species without provocation)

(c) fear motivated or induced (no way of escape with attempt at flight)

(d) territorial (intruder violating territory)

(e) irritative (pain stimulus; rage reaction)

(f) maternal (drive to protect and defend newborns)

(g) sex-related (sexual motivation)

except (h) instrumental (previous experience; hostile or overt aggressive behaviour in man) which has no physiological basis except that operating in the learning process since it is learned and an imitative response. Animal behaviour depends upon the activation of several neural circuits according to functional needs resulting in brain plasticity to environmental requirements. It is a dynamically changing continuum with respect to spontaneous and learned responses to environmental stimuli and to neuro-physiological traits involved. Therefore different kinds of aggression may flow from one to another without interruption making it difficult to identify different types of aggressive behaviour.

As noted in the above section, affective behaviour (including aggression) is neuroanatomically identified with the limbic system in the brain layer beneath the neocortical mantle and surrounding the brain stem (i.e. sandwiched between them). The affective emotional feelings or information received by this system guides behavioural patterns necessary for species or self preservation by means of associative and integrative functions. Thus activation or inhibition of one of its components triggers functional chain reactions spreading over most of the brain. Experimentally, limbic system structures have been identified for a series of behavioural patterns (including aggression) in animals noted above. For example, the hypothalamus is important in feeding behaviour which is accompanied by a specific form of aggression (predatory). Stimulation of various areas within the limbic system or lesions have elicited or suppressed the different kinds of aggressive responses noted above; various nuclei within a particular area having opposite effects on aggressive behaviour. In humans, stimulation of implanted electrodes in the amygdala area resulted in angry verbally hostile threatening behaviour whereas lesioning of the area abolished or decreased outbursts of destructive violence with subjective reports of inability to become angry even if wished to do so. However each amygdala has a cluster of nuclei with several different functions, initiating and suppressing aggressive behaviour. Uncontrollable hostility and aggressiveness have been decreased with lesions in various other areas in the limbic system. Stimulation of the septal region decreases agitated psychotic and violent human behaviour, changing disorganized rage into happiness and mild euphoria vs bilateral medial amygdala stimulation which elicits overt assaultive behaviour. Brain tumors with irritative focus (hypothalamus) induce increased irritability and attacks of rage. About one-half of the epileptics with an anterior temporal focus of abnormal firing have psychiatric disorders with a propensity to be provoked into explosive and violent behaviour. To relieve uncontrollable epilepsy, lesions have been made in the temporal lobe resulting in seizure control as well as in decreased anger, hostility, and overt aggressiveness.

Hormones sensitize the neurological system for aggressive behaviour. For example, castration decreases fighting behaviour as does estrogen (anti-androgen) in animals. In humans, castration has been effective in controlling some violent sex crimes while stilbesterol (estrogen) controls aggressive behaviour in adolescents and young adults. Androgens (male sex hormones) increase self-confidence and may induce aggressive-like responses in those with feelings of insecurity and inferiority. Thus animals and man are equipped neurophysiologically to aggressively respond to biological condition requirements for self and species preservation. Violent thoughts and acts peculiar to man may be triggered by pathological conditions, a wrong environment, and bad imitative learning necessitating further knowledge of neuroanatomical biochemistry of the brain to avoid wrong tuning of this complex system.

Aggression, an intentional behaviour giving rise to physical injury to others, may become part of a coping mechanism in some deviant individuals regardless of drug use. However, this does not mean that drugs do not affect behaviour (Tinklenberg, 1974). Marihuana, as any other drug, may induce alteration in perception and reinforcement enhancing or diminishing possible violence. Aggressive acts may be influenced by age, sex, race, location of encounter or environment (includes laboratory setting with selection of normal subjects and field studies with admitted marihuana users), available weapons, presence of drugs and level of usage noting their pharmacological properties (e.g. marihuana decreases physical strength in tasks requiring sustained effort and has a wide range of effects such as euphoria, sedation, hallucinogen) as well as drug interactions. Both laboratory and field studies (both with limitations) are necessary to obtain useful information pertaining to the possible relation between marihuana use and aggressive behaviour.

In an attempt to determine whether marihuana is dangerous, personality patterns of marihuana users have been studied to determine if marihuana use is associated with adjustment problems, psychopathology, or violence. One such study evaluated personality patterns associated with varying degrees of marihuana use in 96 youthful offenders (18-28 years of age) divided into 4 groups, each with 19 white and 5 blacks, excluding those with a college education or physically addicted to drugs (McGuire and Megargee, 1974). The 4 groups included non-users (except alcohol), occasional users (1-2x or sometime but no other drugs), regular users (more than 1x/week, marihuana only) and heavy users (daily marihuana use plus other drugs). An objective personality test battery consisted of MMPI (Minnesota Multiphasic Personality Inventory), CPI (California Psychological Inventory) and STAI (State-Trait Anxiety Inventory) with records being kept on the highest grade level achieved, revised beta IQ, and whether the offense was drug related. Results obtained were compared with previous results obtained in college students and were found to differ somewhat especially on personality scales related to antisocial behaviour and moral values. Personality profiles were similar in non and occasional users while regular users had the best overall adjustment and heavy users the poorest. The nonusers had a strong tendency to more rigid authoritarian attitudes and conventional conservative thought patterns. The occasional users were more prone to impulsive asocial acting out so that this restless reckless behaviour could have led to experimentation with marihuana. Heavy and regular users differed the most in the tests indicating that both were more likely to be individualistic and think for themselves. The heavy users were the most maladjusted with strong sociopathic tendencies including serious alienations from authority figures in general and their family in particular. Test profiles suggested egocentric values emphasizing hedonism with little concern for others, and, despite the superficial charm, a pattern of shallow and exploitative interpersonal relationships. Regular users were the best adjusted with least deviant values. Non and occasional users were composed of normal thieves vs heavy users whose offences resulted from psychopathology and intrapersonal conflicts vs regular users who were imprisoned for drug-related charges (possession and transportation of marihuana). There appears to be an association between heavy use of marihuana in conjunction with other drugs, and personality test scores indicative of maladjustment found in prisoners and college students. Those using only marihuana did not display serious psychopathology but did appear to be less mature and more socially deviant. Their test profiles were almost identical to those of early adolescents (perhaps not outgrown youthful rebelliousness).

The relation between marihuana and hostility was assessed in 60 healthy male volunteers (21-30 years of age without evident psychological impairment) with prior marihuana experience and social use (1x/week) in more than half the subjects (half experimented with other drugs) (Salzman et al., 1976). Groups of 3 persons each were given either a marihuana (2.2% THC) or placebo cigarette to smoke completely on a double-blind basis. Individual hostility levels were assessed prior to and following each discussion session while interpersonal behaviour (verbal) hostility was assessed during each session. Marihuana intoxicated subjects reported decreased hostile feelings following a frustration stimulus (vs increase in the placebo group) with a slight increase in sarcasm. That is, the decreased inner affective hostility in conjunction with increased negative verbal behaviour suggests that this dose of marihuana (taken in a group) may have mild disinhibitory effects enabling the individual to feel less internally angry and less externally constricted in interpersonal communication. Thus marihuana intoxication modified the expected hostile response to a frustration stimulus suggesting no association with increased hostility. The relation between marihuana and hostility may be the collective result of an interaction between the drug and other factors such as dose, environment, nature of stimulus (or stress) and individual (adaptive ego defenses). If ego defenses control more serious psychopathology, then higher drug doses in the presence of a stronger stimulus and non-supportive environment might lead to decompensation rather than disinhibition possibly resulting in panic, psychosis, and aggressive behaviour. In this instance, the supportive group structure, modest dose, and mild frustration stimulus was not associated with increased hostility.

Several investigations support the assumption that expression of physical aggression is related to alcohol intake vs the controversial relation between marihuana and aggression. Marihuana and alcohol effects on expression of human aggressive behaviour were therefore compared. Each of 50 male volunteers (over 21 years of age with some experience with alcohol and marihuana) received oral preparations of high and low doses of alcohol (100 proof ethanol; 1.5 or 0.5 oz/40 lbs weight) or THC (0.3 or 0.1 mg kg; a reliable high being obtained with 0.2-0.5 mg/kg p.o.) or a placebo drink (Taylor et al., 1976). Aggression was measured by the intensity of shock a subject set for his opponent to receive in a competative reaction time task. The high dose of alcohol increased whereas the high dose of THC decreased the tendency to initiate aggressive behaviour (Fig. 12); the high dose of both drugs showing greater disruption in performance than lower doses. The high dose of alcohol produced a greater subjective effect than the high THC dose with high doses of both drugs being greater than for low doses. THC did not appear to elicit an irrational impulsive response vs alcohol which increased the expression of aggressive behaviour.

In order to help resolve divergent views on long term marihuana effects, studies were conducted in natural environments with 275 chronic users from India and 17 alienated youths (hippies) from America and Europe (who had come to India) examining immediate marihuana effects and after the effects had worn off (Chopra and Jandu, 1976). The sample included individuals from various education levels (uneducated to university level) with mean age ranging from 17 to 48 years, mean duration of use 2-27 years, and a mean daily THC intake of 40-350 mg. The various cannabis preparations used were marihuana (1.47% THC), bhang (1% THC), ganja (3% THC) and charas (5% THC). Of the 275 users, 43.6% complained of marked degree of impairment in their general health and working capacity, with respiratory disorders being most prevalent. Most took cannabis (to obtain relaxation and release social inhibition) to the point of a mild sense of intoxication (with a mild degree of confusion and loss of time and space sense). Adverse psychic reactions occurred more often in the younger age group (17-19 years), some of whom had childhood histories of neurosis, psychopathic personality, deviancy, anxiety, and who took cannabis to stabilize their condition and regain self-confidence. Adverse psychiatric reactions occurred with excessive daily doses in a group of 85 individuals resulting in acute intoxicated states. These reactions depended upon dose, mood, personality and pre-existing psychopathology and were observed as psychosis in those with low psychotic thresholds as well as hallucinations and psychotomimetic effects of acute intoxication. The drug appears to remove higher control activity in the brain exciting any pre-existing trend of mental aberrations. Prolonged heavy use resulted in lack of initiative, motivation, and interest in work and family. Use of smaller doses lead to a quiet, apathetic, disinterested individual followed by permanent behaviour alterations evident especially during stress as an amotivational syndrome. Excessive use was associated with personality inadequacies found in heavy users as emotional immaturity, low frustration tolerance, and failure to assume responsibility. Behaviourally their traits were seen as unrealistic emphasis on the present vs the future; tendency to drift along in a passive manner; failure to develop long term abilities or skills; and, favour regressive and magical rather than rational thinking process. Depression and apathy may give way to increased locomotor activity and aggressive behaviour with repeated higher doses. However cannabis is really a deterrent to premeditated crime because of its stupefying and depressive effects (vs alcohol) but may be indirectly associated with crime by trying to support a drug habit by stealing. Also, those with personality problems (noted above) may become irritable and violent if their chosen "quiet" life is threatened or disturbed. Passive non-productive individuals are more prone to psychosis than those with regular daily vocation. It appears that cannabis may precipitate latent psychiatric disorders and/or aggravate pre-existing psychiatric problems.

One of the most controversial issues in psychopharmacology is the nature of the relation between marihuana use and violence. It is difficult to compare data from various countries regarding use and violence because of the variation in THC content in plants grown in different geographical areas as well as street marihuana being adulterated with other psychoactive substances (Abel, 1977). Chronic users may respond differently from casual users because of possible cumulative drug effects and polydrug use. The limbic system in the temporal lobes of the brain is considered to be involved in aggressive behaviour. Symptoms common to both marihuana intoxication and temporal lobe epilepsy (which precede loss of impulse control and episodes of aggression) include sense of depersonalization; paranoia; loss of recent memory and speech difficulties; intrusion of thoughts occupying centre of awareness to exclusion of all other conscious activity; changes in mood and affect (increased sense of anxiety, terror, irritability); changes in visual, auditory, and tactile perception; and hallucinatory experiences. Spontaneous activity in the temporal lobe is known to cause subjective feelings of rage and uncontrollable acts of violence. Increased EEG activity noted in the temporal lobe of cannabis induced psychosis might set off neural impulses in brain areas dealing with feelings and aggressive behaviour. Subjects, who had committed acts of violence, given alcohol under laboratory conditions exhibited temporal lobe dysrhythmia. Thus alcohol may not only intoxicate but also facilitate temporal lobe epileptoid states in susceptible individuals. If a link could be established between marihuana neurophysiological effects and neural activity in the temporal lobe, then this locus of action could account for some isolated instances of violence associated with marihuana use. Marihuana may precipitate violent behaviour in unstable individuals with behaviour disorders who are prone to chronic drug use as a means of coping with inferiority feelings and sense of resentment and who are not necessarily violent by nature.

Human investigations have revealed less aggressive feeling with relatively low doses of THC in healthy individuals vs reports of aggression or violence from countries where chronic use of more potent preparations have been used in perhaps less healthy or robust individuals. Animal studies were therefore undertaken in an attempt to explain some of the human findings, keeping in mind that there are 7 basic classical aggressive behaviours (not only one, noted earlier) each with a distinct neurological and endocrinological basis. Cannabis appears to have a differential effect on various kinds of aggression; increasing irritable aggression and decreasing both predatory and inter-male types (Abel, 1975). Any condition causing discomfort (pain, frustration, increased drive) may result in irritable aggression observed as an absence of a prior attempt at escape; an extreme form labelled uncontrollable rage. Destruction of the septal area in the limbic system of animals' brains has produced rage. Predatory aggression involves attacking some natural prey, while inter-male aggression occurs following prolonged isolation. In non-stressed animals, acute cannabis administration decreased aggression (i.e. a depressant effect which may be due to decreased locomotor activity and/or decreased motivation comparable to an amotivational syndrome) vs chronic, when aggression was increased (which may be due to tolerance development to the depressive effects). Previously stressed animals (food deprivation, cold environment, REM sleep deprivation, foot shock) given cannabis, either acutely or chronically, increased their fighting behaviour (Carlini, 1978). The relation between stress and cannabis induced aggression in animals depends upon the kind of stress; state or condition of the subject; prior conditioning to stress; drug dose (may decrease motor activity); frequency and duration of use (acute or chronic); nature and degree of aggressive behaviour; and emotionality.

Laboratory controlled settings lack evidence for increased aggressiveness with acute and chronic marihuana use which appeared to decrease physical interaction, increase positive mood states, and decrease hostility. Field studies in which retrospective case analysis of crimes committed by marihuana users were carried out, indicated that some individuals demonstrate an abnormal susceptibility to marihuana intoxicating effects as irrational poorly controlled behaviour (may entail aggressive actions) and may be idiosyncratic. These idiosyncratic reactions are infrequent occurring in those with prior psychiatric disturbances or when other drugs are used concomitantly. Some youths use marihuana for a "cool" image vs a "rawdy" one seen with alcohol. In a study dealing with incarcerated adolescent delinquents, it was found that the extent of marihuana use was not a positive predictor of assaultive crime and that marihuana may be used for aggression-reducing effects. Thus human hostility and aggression appears to be decreased with cannabis although the effects during various stressful conditions has not been investigated systematically. The generally stated belief that marihuana use is not a major cause of aggression is based on the typical marihuana user and does not consider the at-risk individual (since studies screen out those with psychiatric problems) who may react violently due to exacerbation of pre-existing problems (history of violent behaviour) involving impulse control.

(d) Classification of Psychiatric Conditions

A workable classification of psychiatric conditions associated with cannabis intoxication has been suggested for clinicians enabling them to recognize the various cannabis reactions thereby increasing clinical acumen necessary for appropriate diagnosis and treatment of medical complaints (Hart, 1976). It appears that each and every case of cannabis intoxication falls within the following classification:

      (i) drug dependence;

      (ii) non-psychotic OBS (organic brain syndrome)

      (iii) psychosis; and

      (iv) schizoprenic-like including one of (i), (ii), or (iii).

An organic brain syndrome is characterized by impairment of orientation, memory, intellectual function, judgment as well as labile and shallow affect. Brain syndromes have been designated as either acute, reversible (delirium) or, chronic, irreversible or persistent organic brain syndrome (dementia). However a continuum of the brain syndrome exists as acute, subacute, subchronic and chronic depending upon the duration of persistence of symptoms. Occasional users are those individuals who use cannabis less than 4x/month vs regular users who use the drug at least 4x/month. Since the half-life of THC (time for half the drug to be eliminated) in tissues is 7 days indicating accumulation, then concern is expressed for regular users who would always have some THC and/or metabolites in their bodies. The regular user is often drug dependent (classification (i)) psychologically and may be physiologically (abstinence syndrome due to tolerance development) dependent as well. Such a user would at least suffer from non-psychotic OBS (classification (ii)). Classification (iii) is OBS with psychotic features which may be an acute episode superimposed on (ii). In classification (iv), schizophrenia should be distinguished from psychotic effects due to cannabis and may be superimposed on intellectual deficiency. Mental retardation is thought to facilitate the development of the schizophrenic syndrome in a predisposed person. Also, a dormant schizophrenia may predispose an individual to drug-seeking behaviour as a defense against the emerging process making the brain syndrome associated with cannabis use secondary to the underlying schizophrenia. Cannabis psychosis should not be compared to schizophrenia which is a functional disorder of unknown etiology. When cannabis use is denied by a patient, a diagnosis of acute cannabis use may be reached from a triad of signs and symptoms of tachycardia (increased heart rate), bilateral conjunctival injection (red eyes), and time slowing; chronic use yielding a bradycardia (decreased heart rate). Clinically, each and every use of cannabis produces a toxic state for which it is often used. The minimum observed in an acute intoxicated state is impairment of orientation (temporal distortion), memory impairment (registration defect) and altered affect (some degree of euphoria or dysphoria) with possibly some impairment of intellectual functions and judgment. Thus cannabis experience may be considered an organic brain syndrome keeping in mind that cannabis is fat soluble with a long lifetime in the body (vs alcohol which is water miscible and rapidly metabolized). Most marihuana users are looking for some distortions of reality in addition to euphoria as part of their "high" feeling equivalent to an acute alcohol intoxication (a psychosis or mental derangement with lost contact with reality). Other equivalent alcohol reactions are alcoholism or drug dependence ((i) noted above) and drunkeness or (ii). Longer term cannabis effects are now being considered and are equivalent to Korsakoff's psychosis and alcoholic deterioration. With optimum dose, frequency, and duration of cannabis use, a subchronic OBS can develop in anyone irrespective of premorbid personality and depends upon the individual's metabolic capability to handle THC. Cannabis intoxication may also be compared to CO (carbon monoxide) poisoning which under optimum conditions may result in CO psychosis (iii) or a CO (ii) with the difference that CO poisoning often ends in death. Thus acute cannabis intoxication may occur as crises of delirium or toxic psychosis whereas a chronic state may result in physical and mental deterioration.

4. Psychomotor Function or Performance

Complex psychomotor performance involved in driving a car or flying an aeroplane has been shown to be impaired by social marihuana use, the impairment being similar to alcohol use (Petersen, 1976). The various perceptual, cognitive, and psychomotor functions required in driving ability are not well understood with respect to their relative importance. Cannabis is used to alter cognition (awareness and judgment) or perception (consciousness or mental image). One means of assessing cannabis-related driving risks is by comparing accident rates for users vs non-users. This may be accomplished by screening (RIA) urine specimens for cannabinoids (Fig. 13) in drivers involved in motor accidents (Teale et al., 1976; Teale and Marks, 1976). The incidence of cannabis use appears to be confined to young drivers (17-27 years of age) noted in a limited survey of 66 fatally injured drivers (Fig. 14), 6 of whom showed cannabinoid levels in post-mortem blood (one with a high blood alcohol level) (Teale et al., 1977). Proof of cannabis consumption may be demonstrated by examination of dental deposits obtained via a toothpick with a cotton swab soaked in petroleum ether or chloroform (Noirfalise and Lambert, 1978). A benzene extract of the swab material is cleaned by chromatography and the eluate examined chromatographically resulting in a chromatogram of cannabis constitutents; such information being useful for criminological and clinical toxicological purposes. Since some users imbibe alcohol comcomitantly, attempts are being made to find the contribution made by each drug, by conducting behavioural tasks in laboratories as well as road tests to determine the possible deterioration in driving performance.

Significant human motor and mental performance decrements (also noted under amotivational syndrome) have been noted 30 minutes following the smoking of a marihuana cigarette containing 10 mg THC. Alcohol (15 ml/50 lb weight) with THC (2.5 or 5 mg) increased performance decrements as well as side effect scores, pulse rate, and conjunctival reddening. A linear dose-response relationship has been reported for various doses of THC (6.25, 12.5, 25, 50 μg/kg) on pulse rate, mental and motor performance, static equilibrium (swaying) and subjective effects (Forney and Kiplinger, 1971; Kiplinger et al., 1971). Altered time sense (overestimation) and impaired short term memory in more complex tasks have been observed. The effects appear to depend on drug dose and task demand as well as interaction between the various cannabis constituents (Δ^9 and Δ^8 THC, cannabinol, cannabidiol). Qualitatively, the above acute responses by heavy long term cannabis users are similar to occasional short term users (Dornbush and Kokkevi, 1976). Time sense or sensory perception distortions may be due to the differential effects of THC (vs ethanol and pentobarbital in animals) on the frontal polysensory area of the cerebral cortex where sensory integration occurs (Boyd et al., 1971). At THC doses of 70, 130, 190, and 250 mcg/kg (vs placebo and no smoking control) in 5 volunteers (including one female; 21-31 year old occasional marihuana users of 2 x/week) smoking marihuana (1.5% THC) cigarettes, pulse rate was increased and performance (psychomotor via motor components of simple and complex reaction time tests, psychomotor learning via DSST (digit symbol substitution test), cognitive via WAT (word association test)) impaired with respect to response speed in a dose-related manner with slower overall speed in more complex tasks improving with practice; a greater cognitive involvement improving speed in simple automatic and motor functions in an irregular fashion which may be due to a short-term memory loss (Borg et al., 1975). Distortion of time perception (temporal judgement via time estimation and production) was observed as underproduction of time with overestimation at low doses and underestimation at high doses. Physiological tolerance (decreased acceleration of pulse rate) developed with repeated doses. The effects of oral cannabinoids (215 μg/kg THC, 320 μg/kg CBD and CBN) and ethanol (0.54 gm/kg), alone and in various combinations (as well as placebo) were studied (double-blind) in human volunteers (male and female university students; 18-36 years of age; cannabis use at least once per week/1-13 years duration; alcohol use at least once per week/1-16 years duration; occasionally combining alcohol with cannabis use) noting changes over a 280 minute period in performance, pulse rate, conjunctival condition, BAC, and subjective effects (Bird et al., 1980). THC decreased performance (general, psychomotor, standing steadiness (eyes opened and closed), and reaction speed (visual, auditory, complex)) and increased pulse rate and intoxication with conjunctival hyperemia; the onset being slow with effects still evident at the end of the test period. Ethanol also decreased performance except for psychomotor coordination factor; the onset being rapid with recovery at the end of the experiment. THC combined with ethanol had greater effects on performance and intoxication (without recovery at the end of test period) than THC alone, considered to be additive in nature; BAC (breath analysis via alcometer) being unaffected by cannabinoid pretreatment with peak BAC corresponding to maximal performance decrement. Individuals could identify THC or alcohol with peak intoxication occurring earlier with alcohol (100 mins vs 210 mins for THC); the peak intoxication with THC plus ethanol occurring at 100 mins with effects persisting at the end of the experiment. Pulse rate increased with THC alone and combined with ethanol with a maximum effect at 210 mins; similarily with conjunctival hyperemia (also evident with alcohol alone between 100 to 210 min periods). Several anxiety adverse reactions occurred in subjects receiving cannabinoids. CBD and CBN did not modify the above effects. Remote memory (for one season television shows, aired up to 14 years previously, evaluated by recognition, temporal judgement and detailed factual recall from the shows) was not affected by acute marihuana intoxication (marihuana smoked from a pipe with 0.33 gm marihuana with 6 mg THC vs placebo marihuana with 0.02 mg THC) tested 30-35 minutes post smoking but new learning ability and recall (word list; assessed following remote memory tests) was impaired; heart rate and subjective "high" being significantly greater with marihuana than with placebo (Wetzel et al., 1982). Fewer words have been recalled from recently presented word lists with marihuana (smoked 1 gm cigarette with 1.4% THC) intoxication (assessed by increased pulse rate and subjective effects vs placebo) without affecting processing and retention of different types of linguistic information including orthographic (number of letters per word), phonetic (rhyming or speech sounds), semantic (meaning), and syntactic (sentence formation) information (Belmore and Miller, 1980). Peak effects of oral marihuana or synthetic Δ^9 THC on immediate memory have been observed at the 1.5-2 hour period with a duration of at least 3.5 hours when some discernible effects were still evident. The reported difficulty in performing tasks that require accurate recovery of recent information (Fig. 15) may be due to cannabis effects on memory storage where information is transferred from a short term store (STS) or working memory with limited capacity (conscious awareness of stimulus) to a long term store (LTS) or permanent event-knowledge store of unlimited capacity. Cannabis subjects appear to store less information which may be due to loss of information from STS before it can be transferred to LTS. Codes entered into STS may be irrelevant to a task requirement resulting in less of the relevant codes being transferred to LTS. This storage deficit which also occurs with alcohol may be a persistent problem. Cannabis does not impair retrieval of previously stored information (Fig. 16). Thus, difficult tasks which require information processing in STS are affected by cannabis whereas well-learned automatic tasks for which information is obtained from LTS, are little affected. Since similar perceptual and conceptual stimuli are stored in close proximity in memory, a wider range of codes may enter STS. This could explain the various cognitive, perceptual and subjective effects seen with cannabis (Dornbush, 1974; Tinklenberg and Darley, 1976).

Driving is a situation when attention is divided between a tracking task and a search and recognition task for environmental dangers. The most important behavioural factors involved in accidents are thought to be perception, attention, and information processing. In testing procedures, only some subset of behavioural demands of driving are determined. Actual driving tests on a course as well as actual driving in traffic have indicated impairment following smoking of 8.5 mg Δ^9 THC. In order to find the nature of the deficit, simulator auto-driving tests have been conducted. These tests have shown that marihuana has a greater effect on sensory (speed of response to signals i.e. a recognition test) or perceptual aspects of car control than on the motor aspects (car control performance such as number of gear changes) which is affected by alcohol. Even though marihuana (plasma concentration of 70 ng THC/ml following the smoking of 22.5 mg THC) appears to decrease willingness to take risks (passing a car) vs alcohol, it significantly affects judgment, care and concentration. A decrease in attention has been correlated with decreased input into long term memory storage. Tracking, another important component of driving is impaired, with alcohol having an additive effect. Perceptual-central cognitive aspects as well as motor skills are important in tracking. Visual and auditory thresholds are not affected. However, visual function (detection of peripheral light) is impaired and is dose-related (50-200 µg THC/kg). This occurs with alcohol only when central vision material requires information processing by the brain. Marihuana subjects reported more apparent movement of a pin-point light source vs alcohol (0.8 gm/kg), who did not. Significant decrements occurred in auditory signal detection under concentration and divided attention conditions with marihuana, whereas alcohol (0.69 gm/kg) resulted in impairment only under divided attention. Reaction times to both auditory and visual stimuli were delayed by cannabis. Subjective emotional feelings could affect behaviour with the potential of creating accidents. Self reports have stated fuzzy thinking; slow movements and some discomfort as body heaviness and unsteadiness (somatic); time sense loss; perceptual changes as blurred vision and seeing images with eyes closed; feeling sleepy and high; and impaired cognition. From videotaped data (objective) subjects who had smoked 3 marihuana cigarettes (8 mg THC each) were less active and more fatigued vs alcohol use which revealed individuals who were more tenacious, excitable, dissonant, tense, unfriendly, anxious, and aggressive. The alcohol individual tends to pursue more objects more often and for a longer time thereby limiting the opportunity for concentrating simultaneously on different events (Willette, 1977). In a double-blind placebo controlled study with 10 marihuana (3-5 cigs/week) and alcohol (3-4 x/week) users, marihuana (8 and 15 mg THC) and alcohol (0.75 ml/kg 95% ethanol), alone (dose-dependent and closely related to "high" ratings re marihuana) and in combination (greater "high"), delayed foveal (rodless area of retina affording acute vision) glare recovery (light adaption post intense light exposure) for at least 2 hours post drug(s) returning to pre-drug levels by 5 hours (Adams et al., 1978). The combined effect was slightly greater than either drug alone with peak blood alcohol level being lowered in the presence of marihuana (15 mg THC). Pupil diameter decreased with marihuana but remained unaltered with alcohol. Since light and dark adaptation take place in the retina, both marihuana and alcohol may act directly on the retina producing delayed glare recovery; a suggestion being made that these substances may be inhibiting the resynthesis of photopigment retinaldehyde from retinol. Dizziness reported by marihuana users during "high" states led to an investigation of a possible balance problem evaluated by ataxic (sharpened Romberg, standing on one leg with eyes closed, and walking along a line with eyes closed), vestibular (ENG (electronystagmographic) recording of eye movements noting spontaneous and positional nystagmus; nystagmus is the rapid involuntary movement of eyeballs (as from dizziness) which may be horizontal, vertical, rotatory, or mixed (2 varieties)), oculomotor (to move eyeball; gaze, pendulum, monocular fixation, and convergence tests), and hearing (pure tone threshold, speech reception and discrimination, acoustic impedance) tests performed prior to and following smoking of marihuana (1 gm cigarette with 8 mg THC; estimated intake dose of 50-80 µg THC/kg with inhaling technique used) or placebo in 37 volunteers (including 9 female subjects; 18-35 years of age; marihuana use from 2 cigarettes/yr to 2/week) (Liedgren et al., 1974). The marihuana group performed poorly in ataxic tests (suggesting decreased performance during "high" state for about 2-3 hours) with 47% developing positional vestibular nystagmus usually of the vertical upbeating type. Marihuana effects observed during the study included increased pulse rate with orthostatic hypotension in 3 subjects, conjunctival congestion, dry mouth, hunger, and psychological effects ranging from euphoria to anxiety with a peak "high" occurring 15-25 minutes after smoking and the "high" duration being 0.5-3 hours (2/15 placebo subjects reported a "high"). At low doses of marihuana (3,6,9 µg/kg THC vs placebo) performance impairment was still evident and observed as a dose-dependent linear decrease in stability of stance (measurement of psychomotor function) with decreased tracking ability (increased error scores measuring hand-eye coordination) (Evans et al., 1973). The above investigations have demonstrated marihuana's deleterious effects on tracking ability and motor coordination.

Parameters of impairment for the average driver due to various doses of marihuana alone or with alcohol have not been established. Nor do all drivers respond alike (individual differences). Thus a minimum allowable dose or blood level of cannabinoids may be difficult to determine (Petersen, 1976). A recent study (Hollister, 1979; personal communication) has shown that the kinetics (rate of change) for smoked THC is similar to the intravenous route, the latter curve being higher. The subjective "high" remains elevated by a 30 minute lag after the peak drug plasma level. Experimental subjects exposed to THC were given a sobriety test which did not give any false positives and very few false negatives. It was found that if a detectable plasma level of THC (5 ng/ml) was present, then the individual was unable to pass the test (or some portion of the test). Work is in progress to determine the effects of marihuana and alcohol on performance and driving ability. Deterioration in flying performance (Fig. 17; 18) for at least 2 hours has been noted in experienced pilots operating an aviation instrument flight simulator following the smoking of 0.09 mg Δ^9 THC/kg in a pipe for 10 minutes (Blaine et al., 1976; Janowsky et al., 1976). Problems encountered in this test was that marihuana appeared to affect short term memory and time-sense with alterations in concentration and attention leading to loss of orientation with respect to the navigational fix. That is, marihuana affected cognitive functions necessary for flying. The persistense (several hours) of some perceptual or other performance deficits beyond the subjective "high" may pose a hidden danger. That is, attempts may be made to drive or fly at a time when ability is still impaired even though the "high" has disappeared (Petersen, 1976). Thus, machinery operation should be avoided following the use of any drug that may cause performance deterioration.

An epidemiological investigation of drug prevalence was undertaken in fatally injured drivers (401) and pedestrians (83) (meeting certain criteria), in Ontario Canada (during 1 year from April 1978 to March 1979), who had fluid and tissue specimens analysed for drugs including alcohol which were positive in 328/484 (68%) victims (Cimbura et al., 1980). The most common substance found was alcohol with or without drugs, the most frequently detected of which were cannabinoids, salicylates, and diazepam (others being tranquilizers, andidepressants, antihistamines, and narcotics) (Fig. 19). Cannabinoids were found (in urine with THC in blood (1-5 ng/ml) indicating recent use) in young (mostly male) victims (average age 22 years), many of whom (69%) had also used alcohol (BAC 150 mg %) while diazepam was present in the older age group (average 50 years). Most detected drug concentrations were consistent with therapeutic dosage without evidence of multi-drug use or abuse (other than alcohol).

5.   Tolerance and Dependence

Tolerance to a drug develops when increasing doses are necessary to obtain the initial effect of a lower dose. Dependence may be psychological and/or physical. Psychological dependence refers to a craving (or need) for a drug often leading to compulsive drug use. Physical or physiological dependence is a state whereby withdrawal of drug leads to an abstinence syndrome of undesireable discomforting symptoms such as irritability, restlessness, sleep disturbance, tremor, salivation, sweating, nausea, vomiting, diarrhea, decreased appetite, and weight loss.

Animal studies have revealed rapid marked long-lasting tolerance development to Δ^9 THC in various species accompanied by an increase in the lethal dose and cross-tolerance among tetrahydro-cannabinols (Δ^9 and Δ^8 THC) and other cannabinoids (synthetic THC analogues) (McMillan et al., 1971). Humans exhibit marked tolerance (to subjective "high" and some physiological changes) to modest oral doses of THC (3 mg/kg/day in divided doses q 4 h which is duration of intoxication) which is rapidly acquired (Fig. 20; 21) and quickly lost (Jones et al., 1976). Absent or partial tolerance has been observed (Fig. 22; 23) to weight gain and insulin-induced responses (hypoglycemia; growth hormone) as well as decreased plasma testosterone (male hormone) levels (Jones and Benowitz, 1976). The apparent lack of tolerance development to weight gain is probably due to plasma expansion (with hemodilution or decreased Hb levels) which attempts to overcome the THC vasodilating effect (responsible for orthostatic hypotension) to help maintain normal standing blood pressure thereby decreasing the original THC effects (tachycardia) or tolerance development (see CVS section). In the presence of THC, the amount of GH (growth hormone) necessary to overcome insulin-induced hypoglycemia is less than in the absence of THC (because THC encourages increased blood glucose levels noted in Fig. 23; see final comments section). The consistent testosterone depression during chronic THC was probably due to decreased synthesis because of unavailability of cholesterol precursor (see final comments section). Cross tolerance has been noted between THC and the following substances: cannabidiol, diphenyl-hydantoin, phenobarbital, ethanol, and morphine, but not LSD or mescaline (Hollister, 1979). The objective effects, observed in a placebo controlled double-blind study in former opiate addict volunteers (22-53 years of age) of LSD (0.5 and 1.5 mcg/kg I.M.) and THC (75 and 225 mcg/kg in tobacco cigarettes smoked over a 5 minute period) were different (LSD increased temperature and blood pressure, dilated pupils and caused hyperreflexia not seen with THC which greatly increased pulse rate and produced conjunctival congestion and pseudoptosis) but subjective effects (distortions, mood alterations, hallucinations with higher doses) of the 2 drugs could not be distinguished (2/10 THC subjects experiencing psychotic reactions) (Isbell and Jasinski, 1969). Both drugs were considered to be psychotomimetics (LSD being more potent than THC) without cross tolerance (subjects made tolerant to LSD over a 10 day period confirmed with a LSD test dose and challenged with THC) suggesting different mental mechanisms. Behavioural tolerance to suppressed social interactions or effects as well as tolerance to physiological and subjective effects have been reported in heavy marihuana users (42 cigarettes/month) (Mendelson et al., 1976). Marihuana (1.5% THC; 8,12,15 mg THC/gm plant material or cigarette) (and placebo) cigarettes smoked daily (2 cigarettes/1 hour) by 10 regular users (averge 3.4 years use duration by 21-26 year old men) for 27 days (16 mg THC/day) resulted in a reduction of cannabinoid induced tachycardia suggesting tolerance development (Gibbins et al., 1976). Subjective "high" was also decreased in 30 smokers taking part in a 94 day study (see CVS section) (Nowlan and Cohen, 1977). Light smokers showed greater chronotropic and subjective effects vs heavy smokers with both groups developing tolerance within 14-21 days of daily smoking of at least 2 marihuana cigarettes (20 mg THC/cigarette). Minor withdrawal effects were observed after 64 days of toxication. One week abstinence, especially in heavy smokers, was insufficient for tolerance recovery noted as diminished responses vs first week of smoking. A relatively high level of heart rate and subjective "high" may be maintained with serial smoking being less effective with each successive cigarette. Physical dependence becomes evident following 3-8 weeks of self-injected THC in animals and 10-21 days of chronic oral use in man (Hollister, 1979; Jones et al., 1976). Mild symptoms of withdrawal have been reported following cessation (24-48 hours later) of regular use of marihuana (to the point of chronic intoxication with 5-10 cigarettes/day/week or more) being relieved by alcohol, barbiturates, or marihuana (Jones, 1971). Physical dependence on THC is mild noted by a short-lived mild abstinence syndrome (96 hours) following withdrawal of the drug (Jones and Benowitz, 1976; Jones et al., 1976). Such mild symptoms are often interpreted as mild influenza by users or hangover from alcohol often consumed with cannabis leading to under-reporting of actual cases of physical dependence. There is a relationship between the dose taken during dependence development and the intensity of the withdrawal syndrome. The intensity and pattern of withdrawal symptoms due to cannabis/21 days were similar to moderate doses of opiates (100 mg morphine/day/several weeks) or of alcohol (0.5 litres of 95% ethanol/day in divided doses/1 month). Tolerance may also be missed because it disappears rapidly in light smokers. Psychological dependence has been reported in heavy chronic hashish users (more than 1 gm hashish/time with an average THC content of 3%) who displayed an overpowering desire to continue drug use (Soueif, 1976a).

With the development of tolerance, subjects become hyperirritable and dysphoric (similar to barbiturates, opiates) which subside with a further dose of marihuana but reappear and persist until the next dose. This is often referred to as a psychic withdrawal syndrome or behavioural abstinence phenomenon in chronic users and not noticed in infrequent users. Marihuana is not considered to be a primary pharmacological reinforcer (which may occur with more potent preparations as hashish) but acquires secondary (conditioned) reinforcing properties via social reinforcement. From this social reinforcement, the naive user learns to call the functional disrupting effects of the drug (silliness, things go slower) a "high" (Wikler, 1976). Some of the field chronic studies (e.g. Costa Rica study) have carried out tests when their subjects may have been in withdrawal thereby accounting for their results leading to erroneous conclusions of marihuana effects (e.g. increased rather than decreased testosterone plasma levels). Therefore time of testing in chronic user studies is important in assessing consequences of prolonged use (Jones et al., 1976). Heavy long-term (7.4 years average) ganja (mixed with tobacco containing 4.14% THC) use (2-4 oz/day) by 10 healthy men and women (25-36 years of age) did not appear to impair cognitive function (often seen with intermittent cannabis use) (Schaeffer et al., 1981). Urine samples contained > 50 ng/ml cannabinoid metabolites. Tolerance development may account for the apparent normal cognitive function in these healthy individuals. As noted in the chemistry and metabolism section, reversible pharmacological tolerance was not metabolic but functional or adaptive in nature; e.g., adaptation to marihuana cardiovascular (primary) effects (noted above) may result in so-called tolerance to other effects (see cardiovascular and final comments sections).

A recent pharmacokinetic study (Lindgren et al., 1981) was undertaken in 24 hour abstinent (from marihuana and alcohol) light (8 males, 1 female; occasional use not more than once monthly; urinary absence of drugs; 0-0.2 ng THC/ml plasma) and heavy (8 males, 1 female; more than once daily use; urine with cannabinoid metabolites; 0.1-3.0 ng THC/ml plasma) marihuana (potency?) users (19-36 years of age) following IV (5 mg/2 minutes) and smoking (13 mg average) THC. Intravenous THC resulted in similar plasma THC levels (Fig. 24) in both groups with a trend of lower AUC (0-240 minutes) (area under the curve) for heavy users (which may be due to increased metabolism of drug or increased plasma volume expansion (see CVS section)). Inhalation of THC by smoking revealed higher plasma THC levels in heavy users with systemic availability of 23% (compared with IV AUC (0-240 minutes) vs light users with 10% systemic availability; the differences probably being due to different smoking techniques (deeper inhalation and longer smoke retention in lungs by heavy users). That is, tolerance development in heavy users necessitates more efficient smoking so as to acquire the initial desired "high" (vs light users) obtained prior to tolerance development. Somewhat similar acute clinical responses (HR, "high") occurred in both groups (Fig. 25; 26) with a greater degree of intoxication or "high" reported by light users; IV effects being greater than smoking effects. The authors felt that even though tolerance develops, it did not do so readily in this group of heavy users who may not have used large enough doses of cannabis over a sufficiently long period of time. However the degree of "high" achieved was different for the two groups (greater in light users) and the peak HR was delayed in heavy users following IV THC. It appears that plasma THC levels are more accurate determinations of individual doses vs number of cigarettes (or mg THC) smoked with responses varying due to different degrees of tolerance and/or dependence.

It is generally agreed that tolerance develops with high sustained cannabis doses over prolonged period of time in man (Hollister, 1979). THC appears to be pharmacologically similar to opiate properties, some of which are narcosis, analgesia, respiratory depression, cough suppression, tolerance and dependence in animals and man. THC potentiates and is cross-tolerant with morphine effects in animals. Naloxone (a narcotic antagonist) has precipitated an opiate-like abstinence syndrome in chronically THC-treated animals (Kaymakçalan, 1979). Withdrawal of THC encourages self-administration of THC in animals and marihuana smoking in man (noted under amotivational syndrome) to avoid abstinence effects. THC also reduces (and may block) naloxone precipitated abstinence in morphine dependent animals (and in quasi-withdrawal syndrome (Chesher et al., 1979)) indicating substitution capability of THC and perhaps inadequate naloxone dose to overcome both morphine and THC (substitution) effects with the possibility that THC may indirectly stimulate endorphin (endogenous opiate) release (see final comments section).

6.   Summary

In animals, altered brain function was observed as dose-dependent EEG changes occurring in the limbic system (site of emotion) with cellular brain damage being demonstrated in the form of synaptic cleft alteration and disruption of rough endoplasmic reticulum (thought to be involved in protein synthesis) in the nerve cell. Perhaps such changes may contribute to psychopathology observed in some marihuana users who may have genetically induced altered brain function (i.e. a predisposition to undesireable drug effects and/or disease). The EEG profile of cannabis suggests a classification of a central euphoriant with the psychotropic group of psychodysleptics with morphine-like and hallucinogenic properties.

Emotional response to cannabis varies from pleasant tranquilizer and hypnosis, to euphoria with body sense and time illusions, or, to dysphoria ranging from mild irritability and hypochondriasis to episodic panic and terror resembling paranoid schizophrenia (Gregg et al., 1976b). These differences in response may be due to plasma drug concentration (including metabolism to active metabolites), personality (including psychiatric makeup), and previous drug experience or psychological "set". Those who respond adversely to marihuana are more introverted, hold in anger, are more obsessive and reserved, and use drugs to handle problems. Acute intoxication occurs without objective signs as seen with alcohol and sedatives as loss of motor control, speech impairment (i.e. drunken behaviour) which prevents such individuals from receiving professional help for emotional needs. The social use of cannabis is attractive to some people because of heightened sensation, perceptual distortion and visceral "rushes"; hostility and aggression being reduced. However in potentially threatening situations (stress), a heightened anxiety response occurs which could lead to aggression. THC may induce state-dependent learning such that during a stressful situation acute anxiety and paranoid responses may be elicited, acting as a trigger for former stressful states or flashbacks. It is thought that the limbic system in the brain, especially the hippocampus, persists in an altered state following the withdrawal of the inital stimulus.   Psychotic-like thoughts may be biphasic with simultaneous experiences of euphoria and dysphoria, paranoia and major time disorder (déjà vu, time slowing, flashback). In clinical schizophrenia disentegration of time sense with dramatic slowing or stopping of events, déjà vu, as well as depersonalization (seen with hallucinogens) occur. Temporal distortion may be important in paranoid psychotic-like thoughts which are an added source of anxiety. That is, experiences are drawn out or recur. Thus the development and type of adverse mental or psychological (i.e. mental disorganization) effects appear to depend on the potency of material, extent of use (frequency, duration), premorbid personality (normal (acute and chronic organic toxicity) or pathological (psychiatric-schizoid) pre-disposition), age of individual, literacy, nature of symptoms, and response to treatment (ranging from none except stopping drug use with offered reassurance, to drug treatment with phenothiazines used in natural occurring psychotic reactions).   The possibility exists that marihuana use by adolescents may disrupt normal psychological development resulting in inadequate adult mental functioning or emotional responsiveness. This could lead to a future loss to society in terms of productivity and stability.

Mental and motor performance (including response speed and physical work capacity) are impaired by marihuana (THC), especially in experienced users, in a dose-dependent manner with impaired short term (not remote) memory in complex tasks which may be due to cannabis effects on memory storage where information is transferred from STS (short term store) to LTS (long term store). The loss of information from STS in cannabis users may perhaps be due to synaptic cleft alteration which may delay or prevent information transmission affecting information processing and memory storage. Driving (requiring accurate recovery of recent information) impairment (automobile, aeroplane) has been demonstrated following smoking of (approximately 8 mg) THC. Perceptual aspects of machinery control (response speed to signals) are affected with decreased attention (decreased input into LTS) and reaction times to auditory and visual stimuli. Marihuana and alcohol, alone or in combination, have delayed foveal glare recovery for at least 2 hours thought to be due to a direct retinal action which may affect tracking and recognition of environmental dangers. Dizziness reported by marihuana users during "high" states may alter balance affecting motor coordination. To this may be added altered emotional state for creating potential accidents. Some performance deficits persist after "high" has dissipated posing a danger for those who may attempt to drive (or fly) when ability is still impaired. A minimum allowable blood cannabinoid level has not been established for impaired driving due to marihuana alone or with alcohol. Proof of cannabis consumption has been demonstrated by examination of dental deposits.

Animal tolerance has been observed by an increase in lethal dose; a cross-tolerance occurring between various cannabinoids and with opiates. Tolerance (functional or adaptive in nature) also develops in humans within 14-21 days of daily marihuana smoking of at least 2 cigarettes (20 mg THC/cigarette) with cross tolerance between THC and other CNS depressant drugs. Physical dependence occurs in animals (post 3-8 weeks IV THC) and in humans (post 10-21 days chronic oral THC) with mild withdrawal symptoms (96 hours) observed in man which may be relieved by alcohol, barbiturates, or marihuana. Compulsive drug use or psychological dependence has been reported in heavy chronic hashish users; a psychic withdrawal (dysphoria) being observed between drug doses after tolerance development. Heavy users smoke marihuana more efficiently since more is required for a desired effect because of tolerance development (vs casual smokers). This would indicate that in a study where a similar number of cigarettes are smoked, the plasma drug level achieved would not necessarily be the same in all the study subjects because of different degrees of drug tolerance (aside from individual differences in drug metabolism). A greater depth of smoke inhalation with longer retention in the lungs would increase the absorption of cannabinoids. Thus, plasma drug levels are a better indicator of actual drug dose for a particular individual; the response occurring depending upon the degree of drug tolerance and/or dependence.

Existing controversies are probably due to various conditions under which marihuana use is studied such as drug route; drug potency; dose range (plasma drug levels); frequency, pattern (including depth of inhalation and smoke retention in lungs) and duration of use (tolerance and/or dependence); type of subjects observed including controls; different motivational factors; simple or complex tasks; environmental stress factors; and use of other drugs (including alcohol and tobacco). Most smokers titrate their rate of smoking to achieve individualistic desired effect(s) ("high") making actual drug concentration estimations difficult unless blood drug level concentrations are determined. Frequent prolonged marihuana use is probably intertwined with other deviant behaviour and characteristics causing difficulties in determining probable causes and effects. The lack of evidence of neuropsychological deficits in some studies does not necessarily lead to the conclusion that no organic changes occured because psychological test data are inferential and definitive statements as to organic changes can only be based on radiological and pathological evidence (Petersen, 1976).

The issues with psychic phenomenon due to cannabis use are the extent to which the drug impairs individual development and social development, the incidence of that impairment, and the prognosis. There is no doubt that cannabis can produce serious psychic effects and disrupt an individual's social framework; the prognosis of the psychic effect following cessation of drug use being dependent on the duration of drug use (Paton et al., 1973). However, the frequency of the phenomenon is uncertain because many people taking drugs (including alcohol) live with incurred disabilities not brought to the attention of the medical community. It could be that breakdown of a schizophrenic type is being increased due to cannabis use. Opiates do not produce a psychosis and withdrawal effects are avoided with a further dose of opiates; whereas cannabis and LSD psychotic responses are made worse by further exposure (both drugs sharing the phenomenon of flashback; a conditioned reflex to stress?).

II. 3. C. Central Nervous System

List of Figures

Fig. 1.   Central sense areas   107
Fig. 2.   EEG sleep measures   108
Fig. 3.   Three basic cerebral types   109
Fig. 4.   Limbic cortical (ring) system   109
Fig. 5.   Plasma THC in primates   110
Fig. 6.   EEG wave frequency distribution differences   111
Fig. 7.   EEG wave frequency distribution differences   112
Fig. 8.   EEG wave frequency distribution differences   112
Fig. 9.   Anxiety state score   113
Fig. 10.   Anxiety state score   114
Fig. 11.   Performance efficiency   115
Fig. 12.   Aggression   117
Fig. 13.   Urine sample screening for cannabinoids   116
Fig. 14.   Blood sample screening for cannabinoids   117
Fig. 15.   Word recall   118
Fig. 16.   Word recall   119
Fig. 17.   Flying performance errors   120
Fig. 18.   Flying performance errors   121
Fig. 19.   Drug detection in fluid and tissues   122
Fig. 20.   Tolerance development   122
Fig. 21.   Cross tolerance development   123
Fig. 22.   Absent or partial tolerance development   123
Fig. 23.   Absent or partial tolerance development   124
Fig. 24.   Plasma THC in light and heavy marihuana users   125
Fig. 25.   Heart rate in light and heavy marihuana users   126
Fig. 26.   Subjective "high" in light and heavy marihuana users   127

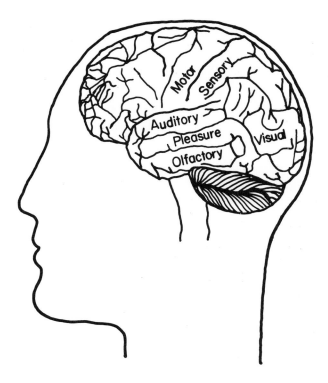

Fig. 1.   Major sense areas of the brain.
II.3.C

Adapted from Swanson, 1975-76.

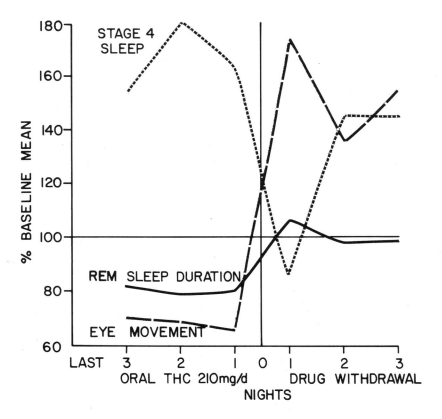

Fig. 2.   THC effect on EEG sleep measures during last 3 days of a 2 week drug
II.3.C   treatment and during first 3 days post drug cessation.

Adapted from Feinberg et al., 1975.

THE BRAIN

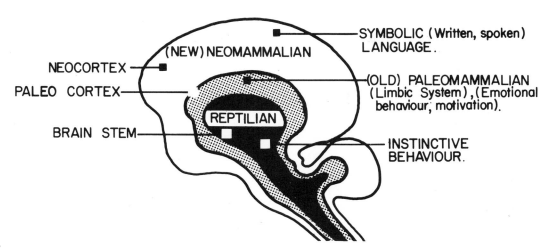

NEOCORTEX

PALEO CORTEX

BRAIN STEM

(NEW) NEOMAMMALIAN

REPTILIAN

SYMBOLIC (Written, spoken) LANGUAGE.

(OLD) PALEOMAMMALIAN (Limbic System), (Emotional behaviour, motivation).

INSTINCTIVE BEHAVIOUR.

Fig. 3.
II.3.C

Three basic cerebral types in the brain.

Adapted from MacLean, 1970.

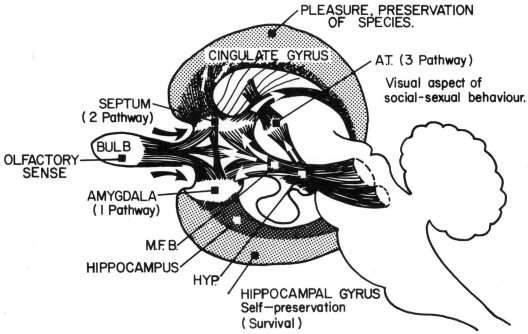

PLEASURE, PRESERVATION OF SPECIES.

CINGULATE GYRUS

A.T. (3 Pathway)

Visual aspect of social-sexual behaviour.

SEPTUM
(2 Pathway)

OLFACTORY SENSE

BULB

AMYGDALA
(I Pathway)

M.F.B.

HIPPOCAMPUS

HYP.

HIPPOCAMPAL GYRUS
Self—preservation
(Survival)

Fig. 4.
II.3.C

The limbic cortical (ring) system with 3 subdivisions linked by 3 (1,2,3) pathways to the brain stem (A.T. - anterior thalamic nuclei; HYP. - hypothalamus; M.F.B. - medial forebrain bundle).

Adapted from MacLean, 1970.

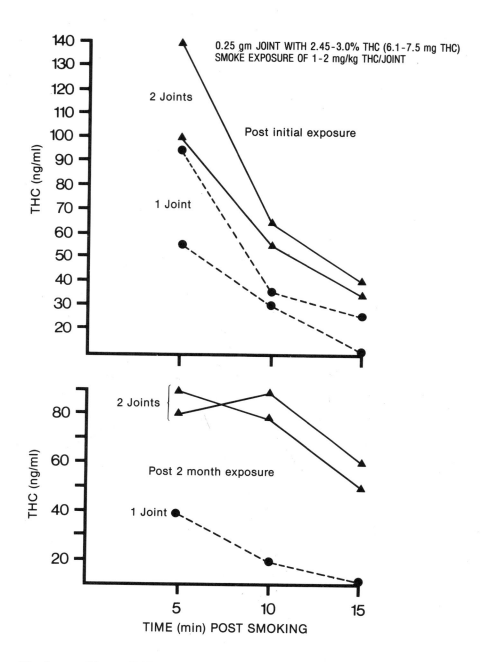

Fig. 5. Plasma THC in primate animals equivalent to plasma levels in human
II.3.C marihuana smokers using a standard 1 gm joint with 3% THC.

Adapted from Heath et al., 1980.

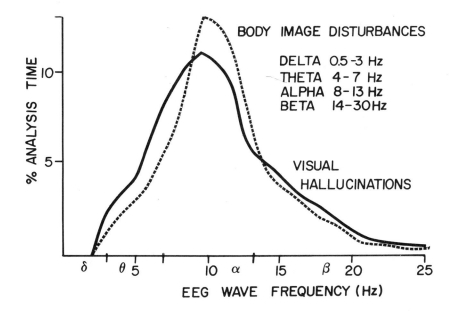

Fig. 6.   Differences between EEG wave frequency distributions during 2 types
II.3.C   of THC experiences.

Adapted from Koukkou and Lehman, 1976.

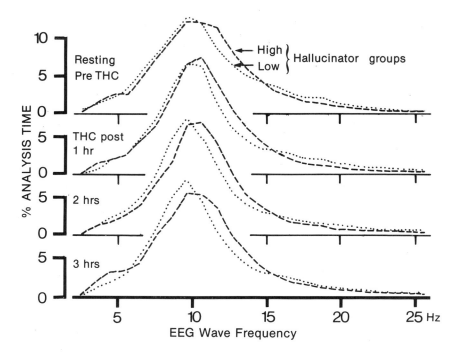

Fig. 7.   Differences between EEG wave frequency distributions between high
II.3.C   (frequency) THC experiences (both types) and low experience
            (hallucinators) groups pre and post oral THC (200 µg/kg).

            Adapted from Koukkou and Lehman, 1976.

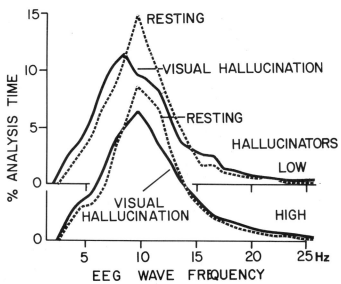

Fig. 8.   Differences between EEG wave frequency distributions during visual
II.3.C   hallucinations and during resting periods in high and low experience
            (hallucinators) groups.

            Adapted from Koukkou and Lehman, 1976.

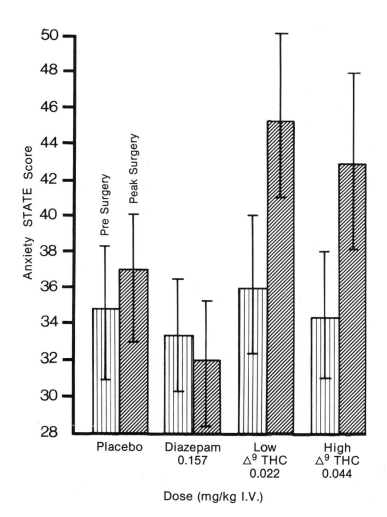

Fig. 9.
II.3.C

The effects of THC, diazepam, or placebo on the anxiety state of moderate marihuana users during oral surgery. Placebo - 5% dextrose in 0.9% NaCl.

Adapted from Gregg et al., 1976b.

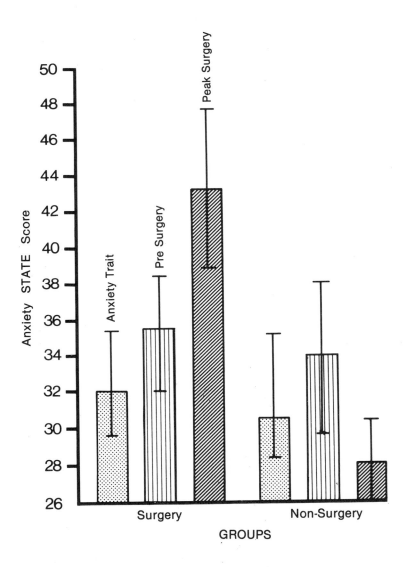

Fig. 10.   The effect of THC (0.044 mg/kg IV) on anxiety traits and states in
II.3.C   surgical and non-surgical groups.

Adapted from Gregg et al., 1976b.

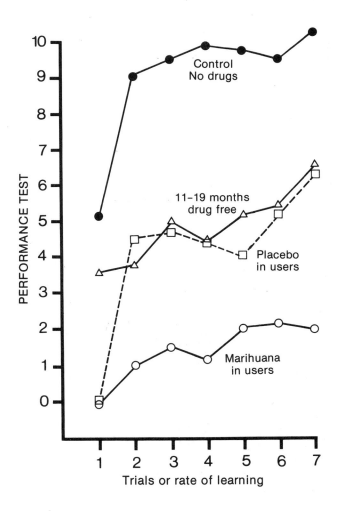

Fig. 11.   Performance efficiency of marihuana users vs non-users.
II.3.C
              Adapted from Salvendy and McCabe, 1975.

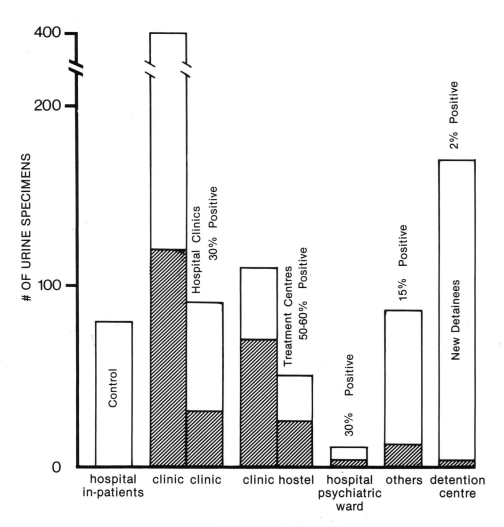

Fig. 13.   Screening (RIA) of 1002 urine samples from various sources for
II.3.C   cannabinoids.

Adapted from Teale et al., 1976.

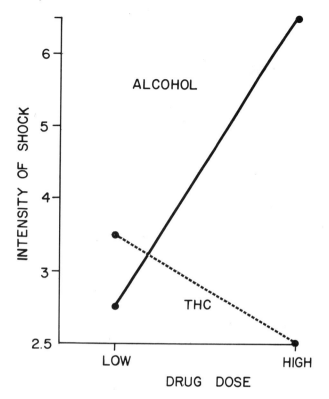

Fig. 12.   Aggression (intensity of shock given to opponent) under influence of
II.3.C   alcohol or oral THC.

Adapted from Taylor et al., 1976.

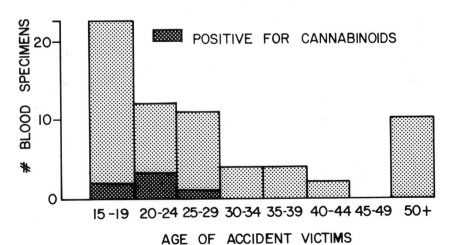

Fig. 14.   Screening (RIA) of blood samples from fatally injured vehicle drivers
II.3.C   for cannabinoids.

Adapted from Teale et al., 1977.

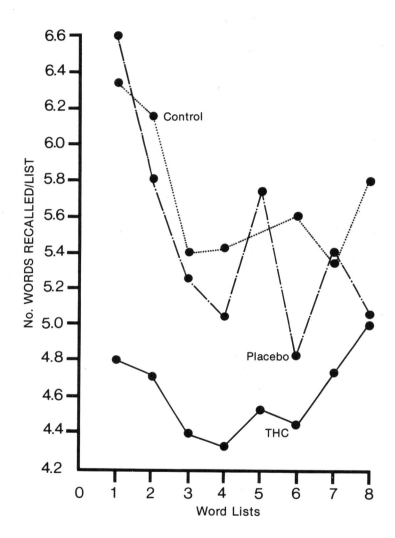

Fig. 15.   Recall of material learned after smoking marihuana (20 mg THC) or
II.3.C   placebo or no smoking (control) in experienced users.

Adapted from Dornbush, 1974.

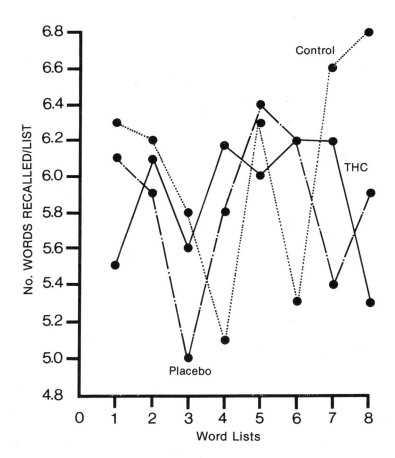

Fig. 16.   Recall of material learned prior to smoking marihuana (20 mg THC) or
II.3.C   placebo or no smoking (control) in experienced users.

Adapted from Dornbush, 1974.

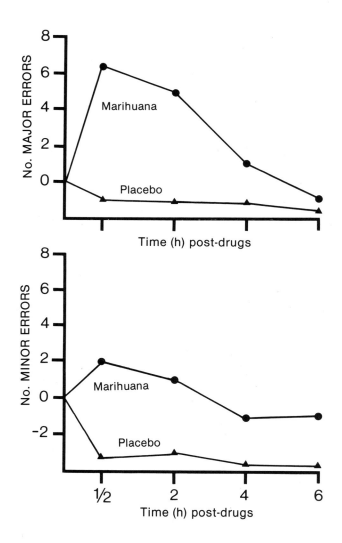

Fig. 17.   Errors in simulated instrument flying performance (16 min. flight
II.3.C   time) pre and post marihuana (2.1% or 0.09 mg/kg THC) or placebo
             smoking.

Adapted from Janowsky et al., 1976.

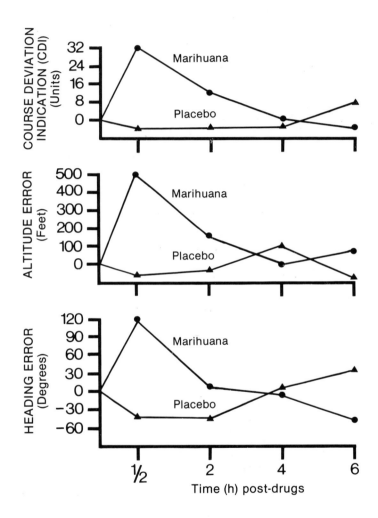

Fig. 18. Deviations from assigned standardized flight pattern pre and post
II.3.C marihuana (2.1% or 0.09 mg/kg THC) or placebo smoking.

Adapted from Janowsky et al., 1976.

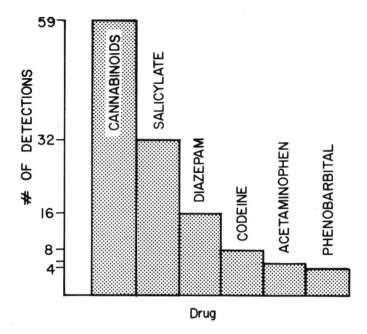

Fig. 19.   Most frequently detected drugs in fluid and tissues from fatally injured
II.3.C   drivers and pedestrians over a one year period.

Adapted from Cimbura et al., 1980.

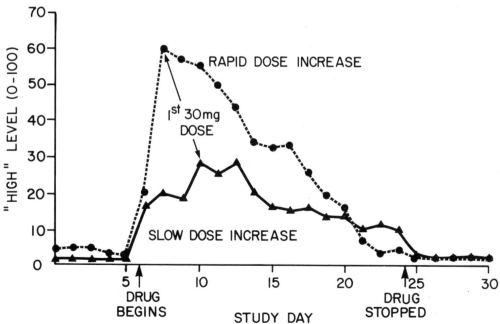

Fig. 20.   Rapid tolerance development to self-reported cannabis "high" in
II.3.C   experienced users; 10 mg THC p.o. q 4 h prior to 30 mg q 4 h.

Adapted from Jones et al., 1976.

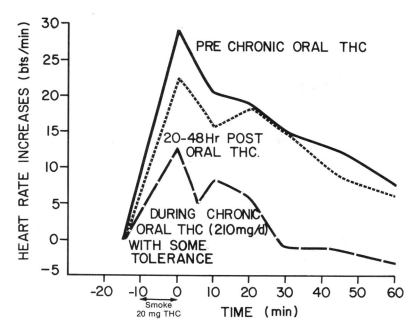

Fig. 21.   Development and cross tolerance between smoked marihuana and oral
II.3.C   THC as measured by heart rate changes in experienced users.

Adapted from Jones et al., 1976.

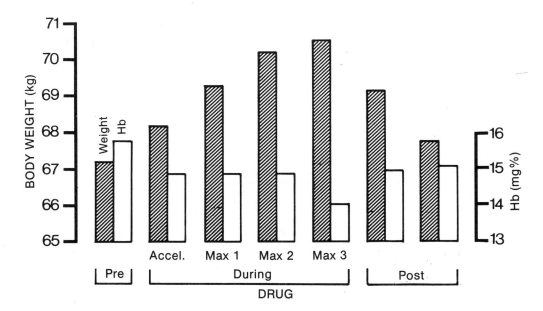

Fig. 22.   Absence of (or partial) tolerance to weight gain and Hb levels
II.3.C   following chronic oral THC (210 mg/d) in experienced users.

Adapted from Jones and Benowitz, 1976.

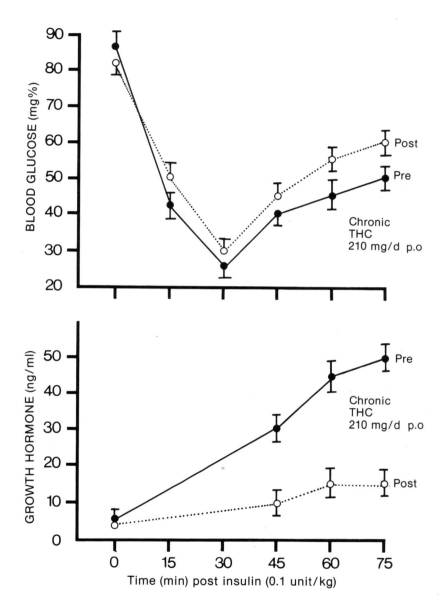

Fig. 23.   Absence of (or partial) tolerance to insulin-induced responses (blood
II.3.C   glucose and serum growth hormone levels) following chronic oral THC
            (210 mg/d) in experienced users.

Adapted from Jones and Benowitz, 1976.

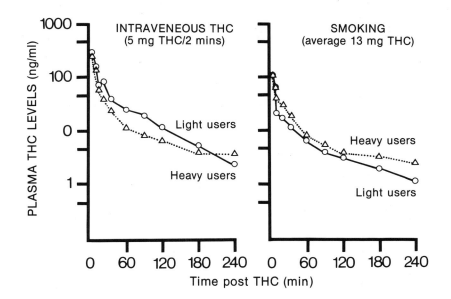

Fig. 24.   Plasma THC levels following intravenous or inhalation (smoking)
II.3.C   administration.

Adapted from Lindgren et al., 1981.

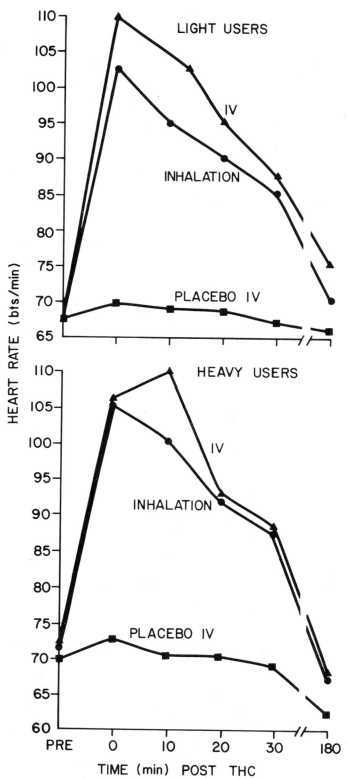

Fig. 25.   Heart rate following inhalation (smoking) or intravenous injection of
II.3.C   THC (or placebo).

Adapted from Lindgren et al., 1981.

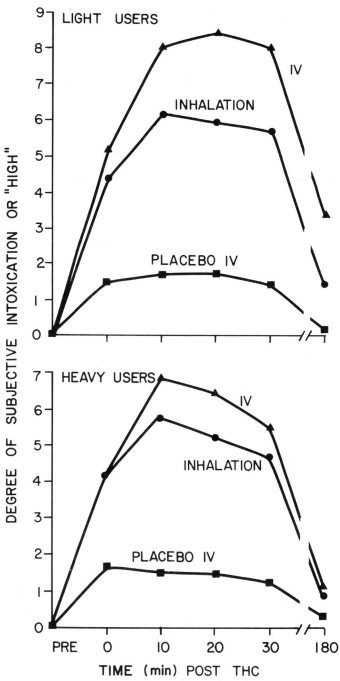

Fig. 26.
II.3.C
Degree of subjective "high" following inhalation (smoking) or intra-venous injection of THC (or placebo).

Adapted from Lindgren et al., 1981.

II. 3. D. Cardiopulmonary System

Contents

	Abstract	128
1.	Introduction	129
2.	Pulmonary System Disorders	130
3.	Cardiovascular System Dysfunction	131
4.	Marihuana Effects on Pulmonary System	
	(a) Smoke Constituents	133
	(b) Acute Effects	137
	(c) Chronic Effects	138
	(d) Pulmonary Defense System Effects	141
	(e) Discussion and Summary	144
	(f) Figures D_1	147
5.	Marihuana Effects on Cardiovascular System	
	(a) Acute and Short Term Effects	164
	(b) Possible Mechanism of Action	166
	(c) Chronic Effects	171
	(d) Cardiac Toxicity	174
	(e) Interactions	178
	(f) Discussion and Summary	182
	(g) Figures D_2	188

Abstract

1. Cardiopulmonary dysfunction due to tobacco smoke is discussed prior to marihuana smoking effects.

2. Marihuana pulmonary effects are presented including effects of smoke constituents, and, acute and chronic pharmacological effects as well as effects on the pulmonary defense system; some effects being similar to tobacco smoking.

3. Marihuana cardiovascular effects are recorded noting acute and chronic effects including drug interactions, cardiac toxicity, and possible mechanism of action; some effects being reminiscent of nitrites.

Keywords: cannabis, cardiovascular effects, nitrites, pulmonary effects, smoking, tobacco.

Abbreviations: adenosine diphosphate (ADP); airway resistance (Raw); alpha-1 (α_1); arterial partial pressure or tension in mm Hg of CO_2 or O_2 (Pa(co_2) or Pa(o_2)); aryl hydrocarbon hydroxylase (AHH); atrio-His bundle (A-H); atrio-ventricular (A-V); beta (β); bipolar limb and precordial leads for ECG recording (I, II, III and V_{1-6}); blood pressure (b.p.); calcium (Ca); cannabidiol (CBD); cannabinol (CBN); carbon dioxide (CO_2); carbon monoxide or cardiac output (CO); carboxy hemoglobin (COHb); cardiac index (CI); cardiovascular system (CVS); central nervous system (CNS); central venous pressure (CVP); cerebral spinal fluid (CSF); cervical level of spinal cord (C_1); chronic obstructive pulmonary disease (COPD); closing volume (CV); cubic (cu); day (d); delta-6a, 10a-dimethylheptyl THC (DMHP); diffusing capacity for carbon monoxide as ml/min/mm Hg (DLco); 7,12 - dimethylbenz [a] anthracene (DMBA); dimethyl sulfoxide (DMSO); ejection fraction (EF); electrocardiogram (ECG); end tidal CO_2 tension (PETco_2); equal to (=); every--hour(s) (q.--h.); for example (e.g.); forced expiratory volume in 1 second in litres (FEV_1); forced expiratory flow over middle half of FVC (FEF_{25-75}%); forced vital capacity in cubic centimetres (FVC); forearm blood blow (FBF); forearm conductance (FC); gram(s) (gm); heart rate (HR); hemoglobin (Hb); hydrogen ion concentration (pH); hydrogen sulphide (H_2S); hydroxy-THC (OH-THC); interval and segment in ECG tracing (PR and ST); interval from onset of QRS to second heart sound (Q.S_2); intraocular pressure (IOP); intravenous (IV); kilogram(s) (kg); left ventricular ejection time (LVET); left ventricular end systolic (diastolic) diameters or volumes (LVES(D) or LVES(D)V); litre(s) (L); lysergic acid diethylamide (LSD); maximal mid-expiratory flow in litres/second (MMEF); maximal voluntary ventilation in litres/minute (MVV); mean arterial blood pressure (MA(B)P); mercury (Hg); microgram (μg or mcg); milligram(s) (mg); millilitre(s) (ml); millimetre(s) (mm); minute(s) (min); nanogram(s) (ng); nitrogen concentration change between 750 and 1250 ml expired volume (ΔN_2 750-1250 ml); norepinephrine (NE); oxygen (O_2); oxygen consumption ($\dot{V}o_2$); package (pkg); parts per million (ppm); peak expiratory flow rate in litres/second (PFR or PEF); per os or oral (p.o.); percent (%); periodic acid-Schiff stain (PAS); polycyclic aromatic hydrocarbons (PAH); premature ventricular contraction (PVC); pressure unit = 1/760 of an atmosphere (torr); reflex venoconstriction (RVC); residual volume (RV); respiratory minute volume or pulmonary ventilation ($\dot{V}_E$ or e); ribonucleic acid (RNA); similar to ($\equiv$); sino-auricular or atrial (SA); sodium (Na); specific airways conductance (SGaw); stroke volume (SV); subscript "c" (corrected for HR); systolic posterior wall excursion (Vpw); systolic time intervals (STI); tetrahydrocannabinol (THC); threshold limit value (TLV); times or multiplied by (x); total lung capacity (TLC); total particulate matter (TPM); total peripheral resistance (TPR); unit(s) (U); United States of America (U.S.A.); velocity or mean rate of internal cardiac diameter or circumferential fibre shortening (Vcf or VCF); venous tone (VT); ventricular pre-ejection period (PEP); vital capacity in cubic centimetres (VC); wave components of ECG tracing (P, QRS, and T waves); white blood cell (WBC).

1. Introduction

Since marihuana is usually smoked, some effects of cigarette (tobacco) smoking shall be discussed with respect to smoke effect on the lungs and cardiovascular system.

Smokers have an increased risk of premature death from bronchopulmonary and/or cardiovascular disease. Tobacco smoke is a mixture of gases and minute droplets of tar. Some components of smoke are filtered off as the smoke is drawn through the unburned tobacco but redistilled as the burning ember advances such that with each successive puff the smoke becomes more concentrated. The clinically important substances in smoke include:

(1) carcinogens (polycyclic aromatic alcohols) and cocarcinogens (phenols, fatty acids, free fatty acids) in tar which initiate cancer formation,

(2) irritants causing coughing, bronchoconstriction, inhibition of cilial action (predisposing to infection) and mucus secretion,

(3) nicotine (vs marihuana) affecting the nervous system (dependence) and circulation (due to catecholamine release leading to vasoconstriction and increased heart rate, cardiac output and blood pressure), and

(4) toxic gases (CO, H_2S, hydrocyanic acid) with CO (carbon monoxide) impairing O_2 (oxygen) release to tissues and increasing atheroma formation (COHb (carboxyhemoglobin) in smokers of 1 package/day is 5% vs 1% in non-smokers).

Smoke from cigarettes, pipes, cigars, contains 4% CO (Dreisbach, 1974). TLV (threshold limit values for 8 hours/day/5 days/week) of CO is 50 ppm. COHb is incapable of carrying O_2 (Hb affinity for CO is 210x greater than for O_2) and prevents the release of O_2 (due to increased stability of HbO_2 in the presence of CO) leading to tissue anoxia. Inhaling smoke from 20 cigarettes/day results in at least 6% Hb being saturated with CO. Smoke inhalation from one cigarette decreases the amount of O_2 available to tissues by 8% (equivalent to going from sea level to 4000 ft. altitude). Arithmetical errors may occur with 8-10% Hb saturation and pulse rate increases during exercise with 13% Hb saturation while O_2 debt incurred during severe exercise is increased with 4% Hb saturation. Pathological findings in fatal CO poisoning cases include microscopic hemorrhages and necrotic areas throughout the body; intense congestion and edema of the brain, liver, kidneys, spleen; and damage to nerve cells (cerebral cortex, medulla). Clinically, slight headache and shortness of breath occurs with 20% COHb. A blood concentration of 40-50% results in headache, nausea, irritability, increased respiration, chest pain, confusion, impaired judgement, and fainting with increased exertion; the common signs being cyanosis and pallor. A COHb of 50-90% may lead to unconsciousness, respiratory failure, and death (if continued for more than 1 hour). Repeated (chronic) anoxia from CO absorption gradually increases CNS damage with loss of sensation in fingers, poor memory, and mental deterioration.

Some lung and cardiovascular diseases related to smoking are chronic bronchitis and emphysema, lung cancer (with an increased risk of these diseases developing being 20x in smokers of >1 package/day vs non-smokers), accelerated atherosclerosis with doubling the risk of myocardial infarction, development of angina or ischemic ECG changes in coronary artery disease, and risk of cerebrovascular disease, peripheral vascular diseases, and aortic aneurysm.

The following section alludes to a discussion of some pulmonary conditions which are adversely affected by smoking as well as those that develop after prolonged exposure to smoke, followed by consideration of cardiovascular dysfunction before proceeding to marihuana effects on the cardiopulmonary system.

2. Pulmonary System Disorders

The lung is an organ which is able to achieve an efficient exchange of gases as well as having defense mechanisms to remove particulate matter. Pulmonary insufficiency, defined as respiratory gaseous exchange impairment between the circulating blood and environmental air, may be due to:

(1) airway obstruction (resistance to air flow) in the bronchial tree seen in chronic bronchitis, emphysema, asthma, and cystic fibrosis,

(2) lung parenchymal (restrictive) disorders including drug sensitivity, radiation, leukemia, disseminated cancer, and,

(3) defective regulation of ventilation brought about by dysfunction of the respiratory centre in CNS, abnormal musculoskeletal structure, or disordered neuromuscular function; also by obesity, hypo-thyroidism, and functional alveolar hypoventiliation (e.g. sleep, chronic CO_2 exposure).

The above are chronic disorders though respiratory failure may occur in acute disorders as heart failure, pneumonia, and shock lung. Pulmonary function tests reveal characteristic changes in lung volumes and ventilation in the various lung ailments aiding in differential diagnosis. Consequences of respiratory failure may arise from:

(1) hypoxia (< 60 mm Hg or decreased arterial and tissue O_2 tension; normal 75-100 mm Hg) affecting cell metabolism with possible irreversible damage in minutes and increasing pulmonary arterial vascular resistance leading to cor pulmonale (right ventricular hypertrophy) and right ventricular failure, and/or

(2) hypercapnia (> 70 mm Hg or increased arterial and tissue CO_2 tension; normal 35-45 mm Hg) which may occur with pharmacological (drug) suppression of total pulmonary ventilation, affecting the CNS (noted as cerebral vasodilation, increased CSF pressure, sensorial changes as confusion and narcosis, and papilledema with persistent elevations of $Pa(co_2)$) and acid-base balance (resulting in decreased CO_2 stimulation of breathing because of increased buffers produced by the kidneys). A sudden increase in CO_2 tension leads to respiratory acidosis (pH < 7.0) or failure responsible for decreased myocardial contractility, hyperkalemia, decreased blood pressure and cardiac irritability as well as pulmonary arteriolar vasoconstriction. Increased alveolar ventilation lowers $Pa(co_2)$ to normal levels reversing the acidosis. Respiratory failure may be detected by arterial blood analysis for $Pa(o_2)$, $Pa(co_2)$ and pH. Respiratory support for a patient in respiratory failure is accomplished by mechanical ventilation and high O_2 mixtures while other technics (eg. bronchodilators, moisturization, tracheal suction) attack underlying responsible factors. Adequate oxygenation and the state of blood acidosis are of prime importance in treatment and should be monitored.

Drug overdose and inhaled irritants have caused acute respiratory distress syndrome which is respiratory failure associated with acute pulmonary injury in a previously disease-free lung resulting in hypoxemia (decreased $Pa(o_2)$). In bronchial asthma, the bronchial tree appears to be hypersensitive to stress including irritants such as cigarette smoke. The airway obstruction (increased air flow resistance during forced expiration) or narrowing of large and small airways is due to bronchial smooth muscle spasm, inflammation and edema of bronchial mucosal wall, and tenacious mucus production leading to decreased alveolar ventilation resulting in hypoxemia with initially normal $Pa(co_2)$ and pH but later development of respiratory acidosis or failure (increased $Pa(co_2)$ and decreased pH). The alleged bronchial hypersentivity may be due to an adrenergic/cholinergic imbalance in airway diameter control with excessive cholinergic effects being responsible for subclinical levels of bronchoconstriction. As the asthmatic attack (wheezing (disappears when mucus plugs airway), coughing, shortness of breath, tightness or pressure in chest, increased heart rate and systolic blood pressure, eosinophilia with > 250-400 cells/cu mm blood) progresses, air trapping occurrs increasing the residual lung volume with hyperinflation of lungs (squared-off chest wall) and emphysematous lung X-ray pattern. Pulmonary function tests, used for differential diagnosis, are also useful for:

(1) assessment of the degree of airway obstruction (severity) and disturbance in gas exchange

(2) measuring airway response to allergens and chemicals (provocative histamine test)

(3) quantifying response to therapeutic agents, noting the degree of reversibility of airway obstruction (vs pretreatment tests) and

(4) long-term follow-up.

Tobacco or other smoke have been responsible for acute irritative bronchitis (self-limited acute inflammation of the tracheobronchial tree) which may result in airway obstruction due to bronchial wall edema, retained secretions, and bronchial muscle spasm. Cigarette smoking irritates the bronchi often giving rise to a chronic productive cough of chronic bronchitis due to prolonged irritant exposure accompanied by mucus hypersecretion and bronchial (inflammatory) structural alteration. Alveoli are small gas-filled structures covered with lyoprotein (surfactant) which decreases surface tension and gives form and stability to the alveoli. Smoking impairs alveolar macrophage lung defense function allowing chronic low grade inflammation with recurrent release of leukocytic (W.B.C. taking part in inflammatory process) proteolytic enzymes (hydrolyze proteins) affecting alveolar walls (destructive) resulting in emphysema (enlargement of air spaces distal to terminal non-respiratory bronchioles). Most individuals have the capability of neutralizing these enzymes via anti-proteolytic α_1-globulin fraction in the serum (in homozygotic α_1-antitrypsin deficiency, emphysema develops by middle age without substance exposure). Airway obstruction (prolonged expiration with wheezing) may develop from narrowing of the airway secondary to bronchial disease or from airway collapse during forced expiration secondary to pulmonary emphysema. Frequent prolonged heavy smoking may lead to chronic bronchitits and emphysema which often coexist in a clinically signficiant irreversible airways obstruction condition known as COPD (chronic obstructive pulmonary disease with chronic productive cough, exertional dyspnea and disability, slowing of forced expiration (normal < 4 secs) with rate of FEV_1 (forced expiratory volume in 1 sec) decline being twice to 3x that expected from aging), a major cause of disability (second to heart disease) and death (greater than lung cancer). The development of chronic bronchitis, emphysema, and chronic airways obstruction depends upon the balance between individual susceptibility (predisposing factors of pulmonary infection, immunological mechanism, heterozygotic α_1-antitrypsin deficiency or mild impairment to inactivation of proteolytic enzymes, and genetic predispostion) and exposure to provocative agents (including air pollution (Rokaw et al., 1980)). COPD cannot be cured; progression of the disease may be slowed by symptomatic relief and control of potentially fatal exacerbations (infections, heart failure secondary to cor pulmonale due to pulmonary hypertension brought about by excessive hypoxemia often associated with hypercapnia, brochospasm, and avoiding inspissation of bronchial secretions). Curtailment of smoking decreases bronchial irritation and hypersecretion of mucus noted in most smokers. The interrelation between COPD and asthma, if any, is not known.

Lung abscess(es) may develop secondary to bronchial obstruction which may be due to bronchogenic carcinoma especially in male smokers over 55 years of age. A statistical (dose-related) association exists between smoking and both squamous (in larger bronchi) and oat (small undifferentiated) cell bronchogenic carcinomas. Since most primary tumors are endobronchial, cough (increased intensity and intractability in chronic bronchitis) is usually present. Cytological studies of sputum for tumor cells aid in diagnosis as does biopsy and bronchial washings. Prognosis for bronchogenic carcinoma is very poor indicating the importance of prevention via avoidance of substances (e.g. cigarette tobacco smoke) associated with lung cancer. Untreated bronchogenic carcinoma results in 9 months survival; the overall 5 year survival rate for the 25% resectable tumors is less than 10%. Since most environmental chemical carcinogens (e.g. tobacco smoke) require enzymatic activation, and, individual variations exist in carcinogen metabolism, the ratio of metabolic activation/inactivation may help determine cancer risk (Harris et al., 1980). Cocarcinogens (e.g. alcoholic beverages) augment the tumorigenicity of carcinogens (tobacco smoke) increasing the risk of (oesophageal) carcinoma. Asbestos combined with tobacco smoke increases the risk for bronchogenic lung carcinoma. Predisposing host factors to cancer include genetic (gene or chromosomal) and acquired (infections, trauma) diseases. Genes related to malignancy and carcinogenesis have been mapped to individual chromosomes (e.g. Philadelphia chromosome, due to translocation of part of one chromosome to another, is found in malignant bone marrow cells of 80-90% chronic myelogenous leukemias). Environmental chemicals (tobacco, tar, some drugs) are considered to be the major etiologic agents in human cancer (others are viruses, radiation); these are also carcinogenic in experimental animals (target organs and sensitivity may be different). Most become carcinogenic after beng metabolized in the body and are mutagens. Tobacco smoke, a complex mixture of about 2000 different chemicals, has at least 30 chemicals with carcinogenic activity (both in gaseous and particulate phases; N-nitrosamines and polycyclic aromatic hydrocarbons (e.g. benz (a) pyrene) being the major classes of carcinogenic compounds respectively).

3.   Cardiovascular System Dysfunction

The heart depends upon coronary blood flow and oxygen delivery for sustained normal function and extracts more oxygen per unit flow than any other tissue (myocardial oxygen demand = heart rate x systolic blood pressure). Thus factors which decrease coronary blood flow (hypotension, tachycardia, coronary obstruction, increased ventricular wall tension) may compromise ventricular function; myocardial hypoxia leading to increased lactate concentration in the coronary (venous) sinus. Shock secondary to vasodilation may occur with drug intoxication. The incidence of atherosclerosis (thickening of the arterial wall due to localized accumulation of lipids or atheromas) is increased in the presence of certain biochemical, physiological and environmental factors; risk factors being hypertension, increased serum lipids (cholesterol, triglycerides), cigarette smoking, diabetes mellitus, and obesity. Prevention depends on adequate treatment or avoidance of risk factors (discouraging or stopping cigarette smoking to decrease the risk of atherosclerotic heart disease). Treatment of atherosclerosis is directed at its complications such as angina pectoris, myocardial infarction, arrhythmias, heart failure, and peripheral arterial occlusion which is really treating a symptom and not the underlying disease process. Atherosclerosis is of clinical importance due to its predilection for coronary, cerebral, and peripheral arteries; its complications being the major causes of death such as arteriosclerotic and degenerative heart disease being the commonest with cerebrovascular disease being the third most common (cancer being second) cause of death. CO (carbon monoxide) from cigarette smoke may cause anoxic damage to the arterial wall predisposing it to lipid infiltration. The hypoxic effect of COHb in maternal and fetal blood due to CO from smoking during pregnancy may adversely affect the fetus resulting in reduced birth weight and increased perinatal mortality including fatal dose-related (> 10 cigarettes/day during gestation) teratogenic effects (possibly a genetic-environmental (smoke) interaction) such as congenital heart disease (exposure when heart and great vessels forming). Heavy cigarette smoking may be responsible for the development of chronic bronchitis and chronic obstructive pulmonary emphysema leading to chronic cor pulmonale (right ventricular enlargement secondary to lung malfunction), being poorly tolerated in heart disease conditions. COHb levels of 5-9% are also not well tolerated in coronary artery disease (may precipitate anginal attacks upon exertion) (Jackson and Menges, 1980).

4. Marihuana Effects on Pulmonary System

Attempts are being made to determine whether chronic marihuana (or hashish) smoking leads to deleterious pulmonary effects similar to that observed in tobacco smokers especially since marihuana is inhaled more deeply than tobacco smoke for the purpose of obtaining a "high". There have been reports of mediastinal or cervical subcutaneous emphysema (swelling of area due to presence of air commonly occurring spontaneously in those with histories of asthma, chronic bronchitis, protracted coughing, and prolonged repeated shouting) brought about by repeated sustained Valsalva's maneuvers (prolonged intraalveolar hyperpressure or sustained increase in intrabronchial pressure) during marihauna smoking (Mattox, 1976). That is, at the end of a long slow inhalation to maximum thoracic expansion, the glottis is closed with a 20-30 sec forceful Valsalva maneuver, the breath being released slowly against a semi-closed glottis. This maneuver is repeated until the entire marihuana cigarette is smoked.

(a) Smoke Constituents

Marihuana is a crude preparation of the whole plant including flowers, leaves, seeds, stems, and roots rolled into a cigarette or "joint", vs, the more potent (5-10x marihuana re THC content) hashish which is prepared by scraping resin from leaf tops of hemp plant, Cannabis sativa, usually smoked in a pipe. Only 50% cannabinoids present in a marihuana cigarette are delivered to the smoker's lungs. CBD does not form THC when marihuana cigarettes are smoked, but, when applied to tobacco cigarettes (marihuana often mixed with tobacco for cigarette or water pipe smoking), CBD is partially converted to THC due to acidity of tobacco (or when water suspension is acidic) which could be a factor in marihuana toxicology (Quarles et al., 1973). Since hashish smoke is hotter and harsher than tobacco smoke, water pipes are used because they filter and cool the hot burning hashish particles and decrease irritation to the respiratory tract while providing the smoker with the desired intoxicated state. About 9% of cannabis smoked by water pipe forms the sublimate (particulate matter of smoke or tar) inhaled by the smoker containing approximately 24% of the main cannabinoids (THC, CBD, CBN) with an increased amount of CBN in the sublimate (vs reference material) and with CBD being partially converted to THC and CBN (Kephalis et al., 1976). In animal studies, a dose-related inhibition of THC metabolism (as well as its metabolite, 11-hydroxy-THC) in the liver occurred with CBN and CBD which may be partly responsible for accumulation of THC in the lungs (Siemens et al., 1976) suggesting that pulmonary THC build-up in cannabis smokers may depend on the amount of CBD and CBN in the preparation smoked. Induction of pulmonary AHH enzyme (increased pulmonary aryl hydrocarbon hydroxylase activity 2-4x basal activity post 6 hours smoke exposure vs decreased activity with 48 hrs fasting in controls) occurred in animals (Marcotte et al., 1975) exposed to marihuana and marihuana placebo smoke (from 4 cigarettes (or 3.6 gm marihuana)/1 hour period vs non-smoking controls) indicating that cannabinoids are not necessary for enzyme induction. Higher enzyme activity (2x) was noted (Fig. 1) with repeated smoke exposure (vs first time exposure) and with increasing age. This enhanced enzyme activity may be due to PAH (polycyclic aromatic hydrocarbons) or other unidentified substances, brought about by "de novo" synthesis of enzyme molecules requiring normal synthesis of pulmonary protein and RNA. Such induction also occurrs with tobacco smoke. These hydroxylating enzymes are thought to be responsible for the production of THC psychoactive metabolites; any induction thereby enhancing THC biotransformation.

Marihuana smoke has been compared with tobacco smoke re carcinogenic potential using 85 mm long cigarettes without filter tips smoked via a smoking machine (Hoffman et al., 1975). Smoke formation is a chain of oxidations, hydrogenations, crackings (heat breakdown of heavy hydrocarbons), distillations and sublimations (heated solid forming vapour which condenses to form a solid again). Marihuana intake by smoke is preferred because during the smoking process about 20% THC is transferred to the mainstream smoke with an increased THC concentration from 0.61% in the marihuana cigarette to 3.5% in the particulate matter (tar) of smoke. Some toxic volatile organic agents generated in the gas phase include carbon monoxide (CO), nitrogen oxides, ammonia, and hydrogen cyanide. Both marihuana and tobacco smoke had qualitatively similar organic gas phases except for their respective cannabinoid and alkaloid (nicotine 2.85 mg/cigarette) contents. Quantitatively tobacco smoke has higher concentrations of isoprene (3x; due to combustion of high percent of terpenoids in wax-rich layer of tobacco leaves), CO (depends on the amount of waxes in the burning leaf as well as porosity of cigarette paper; paper same for both products) and volatile pyridines (3x; due to precursor tobacco alkaloid) in the gas phase with 50% more of weakly tumor promoting (in animals) volatile phenols in the particulate phase of the mainstream smoke. Marihuana, on the other hand, had 50% more carcinogenic hydrocarbons or PAH (polynuclear aromatic hydrocarbons) in the particulate phase formed during incomplete combustion of organic matter (such as cellulose which content is less in the commercial tobacco cigarette). The 4-6 ring condensed aromatic hydrocarbons (naphthalene, benz (a) pyrene and anthracene) are known carcinogens in animals. Smoke condensates were tested for tumorigenic and tumor promoting activity via mouse skin bioassays (Hoffman et al., 1975). An average of 75 mg "tar" was applied 3x/week/74 weeks to shaved backs of mice observing for persistent papilloma (skin lesion of at least 1 mm diameter) formation after 3 weeks treatment and for transformation to carcinoma (tumor invasion into adjacent skin with continued growth and histological confirmation). Tumor promoting properties were investigated by first applying 75 μg DMBA (7, 12-dimethylbenz [a] anthracene; 1 dose to backs of mice) 10 days prior to tar (or vehicle control) skin application for approximately a 12 month (56 weeks) period. The chronic toxicity of tobacco "tar" was greater than marihuana with survival rate being 20% for tobacco and 34% for marihunana (tar application/74 weeks) animals (Fig. 2). In the skin bioassay, the marihuana smoke condensate appeared to be a weaker tumorigenic agent than tobacco with development of benign papillomas (skin tumors) in 6/100 marihuana group and 14/100 tobacco group; 2 of the latter having developed carcinomas (malignant tumors) at the end of the 74 week treatment period. Tumor initiation with DMBA followed by marihuana or tobacco (50% tar suspension) treatment for 56 weeks resulted in 26/60 marihuana group and 34/60 tobacco group developing skin papillomas and carcinomas indicating tumor promoting properties for both products (marihuana slightly less than tobacco tar) thought to be due to non-volatile phenols and long chain fatty acids (based on short-term tests) (Fig. 3). Thus marihuana smoke contains some volatile N-nitrosamines and some polycyclic hydrocarbon carcino-gens (the latter possibly being tumor initiators). Marihuana "tar" has both weak tumorigenic and tumor promoting activities (mouse skin) which are lower than that of tobacco tar. In a more recent study (Rickert et al., 1982), the tar obtained from machine smoking fully one marihuana cigarette (600-729 mg weight with 1.3 or 4.5% THC) was found to be 38 mg vs 15 mg from a standard reference tobacco cigarette smoked to a butt length of 30 mm with per puff tar deliveries being similar (2.2 mg for marihuana; 1.9 mg/puff tobacco). The CO delivery from a marihuana cigarette (13.2-18.4 mg) was similar to the tobacco cigarette (15.5 mg) with per puff CO delivery being greater for tobacco (> 2 x marihuana or 1.87 vs 0.795 mg/puff marihuana) while the pH of mainstream smoke was higher for marihuana (6.2-7.6 vs tobacco with 5.5-6.3) resulting in a more alkaline irritant smoke to the respiratory tract. Using current smoking behaviour for each product, marihuana yielded 3.8 x more tar/cigarette (103-110 mg) than tobacco (27.8 mg) implying, possibly, a higher health risk (tar) problem with marihuana cigarette use.

Mutagenicity was demonstrated by marihuana and tobacco smoke condensates upon metabolic activation in Salmonella/microsome assays (Wehner et al., 1980) being positively associated with nitrogen content of the products (not with condensate pH and yields, nor with psychoactive cannabinoids in marihuana smoke; rather due to pyrolysis products produced during the smoking process). Pyrolyzates were obtained by smoking 20 gm each of marihuana, commercial cigarettes, and home-grown turkish variety tobacco (Transkei; South Africa) in a smoking device (puffs of 2 sec duration with 35 ml capacity/15 sec). The collected condensate was dissolved in DMSO (dimethyl sulfoxide; 80 mg/ml) and assayed within 24 hours for mutagenicity by means of the Ames test using histidine revertants of S. typhimurium (certain mutants of Salmonella typhimurium can be reverted from a histidine requirement back to prototrophy by various mutagens (Ames et al., 1975)) to detect carcinogens as mutagens (a high percent of carcinogens are mutagens due to somatic mutation). The order of decreasing mutagenicity was Transkei tobacco pyrolyzate, followed by marihuana, and, pipe and cigarette tobaccos; the maximum mutagenic activity occurring at 1000-4000 μg/plate concentration for all condensates with high pyrolyzate concentrations (> 6000 μg/plate) resulting in toxicity or bactericidal action (Fig. 4). It was suggested that carcinogenic risks associated with marihuana smoking may be at least comparable to cigarette and pipe tobacco smoking because of its potent mutagenic effect (deep inhalation observed in marihuana users possibly increasing the mutagenic hazards above that of tobacco users) and its 50% higher condensate yield than that obtained with cigarette and pipe tobaccos.

PAH is the largest known group of chemical carcinogens responsible for the major carcinogenic activity in smoke condensates (Lee et al., 1976). Carcinogenic activity of a compound depends on its chemical structure giving rise to various degrees of potency ranging from nil to very potent tumor initiators. Smoke condensates were collected from 2000 gm Mexican marihuana cigarettes with 2.8% THC and standard tobacco cigarettes smoked in a smoking machine simulating the smoking habits of the average tobacco cigarette smoker and analysed for PAH composition. Some 150 polynuclear components in each smoke material were quantitated and tentatively identified as to parent ring structures and type of alkyl substituents. The concentration of PAH with molecular weights greater than that for chrysene was significantly increased in marihuana (vs tobacco) which could greatly increase the carcinogenic activity of marihuana condensate; the concentration of the potent carcinogen, benz[a]pyrene in marihuana being almost twice (170%) that found in tobacco. A question was raised as to the possibility of pyrolysis products of insecticides (chlorinated pesticides found in the tobacco condensate) accelerating PAH tumor initiating activity.

A means of overcoming or controlling the drug problem is to remove the illicit cultivation of narcotic plants by means of herbicides which would destroy or heavily damage cannabis plants (Horowitz, 1977). A desirable herbicide would have negligible drift to the surrounding crop with limited persistence in soil avoiding residual damage to subsequent crops. Paraquat, a herbicide or general weed killer (1,1' dimethyl-4,4' bipyridinium dichloride) has been used (sprayed) to eradicate Mexican marihuana plants (interaction of defoliant with sunlight results in plant death in 2-5 days depending upon the amount of solar exposure, the leaves dropping off prematurely) (Coffman et al., 1978). Paraquat bound to the clay particles in the soil is not available to plants (not herbicidal). Irrespective of route intake, the substance concentrates in the lung with pulmonary edema developing within 24-48 hours ending in fibrosis (decreased lung volume and capacity to absorb oxygen) in about 8 days in reported fatal outcomes. Combustion of paraquat yields one product, 4,4' bipyridine (similar type substances found in tobacco smoke). A small amount of paraquat (0.2 - 0.3%) is transferred in the smoke (1 µg) of treated marihuana (1 gm cigarette with 500 ppm paraquat), the remainder being converted to bipyridine during pyrolysis. Harvesting of plants prior to plant damage or just after spraying and keeping them from sunlight (i.e. the chemical still present on the leaves since it will not wash off and without altering the appearance of the plant) raised concern about health hazards following use of such contaminated marihuana especially since there is no known effective antidote for paraquat, and lung damage is irreversible. Some confiscated samples (about 20%) showed an average paraquat contamination of 500 ppm (range of 3 to 2264 ppm; 1 ppm = 1 µg) or 0.5 mg paraquat per 1 gm marihuana; the cannabinoid content being 0.09% CBC, a trace (< 0.009%) of CBD, 0.61% THC and 0.23% CBN, the average levels typical of Mexican marihuana. The smoking of 5 such marihuana cigarettes/day/year could lead to the development of permanent lung fibrosis and functional impairment (due to small airway involvement of bronchioles and proximal alveolar ducts) in addition to the other adverse pulmonary effects of chronic marihuana use (decreased pulmonary function, induction of aryl hydrocarbon hydroxylase in lung tissue by PAH being associated with increased lung cancer). Animal studies have suggested that repeated inhalation of 1 µg paraquat without allowing time for lung (small airways and alveoli) repair may result in permanent pulmonary damage (fibrosis), the severity of which would depend on the cumulative dose (single inhalation of 2.5-5 µg paraquat produced adverse changes in animal lungs). There have been no reports of paraquat contaminated marihuana poisoning in the U.S.A. Commerical paraquat is available as a 20% (caustic) solution with corrosive properties causing death in 70% of patients ingesting the product while only 10% die upon oral intake of a 3% paraquat product (Wright et al., 1978). Besides the toxic lung effects of edema, hemorrhage, inflammation and fibrosis (made worse with oxygen administration), renal tubular necrosis as well as myocardial and hepatic necrosis may occur. Animal studies revealed 96% urinary excretion of unchanged paraquat. An estimated human lethal dose is 5 gm p.o. (but may be less). A correlation has been established between clinical outcome of paraquat poisoning and drug urinary excretion rate. All 6 patients who ingested a 20% paraquat product (3-19 gm paraquat) and 1/10 patients having taken a 3% product (1.8 gm paraquat) died within 96 hrs to 12 days showing liver and renal damage. The total amount of paraquat excreted ranged from 0.6 mg to 386 mg with excretion rate falling rapidly during the first 48 hours. The high mortality appeared to be associated with over 1 mg/hr excretion rate more than 8 hours following ingestion (excretion rate being a way of assessing severity of poisoning). Excretion rate was not affected by hemoperfusion nor forced duiresis. The actual cause of death is usually respiratory failure.

A recent (November 1979) U.S. committee hearing (1980 publication) (as to whether paraquat-sprayed marihuana was harmful) questioned the level of human lung tolerance to inhaled paraquat stating that 1000 µg could be tolerated without adverse health effects (based on rat lung data showing that 1 µg paraquat/gm lung did not reveal pulmonary damage; the human lung weighing approximately 1 kg) vs a government agency report of 500 µg/year exposure (an estimate based on literature review) above which irreversible lung damage might develop with lesser lung damage occurring between 100-500 µg exposures (paraquat being the only known herbicide with the selective property of pulmonary fibrosis). The cumulative dose of 500 µg/year may be attained by smoking 7 marihuana cigarettes/day/year contaminated with 111 ppm paraquat with 0.2% paraquat passing unchanged into the smoke (400 ppm paraquat would require > 2 cigarettes/day/year). Animal studies have revealed that acute paraquat lung effects are additive to marihuana effects seen histologically as increased collagen formation (fibrous inelastic scar tissue formed during the repair process or fibrosis which decreases the lung's capacity to absorb O_2, death occurring from respiratory failure). By instillation, paraquat produced pathological lung changes in the 1-10 µg concentration range. A dose-response relationship exists with respect to severity of lung damage. Preliminary studies in hamsters (4 hrs continuous smoke exposure) revealed that airway toxicity of paraquat at 1000 and 5000 ppm in marihuana was no greater than marihuana used alone (but > tobacco smoke) while 10,000 ppm had cytotoxic effects greater than uncontaminated marihuana smoke observed at the light microscope level. Pregnant rats exposed to paraquat during early pregnancy (period of organogenesis similar to 3rd to 8th week human pregnancy) resulted in offspring with cystic deformity of lungs. In Mexico, a surfactant was added to paraquat to increase its absorption by marihuana plants, thereby increasing the amount of paraquat remaining in the smoke. Intermittent puffing of cigarettes yields 3x amount of uncombustible paraquat vs continuous (burning) puffing. With respect to tobacco, no paraquat residue is allowed (by U.S. environmental protection agency) to remain on the leaves after spraying. Some animal studies have shown that instillation (direct application) of droplets with 1 picogram ($1/10^6$ µg) paraquat is sufficient to produce lung damage. Paraquat is known to kill cells on contact so that even though the half-life is relatively short (1.5 days), the damage done is left behind and remains as scar tissue. The question is how much lung damage is necessary to produce breathing problems. A UN report (July 1979) stated that residual sprayed paraquat formulations on marihuana plants would not be sufficient to cause toxic effects in a marihuana user based on animal studies of 3 weeks duration (short term) with daily 6 hour exposures, 5 days/week, using various levels of pure paraquat aerosols. In this same inhalation study, moderate-severe laryngeal changes were noted as ulceration and squamous metaplasia which were considered to be non-specific adaptive responses; there was no evidence of epithelial dysplasia or cancer-in-situ leading to the conclusion that the changes were not considered to be pre-cancerous. One wonders what would have been the progression of the lesions with more prolonged exposure. Squamous metaplasia and hyperplasia are often the first indications of carcinogenicity. A long term study should be undertaken to assess the carcinogenic potential (if any) of paraquat, which if present, would add to the carcinogens present in marihuana smoke. Even though pulmonary fibrosis has occurred following paraquat ingestion, no human case reports (re fibrosis) have appeared following inhalation. A registry is being developed in the U.S. of employees working with paraquat to follow long term effects. A preliminary report of an epidemiological study in Malaysia with workers spraying paraquat from backpacks for 5-10 years revealed no significant clinical effects (including pulmonary function) indicating no inhalation risk by this form of application. It appears that many questions remain to be answered with respect to safe/toxic dose levels of inhaled paraquat via smoke (including frequency and duration of use) in humans necessitating further studies. It must be kept in mind that an acute lethal dose is usually larger than a chronic lethal dose taken over a period of time when cumulative effect(s) occurs. Toxicity may be enhanced by the combined effect(s) of paraquat, smoke, and marihuana ingredients. That is, smoke irritation may set up an inflammatory reaction (capillary dilation) while marihuana (THC) may cause vasodilation, both of which might increase absorption of paraquat. Despite the existing controversy as to the safety (toxicity) of inhaled paraquat contaminated marihuana in humans, concern should still be with the possible health hazards as seen with long term harmful effects of nuclear radiation. It was felt that since a safe paraquat dose for human inhalation was unknown, the herbicide should not be used to eradicate marihuana plants until further studies are done. Not only should long range low level effects of paraquat contaminated marihuana be examined but a safer effective herbicide to control marihuana growth should also be developed. The commercial distributor of paraquat has stated that paraquat was not intended for the purpose of wiping out marihuana plants which may not only be illegal but may be too hazardous because of insufficient data for safe use (Marshall, 1982). Paraquat is used to wither leaves and expose bean pods of soybeans for easy mechanical collection (vs marihuana, leaves of which are harvested). It has been suggested that continued paraquat inhalation may be harmful to lungs with respiratory insufficiency, disability and death.

Another form of marihuana contamination (in addition to the chemical herbicide paraquat) is infectious organisms which could be detrimental to immunosuppressed (increased risk of infection) cancer patients using marihuana cigarettes as an antiemetic during intensive chemotherapy and radiation therapy when gastrointestinal mucosal denudation makes oral drug absorption erratic with profound decreased granulocytes and platelets preventing intramuscular injections and rectal suppository use. Various filamentous fungi (Aspergillus fumigatus, flavus and niger) have been cultured and recovered from smoke of contaminated marihuana cigarettes (Kagen, 1981; Moody et al., 1982). A water pipe will not prevent transmission of potentially pathogenic fungal spores to the smoker who risks fungal infection (especially in patients with profound prolonged granulocytopenia) with possible development of invasive systemic mycoses including invasive pulmonary and allergic bronchopulmonary aspergillosis. It is rare for a lung infection to develop in healthy individuals inhaling bacterial contaminated air because of the enormous capacity of the lung to inactivate bacteria but this may not apply to the cancer patient. Viable potentially pathogenic bacteria (Klebsiella pneumoniae, Enterobacter agglomerans, group D streptococcus (enterococcus), Bacillus species and Enterobacter cloacae) have been found in marihuana cigarettes supplied to alleviate nausea and vomiting associated with chemotherapy or radiation therapy which impair antimicrobial lung defenses increasing infection susceptibility which is further comprised by smoking marihuana cigarettes (noted later as impaired intrapulmonary inactivation of bacteria by gas phase due to decreased phagocytic capacity of alveolar macrophages as well as pulmonary airway abnormalities leading to impaired clearance of particles) (Ungerleider et al., 1982). Such contamination may be avoided by sterilizing marihuana cigarettes to be used by immunosuppressed cancer patients in whom pulmonary infection could be fatal. A Salmonella (common food borne pathogen) muenchen (strain) gastroenteritis (feverish diarrheal illness with nausea and vomiting/8 days with organisms in blood and stool) outbreak in young adults in several states (U.S.A.) was traced (plasmid fingerprinting) to contaminated (with animal manure) marihuana exposure indicating that salmonellosis may be caused by a vehicle that is not primarily ingested (Taylor et al., 1982). Isolates of the organism from fecal and blood specimens were sensitive to all antibiotics. Decreased gastric acidity (gastric acid important barrier to ingested microorganisms) in cannabis users may predispose such individuals to infection following ingestion of smaller inocula.

(b) Acute Effects

Acute effects of marihuana smoke on pulmonary function was investigated in supposedly clinically normal volunteer students (15 males, 2 females, 18-26 years of age) with previous marihuana experience (ranging from heavy or 15 "high"/week-years to light or 2 "high"/week-years; duration of use not stated) and light tobacco cigarette smoking (2 pkg years) in 2 subjects, who inhaled smoke from burning marihuana (3.23 mg/kg) containing 2.6% THC (84 µg/kg for 9 individuals; 8 males, 1 female) or 1.0% THC (32 µg/kg for 8 students, 7 males, 1 female); placebo was not used (Vachon et al., 1973). Pulmonary function tests were performed prior to and following (up to 20 minutes) marihuana smoke exposure. The group inhaling the low THC dose appeared to show some early signs of airway obstruction in the initial screening respiratory function data (increased RV (residual volume), increased TLC (total lung capacity), and decreased MMEF (maximal mid-expiratory flow); authors only mention slight increase in RV in low dose group). This group did not show increased heart rate (tolerance may have developed prior to experimental marihuana exposure) seen in the high dose group (28% increase) 15 minutes following marihuana smoke inhalation. Marihuana smoke (Fig. 5) decreased Raw (airway resistance) in both groups (greater decrease in the high dose group) with a corresponding increase in SGaw (specific airways conductance), the increase in flow rates corresponding to the resistance values with the low dose group having a lower increase in air flow rate (may indicate early airway obstruction in this group noted above and not necessarily due to a lower THC dose). The heart rate change 5 minutes following drug intake correlated with bronchodilator effect at the 20 minute period (very little or no change in heart rate and bronchodilator effect may also indicate tolerance development and airway obstructive disease respectively). Some individuals had decreased ventilatory response to a second pre-drug measurement to increasing inspired CO_2 (carbon dioxide) concentration. Following marihuana, neither group showed significant changes with respect to respiratory centre response to acute drug intake. Since the above 2 groups had varying marihuana experience and placebo was not used, a cross-over design should have been used. Since the low dose group did not respond to the same degree as the high dose group and appeared to use individuals with some respiratory function abnormalities, it is not known whether such response is a truly dose-effect one or due to tolerance development or early airway obstruction effects due to previous marihuana use. The above study, nonetheless demonstrates acute bronchodilator effect of marihuana (vs bronchoconstriction of tobacco). Some of the above uncertainies were cleared up in the following 2 studies as well as in others reported later.

One study (Bellville et al., 1975) determined marihuana smoking effect on respiratory response curve using a rebreathing technique (5% CO_2 in O_2) in 9 healthy male experienced marihuana users (22-28 years of age) who abstained from cannabis use for at least 2 weeks, omitting coffee, tea, alcohol, and marihuana from meals for at least 12 hours prior to testing. Also oral THC (7.5 and 22.5 mg) respiratory effects were compared with alcohol (60 and 180 ml of 80 proof vodka with 6 oz fruit juice) and pentobarbital (50 and 150 mg) in 5 healthy male non-drug users (1 naive marihuana user). A 900 mg marihuana cigarette with 2.2% THC (22 mg) was completely smoked within a 10 minute period inhaling the smoke deeply/2-4 secs, holding the breath/15 secs, and resuming normal breathing/several secs before next smoke inhalation. Respiratory response curves (in torr Pco2) were determined prior to (control) and 15, 30, and 60 minutes following cessation of smoking (or 0.5, 1, 2, 3 hours post oral medication). Pulse rate was taken prior to, while "high", graded (0-7+) and assessed after each determination. The smoking portion of the study was repeated within a 2 week period while placebo cigarettes were used 8 weeks after the initial investigation. Both smoking marihuana and oral THC intake revealed some depression of respiration; smoking having a greater effect (relative potency of inhalation: oral route was 3:1) with greater peak effect and shorter duration. The increased pulse rate and "highs" paralleled the above respiratory effect with varied duration (Fig. 6). Alcohol and pentobarbital depress respiration with alcohol acting as a stimulant in some races and low doses of pentobarbital also acting as a respiratory stimulant (often seen with CNS depressant drugs). The possibility of tolerance developing to respiratory depressant effects because of the lesser reponse seen during the second repeated exposure, led to the next study. It is known that tolerance develops to respiratory depression of opiates during dependence. A similar study of CO_2 respiratory response curves was undertaken in 8 healthy male experienced marihuana users (average 5.2 joints/day and abstinent from drugs for 2 weeks) prior to and following (15, 30, 60 minutes) smoking of 1 (3 subjects) to 2 (5 subjects) marihuana (900 mg) cigarettes (2.2% THC) (Bellville et al., 1976). Re-assessments (at 15, 30, 60 minutes post marihuana) were done at 2-3, 5-6, and 8-9 weeks after onset of marihuana (ad lib) intoxication. Respiratory depression was evident following marihuana smoking seen as a significant change from base-line controls. Tolerance developed to the respiratory depressant effect of marihuana (decreased peak effect and earlier onset of peak with exposure time or duration of intoxication) (Fig. 7) and somewhat to pulse increase over the study period with experienced marihuana users.

(c) Chronic Effects

Clinical observations and investigations have substantiated the suspected undesireable pulmonary effects of chronic cannabis smoking. Field studies done in India (Chopra and Jandu, 1976) and Jamaica (Rubin and Comitas, 1975) have pointed to adverse pulmonary effects. In India the respiratory disorders observed in habitual cannabis users were laryngitis, pharyngitis, asthma, irritative cough, dyspnea and chronic bronchitis. The effects were more pronounced in older individuals (average 48.5 years of age) who had used large drug doses (mean daily THC of 350 mg) over prolonged periods (mean 27.1 years duration of use). The risks of heavy chronic ganja smoking (4-5 spliffs/day up to 31 gm for an average of 17 years duration of use) in Jamaica appeared to parallel that of tobacco smoking noted as altered respiratory function tests ($\downarrow$ FVC, $\downarrow$ FEV, $\downarrow$ PFR (peak expiratory flow rate), which are characteristic changes in lung volume and ventilation in intrathoracic airway obstruction, although the authors thought otherwise interpreting the test results as absence of obstructive ventilatory defects) resulting in functional hypoxia (tissue O_2 deficiency seen as $\downarrow$ Pa(O_2) (arterial blood gas) especially in tobacco smokers of > 20 cigs/day + chronic ganja smoking) which increased the demand on bone marrow for RBC production ($\uparrow$ Hb and PCV). Laryngeal irritation was observed in some marihuana smokers (8/14; 2 x/week to 1 x/day/4 to 8 years use; vs tobacco smokers and non-smokers) as altered vocal cord appearance (darker than normal) seen by indirect (mirror) laryngoscopy (Mueller and Wilcox, 1980). During "high" perids, marihuana smokers reported that their voices seemed to be strained and hoarse with lack of pitch control. The above may be of concern to individuals using their voices professionally (singers, speakers).

Medical manifestations reported by chronic hashish smokers involved chiefly the respiratory system (irritation due to hashish smoke) including sinusitis, rhinopharyngitis, bronchitis, and asthma, with uvular edema (12-24 hour duration) being a useful physical sign of excessive use (Fig. 8); improvement occurring with decreased use (Tennant et al., 1971). These individuals were former male marihuana users (U.S.A.), 19-23 years of age, who smoked more than 100 gm hashish/month/6-15 months (as soldiers in Europe; unknown THC content) on a daily habitual basis; 21/31 subjects also smoked tobacco cigarettes with 20/31 having occasionally used amphetamines and hallucinogens. In 5 patients (3 also smoked tobacco cigarettes) with bronchitis (productive cough with dyspnea onset 3-4 months following regular hashish use), pulmonary function tests revealed a mild obstructive pulmonary defect which was partially corrected by decreased hashish use for 3 days noted as average increases in MVV of 14.4 l/minute, VC of 338 cc, and FEV_1 of 432 cc (maximum voluntary ventilation, vital capacity, and forced expiratory volume in 1 sec, respectively, indicating the condition of large airways including both elastic and non-elastic properties) as well as disappearance of expiratory wheezes in 3/5 individuals. In some men with rhinopharyngitis (nose and throat irritation with increased nasal secretions) sinus X-rays showed opacity of at least one sinus. Since hashish has irritating properties, it may potentiate allergic tendencies in some individuals.

Respiratory tract complaints were followed in another 200 young male soldiers (18-23 years of age) who chronically smoked high doses of hashish (Henderson et al., 1972). Analysed samples of hashish contained 5-10% THC with some samples (2-3%) being contaminated with cocaine, morphine, opium, spices, and feces. Those individuals with pharyngitis smoked less than 25 gm hashish/month while those with bronchitis and asthma used more than 50 gm hashish/month (hashaholics; reported use of up to 600 gm/month). The majority (> 90%) also smoked tobacco cigarettes and had used marihuana previously with a few having smoked opiates while in the Far East. Sore throat (pharyngitis) or "hash throat" was the most common complaint due to smoking without a filter (screen) leading to an inflamed pharynx (often with lymphoid hyperplasia noted on the posterior wall) and a swollen uvula. Persistent rhinitis occurred in 26 smokers appearing as nasal stuffiness and coryza (acute inflammation of nasal mucous membrane with profuse discharge from nostrils) with boggy swollen nasal turbinates. Sinus X-rays revealed various degrees of mucosal thickening with some (8 men) having antral cloudiness. Chronic bronchitis in 20 men presented with dyspnea, productive cough, and decreased exercise tolerance with physical findings of rhonchi, wheezes, and rales. Vital capacity was 15-40% below normal. Bronchoscopy and biopsy were performed in 6 of these patients with bronchitis who had used more than 50 gm hashish/month/5-24 months; 2 had not smoked tobacco cigarettes for a period of 5 and 8 months prior to biopsy (consumption for the 6 subjects was 1 package cigarettes/day/3-7 years). During bronchoscopy the mucosa was observed to be injected with various amounts of mucopurulent material seen on the tracheal and bronchial walls. Biopsies taken from the posterior wall of the trachea near the carina (since no specific lesions were seen) revealed abnormal epithelium with loss of cilia, epithelial cell hyperplasia, atypical cells, and squamous metaplasia (in 1 individual), as well as basement membrane thickening and chronic inflammation. Similar changes are usually found in older heavy tobacco cigarette smokers.

The next project involved the investigation of the possibility of developing emphysema or pulmonary carcinoma (seen with tobacco cigarette smoking) with chronic cannabis use. Both clinical and histopathological respiratory system abnormalities were reported in chronic hashish users (Tennant,

1979). Young soldiers (17-22 years of age) who had smoked hashish (25-150 gm/month/3-24 months) sought medical aid for complaints of cough, shortness of breath (dyspnea), excess sputum production, chest pain, or hemoptysis. There were 7 individuals who used only hashish while 23 also used tobacco cigarettes (at least 1 package/day/1.5-12 years). These 30 patients were compared with 6 control subjects (22-32 years of age), 3 of whom smoked tobacco cigarettes only (1.6 packs/day/10-12 years) and 3 who were non-smokers. All men were bronchoscoped when bronchial-tracheal biopsies were obtained. All hashish users had one or more respiratory symptoms with physical findings of rhonchi, rales and wheezes. Bronchoscopy of the tracheobronchial tree revealed erythema and congestion in 13/23 hashish and cigarette smokers. Biopsies disclosed atypical cells, basal cell hyperplasia, and squamous cell metaplasia in some of the smokers but not in the non-smokers. One of the cigarette (tobacco) smoking controls showing abnormalities had smoked at least 2 packs/day/12 years. The combination of hashish with tobacco cigarette use resulted in more clinical and histopathological abnormalities than the use of either substance alone (absence of abnormalities in non-smokers). The pathological findings in the biopsy materials were similar to those found in tobacco cigarette smokers associated with the development of pulmonary emphysema and carcinoma.

An animal study (Rosenkrantz and Fleischman, 1979) substantiates the above human pathological findings. Rodents were chronically (passively vs human active inhalation) exposed to marihuana smoke (as well as tobacco, placebo, sham) in a standardized automatic manner (50 ml puff volume from each of 3 cigarettes with a THC content of 0.9-2.8%, ie. 150 ml total, in a 2 sec puff period/30 sec exposure in a smoke chamber followed by 30 sec purge with fresh air/each minute or 1 puff/minute/cigarette) via a smoking machine. THC concentration in the smoke varied from 0.4-5 mg/kg (relevant to human use) depending on the number of puffs (4-16) giving rise to COHb levels of 15-48% (indicating smoke dosage) and plasma THC levels (cannabinoid dose) of 34-313 ng/ml (similar to human cannabis users with 20-300 ng/ml). Without acclimatization to smoke, lethality occurred with 1-2 doses of 16 or more puffs from 3 marihuana cigarettes with COHb levels of 35-47% while placebo cigarettes caused 50% animal deaths with 47-58% COHb (no deaths in sham or untreated controls). Some deaths occurred with 8-20 day exposures at 14-16 puffs/day (single exposures) resulting in 20-40% COHb levels for both types of cigarettes. COHb levels were found to be dose-related and cleared from the blood by 2 hours following a single smoke exposure. More CO was produced during pyrolysis with a placebo cigarette necessitating the use of a lower number of puffs than that used with marihuana during the investigation. CO production varies with the puff volume, moisture content, cigarette paper porosity and airflow resistance, being independent of puff duration. Behaviourally, CNS inhibition (depression of voluntary activity; also noted with tobacco and placebo) and stimulation (hypersensitivity and hyperactivity) were observed (dose-dependent) with tolerance development to both states. The higher doses suppressed growth rate. Exposure duration of 14-57 days did not reveal pathology which was evident at 87-360 days exposure. Pulmonary (alveolar) pathology (distinguisable from tobacco and placebo smoke which had less intense changes following 7 day/week exposures vs no changes in non-sham controls) was dose-related (% lung involved depending on THC dose with frequency and duration of exposure influencing pathology) being due to smoke (particulate and gaseous components) and cannabinoids seen as focal alveolitis or pneumonitis progressing from alveolar macrophage mobilization (common response to pulmonary irritation) and foreign body cell inflammation to focal proliferative changes (focal hyperplasia of alveolar lining cells with thickening of alveolar walls and pleura) with tissue destruction of granulomatous inflammation and cholesterol (histochemical analysis) clefts. Cholesterol may play a role in removing THC from the lungs. Tobacco smoke has increased serum cholesterol in animals and man. The above pulmonary abnormalities due to marihuana smoke appear to be similar to tobacco smoke changes reported in animals and man. It was felt that storage and biotransformation of cannabinoids, which have an affinity for pulmonary tissue, may lead to undesirable structural changes in the lung.

Peak expiratory flow (PEF) rates (indicating the status of lung volumes and airways) were studied in 195 young (16-20 years of age) male tobacco cigarette and non (22 men) smokers, pre and post 8 weeks abstinence from smoking; the number of cigarettes smoked varying from 1 to > 40 daily in the previous 3 month period (Backhouse, 1975). Some relation existed between the amount of cigarettes smoked and drug involvement (cannabis, amphetamines, LSD, barbituates, heroin, often used in various combinations) with 15/17 individuals having used cannabis alone or with other drugs as well as being moderate or heavy tobacco smokers. PEF was impaired in tobacco smokers; the degree of impairment being proportional to daily cigarette use. At the end of 8 weeks abstinence, improvement in PEF occurred in all men, especially the heavier smoking group, who did not, however, reach the predicted normal values indicating some bronchial alteration. Non and light smokers had normal PEF values at this time. The 15 cannabis smokers (at least 2x/week/previous 3 months) had mean PEF values of 539 L/minute initially vs 578 L/minute 8 weeks later; improvement being best of all groups studied.

Pulmonary function tests performed in 75 chronic marihuana smokers (> 5 years use with at least 5 joints/week during the previous 6 months with occasional use of other illicit drugs) vs non-marihuana smoking controls (matched for amount and duration of tobacco use, if any) indicated some pulmonary insufficiency (Tashkin et al., 1978a). Those with histories of asthma, COPD, or possible occupational lung disease were excluded from the study. Lower values were obtained for FVC (forced vital capacity, -0.51 ± 11 L), FEV_1 (forced expiratory volume in 1 sec, -0.38 ± 0.08 L) and SGaw (specific airway conductance which takes into account the effect of lung volume on Raw or airway resistance, -0.16 ± 0.02 L/sec/cm H_2O/L) for marihuana users vs controls indicating resistance to airflow in the bronchial tree or airway obstruction in the large airways. Similar test differences were noted in a group (50) of non-tobacco smoking marihuana users vs non-tobacco smoking controls, and a group (25) of tobacco smoking marihuana users vs tobacco smoking controls. Non-tobacco smoking marihuana users vs tobacco smoking controls (> 16 cigarettes/day) again showed lower values in the above tests with a higher CV (closing volume) value, the latter indicating small airways disease which could lead to arterial hypoxia and eventual cor pulmonale (heart disease secondary to lung disease). It appears that chronic marihuana smoking (> 4 joints/week) may have more detrimental pulmonary function effects than chronic tobacco smoking (> 16 cigarettes/day). A more detailed report of this study was published recently (Tashkin et al., 1980) stating that one subject was not used in the analysis because a matched control was difficult to find; duration of marihuana use being > 2-5 years with frequency of 3 days/week to several x/day with hashish having been used by 50 individuals from < 10x/year to < 1x/week; average age 24 years (21-33 range); and the study undertaken 12 hours to 1 week post last marihuana use and 8 hours post tobacco use. Matched controls were not questioned re use of marihuana or other illicit drugs which could negate any actual pulmonary function alterations in the study group of marihuana users. The test results ranged from normal to abnormal (FVC, FEV_1, FEF 25-75%, CV, ΔN_2 (750-1250 ml) (nitrogen concentration change between 750 and 1250 ml expired volume), SGaw). Some group means overshadowed some individual abnormalities resulting in insignificant differences in tests in marihuana users vs matched controls (matched for sex, age, height, and quantity and duration of tobacco smoking) such that only SGaw was statistically significant when comparing group means. There was no difference in SGaw between the 2 control groups of tobacco and non-tobacco smoking healthy young men. Was this lack of difference due to the young population studied (i.e. amount of tobacco smoked of < 1/2 package cigarettes/day to 1 package cigarettes/day and duration of use insufficient for detectable changes to have occurred) or were marihuana smokers present in both groups cancelling out any differences? Some of the control subjects presented with respiratory symptoms while the non-tobacco control group included individuals who never smoked tobacco as well as those who had ceased smoking 6 months previously; the possibility of existing pulmonary alterations not being ruled out judging from the abnormal pulmonary function tests noted in some of the control subjects. Group means are difficult to interpret when there is a variation in drug(s) intake; in essence the whole dose-response curve is being averaged with some points missing, the average being influenced by the largest number of common doses used (which?). Animal studies with pre-determined drug doses (and purity) are therefore used to substantitate or clarify clinical findings especially when it is difficult to find a human sample using an illicit drug with the same potency, dose, pattern, frequency and duration of use. Even though this study cannot be considered a "clean" study (which may be difficult to do clinically because the drug is illicit and it is unethical to test the drug in naive subjects), obviously something undersirable (detectable narrowing of large airways as evidenced by statistically significant increase in Raw) is occurring in the lung following cannabis smoke exposure. Chronic irritation by the smoke may lead to inflammatory changes in the bronchial epithelium somewhat reminiscent of an asthmatic condition or reversible airway obstruction in which alveolar ventilation may eventually be decreased leading to ventilation/perfusion imbalance resulting in hypoxemia.

A study carried out in 17 healthy young male experienced marihuana smokers measured pulmonary function and evaluated sputum cytology; the former measurement, prior to and following 3 (early) and 47 (late intoxication) days of daily marihuana (ad libitum) smoking (mean use of 4.7 joints/day with 900 mg marihuana/joint with 2.2% THC), and the latter, pre and post 16 and 63 days of daily smoking (Tashkin et al., 1975). Chronic heavy marihuana smoking (late intoxication) resulted in airway narrowing noted as decreases in pulmonary function tests vs baseline (FEV_1 3.7 ± 1.3%; MMEF (maximal midexpiratory flow rate) 13.0 ± 1.9%; SGaw 13.9 ± 2.8%) probably due to local irriation by the smoke but not detected by sputum cytology. The airways were able to dilate acutely to the marihuana smoke due to the acute pharmacological bronchodilator effect of THC. A further extension of this study involved 29 healthy young (21-37 years of age) male experienced cannabis users who had used marihuana at least 4x/week, with 8 individuals using it daily, 4, several times a day, and one subject using hashish regularly while 6 smoked < 1/2 package tobacco cigarettes/day; there was one drop-out (Tashkin et al., 1976). Following a detoxification period of 11 days in hospital, marihuana (900 mg with 2.2% THC) cigarettes were allowed ad libitum on a daily basis for a period of 9 weeks (average 5.2 cigarettes/-day/subject). Pulmonary function tests (detect abnormalities or early airway disease) were conducted on detox day 8, during the 4th (early), 47th or 59th days (late intoxication) of smoking, following 1 week of abstinence from heavy use, and 1 month after hospital discharge. Baseline results were essentially normal except for one subject who also used tobacco and hashish (< 1/week). Similar results were obtained as above with a decrease in DLco (diffusing capacity for CO) of 8 ± 2% vs baseline (Fig. 9). The decreases in MMEF and SGaw (pulmonary function tests indicating early airway obstruction) correlated with the amount of marihuana smoked daily (or amount of inhaled irritant in the smoke) indicating that heavy marihuana use for 6-8 weeks may lead to a mild significant airway obstruction (Fig. 10). Abstinence from smoking for 1 week resulted in baseline values for SGaw while MMEF reached baseline values 1 month after hospital discharge (Fig. 11) pointing to reversibility of pulmonary impairment due to decreased amount of inhaled irritants under conditions of this study (heavy smoking/several weeks). Partial pharmacological tolerance appeared to develop to the acute broncho-dilator effect noted above (Fig. 12). In another study of 10 stable bronchial asthmatic patients, bronchodilation (for at least 2 hours) occurred with both smoked marihuana and oral THC; the former reversing induced bronchospasm (Tashkin et al., 1974). The acute effects of 2% marihuana (7 mgm/kg), 15 mgm THC p.o., and placebo (double-blind cross-over design) on Raw and SGaw were compared. The SGaw was not altered by placebo vs smoked marihuana which immediately increased SGaw with a 2 hour duration of action at 33-48% above control levels vs higher peak effect of 1250 µg isoproterenol but with a shorter duration of action. Oral THC increased SGaw at 1 and 2 hours post drug intake with a decreased Raw over 1 to 4 hours vs no placebo effects. Induced bronchospasm (> 25% decrease in SGaw) in 4 patients (via graded exercise on a bicycle ergometer or inhalation of 0.25-1.25 mgm methacholine) was reversed by smoked 2% marihuana or inhaled 1250 µg isoproterenol and not by smoked placebo nor inhaled saline.

Bronchial (airway) reactivity in 6 (including 4 females) asymptomatic (healthy) chronic social marihuana smokers (10.5 joints/week/average 7 years; 24-28 years of age; no tobacco use/at least 2 years in 4) vs 8 healthy non-smokers (4 females; 23-37 years of age) and 9 clinically stable asthmatics (4 females; average 32 years of age; non-smokers) was assessed by a histamine inhalation bronchial challenge test determining the provocative dose capable of causing 50% increase in specific airway resistance (PD_{50} SRaw cumulative breath units of histamine; 1 breath unit of histamine = inhalation of 1 mg/ml histamine) (Hernandez, M.J. et al., 1981). Normal baseline functions were found for marihuana and non-smokers while the asthmatics had the expected expiratory flow decrease and specific resistance increase. Only the asthmatics showed the expected hyperreactivity to inhaled histamine (lower PD_{50} SRaw) which was not observed in marihuana and non-smoking controls. Spirometry and broncho-provocative tests did not reveal airway function abnormalities in this group of healthy long-term social marihuana smokers (tests for small airway disease were not done). One must keep in mind that marihuana may be used daily vs tobacco used at least hourly so that the longer interval between marihuana smoke exposures may reduce lung damage vs intensive smoking which can produce early measurable changes.

(d) Pulmonary Defense System Effects

With marihuana smoking, the lung is the primary target organ and the effects on the pulmonary defense system are essential in assessing any potential hazards. The pulmonary antibacterial defense system is a complex system. Inactivation of bacteria occurs by means of:

(1) physical clearance by mucociliary transport from the airways, and

(2) intrapulmonary bactericidal activity by alveolar macrophage phagocytosis (killing of bacteria); the latter being mostly responsible for bacterial inactivation and may be determined by the difference between total bacterial inactivation and physical clearance of bacteria. The alveolar macrophage is the key host defense cell in the lung, clearing debris from the lung via phagocytosis (engulfing and destroying particulate matter).

Biological effects of marihuana on the lung have been evaluated by studying the effects on alveolar macrophages in both "in-vitro" and "in-vivo" systems. In "in-vitro" studies (Cutting et al., 1974; Huber et al., 1975; McCarthy et al., 1976), alveolar macrophages were obtained from unexposed animals by bronchopulmonary lavage, incubating them with staphlococcus albus and graded amounts (0, 2, 4, 6, 8 ml) of marihuana (2.2% THC) or tobacco smoke for periods of 1, 2, and 3 hours. A dose-dependent depression of alveolar macrophage bactericidal activity occurred with marihuana (78% control vs 67-11%) and with tobacco smoke (50-18% of bacteria killed or inactivation rate) (Fig. 13). There was no difference between macrophages impaired by marihuana placebo, filtered (off particulate matter) gas phase of placebo, and whole marihuana smoke (14, 21,11% inactivation respectively) demonstrating that the macrophage cytotoxin was present in the gas phase of whole smoke. Water filtration of the gas phase removed the cytotoxin from the smoke (the macrophage bactericidal activity being similar to control values) (Fig. 14). The alveolar macrophage water soluble cytotoxin was present in the gas phase of fresh smoke of both marihuana and tobacco products of pyrolysis (chemical change brought about by the action of heat) being inactivated in stale smoke. Thus fresh whole marihuana smoke is cytotoxic to alveolar macrophages (maximum effect within minutes of initial exposure) as well as to staphlococci (Fig. 15) (also observed with marihuana placebo and used as a correction factor in macrophage bactericidal assay) in a dose-dependent manner (with a threshold maximum at 4-6 ml smoke, following which a rapid decrease in cell function to minimum bactericidal acitivity occurs) depressing bactericidal activity by impairing phagocytosis without killing the macrophage cell.   This was also observed with tobacco smoke, the gas phase component of which impairs glycolysis which provides some of the cell energy for phagocytosis.   The alveolar macrophage functional impairment (69% vs control of 74% inactivation rate) was not evident and not related to the psychotomimetic or bronchodilator component of marihuana (tested with 0.10 mg THC in 0.02 ml, (Fig. 16) the amount present in an 8 ml puff of fresh marihuana smoke) suggesting that a route other than smoking may be more useful for potential therapeutic (bronchodilator) effect without host defense impairment.

The "in-vivo" studies (Huber et al., 1976; 1979a, b; 1980) used animals challenged (for 30 minutes) with aerosolized intrapulmonary staphlococcus aureus inoculation followed immediately by acute exposures to graded amounts of fresh whole marihuana smoke (from 3, 6, 10, 15, and 30 cigarettes with 2.2% THC smoked via smoking machine/8-10 minutes/hour/5 hours leading to accumulated smoke exposures from 15 (3 x 5 hours), 30, 50, 75, or 150 cigarettes) noting intrapulmonary bacterial inactivation 6 hours after bacterial inoculation. Each cigarette contained 0.9 gm marihuana per 85 mm unit.   Studies were repeated using smoke from marihuana placebo and reference tobacco (Kentucky) cigarettes, and, intraperitoneally administered THC (4 or 10 mg/kg) (most of THC being present in the particulate phase of marihuana smoke). At the 15 cigarette level, fresh whole marihuana smoke was compared with the gas phase of the partitioned smoke. The puff volume delivered was 35 ml with a duration of 2 seconds and frequency of 1/minute/each cigarette in the machine. Each puff of smoke yielded a mean concentration of marihuana particulate matter of 4.8 µg/ml with a corresponding CO (gas phase) concentration of 2600 p.p.m. for both whole and gas phase smoke. Accumulative marihuana particulate smoke exposure from the various number of cigarettes used (15-150) was 200, 400, 670, 1000 and 2000 µg with corresponding COHb levels of 1, 2, 4, 6 and 10%; placebo marihuana cigarettes had 5% COHb and gas phase smoke 6.5% COHb (post 15 cigarette exposure) with control or sham treated animals having < 0.1%.   Marihuana cigarettes burned more rapidly delivering less (about 1/2) TPM (total particulate matter; 12.8 vs 24 mg) and CO (2600 vs 4100 ppm) than tobacco cigarettes; CO increasing slightly with each successive puff with particle size distribution being similar for both products. Slightly less than 5% of the total smoke delivered to the exposure system was retained by the animals with a retention of 20 µg marihuana/gm lung/puff of cigarette. These animals had a mean COHb level of 6% following marihuana smoke vs 5% following tobacco smoke even though, twice as much TPM was recovered from the tobacco smoke exposed lungs indicating possible differences in respiratory rate or volume, or resistance following smoke exposure due to bronchodilator effect of marihuana vs tobacco pulmonary irritation and bronchoconstriction, as well as differences in ventilation/perfusion ratio due to tachycardia produced by marihuana and bradycardia by nicotine.   A dose-related depression of intrapulmonary antibacterial defense occurred following acute exposure to marihuana or tobacco smoke with marihuana reaching a plateau at 2000 µg accumulative smoke exposure above which mortality increased (Fig. 17; 18). There were no deaths with ≤ 1000 µg for marihuana and < 1900 µg for tobacco accumulative particulate exposure (15 cigarettes) vs acute animal mortality of 43% for marihuana with 2000 µg and 58% for tobacco with 3700 µg exposures (30 cigarettes). Tobacco at lower doses had a stimulatory effect on the defense system as well as a higher threshold response. Antibacterial defense depression was also evident with gas phase of partitioned marihuana smoke (being less than for fresh whole marihuana smoke and supporting the above "in-vitro" study) (Fig. 19), placebo marihuana smoke (Fig. 20), but not with sham exposure nor with systemic THC administration. There was no statistical difference with respect to bacterial airway clearance in animals exposed to both products vs controls, although a trend to decreased clearance was noted following marihuana smoke or its gas phase exposure (Fig. 21). Inactivation of bacteria by normal animal lungs is depicted graphically (Fig. 22) showing that bacterial inactivation fundamentally occurs deep within the lungs (rapid decrease in intrapulmonary bacterial viability) vs physical removal (relatively small change in isotope clearance). Bacteria survived longer in the lungs of marihuana treated animals vs tobacco and vs control (ie. a greater decreased effect in bacterial inactivation by marihuana smoke). Other parameters observed were heart rate (290 beats/minute for marihuana vs 96 beats/minute for tobacco) and respiration (decreased in acute experiments with marihuana with tolerance development in later chronic studies).   Thus the acute exposure of animals to the gas phase of marihuana smoke impairs the pulmonary antibacterial defense system such that dose for dose, the lung toxicity (to alveolar bactericidal activity) of marihuana smoke is greater than for tobacco smoke. The data suggest (based on calculated extrapolation with relevance to human consumption) that exposure conditions used in these experiments ranged from 5 or less marihuana cigrettes per day (200 µg accumulateive exposure) to 50 or more at the sublethal (43% mortality) highest dose (2000 µg accumulative exposure) assuming 12 mg marihuana particulate delivery per cigarette. For tobacco, an exposure equivalent of 1 package/day of unflitered high "tar" cigarettes for each 10 cigarette exposure cycle was estimated on the basis of particulate retention. One must keep in mind the passive exposure to smoke in these experiments vs active inhalation in humans which could indicate a greater deleterious effect upon direct smoke inhalation especially since the smoking of marihuana cigarettes left a gummy residue in the smoke exposure system and, a lesser effect with a water pipe since the cytotoxin present in the gas phase is water soluble, as well as undesirable effects in non-smokers exposed (passively) to an environment with marihuana smoke produced by smokers.

In the above experiments the acute effect of smoke (marihuana or tobacco) exposure on animal alveolar macrophages re bactericidal activity revealed depression of macrophage (phagocytosis) function without killing the cell. Ensuing subchronic studies involved animal smoke exposure (10 marihuana or tobaco cigarettes, t.i.d., smoked daily by machine) for 30 consecutive days following which bronchpulmonary lavage was performed to obtain alveolar macrophages for further study of short term smoke exposure effects vs untreated controls (Drath et al, 1979). The smoking regimen for tobacco (based on animal particulate retention) was equivalent to a human dose of 1.5 packages/day of unfiltered cigarettes; the marihuana equivalent, probably less than 5 cigarettes/day (from the above reports). There was less weight gain with animals exposed to both products vs controls (which may be partly due to the stress of exposure regimen), with the tobacco group weight gain being less than the marihuana group (which may be due to appetite depressant effect of nicotine and the appetite stimulating effect of marihuana, or, merely due to plasma expansion; (see CVS effects)). The number of marcophage cells recovered was similar for both inhalants and controls (vs a report (Mann et al., 1971) on human alveolar macrophages which were decreased in number following 2-26 marihuana cigarette years use compared with tobacco and non-smoking controls; the differences may be due to species, dose, exposure time, the latter two being better controlled in animal models) as was protein content (per 10^6 cells), percent cells adhering to a plastic surface, and ability to phagocytize viable bacteria over a 60 minute period. The smoking regimens did not affect resting metabolism of alveolar macrophages. During phagocytosis, oxygen consumption increased in all 3 groups with the marihuana group having an increase less than the tobacco group (and slightly less than the control group) which had a 50% increase over the control group. Cellular release of superoxide in response to particle stimulation or phagocytosis (being not more than 7% of the total O_2 consumption) was similarly increased in the tobacco and control groups (indicating that tobacco smoke/30 days exposure did not affect superoxide generation) with a much lesser increase by the marihuana group (being practically the same as its resting value ie. inhibition of superoxide release). The direct oxidation of glucose (hexose monophosphate shunt) was not altered by the 2 products (resting) nor by phagocytosis (particles), being similar to the control group. The metabolic alterations (occurring only during phagocytosis and due to components in the gas phase of smoke) did not appear to affect the phagocytic ability of alveolar macrophages over a 30 day exposure period to either marihuana or tobacoo smoke. Chronic exposure (6 months) to tobacco smoke led to a 30% inhibition of particle uptake indicating a cumulative effect. Microscopic (light and electron) examination of these short term (30 days) exposed cells were done including a sterologic (3-dimensional) technique to detect subcellular morphological changes (Davies et al., 1979). Following marihuana smoke exposure, a slight shift to the right of the control frequency distribution curve of alveolar macrophage profile diameters occurred with a mean profile diameter of 11.5 µm while tobacco exposure resulted in a more marked shift to the right with a mean of 13.12 µm; the difference for both products not being statistically significant (Fig. 23). In human alveolar macrophages (Mann et al., 1971) a small increase in maximum cell diameters (from 16 to 17 µm) occurred following marihuana use. The ultrastructural appearance of cell profiles in control and marihuana animal groups were similar; the tobacco group had a large number of electron-lucent lipid inclusions (membrane and non-membrane bound) and lipid clefts in the cytoplasm (Davies et al., 1979). Sterologic results (Fig. 24) revealed that tobacco exposure significantly changed the volume densities of 4 parameters:

(1) slight increase in mitochondria (energy production),

(2) a great increase in lipid inclusions which may be due mostly to utilization of intralysosomal lipids leading to a decrease in

(3) lysosomes, and,

(4) small decrease (though greater than for marihuana) in the remaining cytoplasm (important in metabolic exchange and synthesis), as well as significantly decreasing the surface/volume ratio of the cell (functionally important since the cell membrane is involved in recognition phenomenon and phagocytosis) due, in part, to the loss of cell membrane rather than just to increased cell volume.

Marihuana exposure significantly changed the volume densities of only 2 parameters:

(1) increase from control of lipid inclusions by 3x vs 10x for tobacco, being similar in appearance to the tobacco group (also seen in human alveolar macrophages) and

(2) a small decrease from control of the remaining cytoplasm (control 86, marihuana 83, tobacco 76). The surface/volume ratio of the nucleus (indicating degree of nucleo-cytoplasm exchange) was not altered by smoke exposure from either product. The marihuana exposed (30 days) alveolar

macrophages (animals) had fewer changes than the tobacco exposed cells which parallels the fewer metabolic changes following marihuana exposure noted above. It has been suggested that the differences between marihuana and tobacco may be due to lesser retention of marihuana particulate matter (about 1/2 tobacco) due to bronchodilator effect of marihuana vs bronchoconstriction of tobacco. The smaller particulate load in the lung may lead to smaller changes in the alveolar macrophage environment which may result in smaller changes in structure and metabolism of the macrophages.

Since airway dysfunction has been associated with tobacco smoking seen as chronic bronchitis, which has also been reported for chronic cannabinoid users (Chopra and Jandu, 1976; Henderson et al., 1972; Tennant et al., 1971), the tracheal epithelium of marihuana smoke exposed (30 days as above) animals (8 males and 12 females with corresponding untreated controls) was examined with respect to secretory cell population (making up 35% of epithelium) as to number of cells/unit length, volume density of cells, and glycoprotein content in the cells (ie. analyze morphological response of airway) (Hayashi et al., 1980). The effects of marihuana exposure included (Fig. 25):

(1) increased epithelial thickness (by 19% in males, 16% in females) with a decreased number of total secretory cells (increased number of stained cells with a corresponding decrease in unstained cells due to conversion to stained cells), and

(2) decreased secretory cell density in tracheal epithelium (by 30% in males and 12% in females) but increased volume density of total glycoprotein in secretory cells (by 47% in males, 139% in females vs controls of 6 and 3% total glycoprotein respectively in secretory cell) with a corresponding increase in the number of stained cells/unit length of epithelium as well as a shift in secretory cell mucin production from mostly PAS-positive (stain characteristic) glycoprotein (present as 70% in male and 98% in female controls of total glycoprotein) to production of mixtures of PAS-positive and AB-positive glycoproteins (increase by 70% in males and 987% in females or 10x control mixtures). Similar changes have been seen with tobacco smoke and sulphur dioxide exposures (animals). These changes correspond to some of the changes seen in human chronic bronchitis (mucus hypersecretion with structural alteration in bronchi manifested clinically as chronic productive cough) usually associated with tobacco smoking. Other changes observed were decreased body weight (31% in males, 13% in females), decreased weight of male reproductive organs and increased weight of female adrenal glands. An earlier animal study (Valentine et al., 1976) revealed an increased number and size of debris filled vacuoles in alveolar macrophages and in ciliated cells of bronchiolar epithelium. Such changes have also been noted with tobacco smoke.

A recent survey of tobacco cigarette smokers revealed that tar yield and daily cigarette smoking was related to respiratory symptoms (phlegm production influenced by tar yield) and lung function (decreased FEV_1 indicating airflow obstruction due to irritants in gaseous phase of smoke) (Higgenbottam et al., 1980). Low tar cigarettes (as long as consumption and depth of inhalation are not increased) may decrease mucus hypersecretion and risk of lung cancer (both being due to tar deposition and soluble gas absorption in larger bronchi) but not development of airway obstruction which depends on the number of cigarettes smoked (smaller bronchi being exposed more to soluble gases in the gaseous phase). Ex-smokers never fully recover their normal potential pulmonary function. With respect to marihuana smoking, it is rather difficult to do a survey or epidemiological study of smokers who are using an illegal substance.

(e) Discussion and Summary

The physiology or normal function of the lung is to efficiently exchange gases (O_2 and CO_2) and to remove particulate matter (including bacteria) by defense mechanisms of cilia (physical clearance) and by alveolar macrophages (phagocytosis) the key host defense cells. The technique of prolonged and sustained inhalation of marihuana smoke used by cannabis smokers has led to mediastinal and cervical subcutaneous emphysema. Marihuana is smoked as cigarettes or joints (crude plant preparation) while hasish (a resin with 5-10x THC content of marihuana) is smoked in a water pipe to cool the hot harsh smoke; 50% cannabinoids being delivered to the smoker's lungs. Smoking of cannabis is preferred since 20% THC is transferred to the mainstream smoke with an increased THC concentration found in the tar or particulate matter of smoke (vs percent in original cigarette). Pulmonary accumulation of THC may depend partly on the CBD and CBN content of the preparation used because CBD and CBN inhibit liver metabolism of THC. Marihuana mixed with tobacco results in a partial conversion of CBD to THC because of acidity of tobacco which does not occur with smoking marihuana solely. Repeated smoke exposure induces pulmonary AHH enzyme activity enhancing THC biotransformation to psychoactive metabolite(s). A herbicide, paraquat, has been used as a spray to eradicate marihuana plants by interacting with sunlight which leads to premature defoliation (2-5 days) of plants. Whether a human health hazard occurs following inhalation of paraquat contaminated marihuana smoke has not been resolved although the possibility does exist. Irrespective of the route of administration, the herbicide concentrates in the lungs where its toxic effects lead to pulmonary edema in 24-48 hours resulting in irreversible fibrosis (by 8 days, made worse with O_2 administration) and death (no available antidote) from respiratory failure (mortality being associated with > 1 mg/hour urinary excretion rate, 8 hours following intake). Contamination of marihuana has also occurred with infectious organisms such as various filamentous fungi and pathogenic bacteria which could increase the risk of infection especially in immunosuppressed cancer patients using marihuana as an antiemetic during intensive chemotherapy and/or radiation therapy.

Some pulmonary effects of marihuana are due to the irritating properties of smoke regardless of the active ingredient(s) (THC vs nicotine in tobacco). Smoke contains gaseous products of burning carbonaceous materials made visible by the presence of small particles of carbon, i.e., it is a mixture of tiny particles suspended in gas (mostly CO). The solid particles combine to form a residue called "tar". Smoking facilitiates tar deposition in the lung. Smoke (tobacco) related lung diseases include chronic bronchitis, emphysema, COPD (chronic obstructive pulmonary disease often being a combination of chronic bronchitis and emphysema leading to disability (second to heart disease) and death (greater than lung carcinoma)) and carcinoma. During the smoking of marihuana, usually without a filter and fully consumed, the greater and more prolonged inspiration leads to a greater volume of smoke entering the lung (vs tobacco). Combustion of marihuana cigarettes yield somewhat more residue (or tar) than tobacco cigarettes (Fehr and Kalant, 1971). However, marihauna cigarettes burn more rapidly delivering less (about 1/2) TPM (total particulate matter) and CO than tobacco cigarettes, but, the COHb levels are similar probably due to different effects on respiratory physiology by marihuana (bronchodilation, tachycardia) and by tobacco (bronchoconstriction, bradycardia); the bronchodilator or constrictor effects possibly affecting airway resistance, and the tachy or bradycardia affecting ventilation/perfusion ratios. Marihuana, often used with tobacco, may increase tar inhalation and potentiate tobacco-related changes. The quantitative difference between tobacco and marihuana smoke is that tobacco has a higher concentration of isoprene, CO, and volatile pyridines in the gas phase with 50% more weak tumor promoting volatile phenols in the particulate matter, while marihuana has 50% more PAH (polynuclear aromatic hydrocarbons, the largest group of known chemical carcinogens such as benz (a) pyrene) in the particulate matter. Marihuana tar has weak tumorigenic and tumor promoting activity (animal skin bioassay) being less than tobacco tar which also possesses greater chronic toxicity with respect to survival rate (in animals). A large percent of carcinogens are mutagens, to which marihuana and tobacco belong, being associated with nitrogen content of the products.

Marihuana has acute bronchodilating activity (to which partial tolerance develops) vs bronchoconstriction due to tobacco smoke. Stable bronchial asthmatic patients have responded to the bronchodilating effects of cannabis (smoked marihuana or oral THC) for a period of 2 hours. Smoking marihuana or oral THC depressed respiration (also observed with alcohol and pentobarbital); smoking having a greater peak effect with shorter duration of action. A parallel increase in pulse rate and "highs" (of varied duration) occurred. Tolerance developed to the respiratory depression and increased pulse rate.

Smoke related lung diseases seen with tobacco have also been observed in marihuana smokers. Bronchial changes have been detected (decreased peak expiratory flow rates) in young people (16-20 years of age) smoking (tobacco and/or cannabis) heavily for relatively few years. Chronic marihuana smoking (> 4 joints/week) may have more undesireable pulmonary function effects than chronic tobacco smoking (> 16 cigarettes/day). Routine spirometry and plethysmography may not reveal respiratory function impairment in long term healthy social marihuana users which does not rule out possible small airway disease; impairment depending upon extent (frequency) of smoke exposure. Long term deposition of carbon particles and smoke irritation of bronchial mucosa causing increased mucus secretion and bronchial inflammatory changes results in chronic bronchitis and emphysema. The chronic irritating effects impair lung function leading to airway obstruction (bronchitis) and permanent lung disease (COPD; irreversible airway obstruction) similar to tobacco smoke effects. Airway obstruction may develop from airway narrowing secondary to bronchial disease or from airway collapse during forced expiration secondary to pulmonary emphysema. Functional hypoxia due to airway obstruction, increases the demand on bone marrow for RBC production. Excessive hypoxemia leads to pulmonary hypertension resulting in cor pulmonale and right heart failure (ie. heart disease secondary to lung disease). Cessation of smoking decreases bronchial irritation and mucus hypersecretion. Excessive hashish use has caused inflammation of the whole respiratory tract (irritating properties may potentiate allergic tendencies), the degree of involvement depending on the amount used. Bronchitis and asthma occurred in individuals using large amounts, > 50 gm hashish/month. The histopathological changes were similar to older heavy tobacco smokers associated with the development of pulmonary emphysema and carcinoma (endobronchial or bronchogenic squamous and oat cell carcinoma presenting with a persistent cough having a very poor prognosis). The combined use of hashish and tobacco resulted in more clinical and histopathologicl abnormalities than with the use of either substance alone. Animal studies with marihuana smoke have substantiated these findings. Changes in secretory cells of tracheal epithelium of animals exposed to marihuana smoke (30 days) resembled changes seen in human chronic bronchitis (with mucus hypersecretion and structural alteration in bronchi manifested clinically as productive cough) often associated with tobacco smoking.

Both "in-vitro" and "in-vivo" (animal) studies have revealed a dose dependent depression of alveolar macrophage bactericidal activity (impairing phagocytosis without killing the macrophage cell) by acute exposures to marihuana or tobacco smoke. This was due to a water soluble cytotoxin(s) in the gas phase of fresh whole smoke (impairs glycolysis which provides some of cell energy for phagocytosis) and not due to THC (psychomimetic and bronchodilator). Bacteria survived longer in marihuana treated animals vs tobacco and vs control animals, i.e., the lung toxicity to alveolar bactericidal acitivity of marihuana smoke was greater than for tobacco smoke. A trend to decreased clearance by cilia was noted with marihuana smoke and its gas phase. Impairment of alveolar macrophage function may render the host susceptible to bacterial infection and other pathological processes in the lung such as emphysema. Low grade inflammation with recurrent release of leukocytic proteolytic enzymes destroy alveolar walls leading to emphysema especially in individuals with a relative α_1-antitrypsin (neutralize proteolytic enzymes) deficiency.

Since marihuana is a CNS depressant, an overall depressant effect on function(s) may occur such as suppression of:

(a) respiratory rate,

(b) anti-enzyme activity in the lung leading to relative α_1-antitrypsin deficiency, and/or

(c) antibacterial defense system (cilia and alveolar macrophages).

These together with the irritant properties of smoke, encourages lung damage over a period of time depending on the dose; frequency, duration and pattern of use; as well as genetic (including immunological status and possible α_1-antitrypsin deficiency) predisposition to pulmonary ailments. Whereas tobacco cigarettes may be smoked 1-2x/hour (1 package/day) vs marihuana of 1-2 joints/week (up to daily use) without a filter and to a minimum (if any) butt length, it is conceivable that early undesirable pulmonary changes could occur in some individuals should a marihuana habit approach that of tobacco use. The use of marihuana and tobacco would likely lead to unwarranted pulmonary effects earlier than the use of either substance alone. Those with asthma have a hyperreactive bronchial tree (subclinical level of bronchospasm or constriction) to irritants in smoke while respiratory infection (susceptibility may be increased with marihuana use due to possible decreased immunity and/or depressed alveolar macrophage bactericidal activity) would exacerbate asthma. A family history of allergy, asthma, or a physical sign of clubbing of fingers (pulmonary osteoarthropathy) indicating chronic hypoxemia, should alert such individuals to avoid smoking marihuana and/or tobacco, or being exposed to such smoke.

From the above discussion it appears that marihuana smoking may be capable of altering pulmonary function by:

(1) inefficient gaseous exchange due to airway obstruction brought about by irritant and potential carcinogenic properties of smoke, and

(2) ineffective removal of particulate matter including bacteria (by impairment of alveolar macrophage antibactericidal activity and a tendency to decreased mucociliary clearance), leading to the development of chronic bronchitis, emphysema, and pulmonary carcinoma (as seen with tobacco smoking). Any potential therapeutic bronchodilating effect of cannabis may possibly be achieved by administration routes other than smoking which impairs host defense mechanisms. Irrespective of the source of smoke, repeated chronic anoxia due to CO absorption from the gas phase gradually increases CNS damage with loss of sensation in fingers, poor memory, and mental deterioration.

II. 3. D$_1$. Pulmonary System

List of Figures

Fig. 1	Pulmonary enzyme (AHH) activity	148
Fig. 2.	Chronic toxicity and tumorigenic activity	149
Fig. 3.	Tumor promoting activity	149
Fig. 4.	Mutagenic activity	150
Fig. 5.	Acute pulmonary function	151
Fig. 6.	Pulse rate change and subjective effects	152
Fig. 7.	Respiratory curve displacement	152
Fig. 8.	Hashish respiratory effects	153
Fig. 9.	Altered pulmonary function tests	154
Fig. 10.	Airway obstruction	153
Fig. 11.	Pulmonary impairment reversibility	154
Fig. 12.	Partial bronchodilator tolerance	155
Fig. 13.	Alveolar macrophage bactericidal activity depression	155
Fig. 14.	Alveolar macrophage bactericidal activity depression	156
Fig. 15.	Bacterial growth rate depression	156
Fig. 16.	Alveolar macrophage bactericidal activity depression	157
Fig. 17.	Intrapulmonary antibacterial defense depression	157
Fig. 18.	Intrapulmonary antibacterial defense depression	158
Fig. 19.	Intrapulmonary antibacterial defense depression	158
Fig. 20.	Intrapulmonary antibacterial defense depression	160
Fig. 21.	Bacterial airway clearance depression	159
Fig. 22.	Bacterial inactivation	160
Fig. 23.	Alveolar macrophage profile diameters	161
Fig. 24.	Alveolar macrophage subcellular morphological changes	162
Fig. 25.	Airway morphological response	163

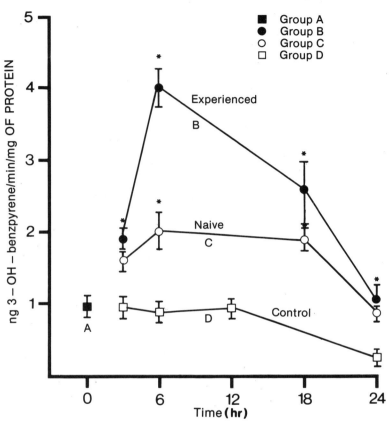

GROUP A - 24 Hr post 3 days marihuana smoke exposure.
GROUP B - Experienced (Ix post 3 days marihuana smoke exposure.)
GROUP C - Naive (only Ix smoke exposure.)
GROUP D - Controls (no exposure) basal AHH activity.

Fig. 1.   Pulmonary AHH activity induction in experienced (B) and naive (C) vs
II.3.D$_1$ control (D) animals.

Adapted from Marcotte et al,1975.

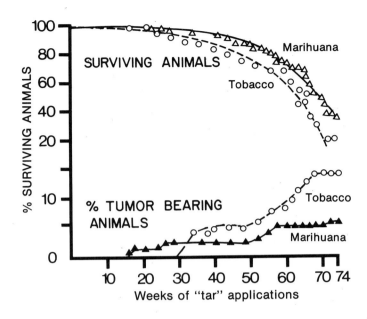

Fig. 2.   Chronic toxicity (survival rate) and tumorigenic activity of smoke
II.3.D$_1$ condensates.

Adapted from Hoffman et al., 1975.

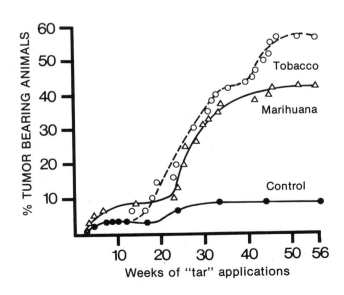

Fig. 3.   Tumor promoting activity of smoke condensates post tumor initiation
II.3.D$_1$ with DMBA.

Adapted from Hoffman et al., 1975.

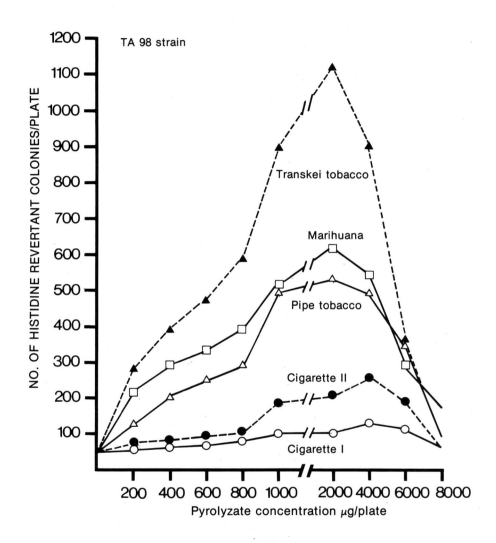

Fig. 4.
II.3.D$_1$ Mutagenic activity via reversion of histidine-requiring strains of S. typhimurium with substance pyrolyzates in the presence of microsomal fraction.

Adapted from Wehner et al., 1980.

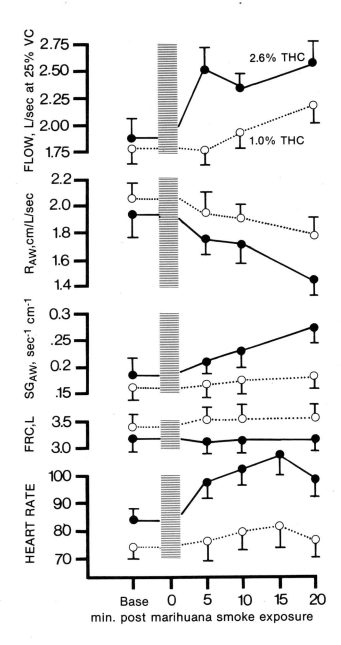

Fig. 5.
II.3.D₁

Acute pulmonary function (and heart rate) effects of marihuana smoke. Definitions: Flow (air flow rate); Raw (airway resistance); SGaw (specific airway conductance); FRC (functional residual capacity); VC (vital capacity).

Adapted from Vachon et al., 1973.

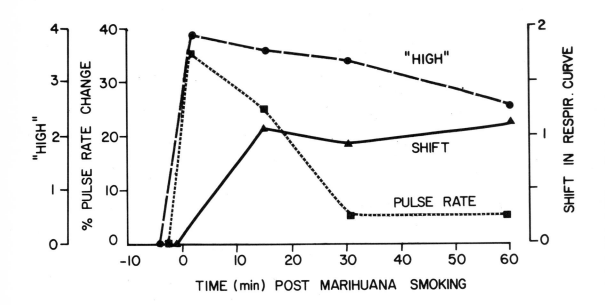

Fig. 6.   Pulse rate change and "high" post marihuana (2.2% THC) smoking with
II.3.D$_1$ displacement (shift) of the respiratory response curves (Torr Pco$_2$).

Adapted from Belleville et al., 1975.

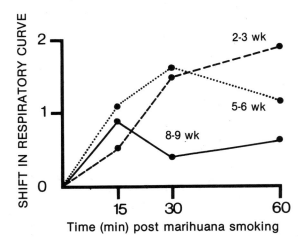

Fig. 7.   Displacement of respiratory curve (Torr Pco$_2$) post marihuana smoking
II.3.D$_1$ following various exposure periods of intoxication.

Adapted from Belleville et al., 1976.

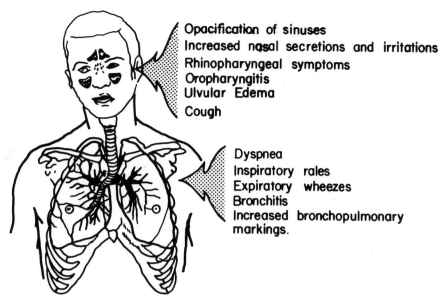

Fig. 8.
II.3.D$_1$

Hashish respiratory effects.

Adapted from Tennant et al., 1971.

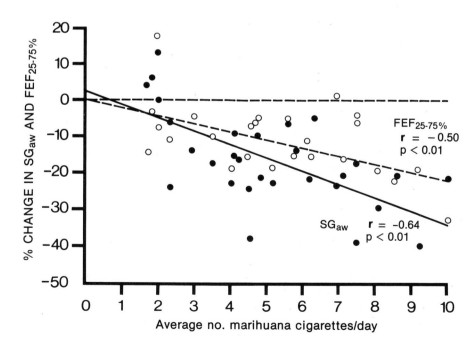

Fig. 10.
II.3.D$_1$

Pulmonary function tests indicating early airway obstruction shown to correlate with amount of marihuana smoked daily for 6-8 weeks.

Adapted from Tashkin et al., 1976.

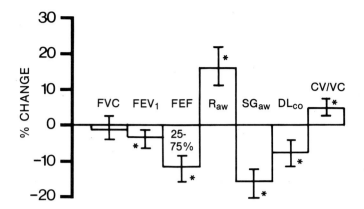

Fig. 9.   Altered pulmonary function tests indicating airway narrowing after
II.3.D$_1$ chronic daily marihuana smoking (47-59 days).
                Definitions: FVC (forced vital capacity); FEV₁ (forced expiratory
                volume/1 sec.); FEF (maximal mid-expiratory flow rate, 25-75%); Raw
                (airway resistance); SGaw (specific airway conductance); DLco (lung
                diffusing capacity for CO); CV/VC, % (closing volume as percent of
                vital capacity); * (significant change).

                Adapted from Tashkin et al., 1976.

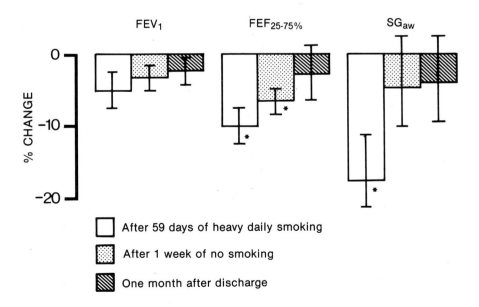

Fig. 11.   Reversibility of pulmonary impairment with cessation of chronic
II.3.D$_1$ marihuana smoking.

                Adapted from Tashkin et al., 1976.

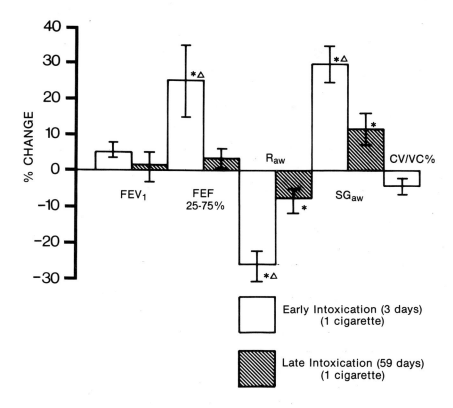

Fig. 12.
II.3.D$_1$
Partial tolerance to acute bronchodilator effect (Raw; SGaw) of marihuana.

Adapted from Tashkin et al., 1976.

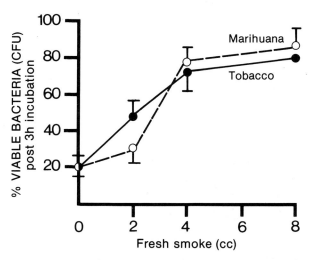

Fig. 13.
II.3.D$_1$
Depression of alveolar macrophage bactericidal activity by marihuana and tobacco. Definition: CFU (colony forming units).

Adapted from Huber et al., 1975.

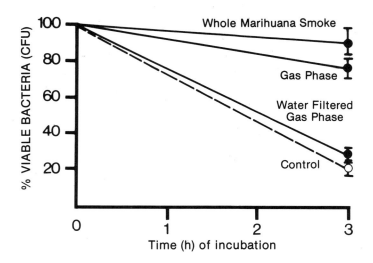

Fig. 14.   Depression of alveolar macrophage bactericidal activity by whole
II.3.D₁   marihuana smoke and its gas phase (8 ml).

Adapted from Huber et al., 1975.

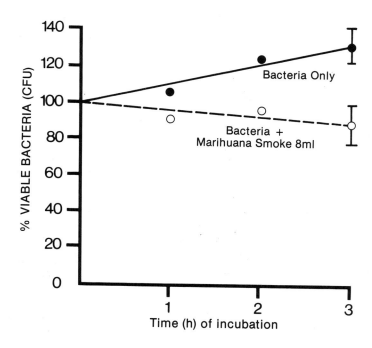

Fig. 15.   Depression of bacterial growth rates by fresh marihuana smoke in the
II.3.D₁   absence of alveolar macrophages.

Adapted from Huber et al., 1975.

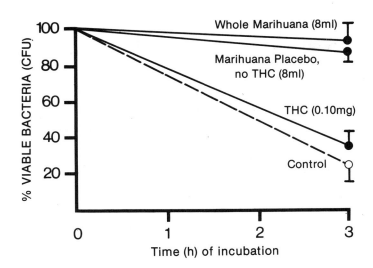

Fig. 16.
II.3.D₁

Depression of alveolar macrophage bactericidal activity by marihuana and placebo smoke, and by THC.

Adapted from Huber et al., 1975.

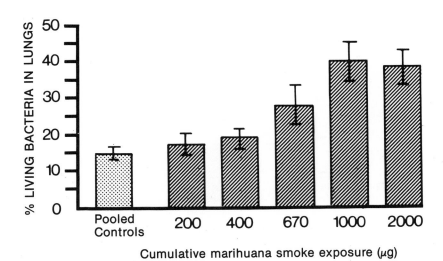

Fig. 17.
II.3.D₁

Depression of intrapulmonary antibacterial defense post acute marihuana smoke exposure.

Adapted from Huber et al., 1980.

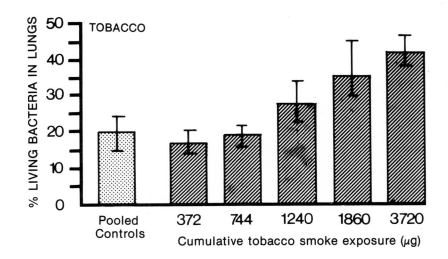

Fig. 18.   Depression of intrapulmonary antibacterial defense post acute tobacco
II.3.D$_1$ smoke exposure.

Adapted from Huber et al., 1979a.

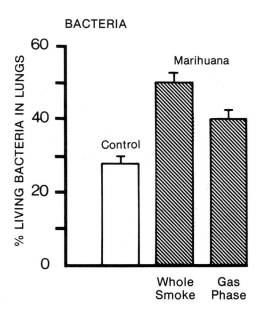

Fig. 19.   Depression of intrapulmonary antibacterial defense post acute
II.3.D$_1$ marihuana smoke and gas phase exposures.

Adapted from Huber et al., 1979b.

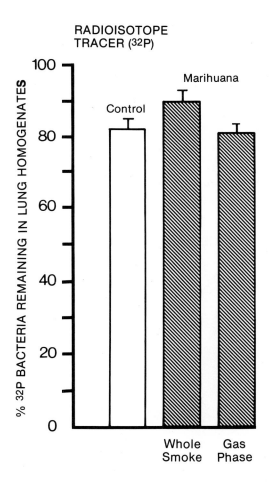

RADIOISOTOPE
TRACER (^{32}P)

Fig. 21.   Depression (slight) of bacterial airway clearance   (mucociliary trans-
II.3.D$_1$ port) post acute marihuana smoke and gas phase exposures.

Adapted from Huber et al., 1979b.

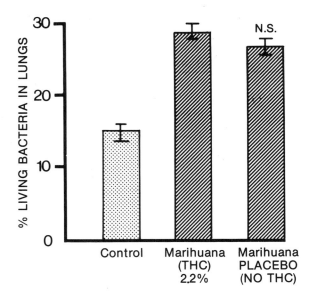

Fig. 20.   Depression of intrapulmonary antibacterial defence post acute
II.3.D$_1$ marihuana and placebo smoke exposures.

Adapted from Huber et al., 1980.

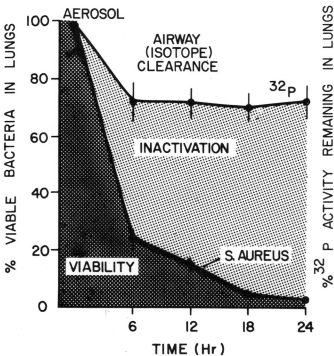

Fig. 22.   Inactivation of bacteria by normal animal lungs occurring primarily
II.3.D$_1$ deep within the lungs.

Adapted from Huber et al., 1979a.

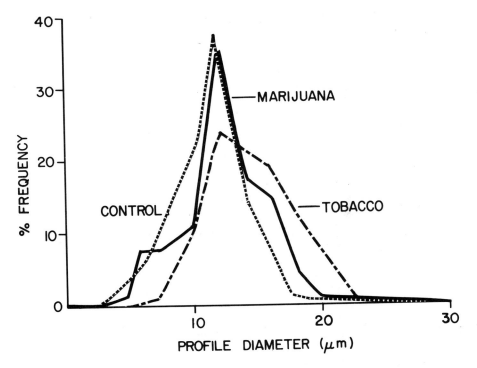

Fig. 23.
II.3.D$_1$

Frequency distribution curves of alveolar macrophage profile diameters post tobacco or marihuana smoke exposures.

Adapted from Davies et al., 1979.

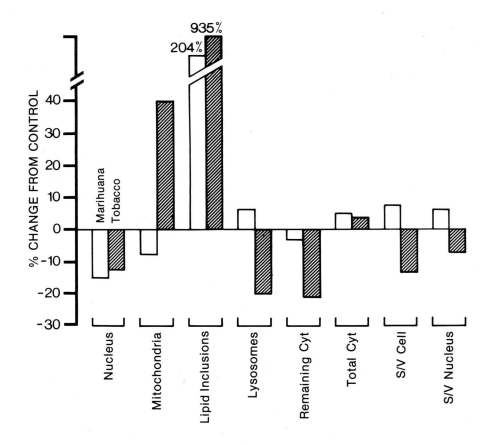

Fig. 24.   Subcellular morphological changes in alveolar macrophages post
II.3.D$_1$ marihuana or tobacco smoke exposure.

Adapted from Davies et al., 1979.

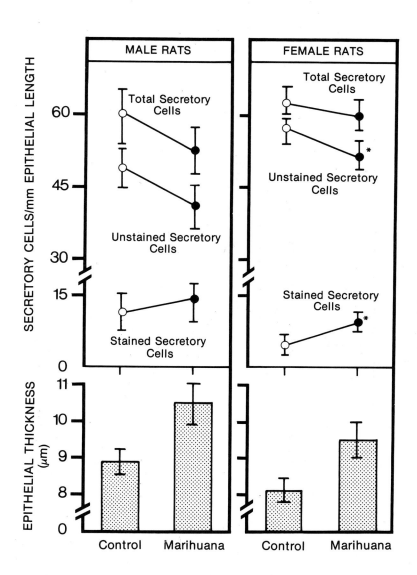

Fig. 25.   Morphological response of airway post marihuana smoke exposure.
II.3.D₁
                Adapted from Hayashi et al., 1980.

5.   Marihuana Effects on Cardiovascular System

Inhalation of materials is comparable to intravenous administration with respect to quick onset of effects and usually short duration of action because substances entering the lung are exposed to a large vascular surface area facilitating rapid absorption and distribution. The respiratory volume at the end of a long slow inhalation (manner in which marihuana is smoked) may enhance drug uptake with the possibility of inducing a rapid profound pharmacological effect(s) so as to upset homeostatic mechanisms with single acute doses while chronic doses may reset such mechanisms to new environmental (drug) conditions. Besides affecting pulmonary epithelial surfaces (e.g. smoke irritation), any active principle(s) entering the pulmonary circulation could affect the blood vessels directly as well as the heart within a short period of time. Such possibilities have been studied in animals and man exposed to marihuana.

Plasma THC profiles were found to be similar following IV THC (5 mg/2 min) and cigarette smoking (19 mg THC/5-7 min) (the smoking curve paralleling but lower (approximately 1/2 concentration) than IV curve) in 11 healthy marihuana experienced men (18-35 years of age) vs oral intake (cookie with 20 mg THC) when low irregular plasma levels were obtained probably due to erratic drug absorption (Ohlsson et al., 1980). The estimated systemic availability of THC post smoking was 18% vs oral of 6%. Both IV and inhalation routes resulted in similar time courses for plasma concentration and "high" with quick onset, declining over a 4 hour period; the "high" appearance lagging behind increasing plasma concentration indicating that brain concentration (increasing) is out of phase with plasma concentration (decreasing). Congested (red) conjunctivae were evident with THC plasma levels above 5 ng/ml, being a sensitive indicator of intoxication and plasma THC. Tachycardia was a less reliable measure of prevailing THC levels and the "high". With oral intake, similar clinical effects occurred at lower plasma concentration, having slower onset with longer duration than with the other 2 administration routes.

(a)   Acute and Short Term Effects

Acute cardiovascular effects of inhaled marihuana, THC (both with 20 mg THC) vs. placebo were studied in 10 young (19-24 years of age) normal male volunteers who had used marihuana previously (Savary et al., 1974). Cardiovascular measurements were made in subjects resting in the supine position prior to and following drug inhalation (40, 70, 130 minutes) in a double-blind fashion, each subject serving as his own control. Placebo had no effects. Both marihuana and THC increased HR (heart rate) by 17 and 9 beats/minute respectively, systolic blood pressure 11 and 6 mm Hg, cardiac output 1.23 and 1.20 l/minute, VCF (mean velocity of ventricular circumferential fiber shortening) 0.34 and 0.12 circumference/second and decreased duration of ventricular diastole 198 and 110 msec, with some decrease in peripheral resistance 8 and 13% suggesting a reflex tachycardia response (via baroreceptors) to peripheral vasodilation effects of the cannabinoids; the inotropic effect being related to HR changes. Marihuana smoking (one cigarette with 20 mg THC) by 8 healthy cannabis experienced men did not affect platelet counts in whole blood or in platelet rich plasma but significantly decreased platelet aggregation (induced by 0.5 and 1 µg ADP) at the 90 minute post smoking period (vs pre-smoking) indicating possible blood coaguability impairment (Schaefer et al., 1979). The expected increased aggregation occurred with increasing ADP doses (0.25, 0.5, 1.0 µg) in both pre and post smoking blood samples.

Short term (64 days intoxication with at least 1 marihuana cigarette with 20 mg THC/day) heart rate effects were studied in 30 young (21-35 years of age) male moderate (3-6 joints/week) and heavy (at least 1 joint/day) marihuana smokers with minimal use of other drugs in the previous 6 months and medically sound (Nowlan and Cohen, 1977). HR (heart rate; radial pulse/minute in sitting position) and subjective "high" feeling were asessed pre and post smoking (0, 15, 30, 60, 120 minutes) of the first compulsory "joint" of each day (9-12 hours abstinent from previous day's use). The daily number of cigarettes smoked ranged from 1.7-10 (average 5.28; each 900 mg marihuana cigarette with 2.2% THC or 19.8 mg THC) or 33.7-198.7 mg THC; 4 groups (7-8 subjects each) of smokers being represented as light (average 2.1 cigarettes/day), low-moderate (4.3 cigarettes/day) with the 2 groups combined to form the light smoker group because of similar parameter changes, high-moderate (6.2 cigarettes/day; became moderate group), and heavy (8.5 cigarettes/day) users. Consumption increased with time except for the lightest smokers; a 1 week abstinence not altering rate of consumption (indicating that tolerance was still present). Development of tolerance was observed as decreased chronotropic (HR) and psychotropic ("high") effects within the first half of the smoking period with decreased peak effects being evident by the second week of intoxication (Fig. 1). It is dose-related with light smokers showing a greater HR change/first week vs heaviest smokers (probably some pre-established tolerance effect); moderate smokers showing an intermediate effect (Fig. 2). Light smokers developed tolerance to HR change gradually over the study period while moderate and heavy smokers showed an abrupt decrease to change within 2-4 weeks of the smoking session. During the 9th week of intoxication the 2 hour post smoking assessment of HR revealed values below pre-intoxication rates for that week (approaching bradycardia seen in animals?). With respect to subjective feeling of euphoria, heavy smokers had a lesser "high" effect than other smokers (Fig. 3). All groups developed tolerance to the "high" by the 5th week noted as reduced intensity and duration of action. Thus tolerance develops to HR changes and euphoria within a relatively short period (14-21 days) of daily smoking of 2 marihuana cigarettes with 20 mg THC/cigarette (critical dose not established). A mild withdrawal was observed during a week of abstinence especially with the heaviest smokers noted as irritability, restlessness, sleeplessness, loss of appetite, mild nausea, which are considered to be physiological and psychological adjustments following 64 days of intoxication. Resumption of smoking did not result in full responsiveness indicating that some acquired tolerance was still present. The suggestion (Schaeffer et al., 1975) that marihuana dosage (as THC) may be controlled via HR is therefore not plausible because of individual variation re tolerance state, difficulty in controlling an involuntary variable, and daily variation in responsiveness.

A dose-response double-blind THC study was conducted in 15 students (8 with prior marihuana experience) who smoked, at weekly intervals, 500 mg marihuana cigarettes with varying concentrations of THC (0, 6.25, 12.5, 25 and 50 µg/kg) (Kiplinger et al., 1971). Linear dose-dependent impairments occurred for motor and mental performance, and stability of stance. Dose-dependent increased scores were obtained for subjective response and conjunctival injection (reddening of eyes), the latter showing a peak effect at 1 hour following smoking (Fig. 4). The increased heart rate (dose-dependent) showed a peak at 20 minutes (time of first measurement) following smoking with a return to normal by 85 minutes with 6.25-25 µg/kg THC doses (Fig. 5). Another study compared placebo marihuana with 10 mg THC (in placebo and natural marihuana) smoked (10 minutes/cigarette) by 12 (male, 21-26 years of age) chronic marihuana users (used 50-500x) revealing a correlation between HR increases and subjective effects (Galanter et al., 1972). HR correlated with plasma THC concentration (both peaking 16 minutes after onset of smoking with the rapid phase of the decline occurring within 2 hours) while subjective effects lagged behind (peaking at 1 hour and declining more slowly over 4 hours) (Fig. 6). In 3 subjects in whom plasma THC levels were followed, peak THC concentrations varied (67, 37, 21 ng/ml) indicating variability in the amount of THC absorbed following smoking even under standardized smoking conditions (probably due to differences in depth of inhalation which is difficult to control). Plasma THC concentration appeared to be more closely related to HR changes than to subjective changes.

Since reddening of eyes commonly occurs with marihuana use, how would it affect diseased eyes such as glaucoma or ocular hypertension considered to be the second most common cause of blindness? Increased pressure within the eyeball or intraocular pressure leads to damage of the optic disc with gradual loss of vision due to restricted outflow of aqueous humor through canal of Schlemm or sinus venosus situated at the angle between the base of the iris and cornea (Fig. 7). Aqueous humor is formed by ciliary processes, passing through the posterior chamber and pupil into the anterior chamber where it is absorbed into the venous system of the canal of Schlemm. A study (Merritt et al., 1980) was undertaken in 18 (12 males, 6 females) glaucoma (31 eyes; 6 patients with secondary glaucoma, 12 with primary open angle glaucoma) patients (28-71 years of age with average 45 years) with normal cardiac, neurological, and psychiatric function (excluding females in child-bearing years), 9 of whom had used marihuana at least once. Medication for glaucoma was discontinued 48 hours prior to the treatment period. Baseline sitting blood pressure, heart rate, and IOP (intraocular pressure via applanation tonometer which eliminates scleral resistance effects) were measured every 5 minutes/15-20 minutes. A 900 mg marihuana cigarette (2% THC) or placebo was smoked/10-20 minutes repeating parameter measurements at 0.25, 0.5, 1, 1.5, 2, 2.5, 3, and 4 hours. Marihuana inhalation resulted in:

(a) tachycardia with onset in 2-3 minutes, peak maximum effect (av 123 beats/minute) at 15 minutes and duration of 1.5-2 hours (Fig. 8;

(b) decreased IOP within the first half hour with maximum effect (av 7mm Hg) at 1.5 hours and duration of at least 4 hours (Fig. 9); and

(c) both systolic and diastolic blood pressures decreasing maximally by 1 hour, systolic (av 11 mm Hg) effect being greater than the diastolic (av 5 mm Hg) effect (Fig. 10).

In 5 cases the maximum decrease in blood pressure (inaudible) occurred within 10-15 minutes of smoking a cigarette with postural hypotension (considered to be a serious side-effect), decreased heart rate (60 beats/minute), and decreased intraocular pressure (in good eye to 1-2 mm Hg and 26 mm Hg in diseased eye) (Fig. 11). When this naive subject was placed in a reclining position, both blood pressure (to 110 mm Hg) and IOP (to 5 mm Hg in good eye, 41 mm Hg in diseased eye) were increased. In a daily marihuana user, 2 marihuana cigarettes precipitated a similar postural hypotensive reaction (Fig. 12). When a compensatory increase in heart rate does not occur readily, postural hypotension results. Other untoward effects (more severe in naive) included anxiety with tachycardia and palpitations (rather than euphoria in 8 naive subjects), alterations in sensorium in 18 (euphoria, hunger, thirst, drowsy, feeling cold), and bulbar conjunctival hyperemia and ptosis in 9 patients. Mechanism (central or direct ocular effect) for decreased IOP is unknown. Bronchodilation was noted in one asthmatic patient. It was felt that frequency and severity of side-effects detracted from the therapeutic use of inhaled or smoked marihuana for glaucoma patients.

Visual function (acuity, glare susceptibility, dark and light adaptation) may be influenced by pupil size. In a study using 10 men (20-32 years of age) acting as their own control, 5 experimental treatments were administered consisting of an alcohol drink/20 minutes (0.75 ml/kg of 95% ethanol in fruit juice), a marihuana cigarette (8 or 15 mg THC), a combination of alcohol and 15 mg THC, and a placebo (Brown et al., 1977). Pupil diameters were measured (double-blind) from eye photographs taken prior to and following drug intake (40, 120 and 300 minutes) as were blood alcohol levels and subjective "high" ratings. At low photopic light levels, alcohol did not significantly affect pupil diameter (insignificant pupil size decrease at the 2 hour interval); the blood alcohol level peaking at 1-2 hours with a similar time course for "high" ratings. A dose-related decrease in pupil diameter occurred with marihuana (7.4% decrease at 40 minutes post 15 mg THC); pulse rate and "high" ratings peaking around the 1 hour interval. Combined alcohol and marihuana produced insignificant pupil changes (very slight decrease at 40 minutes period) with elevated blood alcohol level, pulse rate, and "high"; the pupil perhaps being less responsive to light. Pupil constriction may not only alter visual function but may facilitate fluid drainage from the anterior eye chamber helping to decrease intraocular pressure in glaucoma patients (how significantly?).

(b) Possible Mechanism of Action

The role of adrenergic mechanisms with respect to cardiovascular marihuana effects was studied in 4/10 (9 males, one female) naive volunteers (physicians 30-40 years of age) who had ceased using tobacco (amount and duration of use not stated) one year earlier (Beaconsfield et al., 1972). A 1 gm marihuana cigarette (with 10 mg THC) was smoked/10 minutes through a holder by 10 volunteers. The parameters measured were limb blood flow, blood pressure (b.p.), heart rate (HR), respiratory rate and depth, cardiac activity (ECG), skin and rectosigmoid temperatures, being reported as means/3 minute periods. Control measurements/30 minute period were made at rest after an overnight fast, followed by measurements during and at the end of smoking, and during 1 hour post smoking. One week following the marihuana study in 6 subjects, the effects of tobacco smoke (2 French cigarettes/10 minutes) were investigated in 3/6 subjects while in another 4 individuals the effects of propanolol (40 mg p.o. q. 6 h./48 hours; β-adrenergic blocker), atropine (0.6 mg. s.c.; anticholinergic), or epinephrine (or norephineprine) (IV infusion 10 µg/minute/10 minutes; sympathomimetics) were followed prior to and after smoking 1 marihuana cigarette. Marihuana smoking

(1) increased HR to a maximum of 92 beats/minute at 30 minutes post smoking (89 at 1 hour) vs control of 66 beats/minute,

(2) revealed ECG changes (increased width and decreased amplitude of P-wave in lead 2, inversion of T-wave in lead 3 in 5/6 subjects during and 30 minutes post smoking,

(3) slightly increased b.p. from control (119/74 to 129/78 at 1 minute and 126/78 at 30 minutes post smoking) without respiratory changes,

(4) increased cutaneous toe temperature (from 26.3°C to 27.7°C within 1 minute of having smoked marihuana with 27.8°C noted at the 30 minute period) without rectosigmoid temperature changes,

(5) increased peripheral blood flow (ml/100 ml tissue/minute) in the forearm (control 5.4 → 8.2 at 1 minute → 7.7 at 30 minutes post smoking), calf (2.6 → 5.0 → 3.6), with a small change in hand blood flow (3.1 → 4.6 → 4.0); the latter flow not being influenced by mental arithmetic nor ice, stimulants that normally cause reduced blood flow in the hand. Tobacco smoking

    (a) increased HR by 15 beats/minute (average) during smoking, returning to control values by 30 minutes,

    (b) increased systolic and diastolic pressures by 10 and 5 mm Hg respectively for about 30 minutes,

    (c) insignificantly changed forearm and calf blood flows (mean 4.8 → 5.1 ml/100 ml tissue/minute) with decreased flow in the hand (4.4 → 1.9 with average of 4 ml at 30 minutes),

    (d) decreased cutaneous temperature (25.9 → 23°C/duration of experiment) without rectosigmoid temperature change.

The effects of pharmacological agents on the cardiovascular effects of cannabis smoking included:

(1) propanolol preventing tachycardia and increased forearm blood flow due to cannabis,

(2) atropine enhancing tachycardia and increased b.p.,

(3) epinephrine intensifying HR (100 beats/minute) and forearm blood flow with a greater decrease in diastolic than systolic b.p.; norepinephrine increasing systolic and diastolic b.p., and, decreasing HR and peripheral blood flow prior to and following cannabis use.

The conclusions drawn from this investigation were:

(1) marihuana smoking resulted in peripheral vasodilation (especially in skeletal muscle) with increased cutaneous temperature change, tachycardia, and some E.C.G. changes,

(2) the peripheral vascular responses of tobacco differed from cannabis due to epinephrine release with increased blood levels of some metabolites not seen with marihuana,

(3) reflex vascular response was not as rapid with marihuana during minor stress (arithmetical problems, ice) situations though major stress may overcome sluggish response (i.e. a matter of dose or degree),

(4) β-adrenergic vascular mechanisms were involved in tachycardia (β_1) and increased peripheral blood flow (β_2) produced by cannabis, the former response not being an atropine-like effect,

(5) the suggested clinical significance of these findings included:

(a) suspicion of prior marihuana use in accident victims with persistent tachycardia, and

(b) caution in using atropine or local anesthetics containing epinephrine as premedication in recent marihuana users when tachycardia may be prolonged.

Other possible factors contributing to the above results should be considered. The smoking (burning) of any material emits CO (carbon monoxide) gas, which when inhaled results in COHb (carboxy hemoglobin) leading to hypoxia giving rise to peripheral vasodilation followed by compensatory increased heart rate. The heart is sensitive to hypoxia (with less oxygen available, the heart works harder resulting in increased b.p. & HR) and may be permanently damaged by the presence of COHb in the blood. Chronic CO gas exposure facilitates development of atherosclerosis. Abnormal ECG tracings due to CO have been observed as sinus tachycardia, T-wave abnormalities, ST-segment depression and atrial fibrillation; ischemic changes and subendocardial infarction having been observed. Even passive exposure to CO in those with heart disease places a strain on heart function with possible inability to compensate for hypoxia (vs healthy individuals who respond to hypoxia or stress via increasing cardiac output and increasing blood flow to critical organs). Conditions that lower the threshold to CO effects include drugs, alcohol, cardiac and respiratory disease, pregnancy, and anemia. Since the volunteers in the above study were former tobacco smokers, the possibility of some cardiac and respiratory alterations exists (status of these parameters not reported). The peripheral vascular effects of tobacco smoking (net change being vasoconstriction) differed from marihuana effects (vasodilation) evidenced from peripheral blood flow and temperature recordings. Inhalation of nicotine is known to stimulate the release of epinephrine resulting in increased HR, increased b.p., vasoconstriction (decreasing blood to tissues), increased coronary flow (due to increased cardiac work, increased blood pressure, increased cardiac output), increased blood sugar, and increased tendency for blood to clot. Both propanolol (β-adrenergic blocker) and atropine (anticholinergic) are competative antagonists to adrenergic (β-receptors) and parasympathetic systems respectively meaning that blocks may be overcome by increasing the concentrations of their respective agonists; the former blocking the reflex response to cannabis effects while atropine had additive cardiovascular effects. At the dose, route, and infusion rate of epinephrine used in the above study, a greater β-adrenergic receptor response would be expected which occurred as increased peripheral blood flow (vasodilation) being additive to that of cannabis effect as was increased HR (cardiac stimulation with epinephrine and reflex with marihuana) and significant decrease in diastolic blood pressure (the moderate increase in systolic by epinephrine being offset by the greater effect due to cannabis). (Cardiac electrical changes (ECG) observed with larger epinephrine doses are similar to those of anginal attacks (spontaneous or epinephrine-induced; ST-segment downward deviation) produced by myocardial hypoxia due to the inability of coronary blood flow to keep pace with the increased oxygen requirement of the heart stimulated by epinephrine). Norepinephrine is a purer α-adrenergic substance resulting in vasoconstriction and pressor (increased b.p.) responses overriding cannabis effects. It appears that the adrenergic system is involved as a normal autoregulatory or compensatory mechanism to altered physiological function produced by drug(s) or active constituents in preparations such as marihuana and tobacco which are usually smoked.

Confirmation and extension of the above findings have been reported in a study (Weiss et al., 1972) using oral THC (equivalent to 1 marihuana cigarette) and placebo in regular users (habit not specified). A single blind cross-over study was undertaken in 8 healthy regular marihuana users (23-27 years of age) who abstained from drugs, including marihuana, 1 week prior to the study and who were on a low catecholamine diet 24 hours pre study until its completion. The subjects fasted the night before and during the study period, with 240 ml orange juice given 2 hours before starting the study. The oral dose of THC used was 0.3 mg/kg (dissolved in 1 ml 95% ethanol diluted in cherry syrup and swallowed in 30 secs), the equivalent to smoking 1 marihuana cigarette with 5 mg THC (this would mean 5 mg absorbed according to quoted potency figure of smoked marihuana having 3x oral potency such that an equivalent marihuana cigarette would contain 1% THC (10 mg)). Placebo consisted of ethanol and cherry syrup. Four subjects received radiolabelled THC (C^{14}-THC, 10 µc/0.5 mg added to unlabelled drug). Baseline measurements (2 sets) were taken over a 60 minute period from subjects lying on a tilt table prior to treatment with oral THC or placebo (total study time, 5 hours). The cardiovascular parameters measured as well as their respective results included:

(1) HR (heart rate, beats/minute) calculated from ECG taken q 30 minutes in recumbent position/5 minutes and in head-up tilt to 70° position/5 minutes, expressed as a mean of 4 to 5, 20 second intervals/each 5 minute period, as well as noting the change in HR from the recumbent to tilt position. During recumbent and tilt positions, the HR increased significantly with drug treatment vs placebo and vs control values as it did in changing from recumbent to tilt position (Fig. 13). The maximum effect for the 3 (position) assessments occurred at 3 hours post drug persisting for 4 (upright, changing positions) to 5 (recumbent) hours post drug.

(2) MBP (mean arterial blood pressure, mm Hg = average diastolic pressure + 1/3 average pulse pressure) measured via an ultrasonic device attached to a pneumatic cuff placed over the upper arm registering systolic and diastolic pressures automatically on a mercury manometer, taken q 1 minute beginning 5 minutes pre and continuing 5 minutes post tilt position, repeating q 30 minutes. During the recumbent position, the average MBP increased (maximum at 2 hours) with drug treatment vs placebo and control, while during the tilt position it decreased slightly (lowest at 3 hour interval) with slight increase with placebo vs control (Fig. 14). The change noted from recumbent to tilt position was less for drug than for placebo and control, decreasing with time to a nadir at the 4th hour interval. Orthostatic hypotensive and presyncope manifestations occurred in 7/8 subjects in the first 2-3 minutes post tilt during the 2nd-3rd hour post THC intake (when MBP fell slightly) requiring immediate return to the recumbent position.

(3) PEP (ventricular pre-ejection period, msecs.) measured via simultaneous recording (q 30 minutes in recumbent position) from ECG, phonocardiogram (graphic display of heart sounds), and external carotid (artery) pressure (curve) transducer, and calculated using a mean of 10 cycles uncorrected for HR. PEP = $Q.S_2$ interval - LVET (left ventricular ejection time) (Fig. 15). The $Q.S_2$ interval is the interval from the onset of the QRS complex (ECG) to the first high frequency component of the second heart sound (phonocardiogram). LVET is the interval from the onset of the upstroke of the carotid pressure curve to the trough of the incisura (dicrotic notch). (Systolic time interval measurements are used as an index of left ventricular function). The PEP significantly shortened post THC vs placebo and controls; the greatest shortening occurring within the first hour of drug intake slowly returning toward control values over a 5 hour period with placebo having increased PEP very slightly over time (Fig. 16).

(4) VT (open venous tone) measured via an equilibration technique (q 30 minutes in recumbent position) calculated as a ratio of the increase in venous pressure (mm Hg)/the increase in forearm volume (ml). Statistically significant changes were not evident over time for VT effects, although a slight increase occurred post THC vs placebo (Fig. 17).

(5) RVC (reflex venoconstriction) expressed as increase in venous pressure (mm Hg) post maximal deep breath (done immediately after each VT) was used as index of venomotor reactivity. Following THC intake, RVC was attenuated in all and transiently abolished in 4 subjects with the greatest fall occurring during the second and third hours followed by a very slow recovery (Fig. 17).

(6) FBF (forearm blood flow, ml/100 gm/minute) measured by a venous occlusion technique as percent change in forearm circumference in recumbent and head-up tilt positions (q 30 minutes x 4) with HR and blood pressure being monitored. FBF, post THC, increased linearly over time vs placebo and control when in the recumbent position, not evident during the upright position (tilt). The decrease in FBF observed in changing from recumbent to upright positions became greater with time vs placebo and control (Fig. 18).

(7) FC (forearm conductance) = 1/forearm vascular resistance or FBF/MBP x 10^{-3} U (units). The FC results resembled those of FBF with the decrease in FC occurring with changing from recumbent to tilt positions being linear with time (Fig. 19).

To evaluate the gastrointestinal absorption of oral THC, plasma THC and its metabolites were determined in blood samples from 4 subjects obtained 0, 0.5, 1, 2, 3, 4, 8 and 24 hours following oral intake of C^{14}-THC. The time course of THC (and metabolites) plasma levels revealed a peak level at 3 hours (associated with peak circulatory changes) with a gradual decline over the next 21 hours (associated with persistence of circulatory effects consistent with the long plasma half-life of THC) (Fig. 20). Gastrointestinal absorption was 95% (5% unchanged in feces). Urinary catecholamines (free epinephrine and norepinephrine) were determined in urine samples obtained over a 24 hour period (two 6 hour aliquots and one 12 hour aliquot). Epinephrine excretion during the first 6 hour period following THC intake was greater than for placebo and for the other three 6 hour periods whereas norepinephrine was not significantly altered by THC. No significant intersubject correlations were evident between epinephrine excretion and circulatory effects known to be affected by intravenous epinephrine (HR, PEP, FBF, FC, MBP). To establish that the THC dose used had pharmacological activity, the psychological effects of THC were assessed by subjective reports of time of onset, peak, duration, and characteristics of drug effect (which would probably depend upon previous cannabis experience); objective observations of behavioural changes; and quantitative evaluation via symptom-sign questionnaire (5 subjects) at the end of each study period. The time of onset of subjective effects averaged 45 minutes (30-60 minutes), peaking at 2.4 hours average (1-3.5 hour; about 0.5 hours prior to peak plasma level) with a duration of 3 to more than 6 hours. The symptom-sign test scores post THC were higher than for placebo. It was concluded that following a pharmacologically active oral dose of THC (adequately absorbed noted by THC plasma levels and psychological effects), the cardiovascular effects elicited (shorten PEP, ↑ HR, ↑ FBF, ↑ VT) were similar to those observed with epinephrine intravenous infusion and could involve the sympathoadrenal system (inferred from increased epinephrine excretion). Blood pressure changes varied with posture, increasing in the recumbent position and deceasing in the upright (tilt) position; peak effects occurring at 2-3 hours with 7/8 subjects presenting with orthostatic hypotension and presyncope. Arteriolar constriction noted in the upright position (↓ FBF, ↓ FC, ↑ HR) was not opposed by THC. The shortened PEP with increased heart rate is a reflection of covariation of atrial chronotropic and ventricular inotropic influences. Since the RVC results could not be explained, it was felt that THC circulatory effects may be due to something other than increased sympathoadrenal activity (perhaps a non-specific smooth muscle relaxant?; however the effects of upright position was not tested on this parameter thereby not ruling out sympathoadrenal system completely). Individual variation re responses noted in statistical analysis used, indicated drug-subject interaction (could indicate a difference in degree of tolerance (or habit) to the drug THC).

Another investigation studied STI (systolic time intervals; left ventricular) in 10 resting (supine and fasting basal state) normal males (22-30 years of age with a habit of less than 1x/week marihuana use; 3 individuals never having used the drug) receiving THC intravenously at 1 mg/minute (25 ug/kg dose ≡ smoking 1 marihuana cigarette with approximately 5 mg THC in a 70-80 kg person) as well as noting if prior β-adrenergic blockade (0.1 mg/kg propanolol IV) altered marihuana cardiovascular responses in another 9 age-matched individuals (Kanakis et al., 1976). Medication was injected into tubing connected to an indwelling needle in the dorsum of the left hand out of sight of the subject so that time of injection was unknown to the individual. As in the preceding study, simultaneous recordings were obtained of ECG, phonocardiogram and carotid pulse tracings; arterial pressure being measured with a cuff sphygmomanometer. STI (QS_2, LVET, PEP) represented an average of 10 consecutive beats corrected (Q_{2_c}, $LVET_c$) for effects of HR (heart rate) which was measured from the ECG (60/R-R interval). Control measurements were an average of 3 recordings taken at 5 minute intervals prior to drug administration. THC effects were noted at 5, 10, 15, 30, 60, 90 and 120 minutes post injection with and without prior propanolol injection (propanolol effects noted at 5, 6, and 7 minutes post injection but pre THC injection). At the end of the study adequacy of β-blockade was tested in 8 subjects with isoproterenol (2.5 µg/minute/5 minutes), a β-adrenergic, which did not alter HR. THC peak effects for STI and HR occurred 5-25 minutes post injection with HR returning to control values at 30-120 minutes (90 minutes average) (Fig. 21). Mean peak HR increased 32 ± 7 beats/minute with insignificant b.p. (blood pressure) changes (slight increase in systolic, negligible re diastolic) post THC. Mean STI changes included Q_{2_c} increase of 17 ± 4.2 msecs, $LVET_c$ increase by 24 ± 4.0 msecs. and PEP decrease of 19 ± 5.1 msecs. Propanolol caused a slight decrease in HR and systolic b.p. with increases in QS_2 and PEP without a significant $LVET_c$ change. THC effects in β-adrenergic blocked subjects were HR increase by 19 ± 1.8 beats/minute with insignificant b.p. changes (very slight increase in diastolic), QS_{2_c} increase by 15 ± 3.8 msecs., $LVET_c$ increase of 14 ± 3.4 msecs and insignificant PEP decrease of 7 msecs (Fig. 22). Prior β-adrenergic blockade lessened THC cardiovascular effects; the dose of the blocker perhaps being insufficient to block completely the possible reflex sympathetic activity (secondary to decreased peripheral resistance) induced by THC (or other mechanisms may also be involved). Since PEP change (decrease) post THC is consistent with increased rate of isovolumic pressure rise with constant afterload (insignificant b.p.   change), the increased LVET may be due to increased venous return with increased cardiac output and stroke volume.   That is, the increase in preload could explain the enhanced cardiac performance noted as decreased PEP post THC.

In two other studies in which β-adrenergic blockade was used, results were contradictory. In one study (Bright et al., 1971), oral propanolol (40 mg q.i.d.) was used 24 hours prior to marihuana test while in the other (Tashkin et al., 1978b) intraveous propanolol (0.2 mg/kg) was used 10 minutes prior to marihuana smoking. In the former study (Bright et al., 1971), the increased heart rate due to marihuana was blocked (agreeing with the above oral propanolol study) while in the latter study (Tashkin et al., 1978b), a block was not evident (partial block reported in above IV propanolol study). With respect to the intravenous (propanolol or saline; directly into vein or via tubing?) study (Tashkin et al., 1978b) (unpublished data presented at a conference), 11 male experienced marihuana users (degree of tolerance nor posture?) smoked either a marihuana cigarette with 10 mg THC or a placebo cigarette 10 minutes after IV injections, noting the effects on HR (heart rate). In the other study (Bright et al., 1971), the maximum increase in HR by 17-20 beats/minute occurred at 20 minutes post marihuana (25 μg THC/kg) smoking in 3 resting recumbent normal healthy males (21-34 years of age, previous marihuana use?) while following IV (via tubing of continual IV drip) isoproterenol (3 μg/15 seconds) (pure β-adrenergic drug), the HR increased by 20-35 beats/minute.   The parameters studied were obtained from ECG, phono-cardiogram and carotid pulse wave tracings. One of the subjects was excluded from the propanolol test because of development of a cardiac arrhythmia of bigeminy (a premature ventricular contraction after each normal heart beat or 2 beats close together with a pause after each pair of beats) following isoproterenol or marihuana (Fig. 23). In the other 2 subjects the resting Weissler ratio (PEP/LVET; non-invasive estimation of cardiac output change which depends on the duration of certain phases (time intervals) of the heart's electromechanical cycle, i.e., an index of left ventricular function) was normal (0.345), decreasing at peak HR due to isoproterenol (correlating with increased ventricular function) which was absent with prior propanolol treatment. Propanolol, which did not alter normal baseline ratios, increased the ratio in 1 subject post marihuana use (little change in other subject) indicating decreased cardiac output (or stroke volume). Conjunctival reddening seen post marihuana was much less with prior propanolol administration to marihuana use. Again a β-adrenergic mechanism was implicated in both HR and conjunctival reddening changes but cardiac function (different ratios) intimated another mechanism other than a β-effect (perhaps an α-effect?).

From the above examples of studies dealing with possible mechanism of marihuana cardio-vascular effects, differences in marihuana (THC) response following β-adrenergic blockade may be due to route (oral, IV, stress of needle), frequency and duration of β-blocker administration, tolerance of subjects to marihuana (THC) (naive, degree of experience), as well as the possibility of the existence of another mechanism in addition to or simulating β-adrenergic effects.

Ultrasound measures of left ventricular function (Vcf; mean rate of internal cardiac diameter shortening) via (serial) echocardiograms were obtained from 14 supine healthy men (22-31 years of age with casual marihuana experience) prior to (control; tobacco abstinence for several hours and 2 hours post caffeine-free liquid meal) and following (standardized) smoking (over 10 minute period) of marihuana (2.1% THC stated to be equivalent to 6 mg THC(?)) or placebo cigarettes (1 week apart in double-blind cross-over design) at 0, 10, 30, 60, 120 and 180 minutes (Gash et al., 1978). Simultaneous carotid pulse tracings and ECG (lead II) recordings were also obtained; b.p. being measured by cuff sphygmomanometer. Plasma NE (norepinephrine) levels were determined in 8 subjects   (4/14 + 4 additional subjects) in the supine and standing positions pre (control) and post (10, 30, 120 minutes) smoking marihuana or placebo cigarettes. HR increased significantly over control and placebo values for up to 120 minutes post marihuana with systolic and diastolic b.p. increases being statistically insignificant. Echo measures of Vcf and Vpw (systolic posterior wall excursion) increased (vs control and placebo) at 10, 30, and 60 minutes post marihuana, this alteration in left ventricular performance being due to decreased LVET (left ventricular ejection time). Thus, the increased HR in healthy casual marihuana users appears to have a positive inotropic effect resulting in increased ventricular per-formance (1 hour) which was due to decreased LVET with little change in left ventricular dimensions. An increase in plasma NE levels (supine position) was noted 30 and 120 minutes post acute marihuana use vs control and placebo, a similar effect being seen with smoking of 2 nicotine cigarettes with lower plasma NE levels (vs marihuana) lasting 20 minutes. COHb increase is common for both nicotine and marihuana smoking effects. After standing, both placebo and marihuana smoking produced increased plasma NE levels indicating sympathetic nervous system capability of responding to position changes. Postural hypotension did not occur in this group of subjects. ECG alterations (e.g. PVCs) also did not occur. It was suggested that the alterations of increased plasma NE levels and tachycardia, being similar to nicotine-cigarette effects, could be harmful in cardiovascular diseased states.

Some drugs (pentobarbital, quinidine, propanolol) which depress cardiac contractility "in-vitro", alter cardiac microsomal CaATPase (membrane bound enzyme) activity; cardiac function being related to intracellular ATPase activity. CaATPase is associated with Ca (calcium) transport; intracellular myocardial Ca availability being related to cardiac function. Concentration dependent inhibition of cardiac microsomal CaATPase activity was found with cannabinoids (the order of potency being CBD > THC > DMHP) without shifting Ca dependency relation or availability with Ca uptake inhibition by CBD and THC. Since cardiac contractile dysfunction is associated with lower availability of Ca, inhibition of cardiac microsomal Ca uptake may depress cardiac contractility (Collins and Haavik, 1979).

(c) Chronic Effects

Left ventricular (cardiac) function was assessed in 21 healthy young (21-29 years of age) resting heavy cannabis users (use at least 3x/week during the previous year) prior to and following smoking (0, 15, 30 minutes post) of 1 (over a 10 minute period) to 3 marihuana cigarettes (900 mg marihuana cigarette with 2.2% THC) during various periods of a 94 day hospital stay (when marihuana was smoked ad lib with abstinent periods at the beginning of the study (1st 11 days) and toward the end of the study (76th to 82nd day)) via an indicator dye dilution technique in 6 fasting subjects (for CO (cardiac output) estimation during early intoxication period of the 1st 11 days of heavy smoking (amount?)) and via simultaneous recordings of echocardiogram (CO and stroke volume), ECG, phonocardiogram and indirect carotid pulse (HR and STI (systolic time intervals)) tracings in 2/6 + 15 other subjects during early (1-11 days) and late (37-57 days) marihuana intoxication periods; b.p. (blood pressure) being measured with a sphygmomanometer (in the echocardiographic studies, 17 age-matched experienced users (posture ?) had b.p. measured prior to and following smoking of 1 marihuana cigarette at the 3rd and 27th day of daily marihuana intoxication) (Tashkin et al., 1977). This investigation was attempting to assess the effect of long term marihuana smoking on short term cardiac response (CO and myocardial contractility) to cannabis intoxication. The results were reported as percent change from baseline values. The indicator dye dilution technique revealed the following changes after smoking 1 marihuana cigarette/10 minutes during the early intoxication period (1-11 days daily ad lib marihuana smoking) (Fig. 24):

(1) HR increased 53% immediately post smoking, **decreasing** with time but remaining elevated at the 30 minute-period,

(2) a slight decrease in stroke volume,

(3) CO increased 24-28%/1st 15 minutes, the increase not being as great as with HR due to a decrease in stroke volume (CO = HR x stroke volume), and

(4) insignificant changes in systolic and diastolic b.p.

Echocardiographic and STI determinations (immediately prior to and following smoking a cigarette(s) as well as 15 minutes later) done in different groups of individuals smoking 1, 2, or 3 marihuana cigarettes after early and late intoxication periods as well as smoking 3 cigarettes after 7 days abstinence, altered some of the parameters as follows (Fig. 25):

(1) the HR increase had a tendency to decrease with the number of cigarettes smoked/session and with duration of the intoxication period (tolerance development) when the tachycardia response declined more rapidly following smoking (i.e. immediate effect vs 15 minutes post smoking period). Tolerance development to tachycardia was confirmed in 11/17 subjects in whom HR increase, following smoking of 1 marihuana cigarette, was 37.5 and 13.8 beats/minute after early (3 days) and late (59 days) intoxication periods respectively with subjective intoxication levels being maintained. Following 7 days abstinence from marihuana intoxication, the HR response (increase and duration) was increased after smoking 3 marihuana cigarettes vs response in early and late intoxication periods,

(2) systolic b.p. essentially did not change following smoking of 1 marihuana cigarette nor with time of intoxication but a small increase (7.6-7.8% change) occurred in diastolic b.p. (noted at 3rd and 27th day of intoxication),

(3) stroke volume changes (decrease) were more evident at the 15 minute post smoking period (1, 2, or 3 marihuana cigarettes) during both the intoxication and abstinence periods,

(4) CO changes (increase) followed HR changes with respect to tolerance development; the degree of increase being less than HR increase especially when stroke volume decreased (including abstinence period), and

(5) changes in left ventricular performance measurements during intoxication and abstinence periods included:

(a)   ejection fraction which followed directional changes of stroke volume and were slight,

(b)   PEP/LVET ratio which varied, the overall change (Tashkin et al., 1978b) being an insignificant increase (which is usually proportional to decreased stroke volume in non-valvular heart disease), and

(c)   Vcf (velocity of circumferential fibre shortening) response which also varied; a significant increase occurring during the abstinence period thought to be associated with the increased HR.

      Tolerance developed to the marihuana tachycardia and increased CO effects (the degree of the latter changes appearing to be influenced by stroke volume changes). Marihuana does not appear to have a β-adrenergc stimulating effect on myocardial contractility (usually observed as increased CO, Vcf, ejection fraction, variable stroke volume changes and decreased ratio PEP/LVET) during long term drug use (plasma expansion (see later) may be part of explanation). It was felt that the increased CO following marihuana smoking was related to the increased heart rate thought to be brought about by a mechanism other than β-adrenergic stimulation. Perhaps the variability or trends noted in the results could be firmed up by following the same individual (serving as own control) throughout such a study with plasma THC level determinations (because of individual variation with respect to degree (depth and duration) of smoke inhalation and drug metabolism). It is possible that the increased HR is a reflex response to peripheral vasodilation (due to THC) with increased CO being due to increased venous return irrespective of the small stroke volume changes (a decrease in stroke volume would be relfected in a smaller pulse pressure which is indicated in the report by an increased diastolic pressure during intoxication).

      Circulatory changes occurring with prolonged (up to 20 days) THC ingestion (increasing oral doses over 2-4 days to a maximum of 210 mg/day given at regular intervals of q4h with a double dose at the midnight interval resulting in 2.6-3.9 mg/KgTHC/day (average 3.2 ± 0.4)) were examined in 12 healthy male volunteers (average 25 years of age (20-27), previous cannabis use of 9 marihuana cigarettes/week/4 years (2-21 cigarettes/week/2-6 years)) abstaining from drugs 1 week prior to hospitalization for a 30 day double blind study; placebo being used at the beginning (control) and end (abstinence) of the study while marihuana cigarettes (20 mg THC) were used to test cross-tolerance between routes (oral caps, smoke) of administration (Benowitz and Jones, 1975). Weekly blood samples were obtained for various laboratory tests and body weight was checked each morning. Cardiovascular parameters measured 2 hours following the early morning THC oral dose included:

(1)   HR (radial pulse, ECG) and b.p. (supine, standing, exercise for 1 minute, during Valsalva maneuver, cold pressor test) to provide information re mechanism of action and evaluate functional capacity during chronic drug intake,

(2)   ECG,

(3)   HR (sitting position) pre and post smoking/10 minutes a marihuana cigarette at the end of

      (a)   first placebo period

      (b)   maximum THC ingestion

      (c)   second placebo period, and

(4)   plasma volume (via dye method) in 3 additional subjects pre and post 14 days of oral THC intake.

      During the acceleration phase of drug administration, the resting supine HR and b.p. did not change significantly (although 1 subject developed increased b.p. and HR associated with anxiety) while during maximal oral THC dosing, systolic and diastolic blood pressures decreased as did HR (Fig. 26). Withdrawal of THC resulted in pre-drug levels of systolic and diastolic b.p. with HR remaining slightly lower after 4-6 days of placebo intake. Changing the position from supine to standing resulted in small changes during the pre-drug period noted as a slight decrease in systolic and very slight increase in diastolic b.p., stabilizing with occurrence of increase in HR, while post drug effects revealed systolic b.p. decrease being greater than diastolic b.p. decrease without stabilization/3 minutes with HR increase (Fig. 27). During the early maximum drug dose phase postural hypotension (7 with dizziness) occurred becoming less with time (3 unable to stand/3 minutes without syncope in mid phase maximal dosing period) (Fig. 28). Normally, standing produces cardiovascular adjustment of sympathetic reflex arteriolar constriction and cardiac stimulation via pressure on carotid baroreceptor. Chronic THC intake lowers the acute tachycardia and hypotensive effects with time. The orthostatic hypotension with inadequate HR increase occurring in some individuals indicates sympathetic insufficiency. Tolerance did not develop to decreased supine b.p. but did develop to orthostatic hypotension due to compensatory plasma expansion to which tolerance did not appear to develop. Exercise (1 minute) during the pre-drug phase increased systolic b.p. and HR with a large decrease in diastolic b.p., returning to baseline/3 minutes post exercise (Fig. 29). During early drug phase, a lowered baseline and blunting of systolic b.p. increase occurred with increased HR ($\equiv$ pre-drug) and decreased diastolic b.p. ($\equiv$ pre-drug though lower level), returning to pre-drug levels following drug withdrawal; 2 subjects were unable to exercise due to dizziness. Normally during exercise, cardiac output is increased due to cardiac stimulation and skeletal muscle venocontriction with decreased systemic resistance due to arteriolar vasodilation. THC impairs the usual systolic b.p. increase without affecting diastolic b.p. decrease and HR increase which (HR) is insufficient to keep b.p. at normal levels suggesting either a direct THC venodilation or sympathetic inhibition of the heart and peripheral vessels. THC impaired the degree and onset of bradycardia following release of Valsalva (the HR decrease being a parasympathetic mediated response to b.p. overshoot); the increased HR during straining was not impaired. It was suggested that this effect could be due to sympathetic inhibition or impaired venous return due to venodilation or impaired cardiac output due to myocardial depression. THC also impaired systolic b.p. increase following immersion of the hand in ice water (cold pressor test) returning toward baseline levels with continued drug use (again a suggestion of sympathetic inhibition being made). ECG tracings revealed HR slowing with prolonged drug intake. Abnormalities noted in ECG included premature beats in 2 subjects, P-wave changes in 5, and T-wave inversion in lead III in 3. The resting ECG changes reverted to normal upon drug withdrawal. The smoking of a marihuana cigarette during pre-drug (THC) phase resulted in a significant HR increase by 44.6 ± 13.5 beats/minute while during THC intake the HR increase was significantly reduced (increase by 6.6 ± 6.9 beats/minute) with decreased subjective effects; withdrawal of THC returning HR and subjective responses to pre-drug levels. Thus cross-tolerance to tachycardia and subjective effects occurs with marihuana smoking especially when the THC level is maintained throughout 24 hours as in this study. Body weight and plasma volume increased during the drug phase while Hb (hemoglobin) decreased suggesting an association of body weight and plasma volume increases (Fig. 30). The change in plasma volume/change in body weight = $20.7 \pm 1.6\%$ being comparable to plasma volume/extracellular fluid volume, indicated that weight gain was due to extracellular fluid expansion, a possible compensatory response to chronic b.p. decrease (as occurrs with sympathetic-blocking antihypertensives). The cardiovascular changes due to THC did not appear to be significantly influenced by differences in prior marihuana use nor by differing mg/kg THC doses used. During the first week of drug intake, the subjects were sedated, lethargic, sluggish with poor concentrating ability, slowed speech and motor activity, and ataxic. Almost complete tolerance to these intoxicating effects were evident after 20 days drug use noted as normal performance in various motor and psychological tests. A mild abstinence syndrome appeared upon THC withdrawal being reported as insomnia, anorexia, irritability and sweating. However rebound cardiovascular activity did not occur indicating that adequate THC levels are necessary for cardiovascular effects (which could indicate a direct THC effect resulting in reflex responses). Thus with a maintained THC level (20 days), tolerance begins to develop to tachycardia and hypotension, the latter leading to compensatory plasma volume expansion (responsible for weight gain), with circulatory impairment following exercise and Valsalva maneuver; the suggestion being made that sympathetic insufficiency (or parasympathetic or direct myocardial effects) occurs. (Or does the THC maintained level overcome the reflex sympathetic activity (i.e. competetive inhibition) necessitating plasma volume expansion to offset standing b.p. decrease as a sort of secondary line of defence).

To test some of the hypotheses noted above re sympathetic effects as mechanism of action for THC effects, the same investigators undertook to study effects of prolonged oral THC intake on autonomic nervous system function, noting the cardiovascular effects of sympathomimetic amines (IV isoproterenol, a β-adrenergic agonist, 0.08-0.64 μg/kg/0.5 ml volume; phenylephrine, an α-adrenergic agonist, 20-160 μg/minute/5 minutes; 10 minutes between injections) and autonomic blockers (IV atropine, a parasympathetic blocker, total dose of 0.04 mg/kg in 4 divided doses/3 minute intervals; followed by propanolol, a β-adrenergic blocker, total dose of 0.20 mg/kg in 4 divided doses/3 minute intervals) pre and post 14 days of oral THC (maximum 60, 180, 210 mg/day) in 10 resting hospitalized (30 days) healthy male volunteers (21-31 years of age; regular marihuana users with a habit of 3x/week use and no other drugs) (Benowitz and Jones, 1977). Subjects were abstinent from drugs one week prior to hospital admission. Control measurements were taken following the initial placebo period with retesting after 14 days of THC ingestion with a mean 24 hour dose of 2.57 mg/kg $\pm$ 0.78 S.D. HR was determined from an ECG tracing and b.p. via mercury manometer. The tests were carried out in THC tolerant individuals (to psychological and behavioural effects, orthostatic hypotension and tachycardia of smoked marihuana). Isoproterenol and phenyleprine did not alter resting HR and b.p. values of pre and post THC periods which were similar; one subject exhibiting an exaggerated pressor response to high infusion rates of phenylephrine. Atropine (cumulative doses) significantly increased HR as well as systolic and diastolic b.p. during THC intake, while propanolol (cumulative doses to atropinized subjects) decreased HR in the pre-THC period more than during the THC session (partial block?) without affecting resting b.p.; the absolute HR during THC intake being greater than pre-THC values. The authors propose a sympathetic insufficiency (from previous study) and enhanced parasympathetic activity (on basis of atropine (blocker)

HR response) with prolonged THC intake (but propanolol effect not explained; would the sympathetic insufficiency include competative inhibition?). Clinically, atropine (often used as pre-operative medication) may have a deleterious b.p. effect (increase) in long-term high dose cannabis users.

(d) Cardiac Toxicity

The effect of marihuana (vs placebo) on exercise performance was studied in 10 healthy male volunteers (drug use?) in a single blind fashion on 2 separate days measuring various respiratory parameters and ECG responses pre and post smoking (Shapiro et al., 1976b; Tashkin et al., 1978b). After smoking a placebo or a marihuana (20 mg THC) cigarette, measurements were done on resting subjects for 5 minutes. This was followed by exercise on a bicycle ergometer (beginning with a work load of 150 kg m/minute/5 minutes which was increased by a similar amount at 5 minute intervals) to the point of exhaustion (noting the time). The duration of exercise following marihuana smoking was less than placebo time. The respiratory parameters remained essentially unchanged. The HR increase at rest and at all work loads after marihuana smoking was greater than placebo effect (Fig. 31). It appears that marihuana decreases peak exercise performance which may be due to the additive chronotropic (tachycardia) effects of marihuana and exercise, the maximum HR being attained at lower work loads and sooner than with exercise alone. (The tachycardia may be inadequate to sustain normal systolic b.p. noted above (Benowitz and Jones, 1975) with 1 minute exercise, i.e. one moves more slowly and tires more easily (decreased Hb and increased plasma volume, a functional anemia)).

Cardiovascular (HR, b.p.) and respiratory (pulmonary ventilation $\dot{V}e$, oxygen consumption $\dot{V}o_2$) effects of marihuana (500 mg cigarette with 7.5 mg THC) and placebo smoking (10 minute smoking/cigarette + 10 minutes rest for peak drug action pre exercise and vs control of no smoking) were investigated (double-blind) in 6 normal male (21-27 years of age) chronic marihuana users (at least 3 years regular use; no tobacco nor other drugs; abstinent 24 hours pre study) during rest, standardized submaximal exercise (bicycle ergometer at approximately 50% $\dot{V}o_2$ maximum/15 minutes) and recovery (15 minutes) periods (Avakian et al., 1979). Following resting baseline measurements, exercise at work load of 750 kg m/minute began, pedaling the bicycle ergometer at 50 r.p.m. Physiological measurements were taken throughout the exercise and recovery periods in the seated position as during earlier rest period. Even though the study was double-blind, the subjects knew when they were smoking marihuana and investigators saw objective signs of conjunctival vascular congestion and typical behavioural marihuana intoxicating effects. Placebo smoking did not alter any of the physiological parameters measured. Respiratory and b.p. changes were similar for all 3 conditions (control, placebo, marihuana) prior to, during and post exercise periods. HR was the only parameter altered significantly during marihuana smoking, increasing by 34% (26 beats/minute vs control) during the rest period, 16-18% (vs control and placebo) during exercise, and 28-51% during recovery resulting in an increased systolic index (HR x systolic b.p. or myocardial O_2 demand) of 26% (above control) during rest, 15% during exercise and 21-36% during recovery (Fig. 32). (Tachycardia is one of the factors which decreases coronary blood flow which may contribute to hypoxia or increased O_2 demand). It was suggested that since placebo did not alter physiological measurements, the chronotropic (HR) and associated cardiovascular alterations due to marihuana, was not related to increased COHb levels. However the study was conducted in normal healthy (though experienced marihuana users) subjects in whom blood vessels must have been normal and not diseased (atherosclerotic) seen by absence of b.p. alterations, i.e., the HR increase could be handled by the individuals and was sufficient to keep the b.p. similar to control values. Subjectively, work effort was greater while under marihuana effects (which could mean less efficient and/or decreased work output in such individuals).

Several studies have been conducted in individuals with coronary artery disease. One double blind study (Aronow and Cassidy, 1974) assessed the effects of marihuana smoking (vs. placebo) on cardiovascular function and exercise (bicycle ergometer) induced angina in 10 fasting male patients (47.3 $\pm$ 6.1 years of age with daily tobacco cigarettes consumption of at least 20 cigarettes/day but no marihuana use, abstaining from cigarette smoking 10-12 hours per study) with stable exertional angina pectoris (angiographic evidence with > 75% narrowing of at least one major coronary blood vessel). Resting HR (ECG) and b.p. were obtained from patients while sitting on a bicycle ergometer on which they exercised with increasing work loads until onset of anginal pain noting the time as well as HR and b.p. Supine ECG was taken prior to exercise and following onset of angina when Hb and COHb levels (1 hour post exercise) were also determined. Resting HR and b.p. were also obtained prior to and following (when Hb and COHb levels determined) smoking (10 puffs) of a marihuana (19.8 mg THC) or placebo (0.05 mg THC) cigarette. Exercise was performed upon completion of smoking a cigarette, up to the time of angina when ECG tracings were obtained for 6 minutes post angina measuring HR as well as b.p. In resting individuals marihuana caused increased HR and b.p. giving an increased HR x b.p. or increased O_2 demand by the myocardium as well as increased COHb blood level (from inhaled CO (carbon monoxide) in the smoke (due to incomplete combustion during the smoking process) leading to interference with O_2 delivery) or decreased myocardial O_2 delivery. Placebo increased COHb level without altering the resting HR x b.p. (O$_2$ demand) from control. The exercise time to angina following marihuana smoking (1 cigarette) was decreased significantly (48%) being greater than the significant decrease (8.6%) due to placebo vs control. The decrease noted with placebo may be due to increased COHb level since HR and b.p. remained unaltered. At the onset of angina, marihuana and placebo had similar decreasing effects on HR, b.p., HR x b.p. The degree of maximal ischemic ST-segment depression occurring with angina was similar for control, placebo, and marihuana conditions but the onset was earlier and with less exertion post marihuana vs placebo and control. Hb levels remained within normal limits without significant changes being apparent. Thus the increased myocardial O$_2$ demand (↑ HR x b.p.) together with decreased myocardial O$_2$ delivery (↑ COHb) as well as less than normal increase in coronary blood flow in anginal patients due to exercise (↑ HR is also a factor in decreasing coronary blood flow) resulted in decreased exercise performance or earlier angina with less myocardial work following the smoking of one marihuana cigarette.

These investigators also compared marihuana (18.9 mg THC) effects in anginal patients (decreased exercise performance) with the effects of smoking a high-nicotine (1.8 mg nicotine) tobacco cigarette using the same method and similar type patients (10 males, average 49.6 ± 5.8 years of age, with stable exertional angina, at least 20 high-nicotine cigarettes consumption/day; 4 had smoked 2 marihuana cigarettes in the above study, the others had not used marihuana) (Aronow and Cassidy, 1975). As above, Hb remained within normal limits. The resting values revealed that the increased HR due to marihuana was greater than that due to nicotine while the increase in systolic and diastolic pressures, due to marihuana was less than that due to nicotine. However the increase in HR x b.p. (increased myocardial O$_2$ demand) of marihuana was greater than nicotine as was the increase in COHb level (decreased myocardial O$_2$ delivery) resulting in exercise time to angina being decreased (50%) more by marihuana smoking than by tobacco (high-nicotine) smoking (23%). At angina the decreases in HR, b.p., and HR x b.p. were similar for marihuana and high-nicotine cigarettes. The amount of maximal ischemic ST-segment depression post angina was the same for control, marihuana and high-nicotine conditions but the onset was earlier and with less exertion post marihuana vs nicotine which resulted in earlier onset with less exertion than control. It appears that both marihuana and nicotine cigarettes decrease exercise performance with marihuana having the greater effect as well as precipitating angina sooner.

Not only does active smoking result in decreased exercise performance in anginal patients but so does passive smoking reported in a single blind study (in 10 male patients with exertional angina, average age 54.3 ± 8.1 years, 8 of whom were ex-smokers of tobacco and 2 smoked 2-4 cigarettes/day, abstaining for 16 hours pre study and during the study) by one of the above investigators (Aronow, 1978). Passive smoking occurs when inhaled air contains mainstream smoke exhaled by a smoker and sidestream smoke emitted from the burning end of a product. The absorption of pollutants by the non-smoker (passive) depends on the amount of smoke produced and released into the air, ventilation, proximity to the source, and duration of exposure. The study method used was essentially the same as above (Aronow and Cassidy, 1974) with conditions of exposure to "no smoke" or smoke (from 5 tobacco cigarettes/2 hours) in ventilated and unventilated rooms followed by exercise to onset of angina. COHb levels were also determined in the individuals who did the smoking (pre and post). Passive smoking gave similar (directionally) results as direct smoking noted above (Aronow and Cassidy, 1975) with effects in the unventilated room being greater than in the ventilated room. Nicotine was thought to be responsible for the increase in resting HR x b.p. (↑ O$_2$ demand while ↓ O$_2$ delivery was due to ↑ COHb) post passive smoke exposure since nicotine has been found in urine (10.7 ng/ml) of non-smokers exposed to a smoke filled room. Premature venticular contractions occurred in 1 subject exposed to smoke in an unventilated room prior to exercise and in 3 subjects after exercise.

Cardiovascular hemodynamic effects of marihuana (18 mg THC) or placebo (0.05 mg THC) cigarette smoking by anginal (stable) patients (10 males, average age 48.9 ± 9.1 years, tobacco cigarette consumption of approximately 1 package cigarettes/day but no marihuana use, abstaining from smoking 12 hours pre study (fasting state) and during the study (supine position)) were evaluated by echocardiogram in a double-blind cross-over study (Prakash et al., 1975). Parameters measured included HR (ECG), b.p., and left ventricular end-systolic (LVES) and end-diastolic (LVED) diameters (echocardiogram) from which the following were determined; LVESV and LVEDV (volumes, via cube of respective ventricular diameters x 1.047), SV (stroke volume = LVEDV - LVESV), CO (cardiac output = HR x SV/1000) and EF (ejection fraction = SV/LVEDV). Following control measurements, marihuana or placebo cigarettes were smoked (10 puffs/cigarette) repeating measurements after smoking at time intervals of 0, 10, 15, 20, 30, 60, 90 and 120 minutes. Maximum changes (vs control) noted following marihuana smoking and not after placebo use included increased HR (by 29.4 beats/minute or 42% above control value) and increased b.p. (systolic increase by 9.2 mm Hg or 8%; diastolic increase by 5.4 mm Hg or 7%) which were due to THC content. LVED diameter was altered (decrease) by both preparations (marihuana, placebo) resulting in maximum marihuana effects being greater and of longer duration than the maximum placebo effects leading to the following parameter changes:

(1)   ↓ LVEDV (marihuana 26.5 ml or 13%; placebo 10.6 ml or 7%)

(2)   ↓ stroke index (marihuana 14.2 ml/beat/m² or 29%; placebo 5.7 ml/beat/m² or 13%)

(3)   ↓ EF (marihuana 9.3% or 19% over control; placebo 4% or 8% over control).

Cardiac index was decreased only by placebo (0.42 l/minute/m² or 13%) which decreased stroke index without compensatory HR increase noted with marihuana. The placebo cardiovascular hemodynamic effects were attributed to increased COHb while marihuana effects involved THC effects in addition to increased COHb levels.

To round out the above series of studies in anginal patients, the effects of marihuana (18 mg THC) vs placebo (0.05 mg THC) smoking (10 puffs) on psychophysiological cardiovascular function was undertaken, i.e., simultaneous examination of cognitive and emotional reactions, and cardiovascular function in 10 fasting male stable anginal (coronary artery disease) patients in the supine positon (average 48 ± 9.1 years of age; 1 package tobacco cigarettes/day habit but no marihuana use; abstinence from smoking 12 hours pre study; only medication was sublingual nitroglycerin 2 weeks before study and no medication pre study) (Gottschalk et al., 1977). Cardiovascular parameter measurements, determinations, and method were similar to the above report (Prakash et al., 1975). In addition, control and post smoking speech analyses (psychological state) were scored blindly for anxiety; hostility (overt or outward, inward, ambivalent), social alienation-personal disorganization and cognitive impairment. Average cognitive impairment was significantly increased (not all subjects showed increase suggesting differences in THC levels which depend on depth of smoke inhalation, absorption and metabolism of drug, being influenced by the state of health of the individual) 30 minutes post marihuana use with a duration of 30 minutes (this type of impairment also seen with temporary (electroshock treatment) or permanent cerebral organic impairment) while a statistically insignificant increase occurred in social alienation-personal disorganization scores (also observed with onset of acute or chronic schizophrenia; both types of impairment being seen with other psychomimetic drugs as LSD-25, psilocybin, and body irradiation). The cognitive-intellectual impairment scores confirm other studies noting mental dysfunction following marihuana smoking. Significant average changes were not evident for anxiety and 3 hostility scales although some subjects did display increased anxiety or hostility post marihuana. Individual variation with respect to psychological responses were large suggesting the possibility of personality and/or THC pharmacokinetic differences. Marihuana erased the significant psychophysiological correlations (seen with placebo) between hostility and b.p., ejection fraction, and, between anxiety and LVEDV. Somewhat similar correlations have been observed in hypertensive women; the correlations being abolished with hydrochlorthiazide (antihypertensive diuretic) drug therapy.

From the above studies, it appears that marihuana smoking by coronary artery diseased individuals (with stable exertional angina) increases O_2 demand (due to ↑ HR and b.p.) and decreases O_2 delivery (due to ↑ COHb) to the myocardium thereby decreasing exercise time to the onset of angina (pain) and, perhaps, being partly responsible for blocking normal (placebo) psychocardiovascular correlations between hostility and b.p., ejection fraction, and, between anxiety and LVEDV. The latter may also be influenced by direct CNS marihuana effects noted as increased cognitive impairment (speech content), i.e., both CNS and peripheral cardiovascular marihuana effects could be responsible for altering psychophysiological correlations. (Or, is it possible that the CNS effects are secondary to the peripheral vascular effects?). In essence marihuana (THC) does not appear to be beneficial to anginal patients in the doses studied.

Several of the above studies have alluded to cardiac arrhythmias (irregularity of heart beat) occurring during marihuana smoking. This problem has been specifically addressed by several investigators. One group of investigators observed PVCs in 2 healthy subjects while studying marihuana effects on other functional parameters and decided to study (single blind) the CVS effects of marihuana (low dose of 0.2-0.5% THC in 10 subjects; high dose of 2.9% THC in 15 subjects vs placebo marihuana) smoking (300 mg cigarettes smoked to shortest possible butt; low dose group smoking 2-5 cigarettes, high dose 1-4 cigarettes, inhaling deeply) in 25 normal healthy male volunteers (21-33 years of age with previous marihuana experience, 6 being daily users with 1 subject in the high dose group able to tolerate 30 mg THC without behavioural (psychic) change) (Johnston and Domino, 1971). Prior to (baseline) and 0.5-1 hour post marihuana or placebo smoking as well as after exercise, ECGs were obtain from 8 subjects (supine position), b.p. measured 3 times, and pulse rate recorded from continuous polygraph in those who did not have complete ECGs. The increased HR was dose-related with maximum effect being reached within 30 minutes with duration of at least 90 minutes; the tolerant subject exhibiting an increase in HR from 55 to 120 beats/minute following the acute large dose of 30 mg THC. Both systolic and diastolic b.p. were increased in a dose-related manner with > 10 mg THC (marihuana) doses (systolic > diastolic increase). However b.p. changes correlated better with HR increases than with dose. (This would indicate that blood THC levels would be a better indictor of actual drug dose for a particular individual eliminating such factors as absorption differences (including smoking pattern differences) and individual variations re drug metabolism). Placebo did not alter HR or b.p. ECG changes included falttening of T-waves in many subjects following marihuana smoking and after exercise (greater effect in experienced users) with 2/15 in the high dose group (> 10 mg THC) developing PVCs at < 1/25 beats (vs none in the control period) which were unnoticed by the subjects. The psychological state of mind may modify HR response noted by anxiety (panic) produced in 1 subject after 25 mg THC resulting in a HR increase of 108 while in another who became sedated (somnolent) the increase was only 36, indicating a possible CNS-mediated effect. It was suggested that certain individuals may be susceptible to PVCs induced by marihuana similar to that seen with nicotine (tobacco) and caffeine, and, that marihuana CVS effects may be harmful to cardiac diseased patients.

The ECG effects of single oral doses of THC (200 µg/kg (equivalent to smoking 1 marihuana cigarette) and 300 µg/kg (with 400 µg/kg in 1 subject) as a large dose; doses given 4 days apart to avoid cumulative effect) vs placebo (vehicle) were studied (single blind) in 7 young (24-28 years of age) healthy male volunteers with varying marihuana use ranging from 3x/week (heavy in 1 subject) to no marihuana exposure in 2 individuals; marihuana was not smoked 2 weeks prior to the study (Kochar and Hosko, 1973). Baseline ECG tracings (normal in all subjects) were obtained from resting subjects pre drug intake and repeated 2.5 and 12 hours post drug. Placebo did not alter the ECG. THC had the usual psychological effects. The small dose of THC (200 µg/kg) resulted in increased HR (by 4 beats/minute) and ST-segment elevation (> 2 mm) in one subject and T-wave flattening in another at 2.5 hours post drug reverting to baseline by 12 hours. The large dose of THC (300 µg/kg and 400 µg/kg in 1 subject) caused increased HR (by 5-12 beats/minute) in 6/7 subjects at 2.5 hours post drug persisting for 12 hours in 5 subjects. ECG changes in 3 volunteers following the large THC dose included ST-segment elevation in 1 man, T-wave flattening in 2 (repolarization abnormalities in moderate drug users also noted with other psychoactive substances as phenothiazines and lithium as well as in pericarditis or epicardial injury) and unifocal PVCs (premature ventricular contractions; 5/minute) in the one heavy smoker returning to baseline by the 12 hour period (Fig. 33). The two non-users did not develop ECG abnormalities suggesting that previous marihuana use may determine the severity of ECG changes due to a certain threshold dose of THC. Cardiac symptoms did not occur with ECG and HR changes. ST-segment elevation denotes current of injury which may be due to a condition of myocardial ischemia (T-wave flattening) brought about by tachycardia and/or functional anemia (↓ Hb noted above) (another cause for ischemia being coronary artery disease), all of which, with the observed PVCs, indicate a form of reversible (unless arteriosclerosis is present) marihuana toxicity in a particular individual (which in time with continued marihuana use may possibly become irreversible with permanent heart damage). Therefore certain ECG abnormalities (especially in a young person) should raise suspicions as to possible drug use (medical or misuse) making it part of a differential diagnosis.

A double-blind study (Roth et al., 1973) used continuous ECG monitoring (single pair of leads ≡ V_4 with additional 12 leads in 4 subjects (q 30 minutes)) of 10 normal young male individuals (average 24 years of age (21-29); used marihuana at least 2x/previous year, with most subjects smoking 1-2x/week but abstaining 5 days prior to and during the study period) during marihuana (1 gm cigarette with 2% or 20 mg THC) or placebo (0.02-0.05% THC) smoking (standardized method resulting in 10 minutes of smoking/cigarette). Pre-drug baseline ECG recordings were obtained from subjects in a sitting position for 10 or 30 minutes during recording sessions of 2 or 4 hour durations respectively, when supine or supine and standing b.p. measurements were taken q 5-10 or 20 minutes respectively. Subjective marihuana effects rated as a "high" of 8.8 (on a scale of 10) included time perception distortion, recent memory defect, bodily sensation preoccupation, but no syncopal effects (vs placebo rating of 1 average). Four subjects developed 5 isolated PVCs (1 subject with 2 PVCs during baseline period; 1 with 1 PVC during placebo; and 2 with 1 PVC each during marihuana day) while 2 individuals had sinus arrhythmias (irregular rhythm) pre (baseline HR 55-60 beats/minute) and during experimental sessions becoming less obvious during tachycardia period. Following marihuana use, the 4 subjects with 12 leads revealed increased HR (by 36 beats/minute) accompanied by increased P-wave amplitude, and increased sitting systolic b.p. (by 12 mm Hg). Maximum HR (mean 127.6 beats/minute) developed 17.8 minutes post marihuana smoking. T-wave changes were insignificant. The normal incidence for PVCs in the young age group is unknown. In older men (average 55 years of age) 62% have ≥ 1 PVC/6 hours and those who have PVCs have them 1/20 minutes vs study group of 1/5 hour during baseline measurements and 1/15 hours with placebo or marihuana smoking. It was felt that marihuana does not increase the incidence of PVCs in young men (but the study subjects had previous marihuana experience which may have contributed to established PVCs prior to the study as noted in previous study when non-users did not develop ECG abnormalities vs users).

THC (25 mcg/kg IV ≡ 5 mg THC marihuana cigarette/70-80 kg man) effects on human cardiac conduction (electrophysiology) was studied via His bundle electrogram recordings and cardiac stimulation (atrial at superior vena cava junction) with simultaneous ECG (I, II, III, V_1 leads) recordings in 6 male volunteer cardiac patients (5 with intraventricular conduction disease, 1 with suspected supraventricular arrhythmia; 18-45 years of age (average 33) in a non-sedated, post-absorptive state and no medication prior to study) (Miller et al., 1977). Control measurements were done before THC administration and electrophysiological studies conducted from 5 to 25 minutes post THC. THC affected the sinus node by significantly decreasing sinus cycle length and recovery time (including maximum recovery time) as well as calculated SA conduction time (by 27%) without affecting intra-atrial conduction. A-V nodal conduction was increased as noted by a decrease in A-H interval, and a decrease in effective and functional refractory periods during sinus rhythm and artrial pacing, requiring increased beats/minute pace rate to develop 2° A-V block (Wenckebach; proximal to His bundle), without affecting intraventricular conduction. Only one patient exhibited multifocal PVCs (enhanced ventricular automaticity) which disappeared 15 minutes post THC. The mean sinus HR increased by 39%. It appears that acute IV THC (equivalent to 1 marihuana cigarette) enhances sinus nodal automaticity and facilitates SA and A-V nodal conduction without affecting intra-atrial and intra-ventricular conduction. It was suggested that electrophysiological effects may be mediated by the central autonomic nervous system since they resemble those of isoproterenol and atropine (both increase sinus rate (HR), decrease sinus recovery time, and facilitate A-V conduction).

A case report has been described in the literature of a young man (25 years of age without a personal or family history of cardiovascular disease but with marihuana exposure (degree ?) during the previous 3 years and less than 10 tobacco cigarettes/day consumption) who developed pulmonary edema and acute myocardial infarction (subendocardial) associated with marihuana smoking (1-2 cigarettes mixed with tobacco; THC content?) (Charles et al., 1979). Several minutes after smoking marihuana, there was an acute onset of constricting chest pain and severe breathlessness with production of pink frothy sputum. Chest X-ray confirmed pulmonary edema which was resolved with conventional treatment (furosemide, diamorphine, O_2) so that neither clinical nor radiological evidence was apparent at the 14th day (discharged). ECG revealed sinus rhythm, a HR of 96 beats/minute, and deep extensive symmetrical T-wave inversion most prominent in the anterior leads reverting to normal by the 6th week without development of pathological Q-waves. The only alteration in blood chemistry was an elevation of serum enzymes (creatine phosphokinase, aspartate aminotransferase). Three months later, cardiac catherization showed normal intracardiac pressures. There was no evidence of atherosclerotic or embolic occlusive disease (via left ventricular cine angiography and selective coronary arteriography). Follow-up disclosed no further use of marihuana nor development of further cardiac problems nor ECG abnormalities. Perhaps previous marihuana exposure may affect the severity of ECG changes especially if the cardiac effects are cumulative, making it hazardous (cardiotoxicity) to susceptible individuals. (Opiate overdose may result in acute pulmonary edema (the etiology of which is thought not to be fluid overload or frank congestive heart failure) with the most common arrhythmia being transient atrial fibrillation. Most acute drug reactions give rise to nonspecific tachycardias. Hypoxia appears to be primarily responsible). Or the CVS events may have been due to the combined effects of marihuana (THC) and tobacco (nicotine) on the cardiovascular system. Pulmonary edema may be an excessive adrenergic effect observed with toxic epinephrine doses.

(e) Interactions

Since some individuals approaching elective or emergency surgical anesthesia will be marihuana users and will in essence have "premedicated" themselves and since the incidence of arrhythmias during oral surgery with local anesthesics alone is quite high (> 45%), the cardiovascular effects of combined stressful oral surgery and systemic cannabinols were determined in 55 clinical trails (Gregg et al., 1976a). In one set of trials THC (IV 0.044 mg/kg (with consistent "high"); 0.022 mg/kg (with minimum "high")) was used as premedication vs diazepam (0.157 mg/kg) or placebo (5% dextrose in saline) in 10 healthy male former marihuana users (habit?; 2 having used LSD and mescaline; average 26 years of age (19-28 years)) requiring elective surgery for removal of 4 impacted 3rd molars and serving as own controls (re CVS effects) in a double-blind study (abstaining from smoking 24 hours pre trial) compared with a non-surgical control group of 5 healthy males (average 26 years of age (21-34 years)) in whom one trial ofTHC (0.044 mg/kg) was used to separate drug effect from drug-surgical stress interaction. With the patient in a 30° reclining sitting position, cardiovascular monitoring involved continuous ECG (modified lead II) recording and b.p. q2 minutes via phonosensor, as well as psychological drug effects being noted. Following 30 minutes of baseline monitoring, premedication was given via an indwelling venous catheter over a 5 minute period when a local anesthetic block (peripheral trigeminal) was done with 2% lidocaine (2-4 ml or 40-80 mg) with 1:100,000 epinephrine (40-60 mcg). Removal of a molar was spaced over a 30 minute period followed by further monitoring during additional 60 minutes in the chair and 60 minutes in the recovery room. Average b.p. (and diastolic) was similar for THC, baseline and placebo vs diazepam which resulted in consistent mild systolic hypotension (7-15 torr) throughout the trial (including diastolic b.p.) (Fig. 34). However both doses of THC caused a slight increase in systolic b.p. (8-9 torr) peaking at 25 minutes post drug injection; the large dose ending in a hypotensive effect at the end of surgery (maximum effects of 12 and 14 torr below pre-op baseline and placebo respectively) at 55 minutes post THC returning to placebo levels 70 minutes post drug. In 3/10 subjects, transient mild hypotension (20-40 torr, systolic and diastolic) occurred 4-8 minutes post THC resulting in typical syncope with nausea, dizziness, anxiety, and loss of consciousness in 2 individuals; diazepam and placebo lacked this effect. During and immediately post local anesthesia, b.p. was similar for THC, diazepam and placebo. The peak increased HR with THC varied with dose, the large dose being 69% above baseline and 36% above placebo peak occurring at 18 minutes post drug with a HR change duration of 100 minutes vs low dose being 53% above baseline and 26% above placebo peak at 15 minutes post drug with duration (HR change) of 75 minutes; local anesthesia did not affect HR (Fig. 35). The time course of HR change preceded subjective "high" feeling, i.e., peak tachycardia occurred 12 minutes before peak "high" returning to placebo levels 30 minutes before normal psychic state achieved (Fig. 36). ECG changes due to THC included shortening of P-R interval (> 33%) and decreased T-wave amplitude (> 33%) at peak drug effect in 60-70% of the subjects vs 30% with diazepam and 10% placebo; local anesthesia did not alter ECG changes. Arrhythmias or functional PVCs (premature ventricular contractions) occurred in 11/40 clinical trials during baseline pre-op period. During intra-op with placebo, 2/10 exhibited PVCs. Low dose THC increased the frequency of baseline pre-op PVCs in 2 subjects during intra-op while 2 other subjects developed PVCs during intra-op (none being present during baseline pre-op) (Fig. 37). Only one subject receiving a large THC dose exhibited PVCs during baseline pre-op which disappeared for one hour post drug (and intra-op) (a possible antiarrhythmic in healthy but ? in chronic cardiopathy). The only significant difference between surgical vs non-surgical groups was that peak HR in surgical group > non-surgical group (by 24.1%) with THC indicating a synergistic effect of THC to surgical stress. It was suggested that this supports the theory of CNS-activated sympathoadrenal response to THC with β-adrenergic receptors being the final common pathway. Subjective psychological effects were observed in anxiety scores being significantly increased in THC medicated surgical patients vs placebo, diazepam and non-surgical THC groups with dysphoria and "low" moods predominating during syncopal hypotension post THC. In another (retrospective) study (healthy 7 females, 3 males, 21-30 years of age (average 25)) general anesthesia (including 0.4 mg atropine IV as one of premedications) was given within 72 hours of smoking marihuana (5/10 subjects) and compared with a non-smoking control group undergoing outpatient oral surgery (removal of 2-4 third molars) in a 30° upright position in an operating chair with CVS monitoring similar to the first study noting respiratory rate and measuring (serial) blood gases prior to and during the operation. The only significant difference between the groups occurred in the post anesthetic period with the peak increased HR at the 7 minute period being greater for the marihuana group (64.8% above baseline vs 39% in non-smoker group) returning to baseline levels later (39 minutes vs 19 minutes non-smoker) (Fig. 38). This prolongation of tachycardia due to THC (in part may be due to atropine additive effects) in the post-op period could result in medical mismanagement if the anesthetist is not alert to a possible marihuana habit by a patient. That is, potential drug interactions may occur hours or days after marihuana smoking due to cannabinol metabolism and enterohepatic circulation of active components (plasma half-life of THC being 36 hours and 11-hydroxy THC 40 hours with complete excretion requiring approximately 8 days following one dose). Thus THC has no advantage over known pre-op medications, and, anesthestists should be alert to marihuana consumption by patients to avoid undesirable CVS responses.

Another study (Johnstone et al., 1975) which confirms this alert was done in 15 healthy male volunteers (previous cannabinoid experience-extent?) using large doses of THC (27, 40, 60, 90, 134 µg/kg IV via venous catheter) combined with oxymorphone (1 mg IV in 8 subjects; average 24 years of age) or with pentobarbital (100 mg IV in 7 subjects; average 22 years of age) pretreatment noting psychological, respiratory and cardiovascular effects. Some individuals in the pentobarbital group (4/7) did not receive all THC doses due to severe mental effects noted as anxiety and hallucinations in 5/7 subjects. The sedation and ventilatory depression (24.9 → 14.1 L/minute) seen with oxymorphone was further augmented with the addition of THC (ventilation declining to 6.6 L/minute at 134 µg/kg dose) while pentobarbital and THC did not appear to affect the mean ventilation (although large individual variation) (Fig. 39). The pre and post drug (oxymorphone + THC) ventilatory responses to CO_2 expressed as slope were 2.23 L/minute/torr and 0.88 L/minute/torr respectively (Fig. 40) but were identical for pentobarbital + THC. It was felt that change in slope indicates change in level of consciousness. Normal pre drug (oxymorphone + THC group of 8 subjects) CVS (cardiovascular) responses to CO_2 change (i.e. increase PET_{CO_2} (end tidal CO_2 tension) from 43 to 50 torr since respiratory depression noted above) were observed as increased CI (cardiac index; 2.98 → 3.52 L/minute/m^2), increased HR (60 → 68 beats/minute), increased MAP (mean arterial pressure; 94 → 98 torr) and decreased TPR (total peripheral resistance; 1280 → 1150 dynes. sec/cm^5). The introduction of oxymorphone (at constant PET_{CO_2} of 50 torr) did not alter CVS function significantly. However the addition of THC to oxymorphone resulted in increased CI (4.1 → 5.9 L/min/m^2) and HR (heart rate 66 → 107 beats/minute; > 150 beats/minute in 2 subjects post 27 and 134 µg/kg THC) with decreased TPR (1030 → 660 dynes. second/cm^5). One individual developed supraventricular tachyarrhythmia, probably junctional tachycardia with variable block. At the end of oxymorphone + THC dosing, an increase in CO_2 (from 50 to 62 torr) produced insignificant CVS changes (decreased CI of 6.40 → 6.27 L/minute/m^2; decreased HR of 96 → 94 beats/minute; decreased TPR from 650 → 620 dynes. second/cm^5) indicating reversal or negation of CO_2-mediated CVS changes. In the other 7 subjects (pentobarbital + THC group) the pre-drug CVS responses to CO_2 change (from 45 → 52 torr) were also normal (increased CI from 3.5 → 4.4; increased HR 64 → 75; increased MAP 95 → 102; decreased TPR 1150 → 980). Pentobarbital did not alter CVS function at constant $PETco_2$ (50 torr). Pentobarbital with various doses of THC increased HR (76 → 130 beats/minute; 3 subjects had >150 beats/minute with 27 (in 2 subjects) and 90 (in 1) µg/kg THC, the rate decreasing with subsequent THC doses), increased CI (3.8 → 5.6 L/minute/m²) and decreased TPR (1070 → 720 dynes. second/cm⁵). Arrhythmias did not develop in this group of volunteers. At the end of pentobarbital + THC dosing, a decrease in $PETco_2$ (from 50 → 44 torr since ventilation not depressed or still high noted above) resulted in decreased CI (5.69 → 5.33) decreased HR (123 → 108), decreased MAP (99 → 97) without TPR change suggesting lack of interference with CO_2-mediated CVS control. The increased HR occurring with THC + oxymorphone or pentobarbital was responsible for increased CI since stroke index did not change significantly (Fig. 41). The excessive tachycardia would not be desirable in patients with CVS problems. The varied psychological reactions could contribute to the more varied CVS effects of THC with pentobarbital combination. In essence potential hazards exist in attempting to anesthetize a marihuana intoxicated individual. THC alone can produce panic reactions (see below) and psychotic behaviour, the latter being made worse with barbiturates, whereas, with opioids, ventilatory depression occurrs, and, tachycardia (mechanism not established) warrants ECG monitoring.

The same group had investigated the possibility of using THC as a pre anesthetic medication because of its sedative and euphoric properties hoping to find a hypnotic dose (minor degree of CNS depression favouring or inducing natural sleep) (Malit et al., 1975). The effects of cumulative THC doses (1 minute IV dose infusion at 10-12 minutes apart with 27, 40, 60, 90, 134 and 201 µg/kg, the latter 2 doses reached in 4 subjects each) on CO_2 mediated control of ventilation (drive) and on CO_2 stimulated CVS dynamics were studied in 10 healthy male volunteers (21-41 years of age; previous marihuana experience in all but one with extent?; 2 drop-outs due to anxiety or panic reactions) in the supine position. Continuous pressure measurements (MAP, CVP (central venous pressure)) were made, and continuous ECG (lead II), V_E (respiratory minute volume) and $PETco_2$ recorded. Cardiac output was measured with indocyanine green via duplicate dilution curves at 0 and 5% inspired CO_2 pre and 8-10 mins post THC (during isohypercapnia). CVS parameters calculated included CI (cardiac index), stroke index, TPR (total peripheral resistance), and left ventricular minute work index. THC caused a small dose-related decrease in ventilation seen as decreased V_E and tidal volume (noted by the average slope of dose-response (V_E) curve of - 0.49 L/minute/50% increase in THC dose, but with significant individual variation) with constant respiratory rate. Pre-THC ventilatory responses to CO_2 were normal. Post THC ventilatory responses to CO_2 resulted in a slope (from $PETco_2$ vs V_E) similar to pre-drug slope but displaced to the right by 2.7 torr at 20 L/minute (similar displacement reported for 5 mg morphine IM). It appears that a mild dose-related respiratory depression occurs (with irregular episodes of increased breathing in some individuals secondary to psychological effects). The average HR response to CO_2 increase (41 → 48 torr) during the control pre-drug period was 58 → 65 beats/minute. At a constant $PETco_2$ (48 torr), THC caused a dose-related HR increase (average 89 beats/minute with 27 µg/kg to 101 beats/minute with 134 µg/kg, with signficiant individual variation and 5/6 subjects exhibiting >100 beats/minute); the most dramatic increase being 50 → 120 beats/minute with 27 µg/kg and the fastest HR, 133 beats/minute. A dose-related increase in CI (due to increased HR) also occurred (large individual variation) (control with increasing $PETco_2$ (41 → 48 torr) resulted in increased CI from 3.35 → 4.04 L/minute/m² while at constant $PETco_2$ (48 torr) the CI increase was 5.44 with 27 µg/kg and 6.92 with 134 µg/kg THC), with insignificant change in stroke index, a slight increase in MAP (95 torr → 103 with 134 µg/kg) but without signficiant CVP change, an increase in left ventricular minute work index (5140 → 9630 g/m. minute post 134 µg/kg THC due to increased HR), and a slight decrease in TPR (967 → 676 dyne. second/cm⁵ with 134 µg/kg). Arrhythmias did not occur. Some subjective effects post THC noted were drowsiness, "high" drug effect rated as 8 (average) from scale of 10, odd dreams, excited or alert, difficulty in concentrating and thinking logically, dizziness, nausea and vomiting post study, very dry mouth, burning eyes, blurred vision, and anxiety (1 drop-out post 1st THC dose of 27 µg/kg; 2nd post 5th dose of 106 µg/kg). The THC doses of 134 and 201 µg/kg appeared to sedate the volunteers (without causing unconsciousness) who dissociated themselves from surrounding activities seemingly calm but really feeling considerable anxiety. The CVS effects suggest β-adrenergic stimulation; the excessive tachycardia (arrhythmia) being the limiting toxicity of THC in those who can tolerate the psychological effects which themselves add to the adrenergic effect. However it was felt that the undersirable psychological subjective effects deterred the use of THC as an ataractic (calming) drug.

In addition to inter-drug interactions, vehicles in which oral THC is prepared, may also interact. One study (Perez-Reyes et al., 1973) investigated the influence of 5 different vehicles (solutions of 1.5 ml ethanol/7 subjects and 0.85 ml sesame oil/8 subjects; emulsions of 3.5 ml 5.5% Na glycocholate/10 subjects, 1.25 ml 5.5% Na glycocholate + ethanol/9 subjects and Tween-80/6 subjects) on the rate and degree of absorption, duration of action (including CVS effects), and rate of elimination of oral THC (35 mg, tritium labeled, in gelatin capsules) as well as some metabolic data in 40 fasting (12 hours) healthy male marihuana users (not more than once per week use) hospitalized for 24 hours post drug observation. Absorption and metabolic studies required blood samples q 15 minutes/1st 3 hours, and at 6, 24, 48 and 72 hours as well as collection of urine and feces at time intervals of 0-3, 3-6, 6-24, 48 and 72 hours; THC and metabolites being analysed via chromatography and total radioactivity determined via spectrometry. Subjective psychological "highs" (pleasant or unpleasant) were assessed q 15 minutes/1st 6 hours. Continuous HR was recorded via polygraph and b.p. taken q 15 minutes/1st 3 hours. Rate and degree of gastrointestinal absorption (plasma radioactivity levels) varied with vehicle used, being greatest for Na glycocholate, followed by sesame oil, Tween-80, ethanol, and the combination; the onset of maximum plasma level occurring 1-2 hours post oral drug (coinciding with maximum HR and subjective high) with duration of 6 hours, declining rapidly at 24 hours with slower declines at 48 and 72 hours (Fig. 42). Since ethanol and the combination preparations gave the poorest results, then large amounts of oral THC may be given without serious reactions (reported by some investigators). Thus care must be taken with well absorbed preparations in naive subjects in whom intense dysphoria may occur (not more than 35 mg oral THC). Also there is a large individual variation in absorption of the same vehicle noted by plasma radioactivity levels in 22 subjects who were classed as good or poor absorbers (above or below median level) which was a consistent characteristic observed in repeated experiments (reason?). Subjective psychological "highs" had various degrees of euphoria (elation, easy laughing, perception of time distortion, memory lapses, concentration difficulty, grandiose ideation, inability to evalute ideas and judgments critically) and dysphoria (paranoid ideation, apprehension, fear, panic, and frightening visual hallucinations). The intensity of these effects was related to the vehicle (i.e. rate and degree of absorption noted by high plasma radioactivity) and was greater than that experienced with smoked marihuana and hashish (especially with 35 mg THC in Na glycocholate or sesame oil which produced 3 panic and several paranoid reactions (feeling of vulnerability and apprehension) vs mild dysphoria with ethanol or the combination vehicles). The condition of blood sampling was conducive to dysphoria as was the frequent observation of involuntary muscle jerking, the intensity of which paralleled the rapid development of high plasma radioactivity levels; both dysphoria and movements being controlled with diazepam (IV 10 mg) (both conditions may be an indication of a toxic drug level for a particular individual). Coinciding with the subjective "high" was the development of marked conjunctival congestion and increased HR of 39% above basal rate at the peak "high" (the onset occurring earlier than the former 2 effects); HR increase being due to sympathetic stimulation since propanolol (IV 0.5 mg/6 minutes) blocked tachycardia (in 4 subjects) without altering the "high". The decline in tachycardia coincided with the decrease in "high" by the 6th hour with plasma radioactivity levels remaining elevated. It was felt that the onset and degree of tachycardia may serve as a rough estimate of the onset and amount of drug absorption in a particular individual. Moderate increases in b.p. (systolic 12%, diastolic 16%) occurred at peak HR increase, disappearing in 3 hours. Challenging b.p. control via changing posture (erect position) or drawing a pint of blood (blood volume) resulted in decreased b.p. and bradycardia, a vasodepressor syndrome alleviated via Trendelenberg position. Radioactive oral THC was excreted in the feces more than in urine with a biological half-life of < 48 hours (< 30% in plasma at 48 hours). At peak "highs", low plasma levels of THC and 11-OH-THC were found vs high levels of other metabolites (8, 11-di OH-THC) and polar substances. Plasma THC levels remained elevated 12 hours post drug (may be due to enterohepatic circulation) while metabolite levels were decreased. The major urinary metabolites were 8, 11-di OH-THC and polar compounds (with cannabinoid acids being predominate) while an appreciable amount of THC was found in the feces.

It has been suggested that THC has 2 distinct pharmacological actions in the CNS that affect sympathetic control of HR and b.p., with 2 independent sites of action in the CNS that modulate sympathetic outflow to heart and blood vessels (Hosko & Hardman, 1976). In animals (cats under choralose or barbiturate anesthesia), presser responses to threshold electrical stimuli were assessed via electrodes in hypothalamic, reticular formation, and medullary areas pre and post brain stem transections (mid-collicular and spinal cord at mid-C_1 levels) as well as pre and post (30, 60, 120 minutes) 1 mg/kg IV THC or DMHP (synthetic delta-6a, 10a-dimethylheptyl THC with a potency of 2x THC). In the intact animal, the mean b.p. with barbiturate anesthesia was greater than for chloralose anesthesia, not seen with brain stem transections (Fig. 43). Thus inhibitory impulses from higher brain centres (above mid-collicular levels) under barbiturate anesthesia are less active in modulating sympathetic outflow from the brain stem resulting in apparent higher sympathetic tone. However, HR differences were not evident indicating that barbiturates do not affect higher centres modulating cardioaccelerator outflow. Both THC and DMHP decreased b.p. following both anesthetics and mid-collicular transection but not with spinal cord transection (C_1) indicating a site of THC action between mesencephalon and first cervical level of the brain stem (Fig. 44). It appears that THC produces hypotension (decreased b.p.) and bradycardia (decreased HR) in animals primarily by decreasing spontaneous central sympathetic outflow due to the direct effect on brain stem CVS sites. An attempt to find the specific sites and mechanism of THC action at these sites, was done by studying drug effects on evoked b.p. responses from stimulation of brain stem vasomotor centres (hypothalamus, reticular formation, medulla). Under chloralose anesthesia, THC decreased the baseline mean b.p. and attenuated evoked b.p. responses from 3 vasopressor areas. Under barbituate anesthesia, baseline mean b.p. was again decreased (but from controls that were higher than from choralose anesthesia) by THC with evoked b.p. responses being increased above control responses. Thus barbiturate anesthesia suppressed inhibitory modulating mechanism acting on (medullary) vasopressor neurons giving greater than expected pressor responses to electrical stimulation, with THC enhancing this effect (THC additive to barbiturate effect) (Fig. 45). In other words, the second action of THC is to decrease inhibitory influences of higher centres in modulating sympathetic outlfow from brain stem vasomotor centres. With mid-collicular transection, both anesthetic agents gave similar control evoked pressor responses due to removal of inhibitory influences of centres above mid-collicular level (noted as lowered threshold stimuli) (Fig. 46). THC with barbituate anesthesia again attenuated inhibitory influences, while under chloralose anesthesia reduction of evoked responses did not occur. Therefore, THC has 2 specific mechanisms of action in the CNS; one being to suppress inhibitory influences on medullary vasopressor neurons (exaggerated sympathetic discharge to stimuli) and cardio-accelerator neurons resulting in increased sympathetic outflow (seen as increased b.p. and HR in man); the other, to decrease spontaneous rate of discharge of sympathetic neurons in brain stem vasopressor areas leading to decreased central sympathetic outflow (observed as decreased b.p. and HR in animals).   High THC doses or stress (postural change) may unmask the secondary effect of decreased rate of spontaneous sympathetic neuronal discharge resulting in decreased b.p. and HR in man (postural hypotension). Studies in man involved 2 groups of 6 men (scheduled for orthopedic surgery) who received 20 μg/kg THC, IV (in 95% ethanol vehicle); one group 20 minutes pre pentothal anesthesia (without other pre-anesthetic medication) and the other group, post pentothal anesthesia (after HR & b.p. stabilized). CVS responses (ECG (lead II), b.p.) and rectal temperature were determined pre and post THC (q 1 minute/20 minutes). THC increased diastolic b.p. prior to anesthesia but not after anesthesia because the barbiturate removed the inhibitory modulation of central vasopressor outflow thereby increasing sympathetic tone which was not increased further by THC (Fig. 47).   However increased HR brought about by THC was not altered by anesthesia indicating a more resistant sympathetic pathway (controlling HR) to the depressant THC or anesthetic effects than that involved with peripheral vascular resistance.

In the normal animal, b.p. is determined by the level of sympathetic outflow from the CNS which depends upon 3 factors:

(1)   rate of spontaneous neuronal firing in brainstem sympathetic centres;

(2)   inhibitory and facilitory mechanisms at the brain stem level, and

(3)   from higher CNS levels (Fig. 48).

These factors remained relatively constant under chloralose anesthesia while under barbiturate anesthesia an imbalance occurred by decreasing inhibitory mechanisms (especially above diencephalon level) resulting in increased baseline b.p. and exaggerated evoked pressor responses to stimuli. The THCs have 2 actions: they

(1)   act directly on brain stem CVS centres decreasing spontaneous sympathetic efferent activity leading to decreased b.p., and

(2)   also suppress inhibitory mechanisms similar to barbiturates.

Combining THC with barbiturate anesthesia, decreases b.p. due to direct brainstem action while evoked pressor response is increased by further suppression of inhibitory mechanism brought about by the barbiturate (the augmentation indicating that sympathetic pathways are not affected directly per se by the agents). The above hypothesis requires direct monitoring of sympathetic flow to heart and peripheral vessels.

(f) Discussion and Summary

The physiology or normal function of the heart (cor) is to maintain blood circulation carried by blood vessels to and from body tissues supplying O_2 (oxygen) and removing CO_2 (carbon dioxide), both gases being exchanged in the lungs; the cardiac muscle itself requiring O_2 (myocardial O_2 demand = HR x systolic b.p.) which is supplied by coronary blood flow. Factors which decrease O_2 supply or blood flow for tissue needs lead to ischemia (hypoxia or localized tissue anemia) and include decreased b.p., increased HR, coronary vascular obstruction, increased ventricular wall tension, as well as hypoxic effects of COHb (due to CO (carbon monoxide) in smoke).

Studies on the CVS (cardiovascular) effects of marihuana and its constituents (by various routes (inhalation, oral, intravenous), doses, frequency, duration) were conducted in man (normal healthy (naive, former marihuana users), glaucoma and cardiac (angina pectoris) patients) in differenct postures (supine, sitting, standing erect) under different conditions (resting, exercise, surgical stress) noting HR, b.p., blood flow, cardiac performance, electrical activity of the heart via ECG and His bundle recordings (cardiac conduction system) as well as substance interactions and attempting to find the mechanism of action (peripheral and central) for the CVS responses. Plasma THC profiles were found to be similar for IV and inhalation routes while oral intake produced low irregular plasma levels; systemic THC availability being 18% vs oral of 6%.

Marihuana has been shown to have peripheral vasodilating properties noted as:

(a) increased peripheral blood flow in the recumbent position (not evident in the upright position, i.e. reflex mechanisms unopposed by THC) with increased cutaneous temperature,

(b) being able to prevent peripheral vasoconstriction (hand in ice-water) while intensifying β-epinephrine (α and β-adrenergic) effects without altering norepinephrine (α-adrenergic) effects, and

(c) producing conjunctival injection or hyperemia (reddening of eyes) lessened by a β-blocker; the reddening found to be a sensitive indicator of intoxication and prevailing plasma THC level (above 5 ng/ml).

In the supine position, a slight insignificant increase in venous tone has been observed with oral THC, with a significant decrease in reflex venoconstriction (decreased venous pressure following a deep breath). Tobacco smoking on the other hand did not change peripheral blood flow significantly (net change of vasoconstriction) and decreased cutaneous temperature with increased HR, b.p., and coronary flow (due to increased cardiac output and cardiac work) as well as increasing blood sugar and a tendency to blood clotting; the effects being due to epinephrine release by nicotine. Smoke emits CO (carbon monoxide) gas which when inhaled results in COHb (carboxyhemoglobin) leading to hypoxia which causes vasodilation with compensatory HR increase. Since the heart is sensitive to hypoxia, it works harder increasing HR and b.p. with possible permanent damage due to COHb; chronic CO exposure facilitating atherosclerotic development due to anoxic damage to the arterial wall facilitating lipid infiltration.

Following marihuana use, b.p. (blood pressure) change was dose related correlating with HR (heart rate) increase better than with dose suggesting that plasma cannabinoid levels would be a better indicator of dose for a particular individual. Tolerance developed to b.p. change due to compensatory plasma volume expansion accounting for increased body weight and decreased Hb (hemoglobin) concentration resulting in functional anemia. B.p. change varied with posture, increasing during a supine position with variable alteration (no change, decrease, increase) while sitting and decreasing (systolic > diastolic) in the standing erect position with postural hypotension (accompanied by dysphoria and "low" mood) occurring in some individuals (naive and experienced) to the point of unconsciousness (being alleviated when placed in the supine position). The act of assuming the upright position normally leads to compensatory (reflex via carotid baroreceptor) vasoconstriction accompanied by increased b.p. and HR to accomodate adequate cerebral perfusion. A sudden b.p. decrease leads to decreased blood supply to the brain (cerebral anemia or ischemia increasing vagal action resulting in a sharp decrease in HR prior to fainting) causing unconsciousness (temporary); supine positioning increasing venous return. Marihuana appears to interfere with compensatory vascular adjustments (noted above as peripheral vasodilation and cancelling vasoconstriction) encouraging syncope upon standing. Exercising increases systolic b.p. and HR with a large decrease in diastolic pressure. However following oral THC, b.p. baseline is lowered without affecting HR increase or diastolic pressure decrease (but at a lower level) with blunting of systolic pressure increase which may be due to venodilation (direct or sympathetic inhibition), i.e., the HR increase is insufficient to keep b.p. at normal levels.

All studies with cannabinoids revealed a dose-related HR increase (onset 2-3 minutes, peak at 15-30 minutes, duration 1.5-2 hours for inhalation; oral, maximum at 3 hours, duration 4-5 hours) correlating with plasma THC levels. Tolerance developed within a relatively short period of time (14-21 days) with decreased peak effects by the second week of intoxication (smoking 2 marihuana cigarettes with 20 mg THC/cigarette daily); the onset depending upon the degree of marihuana use, developing gradually in light users with abrupt decrease in HR change (2-4 weeks) in heavy marihuana users. HR at such time (tolerance) may be below pre-intoxication levels (tendency towards bradycardia) which may be brought about by plasma volume expansion. Cross tolerance has been demonstrated between smoking marihuana and oral THC. It has been suggested that the onset and degree of tachycardia may serve as a rough estimate of onset and amount of drug absorption in a particular individual (keeping in mind the state of tolerance). Persistent tachycardia (in accident victims) should raise suspicion of recent marihuana use. The psychological state of mind (CNS) may alter or modify HR (increase) response, intensifying the response with anxiety or damping it with sedation (somnolence) associated with marihuana use. Peak subjective "high" (time perception distortion, recent memory defect, bodily sensation preoccupation) occurs about the same time as peak tachycardia (reports of before and 12 minutes after) returning to the normal state concomitantly. Tolerance also develops to the "high". A mild withdrawal (irritability, restlessness, anorexia or loss of appetite, insomnia, mild nausea, sweating) has been observed following one week abstinence especially in the heaviest users.

Peripheral vasodilation with compensatory HR increase may be responsible for other observed CVS changes. The increased cardiac output noted following acute marihuana use may be due to blood from the thoracic reservoir entering the systemic bed or increased preload (inflow volume pressure or venous return) resulting in increased LVET and stroke volume. Then cardiac output decreases due to peripheral venodilation leading to decreased preload with decreased afterload (systolic pressure) with a slight decrease in stroke volume. Systolic time interval measurements used as an index of left ventricular function reveal significant shortening of PEP (ventricular pre-ejection period) indicating enhanced cardiac performance followingTHC (oral, IV) which may be blocked by propanolol, a β-adrenergic blocker when PEP is increased. Inhaled marihuana and THC caused increased VCF (mean velocity of ventricular circumferential fibre shortening) resulting in decreased LVET (left ventricular ejection time) with a slight decrease in ejection fraction and stroke volume as well as decreased ventricular diastolic duration.

While healthy non-marihuana users did not reveal ECG abnormalities, the smoking of marihuana cigarettes or ingestion of oral THC by both naive and experienced users demonstrated varied ECG changes (without cardiac symptoms), the severity of which appeared to depend upon the degree of previous smoking habits. During and following (0.5 hour post smoking) cannabinoid intake, reported ECG alterations included:

(1) P-waves changes; increased width and decreased amplitude in naive subjects while experienced users showed increased amplitude. A sudden increase in right ventricular burden (e.g. acute cor pulmonale) produces sudden widening and peaking of P-waves as well as tachycardia and right ventricular hypertrophy pattern temporarily; chronic pulmonary emphysema may show tall peaked P-waves without hypertrophy pattern. Is there some degree of lung damage present in experienced marihuana smokers to account for P-waves changes (or is the increased amplitude a consequence of tachycardia)?

(2) T-wave or repolarization abnormalities; flattening or decreased amplitude as well as inversion. Alteration in T-wave may be associated with temporary increase in cardiac work load and is observed with epinephrine (adrenergic) as decreased amplitude. T-wave inversion is the result of myocardial ischemia being due to tachycardia and functional anemia brought about by marihuana and is a reversible process unless coronary arteriosclerosis develops. Could T-wave changes be a prodromal sign to PVC development?

(3) ST-segment variation from the isoelectric line; elevation or depression. Epinephrine causes ST-segment changes above or below the isoelectric line of the ECG; the changes often following T-wave direction unless current of injury or myocardial death occurs.

(4) Cardiac arrhythmias or heart beat irregularities - PVCs or premature ventricular contractions (e.g. bigeminy; PVC after each normal beat) occurring at higher THC concentrations or at lower doses in heavy marihuana users. PVCs have been observed in anginal patients exposed passively to tobacco (nicotine) smoke prior to and following exercise. Development of PVCs with marihuana are similar to those seen with nicotine or caffeine. Ischemia (increase O_2 demand and/or decrease O_2 delivery) or excessive catecholamine release in normal hearts may produce PVCs.

All ECG abnormalities reverted to normal upon cessation of drug (cannabinoid) use. THC (IV) facilitated cardiac SA and AV nodal conduction noted as decreased P-R interval (similar to isoproterenol, a β-adrenergic) and increased sinus node automaticity (increased HR) suggesting an adrenergic effect. The marihuana effect of a reflex increase in HR due to peripheral vasodilation may be due to epinephrine release which is known to directly stimulate:

(a) β$_1$-receptors in the myocardium,

(b) cells in the pacemaker (SA node), and

(c) conducting tissues, with ECG alterations of decreased T-wave amplitude along with varied ST-segment changes (above or below isoelectric line).

These electrical changes (similar to angina pectoris) are due to myocardial hypoxia brought about by the inability of coronary blood flow to keep pace with increased O_2 requirement of the heart stimulated by epinephrine (i.e. increased work of the heart and O_2 consumption leading to decreased cardiac efficiency). The effects of CO gas from smoke may be additive to THC since CO is known to cause sinus tachycardia, T-wave abnormalities, ST-segment depression, atrial fibrillation, ischemic changes, and subendocardial infarction. A possible cardiotoxic marihuana effect has been reported as acute subendocardial infarction with pulmonary edema associated with smoking marihuana mixed equally with tobacco by an expereinced marihuana and tobacco user. ECG revealed deep extensive T-wave inversion (ischemia) reverting to normal within 6 weeks without the development of pathological Q-waves (i.e. no myocardial muscle necrosis or death). Subendocardial areas of the myocardium are particularly vulnerable to ischemia. Infarction (subendocardial) may also occur after prolonged hypotension. The possibility exists that cardiac electrical changes due to marihuana effects may become irreversible with continued drug use leading to permanent heart damage.

Pain in angina occurs at a relatively constant level of myocardial work (HR x b.p. or O_2 demand) and may be prevented by avoiding myocardial hypoxia. The relation between pain and hypoxia is identified via exercise tolerance. If a drug decreases hypoxia then the amount of exertion necessary to produce pain and depress ST-segment (in ECG) increases in parallel. Increased sympathetic activity (drugs, emotional factors) increase O_2 myocardial requirement thereby precipitating anginal attacks in susceptible individuals. Exercise performance (duration) was decreased in healthy (may be interpreted as decreased work output noted earlier) and angina (symptom of ischemic heart disease experienced as severe constricting chest pain) patients with marihuana use due to increased HR (which may be insufficient to maintain adequate b.p. level). That is, myocardial O_2 demand (HR x b.p.) was increased and O_2 delivery decreased due to decreased coronary blood flow as well as increased COHb with ischemic ST-segment depression occurring sooner with marihuana use. Similar effects have been observed with nicotine (direct and passive smoking) with the decrease in exercise performance being less than with marihuana which also precipitates angina sooner. Passive CO (carbon monoxide) exposure places a strain on heart function with an inability to compensate for hypoxia by angina patients (healthy individuals respond by increasing cardiac output and blood flow to critical organs). Other conditions that lower the threshold to CO effects are drugs including alcohol, respiratory disease, pregnancy and anemia. A functional anemia (due to decreased Hb brought about by compensatory plasma volume expansion noted above) may contribute to myocardial ischemia (T-wave inversion). THC plus increased COHb levels have been found to be responsible for decreased LVEDV (left ventricular end-diastolic volume, ml), decreased stroke index (ml/beat/m^2) and decreased EF (ejection fraction = stroke volume/LVEDV). Mental (CNS) dysfunction (cognitive; intellectual impairment) was observed following the smoking of marihuana (30 minutes duration) which appeared to block normal psycho-cardiovascular correlations between hostility and b.p., ejection fraction, and, between anxiety and LVEDV. The possibility exists that CNS effects may be secondary to peripheral vascular effects. It may be seen that marihuana would be deleterious or detrimental to the health of angina patients.

Drugs used in glaucoma do not combat the basic disease process (compare to hypertensive treatment) but one of manifestations (ocular hypertension). In glaucoma (ocular hypertension) patients, marihuana decreases IOP (intraocular pressure; onset within 1 hour, peak 1.5 hours, duration 4 hours) and systemic b.p. with HR increase; a further decrease in IOP occurring during postural hypotension when both b.p. and HR decrease. The decrease in IOP may be due to decreased fluid formation and/or increased fluid outflow, the latter perhaps being further facilitated by pupil constriction. However preservation of visual function remains to be assessed. Also marihuana use for glaucoma may be undesireable because b.p. decrease may lead to insufficient blood flow to the optic nerve resulting in possible nerve atrophy or blindness aside from side-effects of anxiety and palpitations.

A history of marihuana use should caution the clinician re use of such premedications as atropine or local anesthetics with epinephrine which may prolong tachycardia. Persistent tachycardia in accident victims as well as ECG abnormalities should arouse suspicion of cannabinoid use. Surgical stress acts synergistically with THC re HR increase effects. Potential hazards of attempting to anesthetize a marihuana intoxicated individual include psychotic behaviour being made worse with barbiturates and augmentation of opioid ventilatory depression; tachycardia warranting ECG monitoring. Possible blood coaguability impairment has been inferred from decreased platelet aggregation following marihuana smoking. Different vehicles which have been used for oral THC preparations influenced the rate and degree of drug absorption (ethanol giving the poorest results). The large individual variation occurring with the same vehicle was due to good or poor (gastrointestinal) absorbers which may account for varied responses such as euphoria or dysphoria (good absorbers) and which may have a greater effect than smoked marihuana.

The mechanism of action has not been established and remains controversial. Propanolol (β-adrenergic blocker; competitive antagonist) prevented tachycardia (β$_1$-adrenergic receptor) and the increased peripheral blood flow (β$_2$-adrenergic receptor), while atropine (anticholinergic) enhanced tachycardia and increased b.p., with epinephrine (α and β-agonist) intensifying HR and peripheral blood flow (decreasing b.p.), and norepinephrine (α-agonist) decreasing blood flow with increased b.p. and decreased HR. A significant increase in urinary epinephrine excretion has been observed 6 hours after oral THC which did not alter norepinephrine excretion. One study revealed increased plasma norepinephrine levels (supine position) after smoking marihuana (0.5-2 hours post); a similar effect being noted with smoking 2 nicotine cigarettes (both types of cigarettes increasing COHb). Standing produced increased plasma norepinephrine with placebo and with marihuana indicating sympathetic nervous system capability of responding to change in position. A possible β-adrenergic peripheral effect (in conjunction with some other unknown mechanism) has been suggested while a central mechanism (affecting sympathetic control of HR and b.p.) may have a primary site of action in the higher CNS area (decreasing inhibitory mechanism leading to increased b.p. and HR) with secondary site in the brain stem (decreasing spontaneous sympathetic outflow leading to decreased b.p. and HR) modulating sympathetic out flow to heart and blood vessels; the sympathetic pathway not being affected directly per se by the drug. It appears that the adrenergic system is involved in the normal autoregulatory or compensatory mechanism to altered physiological function produced by cannabinoids which may activate the CNS sympathoadrenal system with β-adrenergic receptors being the final common pathway. At the cellular level, cannabinoids were found to inhibit CaATPase activity with decreased Ca uptake which may depress cardiac contractility.

Marihuana may relax smooth muscles (peripheral blood vessels including conjunctival vessels, bronchial smooth muscles) non-specifically reminiscent of nitrites which are vasodilators (arterial and venous) used to increase blood flow, especially in large coronary vessels (vs antihypertensives, such as hydralazine, used primarily to decrease b.p.). Nitrites relax all smooth muscle irrespective of innervation and may be antagonized by any drug that activates smooth muscle. That is, they are functional antagonists of autonomic system substances such that the net response (maximum contraction to maximum relaxation) depends on the relative concentration of 2 chemicals (competative inhibition as with nitrite or marihuana and propanolol). A compensatory mechanism (e.g. sympathetic) may overcome the net effect. (Competitive inhibition between cannabis and the adrenergic system has been suggested by at least two studies: 1) THC effects in animals have been reversed with amphetamine or epinephrine (McMillan et al., 1971; in discussion portion of paper); and 2) in tolerance and dependence studies in humans (Jones and Benowitz, 1976; tolerance developed to tachycardia with periods of bradycardia of 45 beats/min, to orthostatic hypotension, and to decreased intraocular pressure) during THC, the CVS responses to exercise, position changes, cold pressor tests, and Valsalve maneuvers, resembled central sympathetic block.) Vascular smooth muscle is particularly affected with CVS response being sensitive to gravitational influences due to changes in venous return (i.e. cerebral ischemia associated with postural hypotension with unconsciousness due to inadequate compensatory tachycardia, accentuated with alcohol). Large blood vessels (arteries and veins) are relaxed more than smaller vessles (arterioles, venules) with a rapid b.p. decrease resulting in rapid reflex compensation (may have a net increase rather than decrease in venous tone in the forearm). The systolic b.p. decrease is greater than the diastolic (small pulse pressure reflecting stroke volume decrease) with compensatory relfex tachycardia which, if marked, may aggravate circulatory inadequacy. In normal individuals, nitrites, at therapeutic doses, decrease O_2 myocardial requirement via decreasing preload (due to venodilation leading to decreased cardiac output) and afterload (due to decreased peripheral arteriolar resistance with a small increase in stroke volume), the net effect being a large b.p. decrease and tachycardia. In congestive heart failure, cardiac output is increased (by appropriately decreasing pre and afterloads with a net reduction of myocardial O_2 demand) which may counterbalance the peripheral resistance decrease with little or no change in b.p. and HR. Benefits for angina patients involve reduction of myocardial ischemia by decreasing myocardial O_2 demand (via decreasing pre and afterloads which affect the stress on the ventricular wall determined by diastolic and systolic ventricular pressures respectively). With high nitrite doses, the reflex tachycardia (due to a large diastolic pressure decrease) and enhanced (adrenergic) contractility increase myocardial O_2 demand overriding the salutary drug effects. That is, the negative O_2 balance effect may aggravate ischemia and potentially initiate anginal attacks. Occasionally, in angina patients, ST-segment depression (seen with exercise) or myocardial hypoxia is observed with a rapid b.p. decrease and is due to reflex sympathetic effects. Tolerance can develop to frequent high nitrite doses. Perhaps non-intoxicating marihuana doses (avoiding tachycardia) may fall within the realm of nitrite therapeutic dose effects(?). It would also be interesting to find out if cannabinoids persist (affinity for) in muscular arterial vessel walls (as occurrs with hydralazine).

Since marihuana is being used for its intoxicating effects (to which tolerance develops), the CVS responses elicited are really toxic (vs therapeutic) dose effects and may be a form or state of shock (depression of vital processes associated with decreased blood pressure and/or volume) secondary to vasodilation occurring with drug intoxication as seen with a large nitrite dose (nitroid shock). The effects alluded to include decreased b.p., increased HR, with postural hypotension (gravitational shock or orthostatic peripheral circulatory failure) including unconsciousness as well as anxiety (primary shock) brought about by derangement of circulatory control producing vasodilation (vasogenic and/or (cerebral) neurogenic shock) with some respiratory depression. Vasodilation (responsible for orthostatic b.p. decrease and conjunctival reddening) stimulates carotid sinus baroreceptors (sensitive to pressure changes) which initiates HR increase (according to Marey's Law; HR varies inversely with b.p.). In time,

O_2 deficiency (including CO gas in smoke) stimulates chemoreceptors (in carotid and especially aortic bodies) resulting also in HR increase. These additive HR increase effects are attempts to move blood through the vessels at sufficient speed to achieve adequate physiological tissue O_2 levels or better tissue perfusion. The possibility exists that decreased body tissue perfusion may lead to anoxic conditions (i.e. severe hypoxia or O_2 deficiency resulting in permanent damage, as, for example, to arterial walls predisposing them to lipid infiltration resulting in atherosclerosis) which may help explain functional depression of the various systems studied (especially with chronic drug use at intoxicating doses, being more detrimental in diseased states such as angina pectoris). It is suggested that marihuana enters the lungs where it is rapidly absorbed into the circulation leading to a direct effect on blood vessels (peripheral vasodilation) resulting in a sudden orthostatic b.p. decrease which initiates a reflex mechanism (implicating the CNS) giving rise to compensatory HR increase. In time, plasma volume expands in response to b.p. decrease due to peripheral vasodilation, bringing both b.p. and HR towards normal (with body weight increase) with prolonged drug use, eventually decreasing HR reflexly. Hb concentration is decreased or diluted with plasma volume expansion resulting in functional anemia with inadequate tissue oxygenation leading to functional depression of body systems (tire easily; cerebral ischemia when not think or function adequately and which may increase vagal activity thereby contributing to HR decrease). Could it be that some of marihuana body system effects may be due to peripheral vasodilation properties with tolerance development due to plasma expansion which is responsible for functional anemia leading to hypoxic tissue effects (to the point of anoxia or permanent damage) which in turn may help explain sluggish functioning (including lack of motivation and mental awareness or state of shock) aside from the direct smoke effects on the lungs? And how would CVS effects vary if marihuana was smoked as tobacco cigarettes, cigars, or pipe are smoked? Perhaps inhalation patterns may explain the difference between human (long slow inhalation encouraging absorption of a large quantity of drug leading to an abrupt b.p. decrease with compensatory HR increase) and animal (rapid shallow respiration with bradycardia post marihuana) CVS effects.

II. 3. D_2 Cardiovascular System

List of Figures

Fig. 1.	Tachycardia and euphoria tolerance development	189
Fig. 2.	Rate of tolerance development to tachycardia	190
Fig. 3.	Degree of tolerance development to euphoria	191
Fig. 4.	Conjunctival reddening post THC smoking	192
Fig. 5.	Pulse rate post THC smoking	193
Fig. 6.	Plasma THC level, pulse, subjective "high"	194
Fig. 7.	The human eye	195
Fig. 8.	Heart rate post marihuana smoking	196
Fig. 9.	Intraocular pressure in glaucoma	196
Fig. 10.	Blood pressure	197
Fig. 11.	Marihuana effects in naive subject	198
Fig. 12.	Marihuana effects in experienced subject	199
Fig. 13.	Varied postures heart rate changes	200
Fig. 14.	Varied postures blood pressure changes	201
Fig. 15.	Systolic time interval measurements	202
Fig. 16.	Ventricular pre-ejection period changes	203
Fig. 17.	Reflex venoconstriction changes	204
Fig. 18.	Forearm blood flow changes	205
Fig. 19.	Forearm conductance changes	206
Fig. 20.	THC + metabolites plasma levels	207
Fig. 21.	Heart rate and systolic time interval changes	208
Fig. 22.	HR and STI changes with and without prior propanolol	209
Fig. 23.	Cardiac arrhythmia	209
Fig. 24.	Cardiovascular changes	210
Fig. 25.	Cardiovascular parameter changes	211
Fig. 26.	Circulatory effects	212
Fig. 27.	Postural change circulatory alterations	213
Fig. 28.	Postural change circulatory alterations	214
Fig. 29.	Circulatory response pre and post exercise	215
Fig. 30.	Weight and hemoglobin modifications	216
Fig. 31.	Heart rate response pre and post exercise	217
Fig. 32.	Heart rate response pre and post exercise	218
Fig. 33.	Premature ventricular contraction	217
Fig. 34.	Surgical premedication effects on blood pressure	219
Fig. 35.	Surgical premedication effects on heart rate	220
Fig. 36.	Circulatory and psychological effects of surgical premedication	221
Fig. 37.	Surgical premedication effects on cardiac arrhythmia development	222
Fig. 38.	General anesthesia effect on heart rate	223
Fig. 39.	Ventilatory effects of combined drugs	224
Fig. 40.	Ventilatory responses to CO_2	224
Fig. 41.	Heart rate effects of combined drugs	225
Fig. 42.	Plasma radioactivity level post oral THC	226
Fig. 43.	Blood pressure in intact and brain stem transected animals	227
Fig. 44.	THC b.p. effects in intact and brain stem transected animals	228
Fig. 45.	THC b.p. evoked responses in intact animals	229
Fig. 46.	THC b.p. evoked responses in brain stem transected animals	230
Fig. 47.	THC b.p. effects pre and post barbiturate anesthesia in man	231
Fig. 48.	Mechanism re THC and barbiturate b.p. effects in animals	232

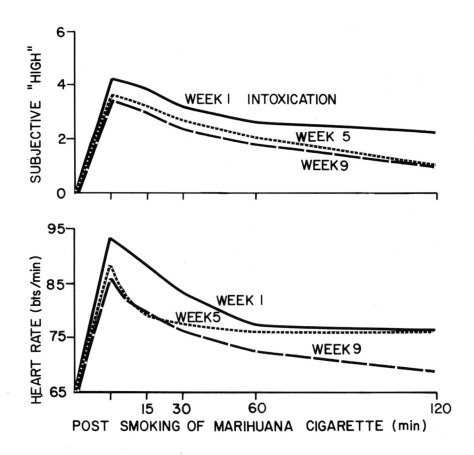

Fig. 1.   Tolerance development to heart rate changes and euphoria.
II.3.D$_2$
Adapted from Nowlan and Cohen, 1977.

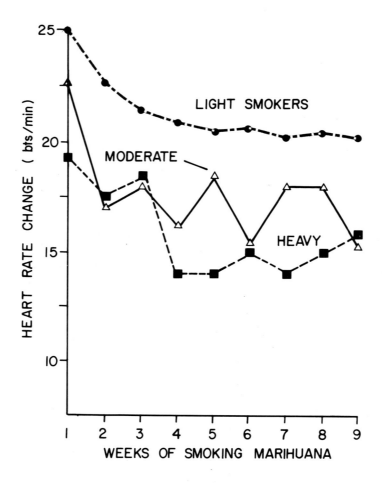

Fig. 2.   Rate of tolerance development to heart rate changes by smoking 1
II.3.D$_2$ marihuana cigarette post weekly (9) intoxication.

Adapted from Nowlan and Cohen, 1977.

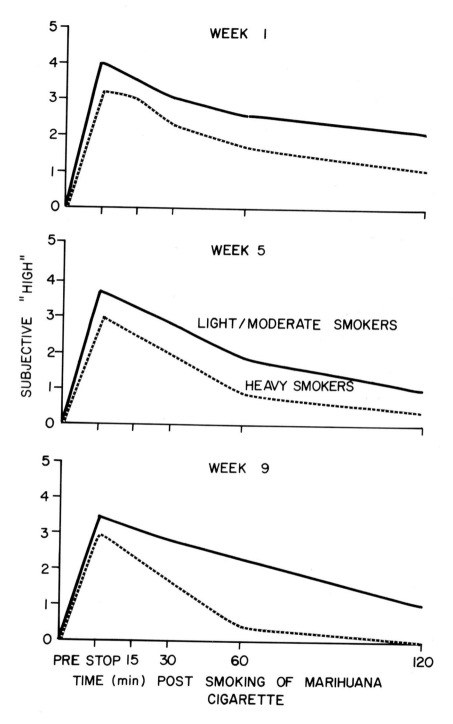

Fig. 3.
II.3.D$_2$ Degree of tolerance development to euphoria.

Adapted from Nowlan and Cohen, 1977.

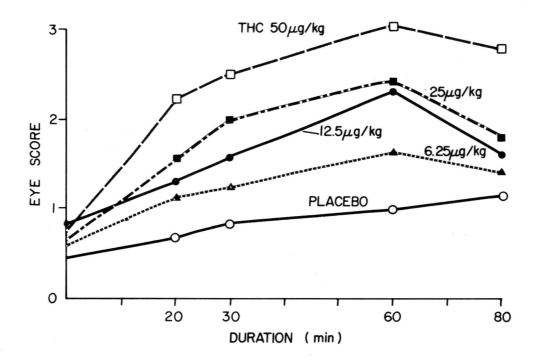

Fig. 4.
II.3.D$_2$ Conjunctival reddening following smoking of THC.

Adapted from Kiplinger et al., 1971.

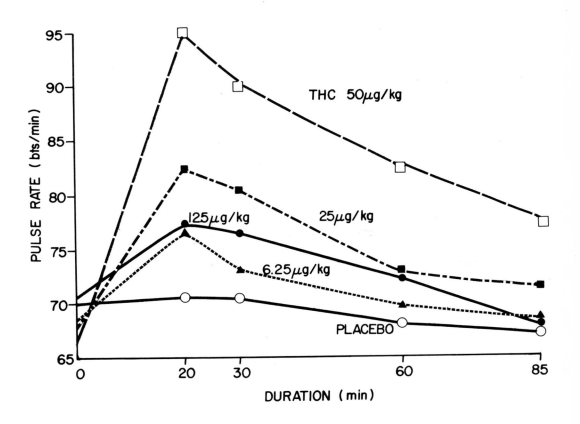

Fig. 5.   Pulse rate following smoking of THC.
II.3.D$_2$
             Adapted from Kiplinger et al., 1971.

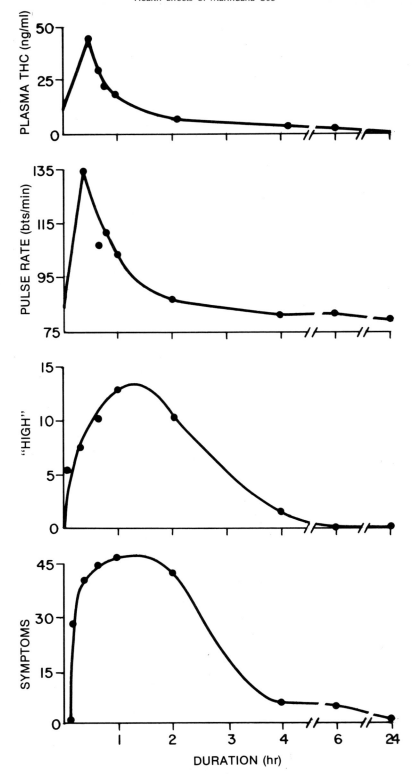

Fig. 6.   Plasma THC concentration, pulse, and subjective "high" post smoking
II.3.D$_2$ of 10 mg synthetic THC.

Adapted from Galanter et al., 1972.

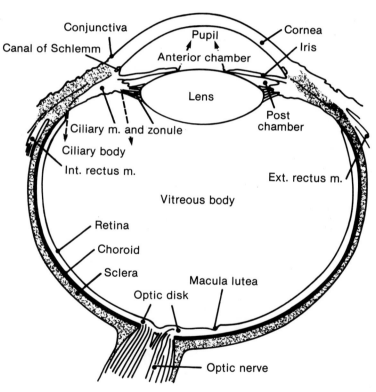

Fig. 7.
II.3.D$_2$

THE HUMAN EYE

Adapted from Stedman's dictionary.

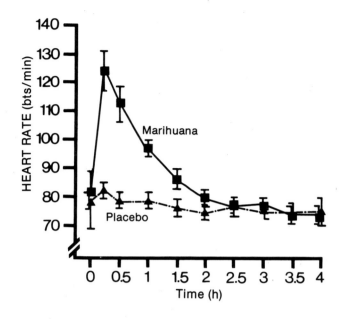

Fig. 8.
II.3.D$_2$

Heart rate post marihuana or placebo smoking.

Adapted from Merritt et al., 1980.

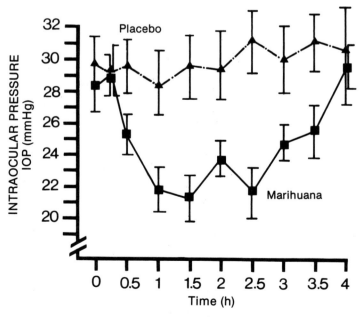

Fig. 9.
II.3.D$_2$

Intraocular pressure in glaucoma eyes post marihuana or placebo smoking.

Adapted from Merritt et al., 1980.

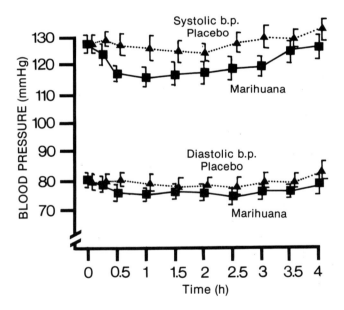

Fig. 10.   Blood pressure post marihuana or placebo smoking.
II.3.D$_2$
                  Adapted from Merritt et al., 1980.

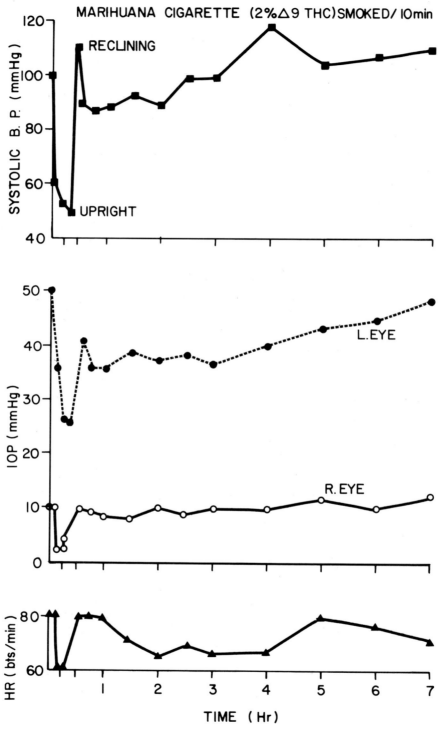

Fig. 11.   Marihuana effect in naive subject.
II.3.D$_2$

Adapted from Merritt et al., 1980.

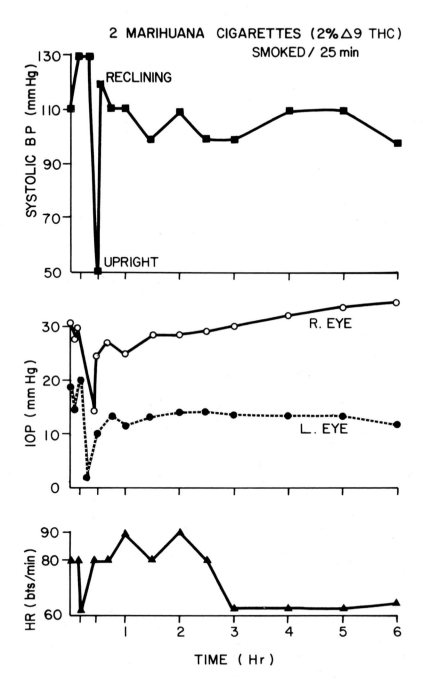

Fig. 12.   Marihuana effect in experienced subject.

II.3.D$_2$

                Adapted from Merritt et al., 1980.

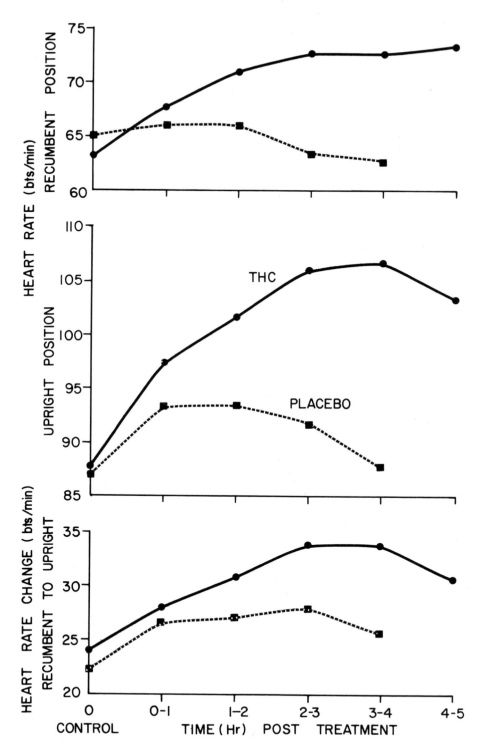

Fig. 13.   Heart rate changes with varied postures due to oral THC or placebo.
II.3.D$_2$
                Adapted from Weiss et al., 1972.

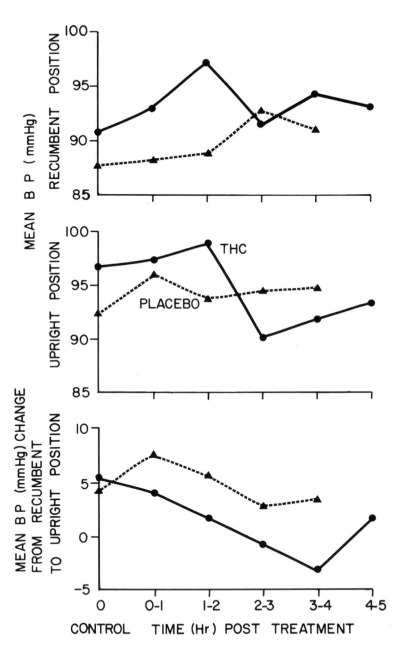

Fig. 14.   Mean arterial blood pressure changes with varied postures due to oral
II.3.D₂   THC or placebo.

Adapted from Weiss et al., 1972.

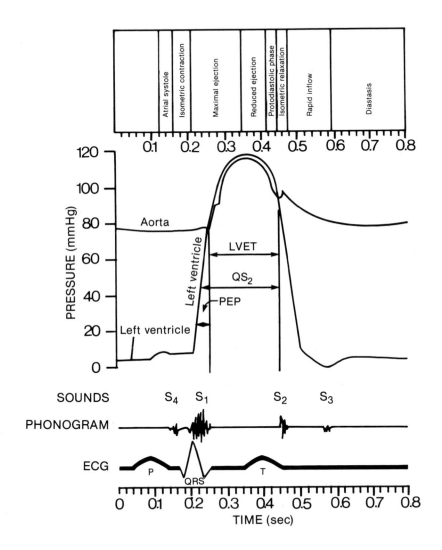

Fig. 15.   Systolic time interval measurements used as an index of left ventri-
II.3.D$_2$ cular function.
             Definition: PEP (ventricular pre-ejection period, m sec.) measurement
             = Q.S$_2$ interval (from onset of QRS of ECG to first high frequency
             component of second sound) - LVET (left ventricular ejection time;
             from onset of upstroke to dicrotic notch of carotid pressure curve).

             Adapted from Merck Manual, 13th edition.

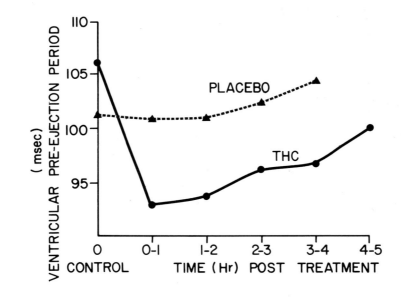

Fig. 16.   Ventricular pre-ejection period changes post oral THC or placebo.
II.3.D$_2$

Adapted from Weiss et al., 1972.

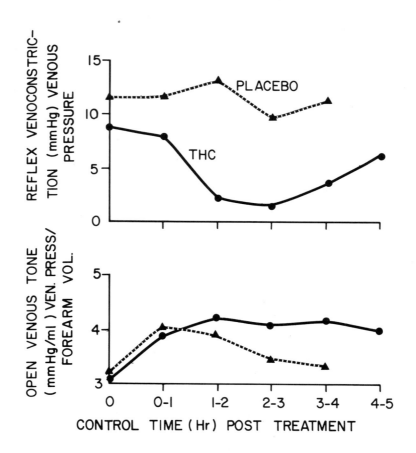

Fig. 17.   Changes in reflex venoconstriction post maximal deep breath and in
II.3.D$_2$ open venous tone due to oral THC or placebo.

Adapted from Weiss et al., 1972.

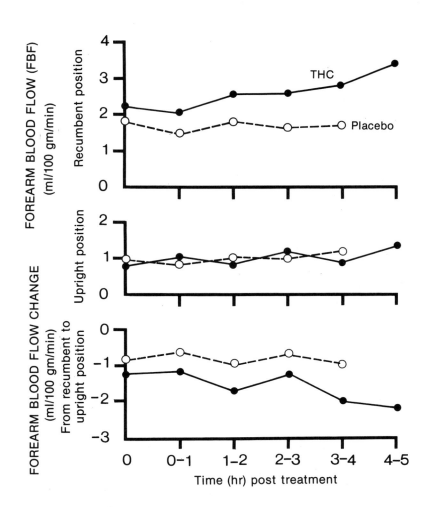

Fig. 18.   Forearm blood flow changes with varied postures due to oral THC or
II.3.D$_2$ placebo.

Adapted from Weiss et al., 1972.

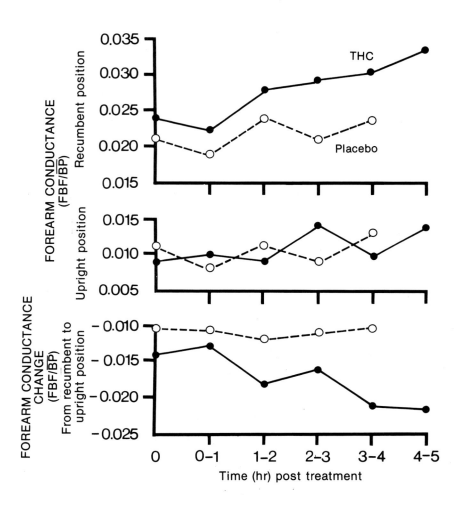

Fig. 19.   Calculated forearm conductance changes with varied postures due to
II.3.D$_2$ oral THC or placebo.

Adapted from Weiss et al., 1972.

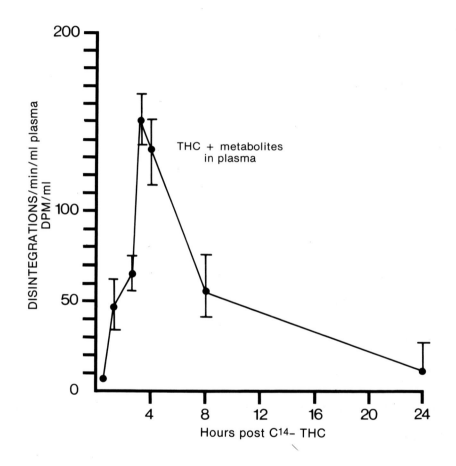

Fig. 20.   THC (and metabolites) plasma levels post oral C^{14}-Δ^9 THC (10 µc).
II.3.D_2

Adapted from Weiss et al., 1972.

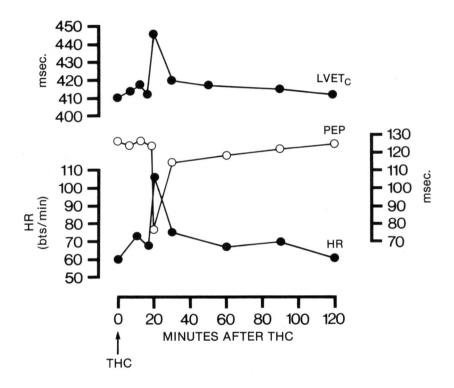

Fig. 21.   Heart (HR) and systolic time interval (PEP; LVET$_c$) changes post THC
II.3.D$_2$ (IV).

Adapted from Kanakis et al., 1976.

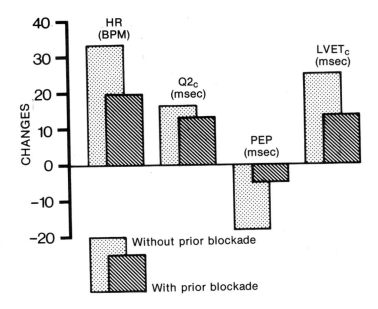

Fig. 22.
II.3.D$_2$

Heart rate (HR) and systolic time interval (Q2c; PEP; LVETc) changes due to THC (IV) with and without prior propanolol (IV; β-adrenergic blocker).

Adapted from Kanakis et al., 1976.

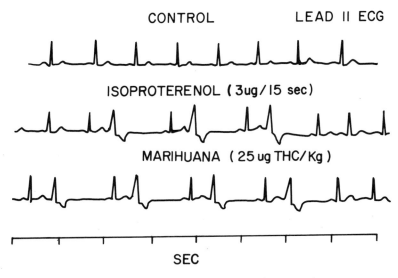

Fig. 23.
II.3.D$_2$

Development of cardiac arrhythmia (bigeminy) in one subject post marihuana smoking or isoproterenol injection (IV; β-adrenergic drug).

Adapted from Bright et al., 1971.

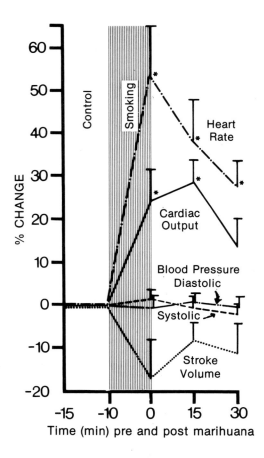

Fig. 24.   Changes post one marihuana cigarette.
II.3.D$_2$
               Adapted from Tashkin et al., 1977.

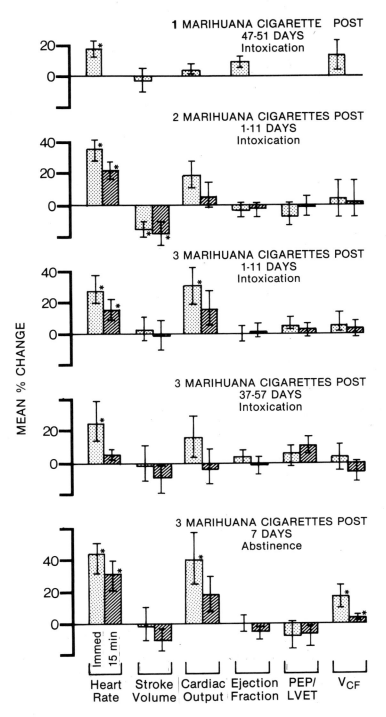

Fig. 25. Parameter changes (immediate; at 15 min) post marihuana cigarettes
II.3.D$_2$ (1-3) after early (1-11 days) and late (37-57 days) intoxication periods,
and after 7 days abstinence.

Adapted from Tashkin et al., 1977.

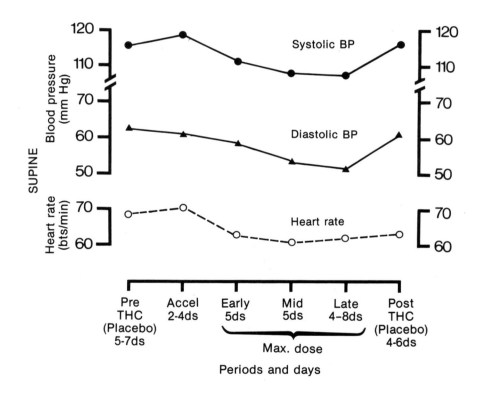

Fig. 26.   Circulatory effects during placebo and oral THC (maximum 210
II.3.D$_2$ mg/d/20 days) intake.

Adapted from Benowitz and Jones, 1975.

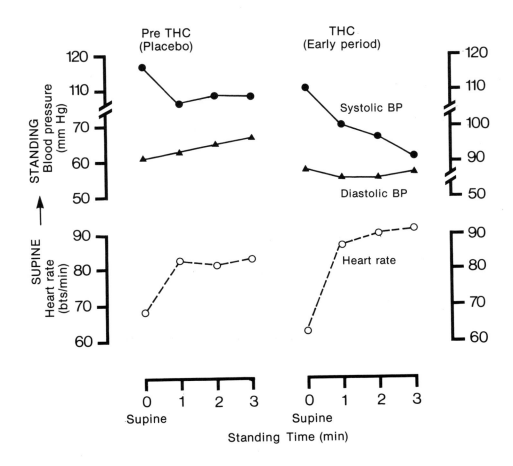

Fig. 27.
II.3.D$_2$

Circulatory alterations with posture change pre and post oral THC
(maximum 210 mg/d/5 days) intake during early period.

Adapted from Benowitz and Jones, 1975.

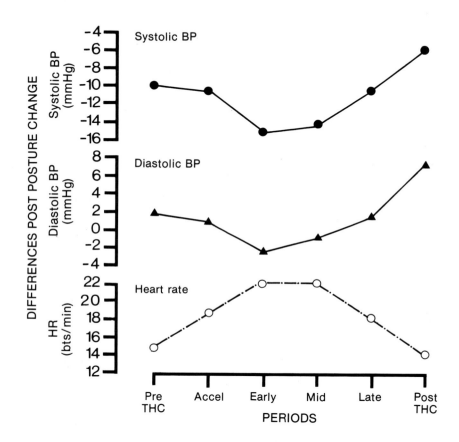

Fig. 28.   Circulatory changes with posture change (supine to standing/1 min)
II.3.D$_2$ pre, during and post oral THC intake.

Adapted from Benowitz and Jones, 1975.

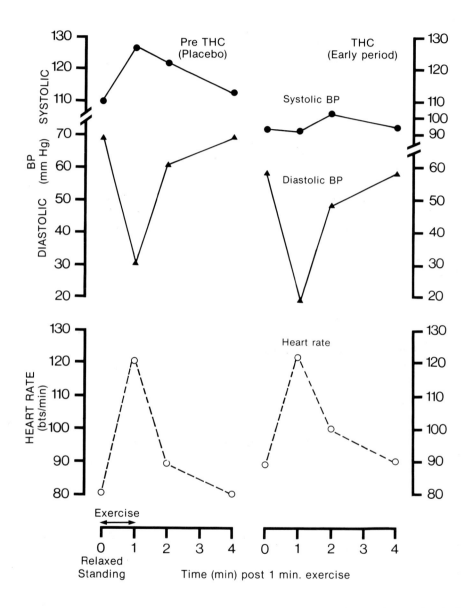

Fig. 29.   Circulatory response pre and post one minute (upright) exercise during
II.3.D$_2$ placebo and early period of oral THC intake.

Adapted from Benowitz and Jones, 1975.

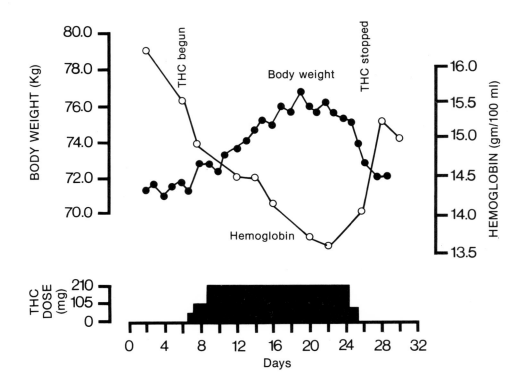

Fig. 30.   Modifications of weight and hemoglobin concentration pre, during and
II.3.D$_2$ post daily THC treatment.

Adapted from Benowitz and Jones, 1975.

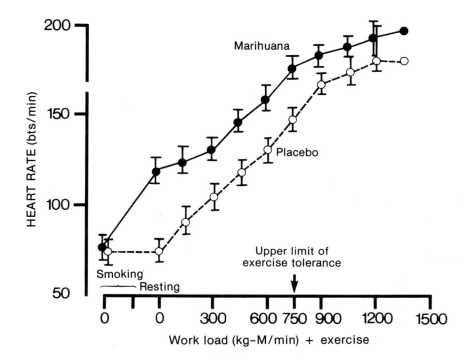

Fig. 31.
II.3.D$_2$

Heart rate response pre and post exercise performance with increasing work loads following placebo or marihuana smoking.

Adapted from Tashkin et al., 1978b

Fig. 33.
II.3.D$_2$

ECG tracing of premature ventricular contraction (3rd irregular shaped wave) followed by compensatory pause recorded 2 1/2 hours post oral THC (300 μg/kg).

Adapted from Kochar and Hosko, 1973.

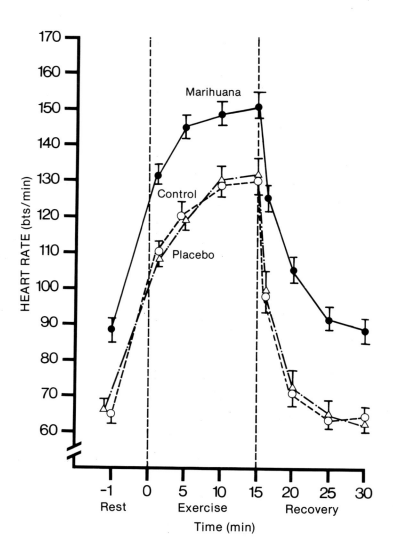

Fig. 32. Heart rate response (in sitting position) pre and post exercise perfor-
II.3.D$_2$ mance (on bicycle ergometer at 50 r.p.m.) at 750 kg.m/min work load
following placebo, marihuana, or no (control) smoking.

Adapted from Avakian et al., 1979.

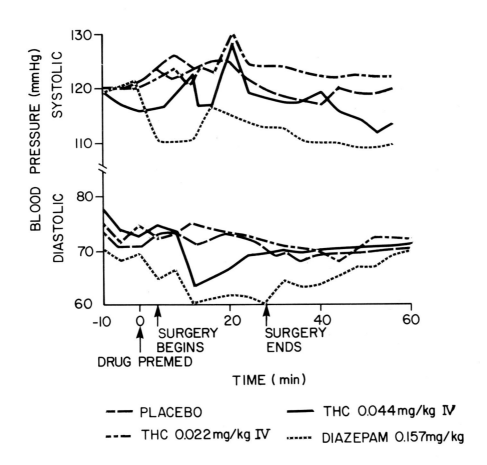

Fig. 34.   Effects of surgical premedication with THC, diazepam or placebo on
II.3.D$_2$ blood pressure.

Adapted from Gregg et al., 1976a.

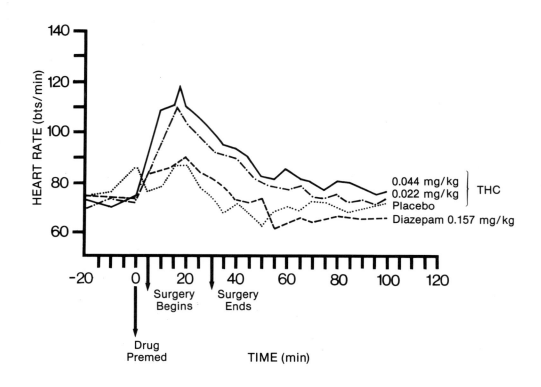

Fig. 35.   Effects of surgical premedication with THC, diazepam or placebo on
II.3.D$_2$ heart rate.

Adapted from Gregg et al., 1976a.

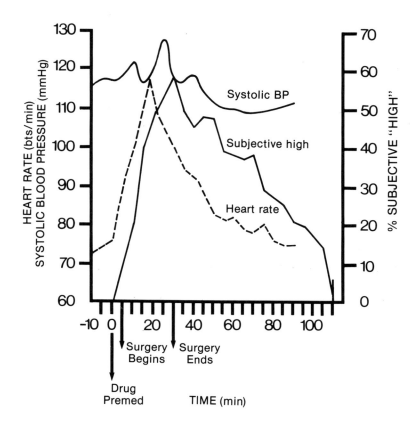

Fig. 36.   Circulatory and psychological effects of surgical premedication with
II.3.D$_2$ THC (0.044 mg/kg).

Adapted from Gregg et al., 1976a.

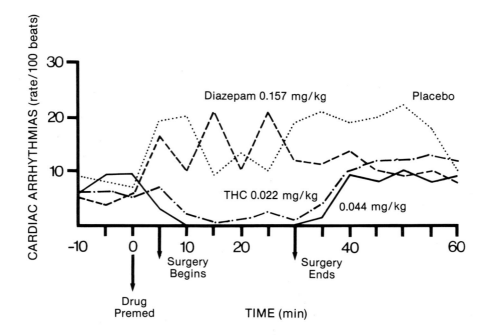

Fig. 37.   Effects of surgical premedication with THC, diazepam or placebo on
II.3.D$_2$ development of cardiac arrhythmias.

Adapted from Gregg et al., 1976 a.

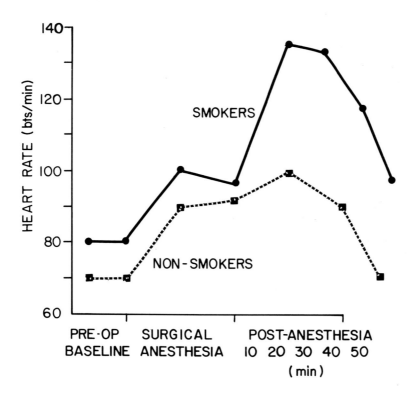

Fig. 38.   Effect of general anesthesia on heart rate in marihuana vs non-
II.3.D$_2$ smokers.

Adapted from Gregg et al., 1976a.

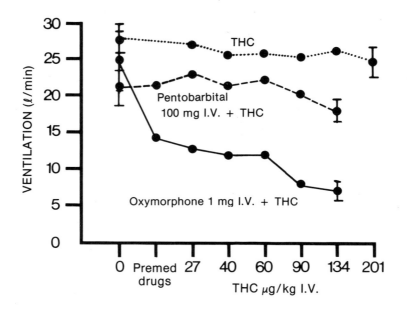

Fig. 39.
II.3.D$_2$

Effects of THC addition to oxymorphone or pentobarbital on ventilation.

Adapted from Johnstone et al., 1975.

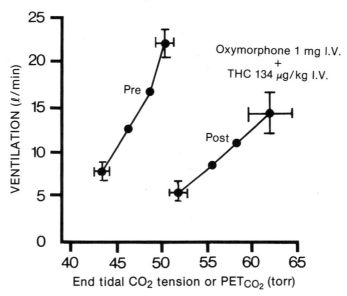

Fig. 40.
II.3.D$_2$

Pre and post drug (oxymorphone + THC) ventilatory responses to CO_2.

Adapted from Johnstone et al., 1975.

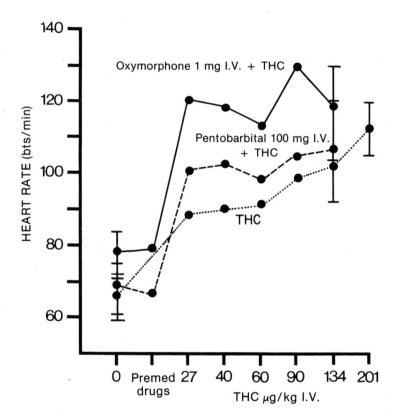

Fig. 41.   Effects of THC addition to oxymorphone or pentobarbital on heart
II.3.D$_2$ rate.

Adapted from Johnstone et al., 1975.

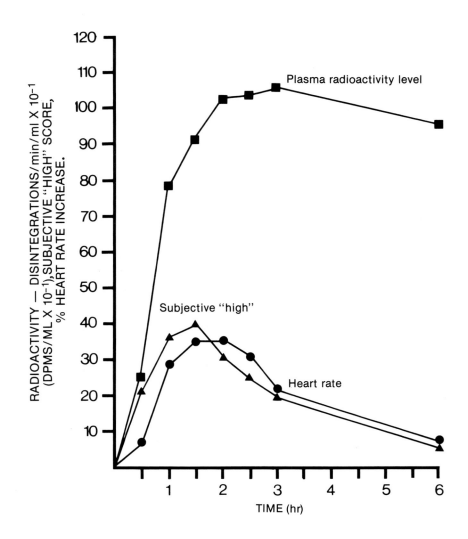

Fig. 42.   Rate and degree of absorption (plasma levels) and duration of action
II.3.D₂   (HR; psychological "high") of oral THC (35 mg).

Adapted from Perez-Reyes et al., 1973.

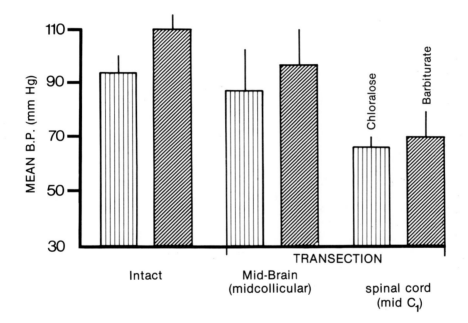

Fig. 43.   Blood pressure effects in anesthesized intact and brain stem trans-
II.3.D$_2$ ected animals.

Adapted from Hosko and Hardman, 1976.

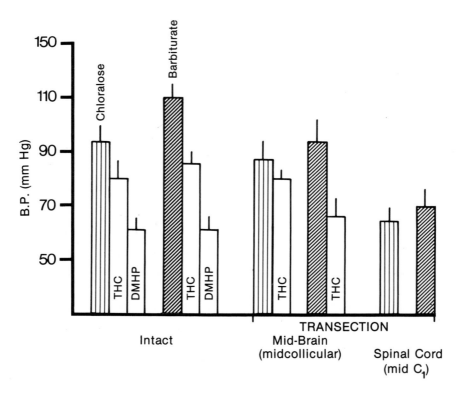

Fig. 44.   Blood pressure effects of THC and DMHP in anesthesized intact and
II.3.D$_2$ brain stem transected animals.

Adapted from Hosko and Hardman, 1976.

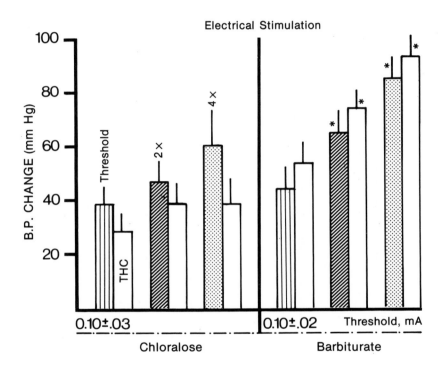

Fig. 45. Pre and post THC effects on evoked blood pressure responses from
II.3.D$_2$ electrical stimulation of medullary vasomotor centre in intact
         anesthesized animals.

Adapted from Hosko and Hardman, 1976.

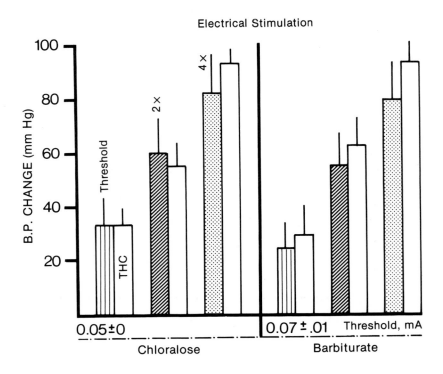

Fig. 46.   Pre and post THC effects on evoked blood pressure responses from
II.3.D$_2$ electrical stimulation of medullary vasomotor centre in mid-collicular
              transected anesthesized animals.

              Adapted from Hosko and Hardman, 1976.

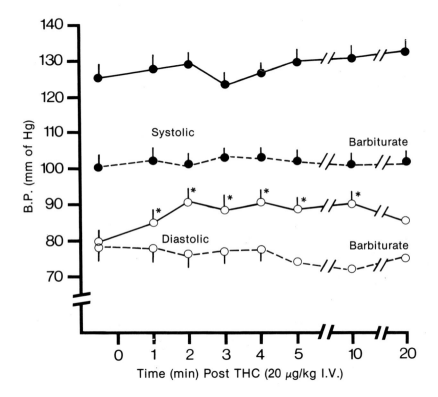

Fig. 47.   THC blood pressure effects pre and post barbiturate (pentothal)
II.3.D$_2$ anesthesia in man.

Adapted from Hosko and Hardman, 1976.

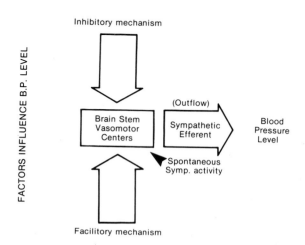

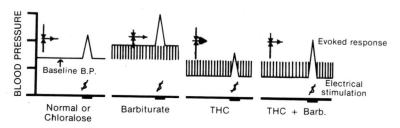

Fig. 48.   Possible mechanism for THC and barbiturate blood pressure effects in
II.3.D$_2$ anesthesized animals.

Adapted from Hosko and Hardman, 1976.

II. 3. E.   Field Studies

Contents

Abstract   233
1.   Introduction   233
2.   In Jamaica   233
3.   In Greece   235
4.   In Costa Rica   236
5.   Discussion and Summary   237

Abstract

Field studies carried out in Jamaica (ganja), Greece (hashish), and Costa Rica (marihuana) in healthy chronic cannabis users did not reveal significant medical alterations although certain individual tendencies were present; other field studies (India, Egypt) being alluded to in the appropriate (eg. CNS) sections in the review.

Keywords: Cannabis field studies, Costa Rican field study, Greek field study, Jamaican field study.

Abbreviations: alpha, beta, theta (α, β, θ); blood pressure (b.p.); cannabidiol (CBD); cannabinol (CBN); central nervous system (CNS); digit symbol substitute task (DSST); electrocardiogram (ECG); electro-encephalogram (EEG); electrooculogram (EOG); heart rate (HR); hematocrit (Hct); hemoglobin (Hb); late VER component (N_3); lysergic acid diethylamide (LSD); packed cell volume (PCV); percent oxygen in blood (pO_2); rapid eye movement (REM); red blood cell (RBC); social economic status (SES); tetra-hydrocannabinol (THC); twice a day (b.i.d.); United States of America (USA); visual evoked response (VER).

1.   Introduction

Field studies were undertaken in several countries where cannabis is traditionally used (illegally) to try to ascertain whether any long term effects could be detected in a small healthy sample of a chronic cannabis using population.

2.   In Jamaica (ganja)

In 1970, a study was undertaken in Jamaica to study the effect of chronic cannabis smoking in a natural setting with objectives aimed at patterns of use and clinical assessment which was hospital based with medical, psychiatric and psychological components (Rubin and Comitas, 1975). The clinical investigation involved 60 men from the working class, 30 of whom were ganja smokers (chronic users smoked a minimum of 3 spliffs/day/for at least 10 years) and 30 were non-smokers or controls with some limited experience in the past, with an average age of 34 years (25-53) and similar SES (social economic status) and residence. It was noted that earlier experience with ganja (Hindu word for cannabis) was predictive of regular use which averaged 18 years (7-37) in the smoker group. Samples of ganja analysed for THC content yielded an average of 3% (0.7-10.3%), the potency depending upon availability, season and grade. THC content of ganja was confirmed independently by chemical analysis of cannabis samples from Jamaica (Marshman et al., 1976). The number of spliffs (1 spliff or joint or cigarette weighed 2-6 gm including 0.5 gm for the paper wrapping) smoked per day averaged 7(1-24) with heavy smokers using more than 8/day, moderate 5-8, light 1-4, and the occasional user less than one. A spliff usually contains ganja mixed with tobacco. Most of the smokers (27) also used tobacco, ganja in teas and tonics, no drugs and less alcohol than the control group. It was found that if the first experience with ganja was unpleasant (nausea, dizzy), then a second trial was refused because "the brain is too light and he can't use it". Thus users are a select group of individuals in Jamaica and do not represent the general population in which more vulnerable subjects are present. Also depending upon the time of the year, intake is varied with frequency of use being increased during the harvest season. At one smoking session about 1 gm of ganja may be a usual dose. Many individuals regulate or titrate their intake because "if you smoke a lot it will ruin your body". Those that work in the field report that they do not smoke to intoxication; the effects ranging from nil to changes in thought patterns lasting from one-half to 5-6 hours.

The test subjects were admitted to the university hospital for 6 days (during which time abstinence from ganja was observed) for medical status determination via medical history, physical examination, and tests which included radiology of heart and lungs, ECG (electrocardiogram), respiratory function, hematology, treponemal serology, chromosome studies, EEG (electroencephalogram) and sleep recordings. Blood and urine samples were analyzed for peripheral thyroid hormone and steroid excretion levels but not for drug levels. Abnormal medical findings in both groups were positive treponemal tests for yaws (chronic nonvenereal spirochetal infection endemic in humid equatorial countries), minor ECG changes indicating cardiomyopathy which may be due to obliterative disease of small coronary vessels (an arteritis seen with heavy tobacco consumption), mild chromatid breakage in 2.5% of subjects, eosinophilia and slight increase in liver enzymes (measure of liver damage). One of 2 smokers presented with bronchial asthma and the other, neuropathy of unknown etiology; 1 control showed scarring of lungs. Smokers were lighter in weight (average 7 lbs) which may be due to appetite suppression (?) or unavailability of precursor building materials (see final comments section). Group differences noted in hematology (increased Hb (hemoglobin) and PCV (packed cell volume) with decreased pO_2 (% oxygen in the blood)) and respiratory function tests indicated that chronic heavy smokers (more than 20 tobacco cigarettes/day plus chronic ganja smoking by spliff and/or pipe) are at greater risk of functional hypoxia (deficiency of oxygen in body tissues) thought to be associated with the duration and frequency of smoking per se. Functional hypoxia leads to increased demand on the bone marrow for RBC (red blood cell) production explaining the hematological alterations. During psychiatric assessment it was noted that tobacco use preceded ganja use. Hallucinations reported by smokers occurred only once during the first smoking of ganja. Family histories of alcoholism and mental illness (including personal history) were found in both groups. There was very little correlation between ganja use and crime. EEGs in some individuals in both groups revealed focal abnormalities and low voltage fast activity records, the significance of which is unknown. The latter may occur in alcoholics, anxiety states, LSD, and acute administration of cannabis. Results of psychological studies with respect to various human abilities lacked evidence that long term use was related to chronic impairment. The major reason for ganja use is the perceived stimulus to energy and work motivation; others being health, relaxation and problem solving. It was felt that personality predisposition of the user rather than ganja is the causative factor in antisocial behaviour including criminal behaviour. Physical dependence or withdrawal effects were minimal noted as considerable discomfort in a heavy smoker during the first hospital stay which cleared by the third day. However, psychic dependence was reported by some smokers but it was difficult to establish tolerance. Individuals who could not tolerate the first ganja experience usually did not become regular users thereby screening out vulnerable personality types and potential "psychotic reactions" avoiding potential social casualties. Alcohol was considered to be more harmful (aggressiveness and loss of control) as was tobacco than ganja (energizer, therapeutic, and socializing effects). It was suggested that there may be less risk to society of work loss from ganja than from alcohol. Ganja in Jamaica is used in a social pragmatic way as required (not hedonistic) vs psychedelic or sought mood altering effects as with marihuana use in the U.S.A. and Canada.

In Jamaica, almost everyone drinks ganja tea, beginning in infancy and childhood, for medicinal purposes to make youngsters healthy and smart. Ganja may be cooked in food (soup) and applied externally as poultices or liniment for relief of pain in open wounds. In adulthood, tea and tonic is thought to strengthen the blood and ward off disease, whereas smoking ganja which enters the lungs and brain has unpredictable effects and makes one sleepy. Women use tea and tonic (few smoke) as do 75% of the men, 50% of whom also smoke. Heavy users smoke 3-8x/day (up to 31 gm), moderate users 1-3x/day (0.5-2 gm), light users 1x/day to 1x/week, and very light users less than 1x/week. The heavy smoker uses at least 4-5 spliffs (joints) daily. Work capacity for labourious tasks reported by workers indicate enhancement which is in contradiction to the reported amotivational syndrome. However, objective measurements contrast with the work productivity perception revealing that following smoking of ganja, the expended kilocalories to complete a task are increased (dose related). This means that cannabis use increases energy requirements as well as decreasing efficiency (more movements are necessary/time). Noted was decreased exercise performance, increased concentration on the work task, a feeling of well-being, and getting along better with a fellow worker. This perception of increased output helps motivate individuals to work in carrying out difficult tasks. That is, work drive may not be diminished, though efficiency or productivity may be.

The conclusion drawn from the above findings was that

(a)   ganja smoking does not affect general physical health aside from the risk that may parallel the risks of chronic tobacco smoking indicated by the medical finding of functional hypoxia in heavy chronic smokers

(b)   there was very little correlation between ganja and crime, and

(c) there was no indication of organic brain damage, chromosome damage nor clinical differences (psychiatric, psychological, or medical) between smokers and controls.

This study reveals some of the difficulties encountered in doing a field study. The sample of smokers is not a representative sample of the population (excluding potentially vulnerable individuals), the controls have used ganja in the form of tea and tonics as well as prior and occasional use, and doses are individually titrated making it difficult to obtain a proper dose-response relationship. At best, the study may be considered a pilot project enabling future investigators to develop better protocols with respect to objective measurements including urinary and blood drug levels, patient population selection including appropriate controls and dose range to be used regularly for extended periods; the latter may be feasible only in animal experimentation, the results to be watched for in humans. Trends noted in a pilot project should be pursued more rigorously.

3. In Greece (hashish)

Hashish is a potent form of cannabis. It is not traditionally used in folk medicine in Greece, being chronically used (illegally) primarily by working class older men (not the young). It has been used as a substitute for alcohol in an attempt to stop alcohol use. Long term (mental and physical health; social function) effects in 47 chronic heavy hashish using Greek men vs 40 matched non-users were studied (Stefanis et al., 1977) over a 3 year period (beginning in 1971) including tolerance and withdrawal effects in 16 hospitalized users (smoking marihuana (2.6% THC or 26 mg THC/cigarette) mixed with tobacco or placebo for 3 days ad libitum (for each preparation) b.i.d. (4.5 hours apart); 8 subjects beginning with marihuana and 8 with placebo) as well as acute physiological (HR, blood pressure, respiratory rate, temperature, EEG, evoked potential, pupil size, plethysmograph), psychological ("high"; tests) and behavioural effects following cannabis inhalation (smoking cigarettes with THC varying from 0 to 180 mg (mixed with tobacco); 2 doses of hashish with 4.5% THC (90 and 180 mg), marihuana with 2.6% THC (78 mg), pure THC (100 mg), and placebo) in 20 users.

The subjects (average 40.7 years of age) reported 10-30 years (average 23 years; beginning use around 17.6 years of age) daily hashish use by water pipe (usually combined with tobacco which was also smoked heavily, approximately 40 cigarettes/day vs 30 cigarettes/day for controls) with a current frequency of 2-3x/day consuming approximately 3 gm/day hashish with 4.5% THC (140 mg THC/day) following which relaxed drowsy states were reached. Abstinence periods had occurred 1.2x with an average duration of 10 months, the unavailability of hashish resulting in irritability, anxiety, and outbursts. Pleasureable subjective experiences were reported more frequently than unpleasant ones following cannabis smoking. The former involved emotions (euphoria, talkative, laughter, relaxation), memory (increased, decreased), thought (slow thinking, thoughtfulness, superiority), perception (increased, floating sensation), motivation (work better and tolerable), and somatic effects (dry mouth, increased appetite, increased sexual arousal). Unpleasant reports consisted of anxiety reactions (panic, agitation, thought block, depression), psychotic symptoms (delusion of persecution, hallucinations), somatic effects (palpitation, sweating, dizzy, sleep disorder, vomiting), and psychomotor retardation with inability to work. The toxic psychotic reactions reported may be due to varied psychoactive substance concentrations in illegal preparations acquired at different times. Even though work was made tolerable (as in Jamaican study) with cannabis use, the work records were irregular (vs controls). Mental deterioration was not demonstrated by psychological tests in chronic hashish users. Mental health status assessed by psychiatrists noted that more users (vs controls) had psychiatric abnormalities (psycho-pathology) especially personality disorders (antisocial); the incidence of abnormalities not being related to hashish consumption. Paranoid (schizophrenic type) psychosis was observed in three smokers. Perhaps an antisocial personality lends itself to cannabis use which in time may influence personality further. Absence of organic dementia suggested lack of gross brain damage. Physical examination revealed more palpable (enlarged) livers in hashish users (due to heavy alcohol use) and higher pulse rates (85 vs 75 bts/minute in controls) with both groups having signs of bronchitis (13/44 users; 6/38 controls). Brain function studies (4/46 users with abnormal resting EEG; neurological examination; echoencephalogram (3rd ventricular size in normal range)) in the chronic users were considered not to show brain damage confirming psychological tests which did not divulge an organic brain syndrome (or psychosis including memory loss, confusion, disorientation, confabulation).

Acute toxic subjective effects were reported in some users following various cannabis preparations tested such as panic reactions, hallucinations, vomiting and dysarthria due to unaccustomed high doses. Aside from practice effects, both THC (180 mg) and marihuana (78 mg THC + other cannabinoids) acutely affected (transiently for about 1 hour post smoking) more complex mental functioning psychological tests (impairment of barrage de signe or alertness test; overestimation of time; impairment of serial 7^s) assessing cognitive (memory, altertness), perceptual (time sense, mental coordination) and motor performance. The ability to smoke 180 mg THC per session without toxicity in some individuals indicated tolerance development to cannabis. The acute transient (about 1 hour) EEG effects of cannabis preparations were increased amount (amplitude) of α-activity with decreased frequency (indicating relaxation), decreased β-activity and ↑ θ-activity/30 minutes; the degree and duration of effects depending upon the relative amounts of CBD (and CBN) present in the preparations used (CBD possibly interferring with THC effect). Brain electrical responses to sensory stimuli or evoked responses in chronic hashish users following high cannabis doses showed small changes in VER (visual evoked response) limited to increased amplitude of negative late (N_3) VER components (in 10/12 subjects studied) which may indicate a possible stimulant effect of THC (perhaps a pre-lethal anoxic toxic effect?). The acute psychological "high" obtained with the smoked cannabis preparations was related to EEG changes (observed above but not to θ-activity) and to increased HR (peak 10 minutes) which was affected by CBD present in the preparations used (the pure 100 mg THC producing the greatest tachycardia. Psychophysiological measurements were used to indicate autonomic changes or level of arousal. Adrenergic effects were observed as increased HR, decreased finger pulse volume and increased pupil size; relaxation being noted as decreased skin conductance level with increased EEG α-activity with decreased fast β-activity.

In the withdrawal studies, more marihuana was smoked following 3 days (placebo) abstinence than preceding an abstinence period suggesting a possible physiological dependence on cannabis which sustains continued use as well as a greater "high" indicating more efficient smoking to achieve a desired "high" with tolerance developing to tachycardia, decreased temperature and b.p. effects depending upon the number of smoked cigarettes. Subjects probably titrate their doses for individualized "high" (not continued intoxication vs oral preparations when doses cannot be controlled) with a greater degree of tolerance and dependence than could be demonstrated by a 3 day abstinent period (inadequate time to deplete body THC). In general, overt physical withdrawal symptoms and signs (including laboratory signs) were not observed. However some tendencies were reported including withdrawal ratings increasing during the second and third days on placebo; greater ratings during withdrawal for constipation, flatulence, appetite, and cramps; and irritability (hostility) being greater with placebo. (Assuming that placebo was also mixed with tobacco, the nicotine in tobacco may have modified the withdrawal effects.) The smoking of marihuana revealed highest fatigue ratings during day one with more abnormal psychopathology (especially in 2/16 subjects showing paranoid behaviour, and, visual and auditory hallucinations) and better hospital ward adjustment (tolerate conditions) being more talkative (11/16). Perhaps cannabinoid blood and urinary levels may have helped to explain some of the order (of drugs, sessions) effects which indicated cumulative (fewer cigarettes smoked with greater "high" during second smoking session in the day) as well as practice effects (psychological test task performance (in barrage de signe, DSST, number ordination) with the second drug or placebo (in drug order) was better than the first except for impairment of serial 7^s which occurred only with the drug marihuana). There was a tendency to slightly overestimate a time period of 5 minutes. In spite of practice effects, cannabis does inhibit test performance since improvement with the marihuana-placebo order is greater than placebo-marihuana order of administration. Performance in these subjects indicates adaptation to cannabis effects over a prolonged period of time; abstinence periods perhaps allowing for repair processes prior to next cannabis consumption.

It was concluded that long term cannabis use in this small sample of healthy individuals did not result in significant medical alterations while personality disorders contributed to continued cannabis use; a suggestion being made that larger population prospective studies are necessary to determine medical consequences or complications including tolerance and withdrawal effects (seen with excessive tobacco and alcohol use).

4. In Costa Rica (marihuana)

In Costa Rica, marihuana is used as a recreational drug together with alcohol and tobacco. Medicinal uses of marihuana have been reported for epilepsy, delirium tremens (substitute for alcohol possibly), retention of urine, and excess menstrual flow. Presently marihuana is used medicinally for relieving coughing and asthma; loss of appetite; hangover and headaches; and is eaten and used in cooking. The available varieties of cannabis have various potencies depending where the plants are grown as well as different implements being used to smoke marihuana (varying pipes including a water pipe; a marihuana butt placed at the end of a tobacco cigarette). Early use of marihuana (1-2 cigarettes/day) has resulted in dizziness and headaches. The average amount of marihuana smoked was 10 cigarettes/day (20-74 mg THC) for an average of 16.9 years duration (beginning regular use around 15 years of age).

Long term effects of chronic marihuana smoking was investigated in marihuana smokers of more than 10 years use (at least 3 cigarettes/week) using a matched sample of 41 marihuana users vs 41 non-users (the smoking group not necessarily representing all marihuana smokers) with examiners not knowing who were users or non-users (single blind study) (Carter, 1980). Medical and physical examinations including laboratory tests (only fasting blood samples taken in the early morning) excluded diseased states and 50 years of age was the upper limit to avoid aging effects. Biomedical studies involved pulmonary function tests, neuropsychological evaluations of personality changes and brain function (EEG (sleep) - EOG (electrooculogram), visual function) and plasma testosterone levels but not chromosome studies.

The cannabinoid content of marihuana samples tested over a 2 year period was THC (1.33-3.72%), CBN (0.02-0.44%), CBD (trace) and cannabichromeme (0.08-0.25%). From a 24 hour recall by 41 marihuana users, the average daily use was 9.6 cigarettes with a daily THC dose of 12.1 to 35 mg (daily dose range of 2.5 to 40 cigarettes/day or 3.18 to 149 mg THC/day): keeping in mind that 50% THC is lost to air or destroyed by burning. Some reported subjective immediate effects following marihuana smoking were: bad for eyes (redness) and heat over whole body (perhaps vasodilation); good for asthma (perhaps bronchodilation); bad for lungs (perhaps due to smoke irritation) and rough throat; dry mouth, hangover; white death or panic reaction (which is treated with a high sugar drink); general "blahs" (with a large amount of marihuana); sleep better, appetite increased, nerves calmed (less aggressive), indure work better; bad for memory; and intoxicating effects similar to alcohol without the drunken behaviour (the mixing of alcohol and marihuana leading to unpleasant experiences). Some chief complaints noted in the medical history of users vs non-users was weight loss, appetite increased and some decreased, indigestion, nausea, abdominal pain, excessive frequent urination, and more frequent use of other drugs including tobacco. Physical examination revealed lowered weight and mean systolic blood pressure, and more unilateral testicular atrophy (thought to be due to mumps or trauma) in users. Both groups had dilation of conjunctival vessels (hyperemia). Laboratory tests in users showed longer prothrombin time; lower Hct, Hb, total bilirubin and serum globulins; with a tendency to decreased glucose tolerance. Visual function did not show detrimental effects except for a mild non-specific irritation of the anterior segment of the eye. Users had the ability to fall asleep more readily with longer REM periods seen in EEG-EOG results. Pulmonary function studies indicated a mild to moderate bronchitis in both groups with a tendency to mild airway changes in users. Both groups had similar plasma testosterone levels. Slightly lower performance by users was noted in the neuropsychological tests. It was felt that no clear pattern of health impairment due to chronic marihuana use could be established under the conditions of this investigation and that further longitudinal research be undertaken.

However the possibility of altered carbohydrate metabolism exists (see final comments) noted by the reports of frequent urination and dry mouth, increased appetite, decreased weight, nausea and abdominal pain, increased prothrombin time, decreased serum globulin levels, and treating panic reaction with a sugar drink (perhaps replenishing liver glycogen being depleted during drug use). Since all 3 drugs (marihuana, alcohol, tobacco) are used, less of each substance may be needed to give a desired effect. The mode of smoking (water pipe) and preparations used (varied THC potency) may not result in overt toxic effects. Since marihuana is illegal, it may not always be available and the potency inconsistent. The subject sample included healthy individuals which may be equated to tobacco smokers who do not develop any of the associated adverse effects (lung carcinoma, cardiovascular disease). Also both groups used other drugs (barbiturates, tranquilizers, hallucinogens, and vaporizing intoxicants (gasoline)) which could nullify differences.

5. Discussion and Summary

Similarities and differences in reported field studies (in Jamaica (ganja), Greece (hashish), Costa Rica (marihuana)) shall be discussed. The purpose of all three studies was to assess the clinical outcome following chronic cannabis use in a small sample of medically healthy smokers vs non-cannabis users; the Greek study also reporting on acute cannabis effects in chronic users due to various preparations (hashish, marihuana, THC) as well as tolerance and withdrawal effects due to marihuana.

Cannabis has been used for medicinal purposes in Jamaica and Costa Rica but not in Greece (except as a substitute for alcohol in an attempt to stop using alcohol; in Costa Rica used in delirium tremens). The uses for urinary retention and loss of appetite indicate a possible cannabis carbohydrate metabolic effect (see final comments section); for excess menstrual flow because of a hormonal imbalance due to cannabis (see reproduction section); relief of asthma due to cannabis bronchodilating effect (see pulmonary section); for epilepsy due to cannabinoids other than THC (see chemistry section); while external use as poultice or liniment for relief of pain in open wounds through which cannabinoids are probably absorbed into the body, may be due to an indirect endorphin effect (see final comments section). Cannabis has also been used in cooking, teas, and tonics with alcohol (oral vs smoking which makes one sleepy). Aside from being used as a recreational drug as tobacco and alcohol, cannabis is utilized as required (not hedonistic) for energy and work motivation or increasing the capacity for laborious work. However efficiency and productivity are decreased without decreasing work drive.

Since cannabis is usually mixed with tobacco and alcohol is also used, the combined effects may require less of each drug to give a desired subjective effect. The potency of smoked cannabis in terms of THC content was determined to be an average of 3% (0.7-10.3%) for ganja, 4.5% for hashish, and a range of 1.33-3.72% for marihuana; the potency depending upon availability, season, and grade. The amount of material mixed with tobacco smoked per day averaged 7(1-24) spliffs or cigarettes of ganja (with 1 gm being a usual dose), 3 gm hashish (140 mg THC) by water pipe, and 10 cigarettes/day marihuana (20-74 mg THC) spanning over an average duration of 18, 23, and 17 years respectively (beginning use at 15 to 18 years of age). Subjective effects reported by smokers (lasting 0.5 to 5-6 hours) were both pleasant and unpleasant which may be due to varied potencies of available material used and state of mental health (personality) of an individual; unavailability leading to irritability, anxiety and outbursts. In Jamaica, if the first cannabis experience is not tolerated (nausea, dizziness, hallucinations), then the individual does not become a ganja smoker thereby naturally screening out vulnerable personality types and potential psychotic reactions; the smokers titrating intake (refraining from continued intoxicated state) to avoid "ruining" the body and to tolerate tedious work. Some of the pleasant effects reported were euphoria, relaxation, well-being, increased appetitie, motivation (work better), sleep better and increased perception. Unpleasant effects included anxiety reactions (panic reactions being treated with a high sugar drink in Costa Rica (see final comments section re carbohydrate metabolic alteration)), psychotic symptoms, psychomotor retardation (inability to work), and symptoms of shock (associated with hypotension due to peripheral vasodilation which was observed as red eyes and heat over whole body).

All 3 clinical assessments were hospital based (ward or out patient department) studying healthy working-class men (30-47 cannabis smokers vs 30-41 non-cannabis users with an average age of 34-40.7 years). No clear health deterioration pattern emerged; physical health risk paralleling tobacco smoking (functional anoxia) with personality disorders contributing to continued cannabis use, thereby necessitating larger population prospective studies. However some trends for potential health damage were observed. Both users and non-users revealed liver alteration (increased size and enzymes) probably due to alcohol use as well as bronchitis due to the smoking process with pulmonary function tests in users showing airway changes. Cardiovascular changes noted in users were a greater increase in heart rate and a lower systolic blood pressure. Brain function studies showed abnormal resting EEG tracings in some individuals and longer REM periods with subjects falling asleep more readily. Laboratory tests revealed lowered Hct and Hb (which may be a dilution effect due to increased plasma volume) in Costa Rican study while in Jamaican study chronic smokers using more than 20 tobacco cigarettes/day plus ganja (spliff or pipe) showed increased Hb and PCV with decreased pO_2 and pulmonary function tests indicating functionl hypoxia responsible for increased demand on bone marrow for RBC production; mild chromosomal breaks in ganja users and controls (significance?); increased prothrombin time with decreased serum globulin levels and a tendency for decreased glucose tolerance indicating altered carbohydrate metabolism (see final comments section) in marihuana users. Other indices suggesting modified carbohydrate metabolism included chief complaints by some chronic cannabis users of weight loss (also noted in physical examination as lower weight by about 7 lbs vs controls) with increased appetite, nausea, abdominal pain, dry mouth, and excessive frequent urination. Complaints of dizziness and headaches may be due to hypotension brought about by peripheral vasodilation due to cannabis. A slight decrease in performance was observed in users (neuropsychological tests) who also had more psychiatric abnormalities (personality disorders; paranoid schizophrenic type in a few subjects). However psychological testing did not show mental deterioration or gross brain damage. Expected effects occurred with acute cannabis smoking in the Greek study such as toxic subjective effects; affecting more complex mental functioning psychological tests; altered EEG consistent with relaxation effects which was related to the psychological "high" and tachycardia; performance inhibition; overestimation of time; and the capability of producing psychopathological paranoid behaviour. Tolerance developed to tachycardia and blood pressure effects; the amount of THC consumed without toxicity in some individuals being 180 mg. Following a placebo abstinent period a greater "high" was achieved (more efficient smoking) with more marihuana being used signifying a physiological dependence (sustains cannabis use); a psychic dependence being reported in the Jamaican study. A tendency toward physical dependence or withdrawal effects were evident in the Greek and Jamaican studies (inadequate time to deplete body THC). There was no correlation between cannabis use and crime.

It appears that individuals traditionally using cannabis in several countries titrate their doses to attain relaxation (without intoxication) without adverse physical effects and to tolerate tedious tasks. That is, depth of cannabis smoke inhalation may not be as great nor prolonged as used for hedonistic purposes (observed above as increased intake post withdrawal phase and some severe acute effects). Since there is variation in type of preparation (including potency) and mode of use (water pipe or cigarette) as well as inhalation pattern (Petersen, 1979), blood and urinary canabinoid levels are necessary to determine what dose effects are being reported (which may be difficult to do since use is illegal with varied unstandardized cannabinoid doses). Episodic drug use may result in fluctuating drug and tolerance levels with sedation occurring with drug levels above tolerance and irritability if below tolerance; tolerance level approaching dependency with continued use of higher cannabis potency. Incidence of cannabis problems may be comparable to alcoholics who do not represent the drinking population or to healthy heavy tobacco smokers who may not show overt medical problems (vs those who may have succumbed to pulmonary carcinoma); the difference being that both alcohol (oral) and tobacco (usually smoked) are legal substances with known percent of active ingredient(s) making it easier to assess health consequences over a period of time. Obviously long term well-planned prospective and epidemiological cannabis studies are necessary to determine the medical outcome of habitul use in a general population (not only in medically healthy individuals).

III. General Summaries

Contents

	Abstract	240
1.	Chemistry and Metabolism	240
2.	Chromosomes, Cell Metabolism, Immunity	242
3.	Reproductive System	245
4.	Central Nervous System	246
5.	Cardiopulmonary System	249

Abstract

1. General summaries are presented to give an overview of each area reviewed; details to be found in the appropriate section in the text.

2. Field studies have been presented as summaries and are not repeated here.

Keywords: cannabinoids, cardiopulmonary system, central nervous system, chemistry, chromosomes, immunity, metabolism, reproductive system.

Abbreviations: alpha (α); antibodies or immunoglobulins (IgG, IgM); aryl hydrocarbon hydroxylase (AHH); atrio-ventricular (AV); beta (β); blood pressure (b.p.); bone marrow lymphocytes (B-cells); cannabi-chromeme (CBC); cannabidiol (CBD); cannabinol (CBN); carbon monoxide (CO); carboxyhemoglobin (COHb); carboxy-THC (C-THC); cardiovascular (CV); central nervous system (CNS); cigarette(s) (cig(s)); computerized transaxial tomography (CTT); crude marihuana extract (CME); day; (d); delayed type hypersensitivity (DTH); deoxyribonucleic acid (DNA); electrocardiogram (ECG); electroencephalogram (EEG); escherichia coli or intestinal bacteria (E. coli); follicle stimulating hormone (FSH); for example (e.g.); forced expiratory volume in 1 second in litres (FEV_1); gas-liquid-chromatography-mass spectrometry (GLC-MS); heart rate (HR); hemoglobin (Hb); high pressure liquid chromatography - mass spectrometry (HPLC-MS); homogeneous enzyme immunoassay (EMIT); human chorionic gonadotropin (HCG); hydroxy (OH); intraperitoneal (IP); intravenous (IV); kilogram (kg); less than (<); luteinizing hormone (LH); lysergic acid diethylamide (LSD); mass spectrometry (MS); micromoles (μM); milligram (mg); millilitre (ml); molar, moles (m); multiple ion detection (MID); nanogram (ng); oxygen (O_2); packed cell volume (PCV); per os or oral (p.o.); percent (%); phytohemagglutinin (PHA); picogram (pc); polynuclear aromatic hydrocarbons (PAH); pre-ejection period (PEP); premature ventricular contraction (PVC); radioimmunoassay (RIA); red blood cell (RBC); ribonucleic acid (RNA); short or long term store (S or (L) TS); sino-auricular or atrial (SA); slow wave sleep (NREM); systemic lupus erythematosus (SLE); tetrahydrocannabinol (THC); that is (i.e.); thin layer chromatography (TLC); thymus dependent lymphocytes (T-cells); times (x); waves and segment in ECG tracing (P, T, ST).

III. 1. Chemistry and Metabolism

Marihuana plants of the genus Cannabis belong to one species (C. sativa) with two subspecies (sativa, a fibre type and indica, a drug type) each with wild and cultivated varieties. There are three known phenotypes with varying concentrations of THC and CBD (I with THC mainly, III with CBD; and II with both CBD (slightly more) and THC); the cannabinoid content being similar in female and male plants in phenotype I with more potent (re THC) female plants in II and III phenotypes.

The chemical composition of cannabis has been reported to contain 421 compounds with 61 known cannabinoids with varied known and unknown pharmacological actions which may be desireable or undesireable. The cannabinoid content of a plant (found mainly in epidermal glands of bracts, leaves and flowering parts) depends upon heredity, type of plant, time of harvest, and part of plant (decreasing from flower portion to roots and seeds). The fibre type (less THC) may change to the resin type (more THC) in hot climates and vice versa in temperate climates after several generations of growth. Air oxidation leads to loss of marihuana potency via conversion of THC (active principle) to CBN (one-tenth activity of THC) while light exposure results in cannabinoid loss. Compounds other than cannabinoids found in the plant and (marihuana) smoke have the possibility of being converted to carcinogenic substances which raises concern as to potential carcinoma development.

Qualitative and quantitative identification (including chemical structure elucidation) of cannabinoids may be accomplished by GLC-MS (gas-liquid-chromatography-mass spectrometry) combination in chloroform extracted marihuana samples (determining geographic origin) or in methanol extracted tissue cannabinoids; mass fragmentography (MID; addition of multiple ion detector) increasing MS sensitivity for ng (nanogram) or pc (picogram) levels. A modification of the above, HPLC-MS (high pressure liquid chromatography - mass spectrometry), has been used to accurately quantify THC (over 1-100 ng/ml range) in human specimens (plasma, breath, saliva, bile, brain); TLC (thin layer chromatography) and MS having been used for cannabinoid detection in saliva and fingertip washings. Qualitative screening for cannabinoids in urine (several days post exposure) has been accomplished with immunoassay methods (RIA or radioimmunoassay and EMIT or homogeneous enzyme immunoassay) (1 ng/ml detection limit) and TLC. Another urinary detection and quantifying method uses a chemical reaction resulting in fluorescent compounds, the intensity of fluorescence emitted being measured against a standard.

Smoking of a marihuana cigarette yields CBD (cannabidiol; partly converted to THC and CBN), CBN (cannabinol), CBC (cannabichromeme), and Δ^9 THC, the active water insoluble (since no nitrogen atom in molecule) principle which is responsible for the psychotomimetic property and observed physiological changes correlating with plasma cannabinoid levels (including metabolites). Since THC binds readily to human plasma lipoproteins, only a small amount of free THC is necessary for activity. With smoking, 50% THC is absorbed into the bloodstream with bioavailability (100 ng/ml plasma post 5 mg THC at 5 minute period) being 10x greater than with oral THC (10 ng/ml plasma post 20 mg THC at 1 hour period). Rapid clearance occurs from the blood (animals) to liver, fat, brain, spleen, lung, kidney and reproductive tissues; chronic dosing resulting in fat and liver accumulation. Drug has been shown to amass in salivary glands, adrenal glands and brain (especially in structures involved in processing visual and acoustic information and in motor control). THC has been found in milk (animals) with suckling infants showing THC in urine and feces. The metabolism of THC (Δ^9, Δ^8), CBD and CBN (found in marihuana smoke) in man occurs in the liver via hydroxylation to active (being responsible for psychological or euphoric effects; analgesia in animals) equipotent 11-OH (hydroxy) metabolites (excreted in feces via bile) with further oxidation to carboxylic acids found in plasma, urine and feces. Hydroxylation may also take place in the side chain and at the 8α, β positions. More than 50 metabolites have been identified. Other sites of THC transformation (animals) occur in heart and lungs, not being as extensive as in the liver. The 11-OH metabolites disappear from plasma (man) more readily than THC, penetrating the brain (animal; THC metabolized to 11-OH metabolite at this site also) faster with quicker onset of action (increased HR). However a lower THC brain concentration is necessary for activity. Metabolic tolerance to THC does not occur; the plasma half-life being 20-30 hours. THC (post IV) accumulates in the body, evidenced by its half-life in tissues being 7 days due to slow release from tissues; 15-17% of the dose appearing as urinary metabolites in 5 days with 40-45% biliary excretion in feces and 15% entero-hepatic recirculation of biliary metabolites. In animals CBD may interfere (inhibit) with THC metabolism and its 11-OH metabolite which may account for varied activities of different cannabis preparations. Repeated THC administration (as well as exposure to other drugs) may induce or stimulate its metabolism. Active immunization (animals) with a THC-protein conjugate neutralized depressed motor activity (a form of prevention?).

Pharmacokinetic studies of THC were made possible by detection methods noted above. Following intravenous THC (4-5 mg), a plasma peak level (50-60 ng/ml was reached at 10-20 minute period coinciding with maximum psychotomimetic activity; the amount of plasma metabolite (11-OH-THC) being 1/20-1/25th THC (2-3 ng/ml at peak level) with an insignificant amount of CBN (which may be an intermediary product of THC metabolism?). Elimination (biphasic) of THC from the blood occurs rapidly at first (15-40 minutes) becoming slower up to 24 hours. The smoking of a marihuana cigarette (19.8 mg THC) by an occasional user results in a peak THC plasma level (10-130 ng/ml) at 15-30 minute period (undetectable at 1-2 hours) with THC being detected in the breath and saliva for the first 60 minutes; brain and bile levels being higher than in plasma of post-mortem samples. A metabolite, C-THC (carboxy-THC) in plasma is present at 30-60 minute period, persisting for several (3) hours and appears in the urine (up to 60 ng/ml) for up to 48 hours. The use of 3 cigarettes increases detection time for plasma THC (peak 100-260 ng/ml) up to 3 hours and C-THC up to 48 hours. Plasma cannabinoid levels attained as well as degree of pharmacological responses vary with THC dose or potency of marihuana smoked, but peak pharmacological effects appear to correlate with peak plasma levels of the inactive metabolite, carboxy-THC. Detectable urinary C-THC levels (17-123 ng/ml) occur in chronic smokers (who metabolize THC more readily) prior to smoking a cigarette, following which a great increase in C-THC levels occurs at the 2-4 hour period. Thus single and multiple marihuana use may be detected in biological fluids; absence of plasma THC indicating no use within the previous hour while the presence of only C-THC suggesting distant exposure. Urinary cannabinoids may be found several days after marihuana exposure with chronic users having detectable levels prior to current use. Cannabinoid detection in saliva occurs 1-2 hours post smoking and in fingertip washings at 1-3 hour periods. Earlier time period plasma THC determinations following IV (5 mg) injection or smoking (19 mg) revealed peak plasma levels of > 200 ng and < 100 ng THC/ml plasma (respectively) occurring at 3 minutes following administration when conjunctival reddening was evident with peak "high" reported at 30 minutes; oral intake (20 mg) resulting in a peak of 6 ng THC/ml plasma at the one hour period with peak "high" at 2-4 hours with noticeable eye reddening at 0.5 to 1 hour. Tachycardia occurred at lower THC plasma concentration following oral intake suggesting a possible additive metabolite effect. Orally, THC is less bioavailable because it reaches the liver directly where THC metabolites are formed vs smoking or IV injection when cannabinoids enter the blood stream, pass through the left side of the heart, being conducted to the brain and other organs before passing through the liver resulting in quicker onset of action. Different routes of THC administration result in plasma levels which correlate with onset, degree and duration of clinical effects depending upon rate of absorption, distribution, and metabolism of administered drug. CBD does not appear to influence THC pharmacokinetics in man while CBN potentiates peak THC plasma levels. CBN is thought to be a thermal degradation product of THC (during smoking) and not a true metabolite. It has been suggested that it may be difficult to interpret cannabinoid levels in terms of intoxication as with alcohol (breathalyser test for impaired driving) because of the varied (different composition) cannabis preparations used, the effects of which may be only partly related to biological THC levels and because of large individual variability re plasma THC concentration (which may not correlate with tissue concentration) and degree of "high" or intoxication achieved which may be due to tolerance development.

III. 2. Chromosomes, Cell Metabolism, Immunity System

Chromosomes

The increased incidence of structural chromosomal abnormalities in polydrug users and psychiatric patients was less than in irradiated subjects while low incidence of aberrations was noted in light marihuana users and controls indicating an apparent absence of a correlation between drug use (or use pattern) and incidence of chromosomal alterations. The sporadic chromosomal abnormalites in drug users differ from irradiated subjects who have a subpopulation of cells with the same abnormality (clone), suggesting that lymphocyte precursors may not be affected in drug users. The observed chromosomal breaks with insignificant abnormal forms following marihuana use may become responsible (in time) for neoplasia and teratogenesis (seen with persistent chromosomal damage due to irradiation (mutagen)). Short term treatment (5-12 days) with cannabinoids (hashish, THC) or placebo did not alter chromosomal damage of peripheral blood leukocytes in experienced marihuana users (who may have developed a persistent change). Heavy hashish users revealed irregular mitoses with varied chromosomal aberrations (asymmetrical, dicentric, breaks, numerical (hypo or hyperploidy)) similar to chemical and irradiation alterations. Heavy marihuana smoking (14 marihuana cigs/day/28-29 days) resulted in an increased incidence of hypoploid cells (nuclei with < 30 chromosomes vs normal of 46 chromosomes) returning to normal baseline with abstinence. THC or olivetol (chemical structure similar to C-ring of cannabinoids) added to normal lymphocyte cultures (from healthy individuals) produced hypoploid nuclei indicating a decreased ability of cells to synthesize proteins or enzymes (growth, inborn error of metabolism). THC in such cultures induced chromosomal segregational errors implicating it as a chromosomal mutagen or mitotic poison. In normal human lung explants, smoke exposure (marihuana, tobacco, for 1-45 days vs controls) initially (1-4 days exposure) decreased DNA synthesis and mitoses (cytotoxic effects; mitotic abnormalities or abnormal chromosomal behaviour including decreased number and breaks within cell nuclei) followed later (7-45 days) by increased DNA synthesis and abnormal mitosis with irregular and disorganized growth pattern (fewer cells with euploid complement of chromosomes and DNA content (i.e. genetic equilibium disturbance)) representing an early stage of malignant transformation. Whole smoke and gas phases from marihuana and tobacco cigarettes enhanced malignant cell transformation in animal lung cultures, which when injected into animals produced fibrosarcoma (a malignant neoplasm) suggesting a possible pulmonary carcinogenic role (human epidemiological data necessary to determine probability re marihuana use). Mutagenic potential (altered hereditary material in germ cells) of marihuana smoking was observed in animals as decreased number of spermatids with a normal haploid amount of DNA with some spermatids having reduced variable amounts of DNA. THC effect on human and animal sperm revealed decreased sperm motility with almost non-existent progressive movement and swelling of mid-portion of the sperm containing mitochondria (principle energy source for cell) with ruptured (outer and inner) membranes. Mutagenic and carcinogenic (tars, benzpyrene) chemicals requiring liver enzymes for their activation were found to be present in marihuana smoke condensate (products of pyrolysis similar to tobacco) as determined from the Ames test.

Cell Metabolism

At certain concentrations (3.2×10^{-7} to 10^{-5}M), THC inhibited the incorporation of precursors (thymidine, uridine, leucine) into DNA, RNA and protein, repressing synthesis of nucleic acids and protein by 15-50% in various animal and human cells, due to a decrease in macromolecular precursor pool size (without affecting rate of precursor transport into the cell and DNA repair synthesis) the reason for which could not be explained (possibilities stated in appropriate section; also see final comments re possible gluconeogenetic effect accounting for decreased pool size). Marihuana smokers (4x/week use) showed a decreased immune response similar to patients with T-cell immunity impairment noted as decreased thymidine uptake (protein synthesis or growth) by lymphocytes indicating inhibition of "in-vitro" blastogenesis (i.e. lymphocytic transformation to lymphoblasts) which may be related to DNA synthesis impairment (leading to a possible T-memory cell deficit); also observed with THC (1.6 uM to 20 uM) in normal human lymphocytes. During DNA synthesis in cultivated (72 hours) lymphocytes from marihuana smokers, the number of cells decreased and the number of chromosomal breaks increased (altered genetic equilibrium of T-cells). Lymphocytic biosynthesis of DNA (thymidine incorporation) was impaired by cannabinoids, THC metabolites, aspirin, caffeine, and other fat soluble psychotropic drugs such as anesthetics and tranquilizers. THC decreased glucose utilization by cells and discouraged protein synthesis. Both psychoactive (THC, 11-OH-THC) and non-psychoactive (CBN) cannabinoids inhibited cell growth rate (dose-related) observed as decreased incorporation of thymidine, uridine, and leucine into macromolecules (DNA, RNA, proteins) with decreased intracellular precursor pool; reversal of growth inhibition occurring 48 hours post cessation of drug treatment. The biochemical effects reflect alteration in gene expression. The nucleoprotein complex of DNA, and histone and non-histone chromosomal proteins make up chromatin (genome in cells). Cannabinoids did not appear to alter the structure (relative composition of histone and non-histone chromosomal proteins) but did decrease function (metabolism or synthesis and turnover rate) of macromolecules comprising the genome (chromosomes with their genes) implying possible impairment of gene expression necessary for regulation of cell proliferation and for biological viability. Proliferative capacity of cells was decreased by cannabinoids due to decreased macromolecular biosynthesis brought about by altered structural (modification of chromosomal proteins observed as decreased histone acetylation and phosphorylation) and functional properties of the genome. Lymphocytes from chronic hashish users showed alteration in histone (chromosomal basic nuclear protein which maintains chromatin structure) ratio with a decrease in arginine and an increase in lysine indicating transcriptional (transfer of genetic information to RNA) arrest (seen as condensed chromatin) implying possible reduced response to antigenic stimulation or decreased cell-mediated immunity. Thus altered chromatin observed in chronic marihuana users represents altered cellular metabolism in the nuclear area (a correlation with overt pathology remaining to be established). The modification of DNA may lead to mutagenesis and carcinogenesis which may be transmissible to future generations (probability?). The possible DNA damage followed by corrective DNA repair resembles antineoplastic alkylating agents and ionizing radiation effects. Cannabinoids may not affect protein synthesis directly but indirectly by making precursors unavailable (see final comments re gluconeogenesis) to the cell. It would be interesting to find out if insulin increases precursor (pool) uptake in a competative inhibitory manner.

Immunity

In chronic marihuana smokers (habit of 1-7x/week/1-8 years), T-cell forming rosettes ("in-vitro" test indicating presence of T-cells) were decreased implying T-cell (immunological) functional disturbance, with decreased B-cell rosette formation in some individuals. Varied delayed hypersensitivity skin tests to several antigens revealed presence of T-memory cells for some antigens suggesting depression of some T-cells; the immunological competence (counteract infection, tumor surveillance, graft rejection) of the remaining active T-cells being unknown. Another group of marihuana users (3x/week/4 years use) showed low early (active) T-cell rosetting levels vs controls (late or total T-cell formation being similar for the 2 groups, i.e., return to normal % with time) which was not due to decreased peripheral blood T-cells indicating an effect on a subpopulation of T-cells. Such rosette formation was not altered by tobacco, alcohol, nor aspirin. It was felt that individuals with impaired (T) cell-mediated immunity (cancer, acute viral infection, uremia) were likely to have decreased active T-cell rosette formation. The number of active rosette forming cells (15% being lower limit of normal) appears to correlate with the clinical status of cancer patients while a low number in high risk families (e.g. gastrointestinal carcinoma history) may signify predisposition to disease. However, the clinical significance of T-cell rosette formation abnormalities in marihuana smokers is unknown (necessary clinical evidence of T-cell deficiency disorders). Marihuana appears to affect T-cell function transiently (decreasing rosette formation for 24-72 hours post smoking) affecting T-memory cells in some individuals (decreasing PHA (phytohemagglutinin) stimulation response for 24-48 hours becoming normal by the 8th day post smoking (approximating the 1/2 life of THC in tissues)]. Early T-cell rosette formation was also decreased in a THC smoking study [5-12 cigs (with 20 mg THC/cig)/day/4 weeks smoked by chronic users with a habit of at least 2x/week] without changes being evident in controls, white blood cells, % circulating lymphocytes, B-cells and late T-cell rosettes. Some investigators could not find altered lymphocyte (T and B) function with respect to immune response capabilities (although initial decreases in T and B cells occurred with increase toward normal by the 63rd day of a 64 day study in one report). Divergent observations may be due to differing investigational methods such as lymphocyte incubation temperature (37 vs 4°C) and time (1 hour vs 3 days), culture media serum (calf vs human), time of blood sampling post marihuana use (minutes; several hours vs 48 hours), cell population (total vs sub or active), smoking technique (cigarette vs water pipe, depth of inhalation, cannabinoid potency), other drugs, and health status including genetic background.

Cannabis was observed to be an antigenic substance(s) capable of eliciting a humoral (antibody) immune response in marihuana smokers which may be associated with subclinical laboratory abnormalities (e.g. reticulocytosis, decreased serum haptoglobin, decreased serum Ig, abnormal liver function). Animal studies revealed decreased plasma IgG and M levels (secondary and primary immune responses respectively) without hypoproteinemia with differences in circulating subpopulation of T-cells (returning to normal levels 1-2 months post smoking cessation) following various THC levels (4.4-22.4 mg) in marijuana smoke (clinical significance re immunological competence unknown). A slight to moderate suppression of DTH (delayed type hypersensitivity) response occurred with Δ^8 THC and CBN vs known immunosuppressive agents (cyclophosphamide, prednisone, azathioprine). Various marihuana components should therefore be tested with various immunological cell types. Younger vs older animals exposed to (IP) THC showed immune system effects of decreased splenic (and body) weight with a decreased number of splenic cells, decreased splenic lymphocytes (cellular immunity), decreased humoral response (circulating IgG antibody production), and decreased rosette formation (T and B cells). The developing cells in a growing animal appears to be affected more than mature cells (probably due to unavailable protein building material noted as decreased pool size (above) which may be due to gluconeogenesis noted in final comments). Also altered sex hormones (noted in reproduction section) in early life (pre and during adolescence) may affect immunological maturation and regulation; a decreased testosterone level possibly encouraging the development of the autoimmune process (e.g. increasing susceptibility to SLE (systemic lupus erythematosus)) via decreasing activity of T-suppressor cells and/or enhancing T-helper cells. THC (p.o.) immunosuppression (without tolerance development post 16 days treatment using 25-200 mg/kg doses) was observed as T (increased graft survival by 30% average) and B (decreased antibody titre by 72%) cell suppression, decreased spleen size (30%) and decreased number of splenic (46%) and peripheral (49%) nucleated cells, which may be due to cellular metabolic inhibition (decreased cell number) and/or THC release of adrenal steroids (decreased immune response; see final comments). THC also suppressed animal neoplastic tissue proliferation (by 50% average) using various tumor systems with different growth characteristics and etiologies without altering normal bone marrow cells prolonging survival (by 30% average); similar effects being observed with Δ^8 THC and CBN but not with CBD which enhanced growth without altering life span. Thymidine uptake (DNA synthesis) was inhibited by THC (Δ^9, Δ^8) and CBN requiring higher concentration; similar inhibition of RNA and protein synthesis occurring with Δ^8 and Δ^9 THCs. However tolerance or resistance developed to tumor growth inhibition within 30 days treatment. It was found that 11-OH THC, a metabolite, inhibits bone marrow myelopoiesis with accelerated lymphocyte maturation following IV THC (50 mg/kg). It is unknown whether the antiproliferative property is species or tumor specific in humans. A cancer cure necessitates the eradication of all neoplastic cells vs antibiotic therapy for infection when the immune system plays a major role. Cannabinoids resemble chemotherapeutic agents (alkylating agents, antimetabolites) used in neoplastic disease with respect to macromolecular synthesis inhibition (i.e., inhibiting DNA synthesis thereby active against rapidly growing tumors), immunosuppression (prevent transplant rejection), antiproliferative (antineoplastic or tumor inhibition with acquired resistance in some due to increased DNA repair activity) and reproductive system impairment, as well as, cytolytic, mutagenic, carcinogenic, and teratogenic but without bone marrow depression (?; may be a matter of dose). Dividing malignant cells are more susceptible to chemotherapy, being attacked at different phases of a cell cycle (depending upon the agent used).

In non-tolerant (vs tolerant or resistant) animals, THC enhanced mortality due to bacterial endotoxin (E. coli); also seen with antineoplastic drugs and steroid hormones which are immunosuppressant inhibitors of protein or RNA synthesis. Host resistance to gram positive bacteria and to herpes simplex virus in animals was also decreased with THC. Susceptibility of human (non-tolerant and tolerant) marihuana users to various infectious diseases has not been established. But a human hypersensitivity reaction (analphylactoid symptoms) to smoking of one marihuana cigarette (2 separate occasions) has been reported in an individual with an allergy (ragweed) medical history and previous passive exposures to marihuana smoke (at parties). Tests established the diagnosis of a marihuana allergy (including THC, CBD, and cannabicyclol). Passive inhalation has led to marihuana intoxication (contact high) with detection of urinary cannabinoid metabolites in a naive subject. The incidence of such allergy is unknown; if unpleasant and severe enough, marihuana smoking would probably be avoided. An occupational immediate type allergy to cannabis sativa pollen and hashish has been documented; an intense positive reaction occurring with pollen rich hashish. Chronic environmental exposure to various pollutants (such as sulphur dioxide, carbon, cigarette smoke) may modify defenses decreasing immune response to inhaled antigens (marihuana) thereby increasing susceptibility to disease (infections, cancer). The risk lowering of disease development associated with cessation of tobacco smoking may be due in part to restoration of immune function which may also occur in marihuana smokers (provided the point of "no return" has not been reached). The immune system also involves pulmonary alveolar macrophages with bactericidal activity against inhaled organisms and particles. In one study marihuana smokers revealed a decreased number of macrophages (vs tobacco with an increased number of macrophages) without decreasing their functional defensive capacity. Animals exposed to marihuana did not show a decreased number of macrophages. Other animal studies (see pulmonary system) showed phagocytic impairment due to the water soluble gas phase of fresh smoke (acute exposure) impairing pulmonary antibacterial defense system; subchronic marihuana smoke exposure (30 days) not altering phagocytic ability while cumulative effect (30% inhibition of particle uptake) was observed with chronic tobacco smoke exposure (6 months).

Stress (surgical trauma, psychological) may depress cellular immunity transiently, the "in-vivo" capability taking longer to return to normal than indicated by "in-vitro" tests. The clincial significance of decreased T-cells (and/or B-cells) is unknown with respect to adequate function (healthy vs marginally immunologically affected individuals) or possible (probability?) development of immunodeficiency disease(s). The incidence and prevalence of hypersensitivity reactions to marihuana are unknown. Diagnostic detection of marihuana use may be determined from antibodies formed against marihuana. Use of cannabis in the treatment of nausea and vomiting due to cancer chemotherapy appears to be illogical because the immunodepressant effect of cannabis may be additive to chemotherapeutic immunosuppression and to an inefficient immune system in the cancer patient. Malignancy suppresses immune responses leading to secondary immunodeficiency states. Deficient cellular and humoral immunities are associated with recurrent and disseminated tumors. A decrease in T-cells may increase the incidence of some tumors. The immunological status and possible genetic alterations in chronic marihuana users remains to be established. Immunodeficiency problems should be watched for clinically in cannabis users.

III. 3. Reproductive System

Hormonal imbalance appears to contribute to gonadal and reproductive malfunction.

Marihuana Effects in the Male

A dose-related decrease in plasma testosterone (male hormone) level has been observed in marihuana smokers (acute and chronic); the testosterone levels increasing with cessation of drug use or following HCG (human chorionic gonadotropin) during marihuana use (indicating normal Leydig cell reserve where testosterone is synthesized). Plasma LH levels were lowered. FSH (involved in development of spermatozoa) levels had a tendency to be lower with higher marihuana intake when oligospermia was demonstrated; a correlation existing between sperm counts and plasma testosterone and FSH levels. Similar effects were observed in animals such as decreased plasma testosterone level due to inhibition of pituitary LH release as well as lowered plasma FSH level. Also a direct gonadal effect by various cannabinoids (re decreased testosterone production) was observed as inhibition of cholesterol esterase (which may be due to decreased protein synthesis) in Leydig cells making precursor cholesterol unavailable for steroidal hormone synthesis..

Marihuana smoking (8-20 cigs/day/4 weeks) by chronic marihuana users revealed alterations in sperm counts (decrease) associated with decreased motility and abnormal morphology without change in semen volume. Loss of motility response in an assay system correlating with fertilizing capacity of sperm, indicates that sperm produced during marihuana exposure may have structural or biochemical functional defects due to Sertoli cell (to which spermatids attached during spermiogenesis) dysfunction. Cessation of marihuana smoking resulted in normal conditions re sperm counts, motility and morphology. A dose-related seminiferous tubular degeneration has been observed in animals following treatment with various cannabinoids. Protamines found in nuclei of normal mature spermatozoa were not detectable in infertile oligospermic patients; testicular biopsy material revealing spermatidic arrest suggesting a maturation defect of spermatogenesis (lack of substitution of histones by protamines in the nucleus of a sperm cell). Chronic hashish users showed a decrease in arginine-rich histones counterbalanced by an increased lysine-rich fraction indicating arrest in spermatic cell maturation (i.e. interference with the sperm's final differentiation via impairment of transition of histones to protamines). Since testosterone is necessary to induce nuclear protein changes during sperm maturation, a decreased level (due to cannabis) may affect (indirectly) protein (arginine) synthesis. The abnormalities observed in cannabis users such as spermatidic maturation arrest, altered acrosomal (cap-like structure over sperm head) morphogenesis, and incomplete chromatin condensation in sperm heads appears to be due to low protamine content brought about by arginine depletion pointing to a possible metabolic disturbance with respect to histones in tissue cells (see final comments). Impaired spermatogenesis with decreased plasma hormonal levels may be due to both local (gonadal; see final comments re gluconeogenesis) and central (hypothalamic; see final comments re endorphins) effects.

Sexual function has varied from normal to impotence (returning to normal within 2 months of drug discontinuance). Occasional drug-induced gynecomastia has been reported with increased plasma prolactin (stimulates lactation) levels (note final comments); breast tenderness and size decreasing with abstinence from marihuana use. Animal studies with THC resulted in stimulation of breast tissue development in males.

Alcohol differs from marihuana only with respect to acute effects when testosterone and LH plasma levels are not affected; chronic alcoholics exhibit decreased testosterone levels and azoospermia (lack of sperm). Stress (psychological; surgery) decreases testosterone levels and sperm counts without significantly decreasing LH levels. Opiates and phenothiazines decrease LH secretion thereby decreasing testosterone plasma levels. Strenuous exercise produces a transient increase in androgen levels.

Potential implications from the above alterations produced in the male by cannabis include decreased aggression; interference with sexual differentiation during the first trimester of pregnancy; delay in onset or completion of puberty with possible adverse psychosocial and sexual maturation; possible interference with spermatogenesis (especially in mild oligospermia) and fertility; and perhaps impotence. Pubertal arrest has been associated with heavy marihuana smoking in a 16 year old boy (at least 5 joints/day since 11 years of age).

Marihuana Effects in the Female

Animals treated with THC revealed altered reproductive hormone levels (inhibiting LH and FSH at the hypothalamic level) and inhibited ovulation associated with subnormal levels of LH and progesterone as well as prolactin. Abnormal menstrual cycles have been observed in humans as anovulatory cycles (failure to ovulate) or inadequate luteal phase (shortened potential fertility period) leading to infertility. Testosterone levels were higher than normal probably due to adrenocortical stimulation by marihuana (also seen with intoxicating doses of alcohol). THC and CBN have inhibited progesterone synthesis ("in-vitro") thought to be due to inhibition of cholesterol precursor release from its ester storage pool via cholesterol esterase inhibition.

Placental transfer of THC has been demonstrated in animals with THC being found in chorionic fluid, amniotic fluid, and all fetal tissues concentrating in fatty tissues (including the brain). In nursing animals, THC, CBN and some metabolites have been found in the milk. Offspring from animal marihuana using mothers revealed altered behavioural effects (slower learning of avoidance behaviour). Heart rate (HR) in the fetus and neonates was decreased (bradycardia) vs increased maternal HR. Placenta from drug treated animals had gross morphological and vascular abnormalities (massively infarcted). Human nursing mothers concentrated THC in their milk which also contained 11-OH-THC and carboxy-THC (also noted in plasma); infant absorption (through the milk) resulting in fecal excretion of THC, 11-OH-THC and carboxy-THC.

In animals, reproductive loss (not surviving to 6 months of age) occurred with THC ingestion ranging from "in-utero" resorption, abortion, to fetal, neonatal, or infant deaths (i.e. embryonic and fetal toxicity). In viable progeny, a decreased birth rate of male infants (who were also smaller or decreased birth weight) was observed. Some reports of teratogenesis or congenital malformations included cleft palate, skeletal abnormalities, and corneal opacities. During the first year of life, hyperactive behaviour was most evident (behavioural teratogen). THC or CBN during late pregnancy and early lactation suppressed adult copulatory activity in male offspring suggesting that male reproductive functional development may be affected. THC and CBN have interfered with testicular cholesterol esterase with accumulation of esterified cholesterol in the testis and concomitant decrease in peripheral testosterone. Decreased fetal androgen production due to maternal cannabinoid exposure may interfere with sexual differentiation in male offspring. Cannabinoids (THC, CBN, CBD, CME) reduced fertility and increased chromosomal abnormalities in adult male animals and their (untreated) male offspring who produced abnormal litters with congenital malformations, i.e., transmissible reproductive effects or mutational changes. A few human reports of prenatal marihuana use indicate some similarities to other prenatal psychotropic CNS depressant drug effects in the progeny (behavioural and possible non-specific malformations) such as decreased birth weight with physical features reminiscent of the fetal alcohol syndrome.

III. 4. Central Nervous System

Behavioural effects of marihuana may be related to THC distribution (frontal cortex, hippocampus, amygdala, lateral geniculate nucleus, cerebellum) and metabolism (77% 15 mins post IV; 51% at 4 hours) in the brain. In infants, the blood-brain barrier (slows absorption) does not develop until the second year of life making the CNS more vulnerable to drug effects (nursing mothers using drugs). In marihuana and hashish smokers, the gross pathology of the brain, visualized by pneumoencephalography, computerized transaxial tomography (CTT) scans and echoencephalography, revealed differing results of possible cerebral atrophy (irreversible brain damage) as well as no structural brain damage (but not ruling out possible subtle impairment of brain function). The subject population used in these studies were polydrug users with differing neurological status using different cannabis preparations and mode of smoking. In non-human primates, structural brain damage was not evident after 2-8 months oral cannabis intake nor were neuropathological lesions observed under the light microscope; varied biochemical changes suggesting glucose utilization defect.

THC effects on the functional condition of the brain assessed by EEG showed changes from vigilance to the drowsy state. The intensity and duration of wave changes were dose-dependent as were the behavioural ("high") and physiological (increased HR) changes; tolerance developing to all effects. Chronic use yielded dysphoria instead of euphoria. The alteration in sleep pattern (significance unknown but may be related to a sedative effect) with high oral doses of THC (up to 210 mg/d) included decreased rapid eye movement and duration of REM sleep with some increase in NREM (slow wave sleep) and, with some tolerance development; a rebound effect occurring with cessation of drug intake observed as more alert or irritable behaviour (withdrawal effect). Sleep disturbances reported during abstinence may contribute to continued drug use. Cannabis may be classified from its EEG profile as a central euphoriant with the psychotropic group of psychodysleptics (induce dream-like or delusional state of mind) with morphine-like and hallucinogenic properties.

Limbic system brain damage would affect emotional behaviour and motivation with possible hormonal disturbances. A correlation has been demonstrated between altered emotion, brain activity, and sensory perception in various disorders. In animals, heavy and moderate marihuana smoking or IV THC (equivalent to 7 and 1 jt/day) resulted in acute behavioural changes (drowsy/1 hour) with changes in brain activity (in sites of emotion especially in the septal area of the limbic system with catatonic behaviour similar to psychotic patients) which persisted for 7 to 8 months after regular chronic use suggesting possible permanent brain function and structural alterations. Sensory relay nuclei changes occurred with hallucinatory behaviour; nuclei associated with chemical transmitters also being affected. Electron microscopic examination of brain tissue from the affected septal area (altered EEG) demonstrated ultrastructural synaptic (axodendrite where message or nerve impulse transmission occurs giving rise to brain activity) changes seen as dense material within the synaptic cleft which was widened (observed in patients with neurological disorders), clumping of vesicles (contain neurotransmitters that carry impulse across the synaptic cleft) in the presynaptic bouton, and various degrees of fragmentation and disruption of rought endoplasmic reticulum (metabolic state of cell; protein synthesis) in the nerve cell with proteinaceous deposits (inclusion bodies) in the cell nucleus. Altered synaptic fine structure may affect impulse transmission explaining EEG changes. The persistent changes in limbic structures in the brain produced by moderate to heavy cannabinoid use may contribute to psychopathological states. There are electrical brain activity characteristics (fast resting α-frequencies of neurotic trait and fast β-activity in schizophrenic conditions) which indicate a predisposition to subjective (THC) drug effects with increased tendency to visual hallucinations.

Stable individuals use cannabis for social purposes (pleasure and intoxicating effects) while unstable persons use the drug as an escape mechanism for emotional problems (relief of stress or substitute for alcohol or narcotics). Pre-existing psychopathology may predispose individuals to adverse psychological reactions. Various acute emotional responses to cannabis may occur when psychological defenses are overwhelmed. The most common adverse psychological reaction to potent material by naive individuals has been acute panic anxiety brought on by acute intoxication resulting in transient drug induced distortions of reality (feelings of impending death and/or loss of mental function). Such a dysphoric effect has persisted for 3-4 days in some cancer patients using 20 mg oral THC for chronic pain indicating undesireable mental changes in some individuals. THC combined with surgical stress increases anxiety, decreases b.p. (with syncope) and increases HR. A transient mild paranoid feeling is another acute reaction occurring in those who have a paranoid defence mechanism helping to prevent acute anxiety reactions. Toxic delirium (acute brain syndrome) is an acute response to high doses and/or potency of marihuana, i.e., a toxic psychosis or poisoning. Cerebral damage has been reversible in reported poisonings in children; other altered parameters in a 4 year old girl being decreased temperature and respiratory rate, and, increased blood sugar of 116 mg %, the alterations clearing up in about a day.

Prolonged undesireable psychological effects or a chronic organic brain syndrome have been reported. A cannabis psychotic effect (pathological organic CNS response) may occur in individuals using marihuana regularly thought to be due to chemical (THC) damage to brain cells (directly or indirectly; reversible biochemical and/or persistent structural change) observed as mental confusion, slowed time sense, difficulty with recent memory, and inability of completing thoughts during a conversation resulting in confused responses. Acute psychosis in heavy hashish users has progressed to a chronic psychosis (in spite of treatment) similar to a schizophrenic reaction in predisposed individuals.

Schizophrenic patients have reported paranoid reactions to occasional or casual use of potent cannabis. Thought disorder (paranoia) is prevalent in schizophrenia vs cannabis psychosis when rapidity of thoughts or flight of ideas occurs with insight into the nature of their illness (i.e. contact with reality); phenothiazine (antipsychotic) treatment in some resulting in complete recovery with relapse occurring with return to drug use. It has been suggested that once a "saturation point" is reached with cannabis (beyond tolerance), further dosage leads to decompensation of mental functioning leading to a functional psychosis (vs toxic psychosis). Thought disorder may be induced by exogenous (psychotomimetic chemicals or endogenous (schizophrenia) substances resulting in malfunctioning subcortical CNS activity leading to disruption of subcortical-cortical homeostasis. Medically controlled psychotic patients risk relapse and exacerbation of their illness with marihuana use. High doses of cannabis may produce schizophrenic-like psychotic states depending upon the personality structure of an individual. Marihuana use during stressful situations in emotionally vulnerable individuals and in those predisposed to developing psychiatric disorders (underlying psychopathology) run the risk of long lasting adverse effects (psychiatric disturbances) which may be considered a subconscious defense mechanism against intolerable anxiety.

Other chronic effects which are non-psychotic include flashbacks, amotivational syndrome and personality (neuropsychological) changes. Etiology of flashbacks (spontaneous recurrent feelings and perceptions similar to the original drug effect) is unknown. They may be due to high drug doses or are hallucinatory experiences of pre-psychotic personalities, perhaps brought about by persistent biochemical effect(s) of marihuana in the limbic system with disorganization of sensory processes and attention systems. Motivation (incentive, drive) may be decreased with excessive use of euphoric-type drugs (including marihuana) with anti-anxiety (reinforcing) property leading to habitual use (tolerate stressful situations). Any neural alteration or damage in the limbic system (noted above) may explain possible decreased drive. An amotivational syndrome has been described following chronic high marihuana doses observed essentially as depression with flattening of affect (apathy) and mental confusion. Performance in various (psychological) tests appeared to be poorer in the better educated heavy marihuana users noted as slower reaction, poorer concentration and time estimation, poor memory, decreased psychomotor activity, greater perceptuo-motor disturbance, and high neuroticism. Heavy marihuana use is correlated with loss of interest in conventional goals with development of lethargy. Discontinuance of drug results in increased psychic discomfort (withdrawal; addictive) with a peak effect at 4 days, gradually subsiding by the 9th-10th day during which time earlier frustrations are relived.

Aggressiveness is a goal directed behaviour with deep biological roots (e.g. wild animal captures prey for food) and may be released by frustration (species and self-preservation). The limbic system in the temporal lobes in the brain deals with affective behaviour, including aggression, necessary for species and self-preservation. Stimulation of the amygdala area in the limbic system brings forth anger while lesioning this area abolishes or decreases violent outbursts with inability to become angry. Stimulation of the septal region decreases agitated psychotic and violent human behaviour changing rage to happiness and mild euphoria. Brain tumors and some epileptics with abnormal firing in the anterior temporal area have a tendency to be provoked into violent behaviour. Lesions in the temporal lobe have controlled such seizures and decreased anger, hostility, and overt agressiveness. Hormones sensitize the neurological system for aggressive behaviour. Castration in humans has been effective in controlling some sex crimes while stilbesterol (estrogen) controls aggressive behaviour in adolescence and young adults. Androgens (male sex hormones) increase self-confidence and may induce aggressive-like responses in those with feelings of insecurity and inferiority. Individuals using only marihuana appear to be less mature (emotionally) and more socially deviant (not grow up); heavy users being maladjusted with possible psychopathology. Marihuana intoxication following a marihuana cigarette with 2.2% THC (vs placebo) modified an expected hostile response to a frustration stimulus suggesting no association with increased hostility. Alcohol increases aggressive behaviour and may facilitate temporal lobe epileptoid state in susceptible individuals. Marihuana may produce violence in unstable individuals or if the septal area of the limbic system is damaged by large doses of cannabis. Low doses of THC in healthy individuals revealed less aggressive feelings while chronic use may eventually increase aggression due to tolerance development. On the whole, human hostility and aggression appears to be reduced with cannabis in the absence of stress in healthy individuals.

A workable clinical classification of psychiatric conditions associated with cannabis intoxication consists of 1) drug dependence, 2) non-psychotic organic brain syndrome, 3) psychosis, and 4) schizophrenic-like with one of the previous three noted. An acute intoxication may occur as crises of delirium or toxic psychosis whereas a chronic state may result in physical and mental deterioration. Different responses may be due to drug concentration and metabolism, duration and frequency of use, as well as personality including psychiatric makeup. The possibility exists that marihuana use in adolescents may disrupt normal psychological development resulting in inadequate adult mental functioning or emotional responsiveness (decreased productivity and stability).

Social marihuana use has been shown to impair psychomotor performance involved in driving a car or flying an aeroplane which require perceptual, cognitive, and psychomotor functions. Cannabis is used to alter cognition (awareness and judgement) or perception (consciousness or mental image). Mental and motor decrements (including response speed and physical work capacity) due to marihuana (THC) were dose-related with more complex tasks especially in experienced users revealing altered time sense (overestimation) and impaired short-term (not remote) memory (peak effect 1.5-2 hours with 3.5 hours duration post oral marihuana or THC). The latter effect may be due to cannabis effects on memory storage where information is transferred from short-term store (STS) to long term store (LTS); this storage deficit also occurring with alcohol. Cannabis does not impair retrieval of previously stored information. Tasks requiring STS information processing would therefore be affected by cannabis vs automatic well-learned tasks with information from LTS which is not affected. During driving attention is divided between tracking and searching for and recognizing environmental dangers. Driving impairment has occurred following smoking of THC (8.5 mg). Attention, perception, and information processing are important behaviour factors in accidents. Tests have shown that perceptual (sensory) aspects of car control (recognition test; response speed to signals) have been affected more than motor aspects (number of gear shifts) which is affected by alcohol. Marihuana decreases judgement, care, and concentration; a decrease in attention being correlated with a decreased input into long term memory storage. Tracking is also impaired; alcohol having an additive effect. In tracking, perceptual-central cognitive aspects and motor skills are important. Even though visual and auditory thresholds were not altered, a dose-related visual function (detect peripheral light) impairment occurred with decreased auditory signal detection (under concentration and divided attention conditions); reaction times to both visual and auditory stimuli being delayed. Foveal glare recovery has been delayed with marihuana or alcohol (alone or in combination) for at least 2 hours (when tracking and recognition of environmental dangers may be affected) probably due to a direct retinal action; light and dark adaptation taking place in the retina. Altered balance, reported as dizziness by marihuana users, may affect motor coordination. Behaviour may be affected by emotional feelings leading to accidents. The minimum allowable blood level (dose) of cannabinoids may be difficult to determine due to varied impaired responses and use with other drugs including alcohol. Proof of cannabis consumption has been demonstrated by examination of dental deposits. Oral THC, alone or combined with alcohol, has decreased performance, increased pulse rate and intoxication with conjunctival hyperemia being observed; the onset being due to alcohol and persistence due to THC (BAC being unaffected by THC presence but THC effects being augmented by alcohol). CBD and CBN did not modify these effects. The persistence of some performance deficits beyond the subjective "high" period (deterioration in flying performance 2 hours post marihuana smoking) may pose a hidden danger (attempt to drive or fly when ability still impaired even though "high" has disappeared).

Animals and humans exhibited tolerance to marihuana effects, being long-lasting in animals with increased lethal dose and cross tolerance among cannabinoids. Humans rapidly acquired (14-21 days smoking 2 marihuana cigarettes daily) and lost tolerance (depending upon dose, frequency, and duration) with partial tolerance developing to weight gain and decreased testosterone, and, cross tolerance occurring with CBD, phenylhydantoin, phenobarbital, ethanol, and morphine (not LSD nor mescaline). Onset of physical (physiological) dependence for THC was 3-8 weeks (post IV) in animals and 10-21 days (chronic oral THC) in man. Marihuana dependence may be mild (depending upon dose) noted by the mild withdrawal symptoms occurring 24-48 hours following regular smoking of 5-10 cigs/day, being relieved by alcohol, barbiturates or marihuana, and lasting 96 hours. Psychological (psychic) dependence has occurred in heavy chronic (hashish) users who become dysphoric and very irritable (psychic withdrawal or behavioural abstinence) between cannabinoid doses because of tolerance development. Heavy marihuana users smoke more efficiently to increase pulmonary absorption of the active principle (THC) to acquire the initial desired effect ("high") obtained prior to tolerance development which is not due to metabolic (drug) tolerance but may be functional or adaptive in nature.

III. 5. Cardiopulmonary System

Pulmonary System

Approximately 50% cannabinoids in a marihuana cigarette are delivered to the smoker's lungs. The smoking of marihuana transfers 20% THC to mainstream smoke with THC concentrating (3.5%) in the tar or particulate matter of smoke (from 0.61% in the cigarette). One of the reasons for individual variation in responses lies in the amounts of CBN and CBD present in the preparations used because they inhibit THC (liver) metabolism causing THC accumulation. Since a tobacco and marihuana mixture is often smoked, CBD is partially converted to THC due to acidity of tobacco which does not occur with smoking only marihuana. Smoke exposure increases AHH (aryl hydrocarbon hydroxylase, a hydroxylating enzyme) activity enhancing THC biotransformation to psychoactive metabolites (OH-THC). The carcinogenic potential of marihuana smoke resides in the tar which has both tumorigenic and tumor-promoting properties. The carcinogenic risks associated with marihuana are comparable to cigarette and pipe tobacco due to a potent mutagenic effect (associated with the nitrogen content of pyrolysis products during smoking process) and higher smoke condensate yield in which PAH (polynuclear aromatic hydrocarbons (eg. benz (a) pyrene) the largest known group of chemical carcinogens) concentration is almost twice that in tobacco. Smoke irritation sets up an inflammatory reaction (capillary dilation) while marihuana (THC) causes vasodilation; the result being increased absorption of inhaled substances including paraquat (a herbicide used to eradicate marihuana plants) and infectious organisms which may be harmful to lungs. An acute lethal dose is larger than a chronic lethal dose which is taken over a period of time with cumulative effects.

The acute pulmonary marihuana effects are bronchodilation and respiratory depression; tolerance developing to both (similar to opiate dependence re tolerance to depression). Smoked marihuana (or THC) has decreased airway resistance in stable asthmatics for a 2 hour period. Chronic cannabinoid use (large dose/long time) has resulted in pulmonary disorders involving the whole respiratory system with altered pulmonary function tests characteristic of intrathoracic airway obstruction (reversed with abstinence) or pulmonary insufficiency which may lead to (decreased) ventilation/perfusion imbalance resulting in hypoxemia which, in turn, increases the demand on bone marrow for RBC (red blood cell) production (observed as increased Hb and PCV). Excessive hypoxemia leads to pulmonary hypertension resulting in cor pulmonale and right heart failure (heart disease secondary to lung disease). Respiratory function impairment may not be revealed by routine spirometry and plethysmography in long term healthy social marihuana smokers but does not rule out possible small airway disease; impairment depending upon extent (frequency) of smoke exposure. Tracheal biopsies have revealed abnormal epithelium similar to that seen in older heavy tobacco users; pathological findings being similar to those found with tobacco associated with the development of emphysema and carcinoma. Similar animal pathology has been observed with prolonged smoke exposure being dose related (THC) as well as being influenced by frequency and duration of exposure; the undesirable structural pulmonary changes thought to be due to storage and biotransformation of cannabinoids which have an affinity for pulmonary tissue.

Acute marihuana smoke exposure ("in-vitro" and "in-vivo" animal systems) decreased alveolar macrophage bactericidal activity by impairing phagocytosis without killing the macrophage cell due to a water soluble cytotoxin in the gas phase of fresh smoke (not THC nor stale smoke) possibly impairing glycolysis necessary for some cell energy for phagocytosis. This, together with a trend to decreased airway clearance by cilia, resulted in bacteria surviving longer in lungs exposed to marihuana vs. tobacco smoke. The ability to phagocytize was not altered by subchronic smoke exposure. (Chronic tobacco smoke exposure (6 months) led to a 30% inhibition of particle uptake indicating a cumulative effect). Subcellular morphological changes with marihuana was less than with tobacco which may be due to marihuana bronchodilating effect resulting in lesser retention of particulate matter leading to smaller environmental changes thereby creating smaller changes in structure and metabolism of the macrophage. Functional impairment of alveolar macrophages may render the host susceptible to bacterial infections with subsequent development of emphysema. Tracheal epithelial thickness was increased with a decrease in secretory cells; changes similar to human chronic bronchitis (mucus hypersecretion with bronchial structural alteration resulting in a chronic cough). Suppression of respiratory rate, (possibly) enzyme (α_1-antitrypsin) activity, and defense system (to bacteria) as well as smoke irritation over a period of time may produce lung damage. With tobacco, tar yield and daily cigarette use is related to respiratory symptoms (phlegm production) and altered lung function (decreased FEV_1 indicating airflow obstruction) respectively. Those with asthma and allergies should avoid smoke exposure.

Thus marihuana smoking is capable of altering pulmonary function observed as airway obstruction (brought about by irritants and carcinogens in smoke) and ineffective removal of particulate matter (including bacteria) leading to the development of bronchitis, emphysema and pulmonary carcinoma. CNS damage (loss of sensation in fingers, poor memory, mental deterioration) develops gradually due to chronic anoxia from CO (gas phase) absorption. Contamination of marihuana with paraquat (chemical herbicide) and/or infectious organisms could add to any lung abnormalities with possible lethal outcome especially in cancer patients using marihuana as an antiemetic during intensive chemotherapy and/or radiation therapy.

Cardiovascular System

Substances entering the lungs are exposed to a large vascular surface area facilitating rapid absorption and distribution. The acute CV (cardiovascular) effect of inhaled marihuana and THC (systemic availability of 18% vs oral of 6%) is peripheral vasodilation resulting in b.p. (blood pressure) changes varying with posture (an increase in the supine position and a decrease in the standing position, with postural hypotension leading to unconsciousness or syncope in some individuals because of cerebral ischemia which increases vagal activity giving a sharp decrease in heart rate prior to fainting), conjunctival reddening (dose-dependent) which is a sensitive indicator of prevailing plasma THC level and intoxication and decreased exercise tolerance (decreased work output). Peripheral vasodilation stimulates baroreceptors to reflexly increase HR (heart rate) which, if inadequate to maintain normal b.p. level, causes fainting i.e., marihuana may interfere with adequate compensatory vascular adjustments necessary for adequate tissue perfusion. B.p. changes parallel dose-related HR changes which correlate with plasma THC levels (being another indicator of absorbed dose for a particular individual) and psychological subjective "highs" with tolerance development within 2-3 weeks of daily chronic drug use; a mild withdrawal syndrome occurring after 1 week abstinence. Tolerance development is accomplished by compensatory plasma volume expansion (observed as increased body weight and decreased Hb concentration) to help attain normal b.p. level resulting in functional anemia which may contribute to inadequate tissue oxygenation leading to functional system(s) depression. The "high" (or dizzy feeling) may be due to hypotension at first and later due to functional anemia in conjunction with hypotension. Initially cardiac output is increased followed by a decrease, with a slight decrease in stroke volume and an increase in cardiac performance (decreased pre-ejection period or PEP). Cardiac contractility may be depressed because of inhibition of cardiac microsomal Ca uptake and CaATPase activity (associated with Ca transport) observed with cannabinoids "in-vitro". Tachycardia may be modified by psychological state of mind; enhancement with anxiety and depression with somnolence. Carbon monoxide gas in smoke produces COHb (carboxyhemoglobin) resulting in hypoxia which leads to vasodilation with compensatory HR increase and which makes the heart work harder increasing b.p. and HR with possible permanent cardiac damage; chronic carbon monoxide exposure facilitating atherosclerotic development. Tobacco causes vasoconstriction (vs vasodilation of mairhuana) with increased HR and b.p. due to epinephrine release by nicotine. The tachycardia in response to vasodilation (due to cannabis) and carbon monoxide gas (hypoxia) is necessary to increase tissue perfusion to prevent anoxic (permanent damage) conditions.

The severity of E.C.G. changes depends upon the extent of cannabinoid use, cessation of which, reverts ECG to a normal pattern. The changes and abnormalities reported may be due to an adrenergic (especially β) effect leading to ischemic (tachycardia, functional anemia) or hypoxic effects and include varied P and T-wave as well as ST-segment changes, PVCs (similar to nicotine and caffeine effects) and, increased sinus nodal automaticity (↑HR) and nodal (SA, AV) conduction (similar to isoproterenol, a β-adrenergic agonist). The electrical changes resemble those seen in angina being due to myocardial hypoxia when coronary blood flow does not keep pace with increased oxygen consumption of the stimulated (by epinephrine) heart. It may be that the adrenergic system responds in a normal autoregulatory (compensatory) fashion to an altered marihuana CV effect (peripheral vasodilation) which may activate the CNS sympathoadrenal system with β-adrenergic receptors being the final common pathway. Carbon monoxide gas enhances THC tachycardia and ischemic cardiac ECG changes with subendocardial areas being particularly vulnerable (to ischemia) leading to (subendocardial) infarction (also due to prolonged b.p. decrease) which has been reported in a marihuana and tobacco smoker who recovered within 6 weeks with a normal ECG pattern (by abstaining from marihuana use). The possibility exists that chronic marihuana use may result in irreversible electrical changes leading to permanent heart damage.

Marihuana decreases exercise performance in anginal patients, percipitating attacks sooner, due to myocardial hypoxia brought about by increased O_2 demand (HR x b.p.), decreased O_2 delivery (coronary blood flow, COHb), and possibly functional anemia, with earlier development of ischemic ST-segment depression. A similar response is seen with nicotine, carbon monoxide exposure (direct, passive), anemia, pregnancy, alcohol, and respiratory disease. The basic disease process of glaucoma is not altered by drugs used to treat ocular hypertension, a disease manifestation (comparable to hypertensive treatment). Cannabinoids decrease intraocular pressure by decreasing fluid formation (β-adrenergic effect) and increasing fluid outflow (α-adrenergic effect), the latter possibly being augmented by pupil constriction produced by THC. However it is unknown whether visual function is preserved. Even though intraocular pressure is decreased in glaucoma patients, the decreased blood pressure may jeopardize the blood supply to the optic nerve giving rise to nerve atrophy and blindness (anxiety and palpatations being undesireable subjective side-effects). Marihuana smoking has decreased platelet aggregation suggesting possible impairment of blood coagulation. A history of marihuana use should alert the physician to avoid medications (as well as surgical stress) that would enhance and prolong tachycardia, worsen psychotic behaviour, increase ventilatory depression and to suspect use in accident victims with persistent tachycardia and ECG abnormalities.

Marihuana appears to relax smooth muscle (peripheral blood vessels including conjunctival; bronchial smooth muscles) similar to that observed with nitrites; the net response depending upon the relative concentration of two chemicals (marihuana and autonomic nervous system chemicals) with the possibility of a compensatory mechanism overcoming the net effect. As with nitroid shock (due to a large nitrite dose), the CV toxicity of marihuana may be a form of shock secondary to vasodilation.

IV. Conclusion and Final Comments

Contents

	Abstract	252
1.	Introduction	252
2.	Marihuana Hypoxic Effects	252
3.	Secondary CVS Adrenergic Reflex Response	253
4.	Metabolic and Hormonal Alterations	254
5.	Altered Blood Glucose Control	255
6.	Adrenergic Blocking Effects	259
7.	Final Statements	260
8.	Final Conclusion	261
9.	Figures	262

Abstract

Possible (probability?) explanations for health consequences of marihuana are offered through marihuana hypoxic and secondary adrenergic effects leading to metabolic (metabolism being defined as chemical changes in living cells providing energy for vital processes and activities with assimilation of new material for waste repair) alterations resulting in multisystem dysfunction.

Keywords: adrenergic effects, blood glucose, cannabis, hormonal alterations, hypoxic effects, metabolic effects.

Abbreviations: acetylcholine (Ach); adenosine triphosphate (ATP); adrenocortical hormone (ACH); adrenocorticotrophic hormone (ACTH); alpha (α); beta (β); blood pressure (b.p.); blood urea nitrogen (BUN); cannabidiol (CBD); cannabinol (CBN); carbohydrate (CHO); carbon dioxide (CO_2); carboxy-hemoglobin (COHb); cardiac output (CO); cardiovascular system (CVS); central nervous system (CNS); chloride (Cl^-); chronic obstructive pulmonary disease (COPD); cigarette (cig); creatine phosphokinase (CPK); cubic millimetres (cu mm); degrees centigrade ($^\circ$C); day (d); delta-6a, 10a-dimethyl heptyl THC (DMHP); 2,3-diphosphoglycerate (2,3 DPG); electrocardiogram (EC (or K) G); electroencephalogram (EEG); fetal alcohol syndrome (FAS); follicle stimulating hormone (FSH); glomerular filtration rate (GFR); gram (gm); growth hormone (GH); heart rate (HR); hemoglobin (Hb); hydroxy (OH); intramuscular (IM); intraocular pressure (IOP); intraperitoneal (IP); intravenous (IV); kilogram (kg); lactic dehydrogenase (LDH); less than (<); luteinizing hormone (LH); lysergic acid diethylamide (LSD); milli (m); milligram (mg); millilitre (ml); minute (min); myocardial infarction (MI); non-esterified fatty acids (NEFA); norepinephrine (NE); oxyhemoglobin (O_2Hb); oxygen (O_2); per os or oral (p.o.); percent (%); phosphate (Ph); potassium (K^+); red blood cell (RBC); serum glutamic oxaloacetic transaminase (SGOT); sodium (Na^+); subcutaneous (S.C.); sympathetic nervous system (symp. n. system); tetrahydrocannabinol (THC); thyroid hormone (TH); thyroid stimulating hormone (TSH); times (x); water (H_2O); white blood cell or leukocyte (WBC).

IV. 1. Introduction

From the foregoing discussions it appears that possible marihuana effects on an individual would involve the CNS (ultrastructural brain damage; psychopathology), immunological system, reproductive system (altered endocrine function), and cardiopulmonary system; while society would be affected by behavioural manifestations of lethargy (lack of motivation) and psychomotor (driving) impairment as well as possible genetic modifications.   Since cell growth is affected by cannabis, the growing child or adolescent (who is in the early phase of physiological and psychological development) would, therefore, be more vulnerable; the emotionally unstable and mentally ill being prone to psychiatric disturbances. Thus marihuana would be especially harmful in immature, unstable and ailing individuals.

IV. 2. Marihuana Hypoxic Effects

The main marihuana effect on various body systems is one of depression which is a sign of toxicity (vs therapeutic and not quite lethal) since marihuana is smoked for and until a "high" feeling is obtained.   Why are all systems affected?   An answer to this would be another question of, what reaches all parts of the body?   The answer is that the nervous and cardiovasculer systems do, with the nervous system requiring the cardiovascular system (CVS) to function properly. Since the mode of death in animals is cardiac arrest, the CVS may be the common denominator. The CVS is primarily affected by marihuana with secondary reflex effects brought about by the nervous system which itself becomes depressed due to hypoxia (sluggish functioning) with eventual damage. Marihuana smoking creates hypoxia by

(1) carbon monoxide gas in the smoke combining with Hb to form COHb thereby displacing O_2,

(2) irritants and carcinogens in the smoke leading to airway obstruction or decreased ventilation,

(3) depressing macrophage activity encouraging recurrent infection or imflammation which may eventually lead to bronchitis, emphysema, and irreversible COPD with ventilation/perfusion imbalance,

(4) peripheral vasodilation decreasing blood pressure (with orthostatic hypotension encouraging syncope) with attendant decreased tissue perfusion (oxygenation), and

(5) compensatory plasma expansion (due to inadequate maintenance of normal b.p. level by compensatory tachycardia) causing functional anemia (decreased Hb) which may also be due to decreased maturation of blood cells in bone marrow affected by sex hormones and by decreased protein synthesis (alteration in histone ratio); i.e. RBCs are necessary to carry O_2 while WBC are necessary to control infection;

4) and 5) indicating marihuana's interference with adequate compensatory vascular adjustment(s). Should this feedback mechanism break down, then the CNS cannot control or regulate the CVS normally leading to CVS damage and CNS deregulation which in turn could lead to mental illness.

IV. 3. Secondary CVS Adrenergic Reflex Response

The secondary CVS reflex effects alluded to above probably involve the adrenergic nervous system. Other evidence (in addition to CVS effects) exists to support an adrenergic mechanism being the main reflex response to peripheral vasodilation due to marihuana and will be mentioned briefly. At the subcellular level of the CNS (in animals), the distribution of cannabinoids (THC and metabolites) was different from other psychotomimetic drugs (morphine, barbiturates, LSD), large amounts being found in cholinergic and non-cholinergic nerve endings especially in synaptosomes and synaptic vesicles indicating interaction with the neuronal segment involved in storing neurotransmitters (Dewey et al., 1976b). Naloxone was found to inhibit the increased catecholamine synthesis induced by THC thought to occur within the neuron (Dewey et al., 1976a). At the cellular level, a temporary arrest of glucose transport from plasma to RBC (erythrocyte or red blood cell) occurred with hashish smoking (Kalofoutis et al., 1980) being augmented by alcohol (Schurr et al., 1974) which is often used to increase the "high" of hashish smoking. ATP, 2,3 DPG, and lactic acid production were decreased in RBCs maximally 30-45 minutes following hashish resin (3.6% THC) smoking by chronic hashish users (with 20-30 years experience having used up to 100 gm crude hashish/time using a narghile pipe) (Kalofoutis et al., 1980). A decrease in 2,3 DPG (intermediary product in glycolysis regulating O_2 release from Hb to tissues shifting O_2Hb curve to right) causes tissue hypoxia (shift curve to left) leading to an adaptive increase in peripheral blood flow. Hashish smoking does not appear to affect Ach esterase activity (involved in cholinergic action) (Coutselinis and Michalodimitrakis, 1981). Under cell metabolism in the text, THC altered metabolism of cultured lymphocytes by decreasing glucose consumption and lactate excretion (i.e. decreased glucose utilization by cells) as well as slowing growth rate or lowering protein synthesis. In animals chronic THC 2 mg/kg IV/day/1 week increased synthesis of H^3-catecholamines (from radioactive precursor tyrosine) in brain and adrenals (not heart) without changing the endogenous content of NE (norepinephrine) and dopamine in the brain, epinephrine and NE in the adrenals and cardiac NE indicating increased turnover of the biogenic amines in the tissues suggesting an increased sympathetic activity which may be a compensatory mechanism (Mazurkiewicz-Kwilecki and Filczewski, 1973). Exogenous copper and zinc (relatively high concentrations of endogenous metals in hypothalamus) antagonized tolerance developed to cannabis induced hypothermia mediated through the noradrenergic system (Singh and Das, 1978). In India, copper is purported to potentiate cannabis effects. In man (noted in the CVS section) electrophysiological (cardiac conduction) THC effects suggested central autonomic nervous system involvement because of similarity to isoproterenol and atropine effects (increase HR, decrease sinus recovery time, and facilitate A-V conduction); an adrenergic effect being observed as synergistic tachycardia with THC and surgical stress or CO_2. Excessive tachycardia may be the limiting toxicity of THC in those who are able to tolerate the psychological effects; propanolol (β-adrenergic blocker) being capable of blocking the tachycardia.

IV. 4. Metabolic and Hormonal Alterations

Metabolic and hormonal alterations by marihuana (THC) have been observed in animals and man. In animals, THC stimulated ACTH (adrenocorticotrophic hormone) secretion (enhanced by pentobarbital) and did not block (but enhanced) ACTH secretion induced by epinephrine (Dewey et al., 1970). Stress increased both plasma ACTH and corticosterone, the latter also being increased by THC. Higher plasma corticosterone levels were obtained with stress (electric shock) combined with THC (5 mg/kg IP) than with either treatment alone (Jacobs et al., 1979). A dose-related increase in blood glucose with concomitant decrease in liver glycogen (Fig. 1) occurred following IP cannabis extract (in rodents) with maximum effects being reached at 300 mg/kg dose indicating that hyperglycemia was due to increased glycogenolysis (Soni and Gupta, 1978). Uterine glycogen was decreased in normal prepubertal rodents by daily subcutaneous cannabis extract (8% THC, 0.8% CBD, 2.2% CBN) injections of 10 mg THC/kg/11 days due to increased glycogen breakdown (increased total phosphorylase activity) and decreased glycogen synthesis (decreased total synthetase activity at the rate limiting step in glucose conversion to glycogen) noted as inhibition of estradiol-induced glycogen accumulation (an anti-estrogen effect); a possible adrenaline involvement being suggested (Chakravarty and Ghosh, 1977). A dose-related decrease in fructose and citric acid contents of male reproductive organs (testis, prostate, seminal vesicle, epididymis) of prepubertal and adult rodents (Chakravarty and Ghosh, 1981) was produced by cannabis (extract effect > THC; s.c. 10-50 mg/kg THC content/day/10 days) again suggesting a possible metabolic carbohydrate alteration such as inadequate glucose utilization, consequences of which are noted later including unavailability of cholesterol necessary for testosterone synthesis (which is thought to be necessary to stimulate fructose and citric acid production and secretion) the secretion of which is controlled by gonadotropins. In canines (fasting or IV glucose fed 90 minutes post drug), different IM doses (2.5,5, 10 mg/kg THC) of cannabis resin (6.3% THC, 3.2% CBD, 1.9% CBN) resulted (observation/4 hours) in (Fig. 2 to 7) increased blood glucose and ammonia levels (gluconeogenesis) with corresponding decrease in plasma insulin level (maximum effects at 90 minute period) as well as decreased glucose tolerance with a corresponding decrease in insulin response (with increased ammonia levels) to a glucose load (de Pasquale et al., 1978). A large increase in blood ammonia and urea levels was observed in another animal (rabbits) study (Ghoneim et al., 1980) following one month of hashish smoke exposure (15 minutes every other day) indicating increased availability of amino acids (due to decreased incorporation into proteins) for catabolic metabolism with increased glutamate dehydrogenase (an enzyme involved in ammonia formation from amino acids). Urea may be formed from ammonia, or be a breakdown product of arginine (amino acid involved in spermatic cell maturation) or be due to renal impairment. As noted in the reproductive section, cannabis effects on animal endocrine glands varied depending upon the cannabinoid tested, dose, route, duration, sex, species and physiological state of the animal. These effects on circulating hormones included decreased testosterone and thyronine (T_3) with decreased as well as increased thyroxine (T_4), estrogens and pituitary hormones (LH, FSH, GH); such imbalance resulting in gonadal and reproductive malfunction. In non-human primates (Dixit, 1981), testicular and liver damage developed following chronic cannabis extract treatment (14 mg/kg/d/90d. p.o.). Male gonadal lesions developed with mass atrophy of spermatogenic elements. Testicular alkaline phosphatase and cholesterol were increased. Leydig cell tissue regression with decreased RNA, protein and sialic acid production is commensurate with the reported suppressed testosterone levels; a decrease in sialic acid having been noted in cryptorchid testes. Low adrenal ascorbic acid indicated ACTH stimulation by cannabis extract. Histological liver changes were observed as cytoplasmic degranulation and vacuolization with decreased liver glycogen. Generalized severe catabolism was indicated by increased SGOT levels while liver damage was reflected in increased SGPT and bilirubin levels with altered lipid metabolism noted as increased NEFA, phospholipids, total and free cholesterol levels. Similar biochemical changes have occurred with other psychotomimetics including LSD and mescaline. In the CNS section, biochemical changes in primates suggested glucose utilization defect following (up to 8 months) oral cannabis intake (0.275 gm-1.38 gm THC/day). In man, acute IV THC (6 mg producing intoxication in 6 casual marihuana users) impaired glucose tolerance (Fig. 8 to 10) but not insulin response (although shape of curve was different) and increased plasma growth hormone levels (Hollister and Reaven, 1974). In four young chronic marihuana users (12-15 hours fasting), glucose tolerance was decreased (Fig. 11 to 15) after 7 days marihuana smoking (1/2-1 cig/day; THC?) with increased plasma catecholamine levels without significant changes in insulin and growth hormone levels (although there was a tendency for an increase in the latter 2 parameters) (Podolsky et al., 1971). In 10 chronic marihuana users (use at least 1/week/1 year; fasting and fed states), 1 gm (1.5% THC) marihuana (post 24-72 hours fasting) smoking (via spirometer/15-30 minutes) did not produce hypoglycemia nor alter glucose tolerance indicating normal carbohydrate (CHO) metabolism in healthy chronic users. That is, glycogenolysis (occuring during starvation due to liver glycogen depletion) was not impaired (vs alcohol) with expected low insulin levels in fasting individuals (without marihuana stimulating insulin release) (Permutt et al., 1976). In 5 naive (drug use 5-6x) and 5 chronic (25-35 years drug use) hashish users (tobacco smokers; 45-55 years of age), the smoking (10 minutes) of a hashish cigarette (2 gm (1.3% THC, 0.4% CBD, 1.1% CBN) mixed with tobacco) after 20 hours of fasting, revealed decreased blood lactic acid levels within 1 hour of smoking (Fig. 16) without alteration of blood glucose levels. The naive group had a greater rate of lactic acid decrease with a minimum level reached by 30 minutes persisting to the end of the study period (210 minutes); the experienced group reaching a minimum level at 90 minutes with persistence for 210 minutes (Papadakis et al., 1974). Thus liver glycogen formation from lactate (decreased levels being due to decreased glucose utilization) was proceeding normally during fasting (maintaining normal blood glucose levels). Growth hormone and cortisol response to acute insulin hypoglycemia were decreased following 14 days oral THC when the insulin-induced hypoglycemia was not as pronounced as in the pre-THC period (Fig. 17). It was suggested that THC depressed hypothalamic function. (It may be that in the presence of THC (acting via an adrenergic mechanism) less growth hormone but somewhat similar amount of cortisol are required to offset the insulin-induced hypo-glycemia) (Benowitz et al., 1976). Impairment of glycolysis (which provides some cell energy for phagocytosis) has been observed (noted in pulmonary system section) with the water-soluble cytotoxin in the gas phase of fresh whole marihuana smoke being responsible for the phagocytic impairment of alveolar macrophages involved in bactericidal activity. Clinically one report (Hughes et al., 1970) suggests an unmasking of a latent diabetes mellitus by marihuana ingestion in a 21 year old man, while in another (Lockhart and Desser, 1970), insulin requirements were increased (3x) in a juvenile diabetic patient because of marihuana and amphetamine use. Poisoning by cannabis resin in a 4 year old girl (having eaten 1.5 gm with 150 mg THC/gm) resulted in a toxic delirium with decreased temperature and respiratory rate, increased blood sugar of 116 mg % and urinary cannabinoid level of 21 mmoles/l; the signs and symptoms subsiding in about one day (Bro et al., 1975). It may be that healthy individuals may be able to handle marihuana effects adequately while those with disease may not (as seen with anginal patients).

IV. 5. Altered Blood Glucose Control

In order to place the above data into perspective, factors controlling blood glucose concen-tration (noted in diagram of blood glucose control) will be discussed with respect to a possible reflex adrenergic mechanism of marihuana action, keeping in mind that any imbalance (competitive inhibition or antagonism) in the various factors will lead to physiological alterations.

Blood sugar level at any given moment represents the equilibrium between various metabolic reactions dependent on the secretions of the thyroid gland, adrenal glands, and pituitary as well as the pancreas with liver's role being one of regulating blood sugar. There is a high demand by the brain for oxygen (O_2) and glucose since it obtains energy (in the form of ATP) via glucose metabolism (glucose + $O_2 \rightarrow CO_2 + H_2O$). The brain is sensitive to O_2 deficiency and has a limited capacity for carbohydrate storage thereby requiring a constant ample blood supply providing O_2 and glucose continually; the rate of cerebral blood flow through a healthy adult brain being 15% of normal resting cardiac output (normal CO/min = 4-5 litres at rest). Most CNS diseases are accompanied by disorder in cerebral metabolism; inadequate glucose resulting in mental confusion, dizziness, convulsions, and even loss of consciousness. The data suggest that marihuana (THC) may be capable of producing a pseudo-diabetic state (observed clinically as an unmasking of a latent diabetic state and an increased insulin requirement in a diabetic patient) the degree of which depends upon the preparation used, dose, route, frequency and duration of use, and individual state of health including nutritional status and genetic predisposition to disease.

Cannabis has been reported to induce catecholamine synthesis (intraneuronally; increased human plasma levels). Sympathetic activity increases blood sugar (hyperglycemia) through glycognenolysis (via tissue β-receptors) observed above as dose-related increased blood glucose, decreased liver glycogen, decreased glucose tolerance, with decreased plasma insulin (or secretion via tissue α-receptors). ACTH secretion is also increased (and observed above) which, via ACH, results in gluconeogenesis (observed as increased ammonia level which also occurs in anoxic states of shock) and decreased glucose utilization by tissues (observed as decreased glucose transport from plasma to RBC, increased GH levels, and decreased blood lactate) to help replenish depleted liver glycogen during glycogenolysis (also observed in fasting individuals) for optimal blood glucose supply for use by the brain and nervous tissue for normal function. Since ACTH is part of a larger molecule, pro-opiocortin, (Krieger and Martin, 1981; Miller and Cuatrecasas, 1978), its release (by stress, epinephrine, sympathetic (adrenergic) nervous system, THC, insulin-induced hypoglycemia) breaks up the large molecule setting free other components such as endogenous opiates, one being β-endorphin (found in the pituitary gland and plasma) considered to be a neurotransmitter along the pain neural pathway in a natural pain relieving system in the brain while enkephalins (leucine and methionine; shorter amino acid chains) are widely distributed in the brain (found especially in the basal ganglia) and spinal cord. These endogenous opiates may be responsible for the reported THC analgesic effects and may explain naloxone (narcotic antagonist) inhibiting effects (noted above) and the suggestion of cannabis use in narcotic detoxification. Naloxone has been observed to precipitate an abstinence syndrome in THC-tolerant animals but was without effect when THC was substituted or used to avoid morphine withdrawal effects (noted in CNS section) suggesting a possible underlying endorphin releasing mechanism by THC. The endogenous

Diagram

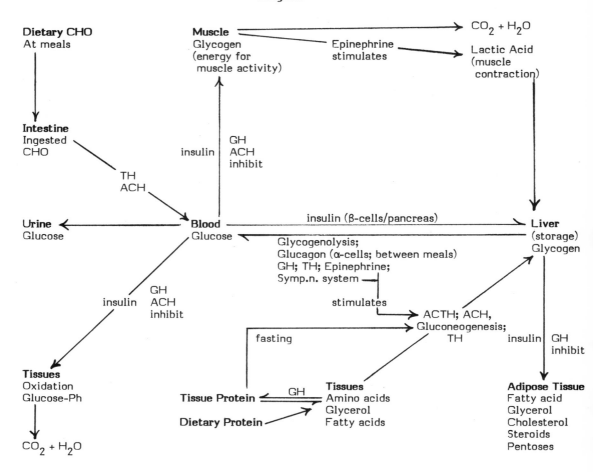

Blood Glucose Control

ACTH-adrenocorticotrophic hormone; ACH-adrenocortical hormone; CHO-carbohydrate; GH-growth hormone; Ph-phosphate; Symp.n. system-sympathetic nervous system; TH-thyroid hormone.

opiates would also explain the mild addiction with cannabis with mild withdrawal effects. Withdrawal may be due to (a) endorphin deficiency produced during the addiction phase when a feedback mechanism shuts off endorphin production, and/or (b) a relative endorphin deficiency produced by a decrease in adrenergic stimulation of ACTH release upon cessation of cannabinoid use. The former (a) occurs with other exogenous drugs decreasing their respective hormone (e.g. thyroid) production which is not needed in the presence of the exogenous source resulting in dependence on the external source i.e. addiction (with possible tolerance development to, e.g. a "high"). The alteration (decreased production) may become permanent with time so that addiction may, perhaps, be equated with metabolic diseases such as diabetes mellitus. In the latter (b), depletion of endorphins may occur more readily in those with inborn endorphin abnormalities. That is, individual variations in hormone levels including endorphins probably occur as observed in those who do not feel pain (possible excess of endorphins); in tic douloureux (severe pain) with less than normal endorphin levels; and possibly in mental illness (noting that the limbic system which deals with emotion (related to emotional disturbances in schizophrenia) has the greatest concentration of opiate receptors; should the limbic system in the brain become damaged, the possibility of high endorphin levels exist via a feedback mechanism from the target limbic area). There may be an endorphin deficiency or aberration (a genetic alteration?) in those who find it difficult to cope with life stresses (a state of depression) encouraging such individuals to rely on exogenous (opioid-like activity) sources leading to drug dependence (addiction). Opioid peptides (endorphins, enkephalins) are known to increase the release of prolactin (noted in reproduction section), GH (noted above), and vasopressin (which also occurs with opioids) but to depress the release of LH (noted in reproduction section) and FSH; naloxone reversing these effects (increasing circulating LH and FSH). β-endorphin has been implicated in states of increased food intake. It has been suggested that ACTH may affect behaviour by increasing attention and perception (via facilitation of selective arousal of limbic-midbrain structures) being involved in memory formation and persistence of learned responses with ACTH fragments being involved in short-term memory processes (vasopression in long term memory). Electrophysiologically, opioid peptides decrease the rate of neuronal firing (spontaneous or glutamate-induced) which does not occur in tolerant animals.

Gluconeogenesis involving amino acids may result in (relative) deficiencies by diversion (e.g. arginine necessary for spermatogenesis) to other tissues where need exists (in this case liver re glycogen) observed in reproduction section as altered spermatogenesis due to lack of (spermatozoan) protamines which contain large amounts of arginine which is decreased resulting in spermatic cell maturation arrest. Stress may also decrease number of sperm; a diet deficient in arginine decreasing spermatozoa production to 1/10th normal. Since gonadotropin (LH, FSH) secretions may be controlled by releasing factors which respond (secreted) to hypothalamic catecholamines, a disruption in hypothalamic amine metabolism may result in the observed THC effect of decreased LH and FSH levels. Decreased progesterone synthesis (ovary) may be due to inhibition of (precursor) cholesterol release from ester storage pool and/or decreased uptake by the cell. Increased ammonia blood levels may cause CNS derangement leading to disturbances in consciousness and EEG abnormalities. Disruption of rough endoplasmic reticulum which is associated with protein synthesis has been observed in the nerve cell (noted in CNS section). The discouragement of protein synthesis (probably due to decreased glucose utilization by cells) by gluconeogenesis would affect the immunological system (by decreasing formation of humoral and cellular components thereby decreasing immunity), chromosomes (irregular mitosis and abnormalities), and, cell metabolism (enzyme deficiency) and proliferation (antineoplastic?) with possible abnormal functioning (including mutagenic potential) leading to irregular growth and tumor formation. Depending upon the physiological and biochemical status at a particular time, GH (growth hormone) may have a diabetogenic effect by stimulating glucagon secretion from α-cells in the pancreas (seen above with insulin-induced hypoglycemia producing increased GH levels which were lowered in the presence of THC when less GH was required) or, a protein synthesizing effect or nitrogen retention (seen in the presence of THC when GH was attempting to replace tissue protein used in gluconeogenesis by, e.g., decreasing arginase activity) when insulin is necessary. Competitive inhibition of insulin (β-cells in the pancreas) by THC (via adrenergic mechanism) in the normal pancreas was observed as a dose-related decrease in insulin response to blood glucose level in the presence of THC.

The decrease in glucose utilization by tissues may make cholesterol unavailable for sex hormone synthesis observed in reproduction section as decreased testosterone in males (with increased esterified cholesterol concentration in animal testis which may also be due to inhibition of cholesterol esterase which in turn may be due to decreased protein synthesis) and decreased estrogen and progesterone in females; pubertal arrest having been associated with heavy marihuana use in a youth. The increase in plasma lipids may encourage atheroma formation in blood vessels leading to arteriosclerosis and heart disease. Inhibition of cholesterol esterification has been observed in cultured normal human dermal fibroblasts and in human aortic medial (smooth muscle) cells by cannabinoids (THC, CBD, CBN) possibly making cholesterol unavailable for cellular cholesterol metabolism (Cornicelli et al., 1981). The unutilized blood glucose a) may exceed the renal threshold resulting in glucose loss in urine with a large amount of water (high osmotic pressure of sugar preventing water reabsorption) leading to polyuria and thirst (due to sugar withdrawing fluid from tissues or dehydration), and b) is unavailable for body needs (essential for normal brain function) producing carbohydrate starvation manifested as hunger (for sweets), weakness (loss of energy (produced from oxidative reactions in Krebs tricarboxylic acid cycle) due to relative lack of insulin), and decreased weight initially (due to urinary glucose loss and gluconeogenesis from proteins and fats (used for sugar and energy supply)). Weakness may contribute to the amotivational syndrome. It has been observed that marihuana decreased physical strength in tasks requiring sustained effort. Acute adverse effects reported frequently by regular marihuana users (5-6 year follow-up) included increased hunger, increased thirst, dry mouth and throat, as well as time slowing (Weller and Halikas, 1982). As in man, rodents preferred sweet calories (sucrose) during acute cannabinoid (2.5 and 5 mg/kg THC, 50 mg/kg for CBN and CBD, I.P.) exposure without total appetite (food and water consumption) being stimulated; food consumption decreased as sucrose concentration increased (Sofia and Knobloch, 1976). This was also observed with IP injections of hashish resin (5 mg/kg or 2.75 mg/kg THC; 10 mg/kg or 5.5 mg/kg THC) in rodents (Corcoran and Amit, 1974). In sheep, food intake was increased at the 30 minute period, then decreased by 24 hours following THC injections (0.125-2 mg IV) (McLaughlin et al., 1979). Dogs, inhaling marihuana smoke (via tracheostomy) daily from 4 marihuana cigarettes/27 months (750 mg marihuana/cigarette with 1.5% THC, 0.09% CBD, 0.05% CBN), increased food intake during the first 3 months with a significant decrease in weight gain up to 9 months when tolerance appeared to develop resulting in weight gain comparable to a control group at the

27 month period (Huy and Roy (1976). A dose-related increase in urinary output due to THC (5-20 mg/kg p.o.) (not observed with CBD nor CBN up to 100 mg/kg) in hydrated rodents has been reported (Sofia et al., 1977) being similar to hydrochlorothiazide in potency (1.25-20 mg/kg) and magnitude; the high THC dose being more effective. Tolerance developed after 15 days of daily dosing (20 mg/kg/25 days for THC; not observed with hydrochlorothiazide 20 mg/kg/25 days) with hypophysectomy or adrenalectomy abolishing the diuretic THC effect. THC did not alter electrolyte excretion significantly whereas hydrochlorothiazide increased Na^+, K^+ and Cl^- excretion (with urinary Na^+/K^+ ratio increase) due to inhibition of Na^+ and Cl^- resorption by distal part of the nephron; the Na^+/K^+ ratio remained unaltered with THC indicating a "water" diuresis. The electrolyte alterations (if any) were similar for acute and chronic dosing.

The decrease in glucose utilization may apply to other addictive-type substances noting that glucose and oxygen are necessary for normal brain function. Parents adopting FAS (fetal alcohol syndrome) children have noted that more frequent daily food intake is necessary to avoid irritability and provide energy for these hyperactive and restless children who lack a normal subcutaneous fat layer seen in normal healthy children. Perhaps the body (cells) is unable to utilize glucose properly for adequate growth (synthesis) and function (including the brain). As noted in the reproductive section, infant toxicity due to prenatal marihuana use appears to be similar to other CNS depressant drugs which may be the result of inadequate carbohydrate utilization thereby diminishing availalbe sugar necessary for CNS function as well as decreased available oxygen due to smoking (carbon monoxide forming COHb displacing oxygen) and placental insufficiency due to maternal hypotension; such factors (decreased sugar; decreased oxygen supply and decreased cerebral perfusion leading to hypoxic tissue effects) possibly affecting adequate fetal CNS development. Alcoholics have been misdiagnosed as diabetics. Such individuals may have been latent diabetics requiring some exogenous stimulus (as alcohol) to expose a diabetic diathesis. Individuals who have stopped tobacco smoking complain of weight gain. Perhaps during the tobacco smoking habit, carbohydrate metabolism was altered such that glucose was not utilized by the body adequately seen as increased blood sugar. In the pulmonary section it was noted that the gas phase of tobacco smoke impairs glycolysis which provides some cell energy for alveolar macrophage phagocytosis which is impaired by the gas phase of marihuana or tobacco smoke.

Fats may not be completely oxidized resulting in ketone bodies (acetoacetic acid, β-OH butyric acid, acetone) appearing in the blood giving acidosis manifested as deep respiration or air hunger (Kussmaul breathing). Fetal mortality may be increased because of acidosis (reported in reproduction section as reproductive loss). An occasional complication of diabetic acidosis is leukocytosis (15,000-25,000/cu mm) due to bone marrow stimulation by organic acids in the blood (associated with abdominal pain and vomiting). An animal study using THC (1 mg/kg/day/30 days s.c. vs controls) in growing rodents (2 days of age) revealed blood granulocytosis and myeloid hyperplasia in bone marrow persisting up to 4 months after treatment (Guisti and Carnevale, 1975). In tobacco cigarette smoking inhalers, a leukocyte (WBC) count of > 9,000/cu mm in middle-aged men was found to be a good predictor of MI (myocardial infarction); the incidence increased with increased WBC being 4x those with < 6,000/cu mm and occurring 4 years (average) earlier (Zolakar et al., 1981). Other causes of leukocytosis are nicotine and increased circulating catecholamines; the latter probably being the primary cause in both tobacco and marihuana users. Individuals with diabetic ketoacidosis are usually hypothermic. Hypothermia (responses from -2 to -7°C) has been observed in animals following parenteral (not with intracerebral injections into hypothalamic areas involved with (fine) thermoregulation) administration (1 to 5 mg/kg; IV effect > IP) of cannabinoids (THC; 11-OH-THC; DMHP (synthetic dimethylheptyl analogue of THC)) with suggested site of (coarse control) hypothermic action being in the caudal brain stem (probably ponto-medullary level; thermoregulatory responses occurring concurrently with CVS and respiratory changes) (Hosko et al., 1981). Patients with diabetic ketoacidosis have severe abdominal pain with ketonemia increasing growth hormone and glucagon. Excessive urinary nitrogen excretion occurs during acidosis due to protein breakdown (gluconeogenesis). Epinephrine is known to increase renal vascular resistance leading to decreased GFR (glomerular filtration rate) resulting in increased renal sodium and water retention or increased plasma volume (observed in CVS section as increased weight); toxic doses having caused pulmonary edema (observed as complication in MI noted in CVS section). Altered glomerular function in kidneys may also be caused by decreased peripheral arterial blood pressure (noted in CVS section) being detected by decreased creatinine clearance which indicates the degree of renal functional loss (< 90 ml/min suggesting decreased GFR). With disturbance in carbohydrate metabolism (decreased liver glycogen noted above) creatinuria may occur with decreased creatinine excretion; also excess ACH interferes with renal tubular reabsorption of creatine.

The above (reversible) multisystem involvement has been reported (Vaziri et al., 1981) as acute toxic manifestations in 2 patients (20 and 22 year old males) 40 hours following the intravenous injection (0.5 and 1.0 ml) of a crude marihuana extract (from a living marihuana plant; sample confirmed by analysis for marihuana). Cardiovascular effects included peripheral vasodilation (diffusely erythematous skin) with a large decrease in b.p. (80/55; 70/50 mm Hg) and tachycardia (HR 104; 120 bts/min) as well as a hematological finding of a large increase in WBC (leukocytosis of 23,000; 27,000/mm^3) associated with gastrointestinal effects of severe vomiting, diarrhea and crampy abdominal pain.   The pulmonary abnormality was essentially pulmonary edema (and possible vascular occlusion due to intravascular coagulation because of IV particles of crude material) with hyperventilation, hypoxemia, and moderate airway obstruction and restriction.   A moderate azotemia (nitrogen retention) associated with a high serum urea nitrogen/creatinine ratio and low fractional excretion of Na occurred.   Renal function improved following fluid and electrolyte replacement observed as increased urinary output and decreased BUN and serum creatinine concentration with reversal of hypotension and tachycardia within 48 hours (oliguria or anuria present 24 hours pre hospital admission). Acute rhabdomyolysis (noted as muscle pain, weakness (moderate decrease in muscle strength), tenderness; increased plasma muscle enzymes (CPK, aldolase, LDH, SGOT), uric acid and inorganic phosphorus) may be due to muscle ischemia brought about by dehydration and prolonged hypotension contributing to acute renal failure development. The use of alcohol (1 gm/kg) with marihuana (18 mg THC) smoking (1 hour later) resulted in severe nausea and vomiting with variable CVS effects (tachycardia with bradycardia in 1/7 subjects, moderate increase in supine b.p., conjunctival reddening), skin pallor, profuse cold sweating, prostration and incapacitation (3-4 hour duration); nausea and vomiting not occurring with 0.5 gm/kg alcohol dose (Sulkowski and Vachon, 1977).

It may be seen that disturbances in the normal balance of factors regulating carbohydrate metabolism (i.e. interference with glycogen storage and cell utilization of glucose) without the pancreas being the chief offender, can lead to a diabetic state (which has occurred with ACTH therapy). Cannabis, via a reflex adrenergic mechanism, appears to cause derangement in the mechanism of blood sugar homeostasis (converting sugar to energy and heat) leading to a pseudo-diabetic state with all its ramifications and complications involving every system in the body. Continued hyperglycemia may lead to "work" exhausted pancreatic β-cells resulting in permanent diabetes. Clinically one should look for renal and visual failures, arteriosclerotic manifestations (gangrene, coronary artery disease or MI, hypertension, cerebral hemorrhage) and infection as possible complications of metabolic disturbances (at autopsy, looking for granules in β-cells of pancreatic islets of Langerhans) which may be due to prolonged frequent marihuana use (to be included in a differential diagnosis).

IV. 6. Adrenergic Blocking Effects

Perhaps investigations will have to be repeated with and without adequate propanolol blockade (β-adrenergic antagonist) to prove or disprove that peripheral vasodilation is primarily responsible for body system alterations (depression) via reflex adrenergic effects brought about by intoxicating doses of marihuana.   One must keep in mind the plasma half-life of propanolol (3 hours in man) which concentrates in the lung (care re use in asthmatics because of bronchoconstriction) and is metabolized in the liver. Some investigators have begun to pursue this path. In one study (Sulkowski et al., 1977) the acute effects (physiological, behavioural, subjective) of propanolol (120 mg p.o. as 3 tabs of 40 mg each) and marihuana smoking (1 gm cigarette with 1% or 10 mg THC/10 mins), alone and in combination (each treatment 3 days apart with p.o. premedication followed by a cigarette 50 mins later; appropriate placebo substitution in single drug determinations) were investigated in 6 experienced marihuana users (use of not more than 2x/week/average 5 years). The drugs alone revealed (Fig. 18; 19; 20) that propanolol decreased HR (Lead II, EKG) and systolic b.p. (slightly) without affecting (behaviour) performance (psychomotor speed, attention, memory, learning), while, marihuana produced a "high" (intensity assessed from a 0-100 point scale; quality as pleasant or unpleasant) with increased HR and systolic b.p., conjunctival reddening, and impaired performance (learning not attention, i.e., impairment of central information processing and integration).   Propanolol premedication effectively blocked marihuana cardiovascular effects (HR, b.p., conjunctival reddening) preventing learning impairment and the "high" (partly; some discernible marihuana effect). It was suggested that THC action may be partly mediated by CNS β-receptors which may be blocked by propanolol (protective action). In another study (Green et al., 1977), cannabinoid derivatives (SP-1, oil soluble analogue of THC; SP-106, water soluble form of SP-1) were compared with THC (0.1% solutions, 2x 50 ul drops (4 hours apart)/day/60 days) re IOP (intraocular pressure) reduction in normal right and left unilateral superior cervical ganglionectomized animal eyes; also noting THC (IV, 5x 10^{-5} mg/ml plasma final concentration) effects in preganglionic sectioned animals. All compounds decreased IOP in the normal eye more than in the ganglionectomized and preganglionectomized eyes indicating central (normal eye) and local (ganglionectomized eye) activity of cannabinoids which acted systemically since responses were bilateral irrespective of which eye was used for drug placement. SP-106 had a greater proportional IOP fall in ganglionectomized eyes (vs normal eyes) than the other 2 drugs indicating a greater local effect (Fig. 21).   Clinically a useful drug would have local effects primarily with minimal central effects. Preganglionic nerve section results were intermediate, between normal and ganglionectomized eyes (re IOP decrease). Optic nerve section did not alter IOP decrease produced in the normal eye. Blocking of IOP decrease in normal and ganglionectomized (direct THC effect) eyes occurred with a β-adrenergic antagonist (sotalol 0.5 mg/kg IV given pre THC), while an α-adrenergic antagonist (phenoxybenzamine 0.1 mg/kg IV) produced a partial block in normal eyes and a total block in ganglionectomized eyes with a block of THC-induced increase in total outflow facility in normal and ganglionectomized eyes (partial block with β-antagonist); an α-adrenergic mechanism probably being responsible for the increase of outflow facility. Responses to IOP and outflow are due to β- and α-receptor involvement in the regulation of these parameters. Atropine (1% topical) did not alter IOP response to THC. Thus the local activity of THC occurs via α- and β-adrenergic mechanisms. Aqueous humor protein concentrations in normal and ganglionectomized eyes are similar. THC increases the protein concentration in the normal eye (due to increased ciliary body permeability), being blocked by α- and β- antagonists, and decreases the concentration in ganglionectomized, being blocked by β-antagonist only, with no change in preganglionic section, all of which may indicate that ciliary body permeability may be controlled by an adrenergic mechanism. The different (protein) responses may indicate a central effect (partly) with the various operative procedures producing different blood vessel physiological status (tone). It appears that cannabinoid ocular effects may be due to both local and central (a site proximal to superior cervical sympathetic ganglia) adrenergic mechanisms.

IV. 7. Final Statements

It seems reasonable that a biochemical modification may be responsible for the reversible systemic alterations observed in healthy individuals because of readily switching back and forth or transient marihuana effect during use with return to adequate normal conditions with cessation of drug use as long as the feedback mechanism is viable and not deregulated (which could occur in time with continual use of an apparent CNS depressant type drug). From the above and in capsule form, it appears that through altered carbohydrate metabolism (brought about by a secondary reflex adrenergic response to THC peripheral vasodilation), the possible depleting effect on liver glycogen stores may lead to decreased uptake of essential building blocks for protein synthesis in cells resulting in abnormal cell formation and/or function in 1) genetic (chromosomes) and immunological (T and B cells; macrophages) systems leading to possible mutagenesis, carcinogenesis, and infections, 2) reproductive system (altered endocrine function; abnormal sperm) possibly affecting fertility and viable life forms, and in 3) CNS, possibly preventing adequate normal brain function; the deleterious respiratory (inadequate oxygenation; hypoxia) and CVS (peripheral vasodilation, decreased blood pressure, increased heart rate) effects altering pulmonary and cardiac function which could lead to chronic disease in susceptible individuals or make an existing disease worse. The brain needs blood to carry oxygen and glucose for proper function which may be compromised by marihuana use because of orthostatic or postural hypotension, carbon monoxide in smoke, and inability of cells to utilize glucose. Alcohol also alters carbohydrate metabolism seen as increased blood glucose levels in adults (mature liver; a decreased level occurring with prolonged fasting) vs decreased levels (hypoglycemia which may cause irreversible brain damage) in the fetus and infants (immature liver with limited supply of glycogen) (Hollstedt, 1981; Hollstedt et al., 1977); the attendant alterations in chronic alcoholics being similar to marihuana users (e.g. chromosomal aberrations; mutagenesis; decreased testosterone levels and azoospermia (Abel, 1980)). Tobacco (nicotine) is thought to affect the CVS via catecholamine release. Another interesting point is that intra-arterial (intracarotid) injection of hypertonic (25%) mannitol (sugar) solution disrupts the blood-brain barrier (up to 30 mins) in humans (i.e. an osmotic blood-brain modification which may increase drug delivery to the brain) which, however, is abolished by steroids.

One final comment. The endorphin system may be the basic mechanism involved in the addiction process (compulsive physiological need for a drug) which may be considered a mental (health) disorder or illness. Schizophrenia may be due to an overabundance of endorphin whereas those who seek and require drugs to soothe their frustrations and conduct their daily lives in a normal fashion (i.e. cope) may have a deficit of endorphins. Thus schizophrenics are made worse with substances promoting endorphin release (e.g. marihuana) whereas those with deficits feel better. Opiates do not produce psychosis because they may be used as replacement therapy by individuals with endorphin deficits (similar to insulin use in diabetics; thyroxine in hypothyroid condition) which eventually could cause a "shuting-off" of endogenous endorphin due to a feedback mechanism observed as severe withdrawal effects upon cessation of opiate use with a prolonged period required for recovery to the normal homeostatic state. Investigations measuring hormonal levels should include circulating endogenous opiates or brain endorphin levels in the blood. The basis for all addictions may be a metabolic one, the degree of addiction depending upon whether the drug effect is a direct one on the endorphin system (e.g. narcotics) or an indirect one (e.g. marihuana, alcohol, tobacco). Individuals with borderline function or metabolic disorders may therefore be more prone to become dependent on or addicted to drugs (iatrogenic or misuse).

The impression gained in reviewing the literature on marihuana is that it is similar to any other natural occurring substance with desireable and undesireable properties (depending upon what is sought by an individual) with a range of pharmacological effects extending into the toxic range (which has mostly been studied with marihuana); the effects being determined by the material used including vehicle; dose; route; pattern; frequency and duration of use; genetic background; age and state of health including stress. Drug blood levels are more accurate for actual dose administered because the dose from smoked marihuana depends upon the amount of THC in the cigarette, amount of smoke inhaled (if any), duration of smoke retention in the lungs, individual variation with respect to drug metabolism (including absorption and excretion), and tolerance development. Since metabolic (drug) tolerance to THC does not occur (noted in chemistry and metabolism section as essentially unaltered pharmacokinetic and THC metabolism following chronic use), functional or adaptive tolerance to marihuana pharmacological effects may be due to compensatory plasma expansion (because of inadequate b.p. maintenance brought about by peripheral vasodilation due to cannabis) which would lessen marihuana effects with chronic use encouraging greater drug use as well as leading to weight gain with functional anemia. Marihuana is composed of many different compounds with varying properties which should be explored as with THC. New synthetic compounds may prove useful clinically. After all, we are still looking for an ideal potent analgesic without addicting properties to act on the pain pathway and not on the limbic system; opium being the parent natural substance containing several opioids.

Thus the potential health hazards of cannabis use noted in the acute or subchronic toxicity studies do not mean that all individuals will be affected equally (as observed with alcohol and tobacco use) but will depend upon genetic makeup of an individual including personality (which may influence the purpose of drug use which, in turn, may alter pre-drug personality in time) and state of health, as well as drug potency, dose (blood and urinary drug levels for actual dose absorbed), route, mode of use (water pipe; cigarette), frequency (whether episodic or continual use of illegal cannabis with varied potencies) and duration of use; the chronic field studies in healthy individuals exemplifying these points. Reliable dose-response curves (including sub-(in)toxic(ation) drug levels when potential therapeutic effect(s) may or may not be discovered) have not been adequately established for the varied cannabinoids present in cannabis preparations in individuals with varied health states or susceptibilities.

IV. 8. Final Conclusion

It appears that marihuana affects all systems in the body primarily by a profound peripheral vasodilation resulting in reflex secondary effects of an adrenergic type mechanism (in a competitive inhibition type manner) which may be responsible for initiating the reported bodily system dysfunctions; being augmented by the effects of smoke and drugs including alcohol and tobacco. Hypotheses (to be proved or disproved) have been proposed to help explain the health consequences of marihuana use and perhaps be extended to other drugs presently known to have CNS depressant and addictive properties.

IV. Conclusion and Final Comments

List of Figures

Fig. 1.   Hyperglycemia and glycogenolysis   263
Fig. 2.   Blood glucose levels   263
Fig. 3.   Plasma ammonia levels   264
Fig. 4.   Plasma insulin levels   264
Fig. 5.   Decreased glucose tolerance   265
Fig. 6.   Decreased insulin response to glucose load   266
Fig. 7.   Plasma ammonia level response to glucose load   267
Fig. 8.   Decreased glucose tolerance in man post THC   265
Fig. 9.   Insulin response to glucose load in man post THC   268
Fig. 10.   Growth hormone response to glucose load in man post THC   269
Fig. 11.   Decreased glucose tolerance in man post marihuana   268
Fig. 12.   Blood glucose increase in man post marihuana   270
Fig. 13.   Insulin response to glucose load in man post marihuana   270
Fig. 14.   Growth hormone response to glucose load in man post marihuana   271
Fig. 15.   Plasma catecholamine response to glucose load in man post marihuana   271
Fig. 16.   Decreased lactic acid post hashish   272
Fig. 17.   Responses to acute insulin hypoglycemia pre and post THC   273
Fig. 18.   Acute physiological effects of marihuana with and without propanolol   274
Fig. 19.   Subjective effects of marihuana with and without propanolol   275
Fig. 20.   Psychomotor performance and behavioural effects pre and post drugs   276
Fig. 21.   Intraocular pressure effects of cannabinoid derivatives   277

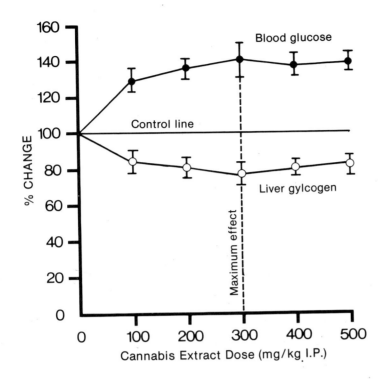

Fig. 1.   Hyperglycemia and glycogenolysis due to cannabis in animals.
IV.

       Adapted from Soni and Gupta, 1978.

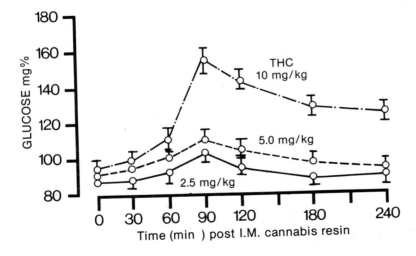

Fig. 2.   Blood glucose levels in animals post various doses of cannabis (THC)
IV.   resin.

       Adapted from de Pasquale et al., 1978.

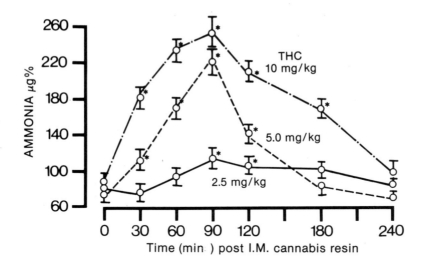

Fig. 3.   Plasma ammonia levels in animals post various doses of cannabis
IV.   (THC) resin.

            Adapted from de Pasquale et al., 1978.

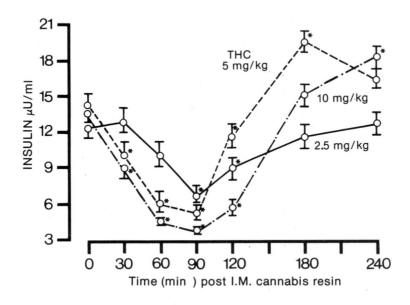

Fig. 4.   Plasma insulin levels in animals post various doses of cannabis (THC)
IV.   resin.

            Adapted from de Pasquale et al., 1978.

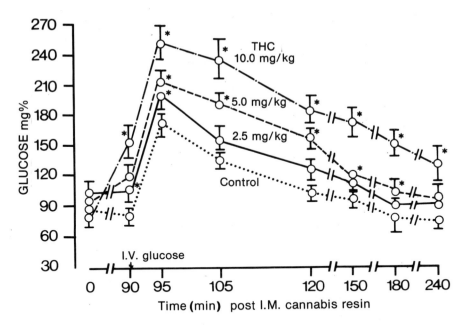

Fig. 5.
IV.

Decreased glucose tolerance in animals post various doses of cannabis (THC) resin.

Adapted from de Pasquale et al., 1978.

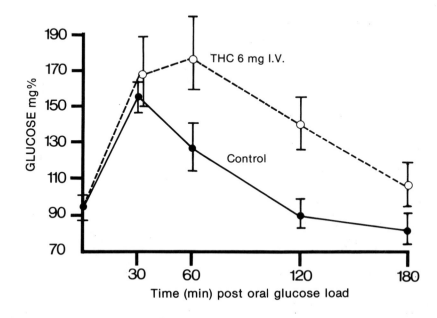

Fig. 8.
IV.

Decreased glucose tolerance in man post THC.

Adapted from Hollister and Reaven, 1974.

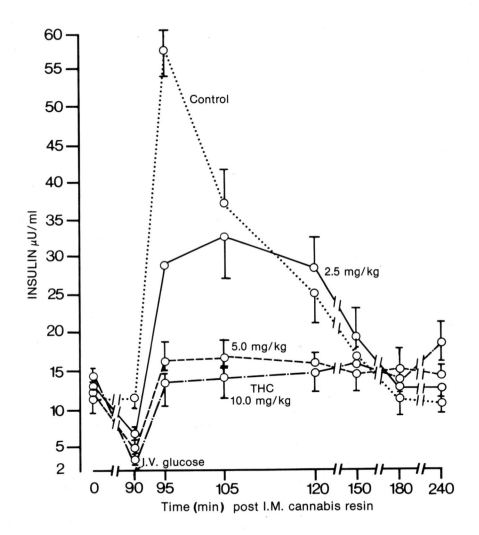

Fig. 6.   Decreased insulin response to glucose load in animals post various
IV.   doses of cannabis (THC) resin.

Adapted from de Pasquale et al., 1978.

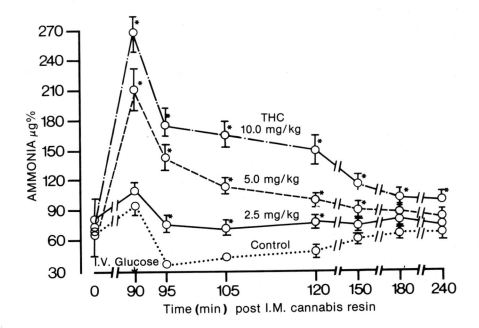

Fig. 7.   Plasma ammonia level responses to glucose load in animals post
IV.   various doses of cannabis (THC) resin.

Adapted from de Pasquale et al., 1978.

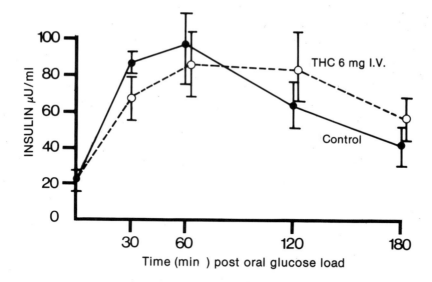

Fig. 9.   Insulin response to glucose load in man post THC.
IV.
               Adapted from Hollister and Reaven, 1974.

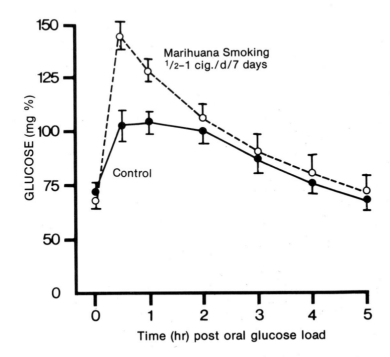

Fig. 11.   Decreased glucose tolerance in man post marihuana.
IV.
               Adapted from Podolsky et al., 1971.

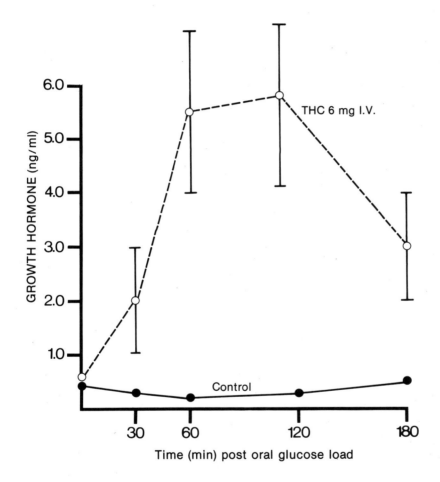

Fig. 10.
IV.

Growth hormone response to glucose load in man post THC.

Adapted from Hollister and Reaven, 1974.

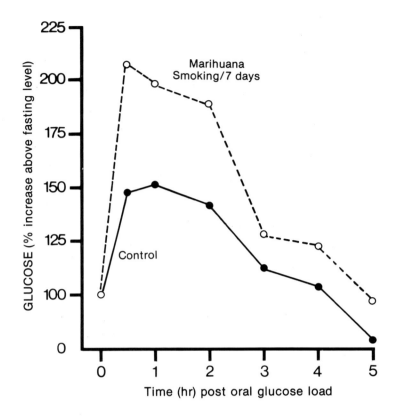

Fig. 12.   Percent increase in blood glucose in man post marihuana.
IV.

Adapted from Podolsky et al., 1971.

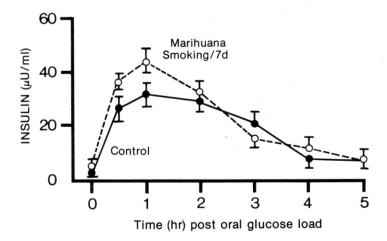

Fig. 13.   Insulin response to glucose load in man post marihuana.
IV.

Adapted from Podolsky et al., 1971.

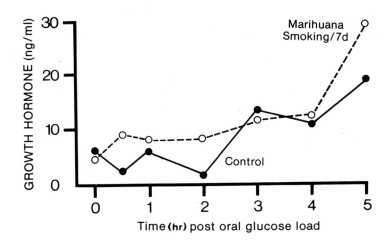

Fig. 14.   Growth hormone response to glucose load in man post marihuana.
IV.
        Adapted from Podolsky et al., 1971.

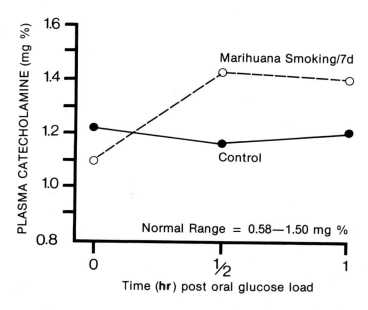

Fig. 15.   Plasma catecholamine response to glucose load in man post marihuana.
IV.
        Adapted from Podolsky et al., 1971.

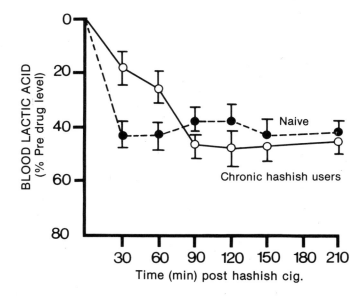

Fig. 16.   Decreased lactic acid post hashish cigarette after 20 hours fasting.
IV.
              Adapted from Papadakis et al., 1974.

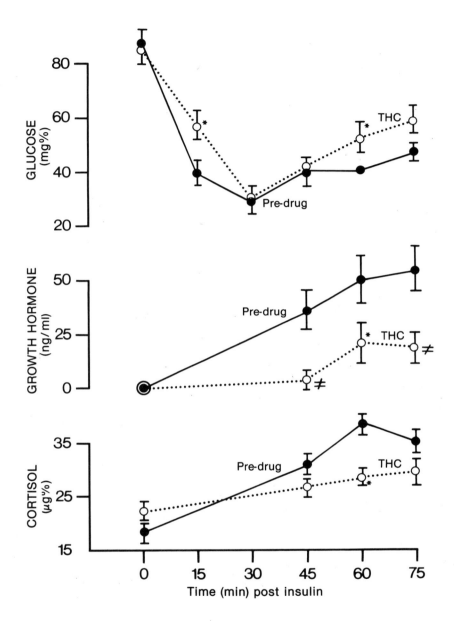

Fig. 17.
IV.

Parameter responses to acute insulin (0.15 U/kg) hypoglycemia pre and post 14 days oral THC (210 mg/d).

Adapted from Benowitz et al., 1976.

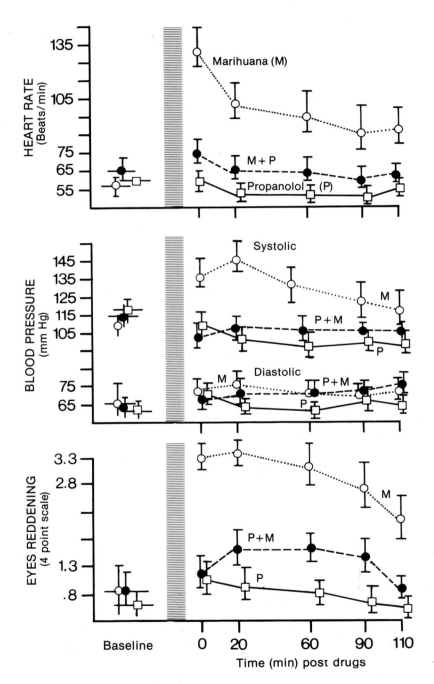

Fig. 18.   Acute physiological effects of propanolol (120 mg p.o.) and marihuana
IV.   smoking (10 mg THC/10 min), alone and in combination, in experienced
              marihuana users.

              Adapted from Sulkowski et al., 1977.

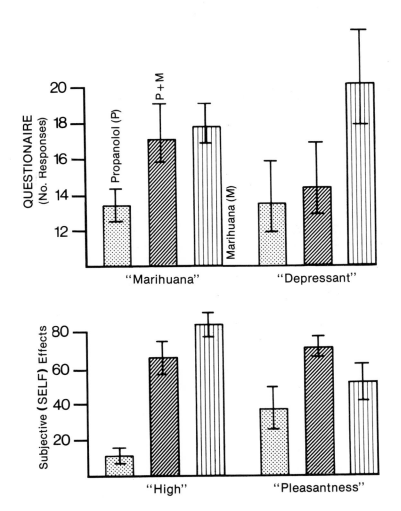

Fig. 19.
IV.   Subjective effects 1.5 hours post drugs.

           Adapted from Sulkowski et al., 1977.

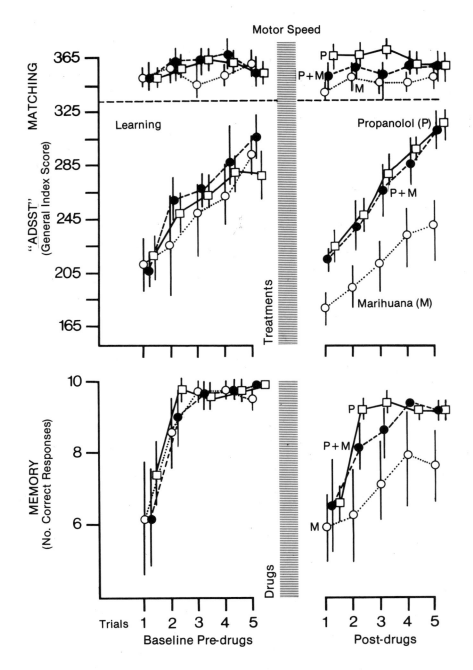

Fig. 20.   Psychomotor performance or behavioural effects pre and post drugs
IV.   (ADSST - automated digit symbol substitution test).

                Adapted from Sulkowski et al., 1977.

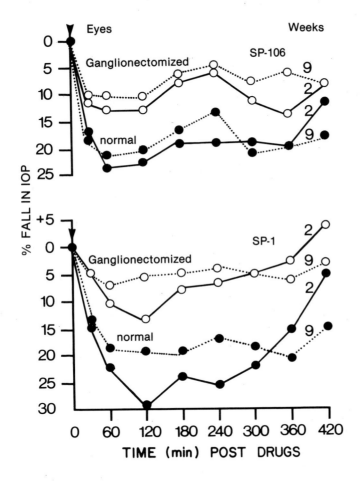

Fig. 21.
IV.

Effects of cannabinoid derivatives (SP-106; SP-1) on intraocular pressure (IOP) in normal and ganglionectomized animal eyes.

Adapted from Green et al., 1977.

V. References

ABEL, E.L. (1975). Cannabis and aggression in animals. Behav. Biol. 14: 1-20.

ABEL, E.L. (1977). The relationship between cannabis and violence. A review. Psychol. Bull. 84: 193-211.

ABEL, E.L. (1979). Behavioral teratology of marihuana extract in rats. Neurobehav. Toxicol. 1: 285-287.

ABEL, E.L. (1980). A review of alcohol's effects on sex and reproduction. Drug and Alcohol Dependence 5: 321-332.

ABEL, E.L., DINTCHEFF, B.A., and DAY, N. (1980). Effects of marihuana on pregnant rats and their offspring. Psychopharmacol. 71: 71-74.

ADAMS, A.J., BROWN, B., HAEGERSTROM-PORTNOY, G., FLOM, M.C., and JONES, R.T. (1978). Marihuana, alcohol, and combined drug effects on the time course of glare recovery. Psychopharmacol. 56: 81-86.

ADAMS, P.M. and BARRATT, E.S. (1975). Effect of chronic marijuana administration on stages of primate sleep-wakefulness. Biol. Psychiat. 10: 315-322.

ADAMS, T.C. Jr., and JONES, L.A. (1975). Phytosterols of cannabis smoke. J. Agr. Food Chem. 23: 352-353.

AGNEW, W.F., RUMBAUGH, C.L., and CHENG, J.T. (1976). The uptake of Δ^9-tetrahydrocannabinol in choroid plexus and brain cortex 'in vitro' and 'in vivo'. Brain Res. 109: 355-366.

AGURELL, S., BINDER, M., FONSEKA, K., LINDGREN, J.-E., LEANDER, K., MARTIN, B., NILSSON, I.M., NORDGVIST, M., OHLSSON, A., and WIDMAN, W. (1976). Cannabinoids: metabolites hydroxylated in the pentyl side chain. In: Marihuana: Chemistry, Biochemistry and Cellular Effects. Ed. G.G. Nahas, Springer-Verlag, New York, p. 141-157.

AGURELL, S., CARLSSON, S., LINDGREN, J.E., OHLSSON, A., GILLESPIE, H., and HOLLISTER, L. (1981). Interactions of Δ^1-tetrahydrocannabinol with cannabinol and cannabidiol following oral administration in man. Assay of cannabinol and cannabidiol by mass fragmentography. Experientia 37: 1090-1092.

AGURELL, S., LEVANDER, S., BINDER, M., BADER-BARTFAI, A., GUSTAFSSON, B., LEANDER, K., LINDGREN, J.-E., OHLSSON, A., and TOBISSON, B. (1976). Pharmacokinetics of Δ^8-tetrahydrocannabinol (Δ^6-tetrahydrocannabinol) in man after smoking - relations to physiological and psychological effects. In: Pharmacol. of Marihuana, M.C. Braude and S. Szara, eds. Raven Press, New York, p. 49-61.

AGURELL, S., LINDGREN, J.-E., and OHLSSON, A. (1979). Introduction to quantification of cannabinoids and their metabolites in biological fluids. In: Marihuana: Biological Effects. G.G. Nahas and W.D.M. Paton, eds. Pergamon Press, Oxford, p. 3-13.

ALTMAN, J., and DAS, G.D. (1965). Autoradiographic and histological evidence of postnatal hippocampal neurogenesis in rats. J. Comp. Neur. 124: 319-335.

AMES, B.N., McCANN, J., and YAMASAKI, E. (1975). Methods for detecting carcinogens and mutagens with the salmonella/mammalian-microsome mutagenecity test. Mutation Res. 31: 347-364.

AMES, F.R., BROWNELL, B., and ZUURMOND, T.J. (1979). Effects of the oral administration of Cannabis sativa (Dagga) on chacma baboons (Papio ursinus). S. Afr. Med. J. 55: 1127-1132.

ARONOW, W.S. (1978). Effect of passive smoking on angina pectoris. N. Engl. J. Med. 299: 21-24.

ARONOW, W.S., and CASSIDY, J. (1974). Effect of marihuana and placebo-marihuana smoking on angina pectoris. N. Engl. J. Med. 291: 65-67.

ARONOW, W.S., and CASSIDY, J. (1975). Effect of smoking marihuana and of a high-nicotine cigarette on angina pectoris. Clin. Pharmacol. Therap. 17: 549-554.

AVAKIAN, E.V., HORVATH, S.M., MICHAEL, E.D., and JACOBS, S. (1979). Effect of marihuana on cardiorespiratory responses to submaximal exercise. Clin. Pharmacol. Therap. 26: 777-781.

BABOR, T.F., MENDELSON, J.H., and KUEHNLE, J. (1976). Marihuana and human physical activity. Psychopharmacology 50: 11-19.

BACKHOUSE, C.I. (1975). Peak expiratory flow in youths with varying cigarette smoking habits. Br. Med. J. 1: 360-362.

BAKER, P.B., GOUGH, T.A., and TAYLOR, B.J. (1980). Illicitly imported Cannabis products: some physical and chemical features indicative of their origin. Bull. Narc. 32(2): 31-40.

BANCHEREAU, J., DESOIZE, B., LÉGER, C., and NAHAS, G. (1979). Inhibitory effects of delta-9-tetrahydrocannabinol and other psychotropic drugs on cultured lymphocytes. In: Marihuana: Biological Effects. G.G. Nahas and W.D.M. Paton, eds. Pergamon Press, Oxford, p. 129-144.

BARRY, H. III, PERHACH, J.L. Jr., and KUBENA, R.K. (1970). Δ^1-tetrahydrocannabinol activation of pituitary-adrenal function. Pharmacologist 12: 327.

BEACONSFIELD, P., GINSBURG, J., and RAINSBURY, R. (1972). Marihuana Smoking. Cardiovascular effects in man and possible mechanisms. New Engl. J. Med. 287: 209-212.

BELLVILLE, J.W., GASSER, J.C., MIYAKE, T., and AQLEH, K. (1976). Tolerance to the respiratory effects of marijuana in man. J. Pharmacol. Exp. Ther. 197: 326-331.

BELLVILLE, J.W., SWANSON, G.D., and AQLEH, K.A. (1975). Respiratory effects of delta-9-tetra-hydrocannabinol Clin. Pharmacol. Exp. Ther. 17: 541-548.

BELMORE, S.M., and MILLER, L.L. (1980). Levels of processing and acute effects of marijuana on memory Pharmacol. Biochem. Bahav. 13: 199-203.

BENOWITZ, N.L., and JONES, R.T. (1975). Cardiovascular effects of prolonged delta-9-tetrahydro-cannabinol ingestion. Clin. Pharmacol. Ther. 18: 287-297.

BENOWITZ, N.L., and JONES, R.T. (1977). Prolonged delta-9-tetrahydrocannabinol. Effects of sympathomimetic amines and autonomic blockades. Clin. Pharmacol. Therap. 21: 336-342.

BENOWITZ, N.L., JONES, R.T., and LERNER, C.B. (1976). Depression of growth hormone and cortisol response to insulin-induced hypoglycemia after prolonged oral delta-9-tetrahydrocannabinol admini-stration in man. J. Clin. Endocrinol. Metab. 42: 938-941.

BEN-ZVI, Z., BERGEN, J.R., BURSTEIN, S., SEHGAL, P.K., and VARANELLI, C. (1976). The metabolism of Δ^1-tetrahydrocannabinol in the rhesus monkey. In: Pharmacol. of Marihuana, M.C. Braude and S. Szara, eds. Raven Press, New York, p. 63-75.

BINITIE, A. (1975). Psychosis following ingestion of hemp in children. Psychopharmacologia 44: 301-302.

BIRD, K.D., BOLEYN, T., CHESHER, G.B., JACKSON, D.M., STARMER, G.A., and TEO, R.K.C. (1980). Intercannabinoid and cannabinoid-ethanol interactions and their effects on human performance. Psychopharmacol. 71: 181-188.

BLAINE, J.D., MEACHAM, M.P., JANOWSKY, D.S. SCHOOR, M., and BOZZETTI, L.P. (1976). Marihuana smoking and simulated flying performance. In: Pharmacol. of Marijuana. Eds.: M.C. Braude and S. Szara, Raven Press, New York, p. 445-447.

BLEVINS, R.D., and REGAN, J.D. (1976). Δ^9-tetrahydrocannabinol. Effect on macromolecular synthesis in human and other mammalian cells. Arch. Toxicol. 35: 127-135.

BORG, J., GERSHON, S., and ALPERT, M. (1975). Dose effects of smoked marihuana on human cognitive and motor functions. Psychopharmacologia (Berl.) 42: 211-218.

BOURDON, R. (1976). Identification and quantification of cannabinoids in urine by gallium chelate formation. In: Marihuana: Chemistry, Biochemistry and Cellular Effects. Ed.: G.G. Nahas, Springer-Verlag, New York, p. 111-121.

BOYD, E.S., BOYD, E.H. and BROWN, L.E. (1971). Effects of tetrahydrocannabinols on evoked responses in polysensory cortex. Ann. N.Y. Acad. Sc. 191: 100-122.

BRADLEY, S.G., MUNSON, A.E., DEWEY, W.L., and HARRIS, L.S. (1977). Enhanced susceptibility of mice to combinations of Δ^9-tetrahydrocannabinol and live or killed gram-negative bacteria. Infect. Immun. 17: 325-329.

BRAUDE, M.C. (1976). Five years of preclinical marihuana research. In: Pharmacol. of Marihuana, M.C. Braude and S. Szara, eds. Raven Press, New York, p. 21-26.

BRIGHT, T.P., KIPLINGER, G.F., BROWN, D., PHILLIPS, J., and FORNEY, R.B. (1971). Effects of beta adrenergic blockade on marihuana induced tachycardia. Reported to the Committee on Problems of Drug Dependence, Natl. Acad. Sci., Natl. Res. Council Publ., Washington, D.C., Proc. p. 1737-1744.

BRILL, N.Q., and CHRISTIE, R.L. (1974). Marihuana use and psychosocial adaptation. Arch. Gen. Psychiat, 31: 713-719.

BRO, P., SCHOU, J., and TOPP, G. (1975). Cannabis poisoning with analytical verification. New Engl. J. Med. 293: 1049-1050.

BROWN, B., ADAMS, A.J., HAEGERSTROM-PORTNOY, G., JONES, R.T., and FLOM, M.C. (1977). Pupil size after use of marijuana and alcohol. Am. J. Ophthalmol. 83: 350-354.

BURSTEIN, S., and KUPFER, D. (1971). Hydroxylation of trans-Δ^1-tetrahydrocannabinol by hepatic microsomal oxygenase. Ann. N.Y. Acad. Sc. 191: 61-67.

BURSTEIN, S., HUNTER, S.A., and SEDOR, C. (1980). Further studies on the inhibition of Leydig cell testosterone production by cannabinoids. Biochem. Pharmacol. 29: 2153-2154.

BURSTEIN, S., HUNTER, S.A., and SHOUPE, T.S. (1978a). Inhibition of cholesterol esterases by Δ^1-tetrahydrocannabinol. Life Sc. 23: 979-982.

BURSTEIN, S., HUNTER, S.A., and SHOUPE, T.S. (1979). Cannabinoid inhibition of rat luteal cell progesterone synthesis. Res. Comm. Chem. Pathol. Pharmacol. 24: 413-416.

BURSTEIN, S., HUNTER, S.A., SHOUPE, T.S., and TAYLOR, P. (1978b). Cannabinoid inhibition of testosterone synthesis by mouse Leydig cells. Res. Commun. Chem. Pathol. Pharmacol. 19: 557-560.

BUSCH, F.W., SEID, D.A., and WEI, E.T. (1979). Mutagenic activity of marihuana smoke condensate. Cancer Lett. 6: 319-324.

CAMPBELL, A.M.G., EVANS, M., THOMSON, J.L.G., and WILLIAMS, M.J. (1971). Cerebral atrophy in young cannabis smokers. Lancet 2: 1219-1224.

CARAKUSHANSKY, G., NEU, R.L., and GARDNER, L.I. (1969). Lysergide and cannabis as possible teratogens in man. Lancet 1: 150-151.

CARCHMAN, R.A., END, D.W., DEWEY, W.L., and WARNER, W. (1979). Marihuana and opiate interactions with hormonal-induced systems in cell culture. Prog. Clin. Biol. Res. 27: 237-252.

CARLIN, A.S., and TRUPIN, E.W. (1977). The effect of long-term chronic marijuana use of neuropsychological functioning. Int. J. Addict. 12: 617-624.

CARLINI, E.A. (1978). Effects of cannabinoid compounds on aggressive behaviour. Med. Probl. Pharmacopsychiatry 13: 82-102.

CARTER, W.E. (1980). Cannabis in Costa Rica. A publication of ISHI, Philadelphia.

CATES, W., and POPE, J.N. (1977). Gynecomastia and cannabis smoking. Am. J. Surg. 134: 613-615.

CHAKRAVARTY, I., and GHOSH, J.J. (1977). Effect of cannabis extract on uterine glycogen metabolism in prepubertal rats under normal and estradiol-treated conditions. Biochem. Pharmacol. 26: 859-862.

CHAKRAVARTY, I. and GHOSH, J.J. (1981). Influence of cannabis and delta-9-tetrahydrocannabinol on the biochemistry of the male reproductive organs. Biochem. Pharmacol 30: 273-276.

CHAKRAVARTY, I., SHETH, A.R. and GHOSH, J.J. (1975). Effect of acute Δ^9-tetrahydrocannabinol treatment on serum luteinizing hormone and prolactin levels in adult female rats. Fertil. Steril. 26: 947-948.

CHAO, F-C., GREEN, D.E., FORREST, I.S., KAPLAN, J.N., WINSHIP-BALL, A., and BRAUDE, M. (1976). The passage of $^{14}C-\Delta^9$-tetrahydrocannabinol into the milk of lactating monkeys. Res. Commun. Chem. Pathol. Pharmacol. 15: 303-317.

CHARLES, R., HOLT, S., and KIRKHAM, N. (1979). Myocardial infarction and marijuana. Clin. Toxicol. 14: 433-438.

CHASE, R.A., KELLEY, P.R., TAUNTON-RIGBY, A., JONES, R.T., and HARWOOD, T. (1976). Quantitation of cannabinoids in biological fluids by radioimmunoassay. In: Cannabinoid Assays in Humans, NIDA Res. Monogr. 7. Ed.: R.E. Willette, p. 1-9.

CHESHER, G.B., ZALUZNY, S.G., JACKSON, D.M., and MALOR, R. (1979). Δ^9-tetrahydrocannabinol and the quasi-morphine withdrawal syndrome. In: Marihuana: Biological Effects. G.G. Nahas and W.D.M. Paton eds. Pergamon Press, Oxford, p. 605-618.

CHOPRA, G.S., and JANDU, B.S. (1976). Psychoclinical effects of long-term marijuana use in 275 Indian chronic users. A comparative assessment of effects in India and USA users. Ann. N.Y. Acad. Sc. 282: 95-108.

CHOPRA, G. S., and SMITH, J.W. (1974). Psychotic reactions following cannabis use in East Indians. Arch. Gen. Psychiat. 30: 24-27.

CIMBURA, G., WARREN, R.A., BENNETT, R.C., LUCAS, D.M., and SIMPSON, M.M. (1980). Drugs detected in fatally injured drivers and pedestrians in the Province of Ontario. TIRF Reports (Traffic Injury Research Foundation of Canada).

CO, B.T., GOODWIN, D.W., GADO, M., MIKHAEL, M., and HILL, S.Y. (1977). Absence of cerebral atrophy in chronic cannabis users. J.A.M.A. 237: 1229-1230.

COFFMAN, C.B., CONIGLIO, W., GENTNER, W.A., HAWKS, R.L., KILBURN, K.H., TURNER, C.E., WALL, M.E., and ZAVALA, D.C. (1978). Chemistry and toxicology of paraquat contaminated marihuana. Final report, June 1978, NIDA, Washington, D.C.

COLEMEN, J.H., TACKER, H.L., EVANS, W.E., LEMMI, H., and Britton, E.L. (1976). Neurological manifestations of chronic marihuana intoxication. Part I: Paresis of the fourth cranial nerve. Dis. Nerv. Syst. 37: 29.

COLLINS, F.G., and HAAVIK, C.O. (1979). Effects of cannabinoids on cardiac microsomal CaATPase activity and calcium uptake. Biochem. Pharmacol. 28: 2303-2306.

COPELAND, K.C., UNDERWOOD, L.E., and VanWyk, J.J. (1980). Marihuana smoking and pubertal arrest. J. Pediatr. 96:1079-1080.

CORCORAN, M.E., and AMIT, Z. (1974). The effects of hashish injections on feeding and drinking in rats. Res. Commun. Chem. Pathol. Pharmacol. 9: 193-196.

CORDOVA, T., AYALON, D., LANDER, N., MECHOULAM, R., NIR, I., PUDER, M., and LINDNER, H.R. (1980). The ovulation blocking effect of cannabinoids: structure activity relationships. Psychoneuroendocrin. 5: 53-62.

CORNICELLI, J.A., GILMAN, S.R., KROM, B.A., and KOTTKE, B.A. (1981). Cannabinoids impair the formation of cholesteryl ester in cultured human cells. Arteriosclerosis 1: 449-454.

COU ˉELINIS, A., and MICHALODIMITRAKIS, M. (1981). Acetylcholinesterase activity after hashish smoking. Clin. Toxicol. 18: 385-387.

COZENS, D.D., CLARK, R., PALMER, A.K., HARDY, N., NAHAS, G.G., and HARVEY, D.J. (1979). The effect of crude marihuana extract on embryonic and foetal development of the rabbit. In: Marihuana: Biological Effects. G.G. Nahas and W.D.M. Paton, eds. Pergamon Press, Oxford, p. 469-477.

CUSHMAN, P., and KHURANA, R. (1976). Marijuana and T-lymphocyte rosettes. Clin. Pharmacol. Ther. 19: 310-317.

CUSHMAN, P., and KHURANA, R. (1977). A controlled cycle of tetrahydrocannabinol smoking: T and B-cell rosette formation. Life. Sci. 20: 971-980.

CUSHMAN, P., GRIECO, M., and GUPTA, S. (1975). Reduction in T-lymphocytes forming active rosettes in chronic marihuana smokers. J. Clin. Pharmacol. 12: 217-220.

CUTTING, M., GOODENOUGH, G., SIMMONS, G., WATSON, A., LAGUARDA, R., and HUBER, G. (1974). Marijuana and pulmonary antibacterial defenses: depression of alveolar macrophage function following experimental exposure. Chest. 66: 321-322.

DACKIS, C.A., POTTASH, A.L.C., ANNITTO, W., and GOLD, M.S. (1982). Presence of urinary marijuana levels after supervised abstinence. Am. J. Psychiat. 139: 1196-1198.

DALEY, J.D., BRANDA, L.A., ROSENFELD, J., and YOUNGLAI, E.V. (1974). Increase of serum prolactin in male rats by (-)-trans- Δ^9-tetrahydrocannabinol. J. Endocr. 63: 415-416.

DALTERIO, S., BADR, F., BARTKE, A., and MAYFIELD, D. (1982). Cannabinoids in male mice: Effects on fertility and spermatogenesis. Science 216: 315-316.

DALTERIO, S., and BARTKE, A. (1979). Perinatal exposure to cannabinoids alters male reproductive function in mice. Science 205: 1420-1422.

DALTERIO, S., and BARTKE, A. (1981). Fetal testosterone in mice: Effect on gestational age and cannabinoid exposure. J. Endocr. 91: 509-514.

DALTERIO, S., BARTKE, A., ROBERSON, C., WATSON, D., and BURSTEIN, S. (1978). Direct and pituitary-mediated effects of Δ^9-THC and cannabinol on the testis. Pharmacol. Biochem. Behav. 8: 673-678.

DAUL, C.B., and HEATH, R.G. (1975). The effect of chronic marihuana usage on the immunological status of rhesus monkeys. Life Sci. 17: 875-881.

DAVIES, P., SORNBERGER, G.C., and HUBER, G.L. (1979). Effects of experimental marijuana and tobacco smoke inhalation on alveolar macrophages. A comparative stereologic study. Lab. Invest. 4: 220-223.

DESOIZE, B., LÉGER, C., JARDILLIER, J.-C., and NAHAS, G. (1979). Inhibition by THC of thymidine transport: a plasma membrane effect. In: Marihuana: Biological Effects. G.G. Nahas and W.D.M. Paton, eds. Pergamon Press, Oxford, p. 145-159.

DEWEY, W.L., JOHNSON, K.M., and BLOOM, A.S. (1976a). Interactions of active constituents of marihuana with other drugs in the neuron. Ann. N.Y. Acad. Sc. 281: 190-197.

DEWEY, W.L., MARTIN, B.R., BECKNER, J.S., and HARRIS, L.S. (1976b). A comparison of subcellular distribution of cannabinoids in brains of tolerant and nontolerant dogs, rats, and mice after injecting radiolabelled Δ^9-tetrahydrocannabinol. In: Marihuana: Chemistry, Biochemistry, and Cellular Effects G.G. Nahas ed., Springer-Verlag, New York, p. 349-365.

DEWEY, W.L., PENG, T-C., and HARRIS, L.S. (1970). The effect of 1-trans- Δ^9-tetrahydrocannabinol on the hypothalamo-hypophyseal-adrenal axis of rats. Europ. J. Pharmacol. 12: 382-384.

DI BENEDETTO, M., McNAMEE, H.B., KUEHNLE, J.C., and MENDELSON, J.H. (1977). Cannabis and the peripheral nervous system. Brit. J. Pschiat. 131: 361-365.

DIXIT, V.P. (1981). Effects of cannabis sativa extract on testicular function of Presbytis entellus entellus. Planta Med. 41: 288-294.

DIXIT, V.P., ARYA, M., and LOHIYA, N.K. (1975). The effect of chronically administered cannabis extract on the female genital tract of mice and rats. Endokrinologie 66: 365-368.

DOORENBOS, N.J., FETTERMAN, P.S., QUIMBY, M.W., and CARLTON, E.T. (1971). Cultivation, extraction, and analysis of cannabis sativa L. Ann. N.Y. Acad. Sc. 191: 3-14.

DORNBUSH, R.L. (1974). Marijuana and memory: effects of smoking on storage. Trans. N.Y. Acad. Sc. 36: 94-100.

DORNBUSH, R.L. and KOKKEVI, A. (1976). The acute effects of various cannabis substances on cognitive, perceptual, and motor performance in very long-term hashish users. In: Pharmacol. of Marihuana. Eds.: M.C. Braude and S. Szara, Raven Press, New York, p. 421-427.

DRATH, D.B., SHOREY, J.M., PRICE, L., and HUBER, G.L. (1979). Metabolic and functional characteristics of alveolar macrophages recovered from rats exposed to marijuana smoke. Infect. Immun. 25: 268-272.

DREISBACH, R.H. (1974). Carbon Monoxide. In: Handbook of Poisoning 8th ed. Lange Medical Publications, Los Altos, California, p. 228-232.

EDERY, H., GRUNFELD, Y., BEN-ZVI, Z., and MECHOULAM, R. (1971). Structural requirements for cannabinoid activity. Ann. N.Y. Acad. Sc. 191: 40-53.

EVANS, M.A., MARTZ, R., BROWN, D.J., RODDA, B.E., KIPLINGER, G.F., LEMBERGER, L., and FORNEY, R.B. (1973). Impairment of performance with low doses of marihuana. Clin. Pharmacol. Therap. 14: 936-940.

EVANS, M.A., STEVENS, M.W., MANTILLA-PLATA, B., and HARBISON, R.D. (1975). Drugs of abuse: teratogenic and mutagenic considerations. Addictive Dis; an Internat. J. 2: 45-61.

FEHR, K.O., and KALANT, H. (1971). Analysis of cannabis smoke obtained under different combustion conditions. Can. J. Physiol. Pharmacol. 50: 761-767.

FEINBERG, I., JONES, R., WALKER, J.M., CAVNESS, C., and FLOYD, T. (1976). Effects of marijuana extract and tetrahydrocannabinol on electroencephalographic sleep patterns. Clin. Pharmacol. Therap. 19: 782-794.

FEINBERG, I., JONES, R., WALKER, J.M., CAVNESS, C., and MARCH, J. (1975). Effects of high dosage delta-9-tetrahydrocannabinol on sleep patterns in man. Clin. Pharmacol. Therap. 17: 458-466.

FINK, M., VOLAVKA, J., PANAYIOTOPOULOS, C.P., and STEFANIS, C. (1976). Quantitative EEG studies of marijuana, Δ^9-tetrahydrocannabinol, and hashish in man. In: Pharmacol. of Marihuana. Eds. M.C. Braude and S. Szara, Raven Press, New York, p. 383-391.

FLEISCHMAN, R.W., NAQVI, R.H., ROSENKRANTZ, H., and HAYDEN, D.W. (1980). The embryotoxic effects of cannabinoids in rats and mice. J. Environ. Pathol. Toxicol. 4: 471-482.

FORNEY, R.B., and KIPLINGER, G.F. (1971). Toxicology and pharmacology of marijuana. Annals. N.Y. Acad. Sc. 191: 74-82.

FOURNIER, E., ROSENBERG, E., HARDY, N., and NAHAS, G. (1976). Teratologic effects of cannabis extracts in rabbits: a preliminary study. In: Marihuana: Chemistry, Biochemistry, and Cellular Effects. G.G. Nahas, ed. Springer-Verlang, New York, Inc., p. 457-468.

FREEMON, F.R., and AL-MARASHI, M.S.H. (1977). Long-term changes in the sleep of normal volunteers administered multiple doses of delta-9-tetrahydrocannabinol. Drug and Alc. Dep. 2: 39-43.

FRIED, P.A. (1976). Short and long term effects of prenatal cannabis inhalation upon rat offspring. Psychopharmacol. 50: 285-291.

FRIED, P.A. (1980). Marihuana use by pregnant women: neurobehavioral effects in neonates. Drug and Alc. Dep. 6: 415-424.

FRIED, P.A. (1982). Marihuana use by pregnant women and effects on offspring: an update. Neurobehav. Toxicol. Terat. 4: 451-454.

FRIED, P.A., and CHARLEBOIS, A.T. (1979). Effects upon rat offspring following cannabis inhalation before and/or after mating. Can. J. Psychol. 33: 125-132.

FRIEDMAN, M.A. (1977). In vivo effects of cannabinoids on macromolecular biosynthesis on Lewis lung carcinomas. Cancer Biochem. Biophys. 2: 51-54.

FRISCHKNECHT, H.R., SIEBER, B., and WASER, P.G. (1980). The feeding of hashish to lactating mice: effects on the development of sucklings. Gen. Pharmac. 11: 469-472.

GALANTER, M., WYATT, R.J., LEMBERGER, L., WEINGARTNER, H., VAUGHAN, T.B., and ROTH, W.T. (1972). Effects on humans of Δ^9-tetrahydrocannabinol administered by smoking. Science 176: 934-936.

GALE, E.N., and GUENTHER, G. (1971). Motivational factors associated with the use of cannabis (marihuana). Br. J. Addict. 66: 188-194.

GARRETT, E.R. (1979). Pharmacokinetics and disposition of Δ^9-tetrahydrocannabinol and its metabolites. In: Marihuana: Biological Effects. G.G. Nahas and W.D.M. Paton, Eds. Pergamon Press, Oxford, p. 105-121.

GASH, A., KARLINER, J.S., JANOWSKY, D., and LAKE, C.R. (1978). Effects of smoking marihuana on left ventricular performance and plasma norepinephrine. Studies in normal men. Ann. Intern. Med. 89: 448-452.

GERSTEN, S.P. (1980). Long-term adverse effects of brief marihuana usage. J. Clin. Psychiat. 41: 60-61.

GHONEIM, M. Th., MIKHAIL, M.M., MAHFOUZ, M., and MAKAR, A.B. (1980). Effect of hashish smoke on some blood and serum parameters in rabbits. Pharmazie 35: 226-228.

GIBBINS, R.J., McDOUGALL, J., MILES, C.G., and MARSHMAN, J.A. (1976). Tolerance to marijuana-induced tachycardia in man. Acta Pharmacol. Toxicol. 39: 65-76.

GILMOUR, D.G., BLOOM, A.D., Lele, K.P., ROBBINS, E.S., and MAXIMILIAN, C. (1971). Chromosomal aberrations in users of psychoactive drugs. Arch. Gen. Psychiat. 24: 268-272.

GIUSTI, G.V., and CARNEVALE, A. (1975). Myeloid hyperplasia in growing rats after chronic treatment with Δ^9-THC at behavioral doses. Arch. Toxicol. 34: 169-172.

GOLDMAN, H., DAGIRMANJIAN, R., DREW, W.G., and MURPHY, S. (1975). Δ^9-tetrahydrocannabinol alters flow of blood to subcortical areas of the conscious rat brain. Life Sci. 17: 477-482.

GOTTSCHALK, L.A., ARONOW, W.S., and PRAKASH, R. (1977). Effect of marijuana and placebo-marijuana smoking on psychological state and on psychophysiological cardiovascular functioning in anginal patients. Biol. Psychiat. 12: 255-266.

GREEN, K., BIGGER, J.F., KIM, K., and BOWMAN, K. (1977). Cannabinoid action on the eye as mediated through the central nervous system and local adrenergic activity. Exp. Eye Res. 24: 189-196.

GREENLAND, S., STAISCH, K.J., BROWN, N., and GROSS, S.J. (1982). The effects of marijuana use during pregnancy. I. A preliminary epidemiologic study. Am. J. Obstet. Gynecol. 143: 408-413.

GREGG, J.M., CAMPBELL, R.L., LEVIN, K.J., GHIA, J., and ELLIOTT, R.A. (1976a). Cardiovascular effects of cannabinol during oral surgery. Anesth. Analg. 55: 203-213.

GREGG, J.M., SMALL, E.W., MOORE, R., RAFT, D., and TOOMEY, T.C. (1976b). Emotional response to intravenous Δ^9-tetrahydrocannabinol during oral surgery. J. Oral Surg. 34: 301-313.

GROSS, S.J., and SOARES, J.R. (1976). Separate radioimmune measurements of body fluid Δ^9-THC and 11-nor-9-carboxy-Δ^9-THC. In: Cannabinoid Assays in Humans, NIDA Res. Mongr. 7. Ed.: R.E. Willette, p. 10-14

GUPTA, S., GRIECO, M.H., and CUSHMAN, P. (1974). Impairment of rosette-forming T lymphocytes in chronic marihuana smokers. N. Engl. J. Med. 291: 874-877.

HALIKAS, J.A. (1974). Marijuana use and psychiatric illness. In: Marijuana: Effects on Human Behavior. Ed. L.L. Miller. Academic Press, New York, p. 265-302.

HALL, F.B., KLEIN, A.L., and WATERS, J.E. (1975-76). Long term effects of marijuana smoking. J. Altered States of Consciousness 2: 161-170.

HARMON, J.W., and ALIAPOULIOS, M.A. (1972). Gynecomastia in marihuana users. N. Engl. J. Med. 287: 936.

HARMON, J.W., and ALIAPOULIOS, M.A. (1974). Marijuana-induced gynecomastia: clinical and laboratory experience. Surg. Forum 25: 423-425.

HARPER, J.W., HEATH, R.G., and MYERS, W.A. (1977). Effects of cannabis sativa on ultrastructure of the synapse in monkey brain. J. Neurosci. Res. 3: 87-93.

HARRIS, C.C., MULVIHILL, J.J., THORGEIRSSON, S.S., and MINNA, J.D. (1980). Individual differences in cancer susceptibility. Ann. Intern. Med. 92: 809-825.

HARRIS, L.S., MUNSON, A.E., and CARCHMAN, R.A. (1976). Antitumor properties of cannabinoids. In: Pharmacol. of Marihuana. M.C. Braude and S. Szara eds. Raven Press, New York, p. 749-762.

HART, R.H. (1976). A psychiatric classification of cannabis intoxication. J. Amer. Acad. Psychiat. Neurol. 1: 83-97.

HARVEY, D.J. and PATON, W.D.M. (1976). Examination of the metabolites of Δ^1-tetrahydrocannabinol in mouse liver, heart, and lung by combined gas chromatography and mass spectrometry. In: Marijuana: Chemistry, Biochemistry and Cellular Effects. Ed. G.G. Nahas, Springer-Verlag, New York, p. 93-109.

HATOUM, N.S., DAVIS, W.M., ELSOHLY, M.A., and TURNER, C.E. (1981). Prenatal exposure to cannabichromene and Δ^9-tetrahydrocannabinol: separate and combined effects on viability of pups and on male reproductive system at maturity. Toxicol. Lett. 8: 141-146.

HAYASHI, M., SORNBERGER, G.C., and HUBER, G.L. (1980). A morphometric analysis of the male and female tracheal epithelium after experimental exposure to marijuana smoke. Lab. Invest. 42: 65-69.

Hearing before the select Committee on Narcotic Abuse and Control (November 29, 1979). Is paraquat-sprayed marihuana harmful or not? U.S. Printing Office, Washington, 1980.

HEATH, R.G. (1975). Brain function and behaviour. I. Emotion and sensory phenomena in psychotic patients and in experimental animals. J. Nerv. Ment. Dis. 160: 159-175.

HEATH, R.G. (1976). Marijuana and Δ^9-tetrahydrocannabinol: acute and chronic effects on brain function of monkeys. In: Pharmacol. of Marihuana. Eds. M.C. Braude and S. Szara, Raven Pres, New York, p. 345-356.

HEATH, R.G., FITZJARRELL, A.T., FONTANA, C.J., and GAREY, R.E. (1980). Cannabis sativa: effects on brain function and ultrastructure in rhesus monkeys. Biol. Psychiat. 15: 657-690.

HECHT, F., BEALS, R.K. LEES, M.H., JOLLY, H., and ROBERTS, P. (1968). Lysergic-acid-diethylamide and cannabis as possible teratogens in man. Lancet 2: 1087.

HEMBREE III, W.C., NAHAS, G.G., ZEIDENBERG, P., and HUANG, H.F.S. (1979). Changes in human spermatozoa associated with high dose marihuana smoking. In: Marihuana: Biological Effects. G.G. Nahas and W.D.M. Paton, eds. Pergamon Press, Oxford, p. 429-439.

HENDERSON, R.L., TENNANT, F.S., and GUERRY, R. (1972). Respiratory manifestations of hashish smoking. Arch Otolaryng. 95: 248-251.

HENRICH, R.T., NOGAWA, T., and MORISHIMA, A. (1980). In vitro induction of segregational errors of chromosomes by natural cannabinoids in normal human lymphocytes. Environ. Mutagenesis 2: 139-147.

HERNANDEZ, M.J., MARTINEZ, F., BLAIR, H.T., and MILLER, W.C. (1981). Airway response to inhaled histamine in asymptomatic long-term marijuana smokers. J. Allergy Clin. Immunol. 67: 153-155.

HIGGENBOTTAM, T., SHIPLEY, M.J., CLARK, T.J.H., and ROSE, G. (1980). Lung function and symptoms of cigarette smokers related to tar yield and number of cigarettes smoked. Lancet 1: 409-412.

HINGSON, R., ALPERT, J.J., DAY, N., DOOLING, E., KAYNE, H., MORELOCK, S., OPPENHEIMER, E., and ZUCKERMAN, B. (1982). Effects of maternal drinking and marijuana use on fetal growth and development. Pediatrics 70: 539-546.

HOFFMAN, D., BRUNNEMANN, K.D., GORI, G.B., and WYNDER, E.L. (1975). On the carcinogenicity of marijuana smoke. Recent. Adv. Phytochem. 9: 63-81.

HOLLISTER, L.E. (1979). Cannabis and the development of tolerance. In: Marihuana: Biological Effects. G.G. Nahas and W.D.M. Paton, eds. Pergamon Press, Oxford, p 585-589.

HOLLISTER, L.E., and REAVEN, G.M. (1974). Delta-9-tetrahydrocannabinol and glucose tolerance. Clin. Pharmacol. Therap. 16: 297-302.

HOLLISTER, L.E., GILLESPIE, H.K., OHLSSON, A., LINDGREN, J-E., WAHLEN, A., and AGURELL, S. (1981). Do plasma concentrations of Δ^9-tetrahydrocannabinol reflect the degree of intoxication? J. Clin. Pharmacol. 21: 171S-177S.

HOLLISTER, L.E., OVERALL, J.E., and GERBER, M.L. (1975). Marihuana and setting. Arch. Gen. Psychiat. 32: 798-801.

HOLLSTEDT, C., (1981). Alcohol and the developing organism. Experimental and clinical studies. Opuscula Medica supplementum LII (52).

HOLLSTEDT, C., OLSSON, O., and RYDBERG, V. (1977). The effect of alcohol on the developing organism. Genetical, teratological, and physiological aspects. Med. Biol. 55: 1-14.

HONG, R., and HOROWITZ, S. (1975). Thymosin therapy creates a "Hassall"(?). N. Engl. J. Med. 292: 104-105.

HOROWITZ, M. (1977). Herbicidal treatments for control of Cannabis sativa L. Bull. Narc. 29: 75-84.

HOSKO, M.J. and HARDMAN, H.F. (1976). Evidence for a dual mechanism of action of cannabis on central cardiovascular control. In: Pharmacol. of Marihuana, M.C. Braude and S. Szara eds. Raven Press, New York, p. 239-253.

HOSKO, M. J.,SCHMELING, W.T., and HARDMAN, H.F. (1981). Evidence for a caudal brainstem site of action for cannabinoid induced hypothermia. Brain Res. Bull. 6: 251-258.

HUBER, G.L., O'CONNELL, D., McCARTHY, C., PEREIRA, W., MAHAJAN, V., and MULLANE, J. (1976). Toxicologic pharmacology of tetrahydrocannabinol (THC) and marijuana (MJ) smoke components. Clin. Res. 24: 255A.

HUBER, G.L., POCHAY, V.E., PEREIRA, W., SHEA, J.W., HINDS, W.C., FIRST, M.W., and SORNBERGER, G.C. (1980). Marijuana, tetrahydrocannabinol, and pulmonary antibacterial defences. Chest 77: 403-410.

HUBER, G.L., POCHAY, V.E., SHEA, J.W., HINDS, W.C., WEKER, R.R.., FIRST, M.W., and SORNBERGER, G.C. (1979a). An experimental animal model for quantifying the biologic effects of marijuana on the defence system of the lung. In: Marihuana: Biological Effects. G.G. Nahas and W.D.M. Paton eds. Pergamon Press, Oxford, p. 301-328.

HUBER, G.L., SHEA, J.W., HINDS, W.C. POCHAY, V.E., WEKER, R.T., FIRST, M.W., and SORNBERGER, G.C. (1979b). The gas phase of marijuana smoke and intrapulmonary bactericidal defences. Bull. europ. Physiopath. resp. 15: 491-503.

HUBER, G.L., SIMMONS, G.A., McCARTHY, C.R., CUTTING, M.B., LAGUARDA, R., and PEREIRA, W. (1975). Depressant effect of marihuana smoke on antibactericidal activity of pulmonary alveolar macrophages. Chest 68: 769-773.

HUGHES, J.E., STEAHLY, L.P., and BIER, M.M. (1970). Marihuana and the diabetic coma. J.A.M.A. 214: 1113-1114.

HUNT, C.A., and JONES, R.T. (1980). Tolerance and disposition of tetrahydrocannabinol in man. J. Pharmacol. Exp. Ther. 215: 35-44.

ISBELL, H., and JASINSKI, D.R. (1969). A comparison of LSD-25 with (-) - Δ^9-trans-tetrahydrocannabinol (THC) and attempted cross tolerance between LSD and THC. Psychopharmacologia (Berl.) 14: 115-123.

ISSIDORIDES, M.R. (1979). Observations in chronic hashish users: nuclear aberrations in blood and sperm and abnormal acrosomes in spermatozoa. In: Marihuana: Biological Effects. G.G. Nahas and W.D.M. Paton, eds. Pergamon Press, Oxford, p. 377-388.

JACKSON, D.L., and MENGES, H. (1980). Accidental carbon monoxide poisoning, J.A.M.A. 243: 772-774.

JACOBS, J.A., DELLARCO, A.J., MANFREDI, R.A., and HARCLERODE, J. (1979). The effects of Δ^9-tetrahydrocannabinol, cannabidiol, and shock on corticosterone concentrations in rats. J. Pharm. Pharmacol. 31: 341-342.

JAKUBOVIC, A., McGEER, E.G., and McGEER, P.L. (1979). Effects of cannabinoids on testosterone and protein synthesis in rat testis Leydig cells in vitro. Mol. Cell. Endocrinol. 15: 41-50.

JANOWSKY, D.S., MEACHAM, M.P., BLAINE, J.D., SCHOOR, J., and BOZZETTI, L.P. (1976). Simulated flying performance after marihuana intoxication. Aviat. Space Environ. Med. 47: 124-128.

JOHNSON, R.J., and WIERSEMA, V. (1974). Effects of Δ^9-tetrahydrocannabinol (Δ^9-THC) metabolite on bone marrow myelopoiesis. Res. Comm. in Chem. Pathol. and Pharmacol. 8: 393-396.

JOHNSTON, S., and DOMINO, E.F. (1971). Some cardiovascular effects of marihuana smoking in normal volunteers. Clin. Pharmacol. Therap. 12: 762-768.

JOHNSTONE, R.E., LIEF, P.L., KULP, R.A., and SMITH, T.C. (1975). Combination of Δ^9-tetrahydrocannabinol with oxymorphone or pentobarbital. Anesthesiology 42: 674-684.

JONEJA, M.G. (1976). A study of teratological effects of intravenous, subcutaneous and intragastric administratin of Δ^9-tetrahydrocannabinol in mice. Toxicol. Appl. Pharmacol. 36: 151-162.

JONES, A.B., ELSOHLY, M.A., BEDFORD, J.A., and TURNER, C.E. (1981). Determination of cannabidiol in plasma by electron-capture gas chromatography. J. Chromatogr. 226: 99-105.

JONES, R.T. (1971). Tetrahydrocannabinol and the marijuana-induced social "high", or the effects of the mind on marijuana. Ann. N.Y. Acad. Sc. 191: 155-165.

JONES, R.T., and BENOWITZ, N. (1976). The 30-day trip - clinical studies of cannabis tolerance and dependence. In: Pharmacol. of Marihuana. M.C. Braude and S. Szara, Eds. Raven Press, New York, p. 627-642.

JONES, R.T., BENOWITZ, N. and BACHMAN, J. (1976). Clinical studies of cannabis tolerance and dependence. Ann. N.Y. Acad. Sc. 282: 221-239.

JUST, W.W., ERDMANN, G., WERNER, G.,WIECHMANN, M., and THIEL, S. (1976). Forensic, metabolic, and autoradiographic studies of Δ^8- and Δ^9-tetrahydrocannabinol. In: Marihuana: Chemistry, Biochemistry and Cellular Effects. Ed. G.G. Nahas, Springer-Verlag, New York, p. 123-138.

JUST, W.W., FILIPOVIC, N. and WERNER, G. (1974). Detection of Δ^9-tetrahydrocannabinol in saliva of men by means of thin-layer chromatography and mass spectrometry. J. Chromatography 96: 189-194.

KAGEN, S.L. (1981). Aspergillus: an inhalable contaminant of marihuana. N. Engl. J. Med. 304: 483-484.

KAKLAMANI, E., TRICHOPOULOS, D., KOUTSELINIS, A., DROUGA, M., and KARALIS, D. (1978). Hashish smoking and T-lymphocytes. Arch. Toxicol. 40: 97-101.

KALOFOUTIS, A., KOUTSELINIS, A., DRONYSSIOU-ASTERIOU, A., and MIRAS, C. (1978). The significance of lymphocyte lipid changes after smoking hashish. Acta. Pharmacol. Toxicol. 43: 81-85.

KALOFOUTIS, A., KOUTSELINIS, A., LEKAKIS, J., and MIRAS, C. (1980). Levels of erythrocyte 2,3 DPG and ATP in heavy hashish smokers. Experimentia 36: 897-898.

KANAKIS, C., POUGET, J.M., and ROSEN, K.M. (1976). The effects of delta-9-tetrahydrocannabinol (cannabis) on cardiac performance with and without beta blockade. Circulation 53: 703-707.

KANTER, S.L., HOLLISTER, L.E., and MUSUMECI, M. (1982a). Marijuana metabolites in urine of man. X. Identification of marijuana use by detection of Δ^9-tetrahydrocannabinol-11-oic acid using thin-layer chromatography. J. Chromatogr. 234: 201-208.

KANTER, S.L., HOLLISTER, L.E., and ZAMORA, J.U. (1982b). Marijuana metabolites in urine of man. XI. Detection of unconjugated and conjugated Δ^9-tetrahydrocannabinol-11-oic acid by thin-layer chromatography. J. Chromatogr. 235: 507-512.

KAWASH, G.F., YEUNG, D.L., and BERG, S.D. (1980). Effects of administration of cannabis resin during pregnancy on emotionality and learning in rats' offspring. Percept. Mot. Skills. 50: 359-365.

KAYMAKÇALAN, S. (1979). Pharmacological similarities and interactions between cannabis and opioids. In: Marihuana: Biological Effects. G.G. Nahas and W.D.M. Paton eds. Pergamon Press, Oxford, p. 591-604.

KEPHALIS, T.A., KIBURIS, J., MICHAEL, C.M., MIRAS, C.J., and PAPADAKIS, D.P. (1976). Some aspects of cannabis smoke chemistry. In: Marihuana: Chemistry, Biochemistry and Cellular Effects. Ed. G.G. Nahas, Springer-Verlag, New York, p. 39-49.

KIPLINGER, G.F., MANNO, J.E., RODDA, B.E., FORNEY, R.B., HAINE, S.E., EAST, R., and RICHARDS, A.B. (1971). Dose-response analysis of effects of tetrahydrocannabinol in man. Clin. Pharmacol. Therap. 12: 650-657.

KOCHAR, M.S., and HOSKO, M.J. (1973). Electrocardiographic effects of marihuana. J.A.M.A. 225: 25-27.

KOLANSKY, H., and MOORE, W.T. (1972). Toxic effects of chronic marihuana use. J.A.M.A. 222: 35-41.

KOLODNY, R.C. (1975). Research issues in the study of marijuana and male reproductive physiology in humans. In: Marijuana and Health Hazards. J.R. Tinklenberg, ed. Academic Press, Inc., New York, p. 71-81.

KOLODNY, R.C., LESSIN, P., TORO, G., MASTERS, W.H., and COHEN, S. (1976). Depression of plasma testosterone with acute marihuana administration. In: Pharmacology of Marihuana. M.C. Braude and S. Szara, eds. Raven Press, New York, p. 217-227.

KOLODNY, R.C., MASTERS, W.H., KOLODNER, R.M. and TORO, G. (1974). Depression of plasma testosterone levels after chronic intensive marihuana use. N. Engl. J. Med. 290: 872-874.

KOSTELLOW, A.B., ZIEGLER, D., KUNAR, J., FUJIMOTO, G.I., and MORRILL, G.A. (1980). Effect of cannabinoids on estrous cycle, ovulation and reproductive capacity of female A/J mice. Pharmacol. 21: 68-75.

KOUKKOU, M., and LEHMANN, D. (1976). Human EEG spectra before and during cannabis hallucinations. Biol. Psychiat. 11: 663-677.

KOUKKOU, M., and LEHMANN, D. (1978). Correlations between cannabis-induced psychopathology and EEG before and after drug ingestion. Pharmakopsychiat. 11: 220-227.

KRIEGER, D.T. and MARTIN, J.B. (1981). Brain peptides. N. Engl. J. Med. 304: 876-885 and 944-951.

KROLL, P. (1975). Psychoses associated with marijuana use in Thailand. J. Nerv. Ment. Dis. 161: 149-156.

KUEHNLE, J., MENDELSON, J.H., DAVIS, K.R., and NEW, P.F.J. (1977). Computed tomographic examination of heavy marijuana smokers. J.A.M.A. 237: 1231-1232.

LARES, A., OCHOA, Y., BOLANOS, A., APONTE, N., and MONTENEGRO, M. (1981). Effects of resin and smoke condensate of cannabis sativa on the oestrous cycle of the rat. Bull. Narc. 33: 55-61.

LAU-CAM, C.A., and PIZZITOLA, V. (1979). Simple field test for marijuana. J. Pharm. Sci. 68(8): 976-978.

LAW, B. (1981). Cases of cannabis abuse detected by analysis of body fluids. J. Forens. Sci. Soc. 21: 31-39.

LAW, B., WILLIAMS, P.L., and MOFFAT, A.C. (1979). The detection and quantification of cannabinoids in blood and urine by RIA, HPLC/RIA and GC/MS. Vet. Hum. Toxicol. 21 Suppl.: 144-147.

LeDAIN, G. (1972). Cannabis: A report of the Commission of Inquiry into the Non-Medical Use of Drugs.

LEE, M.L., NOVOTNY, M., and BARTLE, K.D. (1976). Gas chromatography/mass spectrometric and nuclear magnetic resonance spectrometric studies of carcinogenic polynuclear aromatic hydrocarbons in tobacco and marijuana smoke condensates Anal. Chem. 48: 405-416.

LEFKOWITZ, S.S., and CHIANG, C.Y. (1975). Effects of Δ-9-tetrahydrocannabinol on mouse spleens. Res. Commun. Chem. Pathol. Pharmacol. 11: 659-662.

LEMBERGER, L. (1976). Pharmacokinetics of Δ^9-tetrahydrocannabinol and its metabolites: importance and relationship in developing methods for detecting cannabis in biological fluids. In: Marihuana: Chemistry, Biochemistry and Cellular Effects. Ed. G.G. Nahas, Springer-Verlag, New York, p. 169-178.

LEMBERGER, L., AXELROD, J., and KOPIN, I.J. (1971). Metabolism and disposition of tetrahydrocannabinols in naive subjects and chronic marijuana users. Ann. N.Y. Acad. Sc. 191: 142-154.

LEMBERGER, L., CRABTREE, R., ROWE, H., and CLEMENS, J. (1975). Tetrahydrocannabinols and serum prolactin levels in man. Life Sci. 16: 1339-1343.

LEMBERGER, L., McMAHON, R., and ARCHER, R. (1976). The role of conversion on the mechanism of action of cannabinoids. In: Pharmacol. of Marihuana, M.C. Braude and S. Szara, eds. Raven Press, New York, p. 125-135.

LEUCHTENBERGER, C., and LEUCHTENBERGER, R. (1976). Cytological and cytochemical studies of the effects of fresh marihuana cigarette smoke on growth and DNA metabolism of animal and human lung cultures. In: Pharmacol. of Marihuana. M.C. Braude and S. Szara, eds. Raven Press, New York, p. 595-612.

LEUCHTENBERGER, C., LEUCHTENBERGER, R., and RITTER, U. (1973a). Effects of marijuana and tobacco smoke on DNA and chromosomal complement in human lung explants. Nature 242: 403-404.

LEUCHTENBERGER, C. LEUCHTENBERGER, R., and SCHNEIDER, A. (1973b). Effects of marihuana and tobacco smoke on human lung physiology. Nature 241: 137-139.

LEVY, J.A., and HEPPNER, G.H. (1978-79). Alterations in murine delayed type hypersensitvity responses by delta-8-THC and cannabinol. J. Immunopharmacol. 1: 105-114.

LIEDGREN, S.R.C., ODKVIST, L.M., and FREDRICKSON, J.M. (1974). The effect of marihuana on vestibular, cerebellar, and oculomotor function. Can. J. Otolaryng. 3: 291-301.

LINDEMAYR, von H., and JÄGER, S. (1980). Occupational immediate type allergy to hemp pollen and hashish. Dermat. Beruf Umwelt 28: 17-19.

LINDGREN, J.E., OHLSSON, A., AGURELL, S., HOLLISTER, L., and GILLESPIE, H. (1981). Clinical effects and plasma levels of Δ^9-tetrahydrocannabinol (Δ^9-THC) in heavy and light users of cannabis. Psychopharmacol. 74: 208-212.

LISKOW, B., LISS, J.L., and PARKER, C.W. (1971). Allergy to marihuana. Ann. Intern. Med. 75: 571-573.

LIST, A., NAZAR, B., NYQUIST, S., and HARCLERODE, J. (1977). The effects of Δ^9-tetrahydrocannabinol and cannabidiol on the metabolism of gonadal steroids in the rat. Drug Metab. Dispos. 5: 268-272.

LOCKHART, J.G., and DESSER, K.B. (1970). Effects of "speed" and "pot" on the juvenile diabetic. J.A.M.A. 214: 2065.

LUTZ, E.G. (1979). Marihuana and paranoid disperception. J. Med. Soc. N.J. 76: 253-259.

MacLEAN, P.D. (1970). The limbic brain in relation to the psychoses. In: Physiological Correlates of Emotion. Ed. P. Black, Academic Press, New York and London, p. 129-146.

McLAUGHLIN, C.L., BAILE, C.A., and BENDER, P.E. (1979). Cannabinols and feeding in sheep. Psychopharmacol. 64: 321-323.

MALIT, L.A., JOHNSTONE, R.E., BOURKE, D.I., KULP, R.A., KLEIN, V., and SMITH, T.C. (1975). Intravenous Δ^9-tetrahydrocannabinol. Anesthesiology 42: 666-673.

MANN, P.E.G., COHEN, A.B., FINLEY, T.N., and LADMAN, A.J., (1971). Alevolar macrophages. Structural and functional differences between non smokers and smokers of marijuana and tobacco. Lab. Invest. 25: 111-120.

MANTILLA-PLATA, B., CLEWE, G.L., and HARBISON, R.D. (1975). Δ^9-tetrahydrocannabinol-induced changes in prenatal growth and development of mice. Toxicol. Appl. Pharmacol. 33: 333-340.

MARCOTTE, J., SKELTON, R.S., CÔTÉ, M.G., and WITSCHI, H. (1975). Induction of aryl hydrocarbon hydroxylase in rat lung by marijuana smoke. Toxicol. Appl. Pharmacol. 33: 231-245.

MARKS, V., TEALE, J.D., and KING, L.J. (1976). Radioimmunossay of cannabis products in blood and urine. In: Marihuana: Chemistry, Biochemistry and Cellular Effects. Ed. G.G. Nahas, Springer-Verlag, New York, p. 71-85.

MARSHALL, E. (1982). Pot-spraying plan raises some smoke. Science 217: 429.

MARSHMAN, J.A., POPHAM, R.E., and YAWNEY, C.D. (1976). A note on the cannabinoid content of Jamaican ganja. Bull. Narc. 28: 63-68.

MARTIN, B.R., DEWEY, W.L., HARRIS, L.S., and BECKNER, J.S. (1977). ^{3}H-Δ^9-tetrahydrocannabinol distribution in pregnant dogs and their fetuses. Res. Commun. Chem. Pathol. Pharmacol. 17: 457-470.

MATTOX, K.L. (1976). Pneumomediastinum in heroin and marijuana users. J. Am. Coll. Emerg. Physicians 5: 26-28.

MAZURKIEWICZ-KWILECKI, I.M., and FILCZEWSKI, M. (1973). The effects of chronic treatment with Δ^9-tetrahydrocannabinol on catecholamine synthesis in the rat. Psychopharmacol. (Berl.) 33: 71-79.

McCARTHY, C.R., CUTTING, M.B., SIMMONS, G.A., PEREIRA, W., LAGUARDA, R., and HUBER, G.L. (1976). The effect of marihuana on the 'in vitro' function of pulmonary alveolar macrophages. In: Pharmacol. of Marihuana, M.C. Braude and S. Szara eds. Raven Press, New York, p. 211-216.

McGUIRE, J.S., and MEGARGEE, E.I. (1974). Personality correlates of marijuana use among youthful offenders. J. Consult. Clin. Psychol. 42: 124-133.

McISAAC, W.M., FRITCHIE, G.E., IDANPÄÄN-HEIKKILÄ, J.E., HO, B.T. and ENGLERT, L.F. (1971). Distribution of marihuana in monkey brain and concomitant behavioural effects. Nature 230: 593-594.

McMILLAN, D.E. DEWEY, W.L., and HARRIS, L.S. (1971). Characteristics of tetrahydrocannabinol tolerance. Ann. N.Y. Acad. Sc. 191: 83-99.

MECHOULAM, R. (1973). Cannabinoid chemistry. In: Marihuana: Chemistry, Pharmacology, Metabolism, and Clinical Effects. R. Mechoulam ed. Academic Press, New York, p. 1-99.

MECHOULAM, R., McCALLUM, N.K., and BURSTEIN, S. (1976). Recent advances in the chemistry and biochemistry of cannabis. Chem. Revs. 76: 75-112.

MELEZ, K.A., REEVES, J.P., and STEINBERG, A.D. (1978-79). Regulation of the expression of autoimmunity in NZBxNZW F_1 mice by sex hormones. J. Immunopharmacol. 1: 27-42.

MELLINGER, G.D., SOMERS, R.H., DAVIDSON, S.T., and MANHEIMER, D.I. (1976). The amotivational syndrome and the college students. Ann. N.Y. Acad. Sc. 282: 37-55.

MENDELSON, J.H. BABOR, T.F., KUEHNLE, J.C., ROSSI, A.M., BERNSTEIN, J.G., MELLO, N.K., and GREENBERG, I. (1976). Behavioural and biologic aspects of marijuana use. Ann. N.Y. Acad. Sc. 282: 186-210.

MENDHIRATTA, S.S., WIG, N.N., and VERMA, S.K. (1978). Some psychological correlates of long-term heavy cannabis users. Brit. J. Psychiat. 132: 482-486.

MERRITT, J.C., CRAWFORD, W.J., ALEXANDER, P.C., ANDUZE, A.L., and GELBART, S.S. (1980). Effect of marihuana on intraocular and blood pressure in glaucoma. Ophthamol. 87: 222-228.

MILLER, R.J., and CUATRECASAS, R. (1978). Enkephalins and endorphins. Vitamins and Hormones 36: 297-381.

MILLER, R.H., DHINGRA, R.C., KANAKIS, C., AMAT-Y-LEON, F., and ROSEN, K.M. (1977). The electrophysiological effects of delta-9-tetrahydrocannabinol (cannabis) on cardiac conduction in man. Am. Heart J. 94: 740-747.

MILSTEIN, S.L., MacCANNELL, K., KARR, G., and CLARK, S. (1975). Marijuana-produced impairments in coordination. J. Nerv. Mental Dis. 161: 26-31.

MIRAS, C.J., KYRKOU, K.A., and MARKIDOU, S.G. (1978). Chromosomal abnormalities in heavy hashish users. United Nations Secretariat ST/SOA/SER, S/56: 1-13.

MON, M.J., HAAS, A.E., STEIN, J.L., and STEIN, G.S. (1981a). Influence of psychoactive and nonpsychoactive cannabinoids on cell proliferation and macromolecular biosynthesis in human cells. Biochem. Pharmacol. 30: 31-43.

MON, M.J., HAAS, A.E., STEIN, J.L., and STEIN, G.S. (1981b). Influence of psychoactive and nonpsychoactive cannabinoids on chromatin structure and function in human cells. Biochem. Pharmacol. 30: 45-58.

MOODY, M.M., WHARTON, R.C., SCHNAPER, N., and SCHIMPFF, S.C. (1982). Do water pipes prevent transmission of fungi from contaminated marijuana? N. Engl. J. Med. 306: 1492-1493.

MORAHAN, P.S., KLYKKEN, P.C., SMITH, S.H., HARRIS, L.S., and MUNSON, A.E. (1979). Effects of cannabinoids on host resistance to listeria monocytogenes and herpes simplex virus. Infect. Immun. 23: 670-674.

MORISHIMA, A., HENRICH, R.T., JAYARAMAN, J., and NAHAS, G.G. (1979). Hypoploid metaphases in cultured lymphocytes of marihuana smokers. In: Marihuana: Biological Effects. G.G. Nahas and W.D.M. Paton, eds. Pergamon Press, Oxford, p. 371-376.

MORISHIMA, A., MILSTEIN, M., HENRICH, R.T., and NAHAS, G.G. (1976). Effects of marihuana smoking, cannabinoids and olivetol on replication of human lymphocytes: formation of micronuclei. In: Pharmacol. of Marihuana. M.C. Braude and S. Szara, eds. Raven Press, New York, p. 711-722.

MUELLER, P.B., and WILCOX, J.C. (1980). Effects of marijuana smoking on vocal pitch and quality. Ear Nose Throat J. 59: 506-509.

MUNSON, A.E., LEVY, J.A., HARRIS, L.S., and DEWEY, W.L. (1976). Effects of Δ^9-tetrahydrocannabinol on the immune system. In: Pharmacol. of Marihuana. M.C. Braude and S. Szara, eds. Raven Press, New York, p. 187-197.

MURAD, F., and GILMAN, A.F. (1975). Estrogens and Progestins. Androgens and anabolic steroids. In: Pharmacological Basis of Therapeutics, Fifth edition. Eds. L.S. Goodman and A. Gilman. The MacMillan Company, New York, p. 1423-1471.

MYERS III, W.A., and HEATH, R.G. (1979). Cannabis sativa: ultrastructural changes in organelles of neurons in brain septal region of monkeys. J. Neurosci. Res. 4: 9-17.

NADITCH, M.P. (1974). Acute adverse reactions to psychoactive drugs, drug usage and psychopathology. J. Abnorm. Psychol. 83: 394-403.

NADITCH, M.P. (1975). Relation of motives for drug use and psychopathology in the development of acute adverse reactions to psychoactive drugs. J. Abnorm. Psychol. 84: 374-385.

NAHAS, G., LEGER, C., TOCOQUE, B., and HOELLINGER, H. (1981). The kinetics of cannabinoid distribution and storage with special reference to brain and testis. J. Clin. Pharmacol. 21: 208S-214S.

NAHAS, G.G., MORISHIMA, A., and DESOIZE, B. (1977). Effects of cannabinoids on macromolecular synthesis and replication of cultured lymphocytes. Fed. Proc. 36: 1748-1752.

NAHAS, G.G., SUCIU-FOCA, N., ARMAND, J.-P., and MORISHIMA, A. (1974). Inhibition of cellular mediated immunity in marihuana smokers. Sc. 183: 419-420.

NATH, I., CURTIS, J., BHUTANI, L.K., and TALWAR, G.P. (1974). Reduction of a subpopulation of T lymphocytes in lepromatous leprosy. Clin. Exp. Immunol. 18: 81-87.

NICHOLS, W.W., MILLER, R.C., HENEEN, W., BRADT, C., HOLLISTER, L., and KANTER, S. (1974). Cytogenetic studies on human subjects receiving marihuana and Δ^9-tetrahydrocannabinol. Mutat. Res. 26: 413-417.

NOIRFALISE, A., and LAMBERT, J. (1978). Proof of consumption of cannabis. Bull-Narc. 30: 65-67.

NORDQVIST, M., LINDGREN, J.-E., and AGURELL, S. (1976). A method for the identification of acid metabolites of tetrahydrocannabinol (THC) by mass fragmentography. In: Cannabinoid Assays in Humans, NIDA Res. Monogr. 7. Ed. R.E. Willette, p. 63-69.

NOVOTNY, M., LEE, M.L., and BARTLE, K.D. (1976). A possible chemical basis for the higher mutagenicity of marijuana smoke as compared to tobacco smoke. Experientia 32: 280-282.

NOWLAN, R., and COHEN, S. (1977). Tolerance to marijuana; heart rate and subjective "high" Clin. Pharmacol. Therap. 22: 550-556.

NOYES, R. Jr., BRUNK, S.F., AVERY, D.H., and CANTER, A. (1975). The analgesic properties of delta-9-tetrahydrocannabinol and codeine. Clin. Pharmacol. Therap. 18: 84-89.

NULSEN, A., HOLT, P.G., and KEAST, D. (1974). Cigarette smoking, air pollution, and immunity: a model system. Infection and Immunity 10: 1226-1229.

OHLSSON, A., LINDGREN, J.-E., LEANDER, K., and AGURELL, S. (1976). Detection and quantification of tetrahydrocannabinol in blood plasma. In: Cannabinoid Assays in Humans, NIDA Res. Monogr. 7. Ed. R.E. Willette, p. 48-63.

OHLSSON, A., LINDGREN, J.-E., WAHLEN, A., AGURELL, S., HOLLISTER, L.E., and GILLESPIE, H.K. (1980). Plasma delta-9-tetrahydrocannabinol concentrations and clinical effects after oral and intravenous administration and smoking. Clin. Pharmacol. Ther. 28: 409-416.

OHLSSON, A., LINDGREN, J.-E., WAHLEN, A., AGURELL, S., HOLLISTER, L.E., and GILLESPIE, H.K. (1982). Single dose kinetics of deuterium labelled Δ^1-tetrahydrocannabinol in heavy and light cannabis users. Biomed. Mass Spectrom. 9: 6-10.

OLUSI, S.O. (1980). Hyperprolactinaemia in patients with suspected cannabis-induced gynecomastia. Lancet 2: 255.

PAPADAKIS, D.P., MICHAEL, C.M., KEPHALAS, T.A., and MIRAS, C.J. (1974). Effects of cannabis smoking on blood lactic acid and glucose in humans. Experientia 30: 1183-1184.

PASQUALE (de) A., COSTA, G., and TROVATO, A. (1978). The influence of cannabis on glucoregulation. Bull. Narc. 30: 33-41.

PATON, W.D.M., PERTWEE, R.G., and TYLDEN, E. (1973). Clinical aspects of cannabis action. In: Marijuana: Chemistry, Pharmacology, Metabolism and Clinical Effects. R. Mechoulam, ed. Academic Press, New, York, p. 335-365.

PEREZ-REYES, M., Di GUISEPPI, S., DAVIS, K.H., SCHINDLER, V.H., and COOK, C.E. (1982). Comparison of effects of marihuana cigarettes of three different potencies. Clin. Pharmacol. Ther. 31: 617-624.

PEREZ-REYES, M., LIPTON, M.A., TIMMONS, M.C., WALL, M.E., BRINE, D.R., and DAVIS, K.H. (1973). Pharmacology of orally administered Δ^9-tetrahydrocannabinol. Clin. Pharmacol. Therap. 14: 48-55.

PEREZ-REYES, M., WAGNER, D., BRINE, D., CHRISTENSEN, D.H., Davis, K.H., and WALL, M.E. (1976). Tetrahydrocannabinols; plasma disappearance in man and rate of penetration to mouse brain. In: Pharmacol. of Marihuana, M.C. Braude and S. Szara, eds. Raven Press, New York, p. 117-123.

PEREZ-REYES, M., and WALL, M.E. (1982). Presence of Δ^9-tetrahydrocannabinol in human milk. N. Engl. J. Med. 307: 819-820.

PERMUTT, M.A., GOODWIN, D.W., SCHWIN, R., and HILL, S.Y. (1976). The effect of marijuana on carbohydrate metabolism. Am. J. Psychiat. 133: 220-221.

PETERSEN, R.C. (1976; 1980). Marihuana research findings. NIDA Research Monographs 14 and 31.

PETERSEN, R.C. (1979). Importance of inhalation patterns in determining effects of marihuana use. Lancet 1: 727-728.

PETERSEN, B.H., GRAHAM, J., and LEMBERGER, L. (1976). Marihuana, tetrahydrocannabinol and T-cell function. Life Sci. 19: 395-400.

PIHL, R.O., and SIGAL, H. (1978). Motivation levels and marihuana high. J. Abnorm. Psychol. 87: 280-285.

PODOLSKY, S., PATTAVINA, C.G., and AMARAL, M.A. (1971). Effect of marijuana on the glucose tolerance test. Ann. N.Y. Acad. Sc. 191: 54-60.

PRAKASH, R., ARONOW, W.S., WARREN, M., LAVERTY, W., and GOTTSCHALK, L.A. (1975). Effects of marihuana and placebo marihuana smoking on hemodynamics in coronary disease. Clin. Pharmacol. Therap. 18: 90-95.

PRUESS, M.M., and LEFKOWITZ, S.S. (1978).   Influence of maturity on immunosuppression by
Δ^9-tetrahydrocannabinol. Proc. Soc. Exptl. Biol. Med. 158: 350-353.

QUARLES, W., ELLMAN, G., and JONES, R. (1973). Toxicology of marijuana: conversion of cannabidiol
to THC upon smoking. Clin. Toxicol. 6: 211-216.

RACHELEFSKY, G.S., OPELZ, G., MICKEY, R., LESSIN, P., KIUCHI, M., SILVERSTEIN, M.J., and
STIEHM, E.R. (1976). Intact humoral and cell-mediated immunity in chronic marijuana smoking. J.
Allergy Clin. Immunol. 58: 483-490.

REPETTO, M., MARTINEX, D., SANZ, P., GIMENEZ, Ma.P., and RODRIGUEZ, Ma.A. (1979). Potential
carcinogenicity of cannabis. Vet. Hum. Toxicol. 21: Suppl: 148-150.

RICKERT, W.S., ROBINSON, I.C., and ROGERS, B. (1982). A comparison of tar, carbon monoxide and
pH levels in smoke from marihuana and tobacco cigarettes. Can. J. Publ. Hlth. 73: 386-391.

ROKAW, S.N., DETELS, R., COULSON, A.M., SAYRE, J.W., TASHKIN, D.P., ALLWRIGHT, S.S., and
MASSEY, F.J. (1980). The UCLA population studies of chronic obstructive respiratory disease. Chest
78: 252-262.

ROSE, R.M. (1975). Background paper on testosterone and marijuana. In: Marijuana and Health Hazards.
J.R. Tinklenberg, ed. Academic Press, Inc., New York, p. 63-70.

ROSENKRANTZ, H. (1979).   Effects of cannabis on fetal development of rodents.   In: Marihuana:
Biological Effects. G.G. Nahas and W.D.M. Paton, eds. Pergamon Press, Oxford, p. 479-499.

ROSENKRANTZ, H., and ESBER, H.J. (1980). Cannabinoid-induced hormonal changes in monkeys and
rats. J. Toxicol. Environ. Health 6: 297-313.

ROSENKRANTZ, H., and FLEISCHMAN, R.W. (1979).   Effects of cannabis on lungs.   In: Marihuana:
Biological Effects. G.G. Nahas and W.D.M. Paton eds. Pergamon Press, Oxford, p. 279-299.

ROSENKRANTZ, H., and HAYDEN, D.W. (1979). Acute and subacute inhalation toxicity of Turkish
marihuana, cannabichromene, and cannabidiol in rats. Toxicol. Appl. Pharmacol. 48: 375-386.

ROTH, W.T., TINKLENBERG, J.R., KOPELL, B.S., and HOLLISTER, L.E. (1973). Continuous electrocardiographic monitoring during marihuana intoxication. Clin. Pharmacol. Therap. 14: 533-540.

RUBENSTEIN, K.E. (1979). Determination of cannabinoids in urine by EMIT® homogeneous enzyme
immunoassay. In: Marihuana: Biological Effects. G.G. Nahas and W.D.M. Paton, eds. Pergamon Press,
Oxford, p. 89-99.

RUBIN, V., and COMITAS, L. (1975). Ganja in Jamaica. Mouton and Co., Publishers, The Hague, Paris.

SALEMINK, C.A. (1976).   Pyrolysis of cannabinoids.   In: Marihuana: Chemistry, Biochemistry and
Cellular Effects. Ed. G.G. Nahas, Springer-Verlag, New York, p. 31-38.

SALVENDY, G., and McCABE, G.P. Jr. (1975). Marijuana and human performance. Human Factors 17:
229-235.

SALZMAN, C., van der KOLK, B.A., and SHADER, R.I. (1976). Marijuana and hostility in a small-group
setting. Am. J. Psychiat. 133: 1029-1033.

SASSENRATH, E.N., CHAPMAN, L.F., and GOO, G.P. (1979).   Reproduction in rhesus monkeys
chronically exposed to delta-9-tetrahydrocannabinol. In: Marihuana: Biological Effects. G.G. Nahas
and W.D.M. Paton, eds. Pergamon Press, Oxford, p. 501-512.

SAVAKI, H.E., CUNKA, J., and CARLINI, E.A. (1976).   Pharmacological activity of three fractions
obtained by smoking cannabis through a water pipe. Bull. Narc. 28: 49-56.

SAVARY, P., LAURENCEAU, J.L., de LEAN, A., ROY, P., and MARQUIS, Y. (1974).   Acute
cardiovascular effects of inhaled cannabis sativa smoke in man. Int. J. Clin. Pharmacol. 10: 150.

SCHAEFER, C.F., BRACKETT, D.J., GUNN, C.G., and DUBOWSKI, K.M. (1979).   Decreased platelet
aggregation following marhuana smoking in man. J. Okla. State Med. Assoc. 72: 435-436.

SCHAEFFER, C.G., GUNN, C.G., and DUBOWSKI, K.M. (1975). Marihuana dosage control through heart
rate. N. Engl. J. Med. 293:101.

SCHAEFFER, J., ANDRYSIAK, T., and UNGERLEIDER, J.T. (1981). Cognition and long-term use of
ganja (cannabis). Science 213: 465-466.

SCHOOLAR, J.C., HO, B.T., and ESTEVEZ, V.S. (1976). Comparison of various solvent extractions for
the chromatographic analysis of Δ^9-THC and its metabolites. In: Marihuana: Chemistry, Biochemistry
and Cellular Effects. Ed. G.G. Nahas, Springer-Verlag, New York, p. 63-69.

SCHURR, A., SHEFFER, N., GRAZIANI, Y. and LIVINE, A., (1974). Inhibition of glucose efflux from human
erythrocytes by hashish components. Biochem. Pharmacol. 23: 2005-2009.

SHAHAR, A., BINO, T., KALAY, D., and HOMONNAI, T.Z. (1975). Effect of Δ^9-tetrahydrocannabinol
(THC) on the kinetic morphology of spermatozoa. In: Functional Anatomy of the Spermatozoon, B.A.
Alzelius, ed. Pergamon Press, New York, p. 189-193.

SHAPIRO, C.M., ORLINA, A.R., UNGER, P., and BILLINGS, A.A. (1974). Antibody response to cannabis.
J.A.M.A. 230: 81-82.

SHAPIRO, C.M., ORLINA, A.R., UNGER, P.J., TELFER, M., and BILLINGS, A.A. (1976a). Marihuana-
induced antibody response. J. Lab. Clin. Med. 88: 194-201.

SHAPIRO, V.J., REISS, S., SULLIVAN, S.F., TASHKIN, D.P., SIMMONS, M.S., and SMITH, R.T. (1976b).
Cardiopulmonary effects of marihuana smoking during exercise. Chest 70: 441.

SIEMENS, A.J., and KALANT, H. (1974). Metabolism of Δ^1-tetrahydrocannabinol by rats tolerant to
cannabis. Can. J. Physiol. Pharmacol. 52: 1154-1166.

SIEMENS, A.J., KALANT, H., and deNIE, J.C. (1976). Metabolic interactions between Δ^9-tetrahydro-cannabinol and other cannabinoids in rats. In: Pharmacol. of Marihuana, M.C. Braude and S. Szara, eds. Raven Press, New York, p. 77-92.

SILVESTRONI, L., FRAJESE, G., and FABRIZIO, M. (1976). Histones instead of protamines in terminal germ cells of infertile, oligospermic men. Fertil. Steril. 27: 1428-1437.

SINGER, P.R., SCIBETTA, J.J., and ROSEN, M.G. (1973). Simulated marihuana smoking in the maternal and fetal guinea pig. Am. J. Obstet. Gynecol. 117: 331-340.

SINGH, P.P., and DAS, P.K. (1978). Studies on the interactions of copper and cannabis. Psycho-pharmacol. 56: 309-316.

SLADE, M.S., GREENBERG, L.J., YUNIS, E.J., and SIMMONS, R.L. (1974). Integrated immune response to standard major surgical trauma in normal patients. Surg. Forum 25: 425-427.

SMALL, E. (1977). Nomenclature nonsense and legal marijuana plants. The Bulletin: Pacific Tropical Botanical Garden 7: 1-6.

SMALL, E., and BECKSTEAD, H.D. (1973). Cannabinoid phenotypes in Cannabis sativa. Nature 245: 147-148.

SMALL, E., BECKSTEAD, H.D., and CHAN, A. (1975). The evolution of cannabinoid phenotypes in cannabis. Economic Botany 29: 219-232.

SMALL, E., and CRONQUIST, A. (1976). A practical and natural toxonomy for cannabis. Taxon 25: 405-435.

SMALL, E., JUI, P.Y., and LEFKOVITCH, L.P. (1976). A numerical taxonomic analysis of Cannabis with special reference to species delimitation. Systematic Botany 1: 67-84.

SMITH, C.G., SMITH, M.T., BESCH, N.F., SMITH, R.G. and ASCH, R.H. (1979). Effect of Δ^9-tetra-hydrocannabinol (THC) on female reproductive function. In: Marihuana: Biological Effects. G.G. Nahas and W.D.M. Paton, eds. Pergamon Press, Oxford, p. 449-467.

SMITH, H.W. (1978). Effects of set on subjects interpretation of placebo marijuana effects. Soc. Sci. and Med. 12: 107-109.

SMITH, S.H., HARRIS, L.S., UWAYDAH, I.M., and MUNSON, A.E. (1978). Structure-activity relation-ships of natural and synthetic cannabinoids in suppression of humoral and cell-mediated immunity. J. Pharmacol. Exp. Therap. 207: 165-170.

SOFIA, R.D., and KNOBLOCH, L.C. (1976). Comparative effects of various naturally occurring cannabinoids on food, sucrose, and water consumption by rats. Pharmacol. Biochem. Behav. 4: 591-599.

SOFIA, R.D., KNOBLOCH, L.C., HARAKAL, J.J., and ERIKSON, D.J. (1977). Comparative diuretic activity of Δ^9-tetrahydrocannabinol, cannabidiol, cannabinol and hydrochlorothiazide in the rat. Arch. Int. Pharmacodyn, 225: 77-87.

SONI, C.M., and GUPTA, M.L. (1978). Effect of cannabis (bhang) extract on blood glucose and liver glycogen in albino rats. Indian J. Physiol. Pharmacol. 22: 152-154.

SOUEIF, M.I. (1976a). Cannabis-type dependence: the psychology of chronic heavy consumption. Ann. N.Y. Acad. Sc. 282: 121-125.

SOUEIF, M.I. (1976b). Differential association between chronic cannabis use and brain function deficits. Ann. N.Y. Acad. Sc. 282: 323-343.

STANTON, M.D., MINTZ, J., and FRANKLIN, R.M. (1976). Drug flashbacks. II. Some additional findings. Int. J. Addict. 11: 53-69.

STEADWARD, R.D., and SINGH, M. (1975). The effects of smoking marihuana on physcial performance. Med. Sci. Sports 7: 309-311.

STEFANIS, C., BOULOUGOURIS, J., and LIAKOS, A. (1976). Clinical and psycho-physiological effects of cannabis in long-term users. In: Pharmacol. of Marihuana. Eds. M.C. Braude and S. Szara, Raven Press, New York, p. 659-665.

STEFANIS, C., DORNBUSH, R., and FINK, M.J. eds. (1977). Hashish: Studies of long term use. Raven Press, N.Y. 181 pages.

STEFANIS, C.N., and ISSIDORIDES, M.R. (1976). Cellular effects of chronic cannabis use in man. In: Marijuana: Chemistry, Biochemistry and Cellular Effects. G.G. Nahas, ed. Springer-Verlag, New York, p. 533-550.

STEIN, G.S., MON, M.J., HAAS, A.E., JANSING, R.L., and STEIN, J.L. (1979). Cannabinoids: the influence on cell proliferation and macromolecular biosynthesis. In: Marihuana: Biological Effects. G.G. Nahas and W.D.M. Paton, eds. Permagon Press, Oxford, p. 171-208.

STENCHEVER, M.A., KUNYSZ, T.J., and ALLEN, M.A. (1974). Chromosome breakage in users of marihuana. Am. J. Obstet. Gynecol. 118: 106-113.

SULKOWSKI, A., and VACHON, L. (1977). Side effects of simultaneous alcohol and marijuana use. Am. J. Psychiat, 134: 691-692.

SULKOWSKI, A., VACHON, L., and RICH, E.S. Jr. (1977). Propanolol effects on marihuana intoxication in man. Psychopharmacol. 52: 47-53.

SWANSON, J.B. (1975-76). The brain and mind active drugs. Drug Forum 5: 69-73.

SZYMANSKI, H.V. (1981). Prolonged depersonalization after marijuana use. Am. J. Psychiat, 138: 231-233.

TASHKIN, D.P., CALVARESE, B., and SIMMONS, M. (1978a). Respiratory status of 75 chronic marijuana smokers: comparison with matched controls. Am. Rev. Resp. Dis. 117: 261.

TASHKIN, D.P., CALVARESE, B.M., SIMMONS, M.S., and SHAPIRO, B.J. (1980). Respiratory status of seventy-four habitual marijuana smokers. Chest. 78: 699-706.

TASHKIN, D.P., LEVISMAN, J.A., ABBASI, A.S., SHAPIRO, B.J., and ELLIS, N.M. (1977). Short-term effects of smoked marihuana on left ventricular function in man. Chest 72: 20-26.

TASHKIN, D.P., SHAPIRO, B.J., and FRANK, I.M. (1974). Acute bronchial effects of smoked marijuana and oral Δ^9-tetrahydrocannabinol in asthmatic subjects. Clin. Res. 22: 512A.

TASHKIN, D.P., SHAPIRO, B.J., LEE, Y.E., and HARPER, C.E. (1976). Subacute effects of heavy marihuana smoking on pulmonary function in healthy men. N. Engl. J. Med. 294: 125-129.

TASHKIN, D.P., SHAPIRO, B.J., ROSENTHAL, D., and McLATCHIE, C. (1975). Chronic effects of heavy marijuana smoking on pulmonary function and sputum cytology in healthy young men. Am. Rev. Respir. Dis. 111: 895.

TASHKIN, D.P., SOARES, J.R., HEPLER, R.S., SHAPIRO, B.J., and RACHELEFSKY, G.S. (1978b). Cannabis, 1977 (clinical conference). Ann. Intern Med. 89: 539-549.

TAYLOR, D.N., WACHSMUTH, I.K., SHANGKUAN, Y.-H., SCHMIDT, E.V., BARRETT, T.J., SCHRADER, J.S., SCHERACH, C.S., McGEE, H.B., FELDMAN, R.A., and BRENNER, D.J. (1982). Salmonellosis associated with marijuana. A multistate outbreak traced by plasmid fingerprinting. N. Engl. J. Med. 306: 1249-1253.

TAYLOR, S.P., VARDARIS, R.M., RAWITCH, A.B., GAMMON, C.B., CRANSTON, J.W., and LUBETKIN, A.I. (1976). The effects of alcohol and delta-9-tetrahydrocannabinol on human physical aggression. Aggressive Behav. 2: 153-161.

TEALE, J.D. and MARKS, V. (1976). A fatal motor-car accident and cannabis use. Lancet 1: 884-885.

TEALE, J.D., CLOUGH, J.M., FRY, D., BACKHOUSE, C., and MARKS, V. (1976). The use of radioimmunossay in the detection of urinary cannabinoids. In: Clinical toxicology. Eds. W.A. Duncan and B.J. Leonard, p. 252-254.

TEALE, J.D., CLOUGH, J.M. KING, L.J., and MARKS, V. (1977). The incidence of cannabinoids in fatally injured drivers: an investigation of radioimmunossay and high pressure liquid chromatography. J. Forensc. Sci. Soc. 17: 177-183.

TENNANT, F.S. (1979). Histopathologic and clinical abnormalities of the respiratory system in chronic hashish smokers. Problems of Drug Dependence. NIDA Research Monograph 27 Ed: L.S. Harris, p. 309-315.

TENNANT, F.S., and GROESBECK, C.J. (1972). Psychiatric effects of hashish. Arch. Gen. Psychiat. 27: 133-136.

TENNANT, F.S., PREBLE, M., PRENDERGAST, T.J., and VENTRY, P. (1971). Medical manifestations associated with hashish. J.A.M.A. 216: 1965-1969.

THACORE, V.R., and SHUKLA, S.R.P. (1976). Cannabis psychosis and paranoid schizophrenia. Arch. Gen. Psychiat. 33: 383-386.

THOMAS, W., HOLT, P.G., and KEAST, D. (1973). Effect of cigarette smoking on primary and secondary humoral responses of mice. Nature 243: 240-241.

THOMAS, W., HOLT, P.G., and KEAST, D. (1974). Recovery of immune system after cigarette smoking. Nature 248: 358-359.

TINKLENBERG, J.R. (1974). Marijuana and human aggression. In: Marijuana: Effects on Human Behaviour. L.E. Miller, ed. Academic Press, New York, p. 339-359.

TINKLENBERG, J.R. and DARLEY, C.F. (1976). A model of marijuana's cognitive effects. In: Pharmacol. of Marijuana. M.C. Braude and S. Szara, eds. Raven Press, New York, p. 429-443.

TREFFERT, D.A. (1978). Marihuana use in schizophrenia: a clear hazard. Am. J. Psychiat. 135: 1213-1215.

TUCKER, A.N., and FRIEDMAN, M.A. (1977). Effects of cannabinoids on L1210 murine leukemia. 1. Inhibition of DNA synthesis. Res. Comm. in Chem. Pathol. and Pharmacol. 17: 703-714.

TUCKER, A.N., and FRIEDMAN, M.A. (1979). Effects of cannabinoids on L1210 murine leukemia. III. Inhibition of respiration. Res. Comm. in Chem. Pathol. andf Pharmacol. 23: 327-332.

TURNER, C.E., ELSOHLY, M.A., and BOEREN, E.G. (1980). Constituents of cannabis sativa L. XVII. A review of the natural constituents. J. Natural Products 43: 169-234.

TURNER, J.C., HEMPHILL, J.K., and MAHLBERG, P.G. (1981). Interrelationships of glandular trichomes and cannabinoid content. II. Developing vegetative leaves of cannabis sativa L. (cannabaceae). Bull. Narc. 33: 63-71.

UNGERLEIDER, J.T., ANDRYSIAK, T., TASHKIN, D.P., and GALE, R.P. (1982). Contamination of marihuana cigarettes with pathogenic bacteria - possible source of infection in cancer patients. Cancer Treatment Reports 66: 589-591.

VACHON, L., FITZGERALD, M.X., SOLLIDAY, N.H., GOU'D, I.A., and GAENSLER, E.A. (1973). Single-dose effect of marihuana smoke. N. Engl. J. Med. 288: 985-989.

VALENTINE, J.L., BRYANT, P.J., GUTSHALL, P.L., GAN, O.H.M., THOMPSON, E.D., and NIU, H.C. (1976). HPLC-MS determination of Δ^9-tetrahydrocannabinol in human body samples. In: Cannabinoid Assays in Humans, NIDA Res. Monogr. 7. Ed. R.E. Willette, p. 96-106.

VALZELLI, L. (1978). Human and animal studies on the neurophysiology of aggression. Prog. Neuro-Psychopharmacol. 2: 591-610.

VARDARIS, R.M., WEISZ, D.J., FAZEL, A., and RAWITCH, A.B. (1976). Chronic administration of delta-9-tetrahydrocannabinol to pregnant rats: studies of pup behaviour and placental transfer. Pharmacol. Biochem. Behav. 4: 249-254.

VAZIRI, N.D., THOMAS, R., STERLING, M., SEIFF, K., PAHL, M.V., DAVILA, J., and WILSON, A. (1981). Toxicity with intravenous injection of crude marijuana extract. Clin. Toxicol. 18: 353-366.

VORHEES, C.V., BRUNNER, R.L., and BUTCHER, R.E. (1979). Psychotropic drugs as behavioral teratogens. Science 205: 1220-1225.

WAGNER, E.E., and ROMANIK, D.G. (1976). Hand test characteristics of marijuana-experienced and multiple-drug-using college students. Perceptual and Motor Skills 43: 1303-1306.

WAHLIQVIST, M., NILSSON, I.M., SANDBERG, F., and AGURELL, S. (1970). Binding of Δ^1-tetrahydrocannabinol to human plasma proteins. Biochem. Pharmacol. 19: 2579-2584.

WALL, M.E. (1971). The in vitro and in vivo metabolism of tetrahydrocannabinol (THC). Ann. N.Y. Acad. Sc. 191: 23-39.

WALL, M.E., and BRINE, D.R. (1976). Identification of cannabinoids and metabolites in biological materials by combined gas-liquid chromatography-mass spectrometry. In: Marihuana: Chemistry, Biochemistry and Cellular Effects. Ed. G.G. Nahas, Springer-Verlag, New York, p. 51-62.

WALL, M.E., BRINE, D.R., and PEREZ-REYES, M. (1976a). Metabolism of cannabinoids in man. In: Pharmacol. of Marihuana, M.C. Braude and S. Szara, eds. Raven Press, New York, p 93-116.

WALL, M.E., HARVEY, T.M., BURSEY, J.T., BRINE, D.R., and ROSENTHAL, D. (1976b). Analytical methods for the determination of cannabinoids in biological media. In: Cannabinoid Assays in Humans, NIDA Res. Monogr. 7. Ed. R.E. Willette, p. 107-117.

WALL, M.E., and PEREZ-REYES, M. (1981). The metabolism of Δ^9-tetrahydrocannabinol and related cannabinoids in man. J. Clin. Pharmacol. 21: 178S-189S.

WALLACE, L. (1978). Psychoanalytic observations in marijuana use. Am. J. Psychiat. 135: 990-991.

WEHNER, F.C., VAN RENSBURG, S.J., and THIEL, P.G. (1980). Mutagenicity of marijuana and Transkei tobacco smoke condensates in the Salmonella/microsome assay. Mutat. Res. 77: 135-142.

WEISS, J.L., WATANABE, A.M., LEMBERGER, L., TAMARKIN, N.R., and CARDON, P.V. (1972). Cardiovascular effects of delta-9-tetrahydrocannabinol in man. Clin. Pharmacol. Therap. 13: 671-684.

WELLER, R.A., and HALIKAS, J.A. (1982). Change in effects from marijuana: a five to six year follow-up. J. Clin. Psychiat. 43: 362-365.

WETZEL, C.D., JANOWSKY, D.S., and CLOPTON, P.L. (1982). Remote memory during marijuana intoxication. Psychopharmacol. 76: 278-281.

WHITE, S.C., BRIN, S.C., and JANICKI, B.W. (1975). Mitogen-induced blastogenic responses of lymphocytes from marihuana smokers. Sc. 188: 71-72.

WIKLER, A. (1976). Aspects of tolerance to and dependence on cannabis. Ann. N.Y. Acad. Sc. 282: 126-147.

WILLETTE, R.E. (1976). Cannabinoid Assays in Humans. NIDA Research Monograph 7.

WILLETTE, R.E. (1977). Drugs and Driving. NIDA Research Monograph 11, p. 77-99.

WILSON, R.S., and MAY, E.L. (1976). The role of 11-hydroxylation in tetrahydrocannabinol activity. In: Pharmacol. of Marihuana, M.C. Braude and S. Szara, eds. Raven Press, New York, p. 137-138.

WRIGHT, N., YEOMAN, W.B., and HALE, K.A. (1978). Assessment of severity of paraquat poisoning. Br. Med. J. 2: no. 6134: 396.

WYBRAN, J., and FUDENBERG, H.H. (1973). Thymus-derived rosette-forming cells in various human disease states: cancer, lymphoma, bacterial and viral infections, and other diseases. J. Clin. Invest. 52: 1026-1032.

ZEIDENBERG, P., BOURDON, R., and NAHAS, G.G. (1977). Marijuana intoxication by passive inhalation: documentation by detection of urinary metabolites. Am. J. Psychiat. 134: 76-77.

ZIMMERMAN, A.M., BRUCE, W.R., and ZIMMERMAN, S. (1979). Effects of cannabinoids on sperm morphology. Pharmacol. 18: 143-148.

ZOLAKAR, J.B., RICHARD, J.L., and CLAUDE, J.R. (1981). Leukocyte count, smoking, and myocardial infarction. N. Engl. J. Med. 304: 465-468.

HUY, N.D. and ROY, P.E. (1976). Inhalation of Tobacco & Marijuana In Dog over a Period of 30 Months: Effect on Body Weight, Food Intake & Organ Weight. Res. Comm. Chem. Pathol. Pharmacol., Vol.13: page 465-472.

VI. Author Index

Ordinary type page numbers indicate citations in text;
italics, graphs; and bold type, actual references.

Abbasi, A.S. **291**
Abel, E.L. 68, 97, 98, 260, **278**
Adams, A.J. 101, **278, 279**
Adams, P.M. 85, **278**
Adams, T.C. Jr. 8, **278**
Agnew, W.F. 82, **278**
Agurell, S. 9, 11, 22, *278*, **283, 286, 288, 292**
Al-Marashi, M.S.H. 85, **282**
Alexander, P.C. **287**
Aliapoulios, M.A. 64, 75, **283**
Allen, M.A. **290**
Allwright, S.S. **289**
Alpert, J.J. **283**
Alpert, M. **279**
Altman, J. 85, **278**
Amaral, M.A. **288**
Amat-Y-Leon, F. **287**
Ames, B.N. 134, **278**
Ames, F.R. 83, **278**
Amit, Z. 257, **280**
Andrysiak, T. **289, 291**
Anduze, A.L. **287**
Annitto, W. **281**
Aponte, N. **285**
Aqleh, K,(A). **279**
Archer, R. **285**
Armand, J.-P. **288**
Aronow, W.S. 174, 175, **278, 282, 288**
Arya, M. **281**
Asch, R.H. **290**
Avakian, E.V. 174, *218*, **278**
Avery, D.H. **288**
Axelrod, J. **286**
Ayalon, D. **280.**

Babor, T.F. 93, *278*, **287**
Bachman, J. **284**
Backhouse, C.(I). 139, **278, 291**
Bader-Bartfai, A. **278**
Badr, F. **281**
Baile, C.A. **286**
Baker, P.B. 10, **278**
Banchereau, J. 38, *52, 53, 54, 55*, **278**
Barratt, E.S. 85, **278**
Barrett, T.J. **291**
Barry, H. III 65, **278**
Bartke, A. 70, **281**
Bartle, K.D. **285, 288**
Beaconsfield, P. 166, **278**
Beals, R.K. **283**
Beckner, J.S. **281, 286**
Beckstead, H.D. 7, **290**
Bedford, J.A. **284**
Belleville, J.W. 137, *152*, **279**

Belmore, S.M. 100, **279**
Bender, P.E. **286**
Bennett, R.C. **280**
Benowitz, N.(L). 102, 103, *123, 124*, 172, 173, 174, 186, *212, 213, 214, 215, 216*, 255, *273*, **279, 284**
Ben-Zvi, Z. 12, *27*, **279, 281**
Berg, S.D. **285**
Bergen, J.R. **279**
Bernstein, J.G. **287**
Besch, N.F. **290**
Bhutani, L.K. **288**
Bier, M.M. **284**
Bigger, J.F. **282**
Billings, A.A. **289**
Binder, M. **278**
Binitie, A. 88, **279**
Binot, T. **289**
Bird, K.D. 100, **279**
Blaine, J.D. 101, **279, 284**
Blair, H.T. **283**
Blevins, R.D. 37, *50, 51, 52*, **279**
Bloom, A.D. **282**
Bloom, A.S. **281**
Boeren, E.G. **291**
Bolanos, A. **285**
Boleyn, J. **279**
Borg, T. 100, **279**
Boulougouris, J. **290**
Bourdon, R. 10, **279, 292**
Bourke, D.I. **286**
Bowman, K. **282**
Boyd, E.H. **279**
Boyd, E.S. 100, **279**
Bozzetti, L.P. **279, 284**
Brackett, D.J. **289**
Bradley, S.G. 43, **279**
Bradt, C. **288**
Branda, L.A. **281**
Braude, M.C. 11, **279, 280**
Brenner, D.J. **291**
Bright, T.P. 170, *209*, **279**
Brill, N.Q. 93, **279**
Brine, D.R. 11, **288, 292**
Britton, E.L. **280**
Bro, P. 88, 255, **279**
Brown, B. 166, **278, 279**
Brown, D.(J). **279, 281**
Brown, L.E. **279**
Brown, N. **282**
Brownell, B. **278**
Bruce, W.R. **292**
Brunk, S.F. **288**
Brunnemann, K.D. **283**

Brunner, R.L. 292
Bryant, P.J. 291
Bursey, J.T. 292
Burstein, S. 11, 62, 65, 70, *279, 281, 287*
Busch, F.W. 37, **279**
Butcher, R.E. 292

Calvarese, B. 291
Campbell, A.M.G. 82, **279**
Campbell, R.L. 282
Canter, A. 288
Carakushansky, G. 71, **279**
Carchman, R.A. 43, **279, 283**
Cardon, P.V. 292
Carlin, A.S. 92, **280**
Carlini, E.A. 98, **280, 289**
Carlsson, S. 278
Carlton, E.T. 281
Carnevale, A. 258, **282**
Carter, W.E. 237, **280**
Cassidy, J. 174, 175, **278**
Cates, W. 64, **280**
Cavness, C. 281
Chakravarty, I. 25, 65, **280**
Chan, A. 290
Chao, F.-C. 66, *80,* **280**
Chapman, L.F. 289
Charlebois, A.T. 70, **282**
Charles, R. 178, **280**
Chase, R.A. 9, **280**
Cheng, J.T. 278
Chesher, G.B. 104, **279,** 280
Chiang, C.Y. 44, **286**
Chopra, G.S. 89, 97, 138, 144, **280**
Christensen, D.H. 288
Christie, R.L. 93, **279**
Cimbura, G. 102, *122,* **280**
Clark, R. 280
Clark, S. 287
Clark, T.J.H. 283
Claude, J.R. 292
Clemens, J. 286
Clewe, G.L. 286
Clopton, P.L. 292
Clough, J.M. 291
Co, B.T. 83, **280**
Coffman, C.B. 135, **280**
Cohen, A.B. 286
Cohen, S. 102, 164, *189, 190, 191,* **285, 288**
Coleman, J.H. 87, **280**
Collins, F.G. 171
Comitas, L. 138, 233, **289**
Coniglio, W. **280**
Cook, C.E. 288
Copeland, K.C. 63, **280**
Corcoran, M.E. 257, **280**
Cordova, T. 65, **280**
Cornicelli, J.A. 257, **280**
Costa, G. 288
Côté, MG. 286
Coulson, A.M. 289
Coutselinis, A. 253, **280**
Cozens, D.D. 69, **280**
Crabtree, R. 286
Cranston, J.W. 291

Crawford, W.J. 287
Cronquist, A. 7, **290**
Cuatrecasas, R. 255, **287**
Cunka, J. 289
Curtis, J. 288
Cushman, P. 39, 40, *56,* **280, 282**
Cutting, M.(B). 141, **281, 284, 287**

Dackis, C.A. 12, **281**
Dagirmanjian, R. 282
Daley, J.D. 64, **281**
Dalterio, S. 62, 69, 70, **281**
Darley, C.F. 100, **291**
Das, G.D. 85, **278**
Das, P.K. 253, **290**
Daul, C.B. 41, **281**
Davidson, S.T. 287
Davies, P. 143, *161, 162,* **281**
Davila, J. 292
Davis, K.H. 288
Davis, K.R. 285
Davis, W.M. 283
Day, N. 278, 283
Dellarco, A.J. 284
DeNie, J.C. 290
Desoize, B. 38, **278, 281, 288**
Desser, K.B. 255, **286**
Detels, R. 289
Dewey, W.L. 65, 253, 254, **279, 281, 286, 287**
Dhingra, R.C. 287
Di Benedetto, M. 87, **281**
Di Guiseppi, S. 288
Dintcheff, B.A. 278
Dixit, V.P. 65, 254, **281**
Domino, E.F. 176, **284**
Dooling, E. 283
Doorenbos, N.J. 7, 8, **281**
Dornbush, R.(L.) 100, *118, 119,* **281, 290**
Drath, D.B. 45, 143, **281**
Dreisbach, R.H. 129, **281**
Drew, W.G. 282
Dronyssiou-Asteriou, A. 285
Drouga, M. 285
Dubowski, K.M. 289

East, R. 285
Edery, H. 10, **281**
Elliott, R.A. 282
Ellis, N.M. 291
Ellman, G. 289
Elsohly, M.A. 283, 284, 291
End, D.W. 279
Englert, L.F. 287
Erdmann, G. 284
Erikson, D.J. 290
Esber, H.J. 67, **289**
Estevez, V.S. 289
Evans, M. 279
Evans, M.A. 72, 101, **281**
Evans, W.E. 280

Fabrizio, M. 290
Fazel, A. 292
Fehr, K.O. 145, **281**

Feinberg, I. 85, *108*, **281**
Feldman, R.A. **291**
Fetterman, P.S. **281**
Filczewski, M. 253, **286**
Filipovic, N. **285**
Fink, M.(J.) 84, **282**, **290**
Finley, T.N. **286**
First, M.W. **284**
Fitzgerald, M.X. **291**
Fitzjarrell, A.T. **283**
Fleischman, R.W. 68, 139, **282**, **289**
Flom, M.C. **278**, **279**
Floyd, T. **281**
Fonseka, K. **278**
Fontana, C.J. **283**
Forney, R.B. 99, **279**, **282**, **285**
Forrest, I.S. **280**
Fournier, E. 69, **282**
Frajese, G. **290**
Frank, I.M. **291**
Franklin, R.M. **290**
Fredrickson, J.M. **286**
Freemon, 85, **282**
Fried, P.A. 70, 71, **282**
Friedman, M.A. 43, **282**, **291**
Frischknecht, H.R. 68, **282**
Fritchie, G.E. **287**
Fry, D. **291**
Fudenberg, H.H. 39, **292**
Fujimoto, G.I. **285**

Gado, M. **280**
Gaensler, E.A. **291**
Galanter, M. 165, *194*, **282**
Gale, E.N. 93, **282**
Gale, R.P. **291**
Gammon, C.B. **291**
Gan, O.H.M. **291**
Gardner, L.I. **279**
Garey, R.E. **283**
Garrett, E.R. 12, **282**
Gash, A. 170, **282**
Gasser, J.C. **279**
Gelbart, S.S. **287**
Gentner, W.A. **280**
Gerber, M.L. **283**
Gershon, S. **279**
Gersten, S.P. 91, **282**
Ghia, J. **282**
Ghoneim, M.Th. 254, **282**
Ghosh, J.J. 254, **280**
Gibbons, R.J. 102, **282**
Gillespie, H.(K.) **278**, **283**, **286**, **288**
Gilman, A.F. 59, **287**
Gilman, S.R. **280**
Gilmour D.G. 34, **282**
Gimenez, Ma.P. **289**
Ginsburg, J. **278**
Giusti, G.V. 258, **282**
Gold, M.S. **281**
Goldman, H. 85, **282**
Goo, G.P. **289**
Goodenough, G. **281**
Goodwin, D.W. **280**, **288**
Gori, G.B. **283**

Gottschalk, L.A. 176, **282**, **288**
Gough, T.A. **278**
Gould, I.A. **291**
Graham, J. **288**
Graziani, Y. **289**
Green, D.E. **280**
Green, K. 259, *277*, **282**
Greenberg, I. **287**
Greenberg, L.J. **290**
Greenland, S. 71, **282**
Gregg, J.M. 87, 88, 104, *113, 114,* 178, *219, 220, 221, 222, 223,* **282**
Grieco, M.(H.) **280**, **282**
Groesbeck, C.J. 89, **291**
Grunfeld, Y. **281**
Gross, S.J. 9, 10, *20,* **282**
Guenther, G. 93, **282**
Guerry, R. **283**
Gunn, C.G. **289**
Gupta, M.L. 254, **290**
Gupta, S. 39, **280**, **282**
Gustafsson, B. **278**
Gutshall, P.L. **291**

Haas, A.E. **287**, **290**
Haavik, C.O. 171, **280**
Haegerstrom-Portnoy, G. **278**, **279**
Haine, S.E. **285**
Hale, K.A. **292**
Halikas, J.A. 88, 92, 257, **283**, **292**
Hall, F.B. 93, **283**
Harakal, J.J. **290**
Harbison, R.D. **281**, **286**
Harclerode, J. **284**, **286**
Hardman, H.F. 181, *227, 228, 229, 230, 231, 232,* **284**
Hardy, N. **280**, **282**
Harmon, J.W. 64, *75,* **283**
Harper, C.E. **291**
Harper, J.W. 86, **283**
Harris, C.C. 131, **283**
Harris, L.S. 42, **279**, **281**, **283**, **286**, **287**, **290**
Hart, R.H. 98, **283**
Harvey, D.J. 11, **280**, **283**
Harvey, T.M. **292**
Harwood, T. **280**
Hatoum, N.S. 69, **283**
Hawks, R.L. **280**
Hayashi, M. 144, *163,* **283**
Hayden, D.W. 63, **282**, **289**
Hearing - U.S. Committee-paraquat 135, **283**
Heath, R.G. 41, 85, 86, *110,* **281**, **283**, **287**
Hecht, F. 71, **283**
Hembree III, W.C. 63, **283**
Hemphill, J.K. **291**
Henderson, R.L. 138, 144, **283**
Heneen, W. **288**
Henrich, R.T. 36, **283**, **287**
Hepler, R.S. **291**
Heppner, G.H. 41, **286**
Hernandez, M.J. 141, **283**
Higgenbottam, T. 144, **283**
Hill, S.Y. **280**, **288**
Hinds, W.C. **284**
Hingson, R. 71, **283**

Ho, B.T. **287, 289**
Hoellinger, H. **288**
Hoffman, D. 133, *149,* **283**
Hollister, L.(E.) 9, 87, 101, 102, 103, 254, *265,*
 268, 269, **278, 283, 285, 286, 288, 289**
Hollstedt, C. 260, **283, 284**
Holt, P.G. **288, 291**
Holt, S. **280**
Homonnai, T.Z. **289**
Hong, R. 39, **284**
Horowitz, M. 134, **284**
Horowitz, S. 39, **284**
Horvath, S.M. **278**
Hosko, M.J. 177, 181, *217, 227, 228, 229, 230,*
 231, 232, 258, **284, 285**
Huang, H.F.S. **283**
Huber, G.((L.) 141, 142, *155, 156, 157, 158,*
 159, 160, **281, 283, 284, 287**
Hughes, J.E. 255, **284**
Hunt, C.A. 12, **284**
Hunter, S.A. **279**
Huy, N.D. 258, **292**

Indanpään-Heikkilä, J.E. **287**
Isbell, H. 102, **284**
Issidorides, M.R. 39, 63, **284, 290**

Jackson, D.L. 132, **284**
Jackson, D.M. **279, 280**
Jacobs, J.A. 254, **284**
Jacobs, S. **278**
Jäger, S. 44, **286**
Jakubovic, A. 62, **284**
Jandu, B.S. 97, 138, 144, **280**
Janowsky, D.(S.) 101, *120, 121,* **279, 282, 284,**
 292
Jansing, R.L. **290**
Jardillier, J.-C. **281**
Jasinki, D.R. 102, **284**
Jayaraman, J. **287**
Johnson, K.M. **281**
Johnson, R.J. 43, **284**
Johnston, S. 176, **284**
Johnstone, R.E. 179, *224, 225,* **284, 286**
Jolly, H. **283**
Joneja, M.G. 69, **284**
Jones, A.B. 9, **284**
Jones, L.A. 8, **278**
Jones, R.(T.) 12, 102, 103, *122, 123, 124,* 172,
 173, 174, 186, *212, 213, 214, 215, 216,*
 278, 279, 280, 281, 284, 289
Jui, P.Y. **290**
Just, W.W. 10, 11, **284, 285**

Kagen, S.L. 136, **285**
Kaklamani, E. 40, **285**
Kalant, H. 12, 145, **281, 289, 290**
Kalay, D. **289**
Kalofoutis, A. 37, 253, **285**
Kanakis, C. 169, *208, 209,* **285, 287**
Kanter, S.(L.) 10, **285, 288**
Kaplan, J.N. **280**
Karalis, D. **285**
Karliner, J.S. **282**

Karr, G. **287**
Kawash, G.F. 68, **285**
Kaymakçalan, S. 104, **285**
Kayne, H. **283**
Keast, D. **288, 291**
Kelley, P.R. **280**
Kephalis, T.A. 11, 133, **285, 288**
Khurana, R. 39, 40, **280**
Kiburis, T. **285**
Kilburn, K.H. **280**
Kim, K. **282**
King, L.J. **286, 291**
Kiplinger, G.F. 99, 165, *192, 193,* **279, 281, 282,**
 285
Kirkham, N. **280**
Kiuchi, M. **289**
Klein, A.L. **282**
Klein, V. **286**
Klykken, P.C. **287**
Knobloch, L.C. 257, **290**
Kochar, M.S. 177, *217,* **285**
Kokkevi, A. 100, **281**
Kolansky, H. 88, **285**
Kolk (van der) B.A. **289**
Kolodner, R.M. **285**
Kolodny, R.C. 59, 61, 62, 63, 64, 74, **285**
Kopell, B.S. **289**
Kopin, I.J. **286**
Kostellow, A.B. 65, **285**
Kottke, B.A. **280**
Koukkou, M. 86, *111, 112,* **285**
Koutselinis, A. **285**
Krieger, D.T. 225, **285**
Kroll, P. 89, **285**
Krom, B.A. **280**
Kubena, R.K. **278**
Kuehnle, J.(C.) 83, **278, 281, 285, 287**
Kulp, R.A. **284, 286**
Kunar, J. **285**
Kunysz, T.J. **290**
Kupfer, D. 11, **279**
Kyrkou, K.A. **287**

Ladman, A.J. **286**
Laguarda, R. **281, 284, 287**
Lake, C.R. **282**
Lambert, J. 99, **288**
Lander, N. **280**
Lares, A. 65, **285**
Lau-Cam, C.A. 10, **285**
Laurenceau, J.L. **289**
Laverty, W. **288**
Law, B. 9, **285**
Leander, K. **278, 288**
Le Dain, G. 2, **285**
Lean(de) A. **289**
Lee, M.L. 134, **285, 288**
Lee, Y.E. **291**
Lees, M.H. **283**
Lefkovitch, L.P. **290**
Lefkowitz, S.S. 41, 44, **286, 289**
Léger, C. **278, 281, 288**
Lehmann, D. 86, *111, 112,* **285**
Lekakis, J. **285**

Lele, K.P. **282**
Lemberger, L. 8, 9, 10, 11, *21, 23,* 64, *75,* **281, 282, 286, 288, 292**
Lemmi, H. **280**
Lerner, C.B. **279**
Lessin, P **285, 289**
Leuchtenberger, C. 36, *49,* **286**
Leuchtenberger, R. 36, *49,* **286**
Levander, S. **278**
Levin, K.J. **282**
Levine, A. **289**
Levisman, J.A. **291**
Levy, J.A. 41, **286, 287**
Liakos, A. **290**
Liedgren, S.R.C. 101, **286**
Lief, P.L. **284**
Lindemayr, von H. 44, **286**
Lindgren, J.E. 103, *125, 126, 127,* **278, 283, 286, 288**
Lindner, H.R. **280**
Lipton, M.A. **288**
Liskow, B. 43, **286**
Liss, J.L. **286**
List, A. 62, **286**
Lockhart, J.G. 255, **286**
Lohiya, N.K. **281**
Lubetkin, A.I. **291**
Lucas, D.M. **280**
Lutz, E.G. 90, **286**

MacCannell, K. **287**
MacLean, P.D. 85, *109,* **286**
Mahajan, V. **284**
Mahfouz, M. **282**
Mahlberg, P.G. **291**
Makar, A.B. **282**
Malit, L.A. 180, **286**
Malor, R. **280**
Manfredi, R.A. **284**
Manheimer, D.I. **287**
Mann, P.E.G. 44, 143, **286**
Manno, J.E. **285**
Mantilla-Plata, B. 69, **281, 286**
March, J. **281**
Marcotte, J. 133, *148,* **286**
Markidou, S.G. **287**
Marks, V. 9, 99, **286, 291**
Marquis, Y. **289**
Marshall, E. 136, **286**
Marshman, J.A. 233, **282, 286**
Martin, B.(R). **278, 281**
Martin, B.R. 66, **286**
Martin, J.B. 255, **285**
Martinez, D. **289**
Martinez, F. **283**
Martz, R. **281**
Massey, F.J. **289**
Masters, W.H. **285**
Mattox, K.L. 133, **286**
Maximilian, C. **282**
May, E.L. 11, **292**
Mayfield, D. **281**
Mazurkiewicz-Kwilecki, I.M. 253, **286**
McCabe, G.P. 94, *115,* **289**
McCallum, N.K. **287**

McCann, J. **278**
McCarthy, C.(R.) 141, **284, 287**
McDougall, J. **282**
McGee, H.B. **291**
McGreer, E.G. **284**
McGreer, P.L. **284**
McGuire, J.S. 96, **287**
McIsaac, W.M. 82, 87, **287**
McLatchie, C. **291**
McLaughlin, C.L. 257, **286**
McMahon, R. **286**
McMillan, D.E. 102, 186, **287**
McNamee, H.B. **281**
Meacham, M.P. **279, 284**
Mechoulam, R. 8, 10, 12, 44, **280, 281, 287**
Megargee, E.I. 96, **287**
Melez, K.A. 42, **287**
Mellinger, G.D. 92, **287**
Mello, N.K. **287**
Mendelson, J.H. 102, **278, 281, 285, 287**
Mendhiratta, S.S. 92, **287**
Menges, H. 132, **284**
Merritt, J.C. 165, *196, 197, 198, 199,* **287**
Michael, C.M. **285, 288**
Michael, E.D. **278**
Michalodimitrakis, M. 253, **280**
Mickey, R. **289**
Mikhael, M. **280**
Mikhail, M.M. **282**
Miles, C.G. **282**
Miller, L.L. 100, **279**
Miller, R.C. **288**
Miller, R.J. 255, **287**
Miller, R.H. 178, **287**
Miller, W.C. **283**
Milstein, M. **287**
Milstein, S.L. 94, **287**
Minna, J.D. **283**
Mintz, J. **290**
Miras, C.(J.) 35, **285, 287, 288**
Miyake, T. **279**
Moffat, A.C. **285**
Mon, M.J. 38, **287, 290**
Montenegro, M. **285**
Moody, M.M. 136, **287**
Moore, R. **282**
Moore, W.T. 88, **285**
Morahan, P.S. 43, *58,* **287**
Morelock, S. **283**
Morishima, A. 36, **283, 287, 288**
Morrill, G.A. **285**
Mueller, P.B. 138, **287**
Mullane, J. **284**
Mulvihill, J.J. **283**
Munson, A.E. 42, **279, 283, 287, 290**
Murad, F. 59, **287**
Murphy, S. **282**
Musumeci, M. **285**
Myers III, W.A. 86, **283, 287**

Naditch, M.P. 88, **287**
Nahas, G. 11, 38, **278, 280, 281, 282, 283, 287, 288, 292**
Naqvi, R.H. **282**
Nath, I. 39, **288**

Neu, R.L. **279**
New, P.F.J. **285**
Nichols, W.W. 35, **288**
Nilsson, I.M. **278**, **292**
Nir, I. **280**
Niu, H.C. **291**
Nogawa, T. **283**
Noirfalise, A. 99, **288**
Nordqvist, M. 9, **278**, **288**
Novotny, M. 37, **285**, **288**
Nowlan, R. 102, 164, *189, 190, 191,* **288**
Noyes, R. Jr. 87, **288**
Nulsen, A. 44, **288**
Nyquist, S. **286**

Ochoa, Y. **285**
O'Connell, D. **284**
Odkvist, L.M. **286**
Ohlsson, A. 9, 12, *19,* 164, **278, 283, 286, 288**
Olsson, O. **284**
Olusi, S.O. 64, **288**
Opelz, G. **289**
Oppenheimer, E. **283**
Orlina, A.R. **289**
Overall, J.E. **283**

Pahl, M.V. **292**
Palmer, A.K. **280**
Panayiotopoulos, C.P. **282**
Papadakis, D.P. 255, *272,* **285**, **288**
Parker, C.W. **286**
Pasquale (de), A. 254, *263, 264, 265, 266, 267,* **288**
Paton, W.D.M. 11, 91, 105, **283**, **288**
Pattavina, C.G. **288**
Peng, T.C. **281**
Pereira, W. **284**, **287**
Perez-Reyes M. 10, 11, 12, *24, 25, 26,* 67, 180, *226,* **288, 292**
Perhach, J.L. Jr. **278**
Pertwee, R.G. **288**
Permutt, M.A. 254, **288**
Petersen B.H. 40, *57,* **288**
Petersen, R.C. 7, 9, 10, 13, 82, 87, 99, 101, 102, 105, 238, **288**
Phillips, J. **279**
Pihl, R.O. 93, **288**
Pizzitola, V. 10, **285**
Pochay, V.E. **284**
Podolsky, S. 254, *268, 270, 271,* **288**
Pope, J.N. 64, **280**
Popham, R.E. **286**
Pottash, A.L.C. **281**
Pouget, J.M. **285**
Prakash, R. 175, 176, **282**, **288**
Preble, M. **291**
Prendergast, T.J. **291**
Price, L. **281**
Pruess, M.M. 41, **289**
Puder, M. **280**

Quarles, W. 133, **289**
Quimby, MW. **281**

Rachelefsky, G.S. 40, **289, 291**

Raft, D. **282**
Rainsbury, R. **278**
Rawitch, A.B. **291, 292**
Reaven, G.M. 254, *265, 268, 269,* **283**
Reeves, J.P. **287**
Regan, J.D. 37, *50, 51, 52,* **279**
Reiss, S. **289**
Repetto, M. 37, **289**
Rich, E.S. Jr. **290**
Richard, J.L. **292**
Richards, A.B. **285**
Rickert, W.S. 134, **289**
Ritter, U. **286**
Robbins, E.S. **282**
Roberson, C. **281**
Roberts, P. **283**
Robinson, I.C. **289**
Rodda, B.E. **281**, **285**
Rodriguez, Ma.A. **289**
Rogers, B. **289**
Rokaw, S.N. 131, **289**
Romanik, D.G. 94, **292**
Rose, G. **283**
Rose, R.M. 59, **289**
Rosen, K.M. **285**, **287**
Rosen, M.G. **290**
Rosenberg, E. **282**
Rosenfeld, J. **281**
Rosenkrantz, H. 63, 67, 68, 139, **282, 289**
Rosenthal, D. **291, 292**
Rossi, A.M. **287**
Roth, W.T. 177, **282, 289**
Rowe, H. **286**
Roy, P. **289**
Roy, P.E. 258, **292**
Rubenstein, K.E. 10, *21,* **289**
Rubin V. 138, 233, **289**
Rumbaugh, C.L. **278**
Rydberg, V. **284**

Salemink, C.A. 11, **289**
Salvendy, G. 94, *115,* **289**
Salzman, C. 96, **289**
Sandberg, F. **292**
Sanz, P. **289**
Sassenrath, E.N. 67, **289**
Savaki, H.E. 83, **289**
Savary, P. 164, **289**
Sayre, J.W. **289**
Schaefer, C.F. 164, **289**
Schaeffer, C.G. 165, **289**
Schaeffer, J. 103, **289**
Scherach, C.S. **291**
Schimpff, S.C. **287**
Schindler, V.H. **288**
Schmeling, W.T. **284**
Schmidt, E.V. **291**
Schnaper, N. **287**
Schneider, A. **286**
Schoolar J.C. 8, **289**
Schoor, J. **284**
Schoor, M. **279**
Schou, J. **279**
Schrader, J.S. **291**
Schurr, A. 253, **289**

Schwin, R. **288**
Scibetta, J.J. **290**
Sedor, C. **279**
Sehgal, P.K. **279**
Seid, D.A. **279**
Seiff, K. **292**
Shader, R.I. **289**
Shahar, A. 37, **289**
Shangkuan, Y.-H. **291**
Shapiro, B.J. **291**
Shapiro, C.M. 40, 44, **289**
Shapiro, V.J. 174, **289**
Shea, J.W. **284**
Sheffer, N. **289**
Sheth, A.R. **280**
Shipley, M.J. **283**
Shorey, J.M. **281**
Shoupe, T.S. **279**
Shukla, S.R.P. 90, **291**
Sieber, B. **282**
Siemens, A.J. 12, **289, 290**
Sigal, H. 93, **288**
Silverstein, M.J. **289**
Silvestroni, L. 63, **290**
Simmons, G.(A.) **281, 284, 287**
Simmons, M.(S.) **289, 291**
Simmons, R.L. **290**
Simpson, M.M. **280**
Singer, P.R. 66, 79, **290**
Singh, M. 94, **290**
Singh, P.P. 253, **290**
Skelton, R.S. **286**
Slade, M.S. 34, **290**
Small, E. 7, 15, 16, 17, **290**
Small, E.W. **282**
Smith, C.G. 65, 76, 77, 78, **290**
Smith, H.W. 87, **290**
Smith, J.W. 89, **280**
Smith, M.T. **290**
Smith, R.G. **290**
Smith, R.T. **289**
Smith, S.H. 42, **287, 290**
Smith, T.C. **284, 286**
Soares, J.R. 9, 10, 20, **282, 291**
Sofia, R.D. 257, 258, **290**
Solliday, N.H. **291**
Somers, R.H. **287**
Soni, C.M. 254, 263, **290**
Sornberger, G.C. **281, 283**
Soueif, M.I. 92, 103, **290**
Staisch, K.J. **282**
Stanton, M.D. 91, **290**
Starmer, G.A. **279**
Steadward, R.D. 94, **290**
Steahly, L.P. **284**
Stefanis, C.(N.) 39, 63, 83, 235, **282, 290**
Stein, G.S. 38, **287, 290**
Stein, J.L. **287, 290**
Steinberg, A.D. **287**
Stenchever, M.A. 35, 49, **290**
Sterling, M. **292**
Stevens, M.W. **281**
Suciu-Foca, N. **288**
Sulkowski, A. 259, 274, 275, 276, **290**
Sullivan, S.F. **289**

Swanson, G.D. **279**
Swanson, J.B. 82, 107, **290**
Szymanski, H.V. 91, **290**

Tacker, H.L. **280**
Talwar, G.P. **288**
Tamarkin, N.R. **292**
Tashkin, .DP. 140, 141, 153, 154, 155, 170, 171, 172, 174, 210, 211, 217, **289, 291**
Taunton-Rigby, A. **280**
Taylor B.J. **278**
Taylor, D.N. 136, **291**
Taylor, P. **279**
Taylor, S.P. 97, 117, **291**
Teale, (J.)D. 99, 116, 117, **286, 291**
Telfer, M. **289**
Tennant, F.S. 89, 138, 144, 153, **283, 291**
Teo, R.K.C. **279**
Thacore, V.R. 90, **291**
Thiel, P.G. **292**
Thiel, S. **284**
Thomas, R. **292**
Thomas, W. 44, **291**
Thompson, E.D. **291**
Thomson, J.L.G. **299**
Thorgeirsson, S.S. **283**
Timmons, M.C. **288**
Tinklenberg, J.R. 96, 100, **289, 291**
Tobisson, B. **278**
Tocoque, B. **288**
Toomey, T.C. **282**
Topp, G. **279**
Toro, G. **285**
Treffert, D.A. 90, **291**
Trichopoulos, D. **285**
Trovato, A. **288**
Trupin, E.W. 92, **280**
Tucker, A.N. 43, **291**
Turner, C.E. 8, **280, 283, 284, 291**
Turner, J.C. 8, **291**
Tylden, E. **288**

Underwood, L.E. **280**
Unger, P.J. **289**
Ungerleider, J.T. 136, **289, 291**
Uwaydah, I.M. **290**

Vachon, L. 137, 151, 259, **290, 291**
Valentine, J.L. 9, 10, 144, **291**
Valzelli, L. 95, **292**
Van Rensburg, S.J. **292**
Van Wyk, J.J. **280**
Varanelli, C. **279**
Vardaris, R.M. 66, **291, 292**
Vaughan, T.B. **282**
Vaziri, N.D. 258, **292**
Ventry, P. **291**
Verma, S.K. **287**
Volavka, J. **282**
Vorhees, C.V. 70, **292**

Wachsmuth, J.K. **291**
Wagner, D. **288**
Wagner, E.E. 94, **292**
Wahlen, A. **283, 288**

Wahliqvist, M. 44, **292**
Walker, J.M. **281**
Wall, M.E. 9, 11, 12, *18*, 67, **280, 288, 292**
Wallace, L. *93*, **292**
Warner, W. **279**
Warren, M. **288**
Warren, R.A. **280**
Waser, P.G. **282**
Watanabe, A.M. **292**
Waters, J.E. **282**
Watson, A. **281**
Watson, D. **281**
Wehner, F.C. 134, *150*, **292**
Wei, E.T. **279**
Weingartner, H. **282**
Weiss, J.L. 168, *200, 201, 203, 204, 205, 206,*
    207, **292**
Weisz, D.J. **292**
Weker, R.R. **284**
Weller, R.A. 257, **292**
Werner, G. **284, 285**
Wetzel, C.D. 100, **292**
Wharton, R.C. **287**
White, S.C. 40, **292**
Widman, W. **278**
Wiechmann, M. **284**
Wiersema, V. 43, **284**
Wig, N.N. **287**
Wikler, A. 103, **292**
Wilcox, J.C. 138, **287**

Williams, M.J. **279**
Williams, P.L. **285**
Willette, R.E. 9, 101, **292**
Wilson, A. **292**
Wilson, R.S. 11, **292**
Winship-Ball, A. **280**
Witschi, H. **286**
Wright, N. 135, **292**
Wyatt, R.J. **282**
Wybran, J. 39, **292**
Wynder, E.L. **283**

Yamasaki, E. **278**
Yawney, C.D. **286**
Yeoman, W.B. **292**
Yeung, D.L. **285**
Younglai, E.V. **281**
Yunis, E.J. **290**

Zaluzny, S.G. **280**
Zamora, J.U. **285**
Zavala, D.C. **280**
Zeidenberg, P. 44, **283, 292**
Ziegler, D. **285**
Zimmerman, A.M. 63, **292**
Zimmerman, S. **292**
Zolakar, J.B. 258, **292**
Zuckerman, B. **283**
Zuurmond, T.J. **278**

VII. Subject Index

Bold type page numbers indicate topic discussed in studies; italics, graphs.

Abstinence syndrome, ganja **234**
  hashish **235**
  irrational anger **89**
  naloxone precipitated **103-104, 255**
  sleep disturbance **85, 184,** 247
  symptoms **102, 184**
    duration **103**
  THC withdrawal **173**
Accidents
  behavioural factors **100, 101,** 104, 249
  motor 4
    alcohol, blood level **99**
    cannabinoid, blood, post-mortem **99,** *117*
      proof of consumption **99,** 105, 249
      urinary screening **99,** *116*
Accumulation of THC in tissues
  post acute and chronic dosing **11,** 241
  post IV **12**
Act, Canadian Federal Law 2
  Marihuana Tax Act 2
  Schedule of Opium and Narcotic Drug Act 2
  Single Convention on Narcotic Drugs 2
ACTH (adrenocorticotropic hormone),
  behaviour effect **257**
  release **255, 256**
  secretion **65,** 255
    THC effect **254**
  stimulation **254**
Acute effects, short summary, physiological **4**
  psychic **4**
  psychopathological **4**
Administration, route of (see also Vehicle)
  comparison of routes 3, **9-13,** 22, 101, 103,
    123, 125-127, 164, 172, 242
  inhalation 3, **9-13,** *19, 20, 21,* 22, 34-36, 40,
    41, 44, 45, *49, 56, 57, 61, 62, 63,* 66-68, 70,
    74, 79, 83-94, 96, 97, 99-104, *110, 115,
    116-123, 125-127, 133,* 135, 137-146, *148,
    151-155, 161-163,* 164-166, 171, 174-177,
    179, 183-186, *189-194, 196-199, 209-211,
    217, 218, 223, 233, 235, 236,* 242, 243, 244,
    247, 249, 250, *253-255, 257, 259, 268, 270-
    272, 274-276,*
    passive 244
  intramuscular **11,** 65, *76, 77, 78,* 102, 254,
    263-267
  intraperitoneal 41, *43, 58,* 64, 65, 68-70, 142,
    244, 254, 257, 258, *263,*
  intravenous **9-13,** *18, 21, 23-26, 43,* 64, 66,
    69, 75, 82, 85, 86, 87, 103, *113, 114, 125-
    127,* 164, 169, 177-184, *208, 209, 219-222,
    224, 225, 228-231,* 241, 244, 247, 249, 253,
    254, 257, 258, 259, *265, 268, 269*
  intraventricular (brain) **12,** *27*

oral 3, **9-13,** 22, 35, 42, 66-70, 72, 80, 83-88,
    97, 100, 102, 103, *108, 111, 112, 117, 122-
    124,* 137, 141, 145, 164, 168, 172, 173, 177,
    180, 183-186, *200, 201, 203-207, 212-217,
    226,* 244, 247, 249, 250, 254, 255, 258, 259,
    273
  self-injection 103, 258
  subcutaneous 36, 37, 64, 69, 75, 254, 258
  topical, eye drops 259, *277*
    skin scratch test 44
Adrenal glands, ascorbic acid **254**
  blood glucose control **255, 256,**
  cannabinoid accumulation **11-13,** 241
  cholesterol esterase inhibition **65**
  cortex, androgen synthesis 60
    hyperfunction 60
  corticosterone secretion **254**
  cortisol hypoglycemic response **255,** *273*
  immune response **42**
  pituitary-adrenal axis **65**
  stimulation **66, 71,** 246
  THC, adrenalectomy **258**
    steroid release **42**
  weight, female **144**
Adrenergic system, ACTH release **255**
  β-adrenergic stimulation **180,** 186, 251
    propanolol influence **181**
  CNS-activated sympathoadrenal response,
    THC **179,** 186, 187, 251
  compensatory reflex mechanism, marihuana,
    tobacco **167,** 186, 251, **253,** 255, 259, 260,
    261
  electrophysiological effects **178,** *184,* 251
  insulin inhibition, competitive, THC **257**
  marihuana with and without propanolol **259,**
    274-276
  ocular effects **259-260,** *277*
  sympathetic
    increased **253, 254**
      hyperglycemia **255**
    inhibition **173**
    insufficiency **172, 173**
  toxic epinephrine dose **178**
Age, cannabis use **93**
  in drivers **99, 102,** *122*
  immunological maturation **42**
  maturity **96**
  respiratory disorders **138**
  THC effects on immune system **41,** 46
Aggression, male
  alteration **62,** 246
  ganja, chronic use **234,** 238
  hormonal influence **95,** 248
    testosterone **62**

limbic system **97**, 248
    amygdala **95**
    septum **95**, 98
    marihuana use **96-97**, 237, 248
        vs alcohol **97**, *117*, 237, 248
    tolerance development 248
    types of responses **95**, 248
        cannabis effects **98**, 104
            in anginal patients **176**
            stress effects **98**
Airway clearance, cilia 4, **142**, 146, *159*, 250
Airway resistance,
    bronchial asthma 130
        marihuana effect **141**, 145, 250
    in chronic cannabis smokers **138**
    chronic effects 131
    pulmonary function tests 130
        cannabis smoke exposure, acute effects
            137, *151*
            chronic effects **138-141**, 145-146, *153-*
                155, 250, 253
            marihuana vs tobacco **140**, 145
Alcohol, 3, 4, 7, 13, 39, 40, 61, 63, 65, 71, 82,
    86, 92, 93, 96, 104, 233, 234, 235, 236, 237,
    238, 242, 247,
    alcoholism **89**, **99**, **260**
        diabetic misdiagnosis **258**
    blood alcohol **99-102**, 249
        peak time 166
    blood glucose, adult, fetus **260**
    cerebral atrophy **83**
    cocarcinogen 131
    EEG profile 84
    FAS (fetal alcohol syndrome) **258**
    in fatally injured **102**
    with hashish **89**
        glucose transport arrest **253**
    hepatomegaly **83**
    vs marihuana **93**, **99**, **101**, **260**
        aggressive behaviour **97**, *117*, 248
            temporal lobe dysrhythmia **97-98**
        during fasting **254**
        pupil size **166**
        respiratory effects **137**, 145
    with marihuana 259
    memory storage deficit **100**, 249
    performance decrement **100**, **101**, 104, 249
        with THC **100**, **101**, 249
    peripheral neuropathy **87**
    rosette formation **39**, 243
    solubility vs cannabis 99
    testosterone, sperm effects **62**, 246
    treatment of marihuana withdrawl **103**
    weight, birth 68
        maternal 68
    withdrawal vs cannabis, opiates **103**
Allergy (immediate type) 31, 33
    cannabinoid **43-44**, 46, 244
    diagnostic tests **44**, 244
    diathesis **44**, 46, 244
        hashish potentiation **138**, 145
    occupational **44**, 46, 244
Alveoli, emphysema 5, 131
    pathology, marihuana induced **139**

Ames test (mutagenic, carcinogenic potential)
    37, **134**, *150*, 242
Amino acids, hashish effect **254**
Ammonia
    blood level, hashish **254**, *264*, *267*
        CNS derangement **257**
Amnesia, cannabis intoxication **89**
Amotivational syndrome (personality changes)
    chronic cannabis use 5, **92**, **97**, 248
    lethargic effects **93-94**, 101
        weakness, energy loss **257**
    motivation **85**, **86**, **92**
        academic **92-93**
        loss (apathy) **89**, **90**, **93**, 248
    psychoanalytical case report **93**
    psychological characteristics **94**
Amygdala (rage, fear), EEG activity **85-86**
    self-preservation **85**, *109*
    stimulation, lesioning 248
Animal experiments
    active immunization 12, 241
    analgesia **11**
    autoradiographic studies **11**
    behaviour, aggressive **95**, 98
        in female fetus post testosterone 61
        male sexual and aggressive conduct 61
    brain
        11-OH-metabolite **11-12**, 241
        monkey **12**, *27*
        subcellular cannabinoid distribution **253**
        THC hippocampus **85**
            catecholamine synthesis **253**
    cat, THC, CNS pharmacological action **181-**
        182, *227-232*
    dogs
        blood glucose, insulin, ammonia levels **254**,
            263-267
        food intake, chronic marihuana **257**
        pregnant, THC distribution **66**
    guinea pig, placental drug transfer **66**, *79*
    hamster
        lung cultures, malignant transformation **36**,
            242
        paraquat toxicity **135**
    metabolism **11-12**, 241
    mice
        fetal toxicity **68**
        immune system, THC effect **42**
            DTH modification **41**
            maturity re immune system **41**
                autoimmunity (age, sex hormones) **42**
        infection susceptibility **43**, *58*
        lactation **68**
        male fertility **69**
        malignant transformation in lung cultures
            36, 242
        mutagenic potential **37**
        neoplastic tissue proliferation **42**, **43**
            DNA synthesis inhibition **43**
        neuroblastoma cells, cell metabolism **37**
        ovarian function **65**
        pregnancy **68**
        reproductive functional development alter-
            ation **70**

skin bioassay (tumor activity) **133-134**, *149*
sperm toxicity **63**
teratology **69**
testis cultured, mutagenic potential **37**
milk, 11, 241
monkey
  CNS cannabinoid distribution **82**
  EEG sleep pattern, THC **85**
  endocrine effects **67**
  rhesus 10
    brain, THC,
      function, behaviour **85-86**
      metabolism **12**, *27*, 241
    immune system effects **41**
pituitary-adrenal axis **65**
placental drug transfer **66**
primates
  brain damage **83**, 247
  EEG activity **86**, 247
  female hormonal effects **65**, *76-78*
  maternal milk **66-67**, *80*
  plasma THC level, smoke exposure **86**, *110*
  reproductive effects **67-68**, 254
plumonary, AHH enzyme induction **133**, *148*
  alveolar macrophage, functional character-
    istics 45
    intrapulmonary bacterial inactivation
      142-143, *157-162*
    marihuana vs tobacco exposure **143-144**,
      161, 162
  morphological response of airway **144**, *163*
  paraquat toxicity **135**
rabbits
  blood ammonia, urea levels **254**
  teratogenic effects **69**
rodent (rat)
  blood glucose alteration **254**, *263*
  bone marrow myelopoiesis inhibition **43**
  distribution of cannabinoids 11, 241
  endocrine effects in pregnant and lactating
    67
  fetal toxicity **68**
  fructose, citric acid, male reproductive
    organs **254**
  glioma cells **43**
  gonadal effect **62**, *63*, 65
  gynecomastia induction **64**, *75*
  paraquat toxicity **135**
  placental drug transfer **66**
  pregnancy **68**
  pulmonary pathology **139**
  sucrose preference **257**
  THC bone marrow stimulation **258**
  tumor induction **37**
  urinary output, THC vs hydrochlorothiazide
    258
  uterine glycogen alteration **254**
serum prolactin levels **64**
sheep, food intake, THC IV **257**
THC
  ACTH secretion **254**
  catecholamine synthesis **253**
  in feces, suckling infant 11, 241
  hippocampus **85**
  interaction with _____
    CBD **12**, 241
    CBN **12**, 13
  intraocular pressure effects **259-260**, *277*
  intrapulmonary antibacterial defense **142**,
    157-160
  metabolism inhibition **133**
  physical dependence, onset **103**
    abstinence, naloxone **103-104**
  plasma clearance 11, 241
  temperature effects **258**
  testosterone effect **62**
  tolerance development **102**
  tumor suppression **42**
Anoxia, damage, arterial wall 132, 187, 251
  functional 238
  shock, ammonia level **255**
  tissue 129, **187**, 251
    chronic CO absorption 129, 146, 250
Antianxiety property (tranquilizer)
  marihuana 5, **93**, 248
  psychoanalytical case report **93**
Antibodies, autoantibodies 34
  to cannabinoids **44**, 244
    via immunization **12**, 241
  to host tissues 33
  humoral **40-42**, 46, 244
  in hypersensitivity reactions 33
  to marihuana, diagnostic detection 245
  normal circulating 31-32
  production sites (e.g. spleen) **33**, 44
Anxiety, in anginal patients 176
  drug intoxication 4, **87**, **91**, **100**, 186
  in glaucoma patients **165**
  hashish 235, 238
  HR **177**, 183
  vs temporal lobe epilepsy **97**
  THC 180
    with pentobarbital **179**
    with stress **87**, *113, 114*, 179, 247
Appetite, abstinence syndrome 102, 184
  cannabis intoxication **90**
  hashish effect **235**, 238
  hunger **101**
    carbohydrate starvation **257**
    in glaucoma patients **165**
  marihuana effect 5, **237**, 238
Arginine, acrosomes of sperm heads **64**, 245
  cannabis depletion **64**, 245
  gluconeogenesis effect **257**
  in lymphocytes 63
  in spermatic cell nuclei **63**, 245
  testosterone influence **64**, 245
Asphixia, infants **71**
Aspirin, DNA synthesis impairment **38**, 243
  rosette formation **39**, 243
Asthma, bronchial
  bronchial, hypersensitivity 130, 146
    reactivity, histamine test **141**
  bronchodilation, acute cannabis effect, **141**,
    145, 237, 250
  chronic cannabis use **138**, 145
    ganja **234**
  exacerbation, infection 146
Ataxia, tests, marihuana **101**
Atherosclerosis, smoking effects, CO gas exposure **167**, **183**, 187, 251
Atropine (anticholinergic)

effect on cannabis CVS effects **167**, 185
premedication caution in users **167, 174**
in THC tolerant **173**
Attention, in driving **100**, 249
impairment **101, 102**, 249
Availability systemic, post THC
inhalation **12, 13**, 242
IV **12**, 241
oral **13**, 242

Bacteria
alveolar macrophages 32
cytotoxin **141, 143**, 146, *156*, 250
E. coli 244
gram positive 244
staphlococcus **141, 142**, *156-160*
survival post marihuana **142**, 146
Barr body **31**
Behaviour
ACTH effect **257**
adaptive **64**
aggressive, definition **94-95**, 248
hormonal influence **95**, 248
irrational anger 89
limbic system **95**, 97, 248
marihuana use **96-97**
vs alcohol **97**, *117*
alteration (THC) **66, 68, 82, 83, 85-86**
dose-response **82**
relation to CNS drug distribution **82**, 246
catatonic (psychotic) **86**, 247
copulatory **70**, 246
delusional, hallucinatory **90**, 247
destructive **88**
violent **90**, 248
developmental alteration **68**, 72
emotional **85**, *109*
factors in accidents **100-101**, 249
instinctive **85**, *109*
motivation **93**, 248
paranoid **236**, 238
personality predisposition **234**
prenatal cannabis exposure effects **70**, 72, 246
reproductive (teratogen) toxicity 5, **70-71**, 72, 246
socio-sexual **85**, *109*
testosterone during fetal development 60-61
tolerance **102**, 247
abstinence phenomenon **103**, 184, 249
CNS inhibition, stimulation **139**
vigilance **84**, 247
withdrawal **85**, 184, 247
Bile, enterohepatic recirculation **12, 13**, 241
excretion **12**, 241
metabolites in **11**
THC in **9**, 241
Bioavailability of THC, smoking or IV vs oral **9, 11, 12, 13**, 22, 241
Blood, analysis **9-10**, 241
azotemia **259**
brain barrier (drugs) 82, 246
cannabinoids in **11, 102**
coaguability impairment **164**, 185, 251
vs nicotine **167**

eosinophilia, ganja **234**
glucose, ammonia, insulin **254**, *263-267*
granulocytosis, bone marrow stimulation **258**
lactic acid level, hashish post fasting **254, 255**, *272*
leukocytosis **259**
lymphocyte count **33**
NE level post smoking **170**
PCV (packed cell volume) **234**
pharmacokinetics **9-10**, 241-242
plasma, clearance 9, **12**, *18*, 241
glucose transport arrest **253**, 255
levels 9, 13, *18, 19, 20*, 241-242
drug dose 105, 261
THC **9**, 13, *18*, 241-242
11-OH-THC **9**, *18*, 241
CBN **9**, *18*, 241
C-THC 13, 241
lipids **257**
volume expansion **102, 173**, 183 185, 187, 251, **253, 261**
epinephrine effect **258**
RBC, ATP, 2,3 DPG, lactic acid production **253, 255**
glucose transport arrest **253, 255**
production **138, 145, 234**, 250, **253**
serum enzymes, M.I. **178**
Blood flow, peripheral
hashish effect **253**
marihuana **166, 183**, 251
propanolol, epinephrine, NE, atropine influence **167**
vs tobacco **166**, 183
with varied postures, oral THC **168-169**, *205, 206*
Blood pressure, acute effects 4,
atropine, epinephrine, norepinephrine influence **167**, 185
cannabis intoxication **90, 171**, 186, 258, 260
chronic effects **172-173**, *212-215*
changes with varied postures **168, 172**, 181, 183, *201, 213*, 250
bradycardia **181**
CO_2 response **179**
THC **180**
with oxymorphone/pentobarbital **179-180**
coronary artery disease **175**
exercise **174-175**
vs nicotine **175**
correlation with HR **176, 183**, 251
in glaucoma patients (smoking) **165**, 185, *197-199*
marihuana, with alcohol **259**
field study **237**, 238
with propanolol **259**, *274*
orthostatic hypotension 4, **101, 102**, 165, 168, **172, 179**, 183. 186, 187, *198, 199, 214*, 238, 250, **253, 258, 260**
tolerance development **172-173**, 183, **236**, 238, 251
propanolol influence **169**
pulmonary hypertension 130, 131,
resting 94, 164, **165, 166, 172**, 174, 175, 176, *198, 199, 212*
sitting **177**

smoking effects **167**, 183, 253
THC
   CNS sympathetic control **181-182**, *227-232*
   exercise effects **173**, 183, *215*
   with stress **87**, 247
     vs diazepam **178**, *219*
   in various vehicles **181**
Blood vessels
  atherosclerosis, clinical significance 132
   plasma lipids **257**
  inhalation effects **164**
  vasodilation
   marihuana **167**, 183
   smoking effects **167**, 183, 253
   THC effect **136, 164**, 250
  venomotor reactivity **168**, 183, *204*
Body image disturbance
  cannabis induced **86**
   EEG post THC **86**, *111*
Bone marrow lymphocytes (B-cells)
  age influence **41**, 244
  defects 32
  immune rosette impairment **39-41**, 243, 244
  normal function 31
  possible clinical effects of B-cell decrease
   47, 245
  stimulation **258**
  THC effect **42**
Bradycardia, diagnostic sign, chronic use **99**
  fetal **66**, *79*, 246
  marihuana and alcohol **259**
  nicotine **142**, 145
  tendency with tolerance development **171**,
   183, *211*
  THC, animal brain stem effect **181**
   posture change **181**
   Valsalva **173**
Brain (see CNS effects)
  accumulation THC in **11**, 13, 241
   fetal **66**
   maternal **66**
  cannabinoid, detection **9**, 241
   distribution **82**, 87, 246
  CO effects 129
  endogenous opiates **255-257**
  evoked responses in hashish users **235**
  FAS (fetal alcohol syndrome) **258**
  function **82**, *107*
   cannabinoid effects **85-86**, 260
   EEG alterations **84-87**, 104, 247
   hashish **235**, 238
   impairment 5, **87-98**, 185, 260
   limbic system **85, 86, 95**, 104, *109*, 247, 248
  intraventricular THC **12**
  metabolism **82**, 246
   11-OH-metabolite **11-12**, 241
   monkey, THC metabolism **12**, *27*
  nerve cells **82**, 104, 247, 257
  pathology, electron microscopy **86**
   gross **82-84**, 246-247
  requirements, glucose, oxygen **255**
   unavailability **257**, 258
  trochlear (4th cranial) nerve **87**
  tumor, temporal lobe 248

Bronchitis
  chronic cannabis use **138**, 144-146, 237, 250
   bronchoscopy, biopsy **138-139**
   hashish **235**, 238
   mucus hypersecretion 144-146, 250
  smoke effects 131, 238, 253
Bronchodilation
  acute marihuana effect 4, **137, 140**, 145, 146,
   151, 250
   in asthmatic patients, induced bronchospasm
   141, 165
  partial tolerance development **141**, 145, *155*,
   250
  THC effect **142**

Caffeine 71
  DNA synthesis impairment **38**, 243
  PVCs **177**, 184, 251
Calcium, cardiac microsomal CaATPase **171**
  level 33
Cannabichromeme (CBC or CBCH)
  in cigarettes **9, 10**
  in marihuana 9, 10, 241
  maternal and fetal effects **69**
  testicular damage **63**
  testosterone inhibition **62**
  THC antagonism (perinatal effects) **68-69**
Cannabicyclol (CBL or CBCy) 8
  allergic response **44**
  testosterone inhibition **62**
Cannabidiol (CBD)
  allergic response **44**
  antibacterial activity 8
  antibody response **41**
  anticonvulsant property 8
  cardiac microsomal CaATPase **171**
  chromosomal effects 35, 36
  in cigarettes **9, 10**, 37, 41
  conversion **11, 133**, 144, 241, 249
  detection **9**
  gonadotropin effects **67**
  immunosuppression vs CNS activity **43**
  interaction, with THC **9, 12**, 13, **133**, 144, 236,
   241-242, 249
   with 11-OH-THC **12, 13, 133**, 241
  in marihuana **9-11**, 241
  maternal and fetal effects **68-69**
  metabolism **11**, 241
  in plant **7-8**, 240
  sucrose preference **257**
  testosterone synthesis inhibition **62**, 67
  tumor growth enhancement **42**, 46, 244
   DNA synthesis impairment **43**, 244
Cannabigerol (monoethyl ether) (CBG(m))
  antibacterial activity 8
  interaction with pentobarbital 8
  in plant **7-8**
  testosterone inhibition **62**
Cannabinoids (see also individual compounds)
  antineoplastic activity **42**
   DNA synthesis impairment **43**, 46
  carbohydrate preference **257**
  cardiac microsomal CaATPase **171**
  cell proliferation **38**, 45, 243

chemotherapeutic agent similarity **42-43**, 244
cholesterol esterification inhibition 257
detection **8-10**, 12, **99**, *116*, 241
DNA biosynthesis impairment **38**, 45, 243
in fat **11**
in fatally injured **102**, *122*
fetal effects **67-71**, 246
in fingertip washings **10**, 241
immunosuppression vs CNS activity **42**, 43
infection susceptibility **43**, *58*
levels vs intoxication **10**, 242
in liver **11**
loss of 7, 240
metabolism **11-13**, 241
performance impairment **100**
in plant 2, 3, **7-8**, 240
   smoked **133**, 144, 249
in plasma 3, **12**, 83, 241-242
   correlation with tissue concentration **11**
pulmonary disorders 250
pyrolysis products **37**, 45
in resin 2
in saliva **10**, 241
in smoked marihuana **10**, 237
temperature effect **258**
testosterone inhibition **61-62**, *74*, 245
Δ^9 THC 2, **7-13**, 240-242
in urine 3, **10**, 12, *20, 21*, 83, 99, **102**, 241
Cannabinol (CBN)
antibody response **41**
anticonvulsant property 8
anti-inflammatory property 8
cell growth impairment **38**, 243
chromosomal effects **35, 36, 69-70**, 72, 246
in cigarettes **9, 10, 37**, 41
conversion to **7**, 240
DTH modification **41**, 244
interaction, with THC 8, **9**, 12, 13, **133**, 144,
   242, 249
   with 11-OH-THC **133**
in marihuana **9-11**, 235, 241
maternal and fetal effects **68-70**, 246
metabolism **11**, 241
in milk **67**, 246
pituitary-gonadal function **70**
post IV THC
   plasma level **9**, *18*, 241
   thermal degradation product of THC **9**, 242
progesterone inhibition **65**, 246
psychotomimetic activity 8, 240
sucrose preference **257**
testicular damage **63**
testosterone synthesis inhibition **62**, 240
tumor growth inhibition **42, 46**, 244
   DNA synthesis impairment **43**, 244
Cannabis (sativa) (see Marihuana, Hashish,
   Smoking)
allergic response **44**, 244
antigen **40-41**, 244
blood glucose, ammonia, insulin **254**, *263-267*
cannabinoid content 3, **7-8**, 13, 240
chronic smoking in natural setting **233-239**
   carbohydrate metabolic effect 237
classification **84**, 247
clinical use 2

copper potentiation effects 253
EEG effects **84-87**, 247
fructose, citric acid, male organs **254**
memory storage deficit **100**, 249
neurological symptoms **83**
organic brain syndrome **99**, 247-248
other known compounds **8, 37**, 240
ovarian response **65**
plant 2, 3, **7-8**, 13, *15-17*, **41, 133**, 240
   cigarettes **70, 133**
potency 2, 3, 13, **238**, 240, 241
psychopathology **83**
purpose of use **90**
resin 2, **37, 65, 133**
   fetal effects **68, 69**
   poisoning **88**
respiratory disorders **138**
tolerance development **103**
uterine glycogen **254**
Carboxy-THC (C-THC)
in blood 3, **11**, 13, 241
excretion **12**
in feces **11-13**, 241
IV effects **10**
in liver **11**
in maternal milk **67**, 246
plasma level post
   I.V. **12**
   p.o. **12**
   smoking **9-10**, 12, 13, *20*, 67, 241
      relation to pharmacological effects 10,
      13, 241
urinary level
   for forensic purpose 3, **9**
   post I.V. **10**, *21*
   post smoking **9-10**, *20*, 241
in urine 3, **11-13**, 241
Carcinogenesis
benzpyrene **37**, 45, 145, 242, 250
chemical and viral carcinogens 34
chromosomal alterations **35-37**, 45, *49*, 131,
   242
chronic hashish and tobacco **138-139**, *153*
compounds in smoke 4, 8, 37, 45, **133-134**, 145,
   149, 150, 240, 242, 249, 250, 253
   tobacco 129, **133-134**, 145, 250
DNA modification **38**, 45, 243
environmental chemicals, mutagens 131
genetic predisposition 31, 131
gluconeogenesis effect **257**
immunodeficiency diseases 31
T and B-cell deficiencies 34, 260
tars **37**, 45, 145, 242, 249
underactive immune system 31
Cardiac (see Heart, Myocardium)
arrhythmia **170, 176-177**, 184, *209, 217*
conduction, THC IV, cardiac patients **177-178**,
   184, 251, 253
contractility, chronic effects **171-172**, *210,
   211*
   microsomal CaATPase **170-171**, 186, 251
index, CO_2 response **179-180**
   with THC **180**
      with oxymorphone/pentobarbital **179-180**
output **164, 170**, 184, 185, 251

chronic effects 171-172, *210, 211*
  tolerance development 171, *211*
performance THC 170, 251, 260
toxicity 174-178, *217, 218,* 251
  in anginal patients 174-176
  arrythmias 176-178, *217*
    THC, vs diazepam, oral surgical patients 179, *222*
    with oxymorphone 179
  in healthy 174
  myocardial infarction, marihuana and tobacco 178, 185, 251
Catecholamine
  cannabis induced synthesis 255
  excessive, ECG changes 184
  hypothalamic, amine metabolic disruption 257
  leukocytosis 258
  low catecholamine diet 168
  nicotine release 129, 260
  plasma level, glucose load response 254, *271*
  THC induced, chronic 253
    naloxone inhibition 253, 255
  urinary 169
Caution (alert)
  persistent tachycardia 167, 179, 180, 183, 185, *223, 225,* 251
  psychopathological augmentation 179-180, 185, 251
  ventilatory depression 179-180, 185, *224,* 251
Cell
  alveolar macrophage 44-45, 141-144, 146, *155-162,* 250
  B-cells 31-32
  blood, maturation in bone marrow 64
  cytotoxicity, cannabinoid 36, 45, 242
    marihuana and tobacco 36, 45
    psychotropic drugs 38, *53, 54*
    tobacco 36
  developing vs mature 41, 244
  gluconeogenesis effect 257
  growth rate inhibition 38, 55, 243
  lymphocytes cultured 31
    metabolic alterations 38, *52, 55,* 243, 253
  metabolism (macromolecular synthesis) 4, 37-39, 42, 45, 244, 260
    cholesterol 257
  nerve 82, 104, 247, 257
  nucleated peripheral 42, 244
    granulocytosis 258
    leukocytosis 259
  plasma 31-32
  proliferation 38-39, 43, 45, 243
  RBC,
    ATP, 2,3 DPG, lactic acid production 253
    glucose transport arrest, hashish 253, 255
    production 138, 145, 234, 250
  secretary, tracheal epithelial 144, 145, *163,* 250
  T-cells 31-32
Cerebrum
  acute reversible damage 88, 247
  frontal polysensory area 100
  radiological examination 83, 246-247
  psychic functional changes 88-89
    mental disorganization 90

Chelation, cannabinoids in urine 10, 241
Chemical properties of cannabis
  cannabinoid analysis 8-10, 13
  chemical composition 3, 7-8, 13, 240
  detection methods 8-10, 13, 241
  smoke condensate 37
Cholesterol
  steroidal hormone synthesis 60
    inhibition 62, 65, 70, 245, 246, 257
  testicular 254, 257
  unavailability 71, 245, 254, 257
    glucose utilization decrease 257
Chromatin
  alteration (transcriptional arrest) 39, 45, 243
  composition 38-39, 63, 243
  condensation 64, 245
  DNA synthesis impairment 38
Chromatography of cannabinoids, 180
  comparison of methods
    gas (GC) 9, 13
    gas-liquid (GLC) 8-9, 13, 241
    high pressure liquid (HPLC) 9, 13, 241
    thin layer (TLC) 3, 10, 13, 241
Chromosomes
  cytogenetic studies 31, 34-37
  DNA, content post smoke exposure (marihuana, tobacco) 36-37, *49*
    synthesis impairment 38
  gluconeogenesis effect 257
  macromolecular synthesis impairment 38, 45, 260
  mitotic abnormalities due to smoke (marihuana, tobacco) 36, 45
  normal 30
  pathological aberrations 30-31
  proteins, chromosomal 38-39, 243
  rearrangement in male 69-70, 72, 246
  sex 30, 31
    chromosomal complex
      XX (female) 60
      XY (male) 60
        alteration 61, 69
  structural abnormalities due to marihuana 4, 34-38, 45, *49,* 242-243
    ganja 234, 238
    hashish 35, 45
  THC, chromosomal mutagen 36, 45
Chronic effects
  brain function 4, 82-87, 104, *108, 111, 112,* 246-247
  cardiovascular 5, 171-173, 183, *210-215,* 251
  cell metabolism 4, 37-39, 45-46, 50-55, 242-243
  chromosomal 4, 34-37, 45, *49,* 242
  dependence 5, 102-104, 105, *249*
  endocrinological 4, 61-71, *71-72, 74-80,* 245-246
  immunological 4, 39-45, 46, *56-58,* 243-245
  psychiatric 4, 87-99, 104, *113, 114, 117, 118, 119,* 247-248
  psychomotor function 5, 99-102, 104, *115, 120, 121,* 249
  pulmonary 5, 138-141, 145, *153-155,* 250
  tolerance 5, 102-104, 105, *122-127,* 249
Clinical effects, short summary

acute effects **4**
chronic effects **4-5**
Clinical studies with cannabinoids
  alveolar macrophage function **44-45**
  analgesic efficacy, THC **87**
  antianxiety property **93-94**
  behaviour, aggressive **96-97**
    performance **94**
  brain, EEG characteristics **84-87**, *108, 111, 112*
    gross pathology **82-84**
    motivation **93**
    psychiatric assessment **89-91**
  cardiovascular effects, acute **164-166**, *189-194, 196-199*
    adrenergic mechanisms **166-170**, **173**, *200, 201, 203-206, 208, 209*
    cardiac toxicity **174-178**, *217, 218*
    chronic effects **171-173**, *210-215*
    CNS sympathetic control **182, 231**
    in glaucoma patients **165**, *196-199*
    interactions **178-181**, *219-223, 225*
  cell metabolism **38**
    in nuclear area **39**
  chronic canabis use, healthy, field studies **233-239**
  female reproductive function **65, 67, 71**
    prenatal marihuana use **71**
  genetic (chromosomal) effects **34-36**, *49*
  glucose tolerance **254**, *265, 268, 269*
  immunological competence **39-41**, *56, 57*
  male reproductive function **61-64**, *74, 75*
  peripheral nerve conduction **87**
  pharmacokinetic studies **8-13**, *18-26*, **164**, *241-242*
  psychomotor function **99-102**
    visual function **101, 166**
      pupil size **166**
  pulmonary function, acute effects **137**, *151, 152*
    chronic effects **138-141**, *153-155*
  tolerance development **102, 103**, *122, 123, 125*
CNS (central nervous system) effects (see Brain)
  activity alteration **82**
  behavioural changes, THC **68, 71, 82**
  CO effects **129**, **146**, **250**
  depressant **146**
  EEG changes in offspring **70**
  inhibition, THC **68**
  pathological organic response **88-91**, **247**
  prenatal marihuana effects **71, 258**
  subcellular cannabinoid distribution **253**
  sympathetic CVS control **181-182**, *227-232*, **253**
  teratogens **70-71**
CO (carbon monoxide)
  chronic anoxia **146**
  conditions lower threshold to CO effects **167**, **185, 251**
  CVS effects **167**, **183-185, 187, 251**
  fetocidal effect **68**
  marihuana smoke vs placebo **139, 142, 174**, **253, 258**
  passive exposure **185, 251**

poisoning **99**, 129
tobacco smoke 129
  vs marihuana **134, 142, 145**
  during pregnancy 132
Cognition
  alteration 82, 85, **92, 94, 99**, 101, 102, 249
    in anginal patients, onset, duration **176**, 185
  tolerance **103**
COHb (carboxyhemoglobin) 174
  CVS effects **167**, 183, 185, 251
  hypoxia 182, 253, 258
  placebo 174-176
  plasma level 68, **139**
  smoke
    dosage, marihuana vs placebo, lethality **139, 142**
    inhalation tobacco 129
      clinical symptoms 129
      vs marihuana 142, 145, 170, 175
      maternal, fetal 132
Colchicine 31
Cold sensation, in glaucoma patients 165
Concentration (mental) impairment 4, **89**, 90, 92, 101, **102**, 180, 181, 248, 249
  ganja 234
Conception, hormonal maintenance 61
Confusion, mental 89, 247, 248
  inadequate glucose **255**
Conjunctiva, congested (red) (see Eye)
Consciousness
  alteration 99
    ammonia blood levels **257**
  loss **83**, 183, 186, 250
    inadequate glucose **255**
  THC and oxymorphone **179**, *224*
Convulsions, inadequate glucose 255
Coordination impairment **94**, 101
Cough, bronchogenic carcinoma 131, 145, 250
  chronic cannabis use **138**, 145, 250
CVS (cardiovascular system) effects (see Heart, Blood pressure, Hb)
  acute effects **164-166**, *189-194, 196-199*
  adrenergic mechanisms **166-170**, 186, *200, 201, 203-206, 208, 209* 253
    pharmacological agents influence **167**, **173**, 185, 253
    reflex vascular response/stress **166-167**
    β-adrenergic mechanisms **167, 180**, 186
  chronic effects **171-173**, 183, *210-215*, 238, 251
  CO_2 response **179**
    THC and oxymorphone/pentobarbital **179-180**
  disease, tobacco 129, 132
  function in coronary artery disease **174-176**
    hemodynamic effects **175-176**
    psychophysiological CVS function **176**, 185
  marihuana and alcohol 259
  stress and systemic cannabinols **178-179**, 185, *219-223*
  studies 182
  undersirable responses **167**, **179**, 185, *223*
  vasodilation **102, 167**, 182, 184, 186, 187, 238, 250, 253, **258**, 260, 261
    shock 131, **186**

Dependence
  EEG activity **86**
  metabolic basis **260**
  physical (physiological) 5, **93, 102,** 260
    ganja users **234,** 238
    hashish users **236,** 238
    onset **103,** 105, 249
  psychological 5, **102, 103,** 105, 249
    ganja users **234,** 238
    psychic discomfort **93**
  regular cannabis users **99,** 248
  types **102, 256**
Depersonalization
  marihuana use, chronic **90**
    post use and stress **91**
    vs temporal lobe epilepsy **97**
  psychopathology **86**
  THC and stress **88**
  toxic psychosis 85, **89**
Depression, marihuana 92
Derivatives for
  antibody production **12**
  cell metabolic studies **37, 38,** *50-55*
  chelation **10**
  gastrointestinal absorption of oral THC **169,** *207*
  GC-MS **9**
  intraocular pressure **259,** *277*
  maternal milk **66,** *80*
  metabolic tolerance studies **12**
  systemic availability **12**
  THC interaction with vehicles **180,** *226*
  tissue distribution studies **11, 82**
Detection techniques for
  atherosclerosis
    coronary arteriography (angiography) **174, 178**
    left ventricular cineangiography **178**
  brain damage 83
    CTT (computerized transaxial tomography) **83,** 247
    echoencephalography **83,** 247
    pneumoencephalography **83,** 246
  cannabinoids **8-10,** 13, 241
    chelation **10,** 241
    chromatography 181
      GC **9,** 13
      GLC-MS **8-9,** 13, *18,* 241
        and MID **9,** 13, *19,* 241
      HPLC **9,** 13, 241
      TLC 3, **10,** 13, 241
    immunoassay
      EMIT **10,** 12, 13, *21,* 241
      RIA 3, **9,** 13, 99, 241
Diagnosis
  cannabis use **99**
    differential diagnosis **259**
    excessive use **138**
  EEG changes **177**
  hashish use **138**
Diarrhea 259
Diseases
  autoimmune 31, 34, **42, 46**
  chronic, pulmonary, cardiovascular 260
  CNS, cerebral metabolic disorder 255

  diathesis **84**
  gene-environmental interaction 31
  hereditary transmission 31
  hypersensitivity 33-34
  immunodeficiency 31-33
  liability genes 31
  mental 87
    endorphin levels **256**
  metabolic, diabetes mellitus 256
  organic brain **88-99**
  resistance to (susceptibility) 31, **44,** 46
  rhinopharyngitis **89, 138**
  T-cell impairment **38-39**
Distribution of cannabinoids
  autoradiographic studies **11,** 82
  post chronic dosing **11,** 241
  cytogenetic studies 31, **34-37**
  in plant **7-8,** 240
  in rodents 11
  THC and metabolites **8, 12,** 241
  in tissues **8, 11,-13, 66,** 241
    CNS **82**
    correlation with plasma concentration **11,** 242
    maternal and fetal tissues **66**
Diuresis 65, 237, 238, 257, 258
Dizziness
  ganja 233, 238
  hashish 235, 238
  inadequate glucose 255
  marihuana 101, 104, 236, 249, 251
  THC 180
DNA (deoxyribonucleic acid)
  content, THC effect on 36
  normal function 30
  nucleosomes 38
  replication, marihuana effect on 35
  synthesis impairment **36-38,** 45, *49, 52,* 242, 243
    due to aspirin, caffeine 38
    in Lewis lung, L1210 leukemic cells **42, 43**
Driving, cannabis effects on
  accidents 3
  cannabinoid fluid levels 3, 10, 13, 242
  combined with other drugs 3
  drugs in fatally injured **102,** *122*
  impairment **100,** 104, 105, 249
  legal constraints 3, 13
  process **100**
  THC, sobriety test **101**
Drowsiness 2, 4, 69, 84, 86, 247
  EEG wave frequency **86,** 247
  in glaucoma patients **165**
  hashish 235
  THC **180**
Dry mouth
  cannabis intoxication 90
  hashish effect 235, 238
  marihuana effect 101, 237, 238, 257
  THC 180
Dysarthria, cannabis, high dose **235**
Dysphoria
  acute intoxication **99**
  chronic use **84,** 105, 247, 249
  in naive **181,** 183

psychopathology **86**
THC, analgesia 87
    oral, in various vehicles **181**, 185
    and stress **87**, 179
    test for depression **85**
Dyspnea, chronic cannabis use **138**

ECG (electrocardiogram)
  abnormalities, differential diagnosis **177**, 185
  cardiomyopathy, Jamaican field study **234**
  changes, marihuana smoking **166-167**, 177, 184, 251
    anginal onset **175**
  CO gas exposure **167**, 184-185, 251
  myocardial infarction, marihuana and tobacco **178**, 185
  non-users **177**, 184
  THC
    IV, cardiac patients **177-178**
      surgical premedication **179**
    oral, acute **177**, 184, *217*
      chronic **173**, 184
Edema
  CO poisoning **129**
  pulmonary **145**, 178, 185, **258**
  smoke 131
  uvular **138**, *153*
EEG (electroencephalography; brain activity)
  abnormalities, ammonia blood level 257
  cannabis effects 4, **84**, 90, 238, 248
    in ganja users 234
    in hashish users 235, 238
    in marihuana users 237
    profile **84**, 104, 247
    psychosis 97
  characteristics,
    psychopathological **86**, *111*
    psychophysiological (pre-drug) **86**, *112*
  organic brain disease **84**
  sleep pattern **84**, *108*, 247
  type
    depth (within brain) **84-86**
    intracranial (brain surface) **84**
    scalp **84**, 86
      profile **84**
  use **84**
  vigilance **84**, 247
Embryo
  cell differentiation 67
  embryotoxicity **67-69**, 71, 72, 246
  gonad 60
  outgrowth 66
EMIT immunoassay, screening for cannabinoids **10**, *21*, 241
Emotion(al)
  acute toxic response
    acute panic anxiety **87**, 104, 247
      hashish and alcohol **89**
    recurrence 90
    toxic delirium **88**, 247, 248
      hashish and alcohol **89**
    transient mild paranoia **88**, 247
  alteration **85**, 93, 104, 247, 248
    permanent irreversible **86**
  depth EEG acitvity **85-86**, 247

immaturity **97**
unstable **89**, 247
Emphysema
  α_1-antitrypsin **131**, **146**, 250
  mediastinal **133**, 144
  pulmonary 5, **138-139**, 145, 250
    alveolar macrophage functional impairment **142**, 146, 250, 253
    ECG changes **184**
Endocrine (see Hormones)
  cannabis effects **67**, 70, 245-246
  hormones
    hypothalamic 60-61, 65, 245
    ovarian 61, 246
    pituitary 60-64, *74, 75*, 245-246
    placental 61
    testicular 60-64, *74*, 245-246
    thyroid 67
  reproductive functional impairment 4, **61-72**, *74-80*, 245-246, 260
Endorphin (β)
  basic mechanism, addiction **260**
  deficiency, withdrawal **256**
  food intake **257**
  inborn levels **256**, **260**
  pain relief 237
  pro-opiocortin disruption **255**
  THC release 104
Enkephalins, pro-opiocortin disruption **255**
Enterohepatic recirculation of biliary metabolites **12**, 13, 241
Enzymes
  AHH, pulmonary **133**, 144, *148*, 249
  alkaline phosphatase **254**
  α_1-antitrypsin 131, 146, 250
  cholesterol esterase inhibition 62, **65**, **70**, 245, 246
  glutamate dehydrogenase **254**
  hepatic microsomal oxygenase 11
    liver, increase **234**, 238
  liver **254**
  muscle **259**
  phosphorylase, synthetase **254**
  proteolytic (leukocytic) **131**, 146
  serum, M.I. **178**
  synthesis impairment 242
Epileptics
  anterior temporal focus **95**, 248
    vs marihuana intoxication **97**
Epinephrine (sympathomimetic)
  ACTH, secretion **254**
    release 255
  ECG changes **184**
  effect on cannabis CVS effects **167**, 183, 185
  premedication caution in users **167**
  pulmonary edema **178**, 258
  release, nicotine **167**, 183, 251
  urinary excretion, oral THC **169**, 185
Estrogens (female sex hormones)
  alteration **65**, **67**, 71
  biosynthesis 60
    inhibition **66**, 257
  detection, RIA 61
  function 61
  metabolism 61

prolactin post estradiol, THC in males **64, 75**
  in pubertal development 61
  secretion 61
Euphoria (subjective "high"; psychological effect)
  acute intoxication **99**, 177
  chronic ganja **234**, 238
  correlation with
    conjunctival congestion **181**
    EEG changes 235
    HR **165, 181**, 183, *194, 226* 235, 251
    plasma THC **9, 164, 165, 181**, *194, 226,* 242,
      251
  dose-response **82, 84**, 165
  functional disruption **103**
  hashish **235-236**, 238
  "high" 2, 4, *9-11, 23, 25, 93,* **100, 101,** 104,
    137, 145, 165, 241-242, 251
  marihuana and propanolol **259**, *275*
  peak, duration 101, **166**, 179, *221*
    plasma cannabinoids **181**, *226*
  psychopathology **86**
  THC 180
    brain distribution **82**
    oral in various vehicles **181**, 185, *226*
  with 11-OH-THC 11, *23, 25*
  tolerance development **102**, *122,* **164**, 183,
    191, 247, 251
    cross, smoking vs oral **173**
    heavy vs light users **103**, *127,* **164**, *191*
      onset **165**
Exercise
  circulatory response, oral THC **173**, *215*
  ECG changes, marihuana, healthy **177**
    passive, tobacco, angina 184
  performance, marihuana, healthy **174**, 185,
    217, 218, 251
    in coronary artery disease **174-176**, 185,
      251
      vs nicotine **175**
        passive smoke exposure **175**
      vs placebo **175**
  ganja 234
Eye (see Vision)
  burning, THC **180**
  intraocular pressure effects 4
    cannabinoid derivatives vs THC **259-260**,
      277
      β-adrenergic antagonism 259-260
    in glaucoma **165**, 185, *196, 198, 199,* 251
  optic nerve 251, 185
  ptosis, in glaucoma patients **165**
  pupil, constriction 4, **101, 166**, 185, 251
    vs alcohol **166**
    dilation **90**, 236
  reddening (conjunctival hyperemia) 4, 9, 13,
    90, 99, 100, 101, 102, 186, 237, 242, 249
    correlation with, "high" **181**, 251
      plasma THC **9, 164**, 183, 242, 251
    diagnostic sign **9, 99, 164, 174,** 183
    dose response **165**, *192,* 251
    in glaucoma patients **165**
    marihuana, and alcohol **259**
      and propanolol **259**, *274*
      propanolol influence **170**, 183

Fat, accumulation THC in 3, **11-13**, 66, 241
  ketone bodies **258**
  metabolites in **12**
  stress effects 3
Feces, excretion
  cannabinoid **11**, 12, 241
  metabolite **11-13**, 241
  THC, suckling animal infants **11**, 241
Female (see Maternal)
  castration 61
  hormonal imbalance 60-61
  hypothalamic-pituitary-ovarian axis 61
  offspring, performance impairment **68**
  pituitary-adrenal axis 65
Fertility 4, 71
  abnormal ovarian function 61, **65**
  female infertility **65**, 246
  male **69-70**, 246
    fertilizing capacity of sperm **63-64**, 246
Fetus (prenatal)
  development 67
  EEG changes **66**
  HR changes **66**, 79, 246
  mortality, acidosis **258**
  placental drug transfer **66**, 246
  testosterone, excess 60
  THC in tissues **66**, 246
  tobacco smoking 132
  toxicity 4, **67-71**, 72, 246
Field studies in
  Costa Rica (marihuana)
    chronic effects **236-237**, 237-239
    medicinal use **236**, 237
  Egypt, psychological effects **92**
  Greece (hashish)
    chronic effects **235-236**, 237-239
      acute cannabis effects in chronic users
        235-236
      tolerance, withdrawal **236**
  India
    cannabis psychosis **89-90**, 97
    respiratory disorders **138**
  Jamaica (ganja)
    clinical assessment, chronic healthy **233-
      235**, 237-239
    medicinal use, **234**, 237
  Thailand, marihuana psychosis 89, 104, 247
  West Germany, medical, psychiatric assess-
    ment **89**, 104, 247
  respiratory problems **138-139**, 145, 250
Fingertip washings, cannabinoids in **10**, 241
Flashbacks
  cannabis induced 4, 90, **91**, 104, 248
  etiology 248
Flying, marihuana effect **101-102**, 104, *120-121,*
  249
FSH (follicle stimulating hormone)
  hypothalamic catecholamine influence **257**
  marihuana (THC) effects 254
    in females **65**, 77, 246
      pregnant, lactating 67
    in males **61-62, 67, 69**, 71, 245
      pubertal arrest **63**
  normal function 60-61

Gas chromatography-mass spectrometry (GC-MS)
  plasma (fluorinated) CBD **9**
  tetrahydro CBD as internal standard 9
Gas-liquid chromatography-mass spectrometry (GLC-MS)
  for cannabinoid identification **8-9**, 13, 241
  plasma
    CBN **9**, *18*
    THC **9**, 10, *18*
    11-OH-THC **9**, *18*
Genetics
  gene expression impairment **38-39**, 243
  immunodeficiency diseases 32
  marihuana effects **34-37**, 38, *49*
  modification, pathological 30-31
  normal 30
Geographical variation
  cannabinoid biogenesis 8
  in plant growth 8
  origin determination 8, 10
Glaucoma (ocular hypertension)
  intraocular pressure effects **165**, 185, *196, 198, 199*, 251
    onset, peak, duration (smoking) **165**, 185, *196*
    with postural hypotension 185
      good vs diseased eye **165**, *198, 199*
  pupil size **166**, 185, 251
Gluconeogenesis, amine metabolic disruption **257**
    blood ammonia levels **254**, 255, 257, *264, 267*
Glucose, cannabinoid effect on
  altered blood glucose control **255-259**
    pseudo-diabetic state **259**
  blood glucose, insulin, ammonia **254**, 255, *263-267*
  consumption by lymphocytes **38**, *52*, 243, **253**
  diabetes mellitus aggravation 255, **259**
    diabetic acidosis **258**
  glucose
    tolerance 237, 238, **254**, 255, 265, 268, 270
    transport arrest **253**, 255
  hyperglycemia **254**, 259, *263*
  nicotine effect **167**, 183
  poisoning, resin **88**, 247, **255**,
  THC effect on insulin-induced hypoglycemia **255**, *273*
  tolerance, insulin response **102**, *124*
  utilization defect 84, 247, **253-255**, 257-260
    urinary loss 257
Glycogen, gluconeogenesis **257**
  glycogenolysis **254**, 255, *263*
    during fasting **254-255**
  stores 71, 255, 259, 260
  uterine, cannabis effect **254**
Glycolysis
  anaerobic **71**
  hashish resin effects **253**
  impairment, alveolar macrophages 142, 146, 250, **255**
Gonadotropins (see Hormones)
Growth
  androgens, normal 60

cell
  abnormal **36-37**, 45, 242
  malignant transformation, 37, 45, 245
  rate **38**, 55, 243, 253
FAS (fetal alcohol syndrome) **258**
hormone **254**, 255, 269, *271*
  hypoglycemic (insulin-induced) response **255**, *273*
    diabetogenic effect **257**
  nitrogen retention 257
  release, opioid peptides 256-257
  tolerance, insulin response **102**, *124*
intrauterine **71**
puberty
  delayed onset (arrest) **62-63**, 72, 246, 257
  onset, male 60
    female 61
rate, alteration 68, 139
retardation **69**
thyroid hormones 67
tumor **42-43**
Gynecomastia
  adolescence, normal 64
  causes 64
  idiopathic 64
  marihuana (THC) induced **64**, *75*, 246
  prolactin, plasma 62, **64**, *75*, 246

Hallucinations
  chronic cannabis use **97**
    vs temporal lobe epilepsy, 97
  ganja **234**, 238
  hashish **89**, 235-236
  limbic epilepsy **85**
  in perceptual areas, 90
  sensory relay nuclei, EEG **86**, 247
  THC, and pentobarbital **79**
    in various vehicles **181**
  toxic delirium **88**
  visual 89, **91**
    and auditory **90**
    EEG **86-87**, *111, 112*
Hashish
  allergic response **44**, 244
  blood, ammonia, urea 254
    lactic acid 254, *272*
  brain, gross pathology **83**, 246-247
  chromosomal effects **35**, 45, 242
  chronic use, field study **235-236**
  glucose transport arrest **253**
  glycolysis alteration 253
  hash throat 89, **138**
  hashaholic 89, **138**
  during lactation 68
  morphological airway response **138-139**, 145
  performance impairment **92**
  phospholipid effects **37**
  potency 2, 83, **89**, 92, 133, 138, 238, 253
  psychological dependence **103**
  psychosis 247
  from resin **2**, 40, 133
  respiratory effects **138**, *153*
  spermatogenesis impairment **63**
  sucrose preference **257**

water pipe 83, 92, **133**, 238
Hb (hemoglobin)
  coronary artery disease **175**
  decreased, functional anemia **173**, 183, 187,
    216, 237, 238, 251, 253, 261
    ECG changes 184, 185
  ECG changes, functional anemia **177**
  hypoxemic effect **138, 234**, 250
  THC, oral, chronic effect **173**, *216*
  tolerance **102**, *123*
Headache
  cannabis cessation **89**
  frontal and temporal **87**
  marihuana 236, 238
Health aspects of marihuana
  in anginal patients 185
  chronic healthy users in natural setting **233-
    239**, 261
  controversy 3
  legal constraints 3
  physical health **93, 97**
Hearing, auditory signal detection 4, **101**, 104,
  249
Heart (see Cardiac, Myocardium, Tachycardia)
  cardiac, contractilily 171-172, *211*
    output 85, **164**, 170, **171**, 184, *210, 211*
      tolerance development **171-172**, *211*
  CO_2 tension effects 130
  cor pulmonale 130, **140**, 145, 250
  disease, plasma lipids 257
  ECG changes **166-167, 173, 177**, 184, 251
  inotropic (THC) effect 164, 184
  left ventricular function **168, 169, 170-172**,
    184, *202, 203, 208, 209, 211*
    chronic effects **171-172**, *210, 211*
  rate 9-11, *23, 26*, 83, 84, 86, 100, 102, 137,
    145, **164**, 169, 170, **175, 177**, 184, 186, 187,
    208, 209, 235, 236, 238, 247, 249, 251, 260
    in cardiac patients **178**, 185
    changes with varied postures **168**, *200*
    chronic effects **171-173**, *210-215*
    CO_2 response **179**
      THC effect **180**
    correlation with plasma THC, "high" **165**,
      183, *194*, 236, 251
    dose response **165, 176, 179**, 183, *193, 220*
    duration **176, 179**, 183, *220*
    exercise, performance 174, 185, *217, 218*
      coronary artery disease **174-175**, 185
        vs nicotine **175**, 185
    in glaucoma patients **165**, 185
      onset, peak, duration (smoking) **165**, 185,
        196
      with postural hypotension **165**, 185, *198,
        199*
    marihuana and propanolol 259, *274*
    peak time **166, 176, 179**, 183, *220, 221*
    propanolo! influence **169, 170, 181**, 185, *209*
    psychological state **177**, 183, 251
    smokers vs nonsmokers **179**, 223
    vs tobacco **142**, 145, **166**
    THC, vs diazepam 179, *220*
      and oxymorphone/pentobarbital **179-180**,
        225
      and stress 185
  time course, THC **179, 181**, *221, 226*

tolerance development **102**, *123*, 145, **164**,
  171, 172, 183, *189*, **211**, *212*, 236, 247,
  251
  heavy vs light users **103**, *126*, **164**, 176,
    183, *190*
  onset **165**, 183
smoking effects **167**, 183
stroke volume **171, 184**, *210, 211*
THC and metabolites in 13, *241*
Hemp
  allergic response **44**
  plant 2, 3, 133
  toxic delirium, psychosis **88**
  use 2
"High" (see Euphoria)
High pressure liquid chromatography-mass spectrometry (HPLC-MS)
  THC in human specimens 9, 13, *241*
Hippocampus
  chemical property **85**
  memory formation **85**, *109*
  paranoid states **85**, 104
  sclerosis **85**
  THC effect **85**
Histology, pathological
  brain tissue **86**, 247
  chromosomes **34-37**, 45, *242*
  mitochondria in sperm **37**, 45, *242*
Histones (chromosomal proteins)
  in chronic hashish users, sperm **63**, 245
  composition **63**
  function **38**, 243
    alterations **38-39**, 243
  in lymphocytes **63**
  metabolic disturbance **64**, 245
  in oligospermic patients **63**, 245
Hormones
  adrenal
    cortex, corticosterone secretion **254**
      cortisol hypoglycemic response **255**, *273*
    imbalance 71, 72, 85, 237, 245, 247, **254**
      aggression **95**, 248
  hypothalamic
    LHRH, in females 61, **65**, 246
      in males 60, 245
    measurement, RIA 60, 61, 67
  pancreas
    blood glucose control **255-256**
    glucagon 256
      GH stimulation 257
    insulin, during fasting **254**
      hypoglycemic effects pre and post THC
        255, *273*
      plasma level **254**, *264, 266, 268*
      response to glucose load **254**, *266, 268,
        270*
  pituitary, anterior
    ACTH (corticotropin, adrenocorticotropic
      hormone)
      release 255, 256
      secretary stimulation **65, 254**
    fetal **70**
    gonadotropins
      FSH (follicle stimulating hormone) 254
        in female 61

alterations **65, 67,** 77, 246
hypothalamic catecholamine influence
257
in male 60
alterations 60, **63,** 66, **67, 69,** 71, 245
inhibition **71**
LH (luteinizing hormone) 254
in female 61
alterations **65, 67,** *76, 78*
hypothalamic catecholamine influence
257
in male (ICSH interstitial cell stimulating hormone) 60
alterations 60-61 **62, 63,** 66, 67, 69,
71, 74, 245
release, opioid peptides **256-257**
naloxone effects **257**
in oligospermic patients **63**
GH (growth hormone) **254,** 255, *269, 271*
hypoglycemic (insulin-induced) response
255, *273*
diabetogenic effect **257**
nitrogen retention **257**
release opioid peptides 256-257
naloxone effect **257**
tolerance, insulin response **102,** *124*
prolactin 62, **64, 65,** *75,* 246
release, opioid peptides **256-257**
naloxone effect **257**
pituitary, posterior
vasopressin (ADH, pressor)
release, opioid peptides 257
reproductive
immunological maturation **42,** 244
placental; fertilized ovum
HCG (human chorionic gonadotropin)
with marihuana 61, **62,** 245
regulation 61
ovarian
estrogens
alteration 67, 71, 254
cholesterol unavailability 257
biosynthesis, regulation 60, 61
excretion (male, female) 61
progesterone
alteration **65,** 71, 246
cholesterol unavailability 257
biosynthesis; regulation 60, 61
regulation and synthesis 60
testicular (testosterone)
alteration **61-62,** 63, 254
cholesterol unavailability 257
in autoimmune process **42,** 46, 244
biosynthesis; regulation 60
thyroid
triiodothyronine (T3) alteration **67,** 254
thyroxine (T4) alteration **67,** 254
Human
aggressive behaviour **96-97**
alveolar macrophage functional study **44-45**
brain,
EEG,
depth, altered emotion 85
scalp, psychopathology **86**

sleep pattern **84-85**
gross pathology **83**
motivation 93
psychiatric evaluation **89-91**
cannabinoid, blood levels **9-13,** *18-20, 22, 24,*
99, *117,* 164, 241-242
urinary levels **9-10,** *20-21,* 99, *116,* 241
cardiovascular effects, acute **164-166,** *189-*
194, 196-199
adrenergic mechanisms **166-170,** *173, 200,*
201, 203-206, 208, 209
cardiac toxicity **174-178,** *217, 218*
chronic effects **171-173,** *210-215*
CNS sympathetic control **182,** *231*
in glaucoma patients **165,** *196-199*
interactions **178-181,** *219-223, 225*
cell metabolism **37-39**
clinical assessment, chronic use, healthy **233-**
239
cytogenetic studies 31, **34-36**
diagnosis of marihuana allergy **44**
dose response **10,** 13
glucose tolerance **254,** *265, 268, 269*
hypersensitivity reaction **43-44**
immune system effects **39-41**
immunological tests **33-34**
ovulatory effects **65**
performance tests **94**
peripheral nerves, conduction studies **87**
physical dependence, onset **103**
prenatal marihuana use **71**
psychomotor function **94,** *99-102, 115, 120,*
121
visual function **101, 166**
pupil size **166**
pulmonary function, acute effects **137,** *151*
chronic effects **138-141,** *153-155*
ventilatory response **137,** *152*
serum prolactin **64,** *75*
spermatogenesis **63**
testosterone levels **61-62**
THC, vs LSD **102**
in maternal milk **67**
tolerance development **102, 103,** *122, 123, 125*
tranquilizing effect **93-94**
Hydroxy(11)-THC (11-OH-THC)
analgesia 11, *241*
bone marrow myelopoiesis inhibition **43,** 244
in brain **12,** *27,* 241
cell growth impairment **38,** *243*
DNA synthesis inhibition **43**
fecal excretion **11, 12,** *13,* 241
interaction with CBD **12,** *13,* 241
in liver **11,** *241*
in maternal milk **67,** 246
pharmacological properties **11,** *13,* 241
plasma, clearance **11,** *24,* 241
half-life **179**
level, post inhalation **12,** *13,* 67
post intraventricular (brain) **12,** *27*
post IV THC **9,** *12, 13, 18,* 241
post IV 11-OH-THC **11,** *24*
post p.o. **12,** *13*
in pregnant urine **69**

psychological effect **11**, *23, 25,* 241
  serum prolaction **64**, 75
  tachycardia **11**, *23, 26*
  testosterone synthesis inhibition **62**
Hypercapnia, respiratory acidosis (failure) 130
Hypersensitivity reactions
  allergy (immediate type) 31, 33, **43-44**, 46, 244
    diagnostic tests **44**, 244
  antigen-antibody complex 33
  delayed (tuberculin type) (DTH) 34
    alteration **41**
    skin tests 33
      in marihuana users **39**
  drug 34
  hemolytic anemias (cytotoxic) 33
Hypoglycemia, infants, asphixia **71**
Hypothalamus, cannabinoid effect in
  behaviour, feeding **95**
    rage **95**
  females **65-66**, 71
  fetus **70**
  males **61-62**, 71
Hypoxemia
  acute respiratory distress syndrome 130
  bronchial asthma 130
  cannabis smoke irritation **140**, 146, 250
  chronic 146
  crude marihuana extract **259**
  pulmonary hypertension 145, 250
Hypoxia
  COHb, maternal, fetal 132
  cor pulmonale 130
    marihuana induced **140**, 145, 250
  CVS effects **167, 174,** 183, 185, 251
  functional,
    bone marrow RBC production **138**, 145, 234, 238
    ganja **138**, 145, 234, 238
  ischemic 182
  marihuana smoking **253, 258**, 260
  myocardial 131, 184, 185, 251

Immunization, with THC-protein-conjugate **12**, 241
Immunoassay for cannabinoids
  homogeneous enzyme (EMIT) **10**, 12, 13, 241
  radio (RIA) 3, **9**, 13, 241
Immunodeficiency diseases
  associated clinical features 47
  classification 47
  malignancy risk 31
  non-specific 32
  primary 32
  physiological 32
  secondary 32, 245
  specific 32
Immunoglobulins (Ig)
  IgA 41, **44**
  IgC **41**
  IgE 33, **40**
  IgG 31, 32, **41, 44**, 244
  IgM 31, **41, 44**, 244
Immunology
  development 32
  gluconeogenesis effect 257

hypersensitivity (pathological) reaction 31-32, **33-34**
immune response decrease due to
  marihuana **38**, 63, 243-245, 260
  T-cell impairment **38**, 243-245
immunity
  cellular (T-cell) **31-32** 41, 42
  humoral (B-cell) **31-32, 40-42**, 44
  immunodeficiency diseases 31-33
    malignancy risk 31
  immunosuppressants 34
  normal function 31-32, 46, 64
Immunosuppressants 34, 41, 42
  chemical and viral carcinogens 34
  stress 34, 46
Impairment
  brain function **87-98**
    psychic phenomenon 105
  clincal 3
  gene expression **38-39**, 243
  neurological function 82
  psychomotor 3, 82, **99-102**
  reproductive **71**
  stance stability 165
  visual function **101**, 166
In-vitro experiments
  alveolar macrophages **141-142**, 146, *155-157*, 250
  blastogenic response 42
  cell metabolism **37-38**, *50-55*
    cholesterol 257
  cellular immunity test 33, 34
  cytogenetic studies 31, **34-36**, *49*
    lung explant cultures 36, *49*
  immunosuppressive activity **42**
  presence and functional capacity of T and B-cells **39-41**, *56, 57*
  progesterone inhibition 65
  sperm, kinetic morphology 37
  testosterone synthesis **62**
In-vivo experiments (see Animal experiments)
  alveolar macrophages **142**, 146, *157-160*, 250
  Ames test **37, 134**, *150*
  cutaneous delayed hypersensitivity test 33, 34
  cytogenetic studies 31, **34-35**, *49*
  DNA synthesis inhibition (tumor cells) 43
  presence and functional capacity of T and B-cells **39**
  skin allograft survival **42**
Infants
  birth rate, weight **68**, 246
  blood-brain barrier 82
  deaths **68**
    pathological changes **68, 69**
  prenatal marihuana effects **71**, 246, 258
Infarction
  acute myocardial, marihuana and tobacco **178**, 185, 251
  subendocardial, CO gas exposure **167**, 185, 251
    prolonged hypotension 251
Infection
  alveolar macrophage functional impairment 146, 250
  contaminated marihuana, cancer patients **136**, 145, 250

immunological defects 32, 260
   susceptibility **43,** *58*
Inhalation (see Administration, Smoke)
Insulin
   hypoglycemic effects
      ACTH release 255
      pre and post THC **255,** *273*
   plasma level **254,** *264, 266, 268*
      competative inhibition, THC 257
      during fasting 254
      response to glucose load **254,** *266, 268 270*
Interactions of
   CBGM with pentobarbital **8**
   hashish and alcohol **89**
   marihuana and psychotic illness **90-91**
   stress and systemic cannabinols 178-179, *219-223*
   THC, and alcohol **100**
      IV and oxymorphone/pentobarbital **179-180,** *224, 225*
      oral with CBD/CBN **9,** 12, 13, 133, 241-242
      lipoproteins 37
      vehicles 180-181
Irritability
   abstinence **102,** 235, 236, 238, 247, 249
   dysphoric 105
Ischemia (tissue anemia)
   anginal onset **175**
   cerebral 183, 250
   hypoxia 182, 251
   muscle, crude marihuana extract **259**
   myocardial **177,** 185, 251
      ECG changes 184, 185, 251
   smoking effects, CO gas exposure **167**
Isoproterenol (β-adrenergic)
   adequacy of β-blockade **169, 170**
   IV, HR **170**
      PVCs **170,** *209,* 251
   in THC tolerant **173**

Kidney
   CO effect 129
   function, crude marihuana extract **259**
   glomerular function **258**
   THC accumulation in **11,** 241

Laboratory tests
   abnormal **41,** 46, 244
   blood chemistry
      liver 254
      M.I. **178**
   field study,
      Costa Rica **237,** 238
      Jamaica **234,** 238
Lactate, cannabinoid effect on
   excretion by lymphocytes 38, *52,* 253
   hashish, resin effect **253**
   with tobacco, post fasting **254-255,** *272*
Lactation, impairment 65, **68**
   prolactin, plasma 62, **64,** 65, *75*
Laryngitis, vocal cord appearance **138**
Learning, remote vs recent **100,** *118, 119*
Leucine (protein precursor), cannabinoid effects
   on uptake, into
   animal brain cortex slices 8, 13

human diploid fibroblasts (THC) **37,** *51,* 242
   and mouse neuroblastoma cells (THC) **37,** 242
Leukocytes (see Lymphocytes)
   antibacterial activity 64
   chromosomal damage **34-36**
   cultures 34
Leydig cells (testis)
   marihuana with HCG **61, 62,** 245
   testosterone production 60
      cannabinoid inhibition **61-62,** 245
   tissue regression **254**
LH (luteinizing hormone)
   hypothalamic catecholamine influence **257**
   marihuana (THC) effects 254
      in females **65,** 67, *76, 78,* 246
      pregnant, lactating 67
      in males 60-61, **62,** 66, 67, **69, 71,** 74, 245
      pubertal arrest **63**
   normal function 60-61
Limbic cortical system
   behavioural patterns 95, 247
   dysfunction **85- 86,** 104, 247, 248
   function **85,** *109*
   opiate receptors 256
Lipoprotein, binding THC to, 11-13, 241
Liposolubility vs psychotropic effect **38,** *53, 54*
Liver
   blood glucose regulation 255
   cannabinoid metabolism 3, **11-13,** 241-242
   cholesterol esterase inhibition **65**
   CO effect 129
   damage, cannabis **254**
   enzymes, increase 234
   glycogen **254,** 255, 260, *263*
      formation from lactate during fasting 255
      gluconeogenesis **257**
   histological changes 254
   metabolites in **11-13,** 241-242
      inhibition **133**
   palpable 235, 238
   THC, accumulation **11,** 12, 241
      metabolism inhibition **133,** 144, 249
Lungs (see Pulmonary, Respiratory)
   accumulation THC in **11-13, 133,** 241
      metabolites **12, 133,** 241
   bronchodilation, acute effect **137,** 140, *151*
      in asthmatic patients **141**
      partial tolerance **141,** *155*
   bronchogenic carcinoma 131
   cannabinoid absorption 3, 241
   defense function impairment 131
      alveolar macrophage alterations **44-45, 141-143,** 245, 250, 253
   edema 145, 178
   emphysema 90, **138-139,** 145, 250, 253
      ECG changes 184
   fibrosis, paraquat **135-136,** 145, 250
   infection, contaminated marihuana 5, **136,** 145, 250
   morphological response of airway **144,** *163*
   respiratory (rate)
      disorders 97, 130, **138,** 145, 146, 250
         asthmatic wheezing 90

cough 90
  poisoning, resin **88,** 247
tobacco smoke effects 129-131, 250
Lymphocytes
  B-cells 31, 32, **39-42, 44**
  chromosomal alteration **34-36**
  cultures 31 ,34
    metabolic alteration (THC) **38,** *52, 55*
  functional capacity assessment (T-cells) **38**
  hashish users **39,** 243
  lactate excretion **38,** *52*
  lipid changes 37
  marihuana smokers **38,** 243
  patient's, cellular immunity tests 33
  PHA induced blastogenic response **38, 40,** *57*
  rosette formation 31, 33, **39-40**
  T-cells 31, 32, **38-42,** 46, *56, 57*
  THC suppression **42**
  transformation inhibition 8, 33, 38
Lysine
  in lymphocytes **63**
  in spermatic cell nuclei **63,** 245

Macromolecular synthesis, effect on
  CBD 8, 13
  CBG 8, 13
  in cell division **38-39,** 243
  THC 8, 13, **37,** 42, 43, 45, *50, 51, 52*
Macrophages (phagocytes)
  alveolar 141, 253
    bactericidal activity depression **141-142,** 146, *155-160,* 250
    functional study **44-45,** 46
      alterations **44-45,** 46, 245
    impairment (smoke) 4, 131, **142,** *157,* 245, 250, 253, 255
    morphological changes **143-144,** *161, 162,* 250
    normal immunological function 32, 34
  antigen processing 31
  fixed, Kupffer cells in liver **42**
  impairment 33
Maladjustment, heavy use **96,** 248
Male (see Paternal)
  birth weight **68,** 246
  castration 61
  hormonal imbalance **60-62**
    potential implications **62-63,** 246
  hypothalamic-pituitary-testicular axis 60
  offspring, reproductive functional development alteration **70,** 72, 246
Mammary glands
  gynecomastia, THC induced **64,** *75*
  lactation 66
  prolactin, plasma **62, 64, 65,** *75*
Marihuana
  acute effects, alone and with propanolol **259,** *274-276*
  aggressive behaviour **96-98,** 248
    vs alcohol **97,** *117*
  allergic response **43-44,** 46, 244
  alveolar macrophage alterations **44-45, 143,** *161, 162*
    bactericidal activity **141,** *155*
  antigens **40-41, 43-44,** 244

brain, EEG alterations **84-86,** 247
  functional impairment **87-98,** 247
  gross pathology **82-84,** 246-247
  interaction with psychotic illness **90-91**
  motivation **93**
cannabinoids in 2, **8,** 13, 236, 240, 241
  smoked marihuana **10, 133,** 144, 249
  in urine post chronic use **12**
cardiovascular effects, acute **164-166,** 184, *189-194, 196-199,* 251
  adrenergic mechanisms **166-170,** 184, *200, 201, 203-206, 208, 209,* 251
    vascular adjustment interference 183, 251, 253
  cardiac toxicity **174-178,** *217, 218,* 251
  chronic effects **171-172,** *210, 211*
  plasma NE **170**
  premature ventricular contraction **170,** *209*
  tachycardia prolongation **179,** *223,* 251
cell metabolism alteration 4, **39**
chromosomal effects 35, 45, 242
cigarettes 2, 9, 13, 36, 40, 41, 61, 63, 66, 68, 86, 87, 89, 93, 94, 96, 99, 100, 101, 102, 133, 134, 137, 139, 140, 142, 144, 164, 165, 166, 170, 171, 172, 174, 175, 176, 177, 235, 236, 238, 241, 248, 249, 257, 259
  benzpyrene in smoke **37, 133,** 250
  carcinogenic potential **133-134,** *149,* 249-250
  THC content 3, 9, 10, 13, 36, 40, 41, 62, 63, 66, 68, 86, 87, 93, 94, 96, 99, 100, 101, 102, 134, 137, 139, 140, 142, 164, 165, 166, 170, 171, 172, 174, 175, 176, 177, 235, 236-237, 238, 241, 248, 257, 259
  tar content **37, 134,** 145, 249
contamination
  infectious organisms 5, **136,** 145, 250
  paraquat 5, **134-136,** 144, 250
cytotoxic effects **36**
detection 3, 4, **8-10,** 241
  diagnostic 245
DNA synthesis alterations **36**
drug preparation 2
fat retention 3, **11,** 241
hashish 13, 133
health aspects, short summary **3-5**
immune response impairment **38, 39,** 46, 242, 243
intrapulmonary defense effect **142,** *157-160*
maternal and fetal effects **68-69**
metabolic, hormonal alteration **254-255,** *263-273*
  pseudo-diabetes possibility **255**
neurological manifestations **82**
ovarian dysfunction 65
performance **94,** 115
  psychomotor **99-102,** 104, *118-121,* 249
pharmacokinetics **8-13,** *18-24,* 27, 241
pituitary-adrenal axis stimulation **65**
plant 2, **7-8,** 13, *15-17,* 133, 240
possible inheritable alterations post use 47
potency 2, 3, **7,** 13, 240-241
pregnancy suppression, crude extract **65**
prenatal marihuana effects, human **71**
pubertal arrest **63,** 72, 246, 257

pulmonary,
    alveolar macrophage bactericidal activity
        141-142, 146, *155-158, 160*
    function, acute effects **137**, 140, 145, *151,*
        250
        chronic effects **138-141**, *153-155*
    pathology **139**
reproductive function alteration 71
resin 2, 13, 37, **133**, 144
respiratory depression **137**, *152*
sexual function **62**, 246
sperm abnormalities **63**, 245
suspected exposure **9-10**, 13, 241
teratogen **71**
    behavioural 70-71
testicular damage **63**
testosterone levels **61**, 245, 246
THC, in lungs **133**
    in maternal milk **67**
tobacco, combined with **36, 133**, 144, 145, 235,
    249
    myocardial infarction **178**, 251
tolerance development, onset **102**, 105, 249,
    261
    reinforcing (conditioned) property **103**
visual functional impairment **101**, 104
    pupil size **166**
word derviation 2
Mass spectrometry for cannabinoids **8-9**, 13, 181,
    241
    mass fragmentography **9**, 13, 241
    plasma cannabinoid levels
        THC, and CBD/CBN **9**
            post oral intake **9**
            post smoking **9**, *19*
Maternal effects
    anemia **71**
    body weight **68**, 71
    drug ingestion 67
    EEG changes **66**
    HR changes **66**, *79*, 246
    hypotension 258
    reproductive loss **67-68**
    sedation 66
    THC, in milk **66-67**, *80*, 246
        in tissues (maternal, fetal) **66**
Membranes
    phospholipid changes **37**, 45
    psychotropic drugs **38**
    THC effect **38**, 41, 45, 242
    ultrastructural changes (sperm mitochondria)
        37, 242
Memory
    hashish 235
    hippocampus **82, 85, 93**, *109*
    impairment 88, **89**, 92, **93**, 99, 181, 183, 247,
        248
        short term **99-101**
        vs temporal lobe epilepsy 97
    loss 83, **89**
    marihuana and propanolol 259, *276*
    remote vs recent **100**, 104, *118, 119*, 177, 249
    storage deficit **100**, 104, 249
Mental (psychic) changes
    drowsiness 2, 4, **86**, 165, 180, 247

dysfunction 185, 260
euphoria 2, 4, **9-11**, *23, 25*, 241-242
hallucinations 2, **85, 86-87, 91**, *111, 112*, **179,
    181**
Menstrual cycle
    abnormal ovarian function 61
    anovulatory cycle **65**, *78*, 246
    normal 61
    urinary estrogen excretion 61
Metabolism, cannabinoid
    cannabinoid **10-13**, *18-27*, 241-242
    of marihuana 3
    metabolic carbohydrate alteration 254, **255-
        259**, 260, *263-273*
    men vs women **12**, 13
    naive vs chronic user 9
    route comparison **12**
    short summary 3
    Δ⁹THC 3, **12**, 13
Metabolites of cannabis
    accumulation, tissue 3
    analgesia 11
    biliary metabolism **12**
        enterohepatic recirculation **12**, 13, 241
    in brain **12**, *27*
    C-THC 3, **9, 11, 12**, *20*, 241
    DNA synthesis impairment **38**, 243
    elimination half-life **12**
    fecal excretion **11, 12**
    hepatic levels 11
    11-OH (11-hydroxy) **11-12**
    of marihuana 3, **133**, 144, 249
    in maternal milk **67**, 246
    pharmacological activity 9, 241
    polar acids **11, 12**, 13
    psychotomimetic activity 11
    side chain hydroxylation 11, 12, 241
    species differences **11**
    tachycardia 11, 242
    testosterone synthesis inhibition **62**
    11-OH-THC **9, 11, 12, 13**, *18, 27*, 43, 241, 249
        plasma half-life **179**
    tolerance, plasma time course 12
    transformation sites **11**
    urinary **12**, 241
        excretion post IV THC **10, 12**, *21*, 241
        levels **9-10**, *20*, 241
        post passive inhalation **44**
Milk, THC, in animal **11**, 241
    in human **67**, 246
    in primates **66-67**, *80*, 246
Mitochondria, ultrastructural changes **37**, 45, 242
Mitosis
    abnormal
        cannabinoids **36**, 45, 242
        hashish **35**, 45, 242
        smoke **36**
    arrest by colchicine 31
Monkey (see Animal experiments)
    brain, THC,
        function, behaviour **85-86**
        metabolism **12**, *27*, 241
Mood
    changes **82**, 84
    marihuana vs temporal lobe epilepsy **97**

toxic psychosis **85, 89**
Motivation, cannabis effect **92-93**, 235
Mutagenesis via
　cannabinoids **69-70**, 72, 246
　DNA modification **38**, 243
　environmental changes 31
　marihuana 35, **37**, 45
　smoke condensate **37**, 45, **134**, 145, *150*
　THC **36**, 38, 45, 242, 260
Myocardium (see Heart)
　acute infarction **178**, 185, 251
　contractility **171**
　epinephrine effect 184
　ischemia **177**, 185, 251
　　ECG changes **166-167**, **173**, **177**, 184, 251
　O₂, delivery **174-176**, 185
　　vs nicotine **175**
　　demand **174-176**, 182, 184, 185
　　　vs nicotine **175**
　THC and metabolites in **12**, 241

Nausea and vomiting,
　abstinence 184
　diabetic acidosis **258**
　ganja **233**, 238
　hashish **235**, 238
　marihuana **237**, 238, 259
　THC **180**
NE (norepinephrine, sympathomimetic)
　effect on cannabis CVS effects **167**, 183, 185
　plasma level,
　　vs nicotine **170**, 186
　　position change response **170**, 186
　　post smoking **170**, 186
Neonates
　birth weight **68, 70, 71**
　　tobacco effect 132
　deaths **68-69**
　　pathological changes **68**
　HR changes **66**, 246
　hypersensitivity **68**
　meconium staining (fetal distress) **71**
　sedation **66**
　suckling
　　hashish, weight **68**
　　THC and metabolites excretion **66-67**
　THC in tissues **66**
Nerves
　neuropathy 234
　optic nerve 185, 251
　peripheral nerve conduction **87**
　trochlear **87**
Nicotine
　bradycardia **142**
　catecholamine release **129**, 260
　content **133**
　CVS effects **129**, **167**, 183, 251
　　anginal onset, vs marihuana **175**, 251
　　　passive smoke exposure **175**, 251
　　　　PVCs **175**, 184, 251
　　　　in urine **175**
　leukocytosis **258**
　plasma NE, vs marihuana **170**
　PVCs **177**
Nucleic acids

DNA 30, 35, **36-38**, 42, **43**, 45, *49*, *52*, 242,
　253
RNA 30, **37-38**, **43**, 45, *50*, 242
Nucleus
　altered chromatin **39**, 45, 243
　chemical transmitters **86**
　DNA **38**, **63**
　hypoploid metaphases **36**, 45, 242
　nucleoprotein complex 38, **63**, 243
　　testosterone influence **64**
　sensory relay **86**
　spermatic cell alteration **63**
Nystagmus, positional vestibular **101**

Olivetol, hypoploid nuclei **36**, 242
Opiates
　cross tolerance with cannabinoids 105, 249
　endogenous **255-257**
　　cannabis addiction **256**
　opiate-like **84**, 247
　pulmonary edema **178**
　receptors **85**
　respiratory depression tolerance **137**, 250
　vs THC, naloxone precipitated abstinence **104**
　　withdrawal **103**
　withdrawal avoidance 105
Orientation, impairment 99, **102**
Ovary, androgens 60, 61
　corpus luteum, alteration **65**, 69
　　body temperature elevation **61**
　　cholesterol esterase inhibition **65**
　　development 61
　　function 61
　　progesterone secretion 61
　development 60
　estrogen, inhibition **66**
　　metabolism 61
　　plasma binding 61
　　synthesis 60
　functional regulation 61
　　alteration 61, **65**
　hormonal biosynthesis 60
　　imbalance 60, 71
　ovarian follicle, alteration **65**
　　estrogen secretion, excretion 61
　polycystic ovarian disease 61
Ovulation, induction 61
　inhibition **65**, *78*, 246
Ovum (oocyte), fertilized 61
　production 61
　　inhibition **66**, 71
　removal 61

Pain, abdominal 237, 238, 258, 259
　chest **178**
　　angina **185**
　endorphin levels 256
　epigastric **90**
　perception distortion **87**
　relief 237
Pancreas
　blood glucose control **255, 256, 259**
　glucagon **256**
　　GH stimulation **257**
　insulin, fasting **254**

glucose load response **254,** *266, 268, 270*
    plasma level **254,** *264, 266, 268*
    THC, competitive inhibition **257**
        effect on hypoglycemia **255,** 273
Paranoid reaction
    chronic marihuana use **90,** 104
    THC in various vehicles **181**
    toxic, delirium **88**
    psychosis 85, **89-90**
Paraquat (herbicide), action **134-136,** 144, 250
Paternal effects
    offspring, abnormal **68, 70**
    reproductive loss **67-68**
Pathology, cannabinoid induced
    cerebral
        EEG alterations **84-87,** 104, 247-248
        electron microscopy **86,** 247
        gross **82-84**
        psychopathology **87-99,** 104, 247-248
            aggressive behaviour **94-98,** 248
            limbic damage **86,** 104, 247
    pulmonary, alveolar **139**
    sputum cytology **140**
    tracheobronchial biopsies **138-139,** 145
        tracheal epithelium **144,** *163,* 250
Perception
    alteration **99, 101**
    distortion **85,** 90, 92, **100,** 104, 249
        pain **87**
        sensory **100**
    hashish effect **235,** 238
    marihuana vs temporal lobe epilepsy **97**
    stable 82
    time disruption **82,** 85, **88-90,** 92, 93, **99-102,**
        104, 177, 183, **236, 238**
        diagnostic sign **99**
        THC, brain distribution **82**
        oral in various vehicles 181
Performance
    hashish effects **92,** 235-236, 238
    marihuana effects **93, 94,** 100-102, *115, 118-*
        121, 165, 237, 238, 248
        vs alcohol **97**
        and propanolol **259,** *276*
    THC, alone and with alcohol **100,** 249
Peripheral resistance
    CO_2 response **179**
        THC **180**
    marihuana smoking, blood flow **166**
        vs tobacco **166**
    THC effect **164**
        and oxymorphone/pentobarbital **179-180**
Personality
    chronic cannabis use **97**
    disorders 238
    disturbances **89,** 90
    patterns **96,** 235
    prepsychotic **89,** 104, 248
Pharmacokinetics of cannabis **8-13,** *18-24, 27,*
    241-242
Phenylephrine (α-adrenergic) in THC tolerant
    173
Physiology, normal
    blood glucose control **255, 256**

blood pressure (CNS) regulation, animal **182,**
    232
brain **82,** *107*
    cerebral blood flow 255
    limbic system **85,** *109*
eye, aqueous humor **165,** *195*
heart **131,** 182
    inhalation effects **164**
    systolic time interval measurements **168,**
    202
immune system **31-32**
lung **130,** 144
    alveoli **131**
    COHb **129**
    pulmonary antibacterial defense system
        141, 142, 144, *160,*
    inhalation effects **164**
    medical genetics **30**
    reproductive system **60-61**
    standing, cardiovascular adjustment 172, 183
        exercice 173, 183
Phytohemagglutinin (PHA; mitogen) 31, **38, 40,**
    57, 243
Pituitary gland, cannabinoid effect in
    blood glucose control **255, 256**
    endorphin **255-257**
    females **65**
    fetus **70**
    hormones (see Hormones)
    males 61, **62**
    THC, hypophysectomy **258**
Placenta
    drug transfer **66,** 246
    hormonal secretion 61
        excretion, pregnancy 61
    IgG crossing 31
    insufficiency 258
    maternal nutrition 66
    THC, circulation **68,** 72, 246
        concentration **66,** 246
        effects **68,** 246
Plant, marihuana 2
    cannabinoid content **7-8,** *16, 17,* 240
    growth 7, *15*
    other known compounds **8**
    potency 3, **7,** 240
    type 3, **7-8,** 240
    variants **7-8,** 240
Plasma (see Blood)
Polar acids
    excretion **11, 12,** 13
    plasma levels post
        inhalation **12,** 13
        IV **12,** 13
        oral **12,** 13
Potency of cannabis
    variation
        conditions for 3, **7,** 240
        intersample 2, 3
Prefrontal cortex, insight, foresight 85
Pregnancy
    abnormal, incidence **68**
    drug ingestion **67,** 72
    gestation period **71**

labor, type **71**
marihuana use **71**
maternal hypotension 258
  weight **68, 69, 71**
placental, drug transfer **66**
  insufficiency 258
reproductive loss **67-68**
suppression **65, 68**
tobacco smoking 132
Premedication, THC **180**
  vs diazepam **178-179**, *219, 220, 222*
  and oxymorphone/pentobarbital **179-180**,
    224, 225
Progesterone
  alteration **65**, 71, 246
  biosynthesis 60
  inhibition **65**, 66, 257
  secretion 61
Prolactin
  plasma level 62, **64, 65**, 75, 246
  release, opioid peptides **257**
Propanolol (β-adrenergic blocker)
  acute effects, with and without marihuana
    259, *274-276*
  effect on cannabis CVS effects **167, 170**, 185
    left ventricular function, THC **169-170**, 184
  plasma half-life **259**
  in THC tolerant 173
Protamines
  cannabis users **64**, 245
  chronic hashish users **63**, 245
  gluconeogenesis effect **257**
  normal mature spermatozoa **63**, 246
  oligospermic patients **63**, 245
Protein
  chromosomal (histone and non-histone)
    alterations **38-39**, 243
    function **38**, 243
  glycoprotein in secretary cells, tracheal
    epithelium **144**
  immunoglobulins 31-32, 33-34, **40-41, 44**
  Leydig cell 254
  lipoprotein THC binding **11-13**, 45, 241
  normal function 30
  nucleoproteins 63
  synthesis impairment **36-38, 43**, 45, *51, 55*,
    62, **86**, 242, 243, 244, 253, **257, 260**
  total plasma level 41
Psychiatric aspects of marihuana intoxication
  chronic use **88-91**, 97, 238
    ganja **234**, 238
    hashish **235**, 238
  classification **98-99**, 248
  marihuana and stress **91**, 248
Psychodysleptic property (dream-like, delusional) **84**, 104, 247
Psychological effects (see Euphoria)
  acute emotional response **87-88**, 104, 247
  aggressive behaviour **94-98**, 248
  dependence **103**, 105, 249
  dysfunction or psychopathology **97**, 104, 247
  neuropsychological (personality) changes 89,
    90
  prolonged effects,
    non-psychotic **91-94**, 99, 248

psychotic **88-91**, 99, 104, 247-248
tests, ganja users 234
  hashish users **92**, 235
  marihuana, users 248
    in hashish users **235**, 238
  THC, in hashish users **235**
    IV, subjective, vs diazepam **179**
    oral, onset, peak, duration **169**
    variation with vehicle used **181**
  undesirable **180**
Psychotomimetic property of
  cannabis 2, **10, 11**, 241
  CBN **8**
  Δ **8**-THC **8**, 241
  THC vs LSD **102**
Psychomotor effects
  driving, ability **99, 100**, 104
    risks **99**
    tests **99-101**
  impairment 3, 13, 82, 85, 92, **99**, 101, 104,
    165, 248, 249
    in female offspring **68**
    flying **101-102**, 104, *120, 121*, 249
    hashish **235**, 238
    THC and alcohol **99-100**, 104
  marihuana and propanolol **259**, *276*
Psychotic reaction
  chronic cannibis use **97**, 248
    hashish **235**, 238
    marihuana users **99**, 248
  genesis **90**
  limbic cortex **86**
  pathological organic CNS response **88-91**, 247
    decompensation **90**, 248
    features **91**, 104
    treatment **90**, 104, 248
Psychotropic drugs (including opiates) 82, 83, 84,
  89, 138
  biochemical changes 254
  CVS, respiratory effects **179-180**, *224, 225*
  ECG changes 177
  in fatally injured **102**, *122*
  with hashish **89**
  LH effects 61, 246
  marihuana withdrawal treatment **103**
  peripheral neuropathy **87**
  respiratory depression 137
  thymidine uptake effect **38**, *53, 54*, 243
Pulmonary (see Lungs, Respiratory)
  AHH enzyme **133**, *148*
  edema 145, 178, **259**
    epinephrine effect **258**
  fibrosis, paraquat **135**, 145
  function tests 130
    acute cannabis effects **137**, 145, *151*
    chronic effects **138-141**, 145, *153-155*, 237,
      250
      ganja **138**, 234, 238
      vs tobacco **140**, 145
    insufficiency 130, 253
      COPD 131, 145, 146, **253**
      marihuana induced **139-140**, 250, 260
      reversibility **141**, *154*
  pathology, carcinoma 146
    cholesterol clefts **139**

tracheal epithelium **144**, 145, *163, 250*
THC accumulation **133**, 144, 250
Pulse (see Heart rate)
PVC (premature ventricular contraction)
in cardiac patients **178**, 184
ischemic 184, 251
isoproterenol **170**, *209*
marihuana **170**, **177**, 184, *209*
nicotine **175**, 177, 184
normal incidence **177**
THC,
IV, vs diazepam, oral surgical patients **179**,
222
oral, acute **177**, 184, *217*
chronic **173**
smoking **177**

Radiological examination
cerebral ventricles **83**
chest **178**, 234
sinus **138**
Reaction time
cannabis effects **92**, **93**, **101**, 248
THC response speed **100**, 104, 249
Relaxation, acute cannabis effect in hashish
users **236**, 238
Reproduction
fetal mortality, acidosis **258**
functional (fertility) alteration 71, 254, 260
in females **65-66**
in males **61-62**, 70
genetic mutational effects **69-70**, 72, 246
hormones involved in 60-61
loss, reproductive **67-68**, 72, 246
male organs, fructose, citric acid content **254**
newborn toxicity **37**, 45
THC accumuation in tissues **11**, 13, 241
Research, general comments 6
Respiratory (see Lungs, Pulmonary)
breathlessness **178**
depression **137**, 142, 145, *152*, 180, 186, 250
THC and oxymorphone **179**, *224*
tolerance development **137**, 142, 145, *152*,
250
disorders 137, 145
failure (acidosis) 130
fibrosis, paraquat **135**, 145
Kussmaul breathing **258**
poisoning, cannabis resin **88**, 247, 255
marihuana extract **259**
Reticuloendothelial system 33
alteration in functional activity **42**
RIA immunoassay
hormones 67
testosterone plasma level 60, 61
and HPLC (quantification) **9**
screening for cannabinoids 3, **9-10**, 99, *116*,
241
RNA (ribonucleic acid)
Leydig cell **254**
normal function 30
synthesis impairment **37**, **38**, **43**, 45, *50*, 242,
244
Rosette formation
B-cell detection **39-40**

T-cell detection 31, **39-40**, 46, *56, 57*
Rough endoplasmic reticulum (protein
synthesis)
destruction **86**, 104, 247

Salvia, cannabinoid analysis **9-10**, 241
Salivary gland cannabinoid accumulation **11**, 241
Schizophrenic reaction
EEG wave frequency **86-87**, *111, 112*
hashish and alcohol **89**
latent, pre-existent **89-90**
paranoid vs cannabis psychosis **90**, 104, 247
relapse in psychotic patients **90-91**, 248
schizophreniform derangement **99**, 104, 247-
248
scores on MMPI **88**
Sedation 2, 3, 5, **82**, **85**, 247
HR **177**, 183
THC **180**
and oxymorphone **179**
Semen, volume **63**, 245
Seminiferous tubules (testis)
damage 60
degenerative effect **63**, 245
spermatogenesis induction 60
Septum (pleasure, psychotic behaviour)
cannabis damage 248
EEG activity **85-86**, 247
species preservation **85**, *109*
stimulation 248
ultrastructural changes **86**, 247
Sertoli cell, dysfunction **63**, 245
Sex, sexual
development, abnormal ovarian function 61
differentiation, cannabinoid interference **62**,
70, 246
function, impotence **62**, **63**, 246
hashish effect **235**
Shock
anoxic, ammonia level **255**
secondary to vasodilation **131**, 186, 251, 238
Sleep
cycle reversal **89**
disturbance **102**, 184, 247
hashish **235**
duration **93**
EEG synchronization **84**
marihuana effect **237**, 238
pattern alteration, REM **84**, *108*, 247
THC vs lithium **85**
sleepy feeling **101**
Smoke, cannabis
AHH enzyme induction **133**, 144, *148*, 249
benzpyrene content **37**, 45, **134**, 145, 242, 250
cannabinoid, absorption 3, 241
constituents 10, 11, **133**, 241
carcinogenic potential 8, **37**, 45, **133-134**, 145,
146, *149*, 240, 242, 249-250
chromosomal effects **36**, 45, 242
CO content **134**, 145, 253
condensate, fertility effect 65
constituents **133-136**, 145, 249-250
contaminated,
infectious organisms 5, **136**, 145, 250
paraquat 5, **134-136**, 144, 250

CVS effect **167**, 184-185, 251
fetal toxicity **68**
formation **133**
irritant property **66**, 145
mutagenicity **37**, 45, **134**,145, *150*, 242, 250
organic gas phase 133
  gas vapor phase effects **37**, 242
passive exposure 142-143, 175
pH 134
plasma THC level **9**, *19*, 37, 241
  vs oral **10-11**, *22*, **164**, 241-242
pulmonary
  function,
    acute effects **137**, *151*, *152*, 250
    chronic effects **138-141**, *153-155*
  gas phase macrophage cytotoxin **141**, **143**, 146, *156*, 250, 255
    antibacterial defense 142, *158*, *159*
    intrapulmonary antibacterial defense **142**, *157-160*
    macrophage morphology **143**, *161*, *162*
    pathology, lethality **139**
      tracheal epithelium **144**, *163*
  tar content 8, **37**, 45, **134**, 142, 145, 242, 249
THC, content 133, 144, 238, 249
  exposure **41**
  loss 3, 241
  vs tobacco 8, **36-37**, **129-132**, **133-134**, **142-143**, 145, *149*, *150*, *161*, *162*, 249
Smoking cannabis
  aggressive behaviour **96**, 248
  allergic response **43-44**
  antianxiety property **93-94**, 248
  blood lactic acid **254**, *272*
  brain, EEG alterations **85-86**, 104, 247
    functional impairment **87-98**, 247
      latent psychopathology **91**
    gross pathology **82-84**, 246-247
  bronchodilation **137**, **141**, 142, 150, *151*
    partial tolerance **141**, *155*
  carcinogenic potential 8, **35**, 37, 45, **133-134**, 145, *149*, 240, 242, 249-250
  cardiovascular effects,
    acute **164-166**, *189-194*, *196-199*
    adrenergic mechansims **166-167**, **170**
    cardiac toxicity **174-178**, *217*, *218*
    chronic effects **171-172**, *210*, *211*
    in glaucoma patients **165**, *196-199*
    tachycardia prolongation **179**, *223*
  chromosomal effects 34, **35**, 45, *49*, 242
  chronic, natural setting, healthy **233-239**
    functional hypoxia **234**
  by, cigarette **83**, **133**, 144, **236**, 238
    tar deposition, lung 145
    spirometer 254
    water pipe **83**, **133**, 144, **235**, **236**, 238
  contaminated,
    infectious organisms 5, **136**, 145, 250
    paraquat 5, **134-136**, 144, 250
  fetal toxicity **68**
  glucose metabolic alterations **254**, *268*, *270-272*
  hypoxia **253**, 258
  immune response impairment **38-40**, 46, *56*, *57*

mixed with tobacco 13, **83**, **133**, 145, **235**, 238, 249
  cardiotoxicity **178**, 185
  mutagenicity **35-37**, 45, **134**, 145, *150*, 242, 250
  performance **94**, 104, *115*
    psychomotor function **99-102**, 104, *120*, *121*
  physical dependence **103**
    withdrawal **103-104**
  placental transfer **66**
  prenatal use effects **71**
  psychological dependence **103**, 105
  pubertal arrest **63**, 246
  pulmonary function alteration **138-141**, *153-155*, 250
  respiratory depression **137**, *152*, 250
  sperm alteration **63**, 245
  testosterone levels **61-62**, *74*, 245
  THC, absorption 3, **10**, 241
    variability **165**
    bioavailability 11, 13, *22*, **164**, 241
    loss 3, **10**, 13, 241
    in lungs 133
    in maternal milk **67**
    onset and duration of effects 3, 13, **164**, 241
    plasma levels **9-10**, 13, *19*, *20*, *22*, **37**, **86**, *110*, **164**, 241
      duration 3, **9**, 241
      peak variability **165**
    during smoking process **133**, 144, 249
  tolerance development **102-103**, 105, 249
  urinary metabolite 3, **9**, *20*, 241
Smoking machine (smoke-marihuana, tobacco)
  carcinogenic potential **133-134**, *149*
  intrapulmonary antibacterial defense **142**, *157-160*
    alveolar macrophage effects **143**
  mutagenecity **134**, *150*
  pulmonary pathology **139**
Smooth muscle, relaxation, marihuana vs nitrites **186**, 251
Species differences, metabolism **11**
Speech
  marihuana vs temporal lobe epilepsy **97**
  slowed **89**, *173*
Sperm, cannabinoid effects
  kinetic morphology (animal, human) **37**, 45, 242, 260
    morphological changes **64**, 245
    motility (fertilizing capacity) **63**, 245
  mitochondria **37**, 45, 242
  mutagenic potential **37**, 45
  normal formation, maturation 60, 61
    idiopathic oligospermia **63**
    testosterone influence **64**
  number **37**, 45, **62**, **63**, 242, 245
    concentration **63**
    gluconeogenesis effect **257**
  production decrease **66**, 245
    arginine (diet) deficiency **257**
    gluconeogenesis effect **257**
  toxicity **63**
Spermatogenesis

gluconeogenesis effect **257**
impairment **62, 63, 70,** 245-246
maturation defect **63,** 71, 245
normal formation, maturation of sperm 60,
  61
testosterone influence **64**
Spermiogenesis
  normal spermatidic development **63**
  in oligospermic patients **63,** 245
  sperm production interference **63**
  spermatidic maturation defect **63,** 245
Spleen, antibody production 33
  cells
    lymphocytes **41,** 244
    number **42, 44,** 244
  CO effect 129
  disorder 32
  metabolites in **12**
  size **42,** 244
  THC accumulation in **11-13,** 241
  weight **41,** 244
Stability of THC in solvents **7**
Statute (see Act)
Stimulation, THC 82
Stress, effects of, on
  ACTH, corticosterone secretion **254**
    release **255**
  fat 3
  flashbacks **91,** 104
  HR, with THC **185**
  immunological response **34,** 46, 245
  sperm counts **63,** 246, 255
  testosterone levels **61,** 246
Stroke volume
  marihuana effect **171,** 184, *210,* 251
    chronic effect **171,** *211*
Subjective effects (see Euphoria)
  acute toxic in hashish users **235,** 238
  marihuana, acute **177**
    chronic **90**
  psychological effects **101**
  THC
    vs alcohol **97**
    dose-response **99**
    intoxicating effects **173**
    vs LSD **102**
    tolerance **102,** 173
    visual hallucination predisposition, EEG **86-
    87,** *111, 112,* 247
Synapse
  cannabinoids in **253**
  ultrastructural changes **86,** 247
Syncope
  marihuana 4, 183, 186, 250-251, 253
  THC, IV, oral surgery **179**
    oral, presyncope manifestations **168,**
    and stress **87,** 247
Syndrome
  abstinence **85, 99, 102,** *108,* 173
  acute respiratory distress 130
  amotivational **92-94,** 248
  brain, acute reversible **88, 98-99,** 247
    chronic, organic irreversible **88-91, 98-99,**
    248
  FAS (fetal alcohol syndrome) **258**
  psychic withdrawal **103**

Wernicke-Korsakoff 84, **99**

T-cells (thymus dependent lymphocytes)
  active rosetting impairment **39-41,** 46, *56, 57,*
    243, 244
    cell number vs disease predisposition **39-40,**
    46, 243
    significance in marihuana users **40,** 46, 243
  age influence **41,** 244
  defects 32
  DTH test in marihuana users **39,** 243
  functional capacity assessment **38,** 243
  immunological competence test 31
  in marihuana smokers 46
  normal function 31
  possible clinical effects of T-cell decrease **46-
    47,** 245
  stress effect **34,** 46, 245
  THC effect **42**
Tachycardia **9-11,** *23, 26,* **142, 145,** 167, 170, 238,
  242, 253
  cannabis intoxication **90, 258**
  clinical significance **167, 179-180,** 183, *223-
    225*
  correlation with plasma THC **9, 164,** 181, 183,
    226, 242
  diagnostic sign **99**
  drug absorption estimate **181,** 183
  ECG changes **177,** 184
  exercise performance *174, 217, 218*
  marihuana and alcohol **259**
  onset, peak, duration, smoking **165,** *196*
    THC, IV **179,** *221*
  propanolol, atropine, epinephrine, norepine-
    phrine influence **167,** 181, 185, **253**
  psychological state **177,** 183, 251
  reflex response **164**
  THC **236**
    and CO_2 251, **253**
    and oxymorphone/pentobarbital **179-180,** *225*
    and stress **87, 178-179,** *220, 221, 223,* **253**
  with 11-OH-THC **11,** *23, 26*
  tolerance development **102, 171,** *211,* 236, 238
    cross, smoking vs oral **173,** 183
Talkative, in hashish users **236**
Temperature
  cutaneous (toe) vs rectosigmoid **166-167,** 183
    vs tobacco **166,** 183
  hypothermia, THC **258**
  poisoning, cannabis resin, **88,** 247, 255
  tolerance **236**
Temporal lobe
  cannabis psychosis, EEG **97**
  epilepsy **97,** 248
  lesions **95,** 248
  spontaneous activity **97**
Teratogenesis, teratology
  behavioural teratogens **70-71,** 72
  cannabinoid effects **68-71,** 72, 246
  chromosomal alterations **35, 45,** 242
  FAS similarity **71,** 72, 246
  maternal drug ingestion **67,** 72
  thalidomide 72
  tobacco effect 132
Testis
  atrophy, spermatogenic elements **254**

unilateral **237**
biopsy, oligospermic patients **63**, 245
cholesterol, alkaline phosphatase **254**
cholesterol esterase inhibition **65**, **70**, 245, 257
damage **63**, **254**
development 60
estrogen secretion 61
fetal **70**
fructose, citric acid content **254**
functional regulation 60
hormonal (testosterone) biosynthesis 60
  imbalance 61, 71
microsomes, THC effect **62**
sialic acid production (cryptorchid) **254**
weight **69-70**
Testosterone (male sex hormone)
in autoimmune process 42, 46, 244
binding in hippocampus 85
biosynthesis 60, 254
  cannabinoid inhibition **62**, **66**, **67**, **69-71**, 254, 257
  potential implications **62-63**, 246
deficiency 61
drug effects 61, 246
excess in fetal development 60
exercise effects 61, 246
exogenous 61
in females 60, **65**, 246
fetal production alteration **70**
hypogonadism 61
metabolism 60
in oligospermic patients 63
plasma, binding 60
  levels, detection, RIA 60
    normal 60, **61**, **62**
    post marihuana (THC) **61-62**, *74*, 245
      with HCG **61-62**
pubertal, arrest **63**
  development 60
secretion 60
stress effects 61, 246
tolerance **102**, 249
Δ**8**-THC (Δ**8**-tetrahydrocannabinol) and derivatives
DTH modification **41**, 244
immunosuppression vs CNS activity **42-43**
metabolism **11**, 241
psychotomimetic property **8**
RNA and protein synthesis impairment **43**, 244
testosterone synthesis inhibition **62**
tumor growth inhibition **42**, **46**, 244
  DNA synthesis impairment **43**, 244
Δ**9**-THC (Δ**9**-tetrahydrocannabinol)
ACTH, corticosterone secretion **254**
  release **255**
adrenal steroid release **42**, 244
allergic response **44**, **46**, 244
antineoplastic property **42**, **46**, 244
  DNA synthesis impairment **43**
behaviour **85**, **93**, 247
  aggressive **96-97**, 248
  vs alcohol **97**, *117*, 248
in bile **9**, 241
bioavailability **9-12**, 13, *22*, **164**, 241, 242

in brain **9**, **12**, *27*, **82**, 241, 246
  blood flow **85**
  function, behaviour **85-86**
in breath, saliva **9**, 13, 241
cardiovascular effects, acute **164-166**, 250-251
  adrenergic mechanisms **168-170**, **173**, *200*, *201*, *203-206*, *208*, *209*, 251
    left ventricular function **169**, *208*, *209*
  anginal patients, hemodynamic effects **175-176**, 251
  cardiac conduction **177-178**, 251
  cardiac microsomal CaATPase **171**, 251
  chronic effects **172-173**, *212-215*
  CNS sympathetic control **181-182**, *228-232*, 251
  CO$_2$ response, and oxymorphone/pentobarbital **179-180**, *225*
  ECG changes **177-178**, *217*, 251
  stress, oral surgery **178-179**, **185**, *219-223*
cellular metabolic effects **37**, **38**, **45**, **50**, **51**, *52*, *55*, 242, 243
chromosomal effects **35-36**, **45**, 242
in cigarettes (see marihuana cigarettes)
consumption, 3 different potencies **10**
dependence, psychological **103**
  physical, onset **103**, 249
    abstinence, naloxone **103-104**, **255**
    withdrawal **104**
derivatives **62**, **65**
detection 3, **9-10**, 13, 181, 241
EEG changes **84**, 247
  visual hallucinations **86-87**, *111*, *112*, 247
effects, onset, peak, duration
  inhalation, vs IV **103**, *126*, *127*
    vs oral 3, **9**, **10**, **164**, 241-242
endocrine effects in pregnancy **67**
endorphin release **104**, **255**
excretion
  complete **179**
  in excreta of suckling animal infants **11**, 241
  fecal **181**
fetal toxicity **68**, **70**, 246
  teratological effects **68-69**, 246
in fingertip washings **10**, 13, 241
glucose metabolism **254-255**, *263-269*, *273*
  carbohydrate starvation (preference) **257**
  fat oxidation alteration **258**
  gluconeogenesis effect **257**
immune response **40**, **42**, **46**, 243, 244
  vs age **41**, **46**, 244
  immunosuppressive activity **42**, **44**, **46**, 244
immunization with protein conjugate **12**, 241
infection susceptibility **43**, **46**, **58**, 244
intraocular pressure effects, **259-260**, *277*
interaction with CBD/CBN **9**, **12**, 13, **133**, **144**, 241-242
vs LSD **102**
in lungs **133**, **144**
  bronchodilation **137**, **141**, **142**, *151*, 250
    partial tolerance **141**, *155*
  disorders **138**
  pulmonary, function,
    acute effects **137**, *151*, 250
    chronic effects **138-141**, *153-155*
  pathology **139**
respiratory depression **137**, *152*, **180**, 250

major active principle 2, 3, **10**, 241
mammotrophic property **64**, *75*
  serum prolactin **64**, *75*
membrane modification 38, 45, 242
metabolism, liver 3, **11-12**, 13, 144, 241, 249
in milk, animal **11**, **66-67**, *80*, 241, 246
  human **67**, 246
molecular weight **10**
vs opiates **103**
oral activity **10-11**, **164**, 241-242
  absorption **169**
  chronic **172-173**
ovulatory effects **65**, 246
  possible abortive effects **65**
pharmacokinetics 9-12, 13, **103**, **164**, 241-242
  influence of CBD/CBN 9, 13, 242
pituitary-gonadal function **70**
placental transfer to fetus **66**, 246
in plant 2, 3, **7-8**, 13, 240, 241
  ganja **233**
plasma, clearance **11**, **12**, 241
  elimination, half-life post IV **12**
    rate 9, 241
  half-life, post IV, THC 9, **12**, 13, **179**, 241
    post oral THC **12**
  level vs cigarettes re dose **103**, 105, 176
    correlation with tissue concentration **11**, 242
      HR changes **165**
    for forensic purposes 3, 9, 13, 242
    post IV 9, **11**, **12**, *18*, *24*, **103**, *125*, **164**, 241
    post oral 9-12, *22*, **164**, **181**, 242
      time course 169, **181**, *207*, *226*
    post smoking 9, **10**, **12**, 13, *19*, *20*, *22*, **37**, **86**, **101**, **103**, *110*, *125*, **139**, **164**, 241
      correlation with physiological changes **10**, **164**, 241-242
      peak variability **165**, *194*
      women vs men **10**, **12**
  lipoprotein binding **11-12**, **13**, 241
potency 7, 13, **133**, 144, 240, 249
progesterone inhibition **65**, *78*, 246
psychomotor effects **99-102**, 104, 249
  with alcohol **99**, 249
  dose response **99**, 104, 249
  impairment, driving **100**, 104
    flying **101**, *120*, *121*
    sobriety test **101**
    visual function **101**, 166
      pupil size **166**
  performance alteration **100**, 104, 248, 249
    with alcohol **100**, 249
psychotomimetic activity 2, **9-11**, *23*, *25*, 241
reproductive loss **67-68**, 246
RNA and protein synthesis impairment **38-39**, 244
sites for transformation **11**, 241
in smoked marihuana **10**, 237
sperm alterations **37**, 45, **63**, 242
stability in solvents 7
  water solubility **10**, 13, 241
structure **10**, **11**
tachycardia **11**, *23*, *26*, **164**, **172-173**, 242

correlation with plasma THC, high **165**, *194*
  dose response **165**, **179**,*193*, *220*
  propanolol influence **169-170**, *209*
testosterone effect **62**, 246
tissue, accumulation **11**, **12**, **99**, 241
  distribution **11**, **12**, 13, **82**, 241
  half-life post IV **12**, 13, **99**, 241
tolerance, cross **102**, **103**
  functional **12**, 13, **102**, *122*, *123*, *124*, **164**, **173**, **236**, 261
  metabolic **12**, 13, 241
  plasma THC time course **12**, **103**, *125*
  response variation **103**
urinary, catecholamines **169**
  output, vs hydrochlorothiazide **258**
  THC metabolites **9-10**, 13, *20*, *21*, **181**, 241
vasodilation **102**
Therapeutic possibilities
  analgesia 5, **11**, **87**, 247
    endogenous opiates **255**
    narcotic detoxification **255**
  antianxiety 5, **93**, 248
  antiarrhythmic, healthy **179**, *222*
  antibacterial 5, **8**
  anticonvulsant property 5, **8**, 237
  antiemetic (cancer chemotherapy) 5, **46-47**, 145, 245, 250
  antiinflammatory property 5, **8**
  antineoplastic property 5, **42**, 46
  bipolar depression **85**
  bronchodilator **141**, **142**, 146, **165**, 237
  diuretic **258**
  in glaucoma **165-166**, *185*, *196*, *198*, *199*, 251
  immunosuppressant 5, **42**, 46, 47
  medicinal uses, field studies **234**, **236**
  short summary 5
Thirst, dehydration, glucose effect **257**
  in glaucoma patients **165**
Thought, hashish effect **235**
Thymidine (DNA precursor), cannabinoid effects on uptake, into, 244
  Lewis lung cells (animal) **42**
  lymphocytes, normal 36
  human, diploid fibroblasts (THC) **37**, *52*, 242
    lymphocytes **38**, 243
      metabolic alterations **38**, *55*, 243
      and mouse neuroblastoma cells (THC) **37**, 242
Thymus gland 32-33
Thyroid gland, blood glucose control **255**, 256
  hormone alteration **67**, **254**, 255
Tissues, anoxia **129**, *187*, 251
  biogenic amine turnover **253**
  cannabinoid distribution in 8, **11-12**, 13, 241
  metabolite accumulation in **11-12**, 13
  oxygen deficiency **234**, **253**, 258
  THC accumulation **11**,**12**, 241
  transplantation 31
Tobacco 3, 4, 7, 39, 40, 61, 63, 71, 83, 129, 137-139, 233-237
  benzpyrene **37**, 45, **134**, 242
  blood glucose **258**
  body weight **258**
  bronchoconstriction 145
  chromosomal effects **36**

cytotoxic effects **36**
disease, bronchopulmonary **129-131, 144,** 145
 pathology **139,** 145, 250
  respiratory symptoms **144,** 250
 cardiovascular 129, **131-132**
gas vapor phase effects **37, 129, 144,** 242
and hashish **138-139**
leukocytosis, MI predictor **258**
mutagenicity **37, 45, 134,** 145, *150,* 242
nicotine, bradycardia 142
 content **133**
 effects **129,** 183, 251, **260**
 PVCs **177,** 184
organ immune response (humoral) **44**
paraquat, sprayed **135**
rosette formation **39,** 243
smoke vs marihuana **8, 129, 133-134,** *149, 150*
 AHH enzyme induction **133**
 alveolar macrophages **141, 143,** 146, *161, 162,* 250
 glycolysis impairment **142,** 146, 258
 antigen 44
 bronchial alterations **139-140**
 carcinogenic, with alcohol (cocarcinogen) **131**
  with asbestos **131**
  genes **131**
  substances **8,** 45, **129, 133-134, 144,** 145, *149,* 242, 250
 chromosomal DNA content **36,** *49*
 CO content **134**
 CVS effects, adrenergic mechanism **166-167,** 251
  anginal onset **175**
   passive smoke exposure **175**
  blood pressure **166,** 183
   flow, peripheral **166-167,** 183
 formation **133**
 HR **142, 166,** 183, 251
 intrapulmonary defense **142,** *158*
 malignant transformation **36,** 45
 mixed with, ganja **138,** 233
  hashish 13, **235,** 254
  marihuana **36, 133,** 145, **235,** 238, 249
   myocardial infarction **178,** 185, 251
  THC **102**
 organic gas phase **133**
 pH **134**
 plasma NE **170**
 tar content 8, **37,** 45, **129, 134, 142, 144,** 242
toxic effects **84,** 129
Tolerance
 absence or partial **102,** *123, 124,* 249
 antineoplastic property **42,** 244
 bronchodilation **141,** *155*
 cardiovascular effects **171-172,** *211*
 cross-tolerance **102, 103,** 105, *123,* 249
  smoking vs oral **173,** 183
 definition **102**
 development 12, **84, 85, 99,** 105, **173,** 187, 242, 251, 255
  in animals **102,** 105, 249
  in humans **102, 103,** 105, *122, 123,* 249
   heavy vs light users **103,** *125-127*
   onset **102,** 105, 249, 251

 symptoms **103**
  in offspring **70**
 diuretic, THC **258**
 functional (adaptive) **12,** 13, **103,** 105, 187, 249, 261
 hypothermia, antagonism **253**
 immunosuppression **42**
 metabolic **12,** 13, 241
 plasma, drug level **103,** 105
  time course,
   metabolites **12**
   THC **12**
 volume expansion **102, 173,** 251
 physiological **100, 102, 103, 236,** 238, 247
 respiratory depression **137,** *152*
 saturation point **90,** 248
Toxicity, cannabinoid
 vs alcohol **83,** 100
 behavioural, reproductive **70-71**
 carcinogenic potential **8, 34, 35, 37, 45, 133-134,** 145, *149,* 240, 249-250
 cardiac **174-178,** *217, 218,* 251
 chromosomal alterations **35,** 45, *49*
 contamination,
  infectious organisms 5, **136,** 145, 250
  paraquat 5, **134-136,** 144 ,250
 cytotoxicity **36,** 45
 DNA synthesis **36,** 45
 enhanced with bacteria in non-tolerant **43,** 46, 244
 fetal toxicity **67-71**
 immunodeficiency disease 46
 immunosuppressive property **42**
 intoxication **99, 100,** 104, 247, 249
  vs cannabinoid levels **10,** 13, 242
  chronic **89**
  passive inhalation **44**
  psychiatric aspects **87-98,** 247-248
 involuntary muscle movements **181**
 lung, alveolar macrophages **141-142,** 146, *155-158, 160*
 mutagenicity **37, 45, 134, 145,** *150,* 242, 250
 newborn toxicity **37,** 45
 poisoning **88,** 247, **255, 258-259**
 sperm **63**
 tachycardia, excessive **180,** 253
 teratogenic potential **35,** 45
 THC, mitotic poison **36,** 242
 vs tobacco **134,** *149,* 250
 with tobacco, MI **178**
 toxic psychosis 85, **88,** 99, 247, 248
TPM (total particulate matter) in cigarettes
 marihuana vs tobacco **142,** 145
Tracking
 in driving **100,** 249
 impairment **101**
  and alcohol **101,** 104
 process **101,** 249
Transcriptional (genetic info to RNA) arrest
 lymphocytes, hashish users **39**
Translocation, chromosomal 31

Urea
 blood level, hashish **254**
 formation **254**

Uridine (RNA precursor), cannabinoid effects on
  uptake, into
    animal brain cortex slices 8, 13
    human diploid fibroblasts (THC) **37**, *50*, 242
      and mouse neuroblastoma cells (THC) 37,
      242
Urine
  cannabinoid
    analysis **9-10**,241
    levels **9-10**, 13, *20, 21*, 241
      poisoning 255
    catecholamines **169**
  THC metabolites **9-10, 11-12**, 13, 241
  urination, excessive frequent **237**, 238
    polyuria **257**
      THC vs hydrochlorothiazide **258**
      hypophysectomy, adrenalectomy **258**
Uterus
  atrophy 61
  glycogen **254**
  preparation, ovum implantation 61
  THC effect **65**

Vagina, bleeding **68**
  cannabinoid (THC) effect **65**
Vehicle for cannabinoid
  absorption, individual variability **181**, 185
  administration, corn oil **69**
    ethanol (alcohol) **7, 180-181**
    Na glycocholate **180-181**,
    propylene glycol **7**
    saline **69**
    sesame oil **7, 69, 180-181**
    Tween-80, **69, 180-181**
  extraction, chloroform **8**, 241
    methanol **8**, 241
  interaction with oral THC **180-181**, 185
Violence
  heavy cannabis use **90, 97**, 248
    temporal lobe neural activity **98**, 248
  lack **89**, 248

Vision, blurred, THC **180**
  functional impairment (peripheral light) **101**
    249
    foveal glare recovery **101, 104**, 249
  hallucinations, visual **86-87**, *111, 112,* **181**, 247
  infant visual response **71**
  pupil size effects **166**, 185, 251
  socio-sexual behaviour **85,** *109*
  trochlear nerve **87**
Voice, vocal cord appearance **138**

Weight
  adrenal glands, female 144
  birth **68, 70, 71**, 246
  body **41, 83, 102.** 144, *173*, 183, 187, *216,* **234,**
    237, 238, 244, **257, 258, 261**
    tolerance **102,** *123,* 249, 251, **257**
  fetal **69**
  maternal **68, 69, 71**
  pup **69, 70**
  spleen **41**, 244
  testicular **69, 70**, 144
Withdrawal symptoms
  behaviour **85, 102, 104, 165**, 247
  chronic ganja use **234**
  endogenous opiates, deficiency **256**
  post marihuana **93, 102, 165**, 184
    onset **103, 105**, 248, 249, 251
    treatment **103, 105**, 248, 249
  vs opiates, alcohol **103**
  psychic **103, 105**, 248, 249
  ratings **236**, 238
  post THC **173**
Word derivation, marihuana 2
Work capacity
  efficiency decrease, ganja **234** 237
  effort, subjective **174**
  physical impairment **94, 97**, 104, 249, 257
    hashish effect **235**
    weakness, energy loss **257**
  for tedious tasks **237**, 238